Encyclopedia of African American Actresses in Film and Television

Encyclopedia of African American Actresses in Film and Television

BOB MCCANN

McFarland & Company, Inc., Publishers
Jefferson, North Carolina, and London

Publisher's Note: Bob McCann died in 2009, shortly after completing the manuscript for this book.

LIBRARY OF CONGRESS CATALOGUING-IN-PUBLICATION DATA

McCann, Bob, 1948–
Encyclopedia of African American actresses in film and television / Bob McCann.
p. cm.
Includes bibliographical references and index.

ISBN 978-0-7864-3790-0
illustrated case binding : 50# alkaline paper ♾

1. African American actresses — Biography — Dictionaries.
I. Title.
PN1995.9.N4M345 2010 791.4302'8092396073 — dc22 2009037436

British Library cataloguing data are available

Manufactured in the United States of America

McFarland & Company, Inc., Publishers
Box 611, Jefferson, North Carolina 28640
www.mcfarlandpub.com

For Martha

Acknowledgments

My thanks to Tom Lisanti of the New York Public Library Photographic Services and Permissions, Katrina Groover, Mary F. Yearwood and the staff of the Schomburg Center for Research in Black Culture, Astor, Lenox and Tilden Foundations, Adam Robinson, Hattie Winston and Lark Voorhees for that killer head shot!

Contents

Preface

This book focuses on positive achievement. It is a celebration of talent, fortitude, intelligence and beauty. It is not a sociological treatise on the evils of racism or the pitfalls of stereotyping — although it is abundantly clear that these problems have been and continue to be real. Although there are a number of black female superstars in the music business, once you get beyond Halle Berry, the number of highly paid, star-level black film actresses is low. This is clearly not for lack of talent. Race aside, however, the era of the female cinema superstar of any ethnic group has at least temporarily gone into eclipse. The career of a Bette Davis, a Joan Crawford, or a Katharine Hepburn has no contemporary equivalent (with the conspicuous sole exception of Meryl Streep).

Given the broad topic of this encyclopedia, there are a number of reasons why an actress was included (or excluded). Broad-based inclusion criteria are:

- Black actresses who have broadened the opportunities for other black actresses, or who have helped redefine the image of black women on screen.
- All award-winning or well-known black actresses who have sustained film or television careers and those who have worked more prominently in theatre.
- Lesser-known or B-film actresses, especially the actresses of the so-called blaxploitation era of the late 1960s and mid–1970s.
- Only those actresses who fit reasonably into the category of African American. However, many black actresses not born in America have had notable careers in American films or on American TV, and are American citizens or have dual citizenships. This includes a number of British- and Canadian-born actresses. Then there are the Caribbean-born actresses who are or were American citizens and who have done all or most of their acting in the U.S. Also included are African-born actresses who are American citizens and who have primarily focused on U.S. films or TV. A good example is Akosua Busia, born in Ghana, but who is an American citizen (the former wife of director John Singleton), and who has acted extensively in America, including a key role in *The Color Purple*.
- A small but significant group of actresses who, although born in America, spent most of their professional careers in Europe (e.g., Josephine Baker, Olive Moorefield). These actresses are of course considered African American, although much of their work was not done in this country.
- New young actresses who appear to have the potential for sustained careers — e.g., Keke Palmer, Yaya DaCosta, and many others. I excluded some of the new generation of actresses because there was a danger of an imbalance of contemporary entries, since there are so many more opportunities for black actresses these days. Inclusion and exclusion of new genera-

tion actresses is necessarily somewhat subjective.

- Actresses who appeared in one key film (e.g., Lucia Lynn Moses, Geraldine Brock) of historic or artistic value.

The gray areas and exclusions include the following:

- Singers who have appeared in some acting roles, as opposed to just appearing in a film to sing a song (I decided to include Tina Turner and Ella Fitzgerald, but passed on Donna Summer, Gladys Knight, and most reluctantly on Alicia Keys).
- "Adult film" actresses, even if they appeared in a few "straight" films (e.g., Heather Hunter).

I want to emphasize three points. My first goal was to acknowledge the contributions of pioneering black actresses, especially from the silent era to the 1940s, a time when the path to Hollywood stardom was thoroughly blocked. Despite the obstacles, Anita Bush, Evelyn Preer, Etta Moten, Shingzie Howard, Ethel and Lucia Lynn Moses, Nina Mae McKinney, Lena Horne, Francine Everett, Diahann Carroll and others have left a lasting legacy and helped to open many doors — however slowly, however slightly. Fredi Washington should especially be given her due as the first near-breakthrough black star. She was not given the opportunity to showcase her talent and beauty in the Hollywood system after her starring role as Peola in the controversial *Imitation of Life* (1934)—but Washington was not ready to play Hollywood's game, and did not need Hollywood's approval to make a lasting artistic impact. Hattie McDaniel — the first black woman to win an Oscar — was a force of nature who became the preeminent black female film star of her era. As for Dorothy Dandridge, how do you overstate her place in the pantheon of black actresses? The modern era starts with Dandridge. These actresses should be a prominent part of film studies programs, and their achievements should be acknowledged as part of the popular culture.

My second goal was to emphasize those actresses whose work, while acknowledged at the peak of their careers, is now in danger of being ignored, underrated, or forgotten. This group includes Ethel Waters, Diana Sands and Gail Fisher. Their special place in film history should be reconfirmed, reassessed and assured for generations to come.

Finally, I wanted to give a nod to the often unsung B-film actresses who never had a chance to show what they would have been capable of in starring roles in mainstream films: Pam Grier, Marilyn Joi, Carol Speed, Brenda Sykes, Judy Pace, and so many others. Their legacy is an inspiration in its own right.

And for the thousands of black actresses who never made it — whose names don't even languish in obscurity — you too are a part of the struggle and of the celebration.

AFRICAN AMERICAN ACTRESSES, A TO Z

Aaliyah Born in Brooklyn, New York, January 16, 1979; died August 25, 2002.

Aaliyah Dana Haughton's untimely death in a plane crash shouldn't obscure the rewarding career that she enjoyed despite her brief life. On August 25, 2001, at 6:45 P.M., the lives of Aaliyah and seven other people were taken in a crash that happened as the small plane, a Cessna 402B, was leaving Marsh Harbour, Abaco Island, in the Bahamas. The plane was headed to Miami for what would have been approximately a one-hour flight. The total gross weight of the airplane had been exceeded with passengers and equipment, and as it lifted off the runway its nose was down, and the plane impacted in a marsh on the south side of the departure runway.

Born in Brooklyn to Michael and Diane Haughton, Aaliyah was raised in Detroit (graduating from Detroit Performing Arts High School in 1997), but returned frequently to New York with her parents. It was there that she signed with the prestigious Abrams Artists Agency.

Aaliyah sang "My Funny Valentine" at age 10 on the youth vocal competition on *Star Search*, a fairly successful *American Idol*–type talent competition. Although she didn't win, she was in good company: the group that would soon be famous as Destiny's Child was among the losers. At age 11, she landed a five-night stint performing with Gladys Knight in Las Vegas. She was also auditioning for TV roles at the time.

She released her first album (*Age Ain't Nothing But a Number*) in 1994 at age 14. The first single, "Back and Forth," was a top five hit on the *Billboard* Hot 100; her follow-up single "At Your Best (You Are Love)" charted in the top 10 of the Hot 100. But it was her second album that went through the roof: *One in a Million* (1996) was a multi-platinum international hit. The first single, "If Your Girl Only Knew," went double platinum. And in 1998 she had a huge hit with "Are You That Somebody?" from the soundtrack of Eddie Murphy's *Dr. Dolittle*.

Then she recorded the vocal for the Academy Award nominated Song of the Year "Journey to the Past," from the animated feature film *Anastasia* (which she performed at the Oscars). Her final studio album (*Aaliyah*) was posthumously released in July 2001. It sold over 2.4 million copies worldwide and spawned the hit singles "We Need a Resolution," "Rock the Boat," and "More Than a Woman."

Her motion picture debut was a co-starring role in the box office hit *Romeo Must Die* with Jet Li (his first lead role in an American film). This contemporary variant on *Romeo and Juliet* told its unlikely love story amid the conflict of Asian and black gangs vying for mob control of Oakland, California's waterfront. Aaliyah starred as Trish O'Day, the daughter of a crime boss who disowns her father and the crime milieu into which she was born. *Romeo Must Die* didn't impress the critics, but it did well at the box office and remains Li's highest-grossing star vehicle. Perhaps even more popular than the film was the best-selling soundtrack, powered by the hit single "Try Again."

In her last film, released six months after her death, Aaliyah played the title role in *Queen of the Damned*, based on the third novel in Anne Rice's hugely successful *Vampire Chronicles*, with elements taken from *The Vampire Lestat*. Although she had limited screen time as the vampire queen Akasha, Aaliyah delivered a wry, campy performance that was clearly the highlight of the film.

Fans looked forward to her appearance in *The Matrix Reloaded* and *The Matrix Revolutions*, the second and third films in the hugely successful *Matrix* sci-fi series. Although some footage of Aaliyah was shot, there was not enough to be usable, and she was replaced by Nona Gaye. The role was not a substantial or showy one, and the films were a major disappointment. Aaliyah was also slated to appear in *Honey* (which wound up starring Jessica Alba), and in the remake of *Sparkle*, a forerunner to *Dreamgirls*. There was also a starring role on tap in an untitled interracial love story that Aaliyah's agents had successfully pitched to Fox Searchlight.

It is as an archetypal model for today's African American teen music star that Aaliyah will have her place in entertainment history. Aaliyah was a pathfinder for the one-name wonders to follow (including Ashanti, Beyoncé, and other superstars).

In addition to her major singing career and her burgeoning acting career, Aaliyah also had a successful modeling career, most notably for Tommy Hilfiger. Her major awards included the MTV Music Video Award, Best Female Video (2000) ("Try Again"); Best Video from a Film ("Try Again," from *Romeo Must Die*); the NAACP Image Award, Outstanding Female Artist (2002); and American Music Awards for Favorite Female R&B Artist, Favorite R&B Soul Album (2002) and Favorite Female R&B Artist (2003).

Feature Films: *Romeo Must Die* (2000), *Queen of the Damned* (2002).

TV: *Star Search* (1989), *Christmas in Washington* (1997), *New York Undercover* ("Fade Out," 1997), *The 70th Annual Academy Awards* (1998), *MTV Video Music Awards 2000, HBO First Look: Romeo Must Die* (2000), *The Rosie O'Donnell Show* (2 segments; 1997, 2000), *2000 MTV Movie Awards, CNN World Beat* (2001), *BET Tonight Special* (2001), *MTV Icon: Janet Jackson* (2001), *Essence Awards* (2001), *2001 MTV Movie Awards, The Tonight Show with Jay Leno* (2001), *VH1's Behind the Music* (archival footage; "Aaliyah: The Life and Death," 2001).

Video/DVD: *Losing Aaliyah* (archival footage; 2001), *Hip-Hop VIPS* (2002), *The Notorious B.I.G.: Ready to Die—The Remaster* (2004).

Abbott, Diahnne

Born in New York City, January 1, 1945.

Actress and singer Diahnne Abbott is the former wife of Robert De Niro. She married him in 1976, and they were divorced in 1988. De Niro adopted Drena, Abbott's daughter from a previous marriage, and the couple had a child of their own, Raphael. Abbott had roles in some of De Niro's best known collaborations with director Martin Scorsese, including *Taxi Driver* (1976) and *The King of Comedy* (1983). Her career highlight is the sizzling version of Fats Waller's "Honeysuckle Rose" which she sings in Scorsese's lavish musical *New York, New York* (1977).

Her non–De Niro/Scorsese films are not as memorable. *Jo Jo Dancer, Your Life Is Calling* (1986) is a dated Richard Pryor film featuring Abbott as Jo Jo's mother. Heavily influenced by Bob Fosse's *All That Jazz* (1979), it is, like that film, a thinly disguised autobiography, even though Pryor always insisted that it was not autobiographical.

Abbott did have small roles in two prestigious art house productions: *Love Streams* (1984), John Cassavettes' rarely seen penultimate film; and *Before Night Falls* (2000), based on the autobiography of gay Cuban writer Reinaldo Arena. Directed by Julian Schnabel, the film garnered a Best Actor Academy Award nomination for Javier Bardem, and featured Johnny Depp in a memorable supporting role as a drag queen. Her most recent role was in *Soliloquy* (2002), where she appeared with her daughter Drena.

Feature Films: *Taxi Driver* (1976), *Welcome to L.A.* (1976), *New York, New York* (1977), *The King of Comedy* (1983), *Love Streams* (1984), *Jo Jo Dancer, Your Life Is Calling* (1986), *Jonas in the Desert* (documentary; 1994), *Before Night Falls* (aka *Antes que Anochezca*; billed as Diahnne Déa; 2000), *Soliloquy* (2002).

TV: *The Mike Douglas Show* (1977), *Crime Story* (3 episodes in the role of Sonia; "Going Home," "Escape," "Pursuit").

Alexander, Erika

Born in Winslow, Arizona, November 19, 1969.

Best known as one of the stars of the long-running sitcom *Living Single*, Erika Alexander combines a knowing, sarcastic wit with a dynamic screen presence. Alexander studied acting at Freedom Theater at the Philadelphia High School for Girls. She later endowed a $20,000 scholarship for Freedom Theater's performing arts program. She began studying at New York University, but left NYU after only two weeks to perform in Peter Brook's play *The Mahabharata*, which toured in-

Left to right: **Queen Latifah, Morris Chestnut, Erika Alexander and Kim Fields in *Living Single.***

ternationally and was later made into a French TV miniseries (in which she also appeared). The miniseries ran 3 hours and 20 minutes. *The Mahabharata* is a fantastic allegory concerning a violent conflict between two families, the Pandavas and the Kauravas. Both families seek to rule the world.

After this sojourn, Alexander returned to New York and garnered a featured role in Joseph Papp's production of Bill Gunn's *The Forbidden City* (1989). She got her first big mainstream break as Pam Tucker on *The Cosby Show*. She played a teen who is sent to live with the Huxtables when her grandmother becomes ill. At first Pam feels like she doesn't fit in due to all the strict rules, but she learns that the rules are part of the process of tough love. Alexander stayed with the show until it ended its long run in 1992.

The Cosby interlude was followed by her signature role as attorney Maxine "Max" Shaw on *Living Single*, a role she played for five years on the FOX network. Max was an innovative character light years away from the typically sanitized, cheerful roles played by some African American women at that time. Max was compassionate but self-absorbed, a dear friend and confidant to Khadijah James, an independent magazine editor and publisher played by Queen Latifah. Max was a complex character who didn't take any nonsense from anyone, but who had a definite soft side below the surface, and a very appealing sexiness. Alexander won an *Essence* Image Award in 1998 as Outstanding Actress in a Comedy Series.

Living Single centered on six young black people (four women, two men) living in a brownstone in Brooklyn. Max would invariably stop by the brownstone to offer advice and to pillage the refrigerator. Although *Living Single* had a nice run on the FOX network, it died a rather inglorious death. Abruptly revived after first being cancelled (a slot was open because of problems with the Martin Lawrence show, *Martin*), the show was shortly thereafter cancelled for good. *Living Single* was much more than a black version of the long-running NBC sitcom *Friends* (indeed, it predated *Friends* by one season, so it was certainly not a clone). Also, this was not *The Cosby Show*; it was edgier and more urban.

Erika Alexander and Terrence "T.C." Carson — another series regular who played an upwardly mobile stockbroker who lived in the brownstone and began a relationship with Erika's character — reprised their characters of Max and Kyle on an episode of UPN's *Half & Half*. In this episode, they remain together, although still not married, and they have a child. There was another cast member reunion when Queen Latifah and Alexander both starred in the 1998 miniseries *Mama Flora's Family*.

Going to Extremes, which predates *Living Single* by a season, was an unfunny sitcom about American medical students studying at an eccentric medical school on a tropical island (really Jamaica, under the fictional name of "Jantique"). The show had a decent pedigree, produced by the creators of *Northern Exposure* and actually filmed on location in Jamaica in an hour format. Alexander's character was named Cheryl Carter, a bit of a forerunner to Max in that she was pugnacious and "out there." Alexander's most recent attempt to find a new series home was *Side Order of Life* (2007). However, she appeared in the pilot episode only. Her character, Colette, was written out after the pilot.

Her most notable big screen role was with Whoopi Goldberg in 1990's *The Long Walk Home*, a retrospective tale of the great sacrifice and pain required during the civil rights movement. It was set in Montgomery, Alabama, during the 1955 bus boycott by the black community. Sissy Spacek starred as a suburban housewife, and Goldberg was her housekeeper, Odessa, who looks after Spacek's youngest daughter. The two women join forces to take a stand against white bigotry and learn first hand the enormity of the struggle. Alexander played Odessa's daughter.

Alexander's voice is featured on "The Bible Experience" (2007), an audiobook CD set in which numerous black celebrities narrate the Bible. She married artist-screenwriter Tony Puryear on September 27, 1997.

Feature Films Including Video and TV Movies: *George Washington II: The Forging of a Nation* (TV; 1986), *My Little Girl* (1987), *Common Ground* (1990), *The Long Walk Home* (1990), *The Last Best Year* (1990), *He Said, She Said* (1991), *Fathers & Sons* (1992), *Override* (1994), *54* (1998), *Mama Flora's Family* (1998), *30 Years to Life* (2001), *Love Liza* (2002), *Full Frontal* (2002), *Tricks* (2004), *Sixty Minute Man* (2006), *Déjà Vu* (2006), *Mission Street Rhapsody* (2009).

TV: *Le Mahabharata* (French miniseries; 1989), *The Cosby Show* (recurring role of Pam Tucker; 1990–92), *Law & Order* ("Poison Ivy," 1990), *Going to Extremes* (recurring role of Cheryl Carter; 1992), *Living Single* (recurring role of Max Sinclair; 1993–98), *Judging Amy* (recurring role of Fran Winston; 2001), *Street Time* (recurring role of Dee Mulhern; 2002), *The Cosby Show: A Look Back* (2002), *The Zeta Project* ("Absolute Zero," 2002), *LAX* ("Thanksgiving," 2004), *Law & Order: Special Victims Unit* ("Ritual," 2004), *Half & Half* ("The Big Performance Anxiety Episode," 2005), *7th Heaven* ("Leaps of Faith," 2005), *TV Land Confidential* (2005), *In Justice* ("The Ten Percenter," 2006), *Heist* (recurring role of Saundra Johnson; 2006), *ER* ("No Place to Hide," 2006), *Side Order of Life* (pilot; 2007), *Living Single: The Reunion Show* (2008).

Alexander, Khandi Born in New York, New York, September 4, 1957.

Although it seemed early on that her niche would be in musical theater and the dance world, Khandi Alexander turned that around to become much better known for her acting. Alexander was educated at Queensborough Community College and appeared on Broadway in *Chicago*, *Bob Fosse's Dancin'*, and *Dreamgirls*. She was choreographer for Whitney Houston's world tour (1989–92).

Her film career is spotty but not without interest. Alexander appeared in three memorable black-oriented films in 1993. The first was director John Singleton's moody, character-driven love story *Poetic Justice*. Of the cast members, Tupac Shakur stands out most, albeit in understated fashion. *Menace II Society* was directed by Allen and Albert Hughes. Alexander is the heroin-addicted mother of a young hood who robs a liquor store with his friend and eventually succumbs to a drive-by shooting. In the course of the film, the viewer comes to know and care for him. One of the most important and enduring films of its era, *Menace* presented an accurate, unvarnished portrait of life in the L.A. hood. Also that year, Alexander played a club owner in *What's Love Got to Do with It*, the story of the turbulent marriage of Ike and Tina Turner.

Recent films include *Rain* (2006), the story of a piano prodigy who comes to grips with her identity. Raised by an African American family, Latitia Arnold learns that she is the daughter of a white socialite who was paying her family to raise her as their own. Her role as Fran Boyd in the six-episode miniseries *The Corner* (2000) was a career highlight for which she was nominated for an NAACP Image Award for Outstanding Actress in a Television Miniseries. In addition, the miniseries won three Emmy Awards, for Best Miniseries and for Best Direction and Writing of a Miniseries. Based on the nonfiction book *The Corner: A Year in the Life of an Inner City Neighborhood*, the film detailed life in a drug-infested neighborhood in 1990s Baltimore and was directed by Charles S. Dutton.

Alexander has landed one memorable series role after another, reaching a career peak as Dr. Alexx Woods on *CSI: Miami* starting in 2002. The *CSI* franchise — the original series and its various spinoffs — is among the most popular in TV history. But before there was *CSI*, there was the role of Catherine Duke on *NewsRadio* (1995–98). This role was ideally tailored to Alexander's skills. Acerbic and a tad prissy, but always impeccably stylish, Catherine was a great straight woman for the other characters. There was also her role on *ER* as Jackie Robbins (1995–2001), the sister of Dr. Peter Benton (Eriq La Salle).

For her role as Alexx Woods, medical examiner, on *CSI: Miami*, she won the NAACP Image Award for Outstanding Supporting Actress in a Drama Series. While Alexx Woods has echoes of the other no-nonsense characters Alexander has specialized in, this is a role that has allowed her to stretch, to find new emotional levels and to indulge in eccentricities and subtleties. Born into a large family that had to scrape by, Dr. Woods early on learned about responsibility and family. Now a wife and mother herself, she expresses compassion for not only the living but for the dead. Indeed, the character is best known for her habit of talking to the bodies she examines. And, forensically speaking, they talk back to her.

Feature Films Including Video and TV Movies: *Streetwalkin'* (1985), *A Chorus Line* (1985), *Maid to Order* (1987), *CB4* (1993), *Joshua Tree* (aka *Army of One*; 1993), *Poetic Justice* (1993), *Menace II Society* (1993), *What's Love Got to Do with It* (1993), *Shameful Secrets* (aka *Going Underground*; 1993), *House Party 3* (1994), *To My Daughter with Love* (TV; 1994), *Greedy* (1994), *Sugar Hill* (1994), *No Easy Way* (1996), *Terminal* (TV; 1996), *Thick as Thieves* (1998), *There's Something About Mary* (1998), *Spawn 3: Ultimate Battle* (1999), *Partners* (TV; 1999), *Dark Blue* (2002), *Emmett's Mark* (aka *Killing Emmett Young*; 2002), *Fool Proof* (2002), *Rain* (2006), *First Born* (2007).

TV: *FTV* (1985), *The Motown Review Starring Smokey Robinson* (1985), *A Different World* ("Citizen Wayne," 1989), *NewsRadio* (recurring role of Catherine Duke; 1995–98), *ER* (recurring role of Jackie Robbins; 1995–2001), *Spawn* (recurring role of Lakesha; 1997), *La Femme Nikita* ("Soul Sacrifice," 1998), *NYPD Blue* ("What's Up, Chuck?" 1999), *Cosby* ("The Awful Truth," 1999), *X-Chromosome* (1999), *Third Watch* ("History," 2000), *Rude Awakening* ("Star 80 Proof," 2000), *The Corner* (6 episode miniseries; 2000), *Law & Order: Special Victims Unit* ("Paranoia," 2001), *CSI: Crime Scene Investigation* (as Dr. Alexx Woods; "Cross-Jurisdictions," 2002), *CSI: Miami* (recurring role of Dr. Alexx Woods; 2002–08), *Life's a Bitch* (2003), *The Late, Late Show with Craig Kilborn* (2003), *Sharon* (2004), *TV Land Moguls* (2004), *CSI: NY* ("Miami/NYC Non-stop," 2004), *CSI: Miami* (2004), *36th NAACP Image Awards* (2005), *TV Land: Myths and Legends* (2007), *Tavis Smiley* (2007).

Khandi Alexander

Ali, Tatyana Born in North Bellmore, Long Island, January 24, 1979.

Tatyana Marisol Ali is best known for her role as Ashley Banks on *The Fresh Prince of Bel-*

Air. She is the daughter of Sonia, a nurse, and Sheriff Ali, a detective. Her mother is a native of Panama and her father is of Indian descent, from Trinidad and Tobago. Ali has two younger sisters, Anastasia and Kimberly. She attended Marymount High School in West Los Angeles and the Buckley School in Sherman Oaks, Los Angeles, California. In 2002, she graduated with a bachelor's degree in anthropology from Harvard.

Ali was an early bloomer. She began her singing career at age four, appearing with musician Herbie Hancock on a segment of *Sesame Street*. By age seven, she had won the *Star Search* youth competition twice. She also sang on various episodes of *Fresh Prince*. Despite her singing ability, Ali decided to concentrate on her acting skills. She was the understudy on Broadway for the role of Raynall in August Wilson's classic *Fences* (1987–88).

The wildly successful *The Fresh Prince of Bel-Air* ran from September 10, 1990, to May 20, 1996. The basic premise was simple but effective: an inner-city teenager (Will Smith) is sent by his mother to live with his upscale relatives in Bel-Air. Ali played Will's younger cousin Ashley Banks. Sheltered by her family, Ashley sees Will as a role model who truly understands her. But Ashley becomes more questioning and rebellious as a result of her attachment to Will, causing family conflicts, especially with her nurturing dad. Ashley grows both physically and psychologically during the course of the series. *Bel-Air* was a mixture of gentle family sitcom powered by the charm of Will Smith, and deeper, more realistic elements exploring aspects of contemporary black life.

After the series ended, Ali returned to her musical roots, releasing the album *Kiss the Sky*, which was certified gold in 1999. This album spawned the hit song "Daydreamin'" (number 6 on *Billboard*'s Hot 100). She also made an appearance on Will Smith's album *Willennium* ("Who Am I?," with MC Lyte). In addition, she starred in the music video for Nick Cannon and Anthony Hamilton's "Can I Live?"

Jawbreaker (1999) was a black comedy variant on the popular film *Heathers*. Three high school students pretend to kidnap their friend, but things become dicey when she accidentally chokes on a gumball (jawbreaker) and dies. In *Nora's Hair Salon* (2004), Ali is a Dominican girl working in Jenifer Lewis's salon, and who is in an abusive relationship with boyfriend Bobby Brown. In *Back in the Day* (2005), she's a preacher's daughter who falls in love with a young man involved in the murder of her father. *Domino One* is a low-budget mystery thriller shot in 2002 but released in 2005. The film was set at Harvard University (including a network of underground tunnels at the school), from which she garnered a degree. Natalie Portman, who was attending Harvard at the time, stars in the film. *Glory Road* (2006), set in the mid–1960s, is the familiar tale of a basketball team that defies the odds to win the big game. Ali had a throwaway role as the sweetheart of one of the players. *Glory Road* had the unfortunate fate of being released around the same time as the much better *Coach Carter* with Samuel L. Jackson and Ashanti.

Feature Films Including Video and TV Movies: *Eddie Murphy Raw* (1987), *Crocodile Dundee II* (1988), *Kidz in the Wood* (TV; 1996), *Fall into Darkness* (TV; 1996), *Fakin' Da Funk* (1997), *Kiss the Girls* (1997), *The Clown at Midnight* (1998), *Jawbreaker* (1999), *Brother* (2000), *The Brothers* (2001), *Dorm Daze* (2003), *Nora's Hair Salon* (2004), *Back in the Day* (2005), *Domino One* (2005), *Glory Road* (2006), *The List* (2006), *Privileged* (2007), *Nora's Hair Salon II* (2007), *Hotel California* (2008), *Privileged* (2008), *The Misguided Adventures of Three Brothers Dating in Hollywood* (2009), *Locker 13* (2009).

TV: *Sesame Street* (various episodes; 1969), *A Man Called Hawk* ("Life After Death," 1989), *The More You Know* (1989), *The Cosby Show* ("Shall We Dance?" 1989), *The Fresh Prince of Bel-Air* (recurring role of Ashley Banks; 1990–96), *Name Your Adventure* (1993), *Getting By* ("Turnabout Dance," 1993), *Are You Afraid of the Dark?* ("The Tale of the Quicksilver," 1994), *TV's Funniest Families* (1994), *In the House* ("Dog Catchers," 1995), *Living Single* ("Whatever Happened to Baby Sister?" 1996), *413 Hope St.* ("Heartbeat," 1997), *The 26th Annual American Music Awards* (1998), *26th NAACP Image Awards* (1998), *Scenes by the Sea: Takeshi Kitano* (2000), *Fastlane* ("Girls' Own Juice," 2002), *The Other Half* (2003), *Half & Half* ("The Big Condom-nation Episode," 2003), *The Great American Celebrity Spelling Bee* (miniseries; 2004), *100 Greatest Kid Stars* (2005), *BET Awards 2005, Starz Special: On the Set of Glory Road* (2006), *Child Star Confidential* (2006), *On the Lot* (2007), *The Young and the Restless* (recurring role as Roxanne; 2007–08).

Video: *Wow, You're a Cartoonist!* (1988),

Wilted, How to Have a Girl, The Malibu Myth and *First Sight* (short films made for the young filmmaker's reality show *On the Lot* (2007).

Alice, Mary Born in Indianola, Mississippi, December 3, 1941.

Mary Alice is a character actress, best known for her work in the theater, but she has also done substantial work in film and television. Her family moved from Mississippi to Chicago when she was two years old. She attended Chicago Teachers College (now Chicago University), and later taught third, fourth and fifth grades. In 1966, she fell in love with a man who drew her into community theater. Her first acting was in *Days of Absence* and *Happy Endings* by the distinguished playwright, director and actor Douglas Turner Ward. For $200 a week she played three roles, and twice a week washed and ironed the cast's laundry. Ward told her that if she ever decided to come to New York he would discuss a place in the Negro Ensemble Company, the most prestigious black repertory group, with her. She did apply for the NEC but was turned down. But Alice persevered and eventually became one of the most critically acclaimed actresses of her generation.

She received the Tony in 1987 for Best Featured Actress in a Play, for August Wilson's *Fences*. She created the role of Rose in *Fences*, starring with James Earl Jones. *Fences* ran from March 26, 1987, to June 26, 1988, and is considered among Wilson's greatest plays. *Fences* is set in 1957–65. Rose is a central character who has defined her life strictly in the role of wife and mother. After 18 years of marriage, her husband informs her that he has gotten another woman pregnant. How Rose evolves after hearing this news is the play's core. Alice, who never married, devoted most of her energies to her career (her de facto "family"), and thus, as she has noted, felt an affinity with Rose.

Another career-best Broadway highlight was *Having Our Say: The Delany Sisters' First 100 Years*, which ran from April 6 to December 31, 1995, at the Booth Theater. Alice starred with Gloria Foster (whom she later replaced in the third *Matrix* film when Foster passed away). Sadie, 101 years old, played by Alice, and 103-year-old Bessie (Foster) are the Delany sisters of Mount Vernon, New York, two real-life women old enough to have lived during the challenging time for descendants of slaves just after the Civil War. Every year they prepare a dinner in remembrance of their father's birthday and, as they cook and set things up, they recall events in their long lives, taking the story through to contemporary times. They talk about their girlhood, the abuses of the Jim Crow era, and their personal success as pioneering African American professional women. Thus their story becomes a microcosm of the history of black women in America. But as the play goes on, we realize that *Having Our Say* is more than a celebration of black life — it is a celebration of human life.

Alice noted that *The Sty of the Blind Pig* (she appeared in the filmed version in 1974) is the "greatest role I've ever been privileged to play." This play in three acts by Phillip Hayes Dean was first presented by the Negro Ensemble Company at the St. Marks Playhouse in New York on November 23, 1971. "A blind pig" was a house of ill repute where liquor and food were also sold. She appeared in the 1983 25th anniversary revival of *A Raisin in the Sun* at the Yale Repertory Theater. She also appeared in *Richard III* as Queen Margaret at the Delacorte Theater in Central Park. Denzel Washington was Richard in this 1990 production.

More recent theater work includes a revival of James Baldwin's *The Amen Corner* in 1996, as storefront minister Sister Margaret Alexander. Her performance received the lion's share of critical attention, as her interpretation found new layers of depth in the character. She also did a two-week stint in off–Broadway's *The Vagina Monologues*.

Her film work also merits discussion. *The Education of Sonny Carson*, her 1974 film debut, was the raw tale of a controversial Brooklyn activist. During the height of the "blaxploitation" era, it was refreshing to see a film that was trying to seek a deeper level. *Sparkle* (1976) was issued on DVD for the first time in 2007. A critic from *Entertainment Weekly* wrote that it was "an even better movie" than *Dreamgirls*. While this Irene Cara vehicle is certainly no match for *Dreamgirls*, it is an underrated B-film. Especially praiseworthy is Mary Alice's performance as Effie, the single mom who supported her three daughters throughout their childhood and now watches with a mixture of caution and pride as they begin to go places in the world of music (as in *Dreamgirls*, the group more than casually resembles The Supremes). Giving her tired role far more substance that the by-the-numbers script provides, Mary Alice makes Effie by turns dynamic, confused, sweet, consummately giving and, in the final analysis, wise. Only in her mid-thirties when she played the role, Alice beautifully crystallized — and saluted — all the mothers who went the extra mile for their children.

To Sleep with Anger (1990) is a key entry in her filmography. African American writer-director Charles Burnett made it almost 13 years after he created the seminal independent film *Killer of Sheep* (1977), which was released theatrically in 2007 to huge critical acclaim after being essentially unseen in the intervening years. In *To Sleep with Anger*, Mary Alice plays a wife not happy about the intrusion when her husband invites an old friend to stay in his house. The friend begins to insinuate his way into the fabric of their lives.

Down in the Delta (1998) is a meandering character study, a simplistic but well-intentioned drama. Rosa Lynn Sinclair (Mary Alice) sends her drug-addicted daughter Loretta and Loretta's children away from their destructive urban environment and into a backwoods delta region. Predictably, the change in scenery evokes positive psychological changes in Loretta.

Catfish in Black Bean Sauce (1999) shows how two Vietnamese refugee children adopted by an African American family in Los Angeles experience family tensions when the daughter locates her birth mother and convinces the mother to fly to L.A. *The Photographer* (2000), a New York based allegory which had limited distribution, is a fantasy about a photographer who discovers the magic of everyday life. The film alternates color and black and white footage. *The Life* (2002) is another independent film set in New York. Emiline Crane (Mary Alice) is an elderly widow who gets along well with her neighbors but she misses her late husband and prizes a locket she wears that holds his picture. When she dies in a fall, she finds herself at heaven's door where a St. Peter type informs her there's been a mistake — she was called 22 years too soon. Director John Sayles' *Sunshine State* (2002) is set in Florida. Mary Alice plays a mother who gets an unexpected visit from her daughter she hasn't seen in years. The story is centered in a true-life African American beach community.

Notable TV movies include *Lawman Without a Gun* (1979), wherein a civil rights activist becomes involved when a black girl is violated by police officers in rural Alabama, and the highly-rated Oprah Winfrey production *The Women of Brewster Place* (1989), based on the Gloria Naylor novel about a group of strong-willed black women living in a neglected housing project. Alice gives a powerful performance as Fannie Michael, who tries to protect her daughter Mattie (Oprah Winfrey) against her abusive husband. Fannie's most powerful scene comes when she grabs a shotgun and points it at her husband.

Charlotte Forten's Mission: Experiment in Freedom (1985) details the life of a pioneering African American educator, played by Melba Moore. *Road to Freedom: The Vernon Johns Story* (1994) has Alice co-starring with James Earl Jones as a minister and civil rights leader active in the civil rights struggle dating back to the 1920s. *The Last Brickmaker in America* (2001) was a sentimental TV film with Sidney Poitier as a man coping with the loss of his wife and the obsolescence of his job. Redemption comes when he acts as a role model to a 13-year-old.

Alice's Emmy was for Outstanding Supporting Actress in a Drama Series (*I'll Fly Away*, 1993). PBS prefaced its rebroadcast of all 39 episodes of the critically lauded NBC series with a new, final episode in which 60-year-old Lilly (Regina Taylor) recalls to her grandson a horrifying incident that took place during her final days as the Bedford family's housekeeper. In 1962, a young black boy from Detroit who came to stay with Lilly was kidnapped, then murdered, after speaking rudely to a white woman. The only witness to the abduction is Lilly's father, Lewis, who yearns to see justice served, but must also consider his family's well being.

Feature Films Including Video and TV Movies: *The Education of Sonny Carson* (1974), *Just an Old Sweet Song* (TV; 1976), *Sparkle* (1976), *Lawman Without a Gun* (aka *He Who Walks Alone*; 1979), *The Brass Ring* (TV; 1983), *Concealed Enemies* (TV; 1984), *Teachers* (1984), *Beat Street* (1984), *Charlotte Forten's Mission: Experiment in Freedom* (TV; 1985), *To Sleep with Anger* (1990), *The Bonfire of the Vanities* (1990), *Malcolm X* (1992), *Life with Mikey* (1993), *Laurel Avenue* (TV; 1993), *A Perfect World* (1993), *The Vernon Johns Story* (TV; 1994), *The Inkwell* (1994), *Ray Alexander: A Menu for Murder* (TV; 1995), *Heading Home* (1995), *Bed of Roses* (1996), *Down in the Delta* (1998), *The Wishing Tree* (1999), *Catfish in Black Bean Sauce* (1999), *The Photogra-*

pher (2000), *The Last Brickmaker in America* (TV; 2001); *The Life* (2002); *Sunshine State* (2002), *The Matrix: Revolutions* (2003).

TV: *The Sty of the Blind Pig* (1974), *Police Woman* ("Target Black," 1975), *Good Times* ("The Baby," 1975), *Sanford and Son* (2 episodes; "Brother Can You Spare an Act?" "My Brother-in-Law's Keeper," 1975), *Serpico* ("The Traitor in Our Midst," 1976), *Visions* ("Scenes from the Middle Class," 1976), *All My Children* (recurring role of Ellie Grant Hubbard; 1970), *ABC Afterschool Specials* ("The Color of Friendship," 1981), *A Different World* (recurring role of Leticia "Lettie" Bostic; 1988–89), *The Women of Brewster Place* (miniseries; 1989), *L.A. Law* ("Watts a Matter?" 1990), *I'll Fly Away* (3 episodes: "The Third Man," "Desperate Measures," "Hard Lessons," 1992) *Law & Order* ("Mother Love," 1993), *Orleans* ("Baby-Sitting," 1997), *Cosby* (3 episodes; "Afterschool Delight," "Lucas Absentia," "The Awful Truth," 1999), *Providence* ("The Gift," 2000), *Touched by an Angel* ("God Bless the Child," 2000), *Soul Food* ("Sex and Money," 2001), *Oz* ("Visitation," 2002), *What I Want My Words to Do to You* (2003), *Line of Fire* ("The Senator," 2004), *The Jury* ("Memories," 2004), *Kojak* ("All That Glitters," 2005).

Allen, Debbie Born in Houston, Texas, January 16, 1950.

Deborrah Kaye "Debbie" Allen is one of the few black women working as a producer and director in television, film, and theatre. She is also a choreographer, dancer, actress, and a member of the President's Committee on the Arts and Humanities. Allen received a star on the Hollywood Walk of Fame in October 1992 for her consistent career efforts. Her father, Andrew Allen, was a dentist, and her mother, Vivian Ayers Allen, a Pulitzer Prize–nominated writer for her poetry book *Spice of Dawns*.

As a child, Allen tried to take ballet classes at the Houston Foundation for Ballet, but was rejected for what her mother felt were discriminatory reasons. Allen auditioned again in 1964 and was admitted on a full scholarship, becoming the company's first black dancer. She initially began to learn dance by studying with a former member of the Ballet Russes, and later by moving with her family to Mexico City, where she danced with the Ballet Nacional de Mexico. Allen earned a bachelor of arts degree in classical Greek literature, speech and theater from Howard University and holds honorary doctorates from Howard and the North Carolina School for the Arts. During her college years she continued to dance both at the university and with the Michael Malone dance troupe.

After graduating in 1971, she relocated to New York City, where she honed her talents as a dancer, singer and actress. She started her Broadway career in 1971 as a chorus member in *Purlie*, the musical version of Ossie Davis's *Purlie Victorious*. When chorus member George Faison left *Purlie* in 1972 to form the Universal Dance Experience, Debbie became his principal dancer and assistant. In 1973 she returned to Broadway and for two years played the role of Beneatha Younger in *Raisin*, the musical adaptation of Lorraine Hansbury's *A Raisin in the Sun*.

Allen made the stretch to major Broadway stardom in 1980 when she appeared in the role of Anita in the revival of *West Side Story*, which earned her a Tony nomination and a Drama Desk Award. In 1986, she played Charity in the Broadway revival of Bob Fosse's *Sweet Charity*, and received a second Tony nomination. She choreographed the Broadway musical flop *Carrie* (1988), which closed after five performances.

The past decade has seen the return of Debbie Allen to her theatrical roots. Allen has enjoyed a long-standing relationship with the Kennedy Center in Washington, D.C., as artist in residence, and has created seven original musicals for the center. *Pepito's Story* (1996) was loosely based on the classic fairy tale *The Twelve Dancing Princesses*. In 1997, she directed *Brothers of the Knight*, which she turned into a children's book of the same name. Debuts of *Soul Possessed* and *Dreams* were in 2000. *Pearl* followed in 2001, and *Dancing in the Wings* in 2005. The end of 2006 saw the debut of her *The Bayou Legend* at the Glorya Kaufman Hall at the University of California Los Angeles (UCLA). *Alex in Wonderland*, a musical exploring the relevance of fairy tales to older children, premiered at the Kennedy Center in 2007.

Allen made her Broadway directing debut with an all-black production of *Cat on a Hot Tin Roof* (2008). This was the first authorized African American production of the Tennessee Williams classic. James Earl Jones took acting honors as Big Daddy. It was an entertaining if unexceptional take on Williams' compassionate play, which at any rate is starting to show its age.

Debbie Allen

Despite her Broadway and Kennedy Center achievements, Allen is perhaps best known to the mass audience for her role as teacher Lydia Grant in the TV series *Fame*, first appearing as Lydia in the 1980 film that inspired the series. She was lead choreographer for both the film and the series. Allen won two Emmys and a Golden Globe Award for her performance on *Fame*. She eventually served as a director of and producer for the series, and she stayed with *Fame* until it went off the air in 1987. The kinetic program had a large influence on music videos and youth-oriented films. Allen spun off the *Fame* franchise into a reality show competition (2003), but in the era of *American Idol*, it was too much of a carbon copy to be a success.

Allen has choreographed for Sammy Davis Jr., Janet and Michael Jackson, Gwen Verdon, and Mariah Carey. Her choreography for *The Motown 25th Anniversary Special* (1983) won her an Emmy Award. Today she teaches young dancers at her Debbie Allen Dance Academy, a cultural center providing professional training, furthering the artistic development of professional dancers, and fostering youth-focused outreach and education initiatives.

There was abundant life beyond *Fame* for Debbie Allen's television career with *The Cosby Show* spin-off *A Different World*. This was the series that allowed Allen to blossom as a television producer-director. She drew from her own college experiences to accurately portray life on a black campus. Despite the ostensibly light tone of the series, *A Different World* addressed racial and political issues such as apartheid and discrimination, the Persian Gulf War, color issues within the black community, AIDS, the Los Angeles riots, and much else. The late 1980s and early 1990s (and beyond) was a busy time for Allen in television. She hosted her own TV special on ABC in 1989. It received two Emmy nominations for direction and choreography. She also directed the TV musical *Polly* (1989), a remake of Disney's *Pollyanna*, and its sequel *Polly: Comin' Home* (1990). She directed episodes of NBC's *Fresh Prince of Bel-Air* (pilot), *Quantum Leap*, *The Cosby Show*, and later, *The Jamie Foxx Show*, *That's So Raven*, *Girlfriends* and *Everybody Hates Chris*. She produced and directed the TV movie *Stompin' at the Savoy* (1992). And she recently directed *Life Is Not a Fairytale: The Fantasia Barrino Story* (2006), the second highest rated film in Lifetime channel history.

As her career bloomed as a TV director, Allen continued to be a busy actress and choreographer. She appeared in the film version of E.L. Doctorow's *Ragtime* (1981). She played the wife of author Alex Haley in the epochal miniseries *Roots* (1977). She produced *Amistad* with Steven Spielberg (Allen had owned the story for more than 10 years). Allen choreographed the Academy Awards 10 times, including six years in a row. She has been the recipient of 10 NAACP Image Awards. In 1992, she received the *Essence* Award. In 1995, Allen directed an urban action film set in the world of rave music, *Out-of-Sync*, with LL Cool J, Victoria Dillard, and Yaphet Kotto.

Allen's first husband was Wim Wilford; she is now married to former NBA player Norm Nixon. Her daughter, Vivian Nichole, was born in 1984; her son, Norman, Jr., was born in 1987. She is the sister of Phylicia Rashad, well known for her work on Broadway, including her sister's recent production of *Cat on a Hot Tin Roof*, and especially for her role as Claire Huxtable on *The Cosby Show*. She appeared with Debbie in *The Old Settler* (2001), directed by Allen as part of the *PBS Hollywood Presents* series. *The Old Settler* is based on a play by John Henry Redwood. Two middle-aged sisters share a Harlem apartment in 1943, the era of the Harlem Renaissance. A young man boards with the sisters, becomes romantically involved with one, and creates a situation that lays bare many wounds. Rashad and Allen were also the executive producers.

Feature Films Including Video and TV Movies: *Dancing in the Wings* (TV; 1977), *Ebony, Ivory and Jade* (TV; 1979), *The Fish That Saved Pittsburgh* (1979), *Fame* (1980), *Ragtime* (1981), *Alice at the Palace* (TV; 1982), *Women of San Quentin* (TV; 1983), *Jo Jo Dancer, Your Life Is Calling* (1986), *Stompin' at the Savoy* (TV; 1992), *Blank Check* (1994), *Mona Must Die* (1994), *Out-of-Sync* (1995), *Michael Jordan: An American Hero* (TV; 1999), *Everything's Jake* (2000), *All About You* (2001), *The Painting* (video title: *Soldiers of Change*, 2001), *Tournament of Dreams* (2007), *Confessions of an Action Star* (2008), *A Star for Rose* (2008), *Next Day Air* (2009).

TV: *Good Times* ("J.J.'s Fiancée," Parts 1 and 2, 1976), *3 Girls 3* (various episodes; 1979), *Ben Vereen: His Roots* (1978), *Roots: The Next Generations* (miniseries; 1979), *The Hollywood Squares* (1979), *The Love Boat* (3 episodes; 1979–83), *Drawing Power* (voice; 1980), *The 34th Annual Tony Awards* (1980), *The 39th Annual Golden Globe Awards* (1982), *Battle of the Network Stars XII* (1982), *Battle of the Network Stars XIII* (1982), *Fame* (recurring role of Lydia Grant; 1982–87), *The Best of Everything* (1983), *Fame* (3 special episodes; "Fame Looks at Music '83," "The Kids from Fame in Israel," "The Kids from Fame in Concert," 1983–84), *The 11th Annual American Music Awards* (1984), *Star Search* (1984), *Celebrity* (miniseries; 1984), *A Celebration of Life: A Tribute to Martin Luther King, Jr.* (1984), *The 57th Annual Academy Awards* (1985), *The 27th Annual Grammy Awards* (1985), *Disneyland's 30th Anniversary Celebration* (1985), *Motown Returns to the Apollo* (1985), *Night of 100 Stars II* (1985), *Liberty Weekend* (1986), *The 40th Annual Tony Awards* (1986), *Las Vegas: An All-Star 75th Anniversary* (1987), *Happy 100th Birthday, Hollywood* (1987), *Emmanuel Lewis: My Very Own Show* (1987), *Square One TV* (1987), *19th Annual NAACP Image Awards* (1987), *The Cosby Show* ("If the Dress Fits, Wear It," 1988), *The Debbie Allen Special* (1989), *Motown 30: What's Goin' On!* (1990), *Sammy Davis Jr. 60th Anniversary Celebration* (1990), *Story of a People: The Black Road to Hollywood* (1990), *Quantum Leap* ("Private Dancer," 1991), *Sunday in Paris* (unsold TV pilot; 1991), *A Different World* (3 episodes; "Twelve Steps of Christmas," "Ex-communication," "Honeymoon in L.A.," Part 1, 1991–92), *Soul Train Comedy Awards* (1993), *She TV* (series regular; 1994), *The American Teacher Awards* (1994), *The Sinbad Show* ("The Telethon," 1994), *Hollywood Women* (1994), *50 Years of Funny Females* (1995), *Touched by an Angel* ("Sins of the Father," 1996), *C-Bear and Jamal* (voice; 1996), *In the House* (3 episodes; "Come Back, Kid," "Christmas Story," Getting to Know You," 1995–96), *Celebrate the Dream: 50 Years of Ebony Magazine* (1996), *Cosby* ("Dating Games," 1997), *3rd Annual Screen Actors Guild Awards* (1997), *Intimate Portrait* (5 segments; 1998–2000), *Healthy Kids* (series regular; 1998), *The Rosie O'Donnell Show* (1999), *The 71st Annual Academy Awards* (1999), *The Directors* (1999), *Living Positive* (1999), *PBS Hollywood Presents: The Old Settler* (2001), *An Evening of Stars: A Celebration of Educational Excellence* (2001), *Silent Crisis: Diabetes Among Us* (2002), *Inside TV Land: Black Americans in Television* (2002), *It's Black Entertainment* (2002), *The 4th Annual Family Television Awards* (2002), *Inside TV Land: Taboo TV* (2002), *Bill Nye and Debbie Allen Imagine Mars* (2002), *E! True Hollywood Story* ("Gimme a Break," 2003), *The Division* ("Heart of the City," 2003), *Fame* (reality series, as herself; 2003), *9th Annual Soul Train Lady of Soul Awards* (2003), *All of Us* ("Parents Just Don't Understand," 2004), *An Evening of Stars: 25th Anniversary Tribute to Lou Rawls* (2004), *AFI's 100 Years...100 Songs* (2004), *An Evening of Stars: Tribute to Quincy Jones* (2005), *Black in the '80s* (2005), *Mississippi Rising* (2005), *TV Land Confidential* (2 segments; "Being Bad Be-

Debbie Allen in *Jo Jo Dancer, Your Life Is Calling* (1986).

hind the Scenes," "Network Notes," 2005), *Legends Ball* (2006), *I Was a Network Star* (2006), *So You Think You Can Dance* (2007), *The 2007 Miss American Pageant, Broadway: Beyond the Golden Age* (2008), *Silent Rhythm* (2008).

Allen, Jonelle Born in New York, New York, July 18, 1944.

Although her early career highlights were on Broadway, Jonelle Allen has also had a career in films and on television. She was the only child of Marion, a postal worker, and Robert Allen, who worked for the New York City Transit Authority. Her parents divorced when she was five, and she lived with her mother, her aunt Bea, and her maternal grandmother. Her grandfather, the first black post office supervisor in New York City, was a skilled jazz saxophonist who taught neighborhood kid (and future jazz legend) Sonny Rollins how to play. Allen was enrolled by Bea in a children's dance class, where she was discovered by a talent scout from *The Merry Mailman*, a popular local kiddie show seen on WOR-TV, channel 9, and starring Ray Heatherton, who would come on in his postman's suit, do comedy sketches, and introduce Crusader Rabbit cartoons. Allen made recurring appearances on the show. The young Allen also played a Sunday school kid trying to visualize what heaven was like in the *Hallmark Hall of Fame* production of *Green Pastures* (1957). She made her Broadway debut in *The Wisteria Trees* (1950), Joshua Logan's Americanized adaptation of Chekhov's *The Cherry Orchard*, starring Helen Hayes. She returned to Broadway for a 1955 revival of *Finian's Rainbow* (as Honey Lou); it only ran 15 performances. And she appeared in *Small War on Murray Hill* (1957) by Robert E. Sherwood, directed by Garson Kanin. That show closed in nine days.

Allen lived in Harlem's exclusive Sugar Hill section, worked on Broadway, and attended a private school, Walden, on trendy Central Park West. But by age 11, she quickly became too tall for cute little girl roles and her days as a child entertainer were over. At 13, she entered New York's Professional Children's School. In her senior year, an agent told her that Joseph Papp, founder of the New York Shakespeare Festival, was auditioning young singers and dancers for a new, offbeat musical called *Hair*. Papp recognized her talent, and Allen got a role in the landmark production. It was the inaugural offering (1967) at the Public Theater on Lafayette Street, which continues to offer outstanding new plays to this day. *Hair* became a smash international hit and was brought to Broadway by a new production team. Allen decided not to stay with the show, and chose instead to take a role in *George M* (1968–69) starring Joel Gray and Bernadette Peters, which ran for over 400 performances.

Then Allen landed the role that made her a star, *Two Gentlemen of Verona* (1971–73), which was first presented as one of the New York Shakespeare Festival's free productions in Central Park. This irreverent musical version of Shakespeare was a smash hit all summer long. It was given an innovative (for the time) rock score at the suggestion of director Mel Shapiro. It moved indoors to Broadway for a healthy run of 627 performances, and then moved on to Los Angeles. Besides a Tony nomination, Allen received a New York Drama Critics' Circle Award, the Drama Desk and Theater World Awards, and the Outer Critics Circle Award. This has proven to be her last Broadway appearance to date, although she has continued to appear in stage productions elsewhere. These include Shakespeare's *As You Like It* at the Long Beach Theatre (directed by Tony Richardson). In 2007, Allen appeared as the legendary Harlem jazz queen Florence Mills in *Harlem Renaissance* at the Edinburgh Fringe Festival. For this she received some of the best reviews of her career.

After taking *Two Gentlemen of Verona* to L.A., she decided to permanently move there and concentrate on film work, but it wasn't until the spring of 1989 with the premiere of NBC daytime soap *Generations*— the first daytime TV series in which one of the major families was black — that Allen settled in for an extended two-year series run. The show was very controversial for its time and received a huge amount of press.

Despite her numerous appearances on TV, including a recurring role on *Dr. Quinn, Medicine Woman* (the first substantial role for a female black character in a TV western), Allen may be most fondly remembered for her role of the "out there" Doreen Jackson in *Generations*. Allen was outrageous as the pill-popping Doreen, who became pregnant with a baby that was not from her husband. The soap received hate mail, and racism may have helped lead to its early cancellation, but *Generations* did more than its share to integrate daytime TV and entertain viewers with its outrageous melodrama. This was the height of the "blaxploitation" era in films, and action roles were the rage. *Come Back, Charleston Blue* (1972) was the sequel to the popular *Cotton Comes to Harlem* (1970), based on the Chester Himes' novels about hip, seen-it-all black detectives Coffin Ed Johnson and Grave Digger Jones. Allen gets a grapefruit rubbed into her face like Mae Clarke in *Public Enemy*. She also appeared in the 1976 film version of the Negro Ensemble Company's production of Joseph A. Walker's Tony Award–winning play *The River Niger*. The film version of this slice of ghetto life was generally not well received. The central character is Johnny Williams, a house painter who yearns to be a successful poet, struggling to support his wife Mattie, who is suffering from cancer.

TV movies include *Vampire* (1979), wherein the title character's sleep is disturbed by the construction of a new church; and the critically lambasted miniseries version of Aldous Huxley's *Brave New World* (1980). In 1994 she was one of the narrators of the audio cassette *Kwanzaa Folktales*. Allen's husband is Richard Grimmon (they married in 1998).

Feature Films Including Video and TV Movies: *Cotton Comes to Harlem* (1970), *The Cross and the Switchblade* (1970), *Come Back, Charleston Blue* (1972), *Cage Without a Key* (1975), *Foster and Laurie* (TV; 1975), *The River Niger* (1976), *Vampire* (TV; 1979), *Brave New World* (TV; 1980), *Victims* (TV; 1982), *The Hotel New Hampshire* (1984), *The Midnight Hour* (TV; 1985), *The Penalty Phase* (TV; 1986), *Grave Secrets: The Legacy of Hilltop Drive* (TV; 1992), *Next Time* (1998), *Blues for Red* (1999), *Dr. Quinn, Medicine Woman: The Movie* (TV; 1999), *Flossin* (2001), *Mr. Barrington* (2003), *As Seen on TV* (2005), *Float* (2008).

TV: *The Merry Mailman* (various episodes; 1950–56), *Hallmark Hall of Fame* (*Green Pastures*, 1957), *NBC Follies* (1973), *World Wide Mystery* ("Legacy of Blood," 1974), *Police Woman* (2 episodes; "Above and Beyond," "The End Game," 1974), *Barney Miller* ("Hot Dogs," 1975), *Police Story* (2 episodes; "The Company Man," "The Execution," 1975), *Joe Forrester* ("The Boy Next Door," 1976), *The Peter Marshall Variety Show* (1976), *What's Happening!!* ("Rerun Sees the Light," 1978), *The Love Boat* (1978), *All in the Family* ("Archie's Other Wife," 1978), *The White Shadow* ("Airball," 1979), *Battle of the Network Stars VIII* (1980), *Palmerstown U.S.A.* (recurring role of Bessie Freeman; 1980), *Trapper John, M.D.* ("Medicine Man," 1982), *Hill Street Blues* ("The Count of Monty Tasco," 1984), *Cagney & Lacey* (2 episodes; "Open and Shut Case," "A Killer's Dozen," 1983 and 1984), *Body Language* (1984), *Berrenger's* (recurring role of Stacey Russell; 1985), *The Hitchhiker* ("Made for Each Other," 1987), *Werewolf* ("Big Daddy," 1987), *Generations* (recurring role of Doreen Jackson; 1989), *The 11th Annual Black Achievement Awards* (1990), *Dr. Quinn, Medicine Woman* (recurring role of Grace; 1993–97), *The Eddie Files* ("Patterns: The Big Concert," 1997), *Twice in a Lifetime* ("Healing Touch," 1999), *Strong Medicine* ("Stages," 2002), *ER* (2 episodes; "Rescue Me," "Foreign Affairs," 2000 and 2003), *TV in Black: The First Fifty Years* (2004), *Girlfriends* ("Operation Does She Yield," 2007).

Jonelle Allen in *Cagney & Lacey*.

Anderson, Ester (Esther) Born in Kingston, Jamaica, 1945.

Any history of reggae music and Caribbean film would be incomplete without including Ester Anderson. These days Anderson is best known as a photographer whose work recorded the era of Bob Marley and the Wailers in a unique series of candid shots. But this prime mover in the world of reggae also had a decade-long career in films. She co-starred with Sydney Poitier in the romantic cross-cultural love story *A Warm December* (1983).

She worked with Island Records in Jamaica from the late fifties to the early nineties, promoting Jamaican artists abroad (label founder Chris Blackwell launched the international career of Bob Marley). She was personal manager to Millie Small, Jimmy Cliff, and Bob Marley and the Wailers, and had a close relationship with the legendary Marley, the most important figure in Caribbean music. Her career as an actress started in the early sixties with roles in British TV shows, most prominently an episode of *The Avengers*.

Feature Films Including Video and TV Movies: *Genghis Khan* (1965), *Theatre of Death* (1966), *The Touchables* (1968), *Two Gentlemen Sharing* (1969), *One More Time* (1970), *The Harder They Come* (1972), *A Warm December* (1973).

TV: *The Avengers* ("Small Game for Big Hunters," 1966), *Dixon of Dock Green* ("English-Born and Bred," 1968), *The Wednesday Play* ("The Exiles," 1969), *The Rookies* (2 episodes in the role of Pamela Hines; "The Authentic Death of Billy Stomper," "Invitation to a Rumble," 1974 and 1975; her role in "Invitation" consists solely of flashback footage from the first episode, in which her character died).

Anderson, Sylvia Born in St. Louis, Missouri.

The product of a family with nine brothers and sisters, the 6'1" Sylvia Anderson has lived her entire adult life in Los Angeles. She is best known for the "blaxploitation" era film *Ebony, Ivory and Jade* (1976). An American track team arrives in the Philippines for an international competition. Among the competitors are Ginger and Pam (conveniently nicknamed "Ivory" and "Ebony"), who meet up with another friend, Jackie (aka "Jade"). Unfortunately, girls from the team are being kidnapped for ransom. As some fans have pointed out, *Ebony, Ivory and Ebony* would actually have been a better title for the film, since Jade is shot and killed off early in the action. Rosanne Katon, Colleen Camp and Sylvia Anderson make up the trio for the bulk of the movie, and provide most of the martial arts action (as clumsily staged as it may be).

Angels Brigade (1979) is another exploitation film, although not nearly as well known, despite the names in the cast. Peter Lawford and Jack Palance appear as leaders of a drug cartel. Anderson is stuntwoman Terry Grant, part of another avenging female action team, one of seven women who decide to join forces to fight the drug operation. They destroy the processing plant and intercept a shipment, then make a final attack. This was typical action fare inspired by *Charlie's Angels*.

The First Family (1980) is a political satire. Despite being directed and written by the well-regarded (and very hot at the time) Buck Henry, and despite a large name cast (Bob Newhart, Gilda Radner, Fred Willard, and Madeline Khan), this was a total critical and box office failure. It was the last film for Anderson, who had a small role.

Feature Films Including TV Movies: *Ebony, Ivory and Jade* (aka *American Beauty Hostages, Foxforce, She Devils in Chains, Foxfire*, 1976), *Dawn: Portrait of a Teenage Runaway* (TV; 1976), *Angels Brigade* (aka *Angels' Revenge, Seven from Heaven*, 1979), *First Family* (1980).

TV: *Starsky and Hutch* ("The Psychic," 1977).

Andrews, Tina Born in Chicago, Illinois, April 23, 1951.

Tina Andrews was born in the upper middle class section of Chicago known as Pill Hill. She attended New York University, where she majored in film. Although Andrews is now known primarily as a screenwriter and producer, she has been an actress since age 18 and has worked in theater, on television, and in films. She won the title role in *Ermendarde* on Broadway and joined the touring company of *Hello, Dolly!* with Pearl Bailey and Cab Calloway. *Conrack* (1974), with Jon Voight, was her first major film role. She was a regular on the CBS drama series *The Contender* (1980), playing the feisty assistant trainer of a young boxer.

When she was cast in director Martin Ritt's *Carny* (1980), Ritt encouraged her to move to Los Angeles, where she became a cast member of the soap opera *Days of Our Lives*. Her character, Valerie Grant, was involved in daytime TV's first interracial relationship. This pairing received considerable media attention at the time, as well as a flood of negative viewer mail. Her character was written out of the show, and Tina Andrews was out of work and in a financial bind. This is when she decided to embark on the path that eventually saw her become one of the top female TV and film writers.

A role in the historic miniseries *Roots* (1977) forged a life-altering professional relationship with author Alex Haley. Haley read one of the unproduced scripts she had written and hired her to collaborate with him on an eight-part PBS series called *Alex Haley's Great Men of African Descent.* He became not only her literary mentor but also very much a second father to her. Although he died before completion of the PBS project, his tutelage and influence led to Andrews' first screenplay sale at Columbia Pictures, as well as script doctoring chores and other writing assignments.

Her big breakthrough came when she wrote and co-executive produced the CBS miniseries *Sally Hemings: An American Scandal* (2000), which was based on her play *The Mistress of Monticello*, the historic story of the long-hidden, still controversial relationship between Thomas Jefferson, third president of the United States, and his slave Sally Hemings. The miniseries won the Writers Guild of America 2000 award for Outstanding Long Form (television), and the NAACP Image Award for Outstanding Miniseries, TV Movie or Special. Andrews wrote a book about her creative experience, *Sally Hemings, An American Scandal: The Struggle to Tell the Controversial True Story* (2001), a behind-the-scenes memoir of her 15-year struggle to create the miniseries. Among the incidents Andrews recalls in the book are the protestors gathered in front of the CBS affiliate in Philadelphia, picketing the presentation of the series.

She worked on a sequel to *Sally Hemings* called *Daughters of the Declaration*. Andrews also wrote the Warner Bros. film *Why Do Fools Fall in Love* (1998), and co-wrote (and co-executive produced) the CBS miniseries *Jackie Bouvier Kennedy Onassis* (2000). She also created an animated Internet series called *Sistas 'n the City*. Andrews is a popular guest lecturer with speaking engagements at seminars, colleges and universities. She is married to documentary filmmaker and theatrical producer Stephen Gaines.

Feature Films Including TV Movies: *The ABC Saturday Superstar Movie: Willie Mays and the Say-Hey Kid* (voice; 1972), *The Weekend Nun* (1972), *The Girls of Huntington House* (1973), *Hit!* (1973), *Conrack* (1974), *Born Innocent* (TV; 1974),

Tina Andrews in *The Contender*.

McNaughton's Daughter (TV; 1976), *Billy: Portrait of a Street Kid* (TV; 1977), *Carny* (1980), *Off the Mark* (aka *Crazy Legs*; 1987).

TV: *The Brady Bunch* ("Getting Davy Jones," 1971), *The Mod Squad* ("Can You Hear Me Out There?" 1972), *Tenafly* ("Joyride to Nowhere," 1973), *Love Story* ("A Glow of Dying Embers," 1973), *Sanford and Son* (2 episodes; "Here Comes the Bride, There Goes the Bride," "Sanford and Niece," 1972 and 1974), *The Odd Couple* (2 episodes; "The Big Broadcast," "Old Flames Never Die," 1974–75), *The Streets of San Francisco* ("Solitaire," 1975), *Mannix* ("Hardball," 1975), *Good Times* ("Henrietta," 1975), *Police Story* ("Face for a Shadow," 1975), *Days of Our Lives* (recurring role of Valerie Grant; 1975–77), *The Sanford Arms* (recurring role of Angie Wheeler; 1977), *Quincy: M.E.* ("The Thigh Bone's Connected to the Knee Bone," 1977), *Roots* (miniseries; 1977), *The Contender* (recurring role; 1980), *Trapper John, M.D.* ("A Piece of the Action," 1982), *At Ease* ("Valentine's Day," 1983), *Falcon Crest* (recurring role of Valerie: "Solitary Confinement," "Chameleon Charades," "The Double Dealing," "The Betrayal," "Coup d'Etat," 1983), *The Atlanta Child Murders* (miniseries; 1985), *What's Happening Now!* ("Ask Al," 1987), *Charles in Charge* ("Still at

Large," 1989), *Beauty and the Beast* ("A Distant Shore," 1989), *Roots: Celebrating 25 Years* (2002).

Video/DVD: *Sistas 'n the City* (2003).

Arcieri, Leila Born in San Francisco, California, December 18, 1973.

The daughter of an Italian American father and African American mother, Leila Arcieri is a sought-after model as well as an emerging actress. Her mother is an employee of Lucasfilm, the George Lucas company. She spent much of her childhood in Sebastopol, located in California's wine and redwood country. She was a high school cheerleader and an athlete involved in swimming, volleyball, basketball, football, rock climbing and kickboxing, among other activities.

After graduating from high school she moved to San Francisco, where she dabbled in graphic design and photography before becoming a make-up artist. Arcieri made an early foray into the public eye as Miss San Francisco in the 1997 Miss California pageant. Then she started appearing in commercials (1-800 phone spots and Starburst ads), became a spokeswoman for Coors Lite Beer in 2000, and appeared in music videos (Boyz II Men, Q-Tip), which brought her to the attention of producer Timothy Stack and led to her role as Jamaica St. Croix on *Son of the Beach*, a critically lauded parody of *Baywatch*. A lengthy relationship with Jamie Foxx and a prominent role in the direct-to-DVD sequel to *Wild Things* kept her name in the news.

Feature Films Including Video and TV Movies: *Hot Boyz* (1999), *Beverly Hood* (1999), *Foolish* (1999), *Higher Ed* (2001), *xXx* (2002), *Daddy Day Care* (2003), *Double Blade* (2003), *Wild Things 2* (2004), *A Perfect Fit* (2005), *King's Ransom* (2005), *Mammoth* (TV; 2006), *Babylon Fields* (TV; 2007), *Love N' Dancing* (2008), *Buffalo Bushido* (2008), *Death Toll* (2008), *Killing of Wendy* (2008), *Ultimate Champion* (2008).

TV: *MADtv* (1997), *Rescue 77* (pilot; 1999), *Howard Stern Show* (6 segments; 1999–2001), *Cousin Skeeter* ("The Feminine Ms. Skeet," 2000), *Son of the Beach* (recurring role of Jamaica St. Croix; 2000–2002), *Jeremiah* ("The Face in the Mirror," 2003), *Kevin Hill* (recurring role of Monroe McManus; 2004–2005), *CSI: NY* ("City of the Dolls," 2005), *The PTA* (2006), *Prescriptions* (2006), *One on One* ("Fame and the Older Woman," 2006), *Las Vegas* ("Like a Virgin," 2006), *CSI: Miami* ("Shock," 2006).

Arnold, Tichina Born in Queens, New York, June 28, 1971.

Tichina Arnold and her younger sister were born into a middle-class family; her father was a police officer and her mother was a sanitation worker. By age eight, Arnold had already begun auditioning for a show business career and landed her first role in *The Me Nobody Knows* at the Billie Holiday Theater in Brooklyn. This was followed by yeoman work in a lot of theater, supper club and off–Broadway productions. Like so many future celebrities, she attended the High School of Music and Art.

Arnold appeared as Crystal in the 1986 film version of *Little Shop of Horrors* (at age 16), along with future *Martin* cast mate Tisha Campbell. As one of the tongue-in-cheek girl group trio — doubling as a sort of Greek chorus that summarizes the story — she got to cut loose, and looked great in a Supremes-style diva gown. She toured with the stage version of *Little Shop*. She then did two years as the troubled teen character Zena Brown in the daytime soap *Ryan's Hope* (and was nominated for a daytime Emmy Award for her efforts), and during the same period appeared as Sharla Valentine in another soap, *All My Children*.

At 21, Arnold headed west to L.A.; two months later she landed her long-running role on *Martin* (1992–97). For much of the early part of her career, she was best known for the role of Pam, the second female lead on the long-running sitcom, which was centered on the talents of star Martin Lawrence. Although fairly standard sitcom stuff, *Martin* was driven by its strong cast and helped put the fledgling FOX network on the map. Although the role of the caustic but vulnerable Pam was not the most complex of parts, Arnold stole more than her share of scenes.

Arnold is currently featured on the Golden Globe nominated series *Everybody Hates Chris*. She won an NAACP Image Award for the first season of her work as Rochelle Rock, the small screen counterpart to the real-life mother of Chris Rock, upon whose childhood life this poignant, Jean Shepherd–like series is focused. Arnold notes that her character is based more on the women who raised her (her mother, aunt, and grandmother) than it is on herself.

To date, the quality of the theatrical films Arnold has appeared in have not been worthy of her ability. This includes the unfunny romantic comedy *How I Got into College* (1989), which sought to tap the dregs of the *Animal House* audience; *Fakin' Da Funk* (1997), a fish-out-of-water comedy wherein two Asian kids — one adopted by a black family, one an exchange student — try to adapt to life in South Central Los Angeles; and *Civil Brand* (2002), a stereotyped women-in-prison drama in which Arnold is one of the inmates.

Wild Hogs (2007) was an outstanding financial success about four middle-aged suburban friends who decide to fulfill a lifetime dream and take to the road on their motorcycles. It reunited her with *Martin* star Martin Lawrence. She contributed background vocals to *Push*, Tisha Campbell's debut album. The two friends and co-artists also did a duet (1997) on a cover version of The Emotions' "Don't Ask My Neighbor" for the soundtrack of the romantic comedy *Sprung*, which starred Campbell. Arnold has a daughter, Alijah Kai (born 2004), from a relationship with ex-boyfriend Carvin Haggins.

Feature Films Including Video and TV Movies: *The Brass Ring* (TV; 1983), *House of Dies Drear* (TV; 1984), *Little Shop of Horrors* (1986), *Starlight: A Musical Movie* (1988), *How I Got into College* (1989), *Scenes from a Mall* (1991), *Fakin' da Funk* (1997), *Perfect Prey* (TV; 1998), *A Luv Tale* (short; 1999), *Dancing in September* (2000), *Big Momma's House* (2000), *Civil Brand* (2002), *Yo Alien* (short; 2002), *On the One* (aka *Preaching to the Choir*, 2005), *Getting Played* (2005), *Wild Hogs* (2007), *Drillbit Taylor* (2008), *The Lena Baker Story* (2008).

TV: *All My Children* (recurring role of Sharla Valentine; 1989–90), *The Cosby Show* ("Theo's Women," 1989), *Ryan's Hope* (recurring role of Zena Brown; 1989), *Law & Order* ("Out of the Half-Light," 1990), *Martin* (recurring role of Pam James, 1992–97), *The Jamie Foxx Show* ("Soul Mate to Cellmate," 1998), *Pacific Blue* ("Ghost Town," 1999), *The Norm Show* ("Norm vs. the Boxer," 1999), *One on One* (recurring role of Nicole Barnes, 2001–05), *Soul Food* ("Past Imperfect," 2002), *Biography* (2002), *Intimate Portrait* (2002), *Punk'd* (2004), *Listen Up* ("Thanksgiving," 2004), *Everybody BET Comedy Awards* (2005), *Weekends at the DL* (2005), *The Late, Late Show with Craig Ferguson* (2006), *Hi-Jinks* (2006), *Keith Barry: Extraordinary* (2006), *Jimmy Kimmel Live!* (2006), *The Megan Mullally Show* (2007), *Angels Can't Help But Laugh* (2007), *Entertainment Tonight* (2008).

Ashanti (aka Douglas, Ashanti) Born in Glen Cove, Long Island, New York, October 13, 1980.

Pop singer Ashanti has developed into a poised actress working in a variety of film genres. Ashanti Shequoiya Douglas, in addition to being an actress and singer, is a songwriter (for Christina Milian, Ja Rule, Jennifer Lopez, Nas, and Toni Braxton), a record producer, dancer, model and a fashion designer. Her biggest claim to fame to date is her Grammy Award–winning debut album *Ashanti*. It sold over 500,000 copies in its first week of release (April, 2002), and charted three top-10 songs on the *Billboard* Hot 100 chart in the same week. Ashanti was the first female artist to accomplish this feat (and second performer overall, after the Beatles). She was also the first female to hold the top two places in the Hot 100 chart. By 2007, she had sold more than 7 million albums in the U.S. and over 12 million worldwide.

Ashanti is of a racial mix: her mother (a former dance teacher, singer and a computer specialist) is three-fourths African American and one-fourth Dominican; her dad is half African American and half Chinese. Growing up, Ashanti took dance lessons, joined the church choir, and studied at the Bernice Johnson Cultural Arts Center. She danced at Carnegie Hall, the Apollo, the Brooklyn Academy of Music, Avery Fisher Hall, and the Black Spectrum Theater. She also performed at the 1994 Caribbean Awards and danced with Judith Jamison of the Alvin Ailey Dance Company. Her skills in the 100- and 200-meter dash led to offers of athletic scholarships to Princeton and Hampton universities.

Ashanti's huge singing career started when her mother began wooing recording executives and sending demo tapes to record producers. Epic Records offered a contract in 1998, but management changes left Ashanti in the lurch. Undaunted, she continued to sing at local New York clubs and began hanging out at the Murder Inc. recording studio. Murder Inc. guru Irv Gotti noted her abilities as a singer, dancer and actress, and offered her a recording contract. Her second album, *Chapter II*, was released in 2003. Ashanti and her sister Kenashia sang on the first *Disney Mania* CD (2002; "Colors of the Wind"); she went platinum again in 2003 with *Ashanti's Christmas*. *Concrete Rose*, which did not sell the numbers of the prior albums, was released in 2004, and that was followed by *Collectables by*

Ashanti (2005; 4 new songs and 6 remixes of previously released tracks). Her latest album, *Declaration,* was released in 2008, and sold well.

As a child, she danced in the Disney TV movie *Polly* (1989; direction and choreography by Debbie Allen), and was an extra in Spike Lee's *Malcolm X* and the comedy *Who's Da Man?* Her first visible film role was in the 2004 English-language Bollywood film *Bride and Prejudice* in a sexy production number. She sang "My Lips Are Waiting" and "Touch My Body." Her appearance was a satirical homage to the tradition in Bollywood films where a celebrity makes a cameo appearance in a musical number that has no bearing on the film. Her feature film acting debut was in *Coach Carter* (2005) starring Samuel L. Jackson. She played Kyra, a pregnant teenager who has to decide whether to have an abortion.

Then she did the made-for-TV *The Muppets' Wizard of Oz* ('05), a busy but flat take on the original classic. Film roles continued in 2006 with *John Tucker Must Die.* Ashanti played Heather, a cheerleader who participates in a revenge scheme with his other jilted lovers against John Tucker, the school's biggest heartthrob. In the horror film and actioner *Resident Evil: Extinction* (2007), she was a nurse named Betty, but her character became a rather quick victim of the zombies. Hyperion published Ashanti's book of poetry, *Foolish/Unfoolish Reflections on Love,* in 2002.

Feature Films Including TV Movies: *Polly* (1989), *Bride and Prejudice* (2004), *Coach Carter* (2005), *The Muppets' Wizard of Oz* (TV; 2005), *John Tucker Must Die* (2006), *Resident Evil: Extinction* (2007).

TV: *Saturday Night Live* (2001), *V Graham Norton* (2002), *2nd Annual BET Awards* (2002), *Nickelodeon Kids' Choice Awards 2002, American Dreams* ("Silent Night," 2002), *Party in the Park 2002, Top of the Pops* (2002), *Summer Music Mania 2002, The 16th Annual Soul Train Music Awards* (2002), *MTV Video Music Awards 2002, Sabrina, the Teenage Witch* ("Call Me Crazy," 2002), *Diary: Ashanti—Princess of Her Domain* (2002), *The Tonight Show with Jay Leno* (2 segments; 2002 and 2005), *The 31st Annual American Music Awards* (2003), *The 30th Annual American Music Awards* (2003), *The 45th Annual Grammy Awards* (2003), *Buffy the Vampire Slayer* ("First Date," 2003), *2003 Much Music Video Music Awards, MTV Europe Music Awards 2003, VH1 Divas Duets* (2003), *3rd Annual BET Awards* (2003), *MTV Music Video Awards 2003, The Proud Family* (voice; 2003), *Tinseltown TV* (2003), *When I Was 17* (2003), *Entertainment Tonight* (2003), *I Love the '80s Strikes Back* (2003), *Fromage 2003, Punk'd* (2003), *Intimate Portrait* (2003), *Christmas in Washington* (2003), *An Evening of Stars: 25th Anniversary Tribute to Lou Rawls* (2004), *MTV Backstage at the Grammys* (2004), *VH1 Divas 2004, Apollo at 70: A Hot Night in Harlem* (2004), *Maxim Hot 100* (2004), *Ashanti: Custom Concert* (2004), *Live with Regis and Kathie Lee/Live with Regis and Kelly* (4 segments; 2004–06), *Best Hit USA* (2005), *Diamond Life* (2005), *Last Call with Carson Daly* (2005), *GMTV* (2005), *The Ellen DeGeneres Show* (2005), *The Oprah Winfrey Show* (2005), *The 3rd Annual TV Land Awards* (2005), *Las Vegas* ("Magic Carpet Fred," 2005), *The WIN Awards* (2005), *An All-Star Salute to Patti LaBelle* (2005), *2005 American Music Awards, Total Request Live 2005, 106 & Park Top 10 Live* (3 segments; 2005–06), *Legends Ball* (2006), *TV Land's Top Ten* (2006), *Access Granted* (2006), *NFL Football: Jets vs. Cowboys* (sang national anthem; 2007), *The Tonight Show with Jay Leno* (2008), *Jimmy Kimmel Live!* (2008), *Current TV* (2008), *Stand Up to Cancer* (2008).

Video/DVD: *WrestleMania XIX* (2003), *Hip Hop Uncensored, Vol. 5* (2003), *Princess of Hip Hop* (2004), *Kermit: A Frog's Life* (2005), *Kodiak Yearbook* (2006), *Grrrl Power* (2006).

Atkins, Essence

Born February 7, 1972.

Essence Atkins is a comedian with a distinctive style she puts to good use in films and on TV. She appeared in the pilot for *Saved by the Bell: The College Years,* but when Tiffani Amber-Thiessen from the original series opted to return, Atkins was let go. Since that setback, Atkins has enjoyed an upwardly mobile curve of sitcom success. *Under One Roof* (1995) was a six-episode midseason replacement series revolving around the upper middle class Langston family of Seattle, Washington, headed by patriarch Neb (James Earl Jones), a widowed police sergeant who shares a home with his married son Ron and Ron's family Maggie, Charlotte ("Charlie," played by Atkins), her daughter Ayesha, and foster son Marcus. Despite the presence of Jones, the public did not find it compelling.

Malibu Shores (1996) was another short-lived show, a critically lambasted prime time soap that looked like a ratings winner on paper. The multiracial teen cast clashed and fell in love — depending on the story arc — and experienced the generation gap, as well as the cultural and ethnic gap. Atkins portrayed the oldest sibling, Yvette Henderson, sister of Marcus and half-brother T.J., the youngest child in the family, on WB's *The Smart Guy*. *Smart Guy* aired on WB for three seasons (1997–99). Tahj Mowry was the title character with the 180 IQ. Yvette is precocious and intelligent in her own right and a budding women's rights activist. She is in the 10th grade in the first season and graduates from high school at the end of season three. Rejected from Princeton, Yvette is shown going to attend Georgetown University as the series ends.

Atkins is best known for her starring role as Dee Dee Thorne on UPN's *Half & Half*, which had a healthy run from 2002 to 2006 as part of the now defunct UPN black sitcom slate. The series was set in San Francisco and concerned the comedic and sometimes bittersweet lives of half-sisters. The solid cast included Rachel True, Telma Hopkins, Valarie Pettiford, and MC Lyte. Atkins has had several film roles worth noting, including that of the title character in *Nikita Blues* (2001), a 17-year-old high school girl enamored with her teacher; *Looking Through Lillian* (2002), about a beautiful but morally torn Los Angeles girl "kept" by a benefactor; a solid supporting role in *Deliver Us from Eva*, a *Taming of the Shrew* variant; and another supporting role, as an assistant to a Chicago TV talk show host who is faking a marriage, in the light comedy *Love...and Other Four-Letter Words* (2007).

Feature Films Including Video and TV Movies: *Love Song* (TV; 2000), *Nikita Blues* (2001), *XCU: Extreme Close-Up* (2001), *How High* (2001), *Looking Through Lillian* (2002), *Deliver Us from Eva* (2003), *Football Wives* (TV; 2007), *Love...and Other Four-Letter Words* (2007), *Love for Sale* (2008), *The Misguided Adventures of Three Brothers Dating in Hollywood* (2009), *N-Secure* (2009).

TV: *The Cosby Show* (2 episodes; "Vanessa's Rich," "I'm 'In' with the 'In' Crowd," 1986 and 1989), *Charlie Hoover* ("Out of the Frying Pan," 1991), *Sunday in Paris* (1991), *Family Matters* ("Brown Bombshell," 1992), *Saved by the Bell: The College Years* (1993), *Mad TV* (2004), *Under One Roof* (recurring role of "Charlie" Langston, 1995), *The Wayans Bros.* ("Farmer's Daughter," 1995), *The Parent 'Hood* ("One Man and a Baby," 1996),

Essence Atkins in *Smart Guy*.

Malibu Shores (recurring role of Julie Tate, 1996), *The John Larroquette Show* (1996), *Smart Guy* (recurring role of Tasha Yvette Henderson; 1997–99), *Promised Land* ("Mirror Image," 1998), *Moesha* (2 episodes; "Party's Over [Here]," "Unappreciated Interest," 1999), *Sabrina, the Teenage Witch* (2 episodes; "Love in Bloom," "Salem's Daughter," 2000), *Half & Half* (recurring role of Dee Dee Thorne, 2002–06), *The Wayne Brady Show* (2004), *Love, Inc.* ("Mad About You," 2005), *All Shades of Fine: 25 Hottest Women of the Past 25 Years* (2005), *Angels Can't Help But Laugh* (2007), *The Class* ("The Class Has to Go to a Stupid Museum," 2007), *House* ("The Right Stuff," 2007).

Atkinson, Beverly Hope Born in New York, New York, December 9, 1935; died in Los Angeles, California, December 11, 2001.

Although her life was cut short by cancer (she died at 66 at Midway Hospital in Los Angeles), Beverly Hope Atkinson had a career consisting of a combination of offbeat theatrical films and mainstream TV work. Her first film role was as a prostitute who gets in George C. Scott's face in the police drama *The New Centurions* (1972). She later moved on to more complex characterizations (but still as a hooker), such as her poignant drug addict role on Steven Bochco's *Hill Street Blues* (1985–86).

Atkinson attended New York's City College. She studied under Lee Strasberg in the 1960s, later becoming a member of the Actors Studio. She also joined New York's Café LaMama theater troop and Theater West in Los Angeles. While she continued to tour on stage throughout much of her career, she settled in Hollywood in the 1970s, continuing to alternate betweens films, the theater and TV. As a young actress Atkinson toured Scandinavia with *The Skin of Our Teeth* and *Tom Paine*, which played London's West End. At the Seattle Repertory Theater, she performed in *A Midsummer Night's Dream*, *Lysistrata* and *The Blacks*. She was also featured with the Meadowbrook Repertory in Michigan.

While her film roles did not offer the diversity and depth of her theater work, Atkinson had a more varied and interesting big screen career than many of her contemporaries. Although it has fallen into obscurity these days, Ralph Bakshi's raucous animated live-action feature *Heavy Traffic* (1973) caused a definite stir in its day. This was the follow-up to Bakshi's popular *Fritz the Cat* (1972) which, like *Heavy Traffic*, was wildly uneven. In *Heavy Traffic*, inner city life is envisioned as a giant pinball game punctuated by flashes of violence. The metaphor gets tired very quickly. Michael Corleone, a young cartoonist of Italian-Jewish parentage, becomes romantically involved with Carole, a voluptuous black bartender and dancer. Atkinson provided the voice of the animated Carole, as well as appearing as the character in "real" footage.

Cornbread, Earl and Me (1975) is one of the better black-oriented films of the era, telling the poignant tale of a high school student heading out of the ghetto on a college basketball scholarship. Tragedy results when he is accidentally shot by the police. Atkinson's career dwindled down with a series of supporting roles in mediocre TV movies: *Outside Chance* (1978) was a remake of *Jackson County Jail* (1976). *Skag* (1980) was a two-hour pilot film for a short-lived TV series starring Karl Malden as a steel mill foreman who suffers a stroke and is forced to stop and smell the roses amid his medical turmoil. *Maid in America* (1982) was a romantic comedy starring husband and wife Susan Clark and Alex Karras, with Atkinson as a domestic. *Never Forget* (1991) starred Leonard Nimoy as a Holocaust survivor confronting a Holocaust denial organization's allegations in court.

Feature Films Including TV Movies: *Si Volvemos a Vernos* (as Beverly Atkinson; aka *Smashing Up*; Spain; 1968); *The New Centurions* (1972), *Heavy Traffic* (1973), *Hustling* (TV; 1975), *Cornbread, Earl and Me* (1975), *Law & Order* (TV; 1976), *Outside Chance* (TV; 1978), *Skag* (TV; 1980), *Maid in America* (TV; 1982), *UFOria* (1985), *Never Forget* (TV; 1991).

TV: *Dark Shadows* (1968), *Sanford and Son* (2 episodes; "The Return of the Barracuda," "Tyranny, Thy Name Is Grady," 1972 and 1974), *Apple's Way* ("The Temptation," 1974), *Bronk* ("The Fifth Victim," 1975), *Police Story* ("The Cut Man Caper," 1975), *Executive Suite* ("Re: The Trap," 1976), *ABC Afterschool Specials* ("The Pinballs," 1977), *Baretta* ("The Stone Conspiracy," 1978), *Good Times* ("The Witness," 1978), *The White Shadow* ("Out at Home," 1980), *Hill Street Blues* (5 episodes as Vivian DeWitt; "Dr. Hoof and Mouth," "Two Easy Pieces," "Scales of Justice," "I Want My Hill Street Blues," "Larry of Arabia," 1985–86), *thirtysomething* ("The Distance," 1990).

Aubert, K.D. Born in Shreveport, Louisiana, December 6, 1978.

Karen Denise Aubert is an actress of Creole descent (she speaks French). Raised in California, she is one of the original "Fantanas" (the dynamic, sexy Fanta soda girl singing group). Before her modeling career took off, she worked at Macy's. Aubert has modeled for Escada, Noxzema, AT&T, Wilson's Leather, Victoria's Secret and Frederick's of Hollywood. She attended San Diego State University, where she played on the school's softball team. She co-hosted the MTV reality game show *Kidnapped* before making her big screen debut in a small role in *The Scorpion King*. She also appeared in the P. Diddy video "Trade It All, Part II," and the "Def Jam: Icon" video game.

Feature Films Including Video and TV Movies: *The Scorpion King* (2002), *Friday After Next* (2002), *Hollywood Homicide* (2003), *DysEnchanted* (2004), *Soul Plane* (2004), *Frankenfish* (TV; 2004), *In the Mix* (2005), *The Grand* (2007), *Surfer Dude* (2008), *Still Waiting* (2008), *4Chosen* (2008).

TV: *Clueless* (3 episodes as Julie Sinclair; 1999), *Kidnapped* (series co-host; 2002), *Buffy the Vampire Slayer* (2 episodes; "Lies My Parents Told Me," "First Date," 2003), *My Coolest Years* (miniseries; 2004), *Bones* ("The Man in the Bear,"

2005), *2006 Asian Excellence Awards, Inked* ("Crossing the Line," 2006), *CSI: NY* ("You Only Die Once," 2007).

Avery, Margaret Born in Magnum, Oklahoma.

Margaret Avery attended high school in San Diego, California, and graduated from San Francisco State University. She has had a long and varied career in films and on television. She was the sixth black woman ever to be nominated for the Best Actress Oscar. That was for the film she will forever be identified with—*The Color Purple* (1985). Shug Avery was one of the all-time great roles for a black actress.

Based on the Pulitzer Prize-winning novel by Alice Walker, the film was nominated for a total of 11 Academy Awards, but won none of them. Tina Turner reportedly turned down the role of Shug, and Steven Spielberg remembered Margaret Avery from a commercial he had directed and from her appearance in his 1972 TV movie *Something Evil*, when Spielberg was a novice TV director looking to work his way up in the industry. These connections led to Avery's felicitous casting in a film whose reputation has grown with the years.

Avery is marvelous as Shug, the bisexual, worldly blues singer who has an affair with the insecure, "ugly" Celie, and thereby lights the way for Celie to find self-respect. Shug is arrogant and self-centered, but also warm and knowing. Shug is flashy and flamboyant, and yet she knows the blues from the inside out. As guided by the skillful Spielberg, Margaret Avery realizes every facet of the complex role.

An interesting early film Avery was quite good in was *The Folks at Red Wolf Inn* (rechristened *Terror at Red Wolf Inn*; 1972). Billed as "Margret" instead of Margaret, Avery is Edwina, a bookish young woman invited to a free vacation at what turns out to be a house inhabited by cannibals. Although the film is a not always successful blend of dark comedy and conventional horror thriller, Avery's fey performance is charming and detailed. A significant film in Avery's career is the science fiction telefilm *The Lathe of Heaven* (premiered January 9, 1980), based on the

Margaret Avery in *The Color Purple* (1985).

novel by Ursula K. Le Guin. Made for PBS, this was an impossible film to see for many years — a holy grail for genre fans. It is notable for a daring (and for TV, unprecedented in its candor) interracial love scene. Set in the future in Portland, Oregon, it concerns a man (Bruce Davison) whose strange dreams start becoming reality. An immoral psychiatrist seeks to manipulate his mind and harness the power of the dreams. *The Lathe of Heaven* is an unusually adult, cerebral example of the sci-fi genre — the kind of intellectual sci-fi that has all but disappeared from the contemporary scene — although the special effects are crude and cheap by today's CGI standards.

Richard Pryor was at the height of his fame when Avery appeared with him in *Which Way Is Up?* (1977), a remake of the Italian film *The Seduction of Mimi.* An interesting but forgotten title in her filmography is *Blueberry Hill* (1988): a young woman in California circa 1956 learns from her piano teacher (Avery) about her piano player father and about some secrets in her past. The third film in the Superfly series, *The Return of Superfly* (1990), saw Ron O'Neal replaced by Nathan Purdee in the role of Priest. Fortunately, Samuel L. Jackson was around in an early film appearance to add some spark. Avery appeared as Superfly's ill-fated lady friend.

She also appeared in TV movies. *Louis Armstrong — Chicago Style* (1976) depicts the early years of Armstrong's musical career and his rise to fame. *Scott Joplin* (1977) is another bio pic, inaccurate by even Hollywood standards. *For Us the Living: The Medgar Evers Story* (1983), about the life of the inspirational civil rights martyr, had its debut showing on PBS. *Heat Wave* (1990), directed by Kevin Hooks, was a potent look at the Watts race riots in Los Angeles. *The Jacksons: An American Dream* (1992) was a much-hyped ABC telefilm that garnered good ratings and, despite the usual inaccuracies of this genre and some unfortunate miscasting, was an ambitious, moderately successful look at the infamous show business family, with Avery as Martha Jackson, the grandmother of the clan.

In *Lightning in a Bottle* (1993) Avery portrayed a doctor. It was an above average Lifetime TV movie about an alcoholic (Lynda Carter) who drives while drunk. In 1993, Avery appeared in a Los Angeles stage production of Elaine Jackson's *Paper Dolls* with her friend Lillian Lehman, who also appeared with her in the horror film *Mardi Gras for the Devil* that same year. *White Man's Burden* (1995) was neither a financial nor a critical success. This offbeat film envisions a world where black people are the ruling class and whites are the poor underclass. Avery plays the wife of a wealthy magnate (Harry Belafonte) who fires one of his employees (John Travolta) who unintentionally saw the rich man's wife undressing through an open window (a sexually charged scene). The film rather laboriously makes a number of points about race relations in America.

Avery's television series work is of more than passing interest. She was in the *Kolchak: The Night Stalker* episode "The Sentry," about a huge reptilian underground dweller that goes on a rampage when its eggs are stolen. Another TV highlight is her recurring role of Ruby Dome in David Janssen's private eye series *Harry O.* Avery is divorced from Robert Gordon Hunt. The marriage produced a daughter named Aisha.

Feature Films Including Video and TV Movies: *Something Evil* (TV; 1972), *Cool Breeze* (1972), *The Folks at Red Wolf Inn* (aka *Terror at Red Wolf Inn,* 1972), *Hell Up in Harlem* (1973), *Magnum Force* (1973), *An Eye for an Eye* (aka *The Psychopath,* 1975), *Louis Armstrong Chicago Style* (TV; 1976), *Scott Joplin* (1977), *Which Way Is Up?* (1977), *The Fish That Saved Pittsburgh* (1979), *The Sky Is Gray* (TV; 1980), *For Us the Living: The Medgar Evers Story* (*American Playhouse*; TV; 1983), *The Color Purple* (1985), *Blueberry Hill* (1988), *Single Women, Married Men* (TV; 1989), *Riverbend* (TV; 1990), *Malcolm Takes a Shot* (TV; 1990), *Heat Wave* (TV; 1990), *The Return of Superfly* (1990), *The Jacksons: An American Dream* (TV; 1992), *Lightning in a Bottle* (1993), *Mardi Gras for the Devil* (aka *Night Trap,* 1993), *Cyborg 3* (1994), *The Set Up* (1995), *White Man's Burden* (1995), *Love Kills* (1998), *Wie stark muâ eine leibe sein* (TV; 1998), *Waitin' to Live* (2002), *Second to Die* (2002), *Lord Help Us* (aka *A Taste of Us*; 2007), *Meet the Browns* (2008), *Welcome Home, Roscoe Brown* (2008).

TV: *The Rookies* (2 episodes; "The Informant," 1972; "Reign of Terror," 1975), *Ironside* ("The Last Payment," 1973), *The New Dick Van Dyke Show* (1973), *Kojak* ("You Can't Tell a Hurt Man How to Holler," 1974), *Harry O* (recurring role of Ruby Dome, 1974–76), *Sanford and Son* ("Strange Bedfellows," 1975), *Kolchak: The Night Stalker* (1975), *A.E.S. Hudson Street* (recurring role of Nurse Sawyer; 1977), Baby, I'm Back ("Lucky

15 ... Maybe," 1978), *Murder, She Wrote* ("Jessica Behind Bars," 1985), *The 58th Annual Academy Awards* (nominee, Best Actress in a Supporting Role; 1986), *Miami Vice* ("The Afternoon Plane," 1987), *Spenser for Hire* ("One for My Daughter," 1987), *Rags to Riches* ("Marva in the Key of Cee," 1987), *Crime Story* (2 episodes; "Seize the Time," "Moulin Rouge," 1988), *Amen* ("Deacon's Dilemma," 1990), *Roc* ("The Lady Killer," 1991), *MacGyver* ("Gunz 'n Boyz," 1991), *The Cosby Show* ("Claire's Reunion," 1992), *Time Trax* ("The Price of Honor," 1993), *The Roots of Roe* (narration; TV; 1993), *Walker, Texas Ranger* ("The Neighborhood," 1997), *10-8* (2003), *The Black Movie Awards* (2005), *JAG* ("Unknown Soldier," 2005), *Bones* ("The Man in the Fallout Shelter," 2005).

Avery, Shondrella Born April 26, 1971, in Los Angeles, California.

Shondrella Avery is best known for her role as LaFawnduh Lucas in the cult film — and surprise box office smash —*Napoleon Dynamite* (2004). In what could very easily have been a stereotyped role, her LaFawnduh is good-hearted, attractive, delightful — and more than a bit spacey.

The eldest of 10 children, Avery grew up in a section of South Central Los Angeles not for the faint of heart. Her mother has been a foster parent to around 200 other children, many of them crack babies, or the products of abused, neglected, or dysfunctional families. Avery's unusual upbringing inspired her to write and perform the autobiographical one-woman show *Ain't I Enough?* Avery is a graduate of Los Angeles County High School and holds a bachelor's degree in fine arts from Cal State, Los Angeles. She is a member of the famous Groundlings improvisational comedy troupe and has also performed with the legendary improvisational troupe Second City.

On TV, where she has been consistently active, she had a recurring role of the manicurist Candy on the situation comedy *One on One* and later was a cast member of the spin-off series *Cuts* playing the same role. She was also a cast member of the reality-prank TV series *Girls Behaving Badly*— sort of like *Punk'd* with pretty girls — on the Oxygen Network. On the big screen, she played Macy Gray's twin in the female bounty hunter thriller *Domino* (2005). Avery is married to a Nigerian-born banker. They collect Afro-centric art and crafts.

Shondrella Avery.

Feature Films Including Video and TV Movies: *Cyberdorm* (1999), *Trippin'* (1999), *Watermelon Heist* (as Shondrella Akesan; 2003), *Catfish and Gumbo* (2003), *Napoleon Dynamite* (2004), *Domino* (2005), *Community Service* (TV; 2006), *Déjà Vu* (2006), *The Secret Life of Bees* (2008).

TV: *The Jamie Foxx Show* (2000), *For Your Love* (2000), *Girls Behaving Badly* (series regular; 2002), *One on One* (recurring role of Candy, 2002–2005), *Strong Medicine* (2003), *Cedric the Entertainer Presents* (2004), *I Love the 80s* 3-D (2005), *50 Hottest Vegas Moments* (2005), *Cuts* (recurring role of Candy; 2005–06).

Ayola, Rakie Born in Cardiff, Wales, United Kingdom, 1968.

Rakie Ayola, a graduate of the Royal Welsh College of Music and Drama and member of the Made in Wales theater company, is much better known in her native England, where she is a major TV star, than in the United States. Ayola's mother, from Sierra Leone, was the second wife of a wealthy Nigerian. Only three weeks after giving birth to Ayola, she left her in the permanent care of her cousin in Cardiff and his wife. They raised Ayola as their own and, although she has met her real mother a few times over the years, she considers them to be her parents.

Ayola has a rich theatrical background, having appeared in a spectrum of classic and contemporary plays, including *Dido, Queen of Carthage* (2003), August Wilson's *King Hedley the Second* (2002), *Hamlet* (as Ophelia; 2001); and *Twelfth Night, It's a Girl, A Midsummer Night's Dream, Up and Under, Hiawatha,* and *Ashes and Sand,* among many others.

She gained early mass recognition as a regular on the British TV series *Soldier, Soldier* (1993) as soldier's wife Bernie Edwards. However, her outstanding claim to fame is her role on *Holby City* (2003–07) as Kyla Tyson, the steadfast nurse. This is the U.K. equivalent of an *ER* or a *Grey's Anatomy*. The TV role for which she is perhaps best known in America is in the miniseries *Scarlett* (1994), the sequel to *Gone with the Wind*; she plays the role of Pansy. Her most famous theatrical film from a stateside perspective is *Sahara* (2005), a big budget adventure that did fairly well at the box office. Her husband is actor Adam Smethurst; they have a daughter, Tansy.

Feature Films Including TV Movies: *Great Moments in Aviation* (TV; 1993), *Shades of Fear* (1994), *The Secret Laughter of Women* (1999), *Green-Eyed Monster* (TV; 2001), *The I Inside* (2003), *Sahara* (2005), *The Window* (TV; 2006).

TV: *Soldier, Soldier* ("Leaving," 1993), *Nightshift* (1993), *Going Underground: A Better Life Than Mine* (1993), *Scarlett* (miniseries; 1994), *Tiger Bay* (4 episodes; 1997), *Casualty* ("Trapped," 1999), *Maisie Raine* ("Can't See for Looking," 1999), *Double Yellow* (2001), *Waking the Dead* ("A Simple Sacrifice," Parts I and II, 2001), *The Armando Iannucci Shows* (2001), *Being April* (recurring role of Taneshia; 2002), *Offenders* (6 episodes; 2002), Murder in Mind ("Stalkers," 2003), *The Canterbury Tales* ("The Man of Law's Tale," 2003), *Holby City* (recurring role of Kyla Tyson; 2003–2007), *Sea of Souls* ("That Old Black Magic," Parts I and II, 2004), *Children in Need* (appearance as Kyla Tyson; 2006), *The Window* (2006).

Badu, Erykah Born in Dallas, Texas, February 26, 1971.

Erykah Badu holds her own with the iconoclastic idealists of the 1960s ... and then some. She was born Erica Abi Wright. Her music is based in the neo-soul genre. She has recorded for Kedar/Universal, Motown and Umbrella Recordings/Def Jam. As an actress she has appeared in such diverse films as *Blues Brothers 2000* (1998), *Cider House Rules* (1999) and *House of D* (2004). In *Cider House Rules*, a deglamorized Badu gives a natural performance as Rose Rose (one "Rose" was not enough) in this character study of a kindly old doctor (and illegal abortionist) who presides over an orphanage and the young physician he mentors.

Badu and her brother and sister were raised by their mother. Their father, William Wright, Jr., had left the family early in their lives. Their grandmother often looked after the children while their mother (Kollen Maria Gipson-Wright) performed in theatrical productions to provide for the family. Badu had her first taste of show business at age four, singing and dancing with her mother at the Dallas Theater Center. By age 14 she was free-style singing and rapping for a local radio station. Early on, she changed the spelling of her name to Erykah: "kah" means "can do no wrong" in Arabic, and Badu is an African name used by the Ashanti people. She graduated from Booker T. Washington High School for the Performing and Visual Arts and studied theater at Grambling State University, but she left in 1993 before graduating.

She taught drama and dance to children at the South Dallas Cultural Center. She became a freestyle rapper under the name MC Apples and sang in a female rap duo. Around this time she also recorded a multi-song demo, and recorded a duet with singer D'Angelo ("Precious Love"). Eventually she signed a deal with Universal Records. *Baduizm* (1997) was her acclaimed debut album, breaking at number 2 on the *Billboard* charts. The album eventually went triple platinum, and the song "On & On" won a Grammy Award in 1998. Badu had a child named Seven with rapper André 3000 of OutKast in 1997. Their relationship ended later that decade. Her album *Live* was recorded while she was pregnant with Seven. *Live* reached number 4 on the *Billboard* charts, sold double platinum, and spawned another hit single, "Tyrone."

She collaborated with the Roots (who had produced a number of tracks on *Baduizm*) on their 1999 release *Things Fall Apart*. She was featured on the song "You Got Me," which won a Grammy for Best Rap Performance by a Duo or Group. Badu returned to the charts in 2000 with the album *Mama's Gun*. The single "Bag Lady" topped the R&B charts for seven weeks.

Mama's Gun was another platinum-selling success, and the song "Bag Lady" was nominated for a Grammy. She also recorded the single "Love of My Life" with boyfriend Common and was awarded her fourth Grammy for this song in 2003. In September 2003, the EP *Worldwide Underground* was released; it went to number 3 on the *Billboard* charts and was certified gold. Badu received four Grammy nominations for this. Badu gave birth to a daughter, Puma Rose, on July 5, 2004; the father is West Coast rapper The D.O.C. The album *New Amerykah Part One (4th World War)* was released in February 2008. Badu has won American Music Awards (1998, 2003) and Lady of Soul Awards (1997–98). She worked with Curtis Mayfield on the *Eve's Bayou* soundtrack and appeared as a performer on the soap opera *One Life to Live.*

Feature Films including TV Movies: *Blues Brothers 2000* (1998), *The Cider House Rules* (1999), *House of D* (2004), *Block Party* (2005), *Before the Music Dies* (documentary; 2006).

TV: *Vendetta* (1997), *New York Undercover* (1997), *One Life to Live* (1997), *The 40th Annual Grammy Awards* (1998), *The Chris Rock Show* (1998), *One Love: The Bob Marley All-Star Tribute* (1999), *The 72nd Annual Academy Awards* (2000), *Erykah Badu Live* (2001), *2002 Trumpet Awards, Russell Simmons Presents Def Poetry Jam* (2002), *The Award Show Awards Show* (2003), *Essence Awards* (2003), *100 Greatest Videos* (2003), *3rd Annual BET Awards* (2003), *9th Annual Soul Train Lady of Soul Awards* (2003), *The Tonight Show with Jay Leno* (2 segments; 2003–04), *VH1: All Access* (2004), *Chappelle's Show* (2004), *The Late Late Show with Craig Ferguson* (2005), *Tavis Smiley* (2005), *3rd Annual VH1 Hip Hop Honors* (2006), *The Ellen DeGeneres Show* (2008).

Video/DVD: *MTV 20: Jams* (2001).

Bailey, Pearl Born in Southampton County, Virginia, March 29, 1918; died Philadelphia, Pennsylvania, August 17, 1990.

To several generations of fans she was simply "Pearlie Mae." Her folksy stage persona obscured an intellectual, savvy professional. She changed with the times, but somehow was always true to herself. Pearl Bailey was the daughter of the Reverend Joseph and Ella Mae Bailey, and was raised in the Bloodfields neighborhood of Newport News, Virginia. She was married to John Randolph Pinkett (1948–52) and drummer Louie Bellson (1952–90); she and Bellson adopted a son and a daughter. At 15, she made her stage singing debut. Her brother Bill was a tap dancer starting out in show business, and he suggested that she enter an amateur contest being held at Philadelphia's Pearl Theater. She won first prize, and later won an amateur night contest at Harlem's Apollo Theater. That's when she knew she should pursue a career in entertainment.

She started singing and dancing regularly in Philadelphia's black nightclubs in the 1930s. In 1941, during World War II, she toured with the USO, entertaining the troops. After the tour she settled in New York. In addition to success as a solo act, she performed with entertainers like Cab Calloway and sang with the Cootie Williams and Count Basie bands. Bailey tripled as a composer, singer and songwriter, even though she was never formally trained in music. She had notable success as a recording artist (her rendition of "It Takes Two to Tango" was a top 10 hit in 1952).

Bailey made her Broadway debut in *St. Louis Woman* (1946). She also frequently performed at the Old Howard Theater in downtown Washington. She starred in the Broadway musical *House of Flowers* (1954) with the young Diahann Carroll. That same year she was Frankie in Otto Preminger's *Carmen Jones,* starring Dorothy Dandridge. Her performance of "Beat That Rhythm on the Drum" is one of the film's highlights. She was Maria in the 1959 film version of *Porgy and Bess,* with Sidney Poitier and, again, the young Dorothy Dandridge. That same year she was Aunt Hagar in *St. Louis Blues,* the movie biography of W.C. Handy; Eartha Kitt and Nat "King" Cole also starred. She won a special Tony Award for her performance in the title role in the all-black production of *Hello, Dolly!* (1968). In 1987, she won a daytime Emmy Award for her performance as a fairy godmother in the *ABC Afternoon School* special "Cindy Eller: A Modern Fairy Tale."

Bailey had her own short-lived variety show on ABC in 1971. In the latter stage of her career she provided voice work for animated features such as *Tubby the Tuba* and *The Fox and the Hound.* Bailey was the author of a number of books: *The Raw Pearl* (autobiography; 1968), *Talking to Myself* (autobiography; 1971), *Pearl's Kitchen: An Extraordinary Cookbook* (1973), *Between You and Me* (autobiography; 1989). *Pearl Bailey: With a Song in Her Heart,* a biography for children by Keith Brandt, was published in 1992.

In 1975, she served as a special ambassador to the United Nations. She earned a bachelor of arts in theology from Georgetown University in Washington, D.C. in 1985. She was awarded the Presidential Medal of Honor on October 17, 1988. In 1989, she received the Women's International Center Living Legend Award (1989). She died at Thomas Jefferson University Hospital in Philadelphia after collapsing at a local hotel. The cause of death was coronary artery disease. She is buried at Rolling Green Memorial Park in Westchester, Pennsylvania.

Feature Films: *Variety Girl* (1947), *Isn't It Romantic?* (1948), *Carmen Jones* (1954), *That Certain Feeling* (1956), *St. Louis Blues* (1958), *Porgy and Bess* (1959), *All the Fine Young Cannibals* (1960), *The Landlord* (1970), *The Last Generation* (1971), *Tubby the Tuba* (voice; 1976), *Norman ... Is That You?* (1976), *The Fox and the Hound* (voice, 1981), *The Member of the Wedding* (TV; 1982), *Peter Gunn* (TV; 1989).

TV: *Songs for Sale* (1951), *Your Show of Shows* (1951), *The Colgate Comedy Hour* (1954), *The Name's the Same* (1955), *The Nat King Cole Show* (1957), *The Steve Allen Show* (3 segments; 1957), *The Perry Como Show* (2 segments; 1956–58), *The Andy Williams Show* (1963), *What's My Line?* (3 segments; 1955–66), *The Hollywood Squares* (1966), *The Mike Douglas Show* (1967), *The 22nd Annual Tony Awards* (1968), *Toast of the Town/The Ed Sullivan Show* (21 segments; 1949–68), *Personality* (1968), *Carol Channing and Pearl Bailey on Broadway* (1969), *The 23rd Annual Tony Awards* (1969), *The Dick Cavett Show* (1970), *The Pearl Bailey Show* (series host; 1971), *Bing Crosby and His Friends* (1972), *The Flip Wilson Show* (1972), *The Tonight Show Starring Johnny Carson* (2 segments; 1972–73), *Love, American Style* (1973), *The Dean Martin Celebrity Roast: Jack Benny* (1974), *The Merv Griffin Show* (1975), *The 49th Annual Academy Awards* (1977), *The Muppet Show* (1978), *The Love Boat* (1978), *Happy Birthday, Bob* (1978), *All-Star Salute to Pearl Bailey* (1979), *Disneyland* ("Disney Animation: The Illusion of Life," 1981), *All-Star Celebration Opening the Gerald R. Ford Presidential Museum* (1981), *Signature* (2 segments; 1982), *As the World Turns* (1982), *Bob Hope's Women I Love: Beautiful But Funny* (1982), *Night of 100 Stars* (1982), *Broadway Plays Washington on Kennedy Center Tonight* (1982), *ABC Afterschool Specials* ("Cindy Eller: A Modern Fairy Tale," 1985), *Johnny Carson's 29th Anniversary* (archival; 1991), *Mo' Funny: Black Comedy in America* (archival; 1993), *The Carol Burnett Show: A Reunion* (archival; 1993), *The Best of Disney Music: A Legacy in Song, Part I* (archival; 1993), *Mwah! The Best of the Dinah Shore Show* (archival; 2003), *Andy Williams: My Favorite Duets* (archival; 2004), *Broadway: The American Musical* (archival; 2004), *American Masters* ("The World of Nat King Cole"; archival; 2006).

Video/DVD: *Muppet Video: Muppet Moments* (1985), *Passing the Baton* (archival; 2003), *TV in Black: The First Fifty Years* (archival; 2004).

Baker, Josephine Born in St. Louis, Missouri, June 3, 1906; died April 12, 1975, Paris, France.

Born Freda Josephine McDonald, the woman who would grow up to become a lasting icon is perhaps still best known to younger generations through the sincere, touching HBO film version of her life, *The Josephine Baker Story*, starring Lynn Whitfield. Never a major star in America, Baker was a megastar throughout much of Europe and, of course, nowhere more so than in her adopted homeland, France. Her impoverished childhood in St. Louis was marked by domestic instability and a constant struggle against poverty and racism, epitomized by the deadly St. Louis race riots of 1917. She was of mixed Native American and African American background, the descendant of Apalachee Indians and black slaves from South Carolina. Her mother was Carrie McDonald and her father was vaudeville drummer Eddie Carson (Arthur Martin was her stepfather). Her siblings were Richard, Margaret and Willie Mae. Josephine's parents had a song and dance act during their brief marriage. Her mother would dance with a glass of water expertly balanced on top of her head. Josephine was only a year old when her parents introduced her into the finale of their act. Josephine dropped out of school at age 12. She became a street performer — a busker, in the terminology of the day — melding comedic ability with dance talent. She also waited tables and was a babysitter for rich white families.

At age 13 she began her professional career with The Dixie Steppers for the Theater Owners' Booking Association. Her first theatrical appearance was in the chorus line of the Booker T. Washington Theater in St. Louis. It was during this period that she began to slowly define the Josephine Baker that would eventually morph into

Josephine Baker with Jean Galland in *Princesse Tam Tam* (*The Flame of Paris*) (1935).

an iconic international star. She initially performed as the last dancer in the chorus line. It was in this position that the dancer would traditionally perform in a comic manner — much like the Jewish *tummler* of yore in the Borscht belt of upstate New York. This comic relief chorus girl would appear to be unable to remember the steps. But in the encore, she would perform the dance correctly, and outshine the other girls.

Eventually Baker was billed as "the highest-paid chorus girl in vaudeville" and began appearing in legendary shows like Sissle and Blake's *Shuffle Along*. Broadway beckoned with other shows like *Bamville* and *The Chocolate Dandies*. When Baker and her fellow performers took their dance skills to Paris in 1925, it began a journey that would transfigure her life. Paris was ready for the gangly, comical sexuality of Baker in a way that America was not. It was the painter Paul Colin who saw her as the ultimate muse, and greatly contributed to the popularity and the burgeoning legend of Josephine Baker. His masterful posters encapsulated Baker's jazz baby essence in *La Revue Nègre*— her improbable combination of sex goddess, wild child, and human Slinky. The zeitgeist of the Art Deco anything-goes mentality of the era lives forever in Colin's vibrant work. Baker's fame spread so quickly that she was soon able to open her own nightclub, Chez Josephine (a name revived later by her adopted son Jean-Claude for his popular restaurant in New York, which is full of wonderful Baker memorabilia).

Paul Derville, director of the Folies-Bergère, wanted her to star in his next show. A dramatic addition to the show was Baker's pet cheetah, Chiquita, who wore a diamond collar but refused to obey the politer dictates of society. The cheetah, part of the "savage" ambience of the show, often escaped into the orchestra pit, giving the musicians fits, and adding a distinct element to the proceedings, which consisted of Baker dancing in a banana skirt and high heels — and nothing else ("La Danse Souvage"). The banana dance was saluted in a contemporary stage appearance by singer Beyoncé. The banana skirt has become a timeless erotic symbol.

Baker's persona remains controversial to this day: the black woman as insatiable sex goddess. Race and sexuality were the keynotes of her appeal, and she certainly defined perhaps as no woman before or since the "exotic" appeal of women of color. The better part of a century before the emergence of supermodels such as Tyra Banks and Naomi Campbell, and generations before the "dreamgirl" media event created by the appearance of Beyoncé in the *Sports Illustrated* swimsuit issue, Josephine Baker championed an in-your-face sensuality that remains cutting edge. The other side of the coin, however, is that the "sexy savage" image — especially when combined with a "loved-unwisely-and-lost" Madame Butterfly persona — seems as racist to many modern viewers as any other black stereotype of its era. Josephine pined for her white lover, and he, in turn, was attracted to her, but he always returned to the safety and comfort of his white girlfriend or fiancée by the end of the film.

As for Baker, she was sadder but wiser, consoled only by her ability to entertain the crowd — alone amid the applause, the showgirl with little to show in her love life. This formula persists through *La Sirène des Tropiques* (1927; her first feature), *Zou Zou* (1934) and *Princesse Tam-Tam* (1935). Baker is at her most beautiful and most iconic in the wonderful *Zou Zou* (the presence of Jean Gabin adds considerable stature to what is already a polished production). Baker's languorous swing on the trapeze in the "bird in the gilded cage" sequence has an erotic power equal to that of Louise Brooks in *Pandora's Box* (although one plays the victim of men and the other the victimizer). *Princesse Tam Tam* is clearly her great comedic role, and perhaps her greatest, most "Baker-esque" screen role. If you've never seen Baker and would like to know what all the shouting is about, this film is the one to watch.

Baker's music hall act provoked acclaim — and controversy — throughout Europe: Berlin, Vienna, Hungary, Yugoslavia, Denmark, Rumania, and Czechoslovakia. In 1928, Italians, Scandinavians and Central Europeans experienced the Baker phenomenon. An even more potent Josephine emerges in the Casino de Paris show *Paris Qui Remue* (1931–32) — more sophisticated and sexier than ever, and every inch the superstar. As she embarked on a world tour, no doubt the uppermost thought in her mind was to replicate her European success in the United States — to finally find major stardom in her homeland. She signed on as a star of the 1936 Ziegfeld Follies (although it was telling that she had only three numbers to Fanny Brice's seven). This failed version of the Follies garnered neither outstanding reviews nor financial success. Indeed, Baker was replaced by Gypsy Rose Lee later in the show's run. Perhaps it was no coincidence that Baker became a citizen of France in 1937. There she was always welcome.

World War II saw her emerge as a heroine of the French Resistance — very much a Mata Hari of her time. In addition to serving with the French Red Cross and becoming a sub-lieutenant in the Women's Auxiliary Air Force, Baker became a secret agent, smuggling information and transporting messages in occupied territory at the risk of her life. This allowed Baker to show her loyalty to France by participating in the Underground. After the war, she was awarded the Croix de Guerre for her bravery. There is a school of thought that Baker was so renowned and beloved that even the Nazis would have been reluctant to cause her harm. But "reluctance" is not a quality one easily attributes to the Third Reich, and Baker was in fact putting her life in danger.

Throughout much of her career, La Baker's signature song was "J'ai deux amours" ("I Have Two Loves"), her homeland, America, and her adopted home, France. If Baker most strikingly showed her love of France by her participation in the Resistance, she showed her love of America by becoming a notable civil rights advocate. Some of her civil rights activity was personal, such as her reaction to racist mistreatment at the famous New York night spot The Stork Club and her very public feud with columnist and kingmaker Walter Winchell (which is detailed in the HBO bio pic of her life).

Some of her civil rights activity was on a much grander, historic scale. In 1963, she spoke at the historic March on Washington at the side of Martin Luther King, Jr. Wearing her Free French uniform and her Legion of Honor decoration, she was the only woman to speak at the rally. No biographical entry on Baker is complete without mention of the Rainbow Tribe. Not unlike the contemporary multiracial brood adopted by Angelina Jolie (who is most definitely channeling Baker in this regard), the "Tribe," which numbered 12, consisted of children of all nationalities and colors: Akio, Janot, Luis, Jari, Jean-Claude, Moise, Brahim, Marianne, Koffi, Mara, Noel and Stellina. The children were raised at Les Milandes, Baker's chateau in the Dordogne. As she aged, Baker's eccentricity no longer seemed as appealing to the public as it had when combined with the vibrancy of youth. She was no longer in fashion, and her debts began to mount. Thus begins the sad period of her long decline. In February of 1964, Les Milandes was seized to pay debts amounting to 2 million old francs. The sad spectacle of an aging Baker being evicted from her home was pathetic fodder for the tabloid press. The "has-been" was experiencing what many felt was her last gasp of notoriety.

After the debacle of Les Milandes, Baker slowly began a series of comeback attempts that would remind fans old and new what a classic treasure was still in their midst. At age 53, she headlined *Paris Mes Amours* at the Olympia, Paris, in 1959. She returned to the Olympia in 1968. Part of her act involved riding a motorcycle onto the stage. In 1973, she opened at Carnegie Hall to a standing ovation, giving her the popular acceptance in America she had sought for so long. She followed this with the smash Parisienne review *Bobino* in 1975.

She died in Paris after attending a large party in Monaco given in her honor. Josephine Baker was the first American-born woman to receive French military honors at her funeral. Huge throngs surrounded the Arc de Triomphe to see her on her way. Although America never could figure out what to do with her, and never really had a niche for her, "Place Josephine Baker" in the Montparnasse Quarter of Paris was named in her honor. As many around the world celebrated the 100th anniversary of her birth in 2006, it was black women perhaps most of all who had come to realize what a role model she had been. Josephine Baker went through six marriages in her long, peripatetic life — some legal, some not. Her first husband was Willie Wells, her second was Billy Baker. Her third husband was financier Jean Lion. She also married her "manager," Giuseppe "Pepito" Abatino — a Sicilian stonemason who passed himself off as a count. Her marriage to band leader Jo Bouillon, predating and up to the era of the Rainbow Tribe, was in some ways her most satisfying union. Her last "marriage" was to American artist Robert Brady (they exchanged vows in an empty church without being legally married).

Feature Films: *Die Frauen von Folies-Bergères* (1927), *La Revue des Revues* (1927), *La Sirène des Tropiques* (1927), *Le Pompier des Folies-Bergères* (1928), *La Folie du Jour* (1929), *Zou Zou* (1934), *Princesse Tam Tam* (1935), *Moulin-Rouge* (uncredited; 1939), *Fausse Alert* (*The French Way*, 1945), *An jedem Finger Zehn* (1954), *Carosello del Varietà* (1955), *Zelig* (archival; 1983).

TV: *Josephine Baker i København* (1957), *Grüsse aus Zürich* (1963), *Amigos del Martes* (1964), *Sábado 64* (1965), *Aquì el segundo programa* (1966), *The Mike Douglas Show* (197?), *Chasing a Rainbow: The Life of Josephine Baker* (archival; 1986), *The Secret Life of Sergei Eisenstein* (archival; 1987), *The Road to War* (archival; 1989), *Victor Borge's Tivoli* (archival; 1993), *Paris Was a Woman* (archival; 1995), *Intimate Portrait: Josephine Baker* (archival; 1998), *Jazz* (archival; 2001).

Banks, Tyra Born in Los Angeles, California, December 4, 1973.

Supermodels tend to come and go. When their runway career is over, they become the stuff of *Whatever Happened to...?* books. But that has not been the case with Tyra Banks. Born Tyra Lynne Banks, this 5'10" supermodel, producer, talk show host, actress, businesswoman and philanthropist began her ascent to fame by walking the runways in New York, Paris, London, Tokyo, and capitals throughout the world. She is today ranked as one of world's most influential people by *Time* magazine. She is the daughter of Carolyn (a fashion manager and medical photographer who later married Clifford Johnson) and Donald Banks (a computer consultant). They divorced in 1980 when Tyra was six. She has a brother named Devin. Banks grew up in Inglewood, California, and attended Immaculate Heart High School in Los Angeles.

While a high school student, she applied to five colleges with the intention of majoring in film and TV production. Instead she signed with Elite Model Management in her senior year. Although she was accepted at Loyola Marymount College, she moved to Paris for a year, where she modeled for some of the leading designers. Banks has done extensive print and runway work for most of the fashion industry icons, including Tommy Hilfiger, Isaac Mizrahi, Bill Blass, Anna Sui, Cynthia Rowley, Christian Dior, Perry Ellis, Yves Saint Laurent, and Oscar de la Renta. Her advertising accounts are equally legion: Swatch, Coors Light, CoverGirl, Nike, Pepsi, and Victoria's Secret, among others.

Banks was the first black woman on the cover of *GQ*, the *Sports Illustrated* swimsuit issue, and the Victoria's Secret catalogue. She has also been on the cover of *Seventeen*, *Vogue*, *Cosmopolitan*, *Harper's Bazaar*, *Elle*, *Essence*, and dozens of other magazines. She retired from modeling in 2005 to concentrate on *The Tyra Banks Show* (begun in 2005), and *America's Next Top Model* (begun in 2000; spin-offs include *Australia's Next Top Model* and *Canada's Next Top Model*), and her numerous business pursuits. She walked the runway for the final time on the Victoria's Secret 2005 TV special.

She had a relationship in the 1990s with director John Singleton and made her theatrical film debut in his *Higher Learning* (1995); they broke it off in 1996. Banks then dated Sacramento Kings forward Chris Webber, but broke off their two-year romance in 2004. *Higher Learning* was about racism on a college campus at the fictional Columbus University. *Love Stinks* (1999) featured Banks in the second female lead as Holly Garnett, the newlywed best friend of a woman about to marry a sitcom writer. In *Coyote Ugly* (2000) she is Zoe, a sexy bar maid. The TV movie *Life-Size* (2000) gave Banks one of her better roles as a doll named Eve who is brought to life by mistake when a girl, who is trying to resurrect her mother, finds herself with a literal living doll. In *Halloween: Resurrection* (2002), she has a secondary role as Nora Winston, a reality show programmer who eventually runs afoul of mass murderer Michael Myers. Tyra Banks in a horror film is a mind-boggling concept, but she seems to be having fun.

Tyra Banks.

Banks has appeared in a number of musical videos, including *Black or White* (Michael Jackson), *Love Thing* (Tina Turner), *Too Funky* (George Michael), and *Trifle Life* (Mobb Deep). Her own musical career (the single "Shake Ya Body") did not take off, despite the fact that her video (like the song, it wasn't good) debuted on *America's Next Top Model*. She had a recurring role on *The Fresh Prince of Bel-Air* in 1993 as Will's ex-girlfriend, and has acted on other shows including *Just Shoot Me!* and *American Dreams*. She started the Tyra Banks scholarship program in 1994. She also created TZONE, a development program for disadvantaged teenage girls in the Los Angeles. She is the CEO of TYInc., a film and TV production company. In 2007, *Forbes* magazine estimated her earnings for the year at $18 million. Banks is the author of *Tyra's Beauty Inside & Out* (Harper Collins, 1998).

Feature Films including TV Movies: *Inferno!* (TV; 1992), *Extra Terrorestrial Alien Encounter* (short film made for Disney theme park ride, 1994), *Higher Learning* (1995), *A Woman Like That* (1997), *Love Stinks* (1999), *The Apartment Complex* (TV; 1999), *Love & Basketball* (2000), *Life-Size* (TV; 2000), *Coyote Ugly* (2000), *Halloween: Resurrection* (2002), *Eight Crazy Nights* (voice, 2002), *Larceny* (2004), *Mr. Woodcock* (2007), *Tropic Thunder* (2008).

TV: *Soul Train Comedy Awards* (1993), *The Word* (1993), *The Fresh Prince of Bel-Air* (recurring role of Jackie Ames; 1993), *Soul Train* (1994), *Supermodels in the Rainforest* (1995), *Lauren Hutton* (1996), *Sports Illustrated: Swimsuit '97*, *The 39th Annual Grammy Awards* (1997), *New York Undercover* (recurring role of Natasha Claybourne; 1997), *Elmopalooza!* (1998), *Howard Stern* (1998), *Space Ghost Coast to Coast* (1998), *The Oprah Winfrey Show* (6 episodes; 1998–2001), *Just Shoot Me!* ("Nina Sees Red," Parts I and II, 1999), *Wetten, dass...?* (1999), *The Teen Choice Awards 1999*, *The Teen Files* ("The Truth About Drinking," 1999), *The Hughleys* (1999), *Stars and Bras* (2000), *Who Wants to Be a Millionaire?* (2000),

Mad TV (2 episodes; 2000), *Felicity* (recurring role of Jane Scott; 2000), *Late Night with Conan O'Brien* (5 segments; 2000–07), *Soul Food* (2001), *The Victoria's Secret Fashion Show* (2001), *Driven* (2002), *Fashiontrance* (2002), *The Victoria's Secret Fashion Show* (2002), *Cleavage* (2002), *Last Call with Carson Daly* (2003), *Totally Gay!* (2003), *Total Request Live* (2003), *The Victoria's Secret Fashion Show* (2003), *America's Next Top Model* (hostess-producer; 2003-present), *The View* (5 segments; 2003–07), *The 61st Annual Golden Globe Awards* (2004), *Late Late Show with Craig Kilborn* (2004), *The Wayne Brady Show* (2004), *The Daily Show* (2004), *On-Air with Ryan Seacrest* (2 segments; 2004), *Hollywood HD* (2004), *Punk'd* (2004), *The 35th NAACP Image Awards* (2004), *The Teen Choice Awards 2004, Hyppönen Enbuske Experience* (2004), *Live with Regis and Kathie Lee* (2004), *The Tony Danza Show* (2004), *The 2nd Annual Vibe Awards* (2004), *Mad TV* (2004), *All of Us* ("O Brother, Where Art Thou?" 2004), *American Dreams* ("Chasing the Past," 2004), *Jimmy Kimmel Live!* (2 segments; 2004 and 2006), *The Ellen DeGeneres Show* (3 segments; 2004–06), *The Tyra Banks Show* (2005–present), *E! True Hollywood Story* (2005), *The 47th Annual Grammy Awards* (2005), *Good Day Live* (2005), *106 & Park Top 10 Live* (2005), *The Early Show* (2005), *The Fabulous Life of....* ("Today's Hottest Supermodels," 2005), *The 32nd Annual Daytime Emmy Awards* (2005), *The Tonight Show with Jay Leno* (2 episodes; 2005), *The Victoria's Secret Fashion Show* (2005), *The 32nd Annual People's Choice Awards* (2006), *Corazón de...* (2 segments; 2005–06), *Germany's Next Top Model* (2006), *The New Price Is Right* (2006), *The 37th NAACP Image Awards* (2006), *The 20th Annual Soul Train Music Awards* (2006), *Late Late Show with Craig Ferguson* (2 segments; 2005–06), *Legends Ball* (2006), *Kathy Griffin: My Life on the D-List* ("Going, Going, Gone," 2006), *Forbes Celebrity 100: Who Made Bank?* (2006), *The 58th Annual Primetime Emmy Awards* (2006), *Entertainment Tonight* (2 segments; 2006–08), *Howard Stern on Demand* (2006), *Inside Edition* (2006), *Larry King Live* (2 segments; 2006–07), *An Evening of Stars: Tribute to Aretha Franklin* (2007), *The 38th NAACP Image Awards* (2007), *Happy Birthday, Elton!* (2007), *Keeping Up with the Kardashians* (2007), *The View* (2008), *35th Annual Daytime Emmy Awards* (2008).

Video/DVD: *Straight Clownin'* (2002), *Sports Illustrated 40th Anniversary Swimsuit Special* (2004).

Bassett, Angela Born in New York, New York, August 16, 1958.

Angela Bassett is one of seven black actresses to receive a Best Actress Oscar nomination, the others being Dorothy Dandridge, Diana Ross, Cicely Tyson, Diahann Carroll, Whoopi Goldberg and Halle Berry. Bassett has specialized in deeply-realized performances of real-life women. Her interpretation of Tina Turner, whom she had never even seen perform before playing the role, garnered her an Oscar nomination and won her the Golden Globe for Outstanding Lead Actress in a Motion Picture. She won the NAACP Image Award for Outstanding Supporting Actress in a motion picture for her understated, poignant performance as Betty Shabazz, the wife of Malcolm X, in the film of the same name. (She had also played Shabazz in the 1995 film *Panther.*) In addition, she was Emmy nominated for her lead role in the TV movie *The Rosa Parks Story* (2002).

Born in a Harlem housing project, Bassett grew up in St. Petersburg, Florida, with her divorced mother (a social worker) and her sister D'nette. She was an honor student, and at age 15 was chosen to attend an Outward Bound conference in Washington, D.C. While there, she was given a chance to see a performance of John Steinbeck's *Of Mice and Men* starring James Earl Jones. It was a pivotal moment for her, because she knew then that she wanted to get involved in theater. Encouraged by a high school teacher, she applied for Yale and got a scholarship, spending seven years there, including three post-grad years studying drama. She received a bachelor of arts in African American studies from Yale in 1980. In 1983, she earned a master of fine arts degree from the Yale School of Drama.

It was at Yale that she met her future husband, Courtney B. Vance, a 1986 graduate of the drama school. They married in 1997. They have two children, twins Bronwyn Golden and Slater Josiah, born through a surrogate in January 2006. In the early years, she worked as a photo researcher at *U.S. News & World Report* magazine and looked for acting work in the New York theater. She appeared in J.E. Franklin's *Black Girl* at Second Stage Theatre and in two August Wilson plays at the Yale Repertory Theatre (*Ma Rainey's Black Bottom* in 1984; *Joe Turner's Come and Gone* in 1986).

Films include *Strange Days* (as Lornette "Mace" Mason, a dynamic action heroine in an apocalyptic science fiction adventure; 1995); *Waiting to Exhale* (as Bernadine, a wronged wife who clears the house of all of her husband's possessions and holds an instant fire sale on the lawn in a classic scene; 1995); *Vampire in Brooklyn* (Wes Craven's offbeat, critically lambasted romantic horror comedy; 1995); and *How Stella Got Her Groove Back* (from Terry McMillan's best-seller about a successful middle-aged businesswoman who falls in love with a handsome Jamaican man half her age; 1998). In July 2005, she starred with her husband in John Guare's version of *His Girl Friday* at the Guthrie Theater in Minneapolis.

On TV, she appeared on *Alias* (2005) in a recurring role of CIA director Hayden Chase. *ER* bolstered its cast in its final season in the fall of 2008 with the addition of Bassett as emergency room chief Dr. Cate Banfield. She co-authored the book *Friends: A Love Story* with her husband. Bassett received a star on the Hollywood Walk of Fame in March 2008. She has served as a UNICEF goodwill ambassador for the United States.

Feature Films including TV Movies: *F/X* (1986), *Liberty* (TV; 1986), *Family of Spies* (TV; 1990), *Challenger* (TV; 1990), *In the Best Interest of the Child* (TV; 1990), *Perry Mason: The Case of the Silenced Singer* (TV; 1990), *Kindergarten Cop* (1990), *Critters 4* (1991), *Line of Fire: The Morris Dees Story* (TV; 1991), *Fire: Trapped on the 37th Floor* (1991), *Boyz n the Hood* (1991), *The Heroes of Desert Storm* (TV; 1991), *City of Hope* (1991), *Locked Up: A Mother's Rage* (TV, 1991), *One Special Victory* (TV; 1991), *Passion Fish* (1992), *Innocent Blood* (1992), *The Jacksons: An American Dream* (TV; 1992), *Malcolm X* (1992), *What's Love Got to Do with It* (1993), *Vampire in Brooklyn* (1995), *Panther* (1995), *Strange Days* (1995), *Waiting to Exhale* (1995), *Contact* (1997), *How Stella Got Her Groove Back* (1998), *Music of the Heart* (1999), *Supernova* (2000), *Whispers: An Elephant's Tale* (voice; 2000), *Boesman and Lena* (2000), *The Score* (2001), *Ruby's Bucket of Blood* (TV; 2001), *The Rosa Parks Story* (2002), *Sunshine State* (2002), *Masked and Anonymous* (2003), *The Lazarus Child* (2004), *Mr. 3000* (2004), *Mr. & Mrs. Smith* (voice; 2005), *Akeelah and the Bee* (2006), *Time Bomb* (TV; 2006), *Meet the Robinsons* (voice; 2007), *Gospel Hill* (2007), *Meet the Browns* (2008), *Of Boys and Men* (2008), *Nothing But the Truth* (2008), *Toussaint* (2009), *Notorious* (2009).

TV: *26th NAACP Image Awards* (1994), *The 66th Annual Academy Awards* (1994), *A Century of Women* (miniseries; voice; 1994), *The 67th Annual Academy Awards* (1995), *Reading Rainbow* (1995), *The 68th Annual Academy Awards* (1996), *Women in Film Crystal Awards* (1996), *Cinema tres* (1996), *Off the Menu: The Last Days of Chasen's* (1997), *The 69th Annual Academy Awards* (1997), *The 72nd Annual Academy Awards* (2000), *The Rosie O'Donnell Show* (2 episodes; 1998 and 2000), *20th Century–Fox: The Blockbuster Years* (2000), *The 2001 IFP/West Independent Spirit Awards* (2001), *Muhammad Ali's All-Star 60th Birthday Celebration!* (2002), *33rd NAACP Image Awards* (2002), *Essence Awards* (2002), *ESPY Awards* (2002), *The 4th Annual Family Television Awards* (2002), *Independent Lens* (2002), *Unchained Memories: Readings from the Slave Narratives* (2003), *Freedom: A History of Us* (2 episodes; "Let Freedom Ring," "Marching to Freedom Land," 2003), *Hollywood Celebrates Denzel Washington* (2003), *34th NAACP Image Awards* (2003), *When I Was a Girl* ("Singers," 2003), *The Bernie Mac Show* ("Laughing Matters," 2003), *2004 Trumpet Awards, 4th Annual BET Awards* (2004), *Late Late Show with Craig Kilborn* (2004), *Celebrity Poker Showdown* (2004), *Alias* (recurring role of CIA director Hayden Chase; 2005), *Tsunami Aid: A Concert of Hope* (2005), *Party Planner with David Tutera* (2005), *36th NAACP Image Awards* (2005), *The 59th Annual Tony Awards* (2005), *A Capitol Fourth* (2005), *An Evening of Stars: Tribute to Stevie Wonder* (2006), *The 11th Annual Critics' Choice Awards* (2006), *12th Annual Screen Actors Guild Awards* (2006), *The*

Angela Bassett in *Vampire in Brooklyn* (1995).

Oprah Winfrey Show (2006), *106 & Park Top 10 Live* (2006), *Legends Ball* (2006), *AFI's 100 Years ... 100 Cheers: America's Most Inspiring Movies* (2006), *The 2006 Black Movie Awards, Corazón de...* (2006), *Tavis Smiley (2007), The View* (2007), *Rachael Ray* (2007), *ER* (recurring role of Dr. Cate Banfield, 2008).

Video/DVD: *Our Friend, Martin* (voice, 1999).

Beals, Jennifer Born in Chicago, Illinois, December 19, 1963.

Jennifer Beals appeared in high school plays and had a bit part in *My Bodyguard* (1980). She attended the Goodman School of Drama at DePaul University, Chicago. She also studied American literature at Yale, and was still a freshman at Yale when she filmed *Flashdance* (1983), a groundbreaking, very influential film that used music video techniques in a feature film. She starred as the unlikely character Alex, a welder by day and a flashdancer (exotic dancer) by night. Beals was nominated for a Golden Globe (Best Actress, Comedy/Musical), and the title song, stirringly sung by Irene Cara, received an Oscar. After the film was already a smash box office hit it was revealed that Alex's athletic, breathtaking dance moves were performed by dance double Marine Jahan. However, Beal's rough-hewn but charming performance is appealing even if she didn't perform much of the dancing. She won an NAACP Image Award for Best Actress for the role. Strategically ripped, oversized sweaters became a national craze, and suddenly exotic dancers were role models of a sort.

Jennifer Beals in *The Bride* (1985).

Beals also starred in *The Bride* ('85), an interesting if not entirely successful variation on Mary Shelley's *Frankenstein.* She played Eva, an artificial Eve to Dr. Frankenstein's monster. She also starred opposite Nicholas Cage in *Vampire's Kiss* ('89); this strange film is totally dominated by Cage, so it's hard to even remember her in it. In 1995, she co-starred memorably with Denzel Washington in director Carl Franklin's *Devil in a Blue Dress*, a film noir murder mystery featuring Walter Mosley's Easy Rawlins character dealing with a duplicitous Beals.

After graduating from Yale in 1986, Beals married filmmaker Alexandre Rockwell (1986–96) and appeared in several of his films, such as *In the Soup*—which won the 1992 Grand Jury Prize at the Sundance Film Festival and the Audience Award at the Deauville Film Festival—and the less successful *Four Rooms* in 1995. One of her best film roles of more recent vintage is *Roger Dodger* (2002). She plays an arch cynic who skewers the male chauvinist pig title character. In her latter day career, Beals has shown a refreshing interest in quirky, independent films even if they rarely register as a blip on the cultural radar (such as *Mrs. Parker and the Vicious Circle* and *Blood and Concrete*). She is stepmother to her current husband Ken Dixon's two children. She gave birth to her first biological child, a girl, in October 2005.

Today she is best known for her starring role on the popular Showtime series *The L Word*, a sensitive, amusing series in which she plays lesbian art dealer Bette Porter. She is the daughter of an African American father (Alfred Beals, a grocery store owner) and an Irish mother (Jeanne Cohen, an elementary school teacher). Her father died when she was 10 years old, and her mother remarried (Edward Cohen). She has two brothers, Bobby and Gregory. While at Yale, she became friends with David Duchovny, who recommended her for the female lead on *The X Files*, which actually went to Gillian Anderson.

Feature Films including TV and Video Movies: *My Bodyguard* (1980), *Flashdance* (1983), *That's Dancing* (archival; 1985), *The Bride*

(1985), *La Partita* (1988), *Split Decisions* (aka *Kid Gloves,* 1988), *Sons* (1989), *Vampire's Kiss* (1989), *Dr. M* (aka *Club Extinction,* 1990), *La Madonne et le Dragon* (TV; 1990), *Blood and Concrete* (1991), *In the Soup* (1992), *Terror Stalks the Class Reunion* (TV; 1992), *Indecency* (TV; 1992), *Le Grand Pardon II* (1992), *The Princess and the Cobbler* (voice; 1993), *Night Owl* (TV; 1993), *Dead on Sight* (1994), *Mrs. Parker and the Vicious Circle* (1994), *Four Rooms* (1995), *Devil in a Blue Dress* (1995), *Let It Be Me* (1995), *Wishful Thinking* (1997), *The Twilight of the Golds* (1997), *Body and Soul* (1998), *The Prophecy II* (1998), *The Spree* (TV; 1998), *The Last Days of Disco* (1998), *Something More* (1999), *Without Malice* (TV; 2000), *Fear of Flying* (2000), *A House Divided* (TV; 2000), *Militia* (2000), *The Big House* (TV; 2001), *Out of Line* (2001), *The Anniversary Party* (2001), *After the Storm* (TV; 2001), *Feast of All Saints* (TV; 2001), *13 Moons* (2002), *Roger Dodger* (2002), *They Shoot Divas, Don't They?* (TV; 2002), *Runaway Jury* (2003), *Catch That Kid* (2004), *Break a Leg* (2005), *Desolation Sound* (2005), *Troubled Waters* (2006), *The Grudge 2* (2006), *My Name Is Sarah* (TV; 2007), *Joueuse* (2008).

TV: *The 56th Annual Academy Awards* (1984), *Faerie Tale Theatre* ("Cinderella," 1985), *The 57th Annual Academy Awards* (1985), *The Word* (1990), *2000 Malibu Road* (recurring role of Perry Quinn; 1992), *Caro Diario* (1993), *Poetry, Passion—The Postman* (1996), *The Outer Limits* ("Bodies of Evidence," 1997), *Nothing Sacred* ("Kindred Spirits," 1998), *The Hunger* ("And She Laughed," 1999), *The Directors: Adrian Lyne* (2000), *VH1: Where Are They Now?* (2000), *Hollywood Goes to Hell* (2000), *Seitenblicke* (2002), *Dinner for Five* (2002), *Frasier* ("Goodnight, Seattle," Parts I and II, 2004), *The Daily Show* (2004), *Live with Regis and Kathie Lee* (2004), *The Sharon Osbourne Show* (2004), *The L Word* (50 episodes in role of Bette Porter; 2004–08), *Late Late Show with Craig Ferguson* (2 segments; 2005 and 2006), *Law & Order* ("Charity Case," 2007), *Sexo en serie* (archival; 2008), *The View* (2008), *19th Annual GLAAD Media Awards* (2008), *Eigo de Shabera-Night* (2008).

Beauvais, Garcelle Born in St. Marc, Haiti, November 26, 1966.

Garcelle Beauvais' mother, nurse Marie Claire, was a teacher who moved Garcelle and her six older siblings to Massachusetts after she was divorced from her husband, Axel Beauvais, a lawyer. When Beauvais was 16, the family moved again, this time to Miami. She attended North Miami Beach High School and Miami Norland High School. The following year, Beauvais was already pursuing a modeling career in Manhattan. She signed with Ford Models and has modeled for designers Calvin Klein and Isaac Mizrahi. She was a member of the Los Angeles comedy troupe The Groundlings. She got an ongoing role on the Aaron Spelling series *Models Inc.* (1994–95) and appeared on such popular shows as *Miami Vice* and *Hangin' with Mr. Cooper.*

Her first marriage was to producer Daniel Saunders, with whom she had a son, Oliver (1992). She married Mike Nilon in 2001 and had twins, Jax and Jaid, born in 2007. Beauvais is best known for her roles on *NYPD Blue* as Assistant District Attorney Valerie Heywood and on *The Jamie Foxx Show* as Francesca Monroe.

Feature Films including Video and TV Movies: *Manhunter* (1986), *Coming to America* (1988), *Every Breath* (1993), *Wild Wild West* (1999), *Double Take* (2001), *Bad Company* (2002), *Second String* (TV; 2002), *Barbershop 2: Back in Business* (2004), *American Gun* (2005), *10.5: Apocalypse* (TV; 2006), *The Cure* (TV; 2007), *I Know Who Killed Me* (2007), *Women in Trouble* (2009).

TV: *Miami Vice* (2 episodes; "The Maze," "Give a Little, Take a Little," 1984 and 1985), *The Cosby Show* ("An Early Spring," 1985), *Family*

Garcelle Beauvais in *The Jamie Foxx Show.*

Matters (4 episodes; "Old and Alone," "Scenes from a Mall," "To Be or Not to Be, Part II," "A Ham Is Born," 1991–96), *Dream On* ("Red All Over," 1992), *Hangin' with Mr. Cooper* ("Boy Don't Leave," 1993), *The Fresh Prince of Bel Air* (3 episodes; "That's No Lady, That's My Cousin," "For Whom the Wedding Bells Toll," "Not I Barbeque," 1992–95), *Models Inc.* (recurring role of Cynthia Nichols; 1994–95), *The Wayans Bros.* ("Fatal Subtraction," 1995), *The Jamie Foxx Show* (recurring role of Francesca "Fancy" Monroe; 1996–2001), *Arli$$* ("The Cult of Celebrity," 1999), *Opposite Sex* (recurring role of Maya Bradley; 2000), *NYPD Blue* (recurring role of Valerie Heywood; 2001–04), *Titans* ("She Stoops to Conquer," 2001), *The 28th Annual People's Choice Awards* (2002), *Inside NYPD Blue* (2002), *VH1 Big in 2002 Awards* (2002), *The Late Late Show with Craig Kilborn* (2003), *The Bernie Mac Show* ("Bernie Mac Rope-a-Dope," 2003), *Cooking with Mom* (2003), *ABC's 50th Anniversary Celebration* (2003), *I Love the '70s* (2003), *Curb Your Enthusiasm* ("The Surrogate," 2004), *Life with Bonnie* ("Therabeautic," 2004), *Tavis Smiley* (2005), *Jimmy Kimmel Live* (2005), *TV Land's Top Ten* (2005), *Glamour's 50 Biggest Fashion Do's and Don'ts* (2005), *Eyes* (recurring role of Nora Gage; 2005–07), *2006 Independent Spirit Awards*, *Women in Law* (pilot; 2006), *CSI Miami* ("Death Pool 100," 2006), *Entertainment Tonight* (3 segments; 2007–08).

Video/DVD: *Down Low* (2003).

Beavers, Louise Born in Cincinnati, Ohio, March 8, 1902; died October 26, 1962, Hollywood, California.

Louise Beavers was well known for her role in the film version of Fannie Hurst's novel *Imitation of Life* (1934). She played Claudette Colbert's housekeeper Delilah Johnson. Delilah was a doting mother to daughter Peola, a haughty, light-skinned girl passing for white (Fredi Washington). In actuality, Beavers was only a year older than Washington. For white audiences, this was a lesson in racial politics among blacks. For black audiences, it was the same old racial politics.

Beavers moved with her family to the Los Angeles area at age 11 and studied at Pasadena High School. Her mother was a voice teacher. Beavers considered being a nurse, but soon decided on a career in show business. She joined a musical group called Lady Minstrels and took a foray into vaudeville. Beavers became a maid and an assistant to Paramount star Leatrice Joy, and later to Lilyan Tashman. By 1924 she was doing extra work in films and had bit roles in *The Gold Diggers* and *Uncle Tom's Cabin*. She began to attract some notice with maid roles in such major films as *Coquette*, *She Done Him Wrong* starring Mae West, and *Bombshell* with Jean Harlow. These subservient but attention-grabbing roles led to her landmark break in the classic *Imitation of Life*.

In between maid roles, Beavers starred in "race films" such as *Prison Bait* (1939). Although she remained extremely active with roles in major films throughout the 1940s, both "dignified" and wise-cracking servant roles began to peter out in the 1950s, and Beavers turned to television, where she succeeded Ethel Waters and Hattie McDaniel in the title role of *The Beulah Show* (1952–53). Beavers was by far the blandest of the three Beulahs, but it could be argued that the hit show was running out of steam by that time, and the cast was simply going through their paces. She was also a regular as Louise the maid on *The Danny Thomas Show* (1953–54). She followed this with the recurring role of Delia on *The Swamp Fox* (1959–60), a rotating segment of the Disneyland series, alternating with the western *Elfego Baca*.

Beavers made her professional stage debut in 1957 in San Francisco with the short-lived *Praise House*, playing a caregiver who extols the Bible through song. She married late in life to Leroy Moore, a chef, who was her husband from 1952 until her death in 1962. She suffered from obesity throughout her life and contracted diabetes, ultimately succumbing to a heart attack. In 1976, Beavers was inducted into the Black Filmmakers Hall of Fame.

Feature Films including TV Movies: *The Gold Diggers* (1923), *Uncle Tom's Cabin* (1927), *Election Day* (short; 1929), *Coquette* (1929), *Glad Rag Doll* (1929), *Gold Diggers of Broadway* (1929), *Barnum Was Right* (1929), *Follow the Boys* (1944), *Wall Street* (1929), *Nix on Dames* (1929), *Second Choice* (1930), *Wide Open* (1930), *She Couldn't Say No* (1930), *True to the Navy* (1930), *Safety in Numbers* (1930), *Back Pay* (1930), *Recaptured Love* (1930), *Our Blushing Brides* (1930), *Manslaughter* (1930), *Outside the Law* (1930), *Bright Lights* (aka *Adventures in Africa*; 1930), *Paid* (1930), *Scandal Sheet* (1931), *Millie* (1931), *Don't Bet on Women* (1931), *Six Cylinder Love* (1931), *Up for Murder*

Lobby card for *Prison Bait* (*Reform School*) (1939) with Louise Beavers.

(aka *Fires of Youth*; 1931), *Party Husband* (1931), *Annabelle's Affairs* (1931), *Sundown Trail* (1931), *Reckless Living* (1931), *Girls About Town* (1931), *Heaven On Earth* (aka *Mississippi*; 1931), *Good Sport* (1931), *Ladies of the Big House* (1931), *The Greeks Had a Word for Them* (1932), *Freaks* (1932), *The Expert* (1932), *It's Tough to Be Famous* (1932), *You're Telling Me* (1932), *Young America* (1932), *Night World* (1932), *The Midnight Lady* (1932), *The Strange Love of Molly Louvin* (1932), *Street of Women* (1932), *The Dark Horse* (1932), *What Price Hollywood?* (1932), *Unashamed* (1932), *Divorce in the Family* (1932), *Hell's Highway* (1932), *Wild Girl* (1932), *Hesitating Love* (1932), *Too Busy to Work* (aka *Jubilo*; 1932), *She Done Him Wrong* (1933), *Her Splendid Folly* (1933), *42nd Street* (1933), *Girl Missing* (1933), *The Phantom Broadcast* (aka *Phantom of the Air*; 1933), *Pick-up* (1933), *Central Airport* (1933), *The Big Cage* (1933), *The Story of Temple Drake* (1933), *What Price Innocence?* (1933), *Hold Your Man* (1933), *Midnight Mary* (1933), *Her Bodyguard* (1933), *A Shriek in the Night* (1933), *Notorious but Nice* (1933), *Bombshell* (1933), *Only Yesterday* (1933), *In the Money* (1933), *Jimmy and Sally* (1933), *Grin and Bear It* (1933), *Palooka* (1934), *Bedside* (1934), *I've Got Your Number* (1934), *Gambling Lady* (1934), *A Modern Hero* (1934), *The Woman Condemned* (1934), *Registered Nurse* (1934), *Glamour* (1934), *I Believed in You* (1934), *Cheaters* (1934), *Merry Wives of Reno* (1934), *The Merry Frinks* (1934), *Dr. Monica* (1934), *I Give My Love* (1934), *Beggar's Holiday* (1934), *Imitation of Life* (1934), *West of the Pecos* (1934), *Million Dollar Baby* (1934), *Annapolis Farewell* (1935), *Bullets or Ballots* (1936), *The Gorgeous Hussy* (1936), *Wives Never Know* (1936), *General Spanky* (1936), *Rainbow on the River* (1936), *Make Way for Tomorrow* (1937), *Wings Over Honolulu* (1937), *Love in a Bungalow* (1937), *The Last Gangster* (1937), *Scan-*

dal Sheet (1938), *Life Goes On* (1938), *Brother Rat* (1938), *The Headleys at Home* (1938), *Peck's Bad Boy with the Circus* (1938), *Prison Bait* (aka *Reform School*, 1939), *Made for Each Other* (1939), *The Lady's from Kentucky* (1939), *Parole Fixer* (1940), *Women Without Names* (1940), *No Time for Comedy* (aka *Guy with a Grin*; 1940), *I Want a Divorce* (1940), *Virginia* (1941), *Sign of the Wolf* (1941), *Kisses for Breakfast* (1941), *Belle Starr* (1941), *Shadow of the Thin Man* (1941), *The Vanishing Virginian* (1942), *Young America* (1942), *Reap the Wild Wind* (1942), *Holiday Inn* (1942), *The Big Street* (1942), *Seven Sweethearts* (aka *Tulip Time*; 1942), *Tennessee Johnson* (1942), *Good Morning, Judge* (1943), *All By Myself* (1943), *Du Barry Was a Lady* (1943), *Top Man* (1943), *Jack London* (1943), *There's Something About a Soldier* (1943), *South of Dixie* (1944), *Dixie Jamboree* (1944), *Barbary Coast Gent* (1944), *Delightfully Dangerous* (1945), *Young Widow* (1946), *Lover Come Back* (1946), *Banjo* (1947), *Mr. Blandings Builds His Dream House* (1948), *A Southern Yankee* (1948), *For the Love of Mary* (1948), *Good Sam* (1948), *Tell It to the Judge* (1949), *Girls' School* (1950), *The Jackie Robinson Story* (1950), *My Blue Heaven* (1950), *Never Wave at a WAC* (1952), *Colorado Sundown* (1952), *I Dream of Jeannie* (1952), *Goodbye, My Lady* (1956), *You Can't Run Away from It* (1956), *Teenage Rebel* (1956), *Tammy and the Bachelor* (1957), *The Goddess* (1958), *All the Fine Young Cannibals* (1960), *The Facts of Life* (1960).

TV: *The Beulah Show* (in the title role; 1952–53), *Make Room for Daddy* (recurring role as Louise; 1953–54), *Stories of the Century* ("The Younger Brothers," 1954), *GE Theater* ("Amelia," 1955), *Star Stage* ("Cleopatra Collins," 1956), *Playhouse 90* ("The Hostess with the Mostess," 1957), *Frontier Doctor* ("Drifting Sands," 1959), *Bourbon Street Beat* ("The Mourning Cloak," 1959), *The Swamp Fox* (rotating series on *Disneyland*; 5 episodes in the recurring role of Delia; 1959–60), *Brown Sugar* (archival; 1986), *Mo' Funny: Black Comedy in America* (archival; 1993).

Belafonte, Shari (aka Belafonte-Harper, Shari) Born in New York, New York, September 22, 1955.

Shari Belafonte is the daughter of actor, singer and activist Harry Belafonte; her mother is Marguerite Byrd, a psychologist. Her first husband was Robert Harper (1977–88), then she married Sam Behrens in 1989. Belafonte received her master of fine arts in drama from Carnegie Mellon University in 1977. She started as a production assistant and assistant director on public TV. She got work as a cover girl model and appeared in Calvin Klein jeans ads. Aaron Spelling cast her as Julie Gilette on what would prove to be the popular ABC series *Hotel* (1983–88); she stayed for the run of the show.

She made her feature film debuts in *Time Walker* and *If You Could See What I Hear* (both 1982). She also began a music career on Metronome Records, releasing several albums in Europe, and made her theatrical debut in *Tamara*, playing the title role in the Los Angeles production. Later she starred as Dr. Laura Wingate on the USA network series *Beyond Reality* for a two-year run. And she was featured on *With Robin Leach and Shari Belafonte*, an update of Leach's popular show *Lifestyles of the Rich and Famous*. She hosted a travel program in 2006 called *Travels in Mexico and the Caribbean with Shari Belafonte* on NYC-TV.

Most recently, she appeared as Catherine Wicke on the plastic surgery opus *Nip/Tuck*. Belafonte has produced for theater, network and public TV, and feature films. She has done voiceovers, acted as a moderator, and has been a spokesperson for numerous corporate sponsors.

Feature Films including TV Movies: *If You Could See What I Hear* (1982), *Time Walker* (1982), *Overnight Sensation* (1983), *Velvet* (TV; 1984), *The Midnight Hour* (TV; 1985), *Kate's Secret* (TV; 1986), *Speed Zone!* (1989), *Perry Mason: The Case of the All-Star Assassin* (TV; 1989), *Murder by Numbers* (1990), *Feuer, eis & dynamit* (1990), *French Silk* (TV; 1994), *The Heidi Chronicles* (TV; 1995), *Harlequin's Loving Evangeline* (1998), *Mars* (1998), *Babylon 5: Thirdspace* (TV; 1998).

TV: *ABC Weekend Specials* ("The Big Hex of Little Lulu," 1981), *Hart to Hart* ("The Latest in High Fashion Murder," 1981), *Trapper John, M.D.* ("Three on a Mismatch," 1982), *Diff'rent Strokes* ("The Older Woman," 1982), *Hotel* (recurring role of Julie Gillette; 1983–88), *Battle of the Network Stars XV* (1983), *Battle of the Network Star XVI* (1984), *The Love Boat* ("Love Is Blind/ Baby Makers/Lady and the Maid," 1984), *Battle of the Network Stars XVII* (1984), *Matt Houston* ("New Orleans Nightmare," 1985), *Night of 100*

Stars II (1985), *Wetten, dass...?* (1985), *The 7th Annual Black Achievement Awards* (1986), *Square One TV* (1987), *Happy 100th Birthday, Hollywood* (1987), *ZDF Hitparade* (1987), *Battle of the Network Stars XIX* (1988), *The Women of Brewster Place* (miniseries; 1989), *Gravedale High* (voice; 1990), *The Jaleel White Special* (1991), *Beyond Reality* (recurring role of Laura Wingate; 1991–93), *The Player* (1992), *Sonic the Hedgehog* (voice, 2 episodes; 1994), *10th Annual TV Academy Hall of Fame* (1994), *Lifestyles of the Rich and Famous* (co-host with Robin Leach; 1994–95), *Sea World/Busch Gardens Party for the Planet* (1995), *Hey Arnold!* (voice, 3 episodes; 1996–97), *The Real Adventures of Jonny Quest* (voice; 1997), *Intimate Portrait* ("Diahann Carroll," 1998), *Nature* ("The Octopus Show," 2000), *The District* ("The Project," 2001), *Nip/Tuck* ("Lulu Grandiron," 2008).

Bell, Jeannie (aka Bell, Jeanie; Bell, Jean) Born in St. Louis, Missouri, November 23, 1943.

"T.N.T. Jackson, she'll put you in traction!" Or so went the tag line in the trailer for the outrageous 1975 blaxploitation film for which Jeannie Bell is best known today, *T.N.T. Jackson*. Diana "T.N.T." Jackson, a sexy karate expert, searches for her brother's killer in Hong Kong. Even given the intrinsic appeal of an *outre* fight scene where Bell wipes out a squadron of bad guys while clad only in her panties, she had essentially zero knowledge of the martial arts and it shows, but her street charisma (and her *Playboy* Playmate of the Month October 1969 body) gets her through the scene and the film, if barely.

Jeannie Bell in *T.N.T. Jackson* (1975).

She also appeared in a clutch of other blaxploitation films, including *Melinda* (1972), *Trouble Man* (1972), *Black Gunn* (1972), and *Three the Hard Way* (1974), the latter two with Jim Brown. Bell married businessman Gary Judis in 1986; they have a son. She reportedly had an affair with actor Richard Burton.

Feature Films including TV Movies: *Melinda* (1972), *Trouble Man* (1972), *Black Gunn* (1972), *Mean Streets* (1973), *Policewomen* (1974), *Three the Hard Way* (1974), *Negro es un bello color* (1974), *The Klansman* (1974), *T.N.T. Jackson* (1975), *Disco 9000* (1976), *The Muthers* (1976), *Casanova & Co.* (1977), *The Choirboys* (1977).

TV: *The Beverly Hillbillies* (5 episodes in the recurring role of Sugar Jean Bell; "Simon Legree Drysdale," "Hotel for Women," "Three-Day Reprieve," "Shorty Spits the Hook," "Marry Me, Shorty," 1970), *Sanford and Son* ("Lamont, Is That You?" 1973), *Ironside* ("The Last Payment," 1973), *Police Woman* ("Seven-Eleven," 1974), *That's My Mama* ("Clifton's Big Move," 1974), *Kolchak: The Night Stalker* ("Primal Scream," 1975), *Baretta* ("Carla," 1977), *Starsky and Hutch* ("Starsky and Hutch Are Guilty," 1977).

Bell Calloway, Vanessa Born in Cleveland, Ohio, March 20, 1957.

Vanessa Bell Calloway attended Howard University in Washington, D.C.; then she received a bachelor of fine arts degree with an emphasis on dance from Ohio University. She began her illustrious TV career on two soaps: *Days of Our Lives* (as Denise Preston; 1985) and *All My Children* (as Yvonne Caldwell; 1985). Calloway appeared on three episodes of *Boston Public* (as Michele Ronning; 2001), and played Maggie Langston on *Under One Roof* (1995) with James Earl Jones and Earl Morton, an ambitious series about a police officer in Seattle with an extended family. She received NAACP Image Award nominations for both series: Outstanding Lead Actress in a Drama Series for *Under One Roof*, and Outstanding Supporting Actress in a Drama Series for *Boston Public*.

Calloway also received an NAACP Image Award nomination for Outstanding Lead Actress in a Television Movie or Mini-series for *America's Dream* (1996), three stories of black life in America. In her segment, she was the teacher of "The

Boy Who Painted Christ Black." A fourth nomination was for Outstanding Lead Actress in a Television Movie or Mini-series for her role as Johnnie Mae Matthews in *The Temptations*. Her fifth nomination was for Outstanding Lead Actress in a Drama Series for *Orleans* (as District Attorney Rosalee Clark; 1997). And her sixth was for Outstanding Supporting Actress in a Drama Series for *The District* (as Gwen Hendrix; 2004), about life and crime control in Washington, D.C.

A gourmet cook for almost 20 years, Calloway created, wrote, executive produced and starred in a reality TV show that she created for tv one titled *Vanessa Bell Calloway: In the Company of Friends*. Vanessa and her husband of 20 years, Dr. Anthony M. Calloway (they married in 1988, and have two children, Ashley and Alexandra), hosted the show with celebrity guests. Calloway is an accomplished dancer trained by Alvin Ailey, George Faison and Otis Salid. She has generally been relegated to smaller supporting roles when on the big screen, but her film roles have included Eddie Murphy's ill-fated bride-to-be in *Coming to America* (1988), and roles in *What's Love Got to Do with It* (1993) and *Cheaper by the Dozen* (2002). Her daughter Ashley starred in the BET show *Baldwin Hills*.

Feature Films including Video and TV Movies: *Number One with a Bullet* (1987), *Death Spa* (1988), *The Return of the Desperado* (TV; 1988), *Coming to America* (1988), *A Little Bit Strange* (TV; 1989), *Polly* (TV; 1989), *Polly: Comin' Home* (TV; 1990), *Why Colors?* (1992), *Memphis* (TV; 1992), *Stompin' at the Savoy* (TV; 1992), *Bébé's Kids* (voice; 1992), *What's Love Got to Do with It* (1993), *The Inkwell* (1994), *Crimson Tide* (1995), *America's Dream* (TV; 1996), *Daylight* (1996), *The Cherokee Kid* (TV; 1996), *When It Clicks* (1998), *Archibald the Rainbow Painter* (1998), *The Temptations* (TV; 1998), *A Private Affair* (TV; 2000), *Love Song* (TV; 2000), *The Brothers* (2001), *All About You* (2001), *The Red Sneakers* (TV; 2002), *Bad Boy* (2002), *Biker Boyz* (2003), *Love Don't Cost a Thing* (2003), *Cheaper by the Dozen* (2003), *Pryor Offenses* (TV; 2004), *Stompin'* (2007), *Lakeview Terrace* (2008), *Killing of Wendy* (2008), *Aussie and Ted* (2008), *Truly Blessed* (2009).

TV: *Days of Our Lives* (recurring role of Denise Preston; 1985), *All My Children* (recurring role of Yvonne Caldwell; 1985), *The Colbys* ("The Trial," 1986), *Simon & Simon* ("Act Five," 1986), *227* ("The Honeymoon's Over," 1987), *1st & Ten* (2 episodes; "Final Bow," "Out of the Past," 1989), *In the Heat of the Night* ("Accused," 1989), *China Beach* ("One Giant Leap," 1990), *Equal Justice* (in the recurring role of Delia; 1990), *A Different World* (2 episodes; "A Campfire Story," "The Cash Isn't Always Greener") *L.A. Law* ("Splatoon," 1991), *Father Dowling Mysteries* ("Emily," 1991), *The 100 Lives of Black Jack Savage* ("Look for the Union Label," 1991), *Doctor Doctor* ("Butterfields Are Free," 1991), *Rhythm & Blues* (in the recurring role of Colette Hawkins; 1992), *Dream On* (2 episodes; "Red All Over," "The Guilty Party," 1992), *The Sinbad Show* (2 episodes; "My Daughter's Keeper," "The Par-tay," 1993), *Under One Roof* (recurring role of Maggie Langston; 1995), *Touched by an Angel* ("The Driver," 1995), *Orleans* (in the recurring role of Rosalee Clark; 1997), *Sparks* ("Too Hot Not to Cool Down," 1997), *Prey* (2 episodes; "Infiltration," "Revelations," 1998), *Moesha* ("Psyche Your Mind," 1998), *Malcolm & Eddie* ("Daddio," 1999), *Intimate Portrait* ("Star Jones," 2000), *Oh Drama!* (2000), *1st Annual BET Awards* (2001), *Diagnosis Murder* ("No Good Deed," 2001), *Boston Public* (3 episodes; "Chapters 17/18/20," 2001), *The Division* ("The First Hit's Free, Baby," 2001), *One on One* ("The Way You Make Me Feel," 2002), *The Parkers* ("And the Winner Is...," 2002), *10:8: Officers on Duty* (3 episodes; "Blood Sugar Sex Magik," "Late for School," "Love Don't Love Nobody," 2003–04), *The District* (5 episodes in the recurring role of Gwen Hendrix, 2003–04), *CSI: Miami* ("Speed Kills," 2004), *Strong Medicine* ("Foreign Bodies," 2004), *Black in the '80s* (2005), *Joan of Arcadia* ("Shadows and Light," 2005), *The Closer* ("Slippin'," 2006), *All of Us* (2 episodes; "Like Father, Like Son ... Like Hell!," "My Two Dads," 2006).

Berry, Halle Born in Cleveland, Ohio, August 14, 1966.

Halle Marie Berry was the first African American woman to win the Best Actress Oscar (for *Monster's Ball*, 2001). She also won a Screen Actors Guild Award for that poignant film. Her performance as Leticia Musgrove, the wife of an executed murderer who then loses her son in a hit-and-run accident, is by turns poignant and starkly dramatic. Leticia subsequently becomes involved in an interracial affair, which is believably and sensitively delineated. Berry is the offspring of an African American father, Jerome Berry, and a white mother, Judith Anne (née Hawkins; originally from Liverpool, England), a retired psychiatric nurse. She has an older sister named Heidi. Her parents divorced when Berry was four. Berry attended Heskett Middle School in Bedford Heights, Ohio; Bedford High School in Bedford, Ohio; and Cuyahoga Community College in Cleveland. She won the Miss Teen All-American Pageant at age 17 in 1985 and was first runner-up a year later in the Miss USA Pageant.

She became a model after her pageant showings, which led to a recurring role as Emily Franklin on TV's *Living Dolls* (1989). She was the first black American in the Miss World competition. From here she segued into a recurring role on the successful prime time soap opera *Knot's Landing*. Her breakthrough movie role was in Spike Lee's *Jungle Fever* (1991), in which she played a junkie. Other films of the 1990s included *Boomerang* (1992), *The Flintstones* (1994), *Losing Isaiah* (1995), and *Bulworth* (1998).

She first seriously caught the public's attention in the Alex Haley miniseries *Queen* (1993), giving an early sense of her acting ability with her performance as a biracial slave. But her major breakthrough was in another TV movie, *Introducing Dorothy Dandridge* (1999), for which she won an Emmy and a Golden Globe for Best Actress in a TV Movie/Miniseries. Berry neither looked nor acted much like the real Dandridge, but she was intimately aware of how race transfigures the career of a black actress, and she gave a sobering, heart-felt performance. She cemented her career as a box-office star with her performance as mutant super-heroine Storm in *X-Men* (2000), and repeated the role in two sequels, becoming increasingly more comfortable and assured in the part. Berry became a Bond girl (Jinx) in *Die Another Day* (2002); her best scene was when she emerged from the surf in a bikini à la Ursula Andress in *Dr. No*. She won a Razzie Award for Worst Actress for *Catwoman* (2004); although the film was nothing more than a glorified "B" movie unworthy of her talents, her performance in *Catwoman* is quite light and charming and intended to be nothing more. Berry was one of the highest-paid actresses in Hollywood by this time, earning $10 million per film.

In 1993 she married Atlanta Braves' right fielder David Justice; they divorced in 1996. She married singer Eric Bent in 2001 and adopted his daughter India. They separated in 2003 and divorced in 2005. Berry and model Gabriel Aubry became the parents of a girl (Nahla Ariela Aubry) in 2008. Berry is a type 1 diabetic; she is deeply involved with the Juvenile Diabetes Association.

Feature Films including TV Movies: *Jungle Fever* (1991), *Strictly Business* (1991), *The Last Boy Scout* (1991), *Boomerang* (1992), *Queen* (TV; 1993), *Father Hood* (1993), *CB4* (1993), *The Program* (1993), *The Flintstones* (1994), *Solomon & Sheba* (TV; 1995), *Losing Isaiah* (1995), *Executive Decision* (1996), *Race the Sun* (1996), *Girl 6* (1996), *The Rich Man's Wife* (1996), *B*A*P*S* (1997), *The Wedding* (TV; 1998), *Bulworth* (1998), *Why Do Fools Fall in Love* (1998), *Introducing Dorothy Dandridge* (TV; 1999), *X-Men* (2000), *Swordfish* (2001), *Monster's Ball* (2001), *Die Another Day* (2002), X2 (2003), *Gothika* (2003), *Catwoman* (2004), *Their Eyes Were Watching God* (TV; 2005), *Robots* (voice; 2005), *X-Men: The Last Stand* (2006), *This Film Is Not Yet Rated* (archival; 2006), *Perfect Stranger* (2007), *Things We Lost in the Fire* (2007), *Tulia* (2009), *Class Act* (2009).

TV: *Living Dolls* (recurring role of Emily Franklin; 1989), *Amen* ("Unforgettable," 1991), *A*

Halle Berry in *Losing Isaiah* (1995).

Halle Berry with Kurt Russell in *Executive Decision* (1996).

Different World ("Love, Hillman-Style," 1991), *They Came from Outer Space* ("Hair Today—Gone Tomorrow," 1991), *The Tonight Show* (4 segments; 1991–2003), *Knots Landing* (recurring role of Debbie Porter; 1991–92), *MTV Video Music Awards 1992, 25th NAACP Image Awards* (1993), *CB4* (1993), *The Word* (1993), *Hollywood Women* (1994), *A Century of Women* (1994), *Late Night with David Letterman* (4 segments; 1994–2007), *1st Annual Screen Actors Guild Awards* (1995), *Dennis Miller Live* (1995), *E! True Hollywood Story* (1996), *Martin* ("Where the Party At?" 1996), *Celebrate the Dream: 50 Years of Ebony Magazine* (1996), *The Rosie O'Donnell Show* (4 episodes; 1996–2001), *Christmas Miracles* (1997), *Intimate Portrait: Halle Berry* (1998), *AFI's 100 Years ... 100 Movies* (1998), *Behind the Music* ("Lionel Richie," 1998), *Frasier* (voice; 2002), *Mad TV* (2 episodes; 1998 and 2002), *The 51st Annual Primetime Emmy Awards* (1999), *30th NAACP Image Awards* (1999), *The Kennedy Center Honors: A Celebration of the Performing Arts* (1999), *31st NAACP Image Awards* (2000), *2000 Blockbuster Entertainment Awards, 2000 MTV Movie Awards, The 52nd Annual Primetime Emmy Awards* (2000), *Welcome to Hollywood* (2000), *Late Night with Conan O'Brien* (2000–06), *HBO: First Look* (4 segments; 2001–05), *Great Streets: The Champs Elysees with Halle Berry* (2001), *32nd NAACP Image Award* (2001), *The 73rd Annual Academy Awards* (2001), *Headliners & Legends: Halle Berry* (archival; 2001), *America: A Tribute to Heroes* (2001), *Mundo VIP* (2001), *The Concert for New York City* (2001), *The 59th Annual Golden Globe Awards* (2002), *The 74th Annual Academy Awards* (2002), *The Bernie Mac Show* ("Handle Your Business," 2002), *The Orange British Academy Film Awards* (2002), *Seitenblicke* (2002), *Leute heute* (2 segments; 2002), *2002 ABC World Stunt Awards, Essence Awards* (2002), *The 54th Annual Primetime Emmy Awards* (2002), *Bond Girls Are Forever* (2002), *Revealed with Jules Asner* (2002), *Premiere Bond: Die Another Day* (2002), *The Late Late Show with Craig Kilborn* (2002), *James Bond: A BAFTA Tribute* (2002), *The Oprah Winfrey Show* (4 segments; 2002–05), *The 60th Annual Golden Globe Awards* (2003), *Saturday Night Live* (2003), *Love Chain* (archival; 2003), *Biography* (3 segments; 2003–08), *200 Greatest Pop Culture Icons* (archival; 2003), *101 Most Shocking Moments in Entertainment* (archival footage; 2003), *Celebrity Naked Ambition* (archival; 2003), *MTV Europe Music Awards 2003, Ant & Dec's Saturday Night Takeaway* (2003), *Hollywood Celebrates Denzel Washington: An American Cinematheque Tribute* (2003), *34th NAACP Image Awards* (2003), *Celebrities Uncensored* (archival; 2003), *The Screensavers* (archival; 2003), *TV Land Awards* (2003), *Star Style* (2003), *The 75th Annual Academy Awards* (2003), *Women on Top: Hollywood and Power* (2003), *Extra* (2003), *Movie House* (2003), *Punk'd* (2003), *Tinseltown TV* (2003), *Pulse* (2004), *This Morning* (2004), *GMTV* (2004), *T4* (2004), *101 Biggest Celebrity Oops* (archival; 2004), *The Greatest Canadian* (archival; 2004), *Rove Live* (2004), *John Travolta: The Inside Story* (2004), *2004 MTV Movie Awards, 52 Most Irresistible Women* (2004), *4Pop* (2004), *Tsunami Aid: A Concert of Hope* (2005), *The 62nd Annual Golden Globe Awards* (2005), *Good Morning America* (2005), *Good Day Live* (2005), *The 77th Annual Academy Awards* (2005), *Assembling Robots: The Magic, the Music and the Comedy* (2005), *Nickelodeon Kids' Choice Awards '05, BET Awards 2005, Tavis Smiley* (2005), *The Teen Choice Awards 2005, The 57th Annual Primetime Emmy Awards* (2005), *The WIN Awards* (2005), *Corazón de...* (2005–06), *Live with Regis and Kelly* (2005–07), *Blitz!* (2006), *The 78th Annual Academy Awards* (2006), *Celebrity Debut* (archival; 2006), *Boffo! Tinseltown's Bombs and Blockbusters* (archival; 2006), *Le grand jornal de canal+* (2006), *Cannes 2006: Crònica de Carlos Boyero* (archival; 2006), *Cosmetic Surgery Nightmares* (archival; 2006), *Corazòn de...* (2 segments; 2006 and 2007), *Legends Ball* (2006), *Friday Night with Jonathan Ross* (2006), *Forbes' Celebrity 100: Who Made Bank?* (2006), *Just Another Day* (2006), *2006 BAFTA/LA Cunard Britannia Awards, The Insider* (2006), *Entertainment Tonight* (4 segments; 2006–08), *Miradas 2* (2007), *Las mañanas de cuatro* (2007), *The Daily Show* (2007), *The View* (2007), *Stand Up to Cancer* (2008), *For Love of Liberty: The Story of America's Black Patriots* (2009).

Video/DVD: *Christmas from Hollywood* (archival; 2003).

Bey, Marki Born in Philadelphia, Pennsylvania, 1946.

Marki Bey portrayed Lanie in Hal Ashby's film *The Landlord* and Officer Minnie Kaplan in a recurring role on TV's *Starsky and Hutch*. But she is best known for her starring role in the cult film *Sugar Hill*. Diana "Sugar" Hill is the fiancée of a popular Louisiana nightclub owner who is beaten to death when he refuses to sell the operation to a vicious mobster. Seeking revenge, Sugar contacts resident voodoo queen Mama Maitresse, who introduces her to the Lord of the Undead,

Halle Berry in *Introducing Dorothy Dandridge* (1999).

Marki Bey.

Baron Samedi. Samedi resurrects dead slaves buried in the swamp. The zombies make short, violent work of the mobster and his minions. Bey more than holds her own in the by-the-numbers title role, going from loyal girlfriend to avenging black power diva in the course of the action.

Feature Films including TV Movies: *The Landlord* (1970), *Gabriella* (1972), *The Roommates* (1973), *Sugar Hill* (1974), *Hangup* (1974).

TV: *The Merv Griffin Show* (1970), *The Rookies* ("Ladies' Day," 1975), *Bronk* ("Bargain in Blood," 1975), *Baretta* ("Carla," 1977), *Charlie's Angels* ("Pretty Angels All in a Row," 1977), *Starsky and Hutch* (recurring role of Minnie Kaplan; "The Avenger," "The Collector," "Cover Girl," "Birds of a Feather," "Ninety Pounds of Trouble," "Starsky vs. Hutch," 1977–79).

Beyer, Troy Born in New York, New York, November 7, 1964.

Troy Yvette Beyer is a director, screenwriter and an actress. She is the offspring of an African American Muslim mother and a white Jewish father. She has two paternal half-brothers, Jerry and Ryan Beyer; four maternal half-brothers, Mahmoud, Muhammad, Gregory and Jibreel; and three maternal half-sisters, Imani, April and Bahiyyah. Beyer married producer-actor Mark Burg in 1994; they are now divorced. Beyer started her show business career with a role on *Sesame Street* at age four and continued to be associated with the series for seven years. She studied acting at City University of New York's School for the Arts. Then she moved to Los Angeles and took a role on the popular nighttime soap *Dynasty* in 1986, playing Jacqueline, the daughter of Diahann Carroll's character Dominique Deveraux. She had a leading role in the feature film love story *Roof Tops* (1989). She has also been in the features *Weekend at Bernie's II* (1993), *Eddie* (1996) with Whoopi Goldberg, *The Gingerbread Man* (1998), and a small role in the hospital siege drama *John Q* with Denzel Washington (2002). Other roles include the slapstick comedy *Disorderlies* (1987), and the "guy group" musical drama *The Five Heartbeats* (1991), loosely based on the real-life Temptations.

Beyer made her debut as a screenwriter in 1997 with the broad comedy *B*A*P*S* starring Halle Berry. She directed her next screenplay, *Let's Talk About Sex* (1998), in which she had a starring role. It was shown at the Sundance Film Festival. She also wrote and directed the romantic teen comedy *Love Don't Cost a Thing* (2003). Beyer was romantically linked to rock star Prince in the 1990s.

Top: **Marki Bey in *Hangup* (*Super Dude*) (1974).**
Bottom: **Troy Beyer in *Rooftops* (1989).**

Feature Films including Video and TV Movies: *Uncle Tom's Cabin* (TV; 1987), *Disorderlies* (1987), *Rooftops* (1989), *The White Girl* (1990), *The Five Heartbeats* (1991), *The Ryde Divine* (TV;

1991), *Weekend at Bernie's II* (1993), *3 Chains o' Gold* (1994), *The Little Death* (1995), *Alien Avengers* (TV; 1996), *Eddie* (1996), *B*A*P*S* (1997), *The Gingerbread Man* (1998), *Let's Talk About Sex* (aka *Girl Talk*; 1998), *Good Advice* (2001), *Surviving Gilligan's Island* (TV; 2001), *John Q* (2002), *A Light in the Darkness* (2002), *Malevolent* (2002).

TV: *Knots Landing* (recurring role of Whitney; "For Better, for Worse," "Four, No Trump," "A Little Assistance," 1985), *Soul Train* (1986), *Dynasty* (recurring role of Jackie Deveraux; 1986–87), *The 1st Annual Soul Train Music Awards* (1987), *A Different World* ("The Gift of the Magi," 1987), *The Cosby Show* ("No More Mr. Nice Guy," 1991), *Tribeca* ("The Box," 1993), *Walker, Texas Ranger* ("End Run," 1993), *Diagnosis Murder* ("Standing Eight Count," 1994), *Red Shoe Diaries* ("Billy Bar," 1995), *Murder One* (recurring role of Carla Latrell; "Chapters 8–11, Year Two," 1996–97).

Beyoncé (aka Knowles, Beyoncé) Born in Houston, Texas, September 4, 1981.

Beyoncé Giselle Knowles is the former lead singer of Destiny's Child, reportedly the best-selling female group of all time, with over 50 million records sold. She is a 10-time Grammy Award winner and is tied for most Grammys won in a single night by a female artist (five in 2004). She is also a Best Actress Golden Globe nominee for *Dreamgirls* (2006); an Oscar nominee for Best Song ("Listen," *Dreamgirls*); a fashion designer (House of Deréon is her fashion line); and a sought-after model.

Although forgettable films like *Austin Powers in Goldmember* (2002), *The Fighting Temptations* (2003), and an ineffectual remake of *The Pink Panther* made little use of her talents (beyond functioning as eye candy), her role in *Dreamgirls* (2006) convincingly established Beyoncé's right to be considered an actress. Her portrayal of Deena Jones, the reserved and naive young singer who becomes a Diana Ross–like superstar, is a model of understated acting. In the early part of *Dreamgirls*, Beyoncé barely appears to be in the film, but her character gradually, almost imperceptibly, deepens and becomes dominant as the film goes on. Her performance as real-life singer Etta James in *Cadillac Records* (2008) got her the best acting reviews of her career, but the film played fast and loose with the facts, and did poorly at the box office.

Beyoncé is the eldest of two daughters (the younger is Solange) born to Matthew Knowles and Tina Beyince (her first name is a tribute to her mother's maiden name). By age 7, she was attending dance school and was a soloist in the church choir. Her dance instructor took an interest in Beyoncé and entered her in a number of competitions. Beyoncé went on to win over 30 local singing and dancing contests. She attended the High School for the Performing and Visual Arts in Houston, and later went to Alf Hastings High School.

While teenagers, Beyoncé and her best friend Kelly Rowland met LaTavia Roberson and LaToya Luckett. They formed a quartet that performed in back yards and in Tina Knowles' hair salon. After singing in local events, they got their break when they went on the TV show *Star Search*. The group was then known as Girl's Tyme, and they did not win the competition. But Beyoncé's dad, convinced the group had what it takes, quit his six-figure job with Xerox Corporation to manage them. Persistence paid off: they were signed to Columbia Records in 1996. Destiny's Child rose to fame in 1998 with the top 10 hit "No, No, No, Part 2." With much-publicized turmoil arising when Luckett and Roberson left the group, Destiny's Child became a trio, adding Michelle Williams. The new line-up obviously worked, garnering 4 *Billboard* Hot 100 number-one singles and several number-one albums — including *Destiny's Child* (1998); *The Writing's on the Wall* (1999); and *Survivor* (2001) (hits from this album included the title song and "Bootylicious," which added a new word to the lexicon); *8 Days of Christmas* (2001); *Destiny Fulfilled* (2004); and their sixth and final album: *#1's* (2005), a greatest hits album that included three new tracks.

In 2001 Beyoncé won the "Songwriter of the Year" award from the Society of Composers, Authors and Publishers Pop Music Awards. She was the first African American female and second female overall to receive this honor. Beyoncé's debut solo album, *Dangerously in Love* (2003), spawned the number-one singles "Crazy in Love" and "Baby Boy." It was number 1 on *Billboard*'s Top 100 chart, selling 317,000 copies the first week. Her second solo album was the equally successful *B'Day* (2006). It was certified double platinum with over 2.4 million copies sold in the U.S. and 4 million worldwide (hit singles: "Ring the

Alarm," "Déjà Vu"). This was followed by *I Am ... Sasha Fierce* (2008), which took Beyoncé's music in a more personal, confessional direction.

Feature Films including TV Movies: *Carmen: A Hip Hopera* (TV; 2001), *Austin Powers in Goldmember* (2002), *The Fighting Temptations* (2003), *Record of the Year* (TV; 2003), *The Pink Panther* (2005), *Dreamgirls* (2006), *Cadillac Records* (2008), *Obsessed* (2009).

TV: *Smart Guy* ("A Date with Destiny," 1998), *Pacific Blue* ("Ghost Town," 1999), *The Martin Short Show* (1999), *2000 Billboard Music Awards, 2000 Much Music Video Music Awards, 100 Greatest Dance Songs of Rock 'n' Roll* (2000), *Walt Disney World Summer Jam Concert* (2000), *2000 Much Music Video Music Awards, Making the Video* (3 segments; 2000–02), *The Famous Jett Jackson* (2000), *2000 Blockbuster Entertainment Awards, VH1 Divas 2000: A Tribute to Diana Ross, Christmas in Rockefeller Center* (2000), *28th Annual American Music Awards* (2001), *43rd Annual Grammy Awards* (2001), *1st Annual BET Awards* (2001), *MTV Icon: Janet Jackson* (2001), *Concert for New York City* (2001), *Michael Jackson: 30th Anniversary Celebration* (2001), *Christmas in Rockefeller Center* (2001), *Record of the Year* (2001), *Intimate Portrait: Destiny's Child* (2001), *Wetten, dass...?* (2001), *Nobel Peace Prize Concert* (2001), *Smap x Smap* (2001), *Saturday Night Live* (2001–02), *Revealed with Jules Asner* (2001), *E! True Hollywood Story* (2 episodes; 2001 and 2004), *Pop Goes Christmas* (2001), *2001 Teen Choice Awards, I Love the '80s* (2002), *Reel Comedy: Austin Powers in Goldmember* (2002), *Victoria's Secret Fashion Show* (2002), *Star Boulevard* (2002), *The Tonight Show* (2 segments, 2002 and 2003), *MTV Europe Music Awards 2003, Punk'd* (2003), *Pulse* (2003), *Veronica Vibes* (2003), *Entertainment Tonight* (2003–08), *All of Us* (2003), *The Oprah Winfrey Show* (8 segments; 2003–08), *The Tonight Show* (2003), *The Barbara Walters Special* (2003), *The Record of the Year 2003, Essence Awards* (2003), *Tinseltown TV* (2003), *Boogie* (2003), *CD: UK* (2003–04), *Spike TV VGA Video Game Awards* (2003), *MTV Europe Music Awards* (2003), *2003 Radio Music Awards, 2003 MTV Video Music Awards, Macy's 4th of July Spectacular* (2003), *VH1 Divas Duets* (2003), *50 Sexiest Video Moments* (2003), *The 30th Annual American Music Awards* (2003), *American Film Institute Life Achievement Award: A Tribute to Robert De Niro* (2003), *MADtv* (2003), *VH1 Big in 2003, 4Pop* (2003–04), *Diary* (2 segments; 2003 and 2005), *Top of the Pops* (5 segments; 2003–06), *2004 MTV Music Video Awards, 1001 Most Unforgettable SNL Moments* (2004), *52 Most Irresistible Women* (2004), *Maxim Hot 100* (2004), *2004 Radio Music Awards, 18th Annual Soul Train Music Awards* (2004), *35th NAACP Image Awards* (2004), *Brit Awards 2004, The Wayne Brady Show* (2004), *An Evening of Stars: 25th Anniversary Tribute to Lou Rawls* (2004), *46th Annual Grammy Awards* (2004), *MTV Backstage at the Grammys* (2004), *The Record of the Year 2004, Super Bowl XXXVIII* (2004), *Michael Jackson: Number Ones* (2004), *Sing Star Party* (2004), *Fashion Rocks* (2004), *20/20* (2004), *GMTV* (2004), *Fade to Black* (2004), *4th Annual BET Awards* (2004), *Jingle Ball Rock* (2004), *Ant & Dec's Saturday Night Takeaway* (2 segments; 2004 and 2006), *The View* (2 segments; 2004 and 2006), *77th Annual Academy Awards* (2005), *The Kennedy Center Honors: A Celebration of the Performing Arts* (2005), *Jimmy Kimmel Live!* (2005), *2005 World Music Awards, ESPY Awards* (2005), *BET Awards 2005, Rockin' the Corps: An American Thank You* (2005), *106 & Park* (2005), *47th Annual Grammy Awards* (2005), *HBO First Look: Dreamgirls* (2006), *Strictly Come Dancing* (2006), *The Tyra Banks Show* (2006), *The Ellen DeGeneres Show* (2 segments; 2006), *2006 MTV Music Video Awards, Be My Baby: The Girl Group Story* (2006), *The Sharon Osbourne Show* (2006), *The 48th Annual Grammy Awards* (2006), *Late Show with David Letterman* (2006), *BET Awards 2006, Jay Z: Live at the Royal Albert Hall* (2006), *49th Annual Grammy Awards* (2007), *66th Grand Prix of Monaco* (2008), *The Early Show* (2008), *Fashion Rocks* (2008), *Total Request with Carson Daly* (2008), *MTV Europe Music Awards 2008, Stand Up to Cancer* (2008).

Video/DVD: *Live at Wembley* (2004), *Destiny's Child: A Family Affair* (2006), *Destiny's Child: Live in Atlanta* (2006), *Beyoncé: Unauthorized* (2003).

Bingham, Traci

Born in Cambridge, Massachusetts, January 13, 1968.

Traci Bingham was born Julie Anne Smith to an African American and Italian mother and a Native American father. She is the youngest of seven children. Her first husband was Finnian Lozada. Her second husband was musician Robb Valier; they married in 1998 and divorced in 2001.

Bingham attended Harvard Extension School to study psychology after graduating from Cuyahoga Community College. She was very sports oriented in college, participating in swimming, track, pole vaulting, and hurdle jumping, but she also performed in theater while in school (*West Side Story*, *Grease*, *Guys and Dolls*). When Director John Landis was in Boston making the film *Celtic Pride*, he noticed Bingham and offered her a bit part in his basketball film. That's when she decided to become an actress.

Bingham is best known as lifeguard Jordan Tate on *Baywatch* (1996–98). She has also had a recurring role on *The Dream Team* (as Victoria Carrera; 1999); she co-hosted the battling robots show *BattleBots* (2000); was a contestant on *Fear Factor* (2006); and appeared on the reality shows *The Surreal Life* (2003) and *Celebrity Big Brother* (2006). She was Drawna on the sitcom *Strip Mall* (2000), a show that seems to have killed more than one career. Bingham is popular with fans in both the U.S., Europe, especially the United Kingdom, Latin America and Asia (*Baywatch* was syndicated all over the world). She is an outspoken PETA member and a confirmed vegetarian.

Feature Films including Video and TV Movies: *Tales from the Crypt: Demon Knight* (1995), *Beach Movie* (1998), *Foolish* (1999), *Longshot* (aka *Jack of All Trades*; 2000), *Four Fingers of the Dragon* (2003), *More Mercy* (aka *Bad Bizness*; 2003), *Malibooty!* (2003), *Hanging in Hedo* (2007), *Forever Plaid* (2008), *Black Widow* (2008), *Spats* (2009).

TV: *The Fresh Prince of Bel-Air* ("Reality Bites," 1994), *Dream On* ("Am I Blue," 1995), *65th Annual Hollywood Christmas Parade* (1996), *Married with Children* ("The Agony and the Extra C," 1996), *Baywatch* (recurring role of Jordan Tate; 1996–98), *Head Over Heels* ("Vice Guy," 1997), *Light Lunch* ("The World's Best Looking Lifeguards," 1997), *Howard Stern* (2 segments; 1998), *Penn & Teller's Sin City Spectacular* (1998), *Hollywood Squares* (2 segments; 1998 and 2004), *Exploring the Fantasy* (series hostess; 1999), *The Dream Team* (recurring role of Victoria Carrera; 1999), *The Jamie Foxx Show* ("Joy Ride," 1999), *Strip Mall* (recurring role of Dawna; 2000), *BattleBots* (reality show regular; 2000), *To Tell the Truth* (2000), *The Private Public* (2000), *Malcolm & Eddie* ("The Best Men," 2000), *The Parkers* ("Since I Lost My Baby," 2000), *Spy TV* (2001), *1st Annual BET Awards* (2001), *Black Scorpion* ("Life's a Gas," 2001), *The Test* ("The Dating Test," 2001), *Rendez-Vous* ("Blonde Ambition," 2001), *Celebrity Boot Camp* (2002), *Rock Me, Baby* ("A Pain in the Aspen," 2003), *Summer Music Mania 2003, G-Phoria* (2003), *The Surreal Life* (reality series; 2003), *The Proud Family* ("Smackmania 6: Mongo vs. Mama's Boy," 2003), *Lingerie Bowl* (2004), *Girlfriends* ("A Partnerless Partner," 2004), *Reno 911!* ("Department Investigation, Part 2," 2004), *Negermagasinet* (2005), *Celebrity Big Brother* (British version; series regular; 2006), *Big Brother's Efourum* (2006), *Big Brother's Little Brother* (2006), *Fear Factor* (reality series; 2006), *Celebrity Paranormal Project* ("Pearl's Story," 2006), *The Surreal Life: Fame Games* (segments; 2007), *The Tyra Banks Show* (2007).

Video/DVD: *Good Vibrations* (1991), *Exposed: TV's Lifeguard Babes* (1996), *Playboy: Babes of Baywatch* (1998), *Playboy: The Ultimate Pam Anderson* (2002), *Bench Warmer: Behind the Scenes* (2005), *Traci Bingham's Fantasy Fest Uncensored* (2005).

Bledsoe, Tempestt Born in Chicago, Illinois, August 1, 1973.

Tempestt Bledsoe is best known for her role as Vanessa Huxtable on the immensely popular family comedy *The Cosby Show* (1984–92). The character of Vanessa was somewhat based on Cosby's own daughter, Ensa. Vanessa was very much a typical teenager, good in school but prone to having arguments with her younger sister Rudy (Keisha Knight Pulliam), and to occasionally testing the bonds of parental authority. In the final season Vanessa got engaged to an older man, the head of maintenance at Lincoln University, the fictional school Vanessa was then attending. As the series ended, they made it clear they were just friends.

She had her own daytime talk show, *The Tempestt Bledsoe Show* (1995–96), from Tri-Star/Dick Clark Productions. She brought charm to the show, but it only lasted one season in the highly competitive world of daytime TV. She portrayed Roberta Baylor, a single mother, on a three-episode story arc on ABC's legal drama *The Practice*, and did another story arc (as Cicely) on *South of Nowhere* (2006). Recent series work includes an appearance on producer Steven Bochco's law series *Raising the Bar* (2008). Bledsoe, who has kept her options open in the post–Cosby phase of her life, has a degree in finance from New York University.

Feature Films including TV Movies: *Fast Copy* (TV; 1985), *Dance 'Til Dawn* (TV; 1988), *Dream Date* (TV; 1989), *Johnny B. Good* (1998), *Santa and Pete* (TV; 1999), *The Expendables* (TV; 2000), *Fire & Ice* (2001), *Bachelor Man* (2003), *Husband for Hire* (TV; 2008), *N-Secure* (2009).

TV: *One to Grow On* (1982), *The Cosby Show* (recurring role of Vanessa Huxtable; 1984–1992), *Motown Returns to the Apollo* (1985), *Night of 100 Stars II* (1985), *Andy Williams and the NBC Kids Search for Santa* (1985), *The 12th Annual People's Choice Awards* (1986), *NBC 60th Anniversary Celebration* (1986), *ABC Afterschool Specials* (3 episodes; "The Gift of Amazing Grace," "Surviving a Break-up," "I Hate the Way I Look," 1986–94), *Square One TV* (1987), *Walt Disney World 4th of July Spectacular* (1988), *Monsters* ("My Zombie Lover," 1988), *The More You Know* (1989), *The Last Laugh: Memories of the Cosby Show* (1992), *The Fresh Prince of Bel-Air* ("For Whom the Wedding Bells Toll," 1995), *The Tempestt Bledsoe Show* (talk show; 1995–96), *A Different World* ("Risky Business," 1989), *Homeboys in Outer Space* ("The Pleasure Planet Principle, or G Marks the Spot," 1996), *Jenny* ("A Girl's Gotta Live in the Real World," 1997), *The Practice* (recurring role of Roberta Baylor; "Reasons to Believe," "State of Mind," "Love & Honor," 1998), *The Parkers* ("And the Band Plays On," 1999), *E! True Hollywood Story* ("The Cosby Kids," 2001), *The Cosby Show: A Look Back* (2002), *NBC 75th Anniversary Special* (2002), *Pet Star* (3 episodes; 2003), *101 Biggest Celebrity Oops* (archival; 2004), *Rock Me, Baby* ("Pretty Baby," 2004), *100 Greatest Kid Stars* (2005), *Strong Medicine* ("Clinical Risk," 2005), *South of Nowhere* (3 episodes in the role of Cecily; "Play Me or Trade Me," "That Is So Not Mom," "That's the Way the World Crumbles," 2006), *I Was a Network Star* (archival footage; 2006), *The View* (2006), *Fear Factor* (2006), *Celebrity Fit Club* (2006), *The Oprah Winfrey Show* (2008), *Raising the Bar* ("A Leg to Stand On," 2008), *The Replacements* (recurring role of voice of Abbey; 2008).

Tempestt Bledsoe.

Bonet, Lisa Born in San Francisco, California, November 16, 1967.

Lisa Michelle Bonet, the child of a black father and Jewish mother (a music teacher), has lived most of her life in New York and Los Angeles. She attended Reseda High School in Reseda, California, and the Celluloid Actors Studio in North Hollywood. She is undoubtedly best known for playing the role of Denise Huxtable on *The Cosby Show*, but Bonet actually began acting when she was 11, attending many auditions and performing in several television commercials before she achieved stardom. *Cosby* dominated Thursday evenings, ranking first in the ratings for four years. The family was unlike typical black TV households in that it was solidly middle class (this was not *Good Times* or *What's Happening!!*). The show was also unique in that it did not rely on catch phrases or one-liners; the humor was organic and character driven. Lisa Bonet became a major heartthrob for millions of young guys, both black and white, but especially for African American teens, a whole generation of whom grew up with a crush on wholesome, lovely Denise Huxtable.

In 1987, a "new" Lisa Bonet emerged — one that was probably closer in spirit to the real Bonet. She played Epiphany Proudfoot in the film *Angel Heart* (1987) with Mickey Rourke and Robert De Niro. Her appearance generated much controversy (and immense displeasure from Bill Cosby, which led to her removal from the show). Some of Bonet's scenes had to be trimmed to avoid an X rating (even so, the film remains quite explicit, even by today's standards). Unfortunately, *Angel Heart* was a ludicrous mess, featuring De Niro as Satan ("Lou Cipher"). Critics and audiences wisely chose to pass.

In the wake of *Angel Heart* there were *Rolling Stone* and *Interview* magazine photo shoots of Bonet that contained some nudity. The *Rolling Stone* cover photo was even a nude shot. When Bonet threatened legal action against *The Cosby Show*, a compromise was created whereby Denise "went away to school," segueing to a new sitcom, *A Different World*. Bonet left *A Different World* after the first season (due to becoming pregnant), and Jasmine Guy went on to great, long-running success in what had been the secondary role of Whitley. *A Different World* was a different world indeed, focusing on life at Hillman College, a fictitious black Southern college. The show was rightly credited for tackling social and political issues rarely tackled on TV (including the 1992 Los Angeles racial conflict), and opening doors in the television industry for a number of young black actors, writers, producers and directors.

On her 20th birthday, Bonet eloped to Las Vegas with singer Lenny Kravitz, himself the product of an interracial marriage (he is the son of Roxie Roker, famous for her role on *The Jeffersons*, and a Jewish father). Bonet gave birth to a daughter, Zoe Isabella Kravitz, in 1989. Zoe is now a budding film actress. The Kravitzes were divorced in 1993, following a bitter breakup shortly after the baby was born. Bonet later had a son with yoga instructor Brian Kest. More recently, Bonet has done admirable volunteer work with juvenile offenders. And Stephen Frears cast her as a sultry singer who becomes a one-night stand for John Cusack in the cult film *High Fidelity*, which later became an unsuccessful Broadway musical (without any members of the original cast). She also returned to series TV in 2008 with *Life on Mars*, based on a BBC series. In a clever mix of cop show and science fiction elements, a detective is somehow sent back to the 1970s in the wake of a car accident. Bonet appeared as Detective Maya Daniels.

Feature Films including TV Movies: *Angel Heart* (1987), *Bank Robber* (1993), *Dead Connection* (1994), *New Eden* (TV; 1994), *Enemy of the State* (1998), *High Fidelity* (2000), *Lathe of Heaven* (TV; 2002), *Biker Boyz* (2003), *Waking Compton* (2006), *White Paddy* (2006).

TV: *The Cosby Show* (recurring role of

Lisa Bonet and Patrick Dempsey in *Bank Robber* (1993).

Denise Huxtable; 1984–1991), *A Different World* (recurring role of Denise Huxtable; 1987–89), *St. Elsewhere* ("Entrapment," 1983), *Tales from the Darkside* (1985), *Walt Disney World Celebrity Circus* (1987), *Funny, You Don't Look 200: A Constitutional Vaudeville* (1987), *The Cosby Show: Looking Back, Part 1* (1987), *Late Night with David Letterman* (1986), *The 12th Annual People's Choice Awards* (1986), *Andy Williams and the NBC Kids Search for Santa* (1985), *Battle of the Network Stars XVIII* (1985), *Motown Returns to the Apollo* (1985), *Night of 100 Stars II* (1985), *The Last Laugh: Memories of the Cosby Show* (1992), *Behind the Music* (1999), *E! True Hollywood Story* (2001), *The Cosby Show: A Look Back* (2002), *KTLA Morning News* (2006), *100 Greatest Teen Stars* (archival; 2006), *Life on Mars* (recurring role of Detective Maya Daniels; 2008).

Video: *Gentleman Who Fell* (1993).

Lisa Bonet.

Bowman, Laura Born in Quincy, Illinois, October 3, 1881; died March 29, 1957, Los Angeles, California.

Laura Bowman began in theater as a singer and dancer and moved on to dramatic roles with the black theater group The Lafayette Players and in roles on Broadway and touring throughout the United States. She also appeared in films by the seminal black director Oscar Micheaux. Her voice found its way on the soundtrack of Hollywood films, dubbing singing voices. Her on-screen appearances were in black cast films (very much by choice; maid roles were not acceptable to Bowman).

For Micheaux, she joined other Lafayette Players, including star Evelyn Preer, in *The Brute* (1920), a boxing story inspired by the contemporary success of black heavyweight champion Jack Johnson. This was Bowman's first film. Her second screen appearance was in another Micheaux film, *Veiled Aristocrats* (1932), about a young woman (Lucille Lewis) passing for white. Bowman, who was oblivious to sound film techniques, shouted out her dialogue and overacted. *Ten Minutes to Live* (1932), based on unpublished Micheaux short stories, featured three tales interwoven in the narrative. Bowman had a small role in this, but she was prominently featured in the borderline horror film *Drums o' Voodoo* (aka *Louisiana, She Devil*; 1934), her first non–Micheaux film.

She was back with Micheaux in *Lem Hawkins' Confession*, better known now as *Murder in Harlem* (1935). This is a key Micheaux film, and one which has survived. A black night watchman at a factory is accused of murdering a young white secretary who works at the factory, but it turns out the factory owner accidentally killed her when she refused his advances. This was based on a real murder case well covered by the tabloid press. *God's Step Children* (1938) is another Micheaux film that survives. This film returns to Micheaux's obsession for passing characters as white: a young interracial woman tries to reject her black heritage, leading to tragedy. Bowman has a secondary role as Aunt Carrie. *Birthright* (1939) is another Micheaux film, the only of his works based on source material by a white author (T.S. Stribling). Two young people struggle to define their lives in a Jim Crow society. *The Notorious Elinor Lee* (1940) was Bowman's last film for Micheaux. It was a boxing story along the lines of *The Brute*, inspired by the success of black champion Joe Louis.

Son of Ingagi (1940) is a black cast horror film not unlike the white B-horror films of the era. It has virtually nothing to do with the first *Ingagi* (1931), an ape in Africa saga. *Son of Ingagi* is a stateside mad doctor/missing link story. Bowman has the mad doctor role (an unusual role for a woman at the time). Spencer Williams was the director, proving that a black man could create forties-style horror schlock with the best of them.

Bowman lived in the exclusive Sugar Hill section of Harlem with her husband, LeRoi Antoine (they married in 1935). Her first husband was Sidney Kirkpatrick. Bowman co-founded the Negro Art Theatre, along with pastor's son and later congressman Adam Clayton Powell, at the Abyssinean Baptist Church in Harlem in 1929. (There was a second, unrelated Negro Arts Theatre established by actor Clarence Muse in the late 1930s on the west coast.) The first production was *Wade in de Water*, a drama about Southern racial injustice, which opened on June 29, 1929. Bowman was also a member of the Lafayette Players, appearing in productions like *Cheating Cheaters* (as Nell Brockton) with A.B. DeComathiere and her husband Sidney Kirkpatrick. She later appeared in the Los Angeles production of *Anna Lucasta* (1947). Bowman also taught acting. She died at age 75. LeRoi Antoine wrote a book in tribute to his wife titled *Achievement: The Life of Laura Bowman* (Pageant Press, 1961).

Feature Films: *The Brute* (1920), *Veiled Aristocrats* (1932), *Ten Minutes to Live* (1932), *Drums o' Voodoo* (aka *Louisiana, She Devil*; 1934), *Murder in Harlem* (1935), *God's Step Children* (1938), *Birthright* (1939), *Son of Ingagi* (1940), *The Notorious Elinor Lee* (1940), *Miss Susie Slagle's* (1946).

Boyd, Tanya

Born in Detroit, Michigan, March 20, 1951.

Tanya Boyd is best known for her role as the Creole psychic Celeste Perrault on the long-running daytime soap *Days of Our Lives* (starting in 1994). Boyd became a venerable soap opera diva in this campy role. She also had a recurring role on the short-lived sitcom *The Ted Knight Show* (as Philadelphia Phil Brown; 1978). She married smooth jazz pianist Bobby Lyle in 1994, and they were divorced in 1997.

Boyd has had a significant singing career. She traveled around the world as a back-up singer for Anita Baker, husband Bobby Lyle and Natalie Cole. In 1979 she joined the legendary group The Fifth Dimension, replacing Pat Bass, who had replaced Marilyn McCoo replacement Terri Bryant. Boyd was replaced by Joyce Wright Pierce. Boyd's theatrical career has been equally impressive. She's been in regional productions of *Cotton*, *Jelly's Last Jam* and *No Place to Be Somebody*. In 1993 she won a Drama-logue Critics Award for Best Performance for her acting in *Indigo Blues*. In 1993–94 she directed two summer festival Main Stage productions at the Mojo Theater Ensemble Company in Los Angeles. She directed a comedy titled *The Mojo Man* for the NAACP Playwright's Competition. It won first runner-up. Boyd also directed the critically acclaimed play *For You*, based on the life of the late Greg Morris, groundbreaking black star of the original *Mission Impossible* TV series.

Boyd had an earlier career as a queen of the B films, a star of exploitation and blaxploitation films like *Black Shampoo* (1976), a strange rip-off of Warren Beatty's *Shampoo* with a touch of *The Texas Chainsaw Massacre* (1976), and *The Happy Hooker Goes Hollywood* (1980), with TV's Batman Adam West. *Ilsa, Harem Keeper of the Oil Sheiks* (1976) is the best of this outrageous lot. Boyd is Satin, one of Ilsa's enforcers, and the lover of Velvet (Marilyn Joi), her sadistic other half. Boyd and Joi make an iconic pair. She directed the short film *The Gift*; her first feature as a director was *Hold Up*.

Feature Films including Video and TV Movies: *Black Shampoo* (1976), *Ilsa, Harem Keeper of the Oil Sheiks* (1976), *Black Heat* (1976), *Walking Through Fire* (TV; 1979), *Murder Can Hurt You* (TV; 1980), *The Happy Hooker Goes Hollywood* (1980), *Up the Academy* (1980), *Wholly Moses!* (1980), *Jo Jo Dancer, Your Life Is Calling* (1986), *Tricks of the Trade* (TV; 1988), *Loving Lulu* (1993), *The Disappearance of Christina* (TV; 1993), *For da Love of Money* (2002).

TV: *Roots* (miniseries; 1977), *What's Happening!!* ("What's Wrong with Raj?" 1977), *Good Times* ("J.J. and the Boss' Daughter," 1978), *The Paper Chase* ("The Man Who Would Be King," 1978), *The Ted Knight Show* (recurring role of Philadelphia Phil Brown; 1978), *Archie Bunker's Place* ("The Return of Sammy," 1980), *Sanford* ("Cal's Diet: Part II," 1980), *Enos* ("Once and Fur All," 1981), *The Twilight Zone* ("The Junction," 1987), *What's Happening Now!* ("The Older Woman," 1988), *A Different World* ("Great Expectations," 1989), *Parker Lewis Can't Lose* ("Senior Jerry," 1993), *Days of Our Lives* (recurring role of Celeste Perrault; 1994–present), *Under One Roof* (pilot; 1995), *The Good News* ("There's an Old Flame," Parts I and II, 1997), *Life with Bonnie* ("Don't Act Your Age, Just Act," 2002),

Strong Medicine ("Jeaneology," 2003), *Soap Talk* (2005).

Shorts: *Don't Give Me the Finger* (2005).

Brandy (aka Norwood, Brandy) Born in McComb, Mississippi, February 11, 1979.

Brandy Rayana Norwood is one of the best-selling female artists in American recording history, with upward of 11 million sales for her five studio albums in the U.S., and over 25 million worldwide. She is the sister of singer Ray J (William Raymond Norwood, Jr.) and the daughter of Willie (former R&B singer and choir director) and Sonja Norwood. Her mother quit her job with tax preparers H&R Block to manage Brandy and Ray J. She attended Pepperdine University, but dropped out because of professional commitments. Brandy wanted to be a singer since she was four years old, her age when the family moved to Carson, California, in pursuit of show business goals. She released her first single at age eleven.

She was discovered by Atlantic Records when she was a member of a youth singing group and released her self-titled debut album in 1994 at the age of fifteen. She recorded for Atlantic from 1994 to 2005 and with Epic starting in 2008. "I Wanna Be Down" was her first hit single, number 1 on *Billboard*'s Hot R&B singles chart. This was followed by her second number 1 hit, "Baby." Other top 10 hits from the first album were "Best Friend" and "Broken Hearted." The *Brandy* album earned her two Grammy Award nominations for Best New Artist and Best Female R&B Performance. Another huge hit from this era was "Sittin' Up in My Room" (1995), heard on the soundtrack of the film *Waiting to Exhale*.

Brandy's second album, *Never Say Never* (1998), yielded the smash hit single "The Boy Is Mine," a duet with Monica Arnold, which won a Grammy Award for Best R&B Performance by a Duo or Group. It spent thirteen weeks on top of the *Billboard* charts, selling over 14 million copies worldwide. *Full Moon* was her third studio album (2002). Critical approval and sales reaction was not up to par with the first two albums. Brandy began writing and producing for other artists, such as Kelly Rowland and Toni Braxton. Her fourth album, *Afrodisiac* (2005), received a much better critical reception, but sales were mediocre (500,000 copies in the U.S.). It was at this time that Brandy severed her 11-year relationship with Atlantic. Her latest album, with Epic Records, is titled *Human* (2008), and it is a personal, almost confessional record, geared for a more mature generation of fans.

She began her television acting career as Danesha Turrell on the ABC sitcom *Thea* (1993–94). Thea Turrell is a widow making ends meet and struggling to raise her four kids, aided by her brother-in-law and her sister. *Thea* only lasted six months, but many critics and fans liked it, and it paved the way for *Moesha*. Brandy gained major sitcom fame as the star of the UPN Network hit *Moesha* (1996–2001). It soon became the most watched show on the young (and now defunct) network. Moesha learned various life lessons as she made the transition from tween-ager to teenager on the series. Brandy proved herself to be an unaffected, charming actress (a lot of hard work went into that effort).

She had a supporting role in the indifferent 1998 horror film sequel *I Still Know What You Did Last Summer*. It did quite well at the box office, taking in $16.5 million in the first weekend. More memorably, she starred in two highly rated TV movies: *Cinderella* and *Double Platinum*, an inside-the-music-business story co-starring Diana Ross. *Cinderella* was the perfect role for a radiant Brandy, in a cast that included Whitney Houston, Whoopi Goldberg and Bernadette Peters. It was a *Wonderful World of Disney* special that attracted 60 million viewers, and it may well be the apex of Brandy's career to date.

She has a daughter named Sy'rair with Robert Smith, born in 2002. She was engaged to NBA player Quentin Richardson (2004–05). In June, 2006 she was a judge on NBC's *America's Got Talent*, but was replaced by Sharon Osbourne in the second season.

Feature Films including TV Movies: *Arachnophobia* (1990), *Cinderella* (TV; 1997), *I Still Know What You Did Last Summer* (1998), *Double Platinum* (TV; 1999), *Osmosis Jones* (voice; 2001), *Access Granted* (2008).

TV: *Thea* (recurring role of Danesha Turrell; 1993–94), *Rhythm & Jam* (miniseries host; 1993), *Tony Bennett: Here's to the Ladies, A Concert of Hope* (1995), *New York Undercover* ("Digital Underground," 1995), *The 9th Annual Soul Train Music Awards* (1995), *Celebrate the Dream: 50 Years of Ebony Magazine* (1996), *100 Greatest Teen Stars* (archival; 2006), *MTV News: Year in Rock 1996*, *Moesha* (title role; 1996–2001), *The 39th Annual Grammy Awards* (1997), *Ray J in Concert*

The cast of *Moesha* (clockwise from center): Brandy Norwood, Sheryl Lee Ralph, Lamont Bentley, Yvette Wilson, Marcus T. Paulk, Countess Vaughn, William Allen Young.

with Brandy (1997), *Spice Girls: Too Much Is Never Enough* (1997), *The 26th Annual American Music Awards* (1998), *Goodwill Games Opening Celebration* (1998), *MTV Video Music Awards 1998, Celebrity Profile* ("Jennifer Love Hewitt," 1998), *The 51st Annual Primetime Emmy Awards* (1999), *VH1 Divas Live 2* (1999), *The 41st Annual Grammy Awards* (1999), *The 1999 Source Hip-Hop Music Awards, The Howard Stern Show* (1999), *2000 Blockbuster Entertainment Awards, 2000 MLB All-Star Game, Wetten, dass...?* (2001), *1st Annual BET Awards* (2001), *HBO First Look (Osmosis Jones,*

2001), *Intimate Portrait* (2 episodes; "Faith Hill," "Brandy," 2000 and 2002), *The Saturday Show* (2002), *Exclusive* (2002), *The Rosie O'Donnell Show* (5 segments; 1997–2002), *Maybe It's Me* (2002), *American Bandstand's 50th Anniversary Celebration* (2002), *One-Hit Wonders* (2002), *Brandy: Special Delivery* (2002), *MTV Video Music Awards 2002, Total Request Live* (2004), *Punk'd* (2004), *Anke Late Night* (2004), *4th Annual BET Awards* (2004), *The Tonight Show with Jay Leno* (2 segments; 2002–04), *The Late Late Show with Craig Kilborn* (2004), *The Ellen DeGeneres Show* (2004), *MOBO Awards 2004, CD:UK* (2004), *Retrosexual: The '80s* (2004), *Top of the Pops* (2 episodes; 2004), *The View* (2 segments; 2004 and 2006), *I Love the '90s: Part Two* (2005), *House* (2005), *American Idol* (guest judge; 2005), *The Tyra Banks Show* (2 segments; 2005 and 2006), *Last Call with Carson Daly* (2006), *America's Got Talent* (judge; 2006), *Project Runway* (2006), *The Parkers* ("Scary Kim," 2000), *Sabrina, the Teenage Witch* ("Guilty!" 2002), *Reba* ("She Works Hard for Their Money," 2002), *American Dreams* ("Long Shots and Short Skirts," 2004), *One on One* (4 episodes; "Tijuana Break-up?" "Dump Me? Dump You!," "I Love L.A.," Parts 1 and 2, 2006).

Video/DVD: *Sesame Beginnings: Beginning Together* (2006).

Braxton, Toni Born in Severn, Maryland, October 7, 1966.

While her deep, sensual, soaring voice has won her many awards and has sold a ton of records, Toni Braxton has also taken several forays into acting. Acting highlights include starring roles on Broadway in two of the most successful Walt Disney productions, *Beauty and the Beast* (as Belle) in 1998–99, and the title role in *Aida* in 2003. Braxton was the first (and, to date, only) African American to star as Belle, and also the first African American actress to star in a Disney production on Broadway. She made her feature film debut in *Kingdom Come* (2001). She was Juanita Slocumb, an already wealthy woman trying to get her share of the inheritance when mean Bud Slocumb passes away. She was also featured in the TV movie *Play'd: A Hip-Hop* Story (2002), a drama about the sometimes venal world of the hip-hop recording industry.

Braxton is the daughter of an Apostolic minister and a vocalist. She has four sisters: Traci (born in 1971), Towanda (born in 1973), Tamar (born in 1977) and Trina (born in 1978). It was in the church choir that she discovered her vocal talents. Braxton attended Quarterfield Elementary School and Corkran Middle School in Glen Burnie, Maryland. Although anxious to start a singing career, she graduated first from Bowie State University, and although she studied to be a teacher, music was always on her mind. The Braxton sisters formed a group (called, unsurprisingly, the Braxtons), signed a contract with Arista Records, and released a single titled "The Good Life." It was not a hit, but it attracted the attention of top producers Kenneth "Babyface" Edmunds and Antonio "L.A." Reid of LaFace Records. This led to Toni being signed to a contract, and the release of the singles "Give U My Heart," a duet with Babyface) and "Love Shoulda Brought You Home."

Her albums are *Toni Braxton* (1993), *Secrets* (1996), *The Heat* (2000), *Snowflakes* (2001), *More Than a Woman* (2002), *Libra* (2005) and an album due in 2009. She is the winner of six Grammy Awards, including Best New Artist (1993). Hit singles include "Another Sad Long Song," "You Mean the World to Me," and "Breathe Again" (all 1993); and "You're Making Me High," and "Un-break My Heart" (both 1996). "Un-break My Heart," a tribute to love lost and perhaps re-found, is simply one of the most haunting R&B records ever made. This was followed by another hit, "He Wasn't Man Enough" (2000). After winning the 1997 *Billboard* Award for Female R&B of the Year, Braxton shocked the music industry by declaring bankruptcy in 1998 and went into litigation against LaFace Records. She recovered from this nasty financial downturn and continued recording with LaFace when she resolved her conflict early in 1999. But in April 2003, she finally left Arista after 14 years, and released one album on Blackground/Universal, which was not a sales success compared to her earlier releases. She severed her ties with Blackground after filing a $10 million lawsuit in January 2007.

In 2006–07, she headlined an ongoing show ("Toni Braxton: Revealed") at the Riviera Hotel in Las Vegas. (The huge billboard heralding the show was one of the sexiest graphics ever to grace the Strip.) Braxton married Keri Lewis in 2001 and has two children (Denim Cole and Diezel Ky Braxton Lewis). She is a spokeswoman for the

American Heart Association and Autism Speaks (her son Diezel is autistic).

Feature Films including TV Movies: *Kingdom Come* (2001), *Play'd: A Hip-Hop Story* (TV; 2002).

TV: *The 7th Annual Soul Train Music Awards* (1993), *Late Show with David Letterman* (1993), *The 8th Annual Soul Train Music Awards* (1994), *26th NAACP Image Awards* (1994), *1994 MTV Movie Awards, The 21st Annual American Music Awards* (1994), *Roc* ("The Concert," 1994), *Christmas at Home with the Stars* (1994), *MTV Music Video Awards 1996, Celebrate the Dream: 50 Years of Ebony Magazine* (1996), *Top of the Pops* (1996), *The Rosie O'Donnell Show* (1996–98), *The 39th Annual Grammy Awards* (1997), *Songs and Visions* (1997), *The 24th Annual American Music Awards* (1997), *Super Bowl XXXIV* (2000), *The 2000 Billboard Music Awards, MADtv* (2000), *The 43rd Annual Grammy Awards* (2001), *E! True Hollywood Story* (2001), *The 28th Annual American Music Awards* (2001), *Intimate Portrait* (2002), *Inside Out* (2003), *50 Sexiest Video Moments* (2003), *Blue's Clues* ("Bluestock," 2004), *VH1: All Access* (2004), *The 2005 World Music Awards, The Tom Joyner Show* (2005), *The Ellen DeGeneres Show* (2005), *Kevin Hill* (3 episodes in the recurring role of Terry Knox; 2005), *Live with Regis and Kathie Lee* (2006), *2006 FIFA World Cup, American Idol* (2006), *An Evening of Stars: Tribute to Stevie Wonder* (2006), *2007 Trumpet Awards, The View* (2007), *Larry King Live* (2 segments; 2007 and 2008), *Entertainment Tonight* (2008), *Dancing with the Stars* (competitor; 2008).

Video/DVD: *From Toni with Love: The Video Collection* (2001).

Bridgewater, Dee Dee Born in Memphis, Tennessee, May 27, 1950.

Dee Dee Bridgewater was born Denise Eileen Garrett; her parents were Marion and Matthew Garrett (her father was a trumpeter who taught music at Manassas High School). The family relocated to Flint, Michigan, where Bridgewater lived until completing high school. During her first years in college she began singing with big bands, leading to her work with the Thad Jones–Mel Lewis Band. She met and married trumpeter-composer Cecil Bridgewater. They toured the U.S., Europe, the U.S.S.R. and Japan, and had a child, but subsequently divorced. After the divorce, Bridgewater won the role of Glinda the Good Witch in Broadway's black reworking of *The Wizard of Oz*, called *The Wiz*. She received the Tony Award for her work in the show (Best Supporting or Featured Actress in a Musical 1975). *The Wiz* also won the 1976 Grammy Award for Best Musical Show Album. She also appeared in the 1978 film version of the play.

After winning the Tony, she married director Gilbert Moses, had a child, and moved to Los Angeles. There she got a role on the daytime soap *Another Life* (as Samantha Marshall; 1981). When she separated from Moses, she moved to Paris, where she met her third husband, Jean-Marie Durand (1991–present). They have three children: China Moses, Tulani, and Gilbert. She was nominated for the Laurence Olivier Award for London's West End production *Lady Day*, playing Billie Holliday (1987). She starred in the Los Angeles production of *Sophisticated Ladies*, with Gregory Hines and Hinton Battle, and stayed with the show when it went on world tour. She also appeared in *Cosmopolitan Greetings*, *Black Ballad*, *Carmen Jazz* and *Cabaret*.

Albums include *Afro Blue* (1974), *Live in Paris* (1989), *Love and Peace: A Tribute to Horace Silver* (1995), *Dear Ella* (a tribute to her idol Ella Fitzgerald; 1997), *Live at Yoshi's* (2000), *J'ai Deux Amours* (Josephine Baker's anthem; 2005), and *Red Earth* (2007). Bridgewater is the winner of two Grammy Awards (1998's Best Jazz Vocal Performance and Best Arrangement Accompanying a Vocal). She also received France's top musical honor, the Victoire de la Musique (Best Jazz Vocal Album, 1998). She is the first American to be inducted into the Haut Conseil de la Francophonie, and she has received the Award of Arts and Letters in France.

She has also excelled as a film and TV actress in a variety of roles. Her best film role is probably in John Sayles' *The Brother from Another Planet* (1984). She plays a singer who encounters the spaced-out alien of the film's title, and who is intrigued and puzzled by the eccentric stranger. Bridgewater gives a natural, wry performance. Her TV work includes appearances on such shows as *Benson* and the cult fantasy series *Highlander*. As hostess of National Public Radio's Jazz Set, Bridgewater presents premium jazz artists from around the world, from Mali, Africa, to Monterey, California. She is a United Nations ambassador for the Food and Agriculture Organization. She also continues to be a headliner in top jazz clubs throughout the world (an example being her 2008 appearance at New York's Blue Note).

Feature Films including TV Movies: *Everybody Rides the Carousel* (voice; 1975), *The Wiz* (1978), *The Fish That Saved Pittsburgh* (1979), *Night Partners* (TV; 1983), *The Brother from Another Planet* (1984), *Falstaff on the Moon* (1993), *Corps plongés* (TV; 1998), *Tous à l'ouest: Une nouvelle aventure de Lucky Luke* (voice; 2007).

TV: *Dinah!* (1976), *Benson* ("Benson in the Hospital," 1980), *Another Life* (recurring role of Samantha Marshall; 1981), *Highlander* ("The Beast Below," 1993), *Carnegie Hall Salutes the Jazz Masters: Verve Records at 50* (1994), *Kennedy Center's 25th Anniversary* (1996), *Crossroads* (host; 1999), *Im herzen des lichts—die nacht der primadonnen* (2002), *Tout le monde en parle* (2002), *On a tout essayé* (2005), *20h10 pétantes* (2005), *Play Your Own Thing: A Story of Jazz in Europe* (2006), *La nit al dia* (2008).

Brock, Geraldine Born in San Antonio, Texas, July 27, 1929.

Geraldine Brock was a child prodigy, excelling as a singer, dancer and musician. She was a protégé of well-known actress Myra D. Hemmings, and became active in the San Antonio Negro Little Theater Company. Her husband is Benson Benjamin Stain (1952–present). Although she only appeared in a single film, it was a key race film (intended for black audiences and shown in segregated theaters). Brock was the title character in *The Girl in Room 20*, playing a country bumpkin who comes to New York and immediately attracts big city hustlers, leading to tragic circumstances. This film was directed by Spencer Williams, Jr. (Andy of TV's *Amos 'n' Andy*).

Daisy Mae Walker (Brock) is a rube from Prairieville, Texas. She bids her parents and sister farewell before heading to New York City, where she seeks fame and fortune. (Brock's mentor, Myra Hemmings, appears as Mrs. Walker in the film.) Daisy Mae's boyfriend Dunbar does not want her to go and tells her he loves her. Daisy Mae says she loves him too and will return to him after she gives big city life a fling. In New York, Daisy Mae gets a ride from cabbie Joe Phillips (Williams). She gives him the address of her mother's friend Mrs. Jones, but when she gets there it is actually a house of prostitution called Mamie's Place. Despite decent guy Joe's warning, Daisy Mae enters the place and meets Mamie, who tells her Mrs. Jones has relocated to California. But Mamie assures Daisy Mae "there is a place for her" in this establishment. Joe honks his horn, allowing Daisy Mae to make a convenient exit.

He takes her to a real hotel, and she meets some musicians in the lobby, who tell her they have a gig at the Congo Club the following week. She tells the guys she's a singer. She meets the band leader, Duke, and auditions for him right in the hotel. The rehearsal at the club goes well, but the club's manager, Arnold Richardson, makes a play for her and tells her there's a party at Mamie's Place that night. Joe smooth talks Daisy Mae and tells her she's too classy and talented for the Congo Club, and that he will become her agent. He sets her up in an apartment. Joe, who has quickly become Daisy Mae's guardian angel, gets in touch with Dunbar back home, and tells him that his girl is falling in with a bad element. Dunbar heads for New York. Richardson visits Daisy Mae and starts making aggressive overtures to her. By this time, Joe and Dunbar have shown up. Dunbar breaks down the door and starts tussling with Richardson. While this is going on, Mrs. Richardson shows up (she heard two ladies in a beauty parlor discussing her husband's new "client"). She pulls out a gun to shoot her husband, but shoots Daisy Mae instead. Daisy Mae recovers and she and Dunbar agree it's time to head back to Texas, get married, and start raising a family.

Despite its pedestrian plot, *The Girl in Room 20* is a landmark production in that it addresses the social dilemma of "good girls gone bad," and probably had a positive effect on more than one young lady during its play dates.

Feature Film: *The Girl in Room 20* (1946).

Brooks, Golden Born in San Francisco, California, December 1, 1970.

Golden Brooks melds exotic good looks with subtle comic timing and a girl-next-door quality. She has a bachelor of arts in sociology from The University of California–Berkeley and a minor in theater. She also has a master's degree in creative writing from Sarah Lawrence College in Bronxville, New York. She competed in figure skating and won several trophies in her youth. She is also a classically trained dancer and has taught ballet, jazz and modern dance. She has been an active participant in Danny Glover's non-profit Robey Theater Company.

She is best known for her character Maya Wilkes on the long-running sitcom *Girlfriends* (2000–08). Her character has evolved from a secretary to a best-selling author during the course of the program. It's interesting to observe how Brooks has grown in the role, and how much shading she gives to the character, especially in the later seasons. She wrote an episode of the show titled "Snap Back" and played her Maya character in a crossover with the *Moesha* series in 2000. Brooks was nominated for the NAACP Image Award for her work as Maya. She won a BET Comedy Award for Outstanding Supporting Actress in a Comedy Series in 2004. She has also done fine comedic work, appearing on sitcoms such as *Linc's*, *The Parkers*, and *The Jamie Foxx Show*.

Feature Films including Video and TV Movies: *Drive By: A Love Story* (1997), *Hell's Kitchen* (1998), *Timecode* (2000), *Asylum* (2001), *Imposter* (2002), *Motives* (2004), *Beauty Shop* (2005), *Something New* (2006), *A Good Man Is Hard to Find* (2008), *My Place in the Horror* (2009).

TV: *The Adventures of Pete & Pete* (1996), *Promised Land* ("Leaving the Life," 1999), *Linc's* ("What I Did for Love," 1999), *The Parkers* ("Since I Lost My Baby," 2000), *The Jamie Foxx Show* ("Double or Nothing," 2000), *Girlfriends* (recurring role of Maya Wilkes; 2000–08), *Moesha* ("That's My Mama," 2001), Haunted ("Abby," 2002), *35th NAACP Image Awards* (2004), *The Sharon Osbourne Show* (2004), *BET Comedy Awards* (2004), *Star Trek: Enterprise* ("Storm Front," Parts I and II, 2004) *106 & Park* (2005), *Eve* ("Testing, Testing HIV," 2005), *Jimmy Kimmel Live!* (2006), *CSI: Miami* ("How Does That Make You Kill?" 2008).

Brown, Ada Born in Junction City, Kansas, May 1, 1890; died in Kansas City, Missouri, March 30, 1950.

Ada Brown was a blues singer who performed in the features *Stars in Stripes* (1938) and *Stormy Weather* (1943) in a duet with Fats Waller. She is known for her songs "Evil Mama Blues" (considered the first recording of Kansas City jazz), "Crazy 'Bout My Lollipop," "111 Natural Blues," and "That Ain't Right." Brown was active in vaudeville, appearing in musical theater at the London Palladium, and on Broadway in *Brown Buddies* (as Mammy Johnson; 1930–31) and *Memphis Bound!* (as Mrs. Paradise; 1945).

She recorded and toured with the Benny Moten band in the 1920s, and later toured with George E. Lee. She also appeared in the popular revue *Harlem to Hollywood* with pianist Harry Swannagan. Her cousin was ragtime pianist and composer James Scott. Brown was a founding member of the Negro Actors Guild of America (1936).

Feature Films: *Stars in Stripes* (1938), *Stormy Weather* (1943).

Brown, Chelsea Born in Chicago, Illinois, December 6, 1946.

Born Lois Brown, she is best known for dancing in a bikini and wearing body paint in the late sixties on *Rowan & Martin's Laugh-In* (1968–69), the number one show of its era. She was also a series regular in the role of Tag on *Matt Lincoln* (1970–71), a private detective show on ABC starring Vince Edwards. She made her film debut dancing in *Sweet Charity* (1969).

Brown has lived for decades in Sydney, Australia, and was married to actor Vic Rooney, who appeared with her in the Australian soap opera *E Street* (1990–91). Rooney died in 2002.

Feature Films including TV Movies: *Sweet Charity* (1969), *Dial Hot Line* (1970), *The Thing with Two Heads* (1972), *Bronk* (TV; 1975), *Arena* (TV; 1976), *The Return of Captain Invincible* (1983), *Welcome to Woop Woop* (1997).

TV: *Rowan & Martin's Laugh-In* (cast member; 1968–69), *The Flying Nun* ("The Paola Story," 1969), *Love, American Style* ("Love and the Militant," segment, 1969), *Matt Lincoln* (recurring role of Tag, 1970–71), *The Name of the Game* ("The Time Is Now," 1970), *Ironside* ("Accident," 1971), *The Two Ronnies* (1972), *Marcus Welby, M.D.* ("Once There Was a Bantu Prince," 1972), *Police Story* ("Dangerous Games," 1973), *King's Men* (pilot; 1975), *That's My Mama* ("Earl's Girls," 1975), *Bronk* ("The Ordeal," 1976), *Mission: Impossible* ("Reprisal," 1989), *Grass Roots* ("Art," 2003).

Brown, Olivia Born in Frankfurt, Germany, April 10, 1960.

Olivia Margarette Brown spent her early years in Livonia, Michigan, and moved to Sacramento, California, at the age of five. Her brother is NFL player Steve Brown (Houston Oilers, late 1980s). Her first marriage was to actor Mykelti Williamson (1983–85) and her second was to James Okonkwo (they have two children). She had a role in a Chicago production of *Jesus Christ, Superstar* at age 16.

Brown is best known for playing Detective Trudy Joplin on *Miami Vice* (1984–90). The partner of detective Gina Navarro Calabrese, Joplin was a tough but occasionally vulnerable character. She was Vanessa Hargraves, on and off girlfriend of Anthony Bouvier (Meshach Taylor), on *Designing Women* (1990). She was also Patricia Hamilton on *7th Heaven* (1996–2000; 2003) and Barbara Lee on *Moesha* (2001). Her feature films include *48 Hrs.* (1982), *Streets of Fire* (1984) and *Throw Momma from the Train* (1987).

Feature Films including Video and TV Movies: *I Can Jump Puddles* (TV; 1981), *Norman Loves Rose* (1982), *48 Hrs.* (1982), *Streets of Fire* (1984), *Throw Momma from the Train* (1987), *Identity Crisis* (1989), *Memories of Murder* (TV; 1990), *All Tied Up* (1993), *Man's Best Friend* (1993), *Mr. P's Dancing Sushi Bar* (1998).

TV: *The Outsiders* ("Sophie's Mob," 1977), *Bellamy* ("The Siege," 1981), *T.J. Hooker* ("Sweet Sixteen and Dead," 1983), *For Love and Honor* (pilot; 1983), *Hill Street Blues* (3 episodes in the recurring role of Vicki; "Doris in Wonderland," "Praise Dilaudid," "Goodbye, Mr. Scripps," 1983), *The 9th Annual American Black Achievement Awards* (1988), *Paradise* ("All the Pretty Little Horses," 1989), *Monsters* ("Love Hurts," 1989), *Family Matters* ("Stake-Out," 1989), *Miami Vice* (recurring role of Detective Trudy Joplin; 1984–90), *Designing Women* (5 episodes in the recurring role of Vanessa Hargraves; "The First Day of the Last Decade of the Entire Twentieth Century," Parts I and II, "Anthony & Vanessa," "Tornado Watch," "Anthony's Graduation," 1990), *Dear John* (recurring role of Denise; 1990–91), *Roc* ("He's Gotta Have It," 1991), *The Fresh Prince of Bel-Air* ("You Bet Your Life," 1993), *CBS Schoolbreak Special* ("Kids Killing Kids," 1995), *Sister, Sister* ("Dream Lover," 1995), *Lois & Clark: The New Adventures of Superman* (4 episodes in the recurring role of Star; "Contact," "When Irish Eyes are Killing," "Just Say Noah," "Never on Sunday," 1995–96), *7th Heaven* (recurring role of Patricia Hamilton, 1996–2003), *Beverly Hills 90210* (3 episodes in the recurring role of Professor Langely; "All That Jazz," "Mother's Day," "Senior Week," 1997), *The Gregory Hines Show* ("Sofa So Good," 1997), *Murder Call* ("Skin Deep," 1998), *E! True Hollywood Story* ("Miami Vice," 2001), *I Love the '80s* (2001), *Moesha* (4 episodes in the recurring role of Barbara Lee; "Mom," "That's My Mama," "What If...?" "Graduation Day," 2001).

Bryant, Joy Born in the Bronx, New York, October 19, 1976.

Born into modest circumstances to a 15-year-old mother in one of New York's poorer boroughs, Joy Bryant became a Yale graduate, a fashion model, and a successful actress. Determined to improve her circumstances, as a young girl she enrolled in the inner city outreach organization called A Better Chance. A superb student at Westminster High School in Connecticut, she was awarded a full academic scholarship to Yale University. While still at Yale, she was discovered by a scout for Next Models Management and began modeling in Paris. Stateside, she started modeling for Tommy Hilfiger and was featured in the Victoria's Secret lingerie catalogue.

Her acting debut came in 2001 in the role of Nikki in the TV movie *Carmen: A Hip-Hopera*, directed by Robert Townsend and starring Beyoncé. She had a major role in Denzel Washington's directorial debut, the sensitive *Antwone Fisher* (2002). She played Cheryl, Antwone's understanding girlfriend. Antwone is a young sailor who suffers from violent outbursts stemming from a troubled childhood. Subsequent films of note include *Baadasssss!* (2003), Mario van Peebles' excellent film about his father Mario's landmark independent film *Sweet Sweetback's Baadasssss Song*, and how it altered the film industry; *Honey* (2003), a *Flashdance*-like musical starring Jessica Alba; and *Get Rich or Die Tryin'* (2005), as the girlfriend of rapper 50 Cent. She married stuntman David Pope in June 2008.

Feature Films including TV Movies: *Carmen: A Hip Hopera* (TV; 2001), *Kite* (2002), *Showtime* (2002), *Antwone Fisher* (2002), *Baadasssss!* (2003), *Honey* (2003), *Three Way* (2004), *Spider-Man 2* (2004), *Haven* (2004), *The Skeleton Key* (2005), *London* (2005), *Get Rich or Die Tryin'* (2005), *Bobby* (2006), *The Hunting Party* (2007), *Virtuality* (TV; 2007), *Welcome Home, Roscoe Brown* (2008).

TV: *The Making of Antwone Fisher* (2001), *HBO First Look (Antwone Fisher,* 2003), *ER* (3 episodes in the recurring role of Valerie Gallant; "Missing," "Makemba," "Touch and Go," 2003–04), *HypaSpace* (2005), *Late Night with Conan O'Brien* (2005), *The View* (2005), *The Film Programme* (2006).

Video/DVD: *Rhythm City Volume One: Caught Up* (2005).

Shorts: *Kite* (2002).

Bush, Anita Born in Brooklyn, New York, September 1, 1883; died February 16, 1974, New York, New York.

Anita Bush brought to the popular culture (mainly theater, but also films) the notion that black women could be anything they wanted to be (Old West cowgirls included). "The Little Mother of Negro Drama," as she was affectionately known at the height of her popularity, began her love affair with the theater when she and her sister landed roles in a local production of *Antony and Cleopatra*. She was introduced to the world of dance and theater by her father, a theatrical costumer whose clients included many New York actors and performers. Bush and her sister delivered some of these costumes, and it was while doing so that Bush got a taste of the glamorous world of the theater. She and her sister were even able to glimpse white productions blacks weren't allowed to attend.

At age 16, Bush joined the Williams and Walker company as a dancer. The company was the creation of two black minstrels who billed themselves as The Two Real Coons, catering to the popularity of blackface at the time. After Walker and Williams broke up in 1909, Bush formed her own dance company until injury forced her to abandon it in 1913 (she stumbled and fell backstage in a dimly lit theater and a ladder landed on her back). In 1915, looking to increase the presence of blacks in theater — they were banned from acting in white theaters — she formed the Anita Bush Players of Harlem, later known as the Lafayette Players. Black actors such as Charles Gipson and Dooley Wilson (later to achieve immortality in the film *Casablanca*) were given a venue in which to perform. The company survived until January 23, 1932 (at which time it was purchased by a white company), and it was responsible for the training of over 300 black performers and for introducing black theater to many cities across the country. The Lafayette Players was the first professional black dramatic theater ensemble in the United States.

Bush approached Maria Downs, the manager of the poorly attended theater Lincoln Theater in Harlem (vaudeville was already on its way to extinction in the face of the burgeoning film business). She asked Downs if she was interested in an acting company good enough to put some patrons in the seats. Bush said she had a dramatic stock company ready to fill the attendance gap. The problem was, no such company existed at that point. But Bush hit the street and literally rounded up a stock company of blacks interested in giving the project a shot. The Anita Bush Players opened at the Lincoln on November 15, 1915 (it was only one of two theaters blacks were permitted to attend) with what would eventually prove to be a popular production, *The Girl at the Fort*. On-stage photographs of the production show a lively western adventure, with Bush as the beleaguered heroine.

On December 27, following a dispute with Maria Downs, the players moved to the larger Lafayette Theater, and accordingly became the Lafayette Players Stock Company. Offshoot companies were formed in Chicago and Baltimore under Bush's guidance. The great black actress Evelyn Preer was a member of the Chicago troupe, joining the players in 1922, after she had gained renown acting in films for Oscar Micheaux and doing other stage work.

Bush left the Lafayette Players in 1920 and began a short career as a film actress, appearing in *The Bull-Dogger* (1921) and *The Crimson Skull* (1922), the first black westerns, which were produced by the Norman Company and filmed in the all-black town of Boley, Oklahoma. The *Bull-Dogger* prominently featured Bill Pickett, rodeo star and genuine cowboy, and was centered around his roping and riding skills. This was the first time audiences were able to see the black side of the West, including Anita Bush, honorary cowgirl from Brooklyn. *The Crimson Skull* was a serial-style Western melodrama centered around the masked title character, and prominently featuring top-billed heroine Bush going through very much the same paces as Pearl White and yet being quite revolutionary, given her race.

Bush was executive secretary of the Negro Actors Guild in the 1920s. She appeared on Broadway in the popular revue *Swing It* in 1937 in the role of Amy. Although film was a footnote to

Anita Bush and Lawrence Chenault in *The Crimson Skull* (1922). (Photographs and Prints Division, Schomburg Center for Research in Black Culture, The New York Public Library, Astor, Lenox and Tilden Foundations)

Anita Bush's theatrical career, she cracked the door open for all black actresses to come on stage and screen.

Feature Films: *The Bull-Dogger* (1921), *The Crimson Skull* (1922).

Busia, Akosua Born in Ghana, West Africa, December 30, 1966.

Akosua Cyamama Busia is the daughter of Kofi Abrefa Busia, former prime minister of the Republic of Ghana. She is a princess of the royal family of Wenchi, descended from the Ashanti. She was educated at the University of Oxford, England. Her sister is the poet and academic Abena Busia, associate professor of English at Rutgers University, New Brunswick, New Jersey.

Her brief but heart-rending appearance as Nettie in *The Color Purple* (1985) remains the highlight of her career. Nettie is the sister of the main character, Celie (Desreta Jackson plays Celie as a child, and Whoopi Goldberg is the adult Celie). Nettie is banished from the house by her father when she refuses to marry a sadistic neighbor known as Mister (Danny Glover). Nettie joins some missionaries going to Africa and disappears from the film until the climax, although her presence is felt throughout the movie, largely from letters sent to Celie. She returns for an emotionally wrenching finale when the two sisters are reunited. Their separation is a metaphor for the African diaspora.

Busia was Jewel in her director husband John Singleton's racially explosive *Rosewood* (1997), based on the lynch mob attack in 1923 in the African American community of Rosewood, Florida; and she was Patience in Antoine Fuqua's cautionary tale of America's potential military role in Africa, *Tears of the Sun* (2003). She was married to Singleton from 1996 to 1997; they have one child, Hadar Busia-Singleton, who has begun an acting career of her own. Busia is the author of *The Seasons of Beento Blackbird: A Novel* (Washington Square Press, 1997). Set mainly in Ghana and the Caribbean, the novel's protagonist, Simon Wilburforce, is married to two women, loving both but not able to choose between them. The wives begin to form a bond of their own. Busia also collaborated with Richard LaGravenese and Adam Brooks to write the screenplay of *Beloved*, based on Toni Morrison's novel and directed by Jonathan Demme.

Feature Films including Video and TV Movies: *Ashanti* (1979), *Warp Speed* (TV; 1981), *The Final Terror* (1983), *Louisiana* (TV; 1984), *Badge of the Assassin* (TV; 1985), *The Color Purple* (1985), *The George McKenna Story* (TV; 1986), *Crossroads* (1986), *Low Blow* (1986), *Native Son* (1986), *Saxo* (1987), *A Special Friendship* (TV; 1987), *The Seventh Sign* (1988), *Brother Future* (TV; 1991), *New Jack City* (1991), *Rosewood* (1997), *Mad City* (1997), *Ill Gotten Gains* (1997), *Tears of the Sun* (2003), *Ascension Day* (2007).

TV: *Knight Rider* ("Blind Spot," 1983), *Simon & Simon* ("Slither," 1985), *Late Starter* (recurring role of Nicki; 1985), *A.D.* (miniseries; 1985), *CBS Schoolbreak Special* ("Babies Having Babies," 1986), *St. Elsewhere* ("Black's Magic," 1986), *The Twilight Zone* ("Lost and Found," 1986), *Highway to Heaven* ("A Song of Songs," 1987), *A Different World* ("The Hat Makes the Man," 1989), *Dead Man's Walk* (miniseries; 1996), *ER* (5 episodes in the recurring role of Kobe Ikabo; "Choosing Joi," "The Storm," Parts I and II, "Sticks and Stones," "Point of Origin," 1999).

Campbell, Naomi Born in Streatham, London, England, May 22, 1970.

Naomi Campbell's mother is Valerie Campbell (née Morris), an ex-dancer of Jamaican extraction. Campbell has never met her unidentified father, who left her then 18-year-old mother a scant two months after Naomi's birth. Campbell is a mixture of Afro Jamaican and Chinese blood. As a child, Campbell was left in the care of a nanny. Her mother had to travel throughout Europe because she was a member of the dance troupe Fantastica. At age 10, Naomi was accepted into the Italia Conti Academy, where she studied ballet. She also attended Dunraven School, overseen by the London Education Authority in Streatham.

Her first public appearance was at age seven (February 1978) when she was cast to appear in a music video for Bob Marley's song "Is This Love?" In 1982, she appeared in another music video for Culture Club's hit "I'll Tumble 4 Ya." Her many other videos through the years have included George Michael's "Freedom '90" and Madonna's "Erotica" (1992). Campbell also appeared in videos with Michael Jackson, Nelly, The Notorious B.I.G., Jay-Z, Prince, P. Diddy, Macy Gray and Usher.

At 15, and still a student at the Italia Conti Academy, Campbell was spotted in Covent Garden by Beth Boldt, head of the Synchro model agency. She later signed a contract with Elite Model Management as a runway model, but in short order was hired for major advertising campaigns such as Lee Jeans, Ralph Lauren and Olympus. In April 1986, she graced the cover of *Elle*, and in August 1988 became the first black cover girl for *Paris Vogue*. She has appeared on upwards of 700 magazine covers throughout her long modeling career, and remains in worldwide demand as both a model and a product endorser. In 1995, Campbell made her album debut with *Baby Woman* and released the single "Love and Tears." While the album was a success in Japan, it did not do well in England, and wasn't even a blip on the radar screen in the U.S. She is also the titular author of the ghost written semi-biographical novel *Swan* (1994).

The 5'9" supermodel has appeared in a surprising number of films, although often in smaller or walk-on roles, such as in Spike Lee's *Girl 6* (1996), *An Alan Smithee Film: Burn Hollywood Burn* (1997), and *Prisoner of Love* (1999). She has yet to sustain a full-scale, character-driven performance, but certainly has the grace and beauty to be presented effectively on the big screen by the right director. She made her TV acting debut on *The Cosby Show*, playing a girl idolized by Theo (Malcolm Jamal-Warner). She was more recently in a commercial for bottled water dancing with computer-generated lizards.

Feature Films including Video and TV Movies: *Cool as Ice* (1991), *The Night We Never Met* (1993), *Prêt-à-Porter* (1994), *Miami Rhapsody* (1995), *To Wong Foo Thanks for Everything, Julie Newmar* (1995), *Unzipped* (1995), *Girl 6* (1996), *Invasion of Privacy* (1996), *Catwalk* (1996), *An Alan Smithee Film: Burn Hollywood Burn* (1998), *Beautopia* (1998), *Trippin'* (1999), *Prisoner of Love* (1999), *Elvis Lives* (TV; 2002), *Monstrous Bosses and How to Be One* (TV; 2002), *The Rise of the Celebrity Class* (TV; 2004), *Flat Slags* (2004), *Karma, Confessions and Holi* (2008), *The Call* (2006), *Bad Love* (2009).

TV: *Good Morning Britain* (1986), *The Cosby Show* (3 episodes in the role of Julia; "The Birth," Parts I and II, "Cyranoise de Bergington," 1988), *The Fresh Prince of Bel-Air* ("Kiss My Butler," 1990), *Harry Enfield and Chums* (1994), *Wetten dass...?* (3 segments; 1994–2003), *Schönsten frauen der welt* (3 segments; 1995–96), *New York Undercover* (5 episodes in the recurring role of Simone; "Student Affairs," "The Highest Bidder," "Color Lines," "The Finals," "Internal Affairs," 1995), *Saturday Night Live* (1995), *Absolutely Fabulous* (1995), *The 68th Annual Academy Awards* (1996), *Fashion Kingdom* (1998), *For Your Love* ("The Games People Play," 1998), *SexOrama* (1999), *Tout le monde en parle* (2000), *So Graham Norton* (2000), *Esti showder* (2000), *The Orange British Academy Film Awards* (2000), *Miss Universe 2001*, *Intimate Portrait* (2001), *Cleavage* (archival; 2002), *Ali G Indahouse* (2002), *Fashiontrance* (2002), *V Graham Norton* (2002), *The Victoria's Secret Fashion Show* (2002), *Fastlane* ("Asslane," 2003), *Revealed with Jules Asner* (2003), *MTV Europe Music Awards 2003*, *Fashion Mix* (2004), *101 Biggest Celebrity Oops* (archival; 2004), *Favouritism* (archival; 2005), *Silenci?* (2005), *Out of Africa: Heroes and Icons* (2005), *The Fabulous Life of...* ("Today's Hottest Supermodels," 2005), *Fashion in Focus* (2005), *Le grand jornal de canal+* (2005), *The Cut* (2005), *Corazón de...* (3 segments; 2005–06), *The Tyra Banks Show* (2 segments; 2005–06), *E! True Hollywood Story* (2006), *Exclusiv das Star-magazin* (archival footage; 2006), *20 to 1* ("World's Best Love Songs," 2006), *Legends Ball* (2006), *Celebrity Cooking Showdown* (2006), *Taff* (2007), *13 heures le jornal* (2007), *Happy Birthday, Elton! From Madison Square Garden New York* (2007), *Ebony Fashion Fair: 50 Years of Style* (2008), *Ugly Betty* ("Jump," 2008).

Video/DVD: *Models: The Film* (1991), *Sex* (1992), *U2: Numb* (1993), *Michael Jackson — Dangerous: The Short Films* (1993), *Michael Jackson: Video Greatest Hits, HIStory* (1995), *Ladies & Gentlemen: The Best of George Michael* (1999), *U2: The Best of 1990–2000* (2002), *U2: Love Is Blindness* (2003), *Culture Club: Greatest Hits* (2005), *Rhythm City Volume One: Caught Up* (2005).

Shorts: *The Call* (2006).

Campbell, Tisha Born in Oklahoma City, Oklahoma, October 13, 1968.

Tisha Michelle Campbell is the oldest of four children. Her mother, Mona, is her manager. Her first TV appearance was at age six on the PBS show *The Big Blue Marble* (1974), which presented a mini-documentary of her daily life as an aspiring singer and actress. As a child, she won talent shows and appeared on children's programs such as *Kids Are People Too*, *Unicorn Tales* and *Captain Kangaroo*. Campbell graduated from Newark Arts High School in New Jersey. At age 15 she traveled to London to appear as Chiffon, the member of a Supremes-like girl group, in the film version of the off–Broadway hit *Little Shop of Horrors* (1986). She married Duane Martin in 1996. They have a son, Xen Martin, born in 2001.

Campbell's career has been centered in TV sitcoms since her childhood. She is best known for her starring roles in the TV series *Rags to Riches* (as the precocious and ebullient Marva Foley; 1987–88), *Martin* (as Martin's girlfriend, and later as his wife, Gina Waters Payne; 1992–97), *My Wife and Kids* (as Jay Kyle, mother of the family with dad Damon Wayans), and *Linc's* (as Rosalee Lincoln; 1998), Tim Reid's politically savvy Showtime sitcom that came and went far too quickly. Campbell sued her *Martin* co-star Martin Lawrence for sexual harassment in 1992. She abruptly left the show in its last season; her character's disappearance was explained by a change in job venue. Campbell did return to film the last three episodes of the series, but with the proviso that she would not film any scenes with Lawrence.

Campbell released a music album in 1993 (an early CD), including the single "Push." The album was well-produced and well-promoted, but it did not sell well. She produced a short film, *A Luv Tale*, which won an Audience Choice Award at the Black Hollywood Film Festival. She has been nominated for six NAACP Image Awards for Outstanding Actress in a Comedy Series for *Martin* in 1996–97 and for *My Wife and Kids* in 2002 through 2005, with a win in 2003. She was also nominated for an Independent Spirit Award for Best Supporting Actress for the hip-hop comedy *House Party* (1990).

Feature Films including TV Movies: *The Magnificent Major* (1977), *Rags to Riches* (TV; 1986), *Little Shop of Horrors* (1986), *School Daze* (1988), *Rooftops* (1989), *Moe's World* (TV; 1990), *House Party* (1990), *Another 48 Hours* (1990), *House Party 2* (1991), *Boomerang* (1992), *House Party 3* (1994), *Snitch* (1996), *Homeward Bound II: Lost in San Francisco* (voice; 1996), *Sprung* (1997), *The Sweetest Gift* (TV; 1998), *The Last Place on Earth* (2002), *Zack and Mira Make a Porno* (2008), *Pastor Brown* (2009).

TV: *Kids Are People Too, Unicorn Tales, Captain Kangaroo, The Big Blue Marble* (1974), *Rags*

Giancarlo Esposito and Tisha Campbell in *School Daze* (1988).

to Riches (recurring role of Marva Foley, 1987–88), *A Different World* (2 episodes; "How Great Thou Art," "If I Should Die Before I Wake," 1991), *The Fresh Prince of Bel-Air* ("Did the Earth Move for You?" 1991), *Blossom* (2 episodes; "Here Comes the Buzz," "To Tell the Truth," 1991), *Roc* ("A Piece of the Roc," 1992), *Martin* (recurring role of Gina Waters-Payne, 1992–97), *Comic Relief VI* (1994), *Duckman* (voice; "Ebony Baby," 1997), *Between Brothers* ("Dusty's in Love," 1997), *The Rosie O'Donnell Show* (2 segments; 1997 and 2001), *Getting Personal* ("Milo Does the Darndest Things," 1998), *Linc's* (recurring role of Rosalee Lincoln; 1998), *Wasteland* ("The Object of My Affection," 1999), *Intimate Portrait* (2 segments; 1999 and 2002), *Sabrina, the Teenage Witch* ("The Halloween Scene," 2000), *The Victoria's Secret Fashion Show* (archival; 2001), *My Wife and Kids* (recurring role of Janet "Jay" Kyle), *The 28th Annual People's Choice Awards* (2002), *It's Black Entertainment* (2002), *The 30th Annual American Music Awards* (2003), *9th Annual Soul Train Lady of Soul Awards* (2003), *The Wayne Brady Show* (2003), *The Sharon Osbourne Show* (2 episodes; 2003 and 2004), *Retrosexual: The '80s* (archival footage; 2004), *Punk'd* (2004), *BET Comedy Awards* (2004), *Jimmy Kimmel Live!* (2004), *The Late Late Show with Craig Kilborn* (2004), *36th NAACP Image Awards* (2005), *The 2nd Annual BET Comedy Awards* (2005), *All of Us* (recurring role of Carmen; 2006), *The Megan Mullally Show* (2006), *Angels Can't Help but Laugh* (2007), *Rita Rocks* (recurring role as Patty; 2008), *Everybody Hates Chris* ("Everybody Hates Cake," 2008).

Video: *Making a Mark* (2005).

Canty, Marietta Born in Hartford, Connecticut, September 30, 1905; died July 9, 1986, Hartford, Connecticut.

Marietta Canty was known for her performances in theater, radio, motion pictures, and television, and especially for her political and social activities. Often cast as domestic servants, she "held a place" for black actresses in the entertainment industry, all the while working hard to pave the way for more meaningful roles for future generations. Canty's political and social activism, especially in the years following her retirement from the screen (1960s through the 1980s) marked her as an advocate not just for black women but for women in general.

Canty was one of five children born to Henry and Mary Canty. She excelled in singing and oratory at Northeast Elementary School and Hartford Public High School. She got her first taste of acting at age 18 with the Gilpen Players in Hartford, a black theatrical group. This eventually took her all the way to Broadway, even while attending the Lincoln Hospital School of Nursing in New York City. She was in *George White's Sandals* musical revue (1929–30); *Run, Little Chillun* (member of the Pilgrim Choir; March–June 1933); *Co-respondent Unknown* (as Bessie; February–May 1936); *Ring Two* (as Emma; November 1939); and *Horse Fever* (as Virgo; November–December 1940). She also appeared in *The Night of January 16th* (1940) and *No Time for Comedy* (1941).

Her initial screen appearance was a walk-on role in the 1933 film version of *The Emperor Jones*. Canty appeared in 40-plus films, including *The Lady Is Willing* (1942), *The Spoilers* (1942), *Lady in the Dark* (1944), *Words and Music* (1948), *Sea of Grass* (1947), *Father of the Bride* (1950), *The Bad and the Beautiful* (1952), and *Rebel Without a Cause* (her final screen appearance in 1955).

She ended her screen career at age 51, taking a nursing job with the Terry Steam Turbine Corporation in Hartford, a position she held until her retirement in 1971. From 1966 to 1973 she also served as a justice of the peace. In her post-acting years she participated in numerous organizations, served on various boards, and received many awards. She was president of the Hartford Council of the National Council of Negro Women and regional director for the National Conference of Women. She was a co-chair of the Negro College Fund Campaign from 1961 to 1967. Canty received numerous awards and honors, including the Humanitarian Award, Hartford Section of National Council of Women (1969), and the Council Achievement Award, National Council (1972). She died at home at age 80 and is buried in Northwood Cemetery in Wilson, Connecticut.

Feature Films: *The Emperor Jones* (1933), *What's Your IQ?* (1940), *Boom Town* (1940), *The Lady Is Willing* (1942), *The Spoilers* (1942), *Not a Ladies' Man* (1942), *The Magnificent Dope* (1942), *Silver Queen* (1942), *Johnny Doughboy* (1942), *Three Hearts for Julia* (1943), *Mexican Spitfire's Blessed Event* (1943), *Lady in the Dark* (1944), *The Heavenly Body* (1944), *Goin' to Town* (1944), *Irish Eyes Are Smiling* (1944), *Sunday Dinner for a Sol-*

Marietta Canty and Kathryn Grayson in *Toast of New Orleans* (1950).

dier (1944), *Lake Placid Serenade* (aka *Winter Serenade*; 1944), *Johnny Comes Flying Home* (1946), *The Searching Wind* (1946), *Home, Sweet Homicide* (1946), *The Sea of Grass* (1947), *Dear Ruth* (1947), *The Crimson Key* (1947), *Best Man Wins* (1948), *Words and Music* (1948), *Mother Is a Freshman* (1949), *Chicago Deadline* (1949), *Dear Wife* (1949), *My Foolish Heart* (1949), *Father of the Bride* (1950), *Bright Leaf* (1950), *The Toast of New Orleans* (1950), *Belle le Grand* (1951), *Valentino* (1951), *Father's Little Dividend* (1951), *A Streetcar Named Desire* (1951), *Dreamboat* (1952), *The Bad and the Beautiful* (1952), *The "I Don't Care" Girl* (1953), *A Man Called Peter* (1955), *Rebel Without a Cause* (1955).

Capers, Virginia Born in Sumter, South Carolina, September 22, 1925; died May 6, 2004, Los Angeles, California.

Virginia Capers attended Howard University in Washington, D.C., and studied voice at Juilliard in Manhattan. She met bandleader Abe Lyman, who hired her for his radio program and to go on tours with his band. She began performing in the Yiddish theater in the 1950s and then made her way to Broadway. Her Broadway appearances include *Jamaica* (1957; understudy for Adelaide Hall) and the Harold Arlen–Johnny Mercer musical *Saratoga* (1959). She won a Tony Award for her performance as matriarch Lena Younger in the 1974 musical *Raisin*, based on *A Raisin in the Sun*. In 1979 she appeared in a revival of the original dramatic version of Lorraine Hansberry's play.

Capers was not interested in maid roles. She insisted on being cast as a professional, be it a judge, a nurse, or any other high profile job. She appeared on TV in both drama (*Daniel Boone, Mannix, Highway to Heaven, Knot's Landing, Dynasty, St. Elsewhere, ER, The Practice*) and comedy (*Mork & Mindy, Evening Shade, The Fresh Prince of Bel-Air, Married with Children, The Hughleys*). Her best known film roles include Mama Holliday in *Lady Sings the Blues* (1972) and

Nurse Sparrow in *Ferris Bueller's Day Off* (1986). Capers was the recipient of the National Black Theatre Festival Living Legend Award, the Paul Robeson Pioneer Award, and the NAACP's Image Award for Theatre Excellence. She died of pneumonia at age 78.

Feature Films including TV Movies: *House of Women* (1962), *Ride to Hangman's Tree* (1967), *The Lost Man* (1969), *The Great White Hope* (1970), *Norwood* (1970), *Support Your Local Gunfighter* (1971), *Big Jake* (1971), *The Late Liz* (1971), *Lady Sings the Blues* (1972), *Trouble Man* (1972), *The Judge and Jake Wyler* (TV; 1972), *The World's Greatest Athlete* (1973), *Five on the Black Hand Side* (1973), *The North Avenue Irregulars* (1979), *Featherstone's Nest* (TV; 1979), *White Mama* (TV; 1980), *Willow B: Women in Prison* (TV; 1980), *Inmates: A Love Story* (TV; 1981), *Bayou Romance* (TV; 1982), *The Toy* (1982), *Just a Little More Love* (TV; 1983), *Teachers* (1984), *The George McKenna Story* (aka *Hard Lessons*; 1986), *Jo Jo Dancer, Your Life Is Calling* (1986), *Ferris Bueller's Day Off* (1986), *Howard the Duck* (1986), *Backfire* (1987), *Off the Mark* (1987), *Pacific Palisades* (1990), *Burning Bridges* (TV; 1990), *When You Remember Me* (TV; 1990), *Donor* (TV; 1990), *Original Intent* (1992), *What's Love Got to Do with It* (1993), *Beethoven's 2nd* (1993), *The Feminine Touch* (1994), *Everybody Can Float* (1995), *A Last Goodbye* (1995), *Truman* (TV; 1995), *Raven Hawk* (1996), *Bad City Blues* (1999), *For Love of Olivia* (TV; 2001), *Commitments* (TV; 2001), *Taking Back Our Town* (TV; 2001), *Move* (2002).

TV: *Have Gun, Will Travel* ("Odds for Big Red," 1961), *The Untouchables* (2 episodes; "Elegy," "Search for a Dead Man," 1962 and 1963), *Breaking Point* ("A Pelican in the Wilderness," 1963), *Daniel Boone* ("Onatha," 1966), *Insight* ("The Thousand-Mile Journey," 1967), *Judd for the Defense* ("The Name of This Game Is Aquittal," 1968), *Julia* (2 episodes; "Gone with the Draft," "The Doctor's Dilemma," 1969), *Marcus Welby, M.D.* ("Let Ernest Come Over," 1969), *My Three Sons* ("Dodie's Tonsils," 1969), *Dragnet* ("D.H.Q.—The Victims," 1970), *Mannix* (2 episodes; "The World Between," "Out of the Night," 1970 and 1973), *The Rookies* (2 episodes; "The Commitment," "Crossfire," 1972 and 1973), *The Waltons* ("The Collison," 1976), *Jigsaw John* ("Runaway," 1976), *Mork & Mindy* ("Mork in Never-Never Land," 1980), *ABC Afterschool Specials* ("Which Mother Is Mine?" 1979), *Quincy, M.E.* (3 episodes; "House of No Return," "To Kill in Plain Sight," "Memories of Allison," 1979–81), *Amanda's* ("Aunt Sonia," 1983), *Dynasty* ("The Rescue," 1984), *Highway to Heaven* ("One Fresh Batch of Lemonade," Parts I and II, 1984), *St. Elsewhere* ("Homecoming," 1984), *Alfred Hitchcock Presents* ("Arthur, or the Gigolo," 1985), *Murder She Wrote* ("Trial by Error," 1986), *227* ("Fifty Big Ones," 1986), *Downtown* (recurring role of Delia Bonner; 1986), *Starman* ("Fever," 1986), *Frank's Place* ("Frank's Return," 1987), *The Golden Girls* ("Mixed Blessings," 1988), *Unsub* (2 episodes; "And the Dead Shall Rise to Condemn Thee," Parts I and II, 1989), *Booker* (1989), *Gabriel's Fire* (2 episodes; "I'm Nobody," "The Wind Rancher," 1990), *Evening Shade* (2 episodes; "A Day in the Life of Wood Newton," "Goin' to the Chapel," Part I, 1990 and 1992), *The Fresh Prince of Bel-Air* (recurring role of Hattie Banks; 1990–95), *Good Grief* ("The Big Bang Theory," 1991), *Batman* (voice; 1992), *Picket Fences* ("Duty Free Rome," 1993), *Knots Landing* (The Getaway," "Call Waiting," 1993), *The Commish* ("Benny," 1994), *Courthouse* ("Fair-Weathered Friends," 1995), *Married with Children* ("A Bundy Thanksgiving," 1996), *The Pretender* ("Jared's Honor," 1997), *The Practice* (pilot; 1997), *Party of Five* ("I Declare," 1997), *The Hughleys* (3 episodes in the recurring role of M'Dear; "The Thanksgiving Episode," "I Do, I Do Again," Part II, "Roots," Part I, 1998–99), *Snoops* ("The Grinch," 1999), *Poltergeist: The Legacy* ("The Possession," 1999), *The District* ("Worse Block," 2000), *ER* (2 episodes; "Start All Over Again," "Supplies and Demands," 2001), *For Your Love* ("The Enemy Next Door," 2002), *The 11th Annual Screen Actors Guild Awards* (archival footage; 2005).

Cara, Irene Born in the Bronx, New York, March 18, 1959.

This Academy Award–winning singer, composer and actress was born Irene Cara Escalera. She is of black, Cuban and Puerto Rican descent. Her father is Gaspar Cara (who died in 1994); her mother is named Louise. Cara has two sisters and two brothers. Cara was a remarkable music prodigy who began to sing and play the piano by ear at age five and began studying music, acting and dance. At age three, she was one of five the finalists in the Little Miss America pageant. She graduated from the Professional Children's School in Manhattan, but it was LaGuardia High that was the inspiration for the performing arts school in the movie *Fame* (1980), in which Cara starred.

Her professional performing career began as a child on Spanish TV. She also made appearances on *Ted Mack's Original Amateur Hour*, *The Ed Sullivan Show* and *The Tonight Show Starring Johnny Carson*. By age eight she had recorded a Latin-market Spanish language record and an English language album of Christmas songs. She appeared on and off Broadway in the musicals *Maggie Flynn* (as Iris; 1968); *Got to Go Disco* (as Cassette; 1979); the Obie winner *The Me Nobody Knows* (as Little Mae; 1970); and *Via Galactica* (as the Storyteller; 1972). She played Dorothy in the summer of 1980 tour of *The Wiz*.

In 1972 she was the host of *The Everything Show*, which aired locally in New York on NBC, and she played Daisy Allen in the soap *Love of Life* (1970–71). She played a member of the band The Short Circus during the first season of the popular PBS children's educational series *The Electric Company*. She also appeared in two outstanding miniseries: *Roots: The Next Generations* (as Bertha Palmer Haley; 1979) and *Guyana Tragedy: The Story of Jim Jones* (as Alice Jefferson; 1980).

Her film debut was in *Aaron Loves Angela* (1975), followed by her career-making role as Coco Hernandez in the film *Fame*, which led to the popular TV series and generated a multi-platinum album. Cara made a guest appearance on the series in 1983 as an alumna of the performing arts school, singing her then current single "Why Me?" The song "Fame" won the Best Song Oscar (music by Michael Gore, lyrics by Dean Pitchford) and was sung by Cara, along with "Out Here on My Own," another nominated song from the film, on the Oscar telecast. *Fame* earned Cara Grammy nominations in 1980 for Best New Female Artist and Best New Pop Artist, as well as a Golden Globe nomination for Best Motion Picture Artist in a Musical. *Cashbox* magazine awarded her both Most Promising Female Vocalist and Top Female Vocalist.

Irene Cara.

In 1982, Cara won the NAACP Image Award for Best Actress, co-starring with Diahann Carroll and Rosalind Cash in the *NBC Movie of the Week*, Maya Angelou's *Sister, Sister* (1982), as the youngest of three sisters and an accomplished ice skater in a troubled family. She portrayed Myrlie Evers-Williams in the PBS TV movie about martyred civil rights activist Medgar Evers, *For Us the Living: The Medgar Evers Story* (1983), earning an NAACP Image Award Best Actress nomination. She also appeared in 1982's *Killing 'Em Softly*, about a woman who falls in love with the man who killed her former boyfriend. In 1983, she appeared as herself in the film *D.C. Cab*. Cara was hoping to star in her own sitcom, *Irene*, on NBC in 1981. The pilot was aired, but the series didn't sell.

Irene Cara was not just a singer who happened to take a stab at an acting career: she was a sensitive, capable actress. Even in B-films like *A Certain Fury* (1985), she showed an expressive range of emotion. In *City Heat* (also 1984), she co-starred with the two biggest superstars of that era, Clint Eastwood and Burt Reynolds, in a plum role as Ginny Lee, a nightclub singer who witnesses a murder. The film was set in Kansas City during the Prohibition Era.

Cara won the Oscar in 1984 for Best Original Song for co-writing (with Giorgio Moroder and Keith Forsey) "Flashdance ... What a Feeling." The song won every other award in the industry that year, including the Grammy, the Golden Globe, and the American Music Award. Cara also had a major hit with the song.

Her albums include *Anyone Can See* (1982), *What a Feelin'* (1983), and *Carasmatic* (1987). She married Hollywood stuntman Conrad Palmisano in 1986; they divorced in 1991. Cara resides in

Florida, has her own production studio, and is the leader of the all-female band called Hot Caramel.

Feature Films including Video and TV Movies: *Aaron Loves Angela* (1975), *That's Dancing* (archival; 1985), *Apple Pie* (1976), *Sparkle* (1976), *Guyana Tragedy: The Story of Jim Jones* (TV; 1980), *Fame* (1980), *Sister, Sister* (TV; 1982), *Killing 'Em Softly* (1982), *For Us the Living: The Medgar Evers Story* (TV; 1983), *D.C. Cab* (1983), *City Heat* (1984), *Certain Fury* (1985), *Busted Up* (1986), *Caged in Paradiso* (1986), *Die abenteuer von pico und Columbus* (aka *The Magic Voyage*; voice; 1992), *Happily Ever After* (voice; 1993).

TV: *Ted Mack's Original Amateur Hour* (1967), *The Ed Sullivan Show* (1968?), *Love of Life* (recurring role as Daisy Allen; 1970–71), *The Tonight Show Starring Johnny Carson* (1971), *The Electric Company* (series regular as Iris; 1971–72), *The Everything Show* (host; 1972), *Kojak* ("A Hair-Trigger Away," 1976), *What's Happening!!* ("Rerun Gets Married," 1977), *On Location with Fame* (1980), *Midnight Special* (1980), *American Bandstand* (2 segments; 1980–83), *Solid Gold* (2 segments; 1980–84), *The 38th Annual Golden Globe Awards* (1981), *The 53rd Annual Academy Awards* (1981), *Top of the Pops* (1982), *Fame Looks at Music '83* (1984), *The 56th Annual Academy Awards* (1984), *A Celebration of Life: A Tribute to Martin Luther King, Jr.* (1984), *The 11th Annual American Music Awards* (1984), *The 26th Annual Grammy Awards* (1984), 20th NAACP Image Awards (1988), *Sabado noche* (1988), *Gabriel's Fire* ("Birds Gotta Fly," 1991), *Hearts Are Wild* (1992), *VH1: Where Are They Now?* (2000), *I Love the '80s* (2001), *Wetten dass...?* (2001), *Verstehen sie spab?* (1981), *The Disco Ball: A 30-Year Celebration* (2003), *Get Down Tonight: The Disco Explosion* (2004), *Hit Me, Baby, One More Time* (winner of reality show competition; 2005), *Die ultimative chartshow* (2005), *100 Greatest Teen Stars* (archival; 2006), *Any Given Sunday* (2006), *9 am with Dave and Kim* (2006), *My Music: Movie Songs* (2007), *Entertainment Tonight* (2007).

Video/DVD: *Oscar's Greatest Moments* (archival; 1992), *Beyond Awareness to Action: Ending Abuse of Women* (1995).

Shorts: *Snow White and the Magic Mirror* (1994).

Carey, Mariah Born in Huntington, Long Island, New York, March 27, 1970.

Mariah Angela Carey was the third and youngest child of Patricia Hickey, a former opera singer and vocal coach of Irish descent, and Alfred Roy Carey, an aeronautical engineer of African and Venezuelan descent. Her parents divorced when she was three. Carey had little contact with her father after the divorce, while her mother worked several jobs to support the family. Carey turned to music as a palliative to her personal problems. She began singing at age three, inspired by her mother's operatic training. She graduated from Harborfields High School in Greenlawn, New York, and worked as a demo singer for local recording studios. She made her own demo tape and moved to New York City, where she went to beauty school and worked part-time jobs. Then she became a back-up singer for Brenda K. Starr.

She made her recording debut in 1990 under the tutelage of Columbia Records executive Tommy Mottola (Carey gave him her demo tape when she met him at a party). She married Mottola in 1993 and divorced him in 1998. Her first album was the eponymous *Mariah Carey* (1990); she wrote much of the material herself, as she has continued to do throughout her career. It reached the top spot on the *Billboard* chart and stayed there for several weeks. Carey won Grammys for Best New Artist and Best Female Pop Vocal Performance (for the soaring anthem "Vision of Love"). Her first five singles were at the top of the *Billboard* chart; a series of hits established her position as Columbia's number-one artist. *Billboard* called her the most successful recording artist of the 1990s.

After the breakup with Mottola, she developed a more hip-hop oriented sound. Her second album, *Emotions* (1991), was a tribute to the Motown sound. Her third album was *Music Box* (1993), her most successful to that point, with substantial worldwide sales. Her fourth album was the seasonal *Merry Christmas* (1994), which became the best-selling Christmas album of all time, and features what has become a Christmas classic, "All I Want for Christmas Is You." This was followed by *Daydream* (1995), which garnered the best reviews of her career to that point, received six Grammy nominations, and led to a world tour. Her sixth album, *Butterfly* (1997), yielded the hit single "Honey" and continued Carey's move in a hip-hop direction. "My All," a hit from the album, gave her the record for most number ones ever by a female artist. Her seventh album, *Rainbow* (1999), was the lowest-selling of her career, and critical reaction was tepid. Following a *Greatest Hits* album, her next album was *Charmbracelet* (2002), but it too encountered rough waters from critics and fans. *Emancipation of Mimi* (2005), her huge comeback album, was the year's best-seller. Her eleventh album: *E=MC²* (2008) had the misfortune to follow *Mimi*, and simply could not match its success on any level. It did produce the single "Touch My Body," accompanied by a wry music video.

Carey left Columbia in 2001 and was dropped by Virgin records the following year, but rebounded and returned to the pinnacle of the pop charts in 2005. She was named the best-selling female artist of the millennium at the 2000 World Music Awards. She has recorded the most number-one singles — 17 — for a female solo artist in the U.S. She has earned five Grammy Awards. The awards were for Best New Artist and Best Female Pop Vocal Performance (1991); Best R&B Song, Best R&B Female Vocal Performance, and Best Contemporary R&B Album (2006).

Carey's acting career has, to date, not been nearly as stellar as her recording career. *Glitter* (2001) — a semi-autobiographical variant on *A Star Is Born* — is rightfully in the running as one of the worst films ever made (Carey's performance doesn't help). However, her acting in *WiseGirls* (seen mostly on cable TV; 2002), is the best thing about that overwrought film. Here she is in charge of her performance and seems relaxed in front of the camera. Her work in the indie film *Tennessee* (2008) received good advance word from film festival showings. Carey married singer Nick Cannon in 2008.

Feature Films: *The Bachelor* (1999), *Glitter* (2001), *WiseGirls* (2002), *State Property 2* (2005), *Lovers and Haters* (2007), *You Don't Mess with the Zohan* (2008), *Tennessee* (2009).

TV: *Saturday Night Live* (3 segments; 1990–97), *The 18th Annual American Music Awards* (1991), *MTV Video Music Awards 1991, 33rd Annual Grammy Awards* (1991), *Top of the Pops* (20 segments; 1991–2006), *Unplugged* (1992), *34th Annual Grammy Awards* (1992), *Here Is Mariah Carey* (1993), *Verstehen sie spab...?* (1994), *Especial Nochevieja '94, Mariah Carey Rockumentary* (1995), *Fantasy: Mariah Carey at Madison Square Garden* (1995), *38th Annual Grammy Awards* (1996), *1997 VH1 Fashion Awards, The Rosie O'Donnell Show* (1996–2000), *Wetten, dass...?* (3 segments; 1996–2005), *The National Lottery* (1997), *The Gift of Song* (1997), *Nobel Peace Prize Concert* (1997), *VH1 Divas Live* (1998), *1998 Billboard Music Awards, Mariah Carey: Around the World* (1998), *Motown 40: The Music Is Forever* (1998), *Howard Stern* (2 segments; 1998–99), *La llamada de la suerte* (1998), *1998 MTV Music Video Awards, Musica Si* (1998), *When You Believe: Music from The Prince of Egypt* (1998), *Mariah Carey's Homecoming Special* (1999), *Pavarotti and Friends '99 for Guatemala and Kosovo, 71st Annual Academy Awards* (1999), *30th NAACP Image Awards* (1999), *Die lotto-show* (1999), *Sen kvall med luuk* (1999), *VH1 to One* (1999), *1999 MTV Europe Music Awards, 1999 Billboard Music Awards, ABC 2000: The Millennium* (archival; 1999), *Mundo VIP* (2 segments; 1999–2001), *Mariah TV* (2000), *VH1 Divas 2000: A Tribute to Diana Ross, Mad TV* (2000), *TRL Italy* (2000), *Making the Video* (2 segments; 1999–2005), *It's Your New Year's Eve Party* (2001), *Stars 2001: Die AIDS Gala, 2001 Top of the Pops Awards, America: A Tribute to Heroes* (2001), *Rove Live* (2001), *SM:TV Live* (2001–02), *Late Show with David Letterman* (2 segments; 2001–05), *E! True Hollywood Story* (2 segments; 2001–06), *CD:UK* (8 segments; 2001–06), *Children in Need* (2002), *Fame Academy* (2002), *Millionär gesucht!: Die SKL Show* (2002), *8th Annual Walk of Fame Honoring Stevie Wonder* (2002), *Operacion triunfo* (2002), *Exclusif* (2002), *Muhammad Ali's All-Star 60th Birthday Celebration* (2002), *Film Trix 2002, The Oprah Winfrey Show* (4 segments; 2002–05), *Cribs* (2 episodes; 2002 and 2005), *101 Most Shocking Moments in Entertainment* (archival; 2003), *I Love the '80s Strikes Back* (2003), *The Proud Family* (voice; 2003), *Good Day Live* (2003), *Intimate Portrait* (2003), *Death of a Dynasty* (2003), *The National Lottery Wright Ticket* (2003), *V Graham Norton* (2003), *Eurobest* (2003), *17th Annual Soul Train Music Awards* (2003), *50 Sexiest Video Moments* (2003), *It's Good to Be...* (2003), *30th Annual American Music Awards* (2003), *Ant & Dec's Saturday Night Takeaway* (2 segments; 2003–05), *Maxim Hot 100* (2004), *101 Biggest Celebrity Oops* (2004), *2005 Billboard Music Awards, Today with Des and Mel* (2005), *George Michael: A Different Story* (2005), *Store Studio* (2005), *On a tout essayé* (archival; 2005), *Favouritism* (archival; 2005), *Bambi* (2005), *Fashion Rocks* (2005), *Toute le monde en parle* (2005), *Echo-deutscher musikpreis* (2005), *Best Hit USA* (2005), *Total Request Live* (2005), *Stars on Trial* (archival; 2005), *2005 American*

Music Awards, 3rd Annual Vibe Awards (2005), *Gottschalk & Friends* (2005), *BET Awards 2005, Save the Music Concert* (2005), *Uncut Mariah Carey* (2005), *2005 MTV Music Awards, The Paul O'Grady Show* (2005), *Ellen* (2005), *Live 8* (2005), *Macy's 4th of July Fireworks Spectacular* (2005), *The View* (2005), *2005 World Music Awards, 2005 Teen Choice Awards, Live with Regis and Kathie Lee* (2005), *2005 MTV Movie Awards, 2005 MTV Video Music Awards, The Tonight Show with Jay Leno* (2 segments; 2005 and 2006), *Corazon de...* (3 segments; archival; 2005–07), *New Year's Rockin' Eve 2006, Idols!* (2006), *The Advocate Newsmagazine* (2006), *2006 Much Music Video Awards* (archival), *48th Annual Grammy Awards* (2006), *The Tyra Banks Show* (2006), *Legends Ball* (2006), *The Barbara Walters Special* (2006), *Video on Trial* (7 segments; archival; 2006–07), *Taff* (2007), *Happy Birthday, Elton!* (2007), *Corazon, corazon* (2007), *Forbes' 20 Richest Women in Entertainment* (2007), *Live with Regis and Kelly* (2008), *The Teen Choice Awards 2008, Jimmy Kimmel Live!* (2008), *Entertainment Tonight* (2008), *Weekend Sunrise* (2008), *The Ellen DeGeneres Show* (2008), *Stand Up to Cancer* (2008).

Videos/DVDs: *Grammy's Great Moments, Vol. II* (archival; 1994), *Tina Turner: Celebrate Live 1999, #1's* (1999), *Bone Thugs-N-Harmony: Greatest Video Hits* (2000), *Babyface: A Collection of Hit Videos* (2001), *Luthor Vandross: From Luther with Love* (2004), *Definition of a Diva* (2006).

Short: *Lovers and Haters* (2007).

Carroll, Diahann Born in the Bronx, New York, July 17, 1935.

It is difficult to overstate Diahann Carroll's contribution to the advancement of the positive image of black women, especially on television. In the sitcom *Julia* (1968–71), Carroll was TV's first African American professional career woman. It was a tepid but pleasant sitcom that nonetheless provided Carroll with a role that opened doors for black actresses for generations to come. This was the first time since 1952 that a black woman had been cast as the lead in a TV series (Ethel Waters on *The Beulah Show*, later replaced by Hattie McDaniel and Louise Beavers). *Julia* was centered around a widowed nurse raising a young son. Carroll won a Golden Globe for the series and was nominated for an Emmy. *Julia* outlasted its usefulness as the series ran its course. As other young black actresses began to appear with regularity on network television, *Julia* seemed less and less unique — and relevant. The frequent drubbing the show received from the critics was the source of considerable annoyance to Carroll.

Carroll will be remembered for much more than one TV series, given her long list of career highlights. She was a sophisticated, mellifluous jazz and pop vocalist; a Broadway star, most famously for the groundbreaking *No Strings* (1962), which featured a light-years-before-its-time interracial romance; and a Best Actress Academy Award nominee for *Claudine* (1974), in which she depicted a realistic view of an inner city black woman. She was a 1963 Emmy nominee for her acting in an episode of *Naked City* and was nominated as Outstanding Actress in a Comedy Series for *A Different World.*

She was also TV's original black diva in her role as Dominique Deveraux on the immensely successful prime time soap opera *Dynasty*; a guest in the Kennedy and Johnson White House; an impassioned spokeswoman for social issues, including cancer awareness and research; a nominee for an NAACP Image Award for her recurring role as Auntie Ruthie in Showtime's *Soul Food*; and a Grammy nominee.

Diahann Carroll and Pearl Bailey in *Porgy and Bess* (1959).

Carol Diann Johnson was born in the Bronx in a less than stellar neighborhood. Her family moved to Harlem when she was 18 months old. Carol Diann knew she was "different" from other people—smart, talented, motivated—and she credits her parents with providing the shelter, solace and inspiration that got her through a rough environment. Her first public singing experience was at age six as a member of the Tiny Tots choir in Adam Clayton Powell's Abyssinian Baptist Church in Harlem.

Rather than pursue a general education at George Washington High School, Carroll auditioned for and gained entrance to the High School of Music and Art (later known as the New York City High School of the Performing Arts), popularized in the motion picture and subsequent TV series *Fame*. Her first professional job was modeling petticoats for *Ebony* magazine at age 14. By 18, the chanteuse in training was already professionally known as Diahann Carroll. She met with Otto Preminger and landed a supporting role in *Carmen Jones* (1954), the film most remembered today for garnering Dorothy Dandridge a Best Actress Oscar nomination. Carroll's big screen debut was in a rather thankless, fairly small role as one of Pearl Bailey's pals.

Carroll began her professional singing career when she set a record by garnering wins three weeks in a row on the *Chance of a Lifetime* TV show (a variation on *Arthur Godfrey's Talent Scouts*, kind of an early *American Idol*). The prize was a booking at Lou Walters' (TV news legend Barbara's father) legendary Latin Quarter. This launched an enduring career. Carroll sang throughout the world and appeared at all the top supper clubs across the United States, including the Waldorf and the Plaza in New York. She made her professional TV singing debut on *The Red Skelton Show*.

Her Broadway debut was even quite auspicious, in 1954's *House of Flowers*, the Richard Arlen and Truman Capote musical starring Pearl Bailey. Carroll sang two of the show's best songs in the ingénue role: "A Sleeping Bee" and the title song. Audiences and critics were enchanted by the sylph-like young woman with the haunting, evocative, razor-sharp voice. Her most famous Broadway role was as model Barbara Woodruff in the then controversial interracial love story *No Strings*, with Richard Kiley, for which she won the Best Actress in a Musical Tony Award (shared with Anna Maria Alberghetti for *Carnival*).

Carroll looked stunning on stage in the Jackie Kennedy inspired fashions of the day and—at a time when the Civil Rights movement was gaining great momentum—she was the perfect symbol for the new black woman. She received anonymous threats of physical harm during the run of the play, as she did during the filming of *Hurry Sundown* (1967) and at other points in her career and in her private life. Losing the starring role in the proposed film version of *No Strings* to Eurasian actress Nancy Kwan was a devastating blow to Carroll, every bit as personally upsetting as when Lena Horne was denied the role of Julie in the film remake of *Show Boat*. Apparently, Hollywood was not prepared to embrace the reality of interracial relationships as willingly as was Broadway, but the film version fell through and has yet to see the light of day.

Carroll's albums include *The Magic of Diahann Carroll* (with the Andre Previn Trio) and *Fun Life*, with an audaciously sexy cover photo (both 1960). Whether giving a contemporary spin to an Irving Berlin standard, or working her magic on then-contemporary show tunes like "Everything's Coming Up Roses" from *Gypsy*, Carroll was part diva, part waif, and part sophisticated lady. She didn't sound like anyone else—she was an original, much like her contemporary the jazz singer Nancy Wilson.

In 2006, Carroll returned to her roots on the New York cabaret and nightclub scene with a new act called "The Life and Times of Diahann Carroll," which debuted at Feinstein's at the Regency. It was her first New York appearance since her Broadway role in *Agnes of God* with Geraldine Page in 1982. In March 2007 she returned to Feinstein's with a nostalgic cabaret act called "Both Sides Now." This autobiographical show led a reporter for the *New York Post* to write: "Looking impossibly beautiful at 71, and singing with a voice seemingly untouched by age, Carroll performed stirring versions of such standards as 'Come Rain or Come Shine,' 'The Best Is Yet to Come,' and, as part of a Sinatra medley, 'I've Got You Under My Skin.'" The reporter went on to write, "[She] unleashes her full vocal power in a room seemingly too small to contain her." In October of 1995 she starred as Norma Desmond in the Toronto premiere of "Sunset Boulevard." In 2004 she starred onstage in the musical "Bubbling Brown Sugar."

She was successfully treated for breast cancer

in 1998 and is a spokeswoman for the National Women's Cancer Research Alliance. Carroll has been married four times. Her first marriage, to Monte Kay, lasted from 1956 to 1963, and produced one daughter, Suzanne. Other marriages were to Freddie Glusman (married and divorced in 1973); Robert DeLeon (1975, until his death in 1977); and classic pop singer Vic Damone (1987–96). In 1960, she was engaged to Sidney Poitier. In the early 1970s, she had a lengthy engagement to TV talk show host David Frost. Carroll is the author of a recent memoir, *The Legs Are the Last to Go*, dealing with the later stages of her career (Amistad; 2008).

Feature Films including TV Movies: *Carmen Jones* (1954), *Porgy and Bess* (1959), *Paris Blues* (1961), *Goodbye Again* (aka *Aimez-vous Brahms?)* (1961), *Hurry Sundown* (1967), *The Split* (1968), *Claudine* (1974), *Death Scream* (1975; TV), *I Know Why the Caged Bird Sings* (1979; TV), *Roots: The Next Generations* (1979; TV), *Sister, Sister* (1982; TV), *From the Dead of Night* (1989; TV), *Murder in Black and White* (1990; TV), *The Five Heartbeats* (1991), *A Perry Mason Mystery: The Case of the Lethal Lifestyle* (1994; TV), *Eve's Bayou* (1997), *The Sweetest Gift* (1998; TV), *Jackie's Back* (TV; 1999), *Having Our Say: The Delany Sisters' First 100 Years* (1999; TV), *The Courage to Love* (2000; TV), *Sally Hemings: An American Scandal* (2000; TV), *Living for Love: The Natalie Cole Story* (2000; TV), *Takin' Chances* (2006).

TV: *Toast of the Town* (1948), *Chance of a Lifetime* (1952), *The Red Skelton Show* (1956), *The DuPont Show of the Month* (1957), *The Jack Paar Show* (semi-regular; 1958), *GE Theatre* (1959), *Peter Gunn* ("Sing a Song of Murder" 1960), *The Man in the Moon* (1960), *Naked City* (1962), *What's My Line?* (1962), *The Ed Sullivan Show* (various segments, 1962–1968), The *Merv Griffin Show* (1963, 1968), *The Eleventh Hour* ("And God Created Vanity" 1963), *Password* (1963), *The Milton Berle Show* (1966), *Bell Telephone Hour* (two segments, 1964–1966), *The Judy Garland Show* (1964), *The Dean Martin Show* (1965–66), *The Hollywood Palace* (various segments, 1967–1969), *ABC Stage 67* (1967), *Julia* (series lead as Julia Baker, 1968–1971), *The Jackie Gleason Show* (1968), *This Is Tom Jones* (segments in 1969, 1970), *The Julie Andrews Hour* (1972), *Jack Lemmon—Get Happy, a Tribute to Harold Arlen* (1973), *The Tonight Show* (1976), *America Salutes Richard Rodgers: The Sound of His Music* (1976), *Mike Douglas Show* (1977), *The Love Boat* (1977), *The Star Wars Holiday Special* (1978), *Webster* ("Strike Up the Band," 1983), *Dynasty* (recurring role as Dominique Deveraux, 1984–87), *That's Singing: The Best of Broadway* (1984; features Carroll performing "A Sleeping Bee"), *Rockette: A Holiday Tribute to Radio City Music Hall* (1987), *Joan Rivers and Friends Salute Heidi Abromowitz* (1985), *The Colbys* (recurring role as Dominique Deveraux, 1986), *Sammy Davis, Jr. 60th Anniversary Celebration* (1990), *Francis Albert Sinatra Does His Thing* (1991), *Funny Women of Television* (1991), *Color Adjustment* (1991), *Sunday in Paris* (unsold TV pilot; 1991), *A Different World* (recurring role as Marian Gilbert; 1991–1993), *The Sinbad Show* ("My Daughter's Keeper," 1993), *Lonesome Dove: the Series* (1994–95), *Burke's Law* ("Who Killed the Beauty Queen?" 1994), *Evening Shade* ("The Perfect Woman," 1994), *Jirimpimbira: An African Folk Tale* (1995), *Touched by an Angel* ("The Driver," 1995), *Hollywood Squares* (1998; 2004), *Porgy and Bess: An American Voice* (1998), *Ellen/These Friends of Mine* (1998), *Intimate Portrait: Diahann Carroll* (1998), *Motown 40: The Music Is Forever* (1998), *Twice in a Lifetime* ("O'er the Ramparts We Watched," "Double Exposure," 1999), *The Court* (2002), *Half & Half* ("Big Thanks for Forgiving," 2002), *NBC 75th Anniversary Special* (2002), *Strong Medicine* ("Love and Let Die," 2003), *Whoopi* ("Mother's Little Helper," 2003), *Soul Food* ("In the Garden," 2004; "Truth's Consequences," 2003), *TV Land Specials* (2002–2005), *Tavis Smiley* (2 segments; 2005 and 2008), *That's What I'm Talking About* (2006), *The Oprah Winfrey Show* (2006), *Entertainment Tonight* (2006), *Grey's Anatomy* (recurring role as Jane Burke; 2006–07), *Over the River: The Life of Lydia Maria Child, Abolitionist for Freedom* (narrator; 2007), *Back to You* ("Hug and Tell," 2008), *The View* (2008).

Carson, Lisa Nicole Born in Brooklyn, New York, July 12, 1969.

Although born in Brooklyn, Carson spent her teen years in Gainesville, Florida, and graduated from Buchholz High School in 1987. She returned to New York after graduation to live with her grandmother and to pursue an acting career. She attended Hunter College of the City University of New York, appearing in theater productions and working backstage. She became a regular on the syndicated *Apollo Comedy Hour* (1992–

93), a mix of *Showtime at the Apollo* and *Saturday Night Live*. Carson's star burned brightly in the mid–1990s, but she was diagnosed as schizophrenic and has not been active in recent years. She starred as Ally's roommate Renee Radick on FOX's smash hit series *Ally McBeal* (1997–2002). Renee was an unabashedly sexy defense attorney who was Ally's friend and confidant. She also played Carla Reese, Dr. Peter Benton's girlfriend, on *ER* (1996–2001).

Film roles include *Life* (1999), as Sylvia, an eye candy role; *Eve's Bayou* (1997), as Matty Mereaux, the married woman Dr. Louis Baptiste (Samuel L. Jackson) is having a dalliance with; *Love Jones* (1997), and *Devil in a Blue Dress* (1995), as Coretta James, a woman involved in a murder case who soon winds up dead herself. Carson is a skilled vocalist as well as an actress.

Feature Films including TV Movies: *Let's Get Bizzee* (1993), *Jason's Lyric* (1994), *Devil in a Blue Dress* (1995), *Divas* (TV; 1995), *White Lies* (1996), *Love Jones* (1997), *Eve's Bayou* (1997), *Life* (1999), *Aftershock: Earthquake in New York* (TV; 1999).

TV: *Law & Order* ("Aria," 1991), *The Cosby Show* ("And So We Commence," Parts I and II, 1992), *The Apollo Comedy Hour* (series regular; 1992–93), *Lifestories: Families in Crisis* ("No Visible Bruises: The Katie Koestner Story," 1993), *ABC Afterschool Specials* ("Girlfriend," 1993), *Lauren Hutton and...* (1995), *ER* (recurring role of Carla Reese; 1996–2001), *Ally McBeal* (recurring role of Renee Radick; 1997–2002), *Essence Awards* (1998), *Damon* ("The Test," 1998), *Getting Personal* ("Sam I Am," 1998), *The 51st Annual Primetime Emmy Awards* (1999), *The Rosie O'Donnell Show* (1999).

Carter, Nell Born in Birmingham, Alabama, September 13, 1948; died January 23, 2003, Long Beach, California.

Nell Carter's ebullient, confident character on the sitcom *Gimme a Break!* bore little resemblance to the troubled, conflicted woman whose life was steeped in a succession of tragedies. *Gimme a Break!* (1981–87) was a conventional but long-running NBC sitcom with Carter as Nell Harper, housekeeper for a police chief and his three daughters. She eventually becomes head of the household when the chief dies (actor Dolph Sweet really did die of cancer after the 1984–85 season finished filming). Carter had a role on the lowbrow but pleasant *The Misadventures of Sheriff Lobo* (1980–81) before landing her career-making role as Nell Harper on *Gimme a Break!*, for which she earned Golden Globe and Emmy Award nominations.

She was born Nell Ruth Hardy to parents Horace and Edna Mae Hardy, and was one of nine children. Her father was killed in an accident with a power line. Carter was raped at age 16 and became pregnant from the attack, giving birth to her daughter Tracy. She was also mother to two sons, Daniel and Joshua, adopting both as newborns over a four-month period. By age 19, Carter had relocated to New York, where she found work singing in a variety of nightspots (including excellent venues like the Rainbow Room and Sweeney's), and in musical revues.

She studied at Bill Russell's School of Drama from 1970 to 1973 and made her Broadway debut in *Soon* (1971), a two-act musical show that lasted only two days. This was followed by the off–Broadway production *The Wedding of Iphigenia* (1971). Then she was back on Broadway as Suzie Moon in *Dude* (1972). She appeared with Bette Davis in *Miss Moffat* (1974), based on the Davis film *The Corn Is Green*, but the show closed on the road before making it to Broadway. She did two off–Broadway productions in 1975: *Tom Eyen's Dirtiest Musical* and *Be Kind to People Week*.

Carter achieved stardom with *Ain't Misbehavin'* (1978), a revue of the great songs of Fats Waller, for which she won a Best Featured Actress in a Musical Tony Award as well as a Drama Desk Award. She won an Emmy for the same role in a televised performance on NBC in 1982. In 1995 she appeared in an unsuccessful Broadway revival

Lisa Nicole Carson in *Love Jones* (1997).

of *Annie* as Miss Hannigan. Her last theatrical appearance was in the original off–Broadway production of *The Vagina Monologues* in 1999. She appeared in the film version of *Hair* (1979) singing a spirited version of "White Boys." In 1978 she was cast as Effie White in the Broadway musical *Dreamgirls*, but departed the production during development, ostensibly to take a role on the ABC soap *Ryan's Hope*. When the show premiered in late 1981, Jennifer Holliday had taken over the lead.

Carter married mathematician and lumber executive George Krynicki in 1982 and converted from Presbyterianism to Judaism. She attempted suicide in the early 1980s and entered a drug rehabilitation facility around 1985. She divorced Krynicki in 1982 and married Roger Larocque that same year, and in 1993 she divorced Larocque. Carter declared bankruptcy in 1995 and again in 2002. In addition to her marriages, she had a long-standing relationship with domestic partner Ann Kaser.

Carter died from heart disease and diabetes complicated by obesity. At the time of her death, she had been rehearsing for a production of the musical *Raisin*, based on *A Raisin in the Sun*, and filming a movie, *Swing* (2003), a musical fantasy.

Feature Films including TV Movies: *Hair* (1979), *Back Roads* (1981), *Modern Problems* (1981), *Maid for Each Other* (TV; 1992), *Final Shot: The Hank Gathers Story* (TV; 1992), *Bebe's Kids* (voice; 1992), *The Crazysitter* (1995), *The Grass Harp* (1995), *The Proprietor* (1996), *Fakin' Da Funk* (1997), *Special Delivery* (1999), *Perfect Fit* (1999), *We Wish You a Merry Christmas* (voice; 1999), *Sealed with a Kiss* (TV; 1999), *Back by Midnight* (2002), *Swing* (2003).

TV: *Cindy* (1978), *Ryan's Hope* (recurring role of Ethel Green; 1978–79), *The Tonight Show Starring Johnny Carson* (1980), *The Big Show* (3 segments; 1980), *Baryshnikov on Broadway* (1980), *The Misadventures of Sheriff Lobo* (recurring role as Sgt. Hildy Jones; 1980–81), *The 35th Annual Tony Awards* (1981), *Gimme a Break!* (recurring role of Nell Harper; 1981–87), *Night of 100 Stars* (1982), *Ain't Misbehavin'* (1982), *The Billy Crystal Comedy Hour* (1982), *Dean Martin Celebrity Roast: Mr. T* (1984), *The NBC All-Star Hour* (1985), *Night of 100 Stars II* (1985), *Joan Rivers and Friends Salute Heidi Abromowitz* (1985), *Santa Barbara* (2 episodes; 1985), *Circus of the Stars 10* (1985), *Amen* ("The Courtship of Beth Richards," 1986), *The 40th Annual Tony Awards* (1986), *NBC 60th Anniversary Celebration* (1986), *Nell Carter Special* (1986), *19th Annual NAACP Image Awards* (1987), *The 13th Annual People's Choice Awards* (1987), *Las Vegas: An All-Star 75th Anniversary* (1987), *Irving Berlin's 100th Birthday Celebration* (1988), *The 42nd Annual Tony Awards* (1988), *227* ("Take My Diva ... Please," 1989), *The 3rd Annual American Comedy Awards* (1989), *The 43rd Annual Tony Awards* (1989), *The 34th Annual American Comedy Awards* (1990), *The Sammy Davis, Jr. 60th Anniversary Celebration* (1990), *You Take the Kids* (pilot; 1990), *The 48th Annual Golden Globe Awards* (1991), *Voices That Care* (1991), *Jake and the Fatman* ("Ain't Misbehavin'," 1992), *In a New Light: A Call to Action in the War Against AIDS* (1992), *The 65th Annual Academy Awards* (1993), *Hangin' with Mr. Cooper* (2 episodes in the role of P.J. Moore; "Hangin' with Mrs. Cooper," "Call Me Irresponsible," 1993 and 1995), *The 48th Annual Tony Awards* (1994), *Happily Ever After: Fairy Tales for Every Child* (1995), *Spider-Man* (voice; 2 episodes; "Day of the Chameleon," "Partners in Danger: Chapter I," 1995 and 1997), *Marvin Hamlisch and the Pittsburgh Pops* (1996), *Can't Hurry Love* ("The Rent

Nell Carter and John Hoyt in *Gimme a Break!*

Strike," 1996), *The Blues Brothers Animated Series* (voice; 19??), *The Rosie O'Donnell Show* (1996), *The 51st Annual Tony Awards* (1997), *Brotherly Love* ("Paging Nell," 1997), *Sparks* ("Hoop Schemes," 1997), *The 52nd Annual Tony Awards* (1998), *Match Games* (various segments; 1998), *Great Performances* ("My Favorite Broadway: The Leading Ladies," 1999), *The Tulsa Lynching of 1921: A Hidden Story* (2000), *Beyond Tara: The Extraordinary Life of Hattie McDaniel* (2001), *Weakest Link* (2001), *Touched By An Angel* (2 episodes as Cynthia Winslow; "Shallow Water," Parts I and II, 2001), *Seven Days* ("Live from Death Row," 2001), *Reba* (3 episodes as Dr. Susan Peters; pilot, "The Honeymoon's Over, or Now What?" "Someone's at Gyno with Reba," 2001), *Inside TV Land; African Americans in Television* (2002), *Ally McBeal* (2 episodes as Harriet Pumple; "Playing with Matches," "One Hundred Tears," 2002), *E! True Hollywood Story* ("Gimme a Break," 2003), *Great Performances* (archival; "Broadway's Lost Treasures II," 2004).

Cash, Rosalind Born December 31, 1938, in Atlantic City, New Jersey; died October 31, 1995, Los Angeles, California.

Rosalind Cash graduated with honors from Atlantic City High School in 1956 and was a member of an acting workshop at the Harlem YMCA. She began her acting career with the Negro Ensemble Company. She studied English literature at City College in New York. She was the daughter of John O. and Martha E. Cash, and had two brothers and a sister, John, Robert and Helen. She was nominated for an Emmy for the PBS production *Go Tell It on the Mountain* (1985). She played the scheming, venal daughter Goneril in a TV production of *King Lear* (1974), which was Emmy nominated for Outstanding Drama Special.

She was in the made-for-TV movie *Guyana Tragedy: The Story of Jim Jones* (1980). She played the alcoholic sister of Diahann Carroll and Irene Cara in *Sister, Sister* (1982). Cash guest starred on a variety of series, including *Kojak*, *Police Story*, *Barney Miller*, *Mary Tyler Moore*, *Cagney & Lacey*, *China Beach*, and *Hill Street Blues*. Her two most famous film roles centered around interracial relationships. She co-starred with Charlton Heston in the underrated sci-fi thriller *Omega Man* (1971), the second screen version of *I Am Legend*; and was involved with Stacy Keach in the police drama *The New Centurions* (1974).

Cash died of cancer at Cedars-Sinai Medical Center in Los Angeles in the midst of production of *The Matrix* trilogy, and was replaced in the third film by Mary Alice. She was inducted into the Black Filmmakers Hall of Fame in 1992.

Feature Films including TV Movies: *Klute* (1971), *The Omega Man* (1971), *The New Centurions* (1972), *Melinda* (1972), *Hickey & Boggs* (1972), *The All-American Boy* (1973), *Uptown Saturday Night* (1974), *Amazing Grace* (1974), *Cornbread, Earl and Me* (1975), *Dr. Black, Mr. Hyde* (aka *Dr. Black and Mr. Hyde*, 1976), *The Monkey Hu$tle* (1976), *A Killing Affair* (TV; 1977), *The Class of Miss MacMichael* (1978), *Death Drug* (1978), *Flashpoint* (TV; 1979), *Guyana Tragedy: The Story of Jim Jones* (TV; 1980), *Keeping On* (TV; 1981), *The Sophisticated Gents* (TV; 1981), *Wrong Is Right* (1982), *Sister, Sister* (TV; 1982), *Just an Overnight Guest* (TV; 1983), *Special Bulletin* (TV; 1983), *The Adventures of Buckaroo Banzai Across the 8th Dimension* (1984), *Go Tell It on the Mountain* (TV; 1985), *Mighty Pawns* (TV; 1987), *The Offspring* (aka *From a Whisper to a Scream*, 1987), *Death Spa* (1988), *Forced March* (1989), *The Second Coming* (1992), *A Dangerous Affair* (TV; 1995), *Tales from the Hood* (1995), *Circle of Pain* (TV; 1996).

TV: *Harry O* ("Eyewitness," 1974), *The Mary Tyler Moore Show* ("A Girl Like Mary," 1974), *King Lear* (1974), *Ceremonies in Dark Old Men* (1975), *Good Times* ("J.J. and the Older Woman," 1976), *What's Happening!!* (2 episodes in the role of Loretta; "Christmas," "The Sunday Father," 1976 and 1977), *Police Woman* ("Shadow of a Doubt," 1977), *Kojak* ("The Godson," 1977), *Starsky and Hutch* ("The Crying Child," 1977), *Barney Miller* ("Dog Days," 1978), *Benson* ("Rainbow's End," 1981), *Hardcastle and McCormick* ("The Homecoming," 1984), *Trapper John, M.D.* (2 episodes; "Love and Marriage," "School Nurse," 1982 and 1984), *This Is the Life* ("How Shall We Then Live," 1985), *Rip Tide* ("Boz Busters," 1985), *Hill Street Blues* ("Hacked to Pieces," 1985), *Knight Rider* ("Voo Doo Knight," 1986), *The Cosby Show* ("Denise Gets a 'D,'" 1986), *Cagney & Lacey* ("Cost of Living," 1987), *Highway to Heaven* ("A Song of Songs," 1987), *L.A. Law* ("Auld L'Anxiety," 1987), *Frank's Place* ("Dueling Voodoo," 1988), *The Golden Girls* ("Mixed Blessings," 1988), *Knight Watch* ("Knights of the City," 1988), *Family Ties* (2 episodes in the role of Maya Thompson; "All in the Neighborhood," Parts I and II, 1989), *thirtysomething* (3 episodes in the role of Val Shilliday; "Weaning," "We'll Meet Again," "New Job," 1987–89), *Falcon Crest* ("Soul Sacrifice," 1989), *227* ("Gone Fishing," 1990), *Head of the Class* (Billy's Big One," 1990), *China Beach* ("One Small Step," 1990), *A Different World* (4 episodes in the role of Dean Hughes; "Radio Free Hillman," "To Have and Have Not," "Under One Roof," "Ms. Understanding," 1989–91), *Knots Landing* (2 episodes; "Call Me Dmitri," "Upwardly Mobile," 1991), *Wonderworks* ("You Must Remember This," 1992), *Tequila and Bonetti* ("Teach Your Children," 1992), *The Fresh Prince of Bel-Air* ("Six Degrees of Graduation," 1993), *Lois & Clark: The New Adventures of Superman* ("The Man of Steel Bars," 1993), *Roc* (3 episodes in the role of Elenor's mother; "What's Up Roc," "Second Time Around," "God Bless the Child," 1992–93), *General Hospital* (recurring role as Mary Mae Ward; 1994–95).

Rosalind Cash in *The Omega Man* (1971).

Chapman, Lanei Born January 23, 1973.

Lanei Chapman is a graduate of Dartmouth with a bachelor of arts degree in Spanish, and was once a teacher before she became a professional actress. While still in college, Chapman wrote her first play, *Home Run*, which she also produced and directed. She appeared in four episodes of *Star Trek: The Next Generation* (1991–92) as helmsman Ensign Sariel Rager. This role led to a starring role in the sci-fi series *Space: Above and Beyond* (1995–96) as 1st Lieutenant Vanessa Damphousse, a no-nonsense fighter pilot.

Chapman also co-starred with Whoopi Goldberg as her estranged daughter in the film *Rat Race* (2001). In the TV *A Mother's Courage: The Mary Thomas Story* (1989), she appeared as basketball star Isaiah Thomas' mother at age 16 (Alfre Woodard played the adult Mary). She had a recurring role in the series *True Colors*. Chapman acted in episodes of *China Beach* and *The Wonder Years* (both 1988). In the latter, she had one of her best roles as a progressive young teacher who inspires Kevin (Fred Savage) to think outside the box.

Feature Films including Video and TV Movies: *A Mother's Courage: The Mary Thomas Story* (TV; 1989), *White Men Can't Jump* (1992), *The Importance of Being Earnest* (1992), *The Jacksons: An American Dream* (TV; 1992), *Parking* (1996), *Rat Race* (2001), *Dense* (TV; 2004).

TV: *China Beach* ("Souvenirs," 1990), *CBS Schoolbreak Special* ("Lies of the Heart," 1991), *The Wonder Years* ("Kodachrome," 1992), *Martin* ("Things I Do for Love," 1992), *Star Trek: The Next Generation* (recurring role of Ensign Sariel Rager; "Galaxy's Child," "Night Terrors," "Relics," "Schisms," 1991–92), *Seinfeld* (2 episodes; "The Old Man," "The Pilot," 1993), *The Secrets of Lake Success* (miniseries; 1993), *Space: Above and Beyond* (recurring role of Lt. Vanessa Damphousse; 1995–96), *The Pretender* ("Under the Reds," 1997), *C-16: FBI* (2 episodes; "The Art of War," "My Brother's Keeper," 1998), *Judging Amy* (3 episodes in the recurring role of Winnie Van Exel; "Everybody Falls Down," "Between the Wanting and the Getting," "The Frozen Zone," 2001–02), *The District* (2 episodes in the recurring role of Jenny McClure; "Drug Money," "Goodbye, Jenny," 2002 and 2003), *The Division* (2 episodes; "Beyond the Grave," "Wish You Were Here," 2002 and 2003), *Thief* (2 episodes in the recurring role of Sheronda Jones; 2006), *Gray's Anatomy* ("Sometimes a Fantasy," 2006).

Chase, Annazette (aka Annazette; Williams, Annazette) Born May 20, 1943.

Annazette Chase is known for her female lead role as the girlfriend of *Truck Turner* (1974) with Isaac Hayes, and for her role as the hooker China Doll in the blaxploitation classic *The Mack* (1973). She also played Muhammad Ali's wife Belinda in *The Greatest* (1977), in which Ali played himself. She began her film career with uncredited bits in *Don't Worry, We'll Think of a Title* and *Chamber of Horrors* (both 1966). She was also in the barely released sequel *Sounder, Part 2* (1976). Her last film to date was *The Toy* (1982) with Richard Pryor and Jackie Gleason.

Chase was in four episodes of *Burke's Law* with Gene Barry (1964–65) and two episodes of *Ben Casey* (1963–65), as well as guest starring on *Perry Mason*, *The Man from U.N.C.L.E.*, *Get Smart* and *The White Shadow*. She made a guest appearance on *Saturday Night Live* on December 13, 1975, in a sketch with Dan Aykroyd.

Feature Films including TV Movies: *Don't Worry, We'll Think of a Title* (1966), *Chamber of Horrors* (1966), *Marriage: Year One* (TV; 1971), *The Mack* (1973), *Blume in Love* (1973), *Truck Turner* (1974), *Black Fist* (1975), *Sounder, Part 2* (1976), *The Greatest* (1977), *11th Victim* (TV; 1979), *Goldie and the Boxer* (1979), *The Toy* (1982).

TV: *Burke's Law* (4 episodes; "Who Killed WHO IV?" "Who Killed Mr. Cartwright?" "Who Killed Lenore Wingfield?" "Who Killed Mother Goose?" 1964–65), *Ben Casey* (2 episodes; "Allie," "When I Am Grown to Man's Estate," 1963 and 1965), *Kraft Suspense Theatre* ("Four into Zero," 1965), *Perry Mason* ("The Case of the Golden Girls," 1965), *The Man from U.N.C.L.E.* ("The Project Deephole Affair," 1966), *The Green Hornet* ("Deadline for Death," 1966), *Dragnet 1967* ("The Jade Story"), *Get Smart* ("Leadside," 1969), *Sanford and Son* ("Superflyer," 1973), *The Law* (miniseries; 1975), *Harry O* ("Exercise in Fatality," 1975), *Saturday Night Live* (1975), *The Rockford Files* ("The Hammer of C Block," 1976), *The White Shadow* ("Bonus Baby," 1978).

Muhammad Ali and Annazette Chase in *The Greatest* (1977).

Chong, Rae Dawn Born February 28, 1961, in Edmonton, Alberta, Canada.

Rae Dawn Chong is the Afro Asian daughter of comic Tommy Chong and Maxine Sneed; her mother is African American and Amerindian (Cherokee), her comedian father is Scots-Irish and Chinese-Canadian. She is the half-sister of model and actress Robbi Chong and of Marcus, Paris, and Gilbran Chong. Rae Dawn Chong was one of the foremost black actresses of her era, with starring roles in a spate of major films. She was married to Owen Baylis in 1982; they had a son named Morgan and are divorced. In 1989 she married actor C. Thomas Howell and they divorced in 1990.

Chong became an actress at age 12, starring in the *Disneyland* episode "The Whiz Kid and the Mystery at Riverton." She was in the running to play Willis' girlfriend Charlene DuPrey on *Diff'rent Strokes* in 1978, but the producers cast Janet Jackson instead. Her major film roles include *Quest for Fire* (1983), for which Chong won the Genie Award for Best Performance by an Actress in a Leading Role. In *Choose Me* (1984), she gives one of her best performances as Pearl Antoine, a player in the L.A. singles bar scene. In *The Color Purple* (1985) her role as Squeak appears to have been cut, since she has little screen time and her role has little narrative function. In *Commando* (1985), she had very good chemistry with Arnold Schwarzenegger.

She was also in *Soul Man* (1986), where she met co-star and future husband C. Thomas Howell; *American Flyers* (1985), which combined bike racing and romance, with co-starred Kevin Costner; *Cheech & Chong's The Corsican Brothers* (1984), with her father Tommy; *Tales from the Darkside: The Movie* (1990), which was based on the popular TV show and was one of the first films to feature an interracial marriage where race was in no way integral to the plot; *The Principal* (1987), a solid look at high school life with James Belushi; and *Far Out Man* (1990), again with her father.

Chong lives in New England and has been concentrating on TV roles as of late, as well as producing, directing and writing. She wrote and starred in the crime drama *Boulevard* (1994), about a prostitute who witnesses a murder. She played Dr. Peggy Fowler for two years on the TV series *Mysterious Ways* (2000–02), starred in the Canadian series *Wild Card* (2003–04), and acted in the award-winning prison drama *The Visit* (2000), which received the National Board of Review Freedom of Expression Award.

Feature Films including Video and TV Movies: *Stony Island* (1978), *Top of the Hill* (TV; 1980), *Quest for Fire* (1981), *Beat Street* (1984), *Fear City* (1984), *Cheech & Chong's The Corsican Brothers* (1984), *Choose Me* (1984), *American Flyers* (1985), *City Limits* (1985), *Commando* (1985), *Badge of the Assassin* (TV; 1985), *The Color Purple* (1985), *Soul Man* (1986), *Running Out of Luck* (1987), *The Squeeze* (1987), *The Principal* (1987), *Walking After Midnight* (1988), *Rude Awakening* (1989), *Denial* (1990), *Chaindance* (1990), *Tales from the Darkside: The Movie* (1990), *Far Out Man* (1990), *Curiousity Kills* (TV; 1990), *Amazon* (1990), *Prison Stories: Women on the Inside* (TV; 1991), *The Borrower* (1991), *When the Party's Over* (1992), *Father & Son: Dangerous Relations* (TV; 1993), *Time Runner* (1993), *Amberwaves* (1994), *Boca* (1994), *Boulevard* (1994), *Power of Attorney* (1995), *Hideaway* (1995), *The Break* (1995), *Crying Freeman* (1995), *Starlight* (1996), *Mask of Death* (1996), *Small Time* (1996), *For Hope* (TV; 1996), *Alibi* (TV; 1997), *Goodbye America* (TV; 1997), *Highball* (1997), *Valentine's Day* (TV; 1998), *Cosas que olvide recordar* (1999), *Dangerous Attraction* (2000), *The Visit* (2000), *Deadly Skies* (TV; 2005), *Constellation* (2005), *Max Havoc: Ring of Fire* (2006), *When We Were Pirates* (2009).

Rae Dawn Chong.

TV: *Disneyland* ("The Whiz Kid and the Mystery at Riverton," Parts I and II), *Lou Grant* ("Lou," 1980), *St. Elsewhere* (4 episodes; "Monday, Tuesday, Sven's Day," "AIDS & Comfort," "A Pig Too Far," "Whistle, Wyler Works," 1983–85), *Tall Tales and Legends* ("Casey at the Bat," 1986), *The Hitchhiker* ("New Blood," 1991), *Nitecap* (series host; 1992), *Melrose Place* (3 episodes in the recurring role of Carrie Fellows; "Drawing the Line," "Bye, Bye Billy," "End Game," 1992–93), *Lonesome Dove: The Series* ("Firebrand," 1994), *Crazy Love* (1995), *The Outer Limits* ("The Second Soul," 1995), *Highlander* ("Timeless," 1996), *Poltergeist: The Legacy* ("Spirit Thief," 1997), *Mysterious Ways* (recurring role of Dr. Peggy Fowler; 2000–02), *I Love the '80s* (2001), *Judging Amy* ("A Pretty Good Day," 2002), *Alberta Film and Television Awards* (2003), *Wild Card* (recurring role of Sophie Mason; 2003–04), *Open Access* (2004), *Charity Jam* (series hostess; 2005), *That's So Raven* ("The Way They Were," 2007).

Video: *The Subject Is AIDS* (1986).

Shorts: *Mary Stigmata*

Christiani, Rita Born in Trinidad, date N/A.

Rita Christiani danced in avant-garde filmmaker Maya Deren's *Ritual in Transfigured Time* (1946). Deren, who had worked for choreographer Katherine Dunham, choreographed Christiani's movements in the film. Christiani was a dancer with the Katherine Dunham Company, and Deren met her when she toured with Dunham's group in the early 1940s. Footage of Christiani's dance from the film can also be seen in Martina Kudlacek's 2002 documentary *In the Mirror of Maya Deren.*

Christiani also danced in Henry King's *The Black Swan* (1942) with Tyrone Power and Maureen O'Hara, and in Val Lewton's evocative horror classic *I Walked with a Zombie* (1943), and well as in Bob Hope and Bing Crosby's *Road to Morocco* (1942) and musicals such as *Thank Your Lucky Stars* and *Happy Go Lucky* (both 1943).

Feature Films: *Tales of Manhattan* (1942), *Road to Morocco* (1942), *The Black Swan* (1943), *I Walked with a Zombie* (1943), *Thank Your Lucky Stars* (1943), *Happy Go Lucky* (1943), *Ritual in Transfigured Time* (1946), *Im spiegel der Maya Deren (In the Mirror of Maya Deren)* (archival; documentary; 2002).

Clark, Marlene Born in New York, New York, December 19, 1949.

Tall, elegant Marlene Clark was a fashion model before she turned to acting. She was the poster girl for sixties cult film director Robcrt Downcy's *Putney Swope* (1969); this is the famous poster (the original now sells for hundreds of dollars) where Clark appears in the place of an upraised middle finger. Clark is one of the most beautiful women ever to grace the screen. Her prominent cheekbones and gimlet eyes represent the epitome of transcendent exotica.

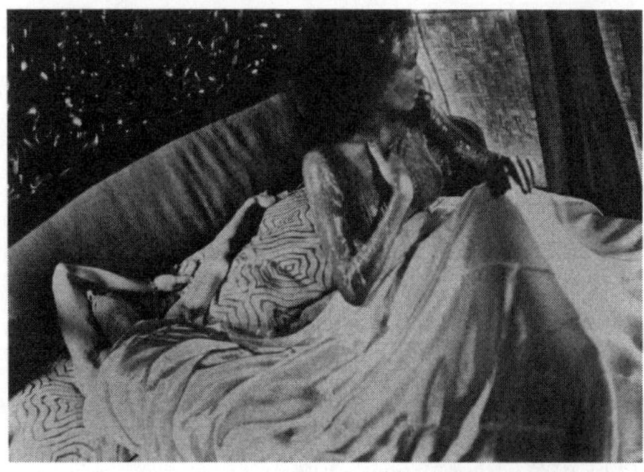

Marlene Clark in *Night of the Cobra Woman* (1972).

A native New Yorker, she made her acting debut on educational TV's *On Being Black* series (1969), and then appeared in a small role in Hal Ashby's *The Landlord* (1970). After her role opposite James Brown in *Slaughter* (1972) she appeared on the brink of a substantial career, especially given the "blaxploitation" film explosion at the time. However, a serious automobile accident called a temporary halt to her career, and it was her appearance in a series of cult horror films that gave her career its definition. The third phase of her career was more television oriented. Her cult horror films include *Night of the Cobra Woman* (1972), *Ganja and Hess* (1973), *The Beast Must Die!* (1974), *Black Mamba* (1974) and *Lord Shango* (1975),

Clark is probably best known for *Ganja and Hess.* Bill Gunn was an actor who, like so many before him, wanted to be a director. His *Ganja and Hess* turned out to resemble an art house rather than a "grindhouse" film. It was taken away from Gunn by the producers, and re-edited and retitled as *Blood Couple.* Clark's co-star, Duane Jones, was best known as the star of the original *Night of the Living Dead* (1968). *Ganja and Hess* is a fever dream of a movie. Dr. Hess Green is an archeologist who has been stabbed by his research assistant with an ancient ceremonial blade. Hess awakens with no wound but he does have an unquenchable desire for human blood. He meets (and then lives with) Ganja, the wife of his assistant. She is concerned about her husband's whereabouts, but soon becomes Hess' lover, as well as his partner in vampirism. *Ganga and Hess* is one of the great horror films of the seventies.

Clark was married to actor Billy Dee Williams. She brought dignity and presence to horror and non-horror roles alike.

Feature Films including TV Movies: *For Love of Ivy* (1968), *Midnight Cowboy* (uncredited; 1969), *Putney Swope* (uncredited; 1969), *Stop* (1970), *The Landlord* (1970), *Clay Pigeon* (1971), *Night of the Cobra Woman* (1972), *Beware! The Blob* (1972), *Slaughter* (1972), *Incident on a Dark Street* (TV; 1973), *Ganja and Hess* (1973), *Enter the Dragon* (1973), *Black Mamba* (1974), *The Beast Must Die!* (1974), *Newman's Law* (1974), *Lord Shango* (aka *The Color of Love*; 1975), *Switchblade*

Sisters (1975), *The Baron* (1977), *Bunco* (TV; 1977).

TV: *On Being Black* (1969), *The Bill Cosby Show* ("How You Play the Game," 1970), *The Governor and J.J.* ("Run, Ballerina, Run," 1970), *Marcus Welby, M.D.* ("Epidemic," 1970), *The Immortal* ("The Return," 1970), *Bonanza* (1971), *The Mod Squad* ("The Wild Weekend," "The Song of Willie," 1972–70), *McCloud* ("The Barefoot Stewardess Caper," 1972), *The Rookies* ("Deliver Me from Innocence," 1976), *Sanford and Son* ("When John Comes Marching Home," "Here Today, Gone Today," "Fred's Extra Cash," "I Dream of Choo Choo Rabinowitz," "The Engagement Man Always Rings Twice," 1976–77), *The Richard Pryor Show* (1977), *What's Happening!!* (1979), *Barnaby Jones* ("Run to Death," 1980), *Flamingo Road* ("The Explosion," 1982), *Highway to Heaven* ("The People Next Door," (1987), *Head of the Class* ("Parent's Day," 1988).

Cleveland, Odessa Born in Winnetka, California, March 3, 1944.

Odessa Cleveland played Lieutenant Ginger Bayliss, a recurring character in the TV series *M*A*S*H*, from 1972 to 1974, plus two more episodes in 1977. She also had a guest role in an episode of the *M*A*S*H* spin-off *Trapper John, MD*. She was the wife of the slave Jim, Huck's bosom companion, in the box office and critical disaster musical film version of *Huckleberry Finn* (1974).

In addition to her acting career, Cleveland is well regarded as an educator and a poet, with poems in both local and national magazines. She is a retired teacher certified by the National Board for Professional Teaching Standards. She has a bachelor of science degree in physical education and English and a master's degree in business management and education. She had has over 30 years of experience with the Los Angeles Unified School District, as well as 13 years as mentor teacher for the district. During the last two years of her career, she worked as a consulting teacher for the United Teachers of Los Angeles.

Feature Films including TV Movies: *Huckleberry Finn* (1974), *Something for Joey* (TV; 1977).

TV: *The Bold Ones: The New Doctors* ("Glass Cage," 1971), *Sanford and Son* ("The Over-Hill Gag," 1975), *M*A*S*H* (recurring role of Lt. Ginger Bayliss; 1972–74), *The Greatest American Hero* ("The Hand-Painted Thai," 1982), *Trapper John, M.D.* ("The Curmudgeon," 1986).

Cole, Natalie Born in Los Angeles, California, February 6, 1950.

Natalie Maria Cole has done her father's legacy proud. Like her father, she's had an acting career on the side. Like Nat King Cole, she will always be better known for her voice, but her acting credits are not insubstantial, and they include the 2000 TV movie *Livin' for Love: The Natalie Cole Story,* in which she starred in her own life story. But her best acting is not in *Livin' for Love,* but *Lily in Winter* (1994), her first feature-length acting job. *Lily in Winter* is the story of Lily Carrington, nanny to a little boy named Michael who accompanies her when she takes a trip home for Christmas. His mother thinks the boy has been kidnapped and the police are informed. Cole is warm and believable as a caring woman with a limited education who acts recklessly but with love. Cole also turns up, looking delightful, to sing a song in the period bio pic about Cole Porter, *De-Lovely* (2004).

Her best TV work as an actress may be the 2006 *Grey's Anatomy* episode in which she played a patient who was stabbed by her husband. Other effective guest star work can be seen on *I'll Fly Away*, *Touched by an Angel*, and *Law & Order: Special Victims Unit.*

Winner of eight Grammy Awards, Cole evolved from an early career as a rhythm and blues

Natalie Cole.

singer to the sophisticated jazz diva of today. As the daughter of a jazz legend, she has been in the spotlight all her life. She was raised in a wealthy Los Angeles neighborhood (her house was only a few doors away from the residence of the governor of California). President John F. Kennedy attended her debutante ball. Growing up in the exalted world of pop music, she began performing at age 11 and was featured on two segments of her dad's landmark TV series (1956–57). She was 15 years old when her father died of cancer, and it fell to her mother Maria to complete the job of raising her. She attended Northfield Mount Hermon School in Northfield, Massachusetts.

Cole has been married three times. Her son Robert, born in 1977, was the product of her marriage to Marvin Yancy. They divorced in 1980. Now a musician, Robert tours with his mother. Cole then married the former drummer of the group Rufus, Andre Fischer, who co-produced her most famous and most awarded album, *Unforgettable ... with Love*, the multi–Grammy Award winning Album of the Year, where old recordings of her dad's classic songs were interspersed with new tracks from his daughter, resulting in a series of hauntingly beautiful duets. This was a very troubled marriage, and they divorced in 1999. Her most recent husband was Kenneth H. Dupree; married in 2001 and divorced in 2004. Her sister, Carol Cole, is an actress; and her adopted brother, who was only six when Nat King Cole died, is named Nat Kelly Cole.

She was already a superstar for many years before *Unforgettable* was released. Her first album, *Inseparable* (1975), was a huge success, highlighted by the R&B classic "This Will Be (An Everlasting Love)," winner of the 1976 Grammy for Best R&B Vocal performance. However, her hit was "I've Got Love on My Mind" (1977). A succession of albums followed: *Natalie* (1976), *Unpredictable* (1977), *Thankful* (1977), *Natalie ... Live!* (1978), *I Love You So* (1979), *We're the Best of Friends* (with Peabo Bryson; 1979), *Don't Look Back* (1980), *Happy Love* (1981), and *I'm Ready* (1983).

Drug problems set her back for a period of time, but Cole came back with the album *Dangerous* (1985), and the even more successful *Everlasting* (1987). *Everlasting* sold two million copies in the U.S. alone and won her a Soul Train Award for R&B Single of the Year ("I Live for Your Love"). Other hits from the album were "Jump Start" and "Pink Cadillac." Albums from the jazz-pop era include *Good to Be Back* (1989), *Take a Look* (1993), *Holly & Ivy* (1994), *Stardust* (1996), *Snowfall on the Sahara* (1999), *Love Songs* (2001), *Ask a Woman Who Knows* (2002), *Anthology* (2003), and *Leavin'* (2006).

Now considered one of the U.S.'s most treasured jazz artists, Cole continues to tour and release albums, the latest being 2008's *Still Unforgettable*, which contains new duets with her dad. In 2000, Cole released her autobiography, *Angel on My Shoulder*, the story of her career triumphs, but also of her life-long battle with drugs. She was hospitalized in New York City in 2008 for complications of hepatitis C, which she acquired from her drug use.

Feature Films including Video and TV Movies: *Lily in Winter* (TV; 1994), *Abducted: A Father's Love* (TV; 1996), *Cats Don't Dance* (voice; 1997), *Always Outnumbered, Always Outgunned* (TV; 1998), *Freak City* (TV; 1999), *Livin' for Love: The Natalie Cole Story* (2000), *De-Lovely* (2004).

TV: *The Nat King Cole Show* (2 segments; 1956–57), *This Is Your Life* ("Nat King Cole," 1960), *Top of the Pops* (1975), *The Tonight Show Starring Johnny Carson* (3 segments; 1975–85), *The 19th Annual Grammy Awards* (1977), *The Captain and Tennille* (1977), *Sinatra and Friends* (1977), *Music My Way* (1977), *The 5th Annual American Music Awards* (1978), *The 20th Annual Grammy Awards* (1978), *The 21st Annual Grammy Awards* (1979), *The 22nd Annual Grammy Awards* (1980), *Uptown: A Tribute to the Apollo Theatre* (1980), *The Grammy Hall of Fame* (1981), *SCTV Network 90* (1981), *Solid Gold* (1984), *Yearbook: Class of 1967* (1985), *Soul Train* (1985), *1986 World Series*, *The 59th Annual Academy Awards* (1987), *The 4th Annual Black Gold Awards* (1987), *It's Showtime at the Apollo* (1987), *Motown Merry Christmas* (1987), *Marblehead Manor* ("An Aunt Hill for Hillary," 1987), *20th NAACP Image Awards* (1988), *The 15th Annual American Music Awards* (1988), *The 2nd Annual Soul Train Music Awards* (1988), *Irving Berlin's 100th Birthday Celebration* (1988), *Nelson Mandela 70th Birthday Tribute* (1988), *Cilla's Goodbye to the '80s* (1989), *Big Break* (series hostess; 1990), *The 11th Annual Black Achievement Awards* (1990), *The 32nd Annual Grammy Awards* (1990), *Nelson Mandela: An International Tribute to a Free South Africa* (1990), *Pero esto que es?* (1990), *Motown 30: What's Goin'*

On! (1990), *Wogan* (1991), *The 19th Annual American Music Awards* (1992), *Aspel & Company* (1992), *The 34th Annual Grammy Awards* (1992), *Danny Kaye International Children's Award for UNICEF* (1992), *Guest Night* (2 segments; 1992 and 1993), *The 7th Annual Soul Train Music Awards* (1993), *I'll Fly Away* ("State," 1993), *The 65th Annual Academy Awards* (1993), *Wrestlemania IX* (1993), *Late Show with David Letterman* (1993), *A Musical Christmas at Walt Disney World* (1993), *Super Bowl XXVIII* (1994), *Legends in Light: The Photography of George Harrell* (1995), *Sinatra: 80 Years My Way* (1995), *Touched by an Angel* ("Reunion," 1995), *The Wizard of Oz in Concert: Dreams Come True* (1995), *The Rosie O'-Donnell Show* (4 segments; 1996–2000), *The 39th Annual Grammy Awards* (1997), *Concert of Hope* (1997), *Tony Bennett Live by Request: An All-Star Tribute* (1998), *To Life! America Celebrates Israel's 50th* (1998), *Goodwill Games* (1998), *Pavarotti and Friends for the Children of Liberia* (1998), *Frank Sinatra: The Very Good Years* (archival; 1998), *Nat King Cole: Loved in Return* (archival; 1998), *Arista Records' 25th Anniversary Celebration* (1999), *Behind the Music* (1999), *Pixelon's iBash* (1999), *Intimate Portrait* (2 segments; "Natalie Cole," "Chaka Khan," 1999–2003), *BET Tonight with Tavis Smiley* (2000), *Wetten, dass...?* (2001), *32nd NAACP Image Awards* (2001), *Muhammad Ali's All-Star 60th Birthday Celebration* (2002), *The Oprah Winfrey Show* (2002), *The Royal Variety Performance 2002, The Nick at Nite Holiday Special* (2003), *Great Performances* (4 segments; "Unforgettable with Love: Natalie Cole Sings the Songs of Nat King Cole," "Natalie Cole: A Woman Who Knows," "30th Anniversary: A Celebration in Song," "We Love Ella! A Tribute to the First Lady of Song," 1992–2007), *Lightning in a Bottle* (2004), *Festival di San Remo* (2004), *Apollo at 70: A Hot Night in Harlem* (2004), *The 8th Annual Soul Train Christmas Starfest* (2005), *American Masters* ("The World of Nat King Cole," 2006), *Legends Ball* (2006), *The View* (2006), *Canada A.M.* (2006), *Ellen* (2006), *Gray's Anatomy* ("Band-Aid Covers the Bullet Hole," 2006), *20 to 1* (archival; "World's Best Love Songs," 2006), *Law & Order: Special Victims Unit* ("Fat," 2006), *The Megan Mullally Show* (2007), *An Evening of Stars: Tribute to Aretha Franklin* (2007), *Studio 60 on the Sunset Strip* (2007), *Ellen* (archival; 2007), *Canal+ en Hollywood* (2007), *22nd Annual Stellar Gospel Music Awards* (2007), *The Tonight Show with Jay Leno* (2007), *National Memorial Day Concert* (2007).

Video/DVD: *The Incomparable Nat King Cole, Vol. I* (1991), *The Incomparable Nat King Cole, Vol. II* (1992), *Can't Forget About You* (2007).

Cole, Olivia Born in Memphis, Tennessee, November 26, 1942.

Olivia Cole is known for her Emmy-winning turn as Mathilda (Outstanding Supporting Actress in a Television Movie), wife of Chicken George (Ben Vereen) and great grandmother of Alex Haley in the ABC miniseries *Roots* (1977). Cole studied acting at London's Royal Academy of Dramatic Arts. She is the daughter of Arvelia (née Cage) and William Cole. Cole married Richard Venture in 1970.

Her other miniseries leads have included Maggie Rogers, the head maid at the executive mansion in *Backstairs at the White House* (1979); and Miss Sophie, the insufferably snoopy neighbor in *The Women of Brewster Place* (1989) and its short-lived series spin-off in 1990. She was Deborah Mehran on the TV soap opera *Guiding Light* (1969–71).

Her Broadway credits include *The School for Scandal* (as Sip; her 1966 stage debut); *Right You Are If You Think You Are* (as an alternate for Dina and Signora Ponza; 1966); *We Comrades Three* (an alternate for Young Woman; 1966); *You Can't Take It with You* (as alternates for Gay Wellington and Reba; 1967); *War and Peace* (as Lisa; 1967), *The Merchant of Venice* (as Nerissa; 1973), and *The National Health* (as Nurse Lake; 1974).

Feature Films including Video and TV Movies: *Heroes* (1977), *Coming Home* (1978), *The Sky Is Gray* (TV; 1980), *Children of Divorce* (TV; 1980), *Fly Away Home* (TV; 1980), *Mistress of Paradise* (TV; 1981), *Some Kind of Hero* (1982), *Something About Amelia* (TV; 1984), *Go Tell It on the Mountain* (TV; 1985), *Big Shots* (1987), *Arly Hanks* (TV; 1993), *First Sunday* (2008).

TV: *The Guiding Light* (recurring role as Deborah Mehran; 1969–71), *Police Woman* ("Glitter with a Bullet," 1975), *Roots* (miniseries; 1977), *Szysznyk* (recurring role as Ms. Harrison; 1977), *Rafferty* ("Brothers & Sons," 1977), *The 29th Annual Primetime Emmy Awards* (1977), *Family* ("Fear of Shadows," 1978), *Backstairs at the White House* (miniseries; 1978), *The 30th Annual Primetime Emmy Awards* (1978), *The Television Annual 1978/'79, Report to Murphy* (recurring role as

Blanche; 1982), *North and South* (miniseries; 1985), *Murder She Wrote* ("Murder to a Jazz Beat," "Judge Not," "Big Easy Murder," 1985–95), *Wonderworks* ("The Fig Tree," 1987), *The Women of Brewster Place* (miniseries; 1989), *L.A. Law* (3 episodes; "America the Beautiful," "Noah's Bark," "Cold Shower," 1989–93), *Brewster Place* (ongoing series; recurring role as Miss Sophie; 1990), *Christy* ("Echoes," 1995), *Roots Remembered* (2007).

Coleman, Monique Born in Orangeburg, South Carolina, November 13, 1980.

Monique Coleman is one of the stars of the Disney Channel movie *High School Musical* (2006), *High School Musical 2* (2007), and the successful theatrical release *High School Musical 3: Senior Year* (2008). She plays Taylor McKessie, best friend of Gabriell Montez (Vanessa Hudgens). Coleman also played Mary-Margaret on *The Suite Life of Zack and Cody* (2005–06). Fans also know her as a competitor on the third season of *Dancing with the Stars* (2006). Coleman, who really got a chance to shine in the spotlight, was the last female to survive the competition.

She started her acting career at a young age in Columbia, South Carolina. Her training began at the Workshop Theater School of Dramatic Arts, where she performed in over 15 plays. She went to Heathwood Hall Episcopal School. Then she attended the Theater School at DePaul University in Chicago, earning her BFA in Acting in 2002. She now lives and works in Los Angeles.

Her first film was the independent feature *Mother of the River* (1995), which won awards at Chicago film festivals. Two years later, Coleman appeared as Young Donna in the Family Channel movie *The Ditchdigger's Daughters* (1997), for which she was nominated for the Young Artists Award of Hollywood. During her sophomore year in high school, she wrote, directed, produced and starred in a one-person play titled *Voices from Within*. In Chicago, she starred in productions of *Noises Off, Polaroid Stories, The Real Thing* and *The Colored Museum*.

In 2005, she played Leesha opposite James Earl Jones in the Hallmark TV movie *The Reading Room*. She was part of the *High School Musical: The Concert Tour* across the country; she also joined the nationwide *Dancing with the Stars* tour in 2007–08.

Feature Films including Video and TV Movies: *Mother of the River* (1995), *The Ditchdigger's Daughters* (TV; 1997), *High School Musical* (TV; 2006), *Online* (2006), *High School Musical 2* (TV; 2007) *High School Musical 3: Senior Year* (2008).

TV: *Strong Medicine* ("Misdiagnosis Murder," 2003), *Gilmore Girls* ("The Nanny and the Professor," 2004), *10–8: Officers on Duty* ("Love Don't Love Nobody," 2004), *Married to the Kellys* ("Chris and Mary Fight," 2004), *Malcolm in the Middle* ("Malcolm Visits College," 2004), *Veronica Mars* ("Lord of the Bling," 2005), *Boston Public* (3 episodes in the recurring role of Molly; 2003–05), *The Reading Room* (2005), *The Suite Life of Zack and Cody* (6 episodes in the recurring role of Mary-Margaret; 2005–06), *The Disney Channel Games* (2006–07), *Ellen* (2006), *Entertainment Tonight* (6 segments; 2006), *The View* (2006), *Dancing with the Stars* (semi-finalist; 2006), *2006 American Music Awards, Macy's Thanksgiving Day Parade* (2006), *Larry King Live* (2007), *What Perez Sez* (2007), *The View* (2008), *Million Dollar Password* (2008), *39th NAACP Image Awards* (2008), *Good Morning America* (2008).

Coles, Kim Born in Brooklyn, New York, January 11, 1966.

Kim Coles' brash but warm comic style has served her well throughout her career. She is most renowned for her roles in two series on the FOX network: *In Living Color*, the cutting-edge sketch comedy series (as a member of the original cast in 1990), and her long-running role as Synclaire James on *Living Single* (1993–98). She was also a regular panelist on the revival of *To Tell the Truth* (2000), and appeared in two episodes of *Frasier* (as Dr. Mary; 2000).

Coles attended Brooklyn Technical High School. She got her start as runner-up in the Big Beautiful Woman Pageant in Atlantic City, after which she became a plus-size model and started doing stand-up comedy in clubs. She was a warm-up comic for *The Cosby Show*. She was the opening act for such performers as The O'Jays, Bobby Brown and Luther Vandross. She was nominated for four NAACP Image Awards: 1996 through 1998 for Best Actress in a TV Program for *Living Single*, and Best Supporting Actress in a TV Program for *Frasier*.

She is the author of the book *I'm Free, but It Will Cost You: The Single Life According to Kim*

Coles (1997). She co-wrote (with Charles Randolph-Wright) and starred in the one-woman stage show *Homework* (1997). She is co-host of *In the Loop with iVillage*, a live interactive daytime program with cutting-edge topics for women. She married Aton Edwards in 1985; they divorced in 1995.

Feature Films including Video and TV Movies: *Strictly Business* (1991), *Kids in America* (2005), *Hell on Earth* (TV; 2007).

TV: *It's Showtime at the Apollo* (2 segments; 1989–91), *In Living Color* (cast regular; 1990), *Sinbad and Friends: All the Way Live ... Almost!* (1991), *Martin* ("Baby You Can Drive My Car," 1993), *Living Single* (recurring role of Synclaire James; 1993–98), *The Crew* (as Synclaire James; "The Worst Noel," 1995), *The Show* ("Deandra and Them," 1996), *MADtv* (1996), *The Rosie O'Donnell Show* (2 segments; 1997–99), *Comics Come Home 4* (1998), *New Attitudes* (host; 1999), *Hollywood Squares* (1999), *To Tell the Truth* (panelist; 2000), *Frasier* (2 episodes as Dr. Mary; "Something About Dr. Mary," "Mary Christmas," 2000), *The Gena Davis Show* (recurring role of Judy; 2000–01), *Headliners & Legends: Halle Berry* (2001), *Biography* ("Kim Fields," 2001), *Weakest Link* (2001), *Six Feet Under* ("The Liar and the Whore," 2002), *Pyramid* (3 segments; 2002–03), *One on One* (5 episodes in the role of Leilani; "Give 'm an Inch, They'll Throw a Rave," "Checkmate Daddy," "PTAmore," "We'll Take Manhattan," "Follow That Car," 2002–04), *The Parkers* ("That's What Friends are For," 2003), *Celebrity Mole: Hawaii* (2003), *Coming to the Stage* (2003), *Good Day Live* (2 segments; 2003 and 2004), *On-Air with Ryan Seacrest* (2004), *BET Comedy Awards* (2004), *Retrosexual: The '80s* (2004), *Steve Harvey's Big Time* (2004), *My Wife and Kids* ("Childcare Class," 2004), *Black in the '80s* (2005), *Celebrity Fit Club* (7 segments; 2005), *101 Even Bigger Celebrity Oops* (2005), *101 Craziest TV Moments* (2005), *Queer Edge* (5 segments as co-host; 2005), *Real Gay* (host; 2005), *The Tom Joyner Show* (2 segments; 2006), *Celebrity Poker Showdown* (2006), *Comics Unleashed* (2 segments; 2006), *The View* (2 segments as co-host; 2007), *Living Single: The Reunion Show* (2008), *The Chelsea Handler Show* (2008), *10 Items or Less* (recurring role as Mercy; 2009).

Conwell, Angell

Born in Orangeburg, South Carolina, August 2, 1983.

Angell Conwell's family moved to Columbia, South Carolina, when she was two. She modeled in South Carolina at age four, then modeled in Atlanta and New York. She moved to Los Angeles with her mother at age 10 and attended Oaks Elementary School in Columbia, where she became the first African American student body president. In 1994 she moved to Los Angeles to film the TV pilot *On Our Own* with Salt and Pepa. Her films include *Baby Boy* (as Kim, Omar Gooding's loyal but opinionated girlfriend; 2001) and *Soul Plane* (as Tamika, a soulful stewardess; 2004).

Feature Films including Video and TV Movies: *Flossin* (2001), *Baby Boy* (2001), *The Wash* (2001), *What About Your Friends: Weekend Getaway* (TV; 2002), *BraceFace Brandi* (2002), *Soul Plane* (2004), *Sugar Valentine* (2004), *Confessions* (aka *Confessions of a Call Girl*, 2006), *Half Past Dead 2* (2007), *Show Stoppers* (2008), *Portal* (2008), *Frankenhood* (2008), *Killing of Wendy* (2008), *Jury of Our Peers* (2008), *Whose Deal?* (2008).

TV: *On Our Own* (pilot; 1994), *Renegade* ("Repo Raines," 1995), *Dave's World* (2 episodes; "Lobster Envy," "Piano, No Strings," 1994 and 1995), *The Faculty* ("Where Is Carlos Garcia?" 1996), *Party Girl* ("Just Say No," 1996), *Sabrina, the Teenage Witch* ("You Bet Your Family," 1998), *NYPD Blue* ("Goodbye, Charlie," 2000), *3rd Rock from the Sun* ("The Big Giant Head Returns Again," Parts I and II, 2000), *City Guys* (5 episodes in the recurring role of Kianna; "Basket Case," "Why Y'all Clippin'?," "Prose and Cons," "Prom-Lems," "Goodbye Manny High," 2000–01), *The Parkers* (2 episodes; "Unforgiven," "It's Showtime," 2000 and 2002), *Moesha* ("Saving Private Rita," 2001), *Web Girl* (2001), *One on One* ("2 Young, 2 Curious," 2003), *My Wife and Kids* ("While Out," 2003), *That's So Raven* (2 episodes; "Dissin' Cousins," "Hearts and Minds," 2003 and 2004), *Cuts* ("Strictly Biz-Nass 2: Biz Nastier," 2006), *Bring that Year Back 2006.*

Video: *Rhythm City Vol. 1: Caught Up* (2005), *You're the One* (2005), *Unappreciated* (2006).

Cox, Deborah

Born in Toronto, Ontario, July 13, 1974.

Deborah Cox is a Canadian R&B singer and songwriter and actress. She began singing for TV commercials at age 12 and entered various talent shows with the help of her mother. She started performing in nightclubs as a teenager, and also started writing music at that time. A breakthrough occurred when she became a back-up singer for Celine Dion.

Her manager was pushing her demo, and this led to a contract with legendary producer Clive Davis in New York. She signed with Arista Records and released her self-titled debut album in 1995. Her second album was 1998's *One Wish*; Cox's hit song from the album, "Nobody's Supposed to Be Here," held the record for longest running number-one single on *Billboard*'s Hot R&B/Hip-Hop songs chart for eight years, until it was broken in 2006. Her third album, *The Morning After*, was released in 2002 on J Records. *Destination Moon*, her fourth studio album (a tribute to singer Dinah Washington) was released in 2007. Cox has achieved nine number-one hits on *Billboard*'s Hot Dance Club Play charts and has been honored with *Soul Train* Awards and Junos (the Canadian version of the Grammy), and was nominated for an *Essence* Award.

She made her Broadway debut in 2004 in the title role of the Elton John–Tim Rice musical *Aida*. Cox has also acted in a number of films and can be heard on various film soundtracks. In 2000, she played Niko Rosen, an attractive young singer who becomes involved with a comedian in *Love Come Down*. In 2005, she was Sharon, the wife of a boxer who finds it hard to leave the fight game behind in *Blood of a Champion* (2006). Her song "Love Come Down" was featured in *Dr. Dolittle 2* (2001). "Nobody Cares" can be heard on the soundtrack of *Hotel Rwanda* (2005), and another Cox song, "Definition of Love," is heard in *Akeelah and the Bee* (2006).

She has traveled to Mozambique and Uganda as a member of the World Vision Tour, helping to promote awareness of AIDS prevention and promoting emergency relief. Cox's parents are of Afro-Guyanese descent. She is married to music producer Lascelles Stephens. They have two children, Isaiah (born July 2003) and Sumayah (June 2006).

Feature Films including TV Movies: *Love Come Down* (2000), *Blood of a Champion* (2006), *A Good Man Is Hard to Find* (2008), *The Grasslands* (2008).

TV: *The 1998 Billboard Music Awards*, *Nash Bridges* ("Hit and Run," 2000), *Soul Food* ("Fly Away Home," 2001), *Michael Jackson: 30th Anniversary Celebration* (2001), *Tonya Lee Williams: Gospel Jubilee* (2004), *Soul Train* (2 segments; 1996–2003), *Black in the '80s* (2005), *Vanity Insanity* (2006), *Vanity Insanity 2* (2007).

Video: *MTV 20: Jams* (2001), *The World According to RZA* (2004).

DaCosta, Yaya Born in Harlem, New York, November, 15, 1982.

Camara Yaya DaCosta Johnson is an actress, model, and scholar. She speaks Portuguese, Spanish and French, and is of African American and Nigerian descent. Her mother teaches the Montessori educational method; her father is a professor of sociology. DaCosta graduated from Brown University, majoring in international relations and African studies. She was first runner-up on season 3 of *America's Next Top Model* (2003), behind Eva Pigford. After her strong showing, she signed to Ford Models and Models 1 London. She has modeled for top designers (such as Isaac Mizrahi) and numerous clients (Sephora, Radio Shack, Target, Olay). She has appeared in many magazines, including *Essence*, *Interview* and *Jewel*.

DaCosta began acting in 2005 with a small role on the series *Eve*. Then she was cast as Cassandra Foster, daughter of Angie Hubbard, on the soap *All My Children* (2008). Her films include director John Sayles' *Honeydripper* (2007), set in the South circa 1950. DaCosta plays China Doll, the naive but well-intentioned 17-year-old daughter of a "juke joint" owner who is desperately trying to save his club. Then she was nominated for a Teen Choice Award for Best Newcomer for *Take the Lead* (2006). She portrayed LaRhette, a problem teen who gains respect for herself thanks to a dance teacher, played by Antonio Banderas. DaCosta made her theatrical debut in 2008 in the revival *First Breeze of Summer* starring Leslie Uggams. Critics were impressed with her performance and the revival's run was extended. "The exquisite Yaya DaCosta makes a lovely New York debut," wrote Ben Brantley in *The New York Times*.

Feature Films including Video and TV Movies: *Take the Lead* (2006), *Honeydripper* (2007), *The Shanghai Hotel* (2008), *Racing for Time* (TV; 2008).

TV: *America's Next Top Model* (contestant; 2004), *Eve* ("Prom Night," 2005), *All My Children* (recurring role as Cassandra Foster; 2008).

Video/DVD and Music Videos: *Gold Dig-*

ger (2005), *Pullin' Me Back* (2006), *Beautiful Girls* (2007).

Dandridge, Dorothy Born in Cleveland, Ohio, November 9, 1922; died September 8, 1965, West Hollywood, California.

Dorothy Dandridge's career epitomizes the evolution of the black actress on screen, spanning the 1940s through the early 1960s. As the first black actress to be nominated for a Best Actress Oscar (*Carmen Jones*, 1954), she is the link between pioneer Fredi Washington and modern day Halle Berry, the first black actress to actually win the Best Actress Oscar (for *Monster's Ball*, 2001), and who played Dandridge in the TV movie *Introducing Dorothy Dandridge* (1999).

The adjective "tragic" is often conjoined with Dandridge's name, but as the years pass, her achievements grow more significant when contrasted to her weaknesses and failures (and the racism she had to fight). She was the first truly mainstream black star, and although this is rarely pointed out, she grew as an actress and gave some of her best performances after *Carmen Jones* (1954). She's poignant in *Island in the Sun* (1957), a story of interracial relationships that set a tasteful standard rarely equaled since. She's dynamic in *Tamango* (1958), showing a new acting maturity. She ably fulfilled the role of Bess in *Porgy and Bess* (1959), a strong point in an uneven film. She won a Best Actress Golden Globe Award for the role. Although looking physically wasted and prematurely aged, she was quite wonderful in the British crime thriller *Malaga* (her last completed film, 1960).

Dorothy Jean Dandridge was the first black woman to headline at major clubs such as the Las Vegas Flamingo and the Waldorf-Astoria in New York. Her mother, Ruby, was an ambitious small-time local performer who sought show business fame and fortune for both herself and her daughters. Ruby walked out on Dorothy's father, Cyrus,

Dorothy Dandridge and Jean Servais in *Tamango* (1958).

five months before Dorothy was born. She created an act for her young daughters, Vivian and Dorothy, and called them The Wonder Children. They toured the South for five years, supervised by Ruby Dandridge's lesbian partner Geneva Williams, who had moved in with the family. They moved to Nashville and the girls signed with the National Baptist Convention to go on tour of Southern churches.

When the Depression came, Ruby moved to Hollywood with the girls, who by this time were known as The Dandridge Sisters, and who were joined by friend Etta Jones, whom they had met at dancing school. Ruby found steady work playing domestics in films and on the radio, and eventually went on to a fairly significant career of her own. The Dandridge Sisters began appearing at major New York venues such as The Cotton Club and the Apollo Theater. This led to Dorothy's first screen appearance, a bit part in an *Our Gang* short (*Teacher's Beau*, 1935). In 1937 she appeared in *A Day at the Races* with the Marx Brothers, singing a solo in the lavish production number "All God's Chillin' Got Rhythm."

As Dorothy grew into womanhood, she enjoyed increasing success in nightclubs throughout the country, and gained her first taste of cinematic fame with a phenomenon called "soundies." Soundies were short films shown on juke boxes, a kind of early forerunner to music videos. Dandridge is seen to attractive effect in *Cow Cow Boogie* (as a miniskirted cowgirl), *Jungle Jig* (as a "native" pin-up girl), *Paper Doll* (with the Mills Brothers), and *Lazybones* (with Hoagy Carmichael).

Dorothy Dandridge in *Tarzan's Peril* (1951).

Her feature film roles were starting to get more interesting as well, especially her turn as the kidnapped African princess Melmendi in *Tarzan's Peril* (1951) with Lex Barker. *Bright Road* (1953) was a well-intentioned film in which Dandridge was a schoolteacher who became romantically involved with Harry Belafonte. It presented a positive, non-stereotyped image of African Americans rarely seen in the films of the era.

In 1954, director Otto Preminger announced that he would be filming an all-black, modernized version of *Carmen* that would be called *Carmen Jones*. He initially rejected Dandridge for the part, offering her instead the lesser role of "good girl" Cindy Lou. The story has it that Dandridge returned to Preminger dressed in a tight-fitting black blouse and red skirt, and it was then that he realized she was indeed right for the role. Her singing voice, needing a more operatic flair, was dubbed by Marilyn Horne. *Carmen Jones* did quite well at the box office, and suddenly for the first time an African American woman was a full-fledged movie star. Even though Grace Kelly won the Oscar for her performance in *The Country Girl*, Dandridge had made Oscar history, and was only the third African American to receive a nomination in any Oscar category (after Hattie McDaniel, winner for Best Supporting Actress for *Gone with the Wind*, and Ethel Waters, a Best Supporting nominee for *Pinky*). Although Preminger was married at the time, he entered into a troubled affair with Dandridge.

She was married to Harold Nicholas (1942–51) of the dancing Nicholas Brothers. The marriage produced her only child, Harolyn Suzanne Nicholas. Her second marriage was to unscrupulous restaurant owner Jack Denison (1959–62). Denison used Dandridge, physically abused her,

***Opposite, top:* Dorothy Dandridge and Harry Belafonte in *Carmen Jones* (1954). *Opposite, bottom:* Ruby Dandridge and George Murphy in *The Arnelo Affair* (1947).**

and ruined her financially. In the divorce settlement, he got half of everything she owned. Dandridge suffered a nervous breakdown. She declared bankruptcy and was forced to sell her home and to put her daughter in a state mental institution (Harolyn had developmental problems since birth).

Dandridge was found dead in 1965 by her manager, Earl Mills, in her West Hollywood apartment, apparently from an overdose of an antidepressant. The death was ruled accidental. Dandridge has a posthumous star on the Hollywood Walk of Fame. Her legacy will continue to be analyzed and evaluated for generations to come.

Feature Films: *The Big Broadcast of 1936* (1936), *Easy to Take* (1936), *A Day at the Races* (1937), *It Can't Last Forever* (1937), *Snow Gets in Your Eyes* (1938), *Going Places* (1938), *Irene* (1940), *Four Shall Die* (1940), *Lady from Louisiana* (1941), *Sun Valley Serenade* (1941), *Sundown* (1941), *Bahama Passage* (1941), *Ride 'Em Cowboy* (1942), *The Night Before the Divorce* (1942), *Night in New Orleans* (1942), *Drums of the Congo* (1942), *Lucky Jordan* (1942), *Happy Go Lucky* (1943), *Hit Parade of 1943* (1943), *Since You Went Away* (1944), *Atlantic City* (1944), *Pillow to Post* (1945), *Ebony Parade* (1947), *Tarzan's Peril* (1951), *The Harlem Globetrotters* (1951), *Bright Road* (1953), *Remains to Be Seen* (1953), *Carmen Jones* (1954), *Island in the Sun* (1957), *The Happy Road* (1957), *Tamango* (1958), *The Decks Ran Red* (1958), *Porgy and Bess* (1959), *Malaga* (aka *Moment of Danger*, 1960), *The Murder Men* (theatrical version of a *Cain's Hundred* TV episode, 1961), *Marco Polo* (unfinished).

TV: *The Colgate Comedy Hour* (2 segments; 1951–53), *The Ed Sullivan Show* (aka *Toast of the Town*; 7 segments; 1952–61), *Light's Diamond Jubilee* (1954), *The 27th Annual Academy Awards* (1955), *Ford Star Jubilee* ("You're the Top," 1956), *The 29th Annual Academy Awards* (1957), *Cain's Hundred* ("Blues for a Junkman," 1962), *Brown Sugar* (archival; 1986), *Small Steps, Big Strides: The Black Experience in Hollywood* (archival; 1998), *It's Black Entertainment* (archival; 2002), *Redeemer* (archival; 2002), *Great Performances* (archival; "The Great American Songbook," 2003), *Dorothy Dandridge: An American Beauty* (2003).

Shorts: *Teacher's Beau* (1935), *Easy Street* (1941), *Jungle Jig* (1941), *Congo Clambake* (1942), *Swing for My Supper* (1941), *Lazybones* (1941), *Yes, Indeed!* (1941), *Cow Cow Boogie* (1942), *Paper Doll* (1942), *A Zoot Suit (With a Reet Pleat)* (1942).

Video/DVD: *Dorothy Dandridge: Singing at Her Best* (archival; 2003), *Harlem Renaissance* (archival; 2004).

Dandridge, Ruby Born in Wichita, Kansas, March 1, 1899; died October 17, 1987, Los Angeles, California.

Born Ruby Jean Butler, Dandridge had a career in films, and on radio and TV. Her parents were Nellie Simon and George Butler. She had three brothers. Dandridge was of Jamaican (her father was born in Jamaica), Mexican and Native American ancestry. Her father was jack of all trades, at various times a minister, a school principal, a janitor, and an entertainer who inspired her to act.

On September 12, 1919, she married Cyrus Dandridge. She moved with her husband to Cleveland, Ohio, where her daughter Vivian was born. A second daughter, Dorothy, was born the following year, five months after Cyrus and Ruby, who had been having marital problems all along, were divorced. Dorothy Dandridge would go on to a major film career and become the first black actress to be nominated for a Best Actress Academy Award. After her divorce, Ruby Dandridge entered into a lesbian relationship with music teacher Geneva Williams, who lived with the family and abused and beat the two daughters.

Ruby Dandridge's career in show business was varied and ambitious. She played a prominent cast member of the *Amos 'n' Andy* radio show (in the roles of Sadie Blake and Harriet Crawford), and appeared in three episodes of the TV series; she was the voice of the sultry Coal Black in the notorious but beautifully animated Bob Clampett cartoon *Coal Black and de Sebben Dwarfs* (1943), and the voice of Grandmother in another Warner Bros. cartoon, *Goldilocks and the Jivin' Bears* (1944).

She had a 20-year career in feature films, ending memorably in 1959 with director Frank Capra's *A Hole in the Head*, as Sally. She also replaced Butterfly McQueen in the role of Oriole on *The Beulah Show* in 1952–53, at the same time Hattie McDaniel replaced Ethel Waters in the title role. Dandridge was apparently told to imitate Butterfly McQueen's voice and mannerisms; the result is annoying and downright bizarre. She was at Dorothy's funeral in 1965 and essentially dropped from sight after that. She died of a heart attack at age 88. She was buried next to Dorothy at Forest Lawn Memorial Park Cemetery in Glendale, California.

Feature Films: *Midnight Shadow* (1939), *Broken Strings* (1940), *The Night Before the Divorce* (1942), *Gallant Lady* (1942), *Tish* (1942), *A Night for Crime* (1943), *Corregidor* (1943), *Cabin in the Sky* (1943), *Melody Parade* (1943), *I Dood It* (1943), *Never a Dull Moment* (1943), *Hat Check Honey* (1944), *Ladies of Washington* (1944), *Carolina Blues* (1944), *Can't Help Singing* (1944), *The Clock* (1945), *Junior Miss* (1945), *Saratoga Trunk* (1945), *Inside Job* (1946), *Three Little Girls in Blue* (1946), *Home in Oklahoma* (1946), *Dead Reckoning* (1947), *The Arnelo Affair* (1947), *My Wild Irish Rose* (1947), *Silly Billy* (1948), *Tap Roots* (1948), *Father Is a Bachelor* (1950), *A Hole in the Head* (1959).

TV: *Amos 'n' Andy* (3 episodes; "Viva La France," "Kingfish's Secretary," "Kingfish Gets Amnesia," 1951), *The Beulah Show* (recurring role of Oriole; 1952–53), *Front Row Center* ("The Human Touch," 1956), *Checkmate* ("A Princess in the Tower," 1960).

Shorts: *Coal Black and de Sebben Dwarfs* (voice; 1942), *Goldilocks and the Jivin' Bears* (1944), *Screen Snapshots* (1945).

Dash, Stacey

Born in the Bronx, New York, January 20, 1966.

Green-eyed Stacey Lauretta Dash will always be known as Dionne Marie Davenport in both the film *Clueless* (1995) and the spin-off UPN series of the same name (1996–99). Dash was in her late twenties when she played 17-year-old Dionne in the original film, and continued to play the ultimate teenage "buppie" into her thirties. Dionne may have been clueless, but she and her friend Cher Horowitz (played by Alicia Silverstone in the original film and Rachel Blanchard in the series) were essentially warm-hearted characters, and they always managed to triumph over adversity—even if "adversity" consisted of figuring out the color of the nail polish du jour.

Dash is of African American and Aztec Native American descent. She was married to Brian Lovell from 1999 to 2006; they have a daughter named Lola. She also has a child with R&B singer Christopher Williams, a son named Austin born in 1991. She is the cousin of music mogul Damon Dash of Rockefella Records and the sister of Darien Dash, Internet maven and CEO of DME Interactive Holdings. She attended Ramapo High School in Spring Valley, New York, and graduated from Paramus High School in New Jersey.

Dash decided on an acting career at an early age. She made appearances as a child on *Sesame Street*, and as a young adult on *The Cosby Show*, *The Fresh Prince of Bel-Air*, and *St. Elsewhere*. She had a recurring role on *TV 101* (1988), which aired for 13 episodes. She was also a regular as Vanessa Weir on the short-lived *The Strip* (1999). More recent guest appearances include *Eve* and *CSI*.

She made her feature film debut at age 22 in the Richard Pryor comedy *Moving* (1988). Other prominent roles were in *Mo' Money* (as Amber Evans; 1992), *Renaissance Man* (as Private Miranda Myers; 1994), and *Illegal in Blue* (1995), an erotically-charged thriller with Dash as femme fatale Kari Truitt. It has deservedly become something of a campy cult classic. Other films include Oliver Stone's *Cold Around the Heart* (as Bec Rosenberg; 1997), *Personals* (aka *Hooked Up*; as Leah; 1999), the interracial love story *The Painting* (as Hallie Gilmore; 2001), and *Paper Soldiers,* directed by Damon Dash (as Tamika; 2002). She was prominently featured in *Gang of Roses* (2003), a Western featuring a rather contemporary-acting group of avenging black cowgirls, but she was killed off too early in the action. She appeared with Michelle Pfeiffer and re-teamed with *Clueless* director Amy Heckerling in *I Could Never Be Your Woman* (2007), a romantic fantasy with Dash in the role of Brianna.

Feature Films including Video and TV Movies: *Farrell for the People* (TV; 1982), *Enemy Territory* (1987), *Moving* (1988), *Black Water* (aka *Tennessee Nights*, 1989), *Mo' Money* (1992), *Renaissance Man* (1994), *Clueless* (1995), *Illegal in Blue* (1995), *Cold Around the Heart* (1997), *Personals* (aka *Hook'd Up*, 1999), *The Painting* (aka *Soldiers of Change*, 2001), *Paper Soldiers* (2002), *View from the Top* (2003), *Gang of Roses* (2003), *Ride or Die* (2003), *Grayson Arms* (aka *Lethal Eviction*, 2005), *Getting Played* (2005), *I Could Never Be Your Woman* (2007), *Nora's Hair Salon II* (2008), *Ghost Image* (2007), *American Primitive* (2007), *Secrets of a Hollywood Nurse* (TV; 2008), *Close Quarters* (2008), *Fashion Victim* (2008), *Phantom Punch* (2008), *The Finest* (2009).

TV: *The Cosby Show* ("Denise's Friend," 1985), *St. Elsewhere* (4 episodes in the role of Penny Franks; "Their Town," "The Naked Civil

Stacey Dash and Damon Wayans in *Mo' Money* (1992).

Surgeon," "Requiem for a Heavyweight," "Split Decision," 1988), *TV 101* (recurring role of Monique; 1988–89), *The Fresh Prince of Bel-Air* ("When You Hit Upon a Star," 1994), *Harts of the West* ("Drive, He Said," 1994), *Soul Train* (1995), *Clueless* (recurring role of Dionne "Dee" Davenport; 1996–99), *Penn & Teller's Sin City Spectacular* (1998), *The Strip* (recurring role of Vanessa Weir; 1999), *Going to California* ("A Pirate Looks at 15 to 20," 2001), *E! True Hollywood Story* ("Clueless," 2001), *Men, Women and Dogs* (pilot; 2001), *CSI: Crime Scene Investigation* ("Slaves of Las Vegas," 2001), *Eve* ("The Ex Factor," 2003), *Duck Dodgers in the 24 1/2th Century* (voice; 2005).

Video/DVD: *Kanye West: College Dropout, Video Anthology* ("All Falls Down" video; 2005), *Emotional* (2001), *All Fall Down* (2004), *Favorite Girl* (2006).

Shorts: *Christmas Break* (2008).

Davis, Dana Born in Davenport, Scott County, Iowa, 1984.

Dana Davis attended Davenport North High School and graduated with a music degree from Loyola Marymount University (she is a skilled violinist). She made her film debut opposite Hilary Duff in *Raise Your Voice* (as Denise Gilmore; 2004). She was also Ashanti's fellow student Peyton in *Coach Carter* (2005) and starred in the remake of the Jamie Lee Curtis horror film *Prom Night* (as Lisa Hines; 2008).

She is best known for recurring roles on two prominent sci-fi series: as Felicia Jones on ABC's *The Nine* and as superheroine Monica Dawson on NBC's *Heroes* (2007–2008). She played an "evolved" woman with adoptive muscle memory. She joined the popular multi-character series in its second season. She has guest starred on other series as well, starting with an appearance on *The Steve Harvey Show* in 2000, followed by *The O.C.*, *Veronica Mars*, *Gilmore Girls* and *Cold Case*. Davis was a singer with the group Necessity.

Feature Films including TV Movies: *Raise Your Voice* (2004), *Testing Bob* (TV; 2005), *Coach Carter* (2005), *Prom Night* (2008), *Relative Stranger* (TV; 2008).

TV: *The Steve Harvey Show* ("Player, Interrupted," 2000), *Boston Public* (2 episodes in the role of Marie Ronning; 2001), *One on One* ("Playing Possum," 2001), *Malcolm in the Middle* ("Poker #2," 2002), *Joan of Arcadia* ("Bringeth It On," 2003), *That's So Raven* ("Theater Queen," 2004), *Point Pleasant* (3 episodes in the role of Lucinda; pilot; "The Lonely Hunter," "Last Dance," 2005), *Cold Case* ("Strange Fruit," 2005), *Gilmore Girls* (2 episodes in the role of Althea; "Say Something," "The UnGraduate," 2005), *The O.C.* (2 episodes in the role of Madison; "The Disconnect," "The Safe Harbor," 2005 and 2006), *Veronica Mars* (2 episodes in the role of Cora Briggs; "Blast from the Past," "Ain't No Magic Mountain High Enough," 2005 and 2006), *CSI: Miami* ("Deviant," 2006), *The Nine* (recurring role of Felicia Jones; 2006–07), *Hidden Palms* (pilot; 2007), *Heroes* (recurring role of Monica Dawson; 2007–08), *Heroes Unmasked* (4 episodes; "New World Disorder," "From Heroes to Villains," "Travelling in Style," "The Casting Couch," 2008), *Pushing Daisies* ("Frescorts," 2008).

Shorts: *No Prom for Cindy* (2002).

Dana Davis.

Davis, Viola Born August 11, 1965, in Saint Matthews, South Carolina.

Viola Davis was nominated for an Academy Award for Best Supporting Actress for her role as Mrs. Miller, a woman whose son may have been molested by a priest, in the film version of John Patrick Shanley's play *Doubt* (2008). She was also nominated for a Golden Globe for Best Supporting Actress, and she won the Breakthrough Performance award from the National Board of Review.

She won the 2001 Tony Award for Best Featured Actress in a Play for August Wilson's *King Hedley II,* with Brian Stokes Mitchell and Leslie Uggams. She played a 35-year-old mother desperately wanting to abort a pregnancy. She also received a Drama Desk Award for her role and received a Drama Desk nomination in 1996 for another August Wilson play, *Seven Guitars*. She also won a 2005 Drama Desk Award and a Los Angeles Drama Critics Circle Award for the off–Broadway play *Intimate Apparel* (2004).

She is the daughter of Mary and Dan Davis. Her father was a horse groomer for the Narragansett and Lincoln Downs racetracks in Rhode Island. Davis grew up in abject poverty. Although she was born in South Carolina, her family moved to Central Falls, Rhode Island, a virtually all-white community where Davis experienced racism. Acting and writing scripts and skits was a way of escaping from this depressing environment. She attended Rhode Island College and majored in theater, graduating in 1968. In 2002 she received an honorary doctor of fine arts degree from the college. She also attended the Juilliard School for four years. Her husband is Julius Tennon; they married in 2003 and have two children.

She has had roles in a number of films, including three for director Steven Soderbergh: *Out of Sight,* as Moselle (1998); *Traffic,* as a social worker (2000); and *Solaris,* as Gordon (2002). Her television work includes a recurring role as Donna Emmett on *Law & Order: Special Victims Unit* (2003–08), and a starring role as Agent Jan Marlowe in the short-lived series *Traveler* (2007). She was also Lynette Peeler in *City of Angels* (2000).

Feature Films including Video and TV Movies: *The Substance of Fire* (1996), *The Pentagon Wars* (TV; 1998), *Out of Sight* (1998), *Grace*

& Glorie (TV; 1998), *Traffic* (2000), *Amy & Isabelle* (TV; 2001), *The Shrink Is In* (2001), *Kate & Leopold* (2001), *Father Lefty* (TV; 2002), *Far from Heaven* (2002), *Antwone Fisher* (2002), *Solaris* (2002), *Stone Cold* (TV; 2005), *Get Rich or Die Tryin'* (2005), *Syriana* (2005), *Jesse Stone: Night Passage* (TV; 2005), *The Architect* (2006), *Jesse Stone: Death in Paradise* (TV; 2006), *World Trade Center* (2006), *Life Is Not a Fairytale: The Fantasia Barrino Story* (TV; 2006), *Ft. Pitt* (TV; 2007), *Disturbia* (2007), *Jesse Stone: Sea Change* (TV; 2007), *The Andromeda Strain* (TV; 2008), *Nights in Rodanthe* (2008), *Doubt* (2008).

TV: *NYPD Blue* ("Moby Greg," 1996), *New York Undercover* ("Smack Is Back," 1996), *Judging Amy* ("Blast from the Past," 2000), *City of Angels* (recurring role as Nurse Lynnette Peeler; 2000), *Providence* ("You Can Count on Me," 2001), *The Guardian* ("The Men from the Boys," 2001), *The 55th Annual Tony Awards* (2001), *Third Watch* ("Act Brave," 2001), *Law & Order: Criminal Intent* ("Badge," 2002), *HBO First Look* ("Inside Solaris," 2002), *Hack* ("Third Strike," 2003), *The Practice* ("We the People," 2003), *Law & Order: Special Victims Unit* (recurring role of Donna Emmett; "Mercy," "Grief," "Birthright," "Doubt," "Cage," 2003–08), *Century City* (recurring role of Hannah Crane; 2004), *The 100 Most Unexpected TV Moments* (2005), *Black Theater Today: 2005*, *Threshold* ("Shock," 2005), *Without a Trace* ("White Balance," 2006), *Traveler* (recurring role of Agent Jan Marlow; 2007), *Brothers and Sisters* ("Double Negative," 2008).

Dawn, Marpessa Born January 3, 1934, in Pittsburgh, Pennsylvania; died August 25, 2008, Paris, France.

Marpessa Dawn's fame rests on a single film, but that film is the Academy Awarding Best Foreign Language Film *Orfeu Negro* (*Black Orpheus*, 1959), a landmark production for a number of reasons. *Black Orpheus* is a film of color, music, and emotion. Director Marcel Camus' palette is one of the most striking uses of color ever seen in a motion picture; the music — composed by Antonio Carlos Jobim — introduced the bossa nova sound to American audiences, and the soundtrack recording was a best seller, featuring numerous songs that went on to become standards and a title theme that haunts audiences to this day. The emotion comes from the story of the doomed lovers of Greek tragedy, Orpheus and Eurydice, here seen as contemporary figures amid the carnival in Rio. In this incarnation, Orpheus is a streetcar conductor and Eurydice a simple country girl from the *favela* (shanty town). Death stalks Eurydice in the form of a man in a skeleton costume — ostensibly, he is simply another carnival reveler.

Dawn brings a fresh beauty and a wonderful innocence to the role, but she would never have the chance to enjoy such a showcase again. This pristine beauty of the Brazilian Carnival was in reality a native of Pittsburgh, Pennsylvania. She moved to England while in her teens and worked as a governess until Marcel Camus tapped her for *Black Orpheus*. Later in life she married a rich businessman and attended New York's Hunter College.

Black Orpheus won the Palme d'Or at the Cannes Film Festival and the Best Foreign Film Oscar in 1959. Critics have pointed out that the film presents a romanticized, unrealistic view of ghetto life in Brazil (which is true); and that, as a French production, it presents an outsider's perspective on Brazilian culture (equally true).

Dawn has about a minute of screen time in the 1958 B-horror film *Womaneater*, released just prior to *Black Orpheus*. She appeared in the play *Chérie Noire* by F. Campoux (1964), which was seen in a televised version in 1966. Most of her later acting career was on French TV and theater productions.

Feature Films including TV Movies: *Elisa* (1957), *Womaneater* (1958), *Orfeu Negro* (*Black Orpheus*; 1959), *El secreto de los hombres azules* (1961), *Le bal du comte d'Orgel* (1970), *Boubou cravate* (1972), *Bel ordure* (1973), *Sweet Movie* (1974), *Les grands ducs* (TV; 1982), *Sept en attente* (1995).

TV: *Discorama* (1961), *Canzoni nel mondo* (1963), *Skaal* (1963), *Au theatre ce soir* ("Chrie Noire," 1966), *Salle no. 8* (1967), *Thibaud* (1968), *Vinicius* (archival; 2005).

Dawson, Rosario Born in New York, New York, May 9, 1979.

A unique, evocative mixture of Puerto Rican, Cuban, African American, Native American and Irish descent, Rosario Dawson has compiled an impressive list of feature film credits for major directors, and in recent years has gotten involved in film production.

Dawson's mother is a professional vocalist, and her father worked in construction. They are now divorced. She has a younger brother named

Clay. She grew up on Manhattan's Lower East Side and was discovered by screenwriters Larry Clark and Harmony Korine while sitting on her stoop. She was asked if she wanted to be in a movie, and the result was *Kids* (1995), featuring Dawson as Ruby, a promiscuous teen whose best friend (Chloe Sevigny) contracts aids. Dawson attended an alternate school in downtown Manhattan and dreamed of becoming a marine biologist. This gave way to an acting career. She became an alumna of the Lee Strasberg Institute.

Dawson has worked in feature films as steadily as any contemporary actress you can name and has wisely varied her projects between mainstream, big budget Hollywood films and edgier, sometimes more challenging independent productions. She was in Spike Lee's *He Got Game* (1998) and *25th Hour* (2002), in which she was excellent in a major role as Naturelle, a precocious schoolgirl who becomes romantically involved with the Ed Norton character, who is on the verge of starting a seven-year jail term. She was Stephanie Williams in *Light It Up* (1999), the story of six New York City high school students who find themselves in an armed standoff with the police. Her big budget misfire was *Josie and the Pussycats* (2001), based on the Archie Comics' all-girl band characters. Dawson played Valerie (the one with the Afro in the original comics). This could have been huge fun, but it fell curiously flat, and Dawson was miscast.

In Oliver Stone's *Alexander* (2004) she was again miscast, this time even more egregiously. She played Roxane, the reluctant bride of Alexander the Great. At least Dawson looked sensational, as she also did in *Rent* (2005), where she was perfectly cast in a faithful film version of the long-running Broadway show. She gave a nice interpretation of Mimi, the exotic dancer with the soul of a poet. She was also part of the ensemble cast in *Sin City* (2005), the gorgeous looking but dramatically overwrought adaptation of Frank Miller's Dark Horse comic book series.

In 2007, Dawson produced and starred in a low-budget film about revenge for a rape called *Descent*. Her revenge leaves the victim feeling curiously empty and the title reflects the fact that she has descended to the level of her rapist. That same year she was in another female revenge film, Quentin Tarantino's *Death Proof*, which was issued as a stand-alone feature on DVD and was originally seen as the second half of the film *Grindhouse* (2007), paired with *Planet Terror*. *Death Proof* worked quite well as a stand-alone feature, and Dawson and Traci Thoms had fun with their funky roles (Thoms also had a cameo in *Descent*). Dawson was nominated for NAACP Image Awards for her work in *Light It Up* and *Rent*.

In August-September 2005, she added theatre to her list of creative achievements, appearing as Julia in the Public Theater revival of Galt McDermott's *Two Gentlemen of Verona* at Central Park's Delacorte Theater.

Feature Films including TV Movies: *Kids* (1995), *Girls Night Out* (1997), *He Got Game* (1998), *Side Streets* (1998), *Light It Up* (1999), *Down to You* (2000), *King of the Jungle* (2000), *Josie and the Pussycats* (2001), *Trigger Happy* (2001), *Chelsea Walls* (2001), *Love in the Time of Money* (2002), *Ash Wednesday* (2002), *The First $20 Million Is Always the Hardest* (2002), *Men in Black II* (2002), *The Adventures of Pluto Nash* (2002), *25th Hour* (2002), *This Girl's Life* (2003), *Shattered Glass* (2003), *The Rundown* (2003), *Alexander* (2004), *This Revolution* (2005), *Sin City* (2005), *Little Black Dress* (2005), *Rent* (2005), *Clerks II* (2005), *A Guide to Recognizing Your Saints* (2006), *Spit* (narrator; 2006), *Grindhouse* (2007), *Descent* (2007), *Death Proof* (feature-length version of the *Grindhouse* segment; 2007), *Killshot* (2008), *Poor Things* (2008), *Eagle Eye* (2008), *The Haunted World of El Superbeasto* (voice; 2008), *Sin City 2* (2009), *Explicit Ills* (2009), *O.C.T.: Occult Crimes Taskforce* (2010).

TV: *The 1999 Source Hip-Hop Music Awards, MTV New Year's Eve 2001, Anatomy of a Scene* ("Sidewalks of New York," 2001), *Backstage Pass* (2001), *The Rosie O'Donnell Show* (2001), *The Tonight Show with Jay Leno* (5 segments; 2001–06), *AFI's 100 Years ... 100 Passions* (2002), *The Late Late Show with Craig Kilborn* (2002), *World VDAY* (2003), *Punk'd* (2003), *Late Night with Conan O'Brien* (2003–07), *The 2004 IFP/West Independent Spirit Awards, E! True Hollywood Story* (archival; "Tara Reid," 2004), *Celebrity Poker Showdown* (2 segments; 2004), *HBO First Look* ("The Making of *Alexander*: Fortune Favors the Bold," 2004), *The Tony Danza Show* (2 segments; 2004–05), *Live with Regis and Kathie Lee* (6 segments; 2004–06), *11th Annual Screen Actors Guild Awards* (2005), *Starz on the Set* ("Sin City," 2005), *Sin City: The Premiere* (2005), *God Sleeps in Rwanda* (voice; 2005), *2005 Taurus World Stunt*

Awards, *The Black Movie Awards* (2005), *The Daily Show* (2005), *Total Request Live* (2005), *Today* (2 segments; 2005), *Ellen* (2005), *The View* (2005), *The 11th Annual Critics Choice Awards* (2006), *Starz on the Set* ("Rent," 2006), *Corazon de...* (2006), *Clerks II: Unauthorized* (2006), *The Film Programme* (2006), *Scream Awards 2006*, *Film Independent's 2007 Spirit Awards*, *Penelope*, *Camino a los Oscar* (archival; 2007), *Jimmy Kimmel Live!* (2 segments; 2007–08), *Sunday Morning Shootout* ("Kevin Costner," 2007), *Robot Chicken* ("More Blood, More Chocolate," 2007), *Aperture* (host; 2008), *Larry King Live* (2008), *Gemini Division* (recurring role as Anna Diaz; 2008), *Women & Power* (documentary; 2009).

Video/DVD: *1999* (remix with Dawson voiceover; 1999), *Out of Control* (1999), *The Train Wreck* (2006).

Shorts: *Girls' Night Out* (1997).

Dee, Ruby

Born in Cleveland, Ohio, October 27, 1924.

While Ruby Dee has had a long and distinguished life in film and theater, any career overview is incomplete without mention of her husband and collaborator, the late Ossie Davis. They were married for 56 years (he passed away on February 4, 2005 at age 87, still very much active at the time). They had three children: blues musician Guy Davis, and daughters Nora Day and Hasna Muhammad.

Dee has been a great civil rights activist, as an individual and with her husband. They wrote an autobiography (*With Ossie and Ruby: In This Life Together*, 1998) in which they discussed their political activism, along with marriage and relationship issues. They were awarded the American National Medal of the Arts in 1995 from the National Endowment of the Arts in Washington, D.C., and were the recipients of Kennedy Center Honors in 2004. They were jointly presented the Academy of Television Arts and Sciences Silver Circle Award in 1994. In 2000, they were given the Screen Actors Guild Life Achievement Award. They are inductees into the Theater Hall of Fame, as well as the NAACP Hall of Fame. In addition, Dee has been inducted into both the Black Filmmakers Hall of Fame (1975) and the Theater Hall of Fame (1988).

Dee was born Ruby Ann Wallace. Her father, Marshall Edward Wallace, was a porter and a waiter on the Pennsylvania Railroad; her biological mother abandoned the family and ran off with another man; her stepmother, Emma Wallace, was a schoolteacher. The family moved to Harlem when Ruby was a baby. Dee attended Hunter College but was asked to leave when her activities with the American Negro Theater (where she met Ossie Davis) took up too much of her time and energy. But she stayed the course and did receive a bachelor's degree from Hunter in 1945. Then she worked briefly as a translator for an import company. Her first husband was Frank Dee; they were briefly married and divorced in 1945.

By this time, Dee had already made her Broadway debut, a walk-on as a native in *South Pacific* (1943). In 1946, she appeared in *Jeb* with Ossie Davis. Her breakthrough role was in the national tour of *Anna Lucasta*, also with Ossie Davis (1946–47). They fell in love on the tour and were married in 1948. Other early Broadway appearances include *A Long Way from Home* (1948) and *The Smile of the World* (1949).

Dee's career in the theater is highlighted by her role as Ruth Younger in Lorraine Hansberry's *A Raisin in the Sun*, often deemed the landmark black play (1959; with the film version, also with Dee, in 1961). *Raisin* is about a Southside Chicago family's struggle for survival. Conflicts arise when the mother receives a check for $10,000 from her husband's life insurance, and the family considers moving to a larger house in a white suburb. *Raisin* depicts contemporary civil rights in microcosm, but it doesn't let us forget that these are real people — individuals — with personal issues.

Other theatrical highlights in the Dee canon include *Purlie Victorious* (1961), written and directed by Ossie Davis, and Athol Fugard's *Boesman and Lena* (1970) with James Earl Jones, for which she won the Obie Award. As Kate in *The Taming of the Shrew* (1965) and Cordelia in *King Lear*, she became the first black woman to play major roles at the American Shakespeare Festival. She won a Drama Desk Award for her role as a woman in an interracial marriage in Alice Childress' play *Wedding Band* (1972), presented by the New York Shakespeare Public Theater, which she reprised for TV; and an Ace Award for her performance in Eugene O'Neill's *Long Day's Journey Into Night* (presented as a 1983 TV production). She also appeared in *Checkmates* (1988), with Denzel Washington and Paul Winfield; *Two Hah Hahs and a Homeboy* (1995), with her husband and son; and

Lobby card for *Take a Giant Step* (1959) with Ruby Dee and Johnny Nash.

St. Lucy's Eyes (2001), as an old woman about to perform an illegal abortion on a 17-year-old girl.

Of special note is the play Dee wrote called *Zora Is My Name!* (seen as a PBS-TV presentation in 1989; released on DVD in 2007), portraying groundbreaking black novelist and folklorist Zora Neale Hurston. She was Amanda Winfield in the *The Glass Menagerie* in Washington, D.C. (1989). She wrote the play *Two-Bit Gardens* (1979), which was later revised and presented as *Take It from the Top*— this was also her stage directing debut.

During the 1950s Ruby Dee appeared in such socially conscious films as *The Jackie Robinson Story* (1950), *Go, Man, Go!* (1954), *Edge of the City* (1957), and the underrated and little seen *Take a Giant Step* (1959). Her 1960s big screen appearances showed no let-up in social commitment or in her desire to choose interesting, challenging roles. *Gone Are the Days* (*Purlie Victorious*; 1963) was a wry satirical look at black social politics. *The Incident* (1967) details the reactions of various subway car passengers to a sociopathic fellow rider. The film version of Jean Genet's *The Balcony* (1963) features what may be Ruby Dee's greatest screen performance. Although her screen time is limited, her role as a prostitute "acting out" for her clients in a courtroom scene manages to be both erotic and heartbreaking. The film, with its "we are all prostitutes" message, provides a key opportunity to see how great an actress Dee is.

She made her screenwriting debut as co-author of *Uptight!* (1968), a remake of John Ford's *The Informer* (1935) from a contemporary African American perspective. It was buried in the plethora of blaxploitation films released that year and did not do well. She has been nominated for eight Emmy Awards, winning twice. She earned her first Emmy nomination for a guest appearance on *East Side/West Side* (1963), the landmark (if short-lived) social drama starring George C.

Scott. Another Emmy went to her performance in the *Hallmark Hall of Fame* production *Decoration Day* (1990). She shared a Grammy Award for Best Spoken Word Album (*With Ossie and Ruby: In This Life Together*) in 2007 with husband Ossie Davis (who was awarded posthumously).

She won a Literary Guild Award in recognition of her plays, poems and children's stories. Her popular book *My One Good Nerve: Rhythms, Rhymes, Reasons* (1986) became a successful one-woman show (as *My One Good Nerve: A Visit with Ruby Dee*). Even radio has been a part of her all-encompassing career. *The Ossie Davis and Ruby Dee Story Hour* ran in nationwide syndication from 1974 to 1978. Dee has survived breast cancer for 30 years and continues to be an active artist, spokeswoman, and role model. She established the Ruby Dee Scholarship in Dramatic Art for talented young black women.

Feature Films including Video and TV Movies: *That Man of Mine* (1947), *What a Guy* (1948), *The Fight Never Ends* (1949), *The Jackie Robinson Story* (1950), *No Way Out* (uncredited; 1950), *The Tall Target* (1951), *The Jackie Robinson Story* (1950), *Go, Man, Go!* (1954), *The Great American Pastime* (uncredited; 1956), *Edge of the City* (1957), *Virgin Island* (1958), *St. Louis Blues* (1958), *Take a Giant Step* (1959), *A Raisin in the Sun* (1961), *The Balcony* (1963), *Gone Are the Days!* (1963), *The Incident* (1967), *Uptight!* (also co-producer and screenplay; 1968), *Deadlock* (TV; 1969), *King: A Filmed Record ... Montgomery to Memphis* (narrator; 1970), *The Sheriff* (TV; 1971), *Buck and the Preacher* (1972), *Black Girl* (1972), *Wattstax* (1973), *Chelsea D.H.O.* (TV; 1973), *It's Good to Be Alive* (TV; 1974), *Cool Red* (1976), *I Know Why the Caged Bird Sings* (TV; 1979), *The Torture of Mothers* (1980), *All God's Children* (TV; 1980), *Cat People* (1982), *Go Tell It on the Mountain* (TV; 1985), *Lincoln* (TV; 1988), *Do the Right Thing* (1989), *Love at Large* (1990), *The Court Martial of Jackie Robinson* (TV; 1990), *Decoration Day* (TV; 1990), *Jungle Fever* (1991), *Jazztime Tale* (1992), *The Ernest Green Story* (TV; 1993), *Cop and a Half* (1993), *Whitewash* (TV; 1994), *Homeward Bound* (TV; 1994), *Tuesday Morning Ride* (1995), *Just Cause* (1995), *Mr. and Mrs. Loving* (TV; 1996), *Captive Heart: The James Mink Story* (TV; 1996), *A Simple Wish* (1997), *The Wall* (TV; 1998), *Passing Glory* (TV; 1999), *Baby Geniuses* (1999), *Having Our Say* (TV; 1999), *A Storm in Summer* (TV; 2000), *Finding Buck McHenry* (TV; 2000), *Freedom Never Dies: The Legacy of Harry T. Moore* (TV; 2001), *The Feast of All Saints* (TV; 2001), *Taking Back Our Town* (TV; 2001), *Baby of the Family* (2002), *Dream Street* (2005), *Their Eyes were Watching God* (TV; 2005), *Number Two* (2006), *The Way Back Home* (2006), *Clarksdale* (2007), *Steamroom* (2007), *Flying Over Purgatory* (2007), *American Gangster* (2007), *Seven Pounds* (2008), *Red and Blue Marbles* (2009), *The Perfect Age of Rock 'n' Roll* (2009).

TV: *Play of the Week* ("Black Monday," "Seven Times Monday," 1960–61), *Frontiers of Faith* ("The Bitter Cup," 1961), *The DuPont Show of the Week* ("The Beauty of a Woman," 1962), *Alcoa Premiere* ("Impact of an Execution," 1963), *The Nurses* ("Express Stop from Lenox Avenue," 1963), *The Fugitive* ("Decision in the Ring," 1963), *The Great Adventure* ("Go Down, Moses," 1963), *East Side/West Side* ("No Hiding Place," 1963), *The Defenders* ("The Sworn Twelve," 1965), *Armchair Theatre* ("Neighbors," 1966), *The Guiding Light* (recurring role, replacing Cicely Tyson; 1967), *The Merv Griffin Show* (1968), *Peyton Place* (various episodes; 1968–69), *To Be Young, Gifted and Black* (1972), *The CBS Festival of Lively Arts for Young People* (1972), *Tenafly* ("The Window That Wasn't," 1973), *Wedding Band* (1974), *Police*

Ruby Dee in *Gone Are the Days!* (*Purlie Victorious*) (1963).

Woman ("Target Black," 1975), *Lorraine Hansberry: The Black Experience in the Creation of Drama* (1975), *America at the Movies* (1976), *Roots: The Next Generations* (miniseries; 1979), *Ossie and Ruby!* (co-host; 1980–81), *American Playhouse* ("Zora Is My Name!" 1981), *Great Performances* (1982), *Long Day's Journey into Night* (1982), *The Atlanta Child Murders* (miniseries; 1985), *Spenser: For Hire* ("Personal Demons," 1987), *Windmills of the Gods* (miniseries; 1988), *Making Do the Right Thing* (1989), *22nd NAACP Image Awards* (1990), *China Beach* ("Skylark," 1990), *The Golden Girls* ("Wham, Bam, Thank You, Mammy," 1990), *Color Adjustment* (narrator; 1992), *Reading Rainbow* (2 episodes, 1984 and 1992), *Middle Ages* (1992), *Evening Shade* ("They Can't Take That Away from Me," 1993), *The Stand* (miniseries; 1994), *American Masters* (narrator; 1995), *Stories from the Edge* (1996), *Sports on the Silver Screen* (1997), *A Time to Dance: The Life and Work of Norma Canner* (narrator; 1998), *Porgy and Bess: An American Voice* (narrator; 1998), *Small Steps, Big Strides: The Black Experience in Hollywood* (1998), *The Directors* (1998), *Promised Land* ("Baptism of Fire," 1998), *The Unfinished Journey* (narrator; 1999), *Little Bill* (voice of Alice the Great; 1999), *Cosby* ("Ol' Betsy," 1999), *Touched by an Angel* ("The Christmas Gift," 1999), *Intimate Portrait: Rosa Parks* (2001), *7th Annual Screen Actors Guild Awards* (2001), *Christianity: The First 2000 Years* (2001), *Inside TV Land: African Americans in Television* (2002), *Hughes' Dream Harlem* (2002), *Unchained Memories: Readings from the Slave Narratives* (2003), *2003 Trumpet Awards, Beah: A Black Woman Speaks* (2003), *Russell Simmons Presents Def Poetry* (2004), *The Kennedy Center Honors: A Celebration of the Performing Arts* (2004), *The History Makers* (2005), *Character Studies* (2005), *The Black Movie Awards* (2005–06), *An Evening of Stars: Tribute to Stevie Wonder* (2006), *Legends Ball* (2006).

Devine, Loretta Born August 21, 1949, in Houston, Texas.

Loretta Devine graduated from the University of Houston in 1971 with a bachelor of arts in speech and drama and from Brandeis University in 1976 with a master of fine arts in theater. On television she is perhaps best known for her role of teacher Marla Hendricks on the FOX drama *Boston Public* (2000–05), for which she won three NAACP Image Awards. Devine appeared in the first season of *A Different World* (1987–88) as Stevie Raillen, dormitory director of the fictional Hillman College. She also has had a recurring role as Adele Webber on ABC's *Grey's Anatomy* (2005–07) and played Patti on the legal drama *Eli Stone* (2007–08).

She appeared in the off–Broadway production *A Broadway Musical* (1978), but it closed after one performance. *Dreamgirls* did considerably better than that. Devine originated the role of Lorell Robinson in *Dreamgirls*. Loosely based on the saga of The Supremes (denials aside), *Dreamgirls* premiered on December 20, 1981, and ran for over 1,500 performances, going on to win six Tony Awards, including Best Musical. Devine had a small but highly visible role as a jazz singer in the film version. Other theater work includes the revival of *Hair* (Member of the Tribe; October–November 1977); the musical *Comin' Uptown* (as Young Mary; December 1979–January 1980); the dance musical *Big Deal* (as Lilly; April–June 1986); and the West Coast revival of *Purlie* (as Missy Johnson; 2005).

Her most prominent film role was in *Waiting to Exhale* (1995). She won the NAACP Image Award for Best Supporting Actress, and won the Image Award again for *The Preacher's Wife* the following year. Devine earned Image Award and Independent Spirit Award nominations for her work in *Woman Thou Art Loosed* (2004). She also appeared in the Academy Award winning Best Picture ensemble drama *Crash* (2005).

Feature Films including Video and TV Movies: *Will* (1981), *Anna to the Infinite Power* (1983), *The Murder of Mary Phagan* (TV; 1988), *Little Nikita* (1988), *Sticky Fingers* (1988), *Parent Trap III* (TV; 1989), *Heart and Soul* (TV; 1989), *Stanley & Iris* (1990), *Livin' Large!* (1991), *Class Act* (1992), *Caged Fear* (1992), *Amos & Andrew* (1993), *The American Clock* (TV; 1993), *The Hard Truth* (1994), *Waiting to Exhale* (1995), *Rebound: The Legend of Earl "The Goat" Manigault* (TV; 1996), *The Preacher's Wife* (1996), *The Price of Kissing* (1997), *Hoodlum* (1997), *Clover* (TV; 1997), *Lover Girl* (1997), *Don King: Only in America* (TV; 1997), *Alyson's Closet* (voice; 1998), *Love Kills* (1998), *Down in the Delta* (1998), *Urban Legend* (1998), *Lillie* (1999), *Operation Splitsville* (1999), *Funny Valentines* (TV; 1999), *The Breaks* (1999), *Jackie's Back!* (TV; 1999), *Introducing Dorothy Dandridge* (1999), *Punks* (2000), *Freedom Song* (TV; 2000), *Best Actress* (TV; 2000), *Urban Leg-*

Left to right: Loretta Devine, Whitney Houston, Angela Bassett and Lela Rochon in *Waiting to Exhale* (1995).

ends: Final Cut (2000), *What Women Want* (2000), *Kingdom Come* (2001), *I Am Sam* (2001), *Baby of the Family* (2002), *The Script* (2002), *Book of Love* (2002), *Woman Thou Art Loosed* (2004), *Crash* (2004), *King's Ransom* (2005), *Life Is Not a Fairytale: The Fantasia Barrino Story* (TV; 2006), *Dirty Laundry* (2006), *Dreamgirls* (2006), *Cougar Club* (2007), *This Christmas* (2007), *First Sunday* (2008), *Touched* (2008).

TV: *The 39th Annual Tony Awards* (1985), *CBS Summer Playhouse* ("Sirens," 1987), *A Different World* (recurring role of Stevie Rallen; 1987–88), *The 42nd Annual Tony Awards* (1988), *Amen* ("Court of Love," 1988), *Sugar and Spice* (recurring role as Loretta Fontaine; 1990), *Murphy Brown* ("The Bitch's Back," 1990), *Cop Rock* ("Marital Blitz," 1990), *Great Performances* ("The Colored Museum," 1991), *Reasonable Doubts* (2 episodes in the role of Valerie Hall; 1991), *Roc* (2 episodes in the role of Cynthia; "Roc Throws Joey Out," "You Don't Send Me No Flowers," 1992 and 1993), *Happily Ever After: Fairy Tales for Every Child* (1995), *Picket Fences* ("Close Encounters," 1995), *Ned and Stacey* ("Reality Check," 1995), *Touched By an Angel* (2 episodes in the role of Tonya Hawkins; "Amazing Grace," Parts I and II, 1997), *Moesha* ("It Takes Two," 1999), *Clueless* ("Graduation," 1999), *The PJs* (recurring role of Muriel Stubbs; 1999–2000), *Family Law* ("Playing God," 2000), *Ally McBeal* ("I Will Survive," 2000), *Boston Public* (recurring role of Marla Hendricks; 2000–05), *Intimate Portrait* ("Lela Rochon," 2001), *Iron Chef USA: Showdown in Las Vegas* (2001), *33rd NAACP Image Awards* (2002), *Headliners & Legends: Denzel Washington* (2002), *34th NAACP Image Awards* (2003), *Pyramid* (2003), *Half & Half* (2 episodes in the role of Erika; "The Big Phat Mouth Episode," Parts I and II, 2003), *Zoe Busiek: Wild Card* (recurring role of M. Pearl McGuire; 2004–05), *The Late Late Show with Craig Ferguson* (2005), *The 20th IFP Independent Spirit Awards* (2005), *Supernatural* ("Home," 2005), *Girlfriends* (2 episodes in the role of Judge Vashti Jackson; "Trial and Errors," "Party Over Here," 2005 and 2006), *Grey's Anatomy* (recurring role of Adele Webber; 2005–07), *HBO First Look* ("The Making of *Dreamgirls*," 2006), *Boston Legal* ("The Nutcrackers," 2006), *Everybody Hates Chris* (2 episodes in the role of Maxine; "Everybody Hates Funerals," "Everybody Hates Math," 2006 and 2007), *Film Independent's 2007 Spirit Awards*, *Eli Stone* (recurring role of Patti; 2007), *Broadway: Beyond the Golden Age* (2008).

Dillard, Victoria

Born September 20, 1969, in New York City, New York.

Victoria Dillard is best known for her co-starring role as Janelle Cooper on the ABC sitcom *Spin City*. She stayed with the show for three seasons before leaving in 2000. As the right-hand woman to the mayor's aide-de-camp, Janelle kept Michael J. Fox's Mike Flaherty on top of his game. Later she got a promotion and became the Mayor's assistant.

Dillard began performing at age five with the Dance Theater of Harlem. She worked with the company until she was 18, appearing in productions such as *Porgy and Bess* at the Metropolitan Opera. Then she went on national tour with Mickey Rooney in the revival of *A Funny Thing Happened on the Way to the Forum*. When the play's run ended in California, she was cast in an episode of *Star Trek: The Next Generation* (1987), which earned her a Screen Actors Guild union card.

Features include her film debut *Coming to America* (1988), and the critically lauded TV movie *The Ditchdigger's Daughters* (1997), in which she portrayed Tass. She was in the espionage thriller *Deep Cover* in 1992 (a former longtime girlfriend of Laurence Fishburne, she first met Fishburne on this set). She was Denzel Washington's wife in *Ricochet* (1991) and Betty Shabazz, the wife of Muhammad Ali, in *Ali* (2001). She was Monica Collins in *Out-of-Sync* (1995), mixing drug pushers, cops and club DJs in a story of the underworld. Dillard still dances in her free time and writes screenplays and theatrical plays.

Feature Films including Video and TV Movies: *Coming to America* (1988), *Internal Affairs* (1990), *Ricochet* (1991), *Deep Cover* (1992), *Killing Obsession* (1994), *The Glass Shield* (aka *The Jenny Johnson Trial*; 1994), *Statistically Speaking* (1995), *Out-of-Sync* (1995), *The Ditchdigger's Daughters* (TV; 1997), *The Best Man* (1999), *Commitments* (TV; 2001), *Ali* (2001).

TV: *Star Trek: The Next Generation* ("Where No One Has Gone Before," 1987), *Seinfeld* ("The Old Man," 1993), *Tribeca* ("The Box," 1993), *L.A. Law* ("Silence Is Golden," 1994), *Roc* ("You Shouldn't Have to Lie," 1994), *Chicago Hope* (2 episodes; "Over the Rainbow," "With the Greatest of Ease," 1994), *Martin* ("Three Homies and a Baby," 1995), *Moesha* ("The List," 1996), *Spin City* (recurring role of Janelle Cooper; 1996–2000), *Family Law* ("Angel's Flight," 2004), *Law & Order* ("C.O.D.," "Self Made," 2004–07).

Dobson, Tamara

Born May 14, 1944, in Baltimore, Maryland; died October 2, 2006, in Baltimore, Maryland.

Tamara "Cleopatra Jones" Dobson was, for a brief, shining moment, an action heroine to challenge Pam Grier. Her two films in the popular action series, *Cleopatra Jones* (1973) and *Cleopatra Jones and the Casino of Gold* (1975), were both fun films, but quite different in tone. The first film was typical blaxploitation, with all the elements of the genre intact; the second film was lighter and more playful — sort of like a tribute to the Saturday matinee serials of the 1940s. Plus, as an Asian co-production, it had more of a kung fu ambience. At 6' 2", with a huge Afro and impeccable taste in clothes (she had Pam beat at least in that regard) Cleopatra Jones was a force to be reckoned with, although Dobson came across better as an iconic figure than she did as an actual actress. Still, the first film in particular caused quite a stir.

Tamara Dobson in *Cleopatra Jones and the Casino of Gold* (1975).

Above: **Mexican lobby card for *Cleopatra Jones.* *Left:* Tamara Dobson as *Cleopatra Jones* (1973).**

Dobson had a degree in fashion illustration from the Maryland Institute College of Art (Cleopatra Jones was very much a fashion illustration come to life). She later became a fashion model who appeared in *Vogue*, *Essence*, *Redbook*, *Ebony* and *Mademoiselle* magazines. She lived much of her adult life in the fashion mecca, New York City. She did print and TV ads for major corporate clients such as Fabergé (Tigress perfume).

She was so typecast as Cleopatra Jones that she appeared in only a handful of other films, most notably *Norman ... Is That You?* (1976) and *Chained Heat* (1983), a women-in-prison melodrama in which she looked considerably older than she had in her Cleopatra days. Dobson made scattered TV appearances, most memorably in the sci-fi series *Jason of Star Command* (a recurring role in 1980–81) and *Buck Rogers in the 25th Century* (1980, as a villainess).

Her premature death was the result of complications from pneumonia and multiple sclerosis, according to her brother, Peter. She is also survived by a sister, Darilyn, who modeled as well. Dobson passed away at Baltimore's Keswick Multi-Care Center, where she had been living for two years. She had been diagnosed with multiple sclerosis in 2000. The Beyoncé Knowles character Foxxy Cleopatra in the spoof *Austin Powers in Goldmember* (2002) was affectionately based on Cleopatra Jones.

Feature Films including TV Movies: *Come Back, Charleston Blue* (1972), *Fuzz* (1972), *Cleopatra Jones* (1973), *Cleopatra Jones and the Casino of Gold* (1975), *Norman ... Is That You?* (1976), *Murder at the World Series* (TV; 1977), *Chained Heat* (1983), *Amazons* (TV; 1984).

TV: *The Tonight Show Starring Johnny Carson* (1973), *The 49th Annual Academy Awards* (1977), *The Mike Douglas Show* (1977), *Jason of Star Command* (recurring role as Samantha; 1979), *Buck Rogers in the 25th Century* ("Happy Birthday, Buck," 1980), *Baadasssss Cinema* (archival; 2002).

Douglass, Suzzanne Born April 12, 1957, in Chicago, Illinois.

Suzzanne Douglass is the daughter of Lois Mae and Donald Douglas, Sr., growing up with three other siblings in a low-income housing project. Her mother always took her to museums and to the theater. When she saw Julie Andrews in *The Sound of Music* (1965), she knew that she wanted to be an actress. She met resistance in her inner-city neighborhood when she started appearing in "white" productions such as *The Nutcracker*, but she knew acting was going to see her through. Her husband is Dr. Roy Jonathon Cobb, a neurological radiologist; they were married in 1989 and have two children, Jordan and Victoria.

She was executive producer of the short film *The Last Weekend* (1998) and appeared in the film as well. She appeared in pilots for *The Knife and Gun Club* (as Ginny Ducette; 1990) and *George* (as Maggie Foster; 1993). She had an ongoing role on *The Parent 'Hood* as solid, supportive wife and mother Jerri Peterson. Robert Townsend was the male lead.

Theater credits include the original off–Broadway production of *Little Shop of Horrors* (understudy, 1982–84; as Chiffon; 1985–86); *The Tap Dance Kid* (understudy; 1983–85); various productions with the Denver Center Theater Company, 1986–87; *Into the Woods* (understudy; 1987–89); *Playboy of the West Indies* (Yale Repertory Theater, New Haven, Connecticut, 1988); *I Ought to Be in Pictures* (as Steffi; New Brunswick, New Jersey, 1991); and *The Threepenny Opera* (Jenny Diver; November–December 1989). She also appeared in *A—My Name Is Alice*, *Sophisticated Ladies*, and in a one-woman show as Harriet Tubman. She appeared at the Paper Mill Playhouse in Milburn, New Jersey, as the fairy godmother in a production of *Cinderella* (2005).

Feature Films including Video and TV Movies: *Tap* (1989), *The Knife and Gun Club* (TV; 1990), *Chain of Desire* (1992), *Condition: Critical* (TV; 1992), *I'll Do Anything* (1994), *The Inkwell* (1994), *Search for Grace* (TV; 1994), *Jason's Lyric* (1994), *Alyson's Closet* (1998), *The Last Weekend* (1998), *How Stella Got Her Groove Back* (1998), *Student Affairs* (TV; 1999), *Sounder* (TV; 2003), *The School of Rock* (2003).

TV: *A Man Called Hawk* ("Vendetta," 1989), *The Cosby Show* ("Live and Learn," 1990), *Against the Law* (recurring role as Yvette Carruthers; 1990), *I'll Fly Away* ("The Kindness of Strangers," 1992), *Story of a People* (miniseries; 1993), *American Playhouse* ("Hallelujah," 1993), *NYPD Blue* ("Where's 'Swaldo?" 1996), *The Promised Land* (4 episodes in the role of Dr. Rebecca Dixon; "Stealing Home," Parts I and II, "A Hand Up Is Not a Hand Out," Parts I and II, 1997–98), *The Parent 'Hood* (recurring role of Jerri Peterson; 1995–99), *Touched by an Angel* ("The Christmas Gift," 1999), *The Parkers* (2 episodes; "It's a Family Affair," "Unforgiven," 1999 and 2000), *Law & Order: Special Victims Unit* ("Secrets," 2001), *It's Black Entertainment* (2002), *Law & Order: Criminal Intent* ("Mad Hops," 2004).

Shorts: *The Last Weekend* (1998).

Du Bois, Ja'Net (aka Du Bois, Jeannette) Born in Philadelphia, Pennsylvania, August 5, 1945.

Jeannette Dubois, better known as Ja'Net Du Bois (Ja-*Nay* Doo-*Bwah*), co-wrote and sang the classic "Movin' on Up" theme of *The Jeffersons*, and further became a part of sitcom history as the nosey, extroverted neighbor Willona on *Good Times*. Du Bois was performing in *Hot L Baltimore* at the Mark Taper Forum in Los Angeles when she captured the attention of Norman Lear, creator of *Good Times*, which aired on CBS from 1973 to 1979. Her role on *Love of Life* as Loretta

Allen (1970–72) was the first time a black female was a regular on a daytime soap. She won a CableACE Award for work in the TV movie *Other Women's Children,* billed as Jeannette Du Bois (1993), based on the Perri Klass novel. She also received two Emmys for her voice work as Mrs. Avery on the animated *The PJs* (1999–2008). She later played the grandmother on *The Wayans Bros.* (1996–98) and guest starred on numerous popular shows, including *A Different World, Home Improvement, Moesha, Martin, Clueless* and *Everybody Loves Raymond.*

Feature films include *A Piece of the Action* (1977), *I'm Gonna Git You Sucka* (1988), and *Charlie's Angel's: Full Throttle* (2003). In the late 1960s she acted in the original Broadway production of Golden Boy with Sammy Davis, Jr. She also appeared in national tours of *A Raisin in the Sun* and *Nobody Loves an Albatross.* Du Bois' love of children caused her to get involved in acting workshops and community projects for the young. She released a CD of songs called *Hidden Treasures* in 2008.

Feature Films including Video and TV Movies: *A Man Called Adam* (1966), *J.T.* (TV; 1969), *Five on the Black Hand Side* (1973), *A Piece of the Action* (1977), *Hellinger's Law* (TV; 1981), *The Sophisticated Gents* (TV; 1981), *Stranded* (TV; 1986), *Kids Like These* (TV; 1987), *I'm Gonna Git You Sucka* (1988), *Penny Ante* (1990), *Heart Condition* (1990), *Hammer, Slammer & Slade* (TV; 1990), *Harlen & Merleen* (TV; 1993), *Other Women's Children* (TV; 1993), *Magic Island* (1995), *Sophie and the Moonhanger* (TV; 1996), *Don't Look Back* (TV; 1996), *Best Friends for Life* (TV; 1998), *Hard Time: Hostage Hotel* (TV; 1999), *Waterproof* (1999), *Charlie's Angel's: Full Throttle* (2003).

Ja'Net Du Bois and Telly Savalas in *Kojak.*

TV: *Love of Life* (recurring role as Loretta Allen; 1970–72), *Sanford and Son* ("Sanford and Son and Sister Makes Three," 1972), *Shaft* ("The Killing," 1973), *The Blue Knight* (1973), *Kojak* ("Loser Takes All," 1974), *Good Times* (recurring role of Willona Woods; 1974–79), *Caribe* ("Flowers of Death," 1975), *Roots: The Next Generations* (miniseries; 1979), *The Love Boat* (1980), *The Facts of Life* ("Brian and Sylvia," 1981), *Good Evening, Captain* (1981), *Crazy Like a Fox* ("Some Day My Prints Will Come," 1985), *Houston Knights* ("Bad Paper," 1988), *Nearly Departed* ("Grant Meets Grandpa," 1989), *Doctor Doctor* ("Ch-Ch-Ch-Changes," 1990), *A Different World* ("Love, Hillman-Style," 1991), *True Colors* ("Favorite Son," 1991), *Dream On* ("Toby or Not Toby," 1991), *Home Improvement* (2 episodes; "Reach Out and Teach Someone," "Her Cheatin' Mind," 1991 and 1995), *Beverly Hills 90210* ("Baby Makes Five," 1992), *The Golden Palace* (2 episodes in the role of Louise Wilson; "Marriage on the Rocks with a Twist," "A New Leash on Life," 1992 and 1993), *Sister, Sister* ("Wedding Bells and Box Boys," 1994), *Hangin' with Mr. Cooper* ("Hangin' with Mrs. Cooper," 1994), *Martin* ("All the Players Came," 1995), *ER* ("A Miracle Happens Here," 1995), *The Wayans Bros.* (recurring role of Grandma; 1996–98), *Moesha* ("Mentor," 1997), *Touched by an Angel* ("Smokescreen," 1997), *Clueless* ("A Test of Character," 1999), *The PJs* (recurring role of Mrs. Avery; 1999–2008), *The Steve Harvey Show* ("Going, Going, Gone," 2000), *E! True Hollywood Story* ("Good Times," 2000), *Everybody Loves Raymond* ("Bully on the Bus," 2000), *As Told by Ginger* (2 episodes in the role of Mrs. Patterson; "Hello Stranger," "Never Can Say Goodbye," 2000 and 2002), *Boomtown* ("Fearless," 2003), *TV Land Awards: A Celebration of Classic TV* (2003), *One on One* ("Meet the Parents," 2003), *BET Comedy Awards* (2004), *The 4th Annual TV Land Awards: A Celebration of Classic TV* (2006), *Crossing Jordan* ("Someone to Watch Over Me," 2006), *TV Land Confidential* (2007), *Random! Cartoons* (voice; "SamSquatch," 2007).

Dunham, Katherine Born in Joliet, Illinois, June 22, 1909; died New York, New York, May 21, 2006.

Dunham was an icon of the dance world,

and for over 30 years she headed and choreographed for the Katherine Dunham Dance Company. At its inception it was the only self-subsidized American black dance troupe. Her father was a black man who owned a dry cleaning business; her mother was of mixed racial parentage. Dunham gave her first public performance at age 15, a charity event for Brown's Methodist Church in Joliet. She moved to Chicago after graduating from Joliet Junior College and eventually began studying in the 1930s at the University of Chicago; her brother Albert also studied there. She studied dance and anthropology, which became the two great passions of her life.

She did graduate work in 1935–36 studying ethnographic dance forms in the Caribbean, and received a bachelor of arts in social anthropology in 1936. She received a grant from the Rockefeller Foundation that led her to abandon her graduate studies and concentrate on dance. Another turning point came in 1939 when she married costume and set designer John Thomas Pratt; they were artistic collaborators throughout their 47-year marriage. They adopted a daughter, Marie-Christine Dunham Pratt.

Katherine Dunham in *Tropical Revue* (1943).

Dunham's professional career began with the dance composition *Negro Rhapsody* at the Beaux Arts Ball in Chicago by the group Ballets Negres, for which Dunham was the choreographer and chief dancer. Dunham advanced to Broadway, where she did the choreography with George Balanchine and played the temptress Georgia Brown in *Cabin in the Sky* (1940), which went on to a 20-week run; Dunham then went with the show to the West Coast. By this time she was also performing in major nightclubs. One of her biggest Broadway triumphs was in 1943's *Tropical Review* at the Martin Beck Theater. It ran for 156 performances, and then toured the U.S. and Canada. In 1945, her Broadway hits were *Carib Song* and *Windy City*, followed by *Bal Negre* in 1946. In 1947, she was one of the first entertainers to appear in what was then a brand new venue called Las Vegas.

The stunning dancer was able to surmount the racial barriers that kept blacks out of mainstream Hollywood productions. Her dancing was featured in *Star Spangled Rhythm* (1941), *Pardon My Sarong* (1942) and, most significantly, in the landmark production *Stormy Weather* (1943), also featuring Lena Horne (who went on to portray Georgia Brown in the screen version of *Stormy Weather*). A later dance appearance is in *Casbah* (1949), also featuring one of her young students, Eartha Kitt. In 1947, she began a 20-year period touring the world: Mexico, Europe, South America, Australia and the Far East. Her *Caribbean Rhapsody* opened at the Prince of Wales Theatre in London. She appeared at the Theatre des Champes Elyses in Paris, and had a Josephine Baker–like impact on the populace.

In 1945 she opened the Katherine Dunham School of Dance and Theater in midtown Manhattan. In 1947 it became the Katherine Dunham School of Cultural Arts. The last Broadway appearance of the Dunham Dance Company was in 1962 in *Bamboche!* In 1963, Dunham became the first African American to choreograph for New York's Metropolitan Opera. She retired the company in 1967 after presenting a farewell show at Harlem's Apollo Theater. However, she continued to choreograph and she directed a revival of Scott Joplin's *Treemonisha* in 1972.

Dunham remained active throughout her later years as an artist-in-residence, teacher, anthropologist, lecturer and writer. She also indulged a lifelong fascination with Haiti by spending an extended period of time there, and was a collector of Haitian artifacts.

Dunham had a defining influence on African American dance. A lifetime of awards included the Albert Schweitzer Music Award (1979), the Kennedy Center Award for the Performing Arts (1983), and the National Medal of Arts (1989).

Feature Films including TV Movies: *Star Spangled Rhythm* (1942), *Stormy Weather* (1943), *Casbah* (1948), *Botta e risposta* (1950), *Die groe starparade* (1954), *Mambo* (1954), *Musica en la noche* (1958), *Im spiegel der Maya Deren* (archival; 2002).

TV: *Toast of the Town* (1950), *The Kennedy Center Honors: A Celebration of the Performing Arts* (1983), *The 9th Annual American Black Achievement Awards* (1988), *The Kennedy Center Honors: Celebration of the Performing Arts* (1988), *Free to Dance* (2001), *Legends Ball* (2006).

Shorts: *Carnival of Rhythm* (1941), *Cuban Episode* (1944).

Echikunwoke, Megalyn Born in Spokane, Washington, May 28, 1983.

Megalyn Echikunwoke was discovered at age 14 while performing in a summer camp play at an arts academy. At age 15, she was cast as in the TV movie *Peter Benchley's Creature* (1988). She starred as Cherish Pardee, a coffee house singer, in the MTV soap opera *Spyder Games* (2001). Echikunwoke is best known for playing the small role of rape victim Nicole Palmer, daughter of the president, in the first season of *24* (2001–02) and Isabelle Tyler in *The 4400* at the beginning of season three (2006–07). The show was cancelled not long after Echikunwoke left it. Another notable character was Danika, the daughter on *Like Family* (2003–04). On *That '70s Show*, she had a recurring role as Angie Barnett, the love interest of Ashton Kutcher's character (2004–05), and she was Claudia Gibson, the district attorney's daughter on the Lifetime series *For the People* (2002).

She has guest starred on *Boston Public*, *ER*, *The Steve Harvey Show*, *Buffy the Vampire Slayer*, *Veronica Mars* and *Supernatural*. She was featured in the BET TV movie *Funny Valentines* (1999), starring Alfre Woodard. It's the story of a woman who rekindles a nurturing relationship with her cousin and was directed by Julie Dash (*Daughters of the Dust*). Her last name is Nigerian and means "leader of men." She is half Nigerian from her father's side. After her father's death, her mother raised her and her three siblings.

Feature Films including Video and TV Movies: *Peter Benchley's Creature* (TV; 1988), *Funny Valentines* (TV; 1999), *B.S.* (TV; 2002), *Great Lengths* (2004), *Hitched* (TV; 2005), *Camjackers* (2005), *Fix* (2008), *Who Do You Love* (2008).

TV: *The Steve Harvey Show* ("Uncle Steve," 1998), *Malibu, CA* ("Three Dudes and a Baby," 2000), *Spyder Games* (recurring role as Cherish Pardee; 2001), *Boston Public* (episode 24; 2001), *24* (recurring role of Nicole Palmer; 2001–02), *Sheena* ("Coming to Africa," 2002), *ER* ("Bygones," 2002), *For the People* (recurring role as Claudia Gibson; 2002), *What I Like About You* ("The Parrot Trap," 2002), *B.S.* (pilot; 2002), *Buffy the Vampire Slayer* ("The Killer in Me," 2003), *Like Family* (recurring role of Danika Ward; 2003–04), *Veronica Mars* ("Drinking the Kool Aid," 2004), *That '70s Show* (recurring role of Angie Barnett; 2004–05), *Supernatural* ("Route 666," 2006), *The 4400* (recurring role of Isabelle Tyler; 2006–07), *The Game* (2 episodes as Cheyenne; "The Commitments," "Take These Vows and Shove 'Em," 2007), *CSI: Miami* (recurring role as Dr. Tara Price; 2008).

Eddy, Sonya Born in Concord, California.

Sonya Eddy graduated from University of California at Davis in 1992 with a bachelor of arts degree, majoring in English and African American studies, with a minor in dramatic arts. Besides being an actress, she is also a singer and improvisational artist. During her studies she began her acting career with a role in the West Coast premiere of *Zora Is My Name!* (written by Ruby Dee). Eddy performed several roles in the play, including Big Sweet, a bawdy blues singer. She then played the role of the Courtesan in *A Comedy of Errors*, as well as roles in *The Crucible*, *Pericles*, and as the witch in *Into the Woods*. She won an Arty Award for her performance as Bloody Mary in *South Pacific*. She appeared in *Cat on a Hot Tin Roof* with John Goodman and Brenda Fricker at the Geffen Playhouse in Los Angeles.

Her TV work includes roles on *ER*, *Joan of Arcadia*, *Seinfeld* and *The Drew Carey Show*. Eddy also appeared on *Everybody Hates Chris*, *Malcolm in the Middle*, *Reba*, *Strong Medicine* and *The Hughleys*. She is a regular on Martin Short's *Primetime Glick* (2001). The recurring role for which she is best known is as no-nonsense head nurse Epiphany Johnson starting in 2006 in the daytime soap *General Hospital*. She also brought the Epiphany character to soapnet's first serialized drama for prime time, *General Hospital: Night Shift* in July 2007 (while maintaining her day job on *General Hospital*). She brings considerable authority to her Epiphany role in that Eddy herself is a licensed vocational nurse.

Feature film appearances include *Nutty Professor II: The Klumps* (2000), *Barbershop* (2002), *Daddy Day Care* (2003), *Surviving Christmas* (2004), *Coach Carter* (2005) with Samuel L. Jackson, and *Bad News Bears* (2005) with Billy Bob Thornton.

Feature Films including Video and TV Movies: *High School High* (1996), *Blast* (1997), *Sour Grapes* (1998), *The Godson* (1998), *Patch Adams* (1998), *Blast from the Past* (1999), *Inspector Gadget* (1999), *Motel Blue* (1999), *Nutty Professor II: The Klumps* (2000), *Dish Dogs* (2000), *Ten Grand* (2000), *Strange Hearts* (2001), *The Jennie Project* (TV; 2001), *Buying the Cow* (2002), *Barbershop* (2002), *The Third Society* (2002), *The Fine Line Between Cute and Creepy* (2002), *One Last Ride* (2003), *A Single Rose* (2003), *Mi Casa, Su Casa* (2003), *Daddy Day Care* (2003), *Matchstick Men* (2003), *Leprechaun: Back 2 Tha Hood* (2003), *Y.M.I.* (2004), *Promised Land* (2004), *Surviving Christmas* (2004), *Lost in Plainview* (2005), *Coach Carter* (2005), *Come Away Home* (2005), *Bad News Bears* (2005), *Gridiron Gang* (2006), *Year of the Dog* (2007), *Player 5150* (2008), *Disfigured* (2008), *The Perfect Game* (2008), *Trim* (2008).

TV: *The Drew Carey Show* ("Drew Meets Lawyers," "Science Names Suck," 1995), *Martin* ("Is You Is or Is You Ain't," 1996), *Married with Children* (2 episodes; "A Shoe Room with a View," "Birthday Boy Toy," 1995 and 1997), *Beverly Hills, 90210* (2 episodes; "Forgive and Forget," "The Way We Weren't," 1997), *Murphy Brown* ("From Here to Jerusalem," 1997), *Tracey Takes On...* ("Smoking," 1998), *3rd Rock from the Sun* ("36! 24! 36! Dick!" Parts I and II, 1998), *Seinfeld* ("The Muffin Tops," "The Bookstore," 1997 and 1998), *Any Day Now* ("Making Music with the Wrong Man," 1998), *Martial Law* ("Shanghai Express," 1998), *To Have and to Hold* (2 episodes in the role of Delilah; 1998), *USA High* ("Goodbye Lazz," 1998), *Home Improvement* ("Love's Labor Lost," Part I, 1999), *Malibu, CA* ("Jason's New Job," 1999), *Touched by an Angel* ("Fighting the Good Fight," 1999), *Arli$$* (2 episodes; "Kirby Carlisle,

Sonya Eddy in *General Hospital*.

Trouble-Shooter," "Cause and Effect," 1997 and 1999), *Providence* ("Sail Away," 1999), *Popular* ("Wild, Wild Mess," 1999), *Strip Mall* ("Burbank Bigfoot," 2000), *Gilmore Girls* ("Kiss and Tell," 2000), *Even Stevens* ("Get a Job," 2001), *Lizzie McGuire* ("Picture Day," 2001), *The Invisible Man* (2 episodes; "Ghost of a Chance," "It's a Small World," 2001), *Diagnosis Murder* ("Deadly Mirage," Part II, 2001), *Primetime Glick* (recurring role as Nurse Frida May; 2001), *Resurrection Blvd.* ("La Agonia y las Extasis," 2001), *Spyder Games* (2001), *The Mind of a Married Man* (pilot; 2001), *ER* (3 episodes; "A Walk in the Woods," "Somebody to Love," "Heart of the Matter," 2001–06), *Felicity* ("Back to the Future," 2002), *Reba* ("Proud Reba," 2002), *Still Standing* ("Still in School," 2002), *Monk* ("Mr. Monk and the Very, Very Old Man," 2003), *MADtv* (2003), *Phil of the Future* ("Future Jock," 2004), *House* ("The Socratic Method," 2004), *Less Than Perfect* ("You Can Leave the Lights On," 2005), *Joan of Arcadia* (3 episodes; "Dive," "Shadows and Light," "Something Wicked This Way Comes," 2004–05), *Inconceivable* (pilot; 2005), *Malcolm in the Middle* ("Bomb Shelter," 2006), *SoapTalk* (2006), *Day Break* ("What If He Can Change the Day," 2006), *General Hospital* (recurring role of Epiphany Johnson; 2006–08), *General Hospital:*

Night Shift (3 episodes in the role of Epiphany Johnson; 2007–08), *In Case of Emergency* ("It's Got to Be the Morning After," 2007), *Everybody Hates Chris* ("Everybody Hates Cutting School," 2007), *CSI* ("The Good, the Bad and the Dominatrix," 2007), *Desperate Housewives* ("The Gun Song," 2008).

Elise, Kimberly Born in Minneapolis, Minnesota, April 17, 1967.

Kimberly Elise Trammel began writing plays and stories at age seven. Elise took filmmaking courses at Minneapolis Community College, getting her communications degree from the University of Minnesota, and then going on to the American Film Institute. She became a member of the Northern Warehouse Artists' Cooperative, a housing development for low-income artists in the warehouse district of downtown St. Paul, Minnesota. She is one of three children. Her father, Marvin Trammel, owns an executive search firm; her mother, Erna Jean (née Johnson) is an elementary school teacher. She was married to Maurice Oldham (1989–2005). They have two children, AjaBleu and Butterfly.

Elise worked as an associate producer for a local public broadcasting station and began acting professionally at age 20. She made her feature film debut in *Set It Off* (1996), the sad story of four diverse women who are desperate enough to join forces to rob a bank. Elise was the meek one, the first to die during the robbery. Then she had featured roles with Denzel Washington in three films: *John Q* (2002), *The Manchurian Candidate* (2004) and *The Great Debaters* (2007). In *Woman Thou Art Loosed* (2004) she was Michele, an abused, addicted young woman who comes to get the help she needs in prison.

Kimberly Elise in *Beloved* (1998).

Elise won the Best Supporting Actress award at the Ace Cable Awards in 1997 for her portrayal of Jeanette in the TV film *The Ditchdigger's Daughters*, about the interaction between a stern father and his six daughters. She was nominated for an NAACP Image Award for the Showtime movie *Bojangles* (2001), with Gregory Hines as Bill "Bojangles" Robinson. She won a Golden Satellite Award and was nominated for an Ace Cable Award and an NAACP Image Award for *Beloved* (1998) for her role of Denver, a woman who takes in a mysterious stranger named Beloved. She won an NAACP Image Award for *Diary of a Mad Black Woman* (2005), another drama of search and redemption. Elise has appeared on series TV, including guest roles on UPN's *Girlfriends* and Showtime's *Soul Food.*

In 2005–07, trying out a glamorous new image, she starred on the CBS crime drama *Close to Home*, as Marion County, Indiana, prosecutor Maureen Scofield. Her character was killed off in the last episode of the 2006–07 season and the show was cancelled in May 2007. She was nominated for an NAACP Image Award for Outstanding Actress in a Drama Series for her work on *Close to Home.*

Feature Films including TV Movies: *Set It Off* (1996), *The Ditchdigger's Daughters* (TV; 1997), *Beloved* (1998), *The Loretta Claiborne Story* (TV; 2000), *Bait* (2000), *Bojangles* (TV; 2001), *John Q* (2002), *Woman Thou Art Loosed* (2004), *The Manchurian Candidate* (2004), *Diary of a Mad Black Woman* (2005), *Pride* (2007), *The Great Debaters* (2007), *Red Soil* (2009).

TV: *In the House* ("Nanna Don't Play," 1995), *Newton's Apple* (1996), *The Sentinel* ("Black or White," 1996), *Headliners & Legends: Denzel Washington* (2002), *Soul Food* (2 episodes in the role of Estella; "Emotional Collateral," "Falling from Grace," 2002 and 2003), *The Twilight Zone*

("Another Life," 2003), *Girlfriends* (2 episodes in the role of Reesie Jackson; "The Pact," "The Fast Track and the Furious," 2003), *Essence Awards* (2003), *Tavis Smiley* (2004), *The View* (2005), *The 20th IFP Independent Spirit Awards* (2005), *The Oprah Winfrey Show* (2005), *36th NAACP Image Awards* (2005), *BET Awards 2005*, *The 2nd Annual BET Comedy Awards* (2005), *The Black Movie Awards* (2005), *Close to Home* (recurring role of Maureen Scofield; 2005–07), *Legends Ball* (2006), *37th NAACP Image Awards* (2006), *38th NAACP Image Awards* (2007), *Masters of Science Fiction* ("Little Brother," (2007), *An Evening of Stars: A Tribute to Smokey Robinson* (2008).

Ellis, Aunjanue Born in San Francisco, California, February 21, 1969.

Aunjanue L. Ellis was raised on her grandmother's farm in Mississippi. She attended Tougaloo College in Tougaloo, Mississippi, before she got her bachelor of arts degree in African American studies from Brown University, and then she studied acting in the graduate program at New York University.

She had prominent roles in *Undercover Brother* (as Sistah Girl; 2002), potent ally of the crime-fighting title character, and in *Ray* (as Mary Ann Fisher; 2004), as Ray Charles' first back-up singer, a composite of several real life women. She was featured in actress Regina Taylor's play *Drowning Crow,* a variation of Chekov's *The Seagull,* at the Manhattan Theater Club in January 2004.

Feature Films including Video and TV Movies: *Girls Town* (1996), *Ed's Next Move* (1996), *Side Streets* (1998), *Desert Blue* (1998), *In Too Deep* (1999), *A Map of the World* (1999), *John John in the Sky* (2000), *Men of Honor* (2000), *The Opponent* (2000), *Disappearing Acts* (TV; 2000), *The Caveman's Valentine* (2000), *Lovely & Amazing* (2001), *I Am Ali* (2002), *Undercover Brother* (2002), *Brother to Brother* (2004), *Racing for Time* (TV; 2008), *The Prince of Motor City* (TV; 2008), *Gifted Hands: The Ben Carson Story* (TV; 2009), *The Hungry Ghosts* (2009), *The Tested* (2009).

TV: *New York Undercover* ("Buster and Claudia," 1995), *High Incident* (recurring role as Officer Leslie Joyner; 1996–97), *The Practice* (4 episodes in the role of Sharon Young; "Target Practice," "Crossfire," "Do Unto Others," "Committed," 1999), *Third Watch* (2 episodes in the role of Gail Moore; "Journey to the Himalayas," "32 Bullets and a Broken Heart," 2000), *Access Granted* ("Snoop Dogg: Undercover Funk," 2001), *100 Centre Street* (3 episodes; 2001), *MDs* (recurring role of Quinn Joyner; 2002), *The D.A.* ("The People vs. Sergius Kovinsky," 2004), *Jonny Zero* (6 episodes in the role of Gloria; 2005), *E-Ring* (recurring role of Master Sergeant Jocelyn Pierce; 2005–06), *Justice* (recurring role of Miranda Lee; 2006), *Law & Order: Criminal Intent* ("Flipped," 2007), *Numb3rs* ("Power," 2008), *True Blood* ("The First Taste," 2008), *The Border* ("Family Values," 2008).

Ellis, Evelyn Born in Boston, Massachusetts, 1894; died 1957, Saranac Lake, New York.

Evelyn Ellis was a pioneering black actress, notable mostly in theater, but with some film work. She had her Broadway debut in *Goat Alley,* a 1927 revival, in the role of Lucy Belle Dorsey. She was Bess in *Porgy* (1927–28 and again in 1929), a non-musical play that was the source material for George Gershwin's *Porgy and Bess.* In Orson Welles' landmark staging of the original production of Richard Wright's novel *Native Son* (1941), her most outstanding Broadway role, she was Hannah, the mother of Bigger Thomas, the doomed murderer from Chicago's South Side. In 1945, she played a housekeeper in *Deep Are the Roots,* and was also in the musical revue *Blue Holiday.* She was Ada Lester in a revival of *Tobacco Road* in 1950. In 1951 she was Della in *The Royal Family,* in which Ossie Davis also appeared. Her final Broadway role was as Aunt Emma in *Touchstone* (1953).

She made her screen debut in Oscar Micheaux's *A Son of Satan* (1924). She was Bessie in Orson Welles's 1947 film noir *The Lady from Shanghai.* In 1953, she was Joe Louis's mother in *The Joe Louis Story.* Her final film was *Interrupted Melody* (1955) with Glenn Ford and Eleanor Parker. She played a maid. In 1957, Ellis died of a heart attack at the Variety Club's Will Rogers Memorial Hospital in New York.

Feature Films including TV Movies: *A Son of Satan* (aka *The Ghost of Tolston's Manor*; 1924), *The Lady from Shanghai* (1947), *The Joe Louis Story* (1953), *Interrupted Melody* (1955).

TV: *Pontiac Playwrights '56* ("Flight," 1956).

Ellis Ross, Tracee Born in Los Angeles, California on October 29, 1972.

Born Tracee Joy Silberstein, Ellis Ross is the

daughter of the legendary lead singer of The Supremes and Academy Award–nominated actress Diana Ross. She has had a significant show business career of her own, specifically as star of the long-running UPN/CW series *Girlfriends*, which was nominated for an Emmy. It won her the NAACP Image Award in 2007 for Outstanding Actress in a Comedy Series. She was nominated six other times for the award, from 2002 to 2008. She has also won a BET Comedy Award and received two BET nominations; two prism Award nominations for Outstanding Comedy Series; and the show received two Women's Image Network awards for best Comedy Series.

Ellis Ross was lawyer (and later, restaurant owner) Joan Carol Clayton in the series, which lasted an impressive eight seasons. Joan's professional success was not matched by her luck with relationships and personal satisfaction, but the character always appeared level-headed and realistic, with a touch of cynicism and an occasional hint of whimsy. Although *Girlfriends* has sometimes been referred to as a black version of *Friends*, it had its own tone and style. Ellis Ross had the honor of directing the final episode of the series. Early TV assignments included hosting chores on Lifetime's *The Dish* (1997), and as part of the comedy ensemble on MTV's *The Lyricist Lounge Show* (2000).

Ellis Ross had a privileged childhood, attending the prestigious Dalton School in Manhattan, and the Institut Le Rosey in Switzerland. She is also a 1994 graduate of Brown University, where she acted in plays. She also studied drama at the William Esper Acting Studio. She worked in the fashion industry as a model (photographed by Francesco Scavullo and Herb Ritts, among other famous names) and was contributing fashion editor at *Mirabella* and *New York* magazine.

She made her feature debut in the independent film *Far Harbor* (1986), in which a group of young people talk about their problems ad infinitum. Later films included another independent, *Sue* (1997), a character study of a disturbed young woman; and she appeared in the TV movie *Race Against Fear: A Moment of Truth* (1998). Her first mainstream big-budget feature was a small role in *Hanging Up* (2000), with Diane Keaton. She was also in Tyler Perry's *Daddy's Little Girls* (2007), about a white collar woman and a blue collar man looking to find love with each other. That same year she was featured in HBO's *Life Support*, about a former crack addict who becomes a community leader.

Ellis Ross has four siblings: Rhonda Ross Kendrick (a half-sister born in 1972); Chudney Lane Silberstein (a sister born in 1975); Ross Arne Naess (a half-brother born in 1987); and Evan Olav Naess (a half-brother born in 1988).

Feature Films including Video and TV Movies: *Fat Harbor* (1996), *Sue* (1997), *A Fare to Remember* (1998), *Race Against Fear: A Moment of Truth* (TV; 1998), *Hanging Up* (2000), *In the Weeds* (2000), *I-See-You.com* (2006), *Life Support* (2007), *Daddy's Little Girls* (2007), *Labor Pains* (2009).

TV: *The Dish* (series host; 1997), *The Lyricist Lounge Show* (2000), *Girlfriends* (recurring role of Joan Clayton; 2000–08), *Cool Women* (2002), *The Isaac Mizrahi Show* (2003), *I Love the '70s* (2003), *Good Day Live* (2003), *Second Time Around* ("A Kiss Is Still a Kiss," 2004), *35th NAACP Image Awards* (2004), *4th Annual BET Awards* (2004), *Life & Style* (2004), *Steve Harvey's Big Time* (2005), *Dennis Miller* (2 episodes; 2004 and 2005), *Tavis Smiley* (2005), *Nick Cannon Presents Wild 'N Out* (2005), *The 2nd Annual BET Comedy Awards* (2005), *The Black Movie Awards* (2005), *An All-Star Salute to Patti LaBelle* (2005), *The 3rd Annual Vibe Awards* (2005), *Turn Up the Heat with G. Garvin* (2005), *The 2006 Black Movie Awards*, *The Late Late Show with Craig Ferguson* (2007), *Late Night with Conan O'Brien* (2007), *Live with Regis and Kathie Lee* (2007), *Entertainment Tonight* (2008).

Video/DVD: *Kanye West: College Dropout: Video Anthology* (2005).

Epps, Shareeka Born in Brooklyn, New York, July 11, 1989.

Shareeka Epps attended William Alexander 51 Junior High School in Brooklyn's Park Slope. Although not a drama student, she was active in dance and music, and performed in school productions of *West Side Story* and *Annie* in her early teens. She starred in the low budget short *Gowanus, Brooklyn* (2004) with Matt Kerr. She was recommended to aspiring filmmakers Ryan Fleck and Anna Bowden by a drama teacher at her middle school and was cast in a 19-minute version of a feature script the pair had written. *Half Nelson* was based on that short. Epps is best known for her multiple award-winning performance as the Brooklyn schoolgirl Drey in *Half Nel-*

son (2006). Drey is a bright, sensitive 13-year-old girl who sees her teacher smoking crack in the girls' locker room. Shot on digital for $1,000, the short went on to win the Grand Jury Prize for short filmmaking at the 2004 Sundance Film Festival. When the feature-length version was being cast in 2006, Epps was still young looking enough to reprise her role, this time opposite Ryan Gosling as the teacher (he went on to be nominated for a Best Actor Oscar).

Epps was nominated for the Black Reel Award for Best Breakthrough Performance and Best Supporting Actress for *Half Nelson* and was the winner of the Boston Society of Film Critics Awards for Best Supporting Actress, The Broadcast Film Critics Association Award for Best Young Actress for *Half Nelson*, The Chicago Film Critics Association Award for Most Promising Performer, The Gotham Awards Breakthrough Award, and The Independent Spirit Awards Best Female Lead.

Epps currently resides in Binghamton, New York; she graduated from Binghamton High School and attends Broome Community College. In 2007 she appeared in the Noah Buschel film *Neal Cassidy* (2007), about the beat generation legend. She made her first TV guest appearance on *Law & Order: Special Victims Unit* in April 2008.

Feature Films including Video and TV Movies: *Half Nelson* (2006), *Neal Cassidy* (2007), *Four* (2008), *The Winning Season* (2009), *Chandelle King* (aka *25/8;* 2009),

TV: *Law & Order: Special Victims Unit* ("Undercover," 2008).

Shorts: *Gowanus, Brooklyn* (2004).

Eve (aka Jeffers, Eve) Born in West Philadelphia, Pennsylvania, November 10, 1978.

Eve Jihan Minnie Jeffers is a rapper, singer, actress and fashion designer. In 2003, she became the star of her own show, *Eve*, in the role of Shelley, a fashion designer. In an instance of life imitating art, Eve has her own fashion line, Fetish. The sales of the rapper-singer's first three albums have inched toward the four million mark. She is the daughter of Julia Wilch, a publishing company supervisor, and Jerry Jeffers, supervisor at a chemical plant. When her parents separated, Eve was raised by her mother and grandmother.

Eve first attracted notice on DMX's *It's Dark and Hell Is Hot*, in addition to other Ruff Ryder label compilations. Her debut album was *Let There Be Eve ... Ruff Ryders' First Lady* (1999). The album entered the *Billboard* 200 at number one. Further success quickly came with the release of the album *Scorpion* (2001), keyed by the singles "Who's That Girl," and "Let Me Blow Ya Mind," with Gwen Stefani of No Doubt. That song won a Grammy Award for Best Rap/Sung Collaboration; the album went platinum, and it was honored with a Grammy nomination. Eve's third album, *Eve-Olution* (2002), was not nearly as successful as the first two. This is when Eve decided to concentrate on acting and signed with UPN to helm a sitcom. *Eve* had a decent run from 2003 to 2006, and she proved to be a surprisingly smooth comedienne, given that she had essentially no acting experience. Her work was acknowledged with an NAACP Image Award nomination for Outstanding Actress in a Comedy series in 2005.

The natural acting talent displayed on her TV series has carried over into feature films. Her best work to date on the big screen was in *Barbershop* (2002), her first film. She played a less than glamorous beautician named Terri who is being abused by her crass boyfriend, and who eventually learns to respect herself and fight back. At the MTV Movie Awards, she was nominated for Best Female Breakthrough Performance for *Barbershop*. Her work was also given an NAACP Image Award nomination for Outstanding Supporting Actress in a Motion Picture.

Other film roles were in the popular Vin Diesel action film *xXx* (2002); *Barbershop 2: Back in Business* (2004), an inferior sequel; a small role in the comedy *The Cookout* (2004), and *The Woodsman* (2004), an excellent dramatic role in a story about the rehabilitation of a pedophile (Kevin Bacon). She made her dramatic television debut on *Third Watch* (2006) in the role of Yvette Powell, in a series about nightshift police, firemen and paramedics. She appeared on the UPN sitcom *One on One* (2004) as a hip-hopper named Ida.

Eve returned to musical prominence with "Rich Girl" (2005), another single with Gwen Stefani. They performed it together with the Harajuku Girls at the Grammy Awards. Her fourth album, *Here I Am*, has been delayed multiple times, but was due to be released in 2009.

Feature Films including Video and TV Movies: *Barbershop* (2002), *xXx* (2002), *Charlie's Angels: Full Throttle* (2003), *The Woodsman* (2004), *Barbershop 2: Back in Business* (2004), *The*

Cookout (2004), *Flashbacks of a Fool* (2008), *Ego* (2008), *Whip It!* (2009).

TV: *One Love: The Bob Marley All-Star Tribute* (1999), *The 1999 Source Hip-Hop Music Awards, Late Night with Conan O'Brien* (1999), *MTV Fashionably Loud: Miami* (1999), *@MTV with Eve* (2000), *Making the Video* ("Eve: Who's That Girl," 2001), *Essence Awards* (2001), *1st Annual BET Awards* (2001), *MTV Video Music Awards 2001, The Teen Choice Awards 2001, Who Wants to Be a Millionaire?* (2001), *Saturday Night Live* (3 segments; 2001–05), *Eve* (recurring role as Shelley; 2003–06), *The 45th Annual Grammy Awards* (2003), *Popworld* (2003), *Tinseltown TV* (2003), *Ellen* (2003), *VH1: Big in '03* (2003), *Third Watch* ("Second Chances," 2003), *E! True Hollywood Story* ("Missy 'Misdemeanor' Elliot," 2004), *Late Show with David Letterman* (2004), *One on One* ("It's a Mad, Mad, Mad, Mad Hip Hop World," 2004), *The Wayne Brady Show* (2004), *VH1 Divas 2004, Punk'd* (2004), *Maxim Hot 100* (2004), *And You Don't Stop: 30 Years of Hip-Hop* (2004), *Live with Regis and Kathie Lee* (2004), *The Late Late Show with Craig Kilborn* (2004), *The 47th Annual Grammy Awards* (2005), *The Apprentice* (2005), *Red Nose Day* (2005), *Ant & Dec's Saturday Night Takeaway* (2005), *Good Morning America* (2005), *CD:UK* (2 segments; 2005), *America's Next Top Model* (2005), *Total Request Live* (2005), *The View* (2005), *2nd Annual VH1 Hip-Hop Honors* (2005), *2005 American Music Awards, Last Call with Carson Daly* (2 segments; 2004–06), *The Tyra Banks Show* (3 segments; 2005–06), *Nickelodeon Kids' Choice Awards 2006, Keith Barry: Extraordinary* (2006), *106 & Park Top 10 Live* (2006), *BET Awards 2007, Movies Rock* (2007), *MTV's Top Pop Group* (2008), *The Upsetter* (documentary; 2008).

Videos/DVD: *Hip-Hop Uncensored, Vol. 2* (2000), *Missy "Misdemeanor" Elliot: Hits of Miss E, Vol. 1* (2001), *Hip-Hop VIPs* (2002), *Slip N' Slide: All-Star Weekend* (2002), *Scarface: Origins of a Hip-Hop Classic* (2003), *Female American Rap Stars* (2004).

Everett, Francine Born April 3, 1920, in Louisburg, North Carolina; died May 27, 1999, New York, New York.

Francine Everett had no use for the maid roles offered black women in mainstream Hollywood films, so she instead concentrated on race movies and other black community show business opportunities. Everett was a well-rounded performer with vibrant girl next door good looks. She was born Franceine Williamson, the daughter of Noah, a tailor, and raised in the town of Henderson, North Carolina. The Williamsons moved to Harlem when she was young. This was the exciting era of the Harlem Renaissance, and it energized Williamson and inspired her to pursue her talents as a singer and dancer.

She was a student at St. Marks School, but dropped out of St. Marks and became a chorus girl at Small's Paradise in Harlem in 1933. That only lasted about a month, and the ambitious Williamson then joined a group called The Four Blacks Cats. It was around this time that she married Harlem resident Booker Everett. He died in a car crash after about a year of marriage, leaving his wife devastated.

In 1936 Francine Everett joined the "Negro unit" of the Federal Theater Project (FTP) in Harlem sponsored by the Works Progress Administration (WPA). She appeared in small roles in their productions *Haiti* and *Black Empire.* She also appeared in "soundies," in the 1940s, short films featuring hit songs that were shown on juke boxes. In addition, she modeled clothes and hairstyles for ads in black-oriented magazines and newspapers and sang in nightclubs. She appeared on Broadway in the shows *Humming Sam* (1931), which opened and closed after one performance, and *Swing It* (1937). The latter had a score by Eubie Blake and Cecil Mack, and was about staging a show on a Mississippi riverboat.

She met and married actor Rex Ingram (best known for his wonderful work in *Green Pastures, Thief of Baghdad* and *Sahara*) in 1933, and they divorced in 1936. Everett was offered a role as one of the angels in *Green Pastures,* but turned it down because it was too stereotypical.

Her film debut was in *Paradise in Harlem* (1939) as Desdemona Jones. The film was a clever updating of *Othello* to a contemporary crime milieu. Everett's other films are *Keep Punching* (opposite boxing champion Henry Armstrong; 1939), *Big Timers* (with Lincoln Perry, better known as Stepin Fetchit; 1945), and the two race films for which she is best known today, *Tall, Tan and Terrific* (1946) and *Dirty Gertie from Harlem, U.S.A.* (1946), an adaptation of Somerset Maugham's *Rain,* also a film with Joan Crawford, and from which the film *Sadie Thompson* with Rita Hayworth was derived. *Dirty Gertie from Harlem, U.S.A.* is a tepid reworking of a standard "bad girl meets a bad fate" story, and Everett is not too believable as a femme fatale (but she is as charming as ever). Gertie LaRue is a nightclub singer and prostitute who flees to a resort hotel on a tropical island to escape her jealous boyfriend. The film was directed by the talented Spencer Williams, who directed a number of efficient race films during this period. *Tall, Tan and Terrific* stars the ever ebullient Mantan Moreland. Everett is a nightclub singer who stands up for her boss after he is framed by gangsters. This was Everett's last race movie.

She appeared in the musical short *Toot That Trumpet* with Louis Jordan (1946) and, more significantly, was also in *Ebony Parade* (1947), a musical revue featuring Dorothy Dandridge, Count Basie, Cab Calloway and the Mills Brothers which premiered in a mainstream Broadway theater. She made a foray into Hollywood films at the end of screen career with *Lost Boundaries* (a small role; 1949) and *No Way Out* (an unbilled walk-on; 1950).

Everett's activism and civil rights activity should not be overlooked. As a member of the Negro Actors' Guild, she often lectured and participated in panels and seminars sponsored by the International Agency for Minority Artists Affairs. Everett retired from show business in the 1950s to take care of her mother, who had suffered a stroke. She lived with her parents and survived off the alimony she received from Rex Ingram (she never married again). Following her mother's death in 1961, she worked at Harlem Hospital, where she held a clerical job until her retirement in 1985.

Feature Films: *Paradise in Harlem* (1939), *Keep Punching* (1939), *Big Timers* (1945), *Tall, Tan and Terrific* (1946), *Dirty Gertie from Harlem, U.S.A.* (1946), *Ebony Parade* (1947), *Lost Boundaries* (1949), *No Way Out* (1950).

Video: *Spencer Williams: Remembrances of an Early Black Film Pioneer* (1996).

Shorts: *Toot That Trumpet* (1946).

Falana, Lola

Born in Camden, New Jersey, September 11, 1942.

It was a different era. The television variety show was alive and well, if in decline. There was a place on the small screen for glitzy, Vegas-style entertainment, although those days were gone on movie screens. And the zeitgeist of the era made it possible for a sexy, dynamic black woman to emerge as one of the top entertainers of the day. Born Loleatha Elayne Falana to Bennett Falana and Cleao Twine, she later moved with her family to Philadelphia. Falana attended Germantown High School there. She was raised as an Episcopalian, but later converted to Roman Catholicism. Her parents were of African Indian and Cuban descent. Her father was an ex-marine and her mother was a seamstress.

By age three she was dancing, and by age five she was singing in the church choir. By the time she was in high school, she was dancing professionally in nightclubs, with her mother as an escort. Pursuing a musical career became so important to Falana that, against her parents' wishes, she left high school a few months before graduation and moved to New York City. She was hired to dance at the famous club Small's Paradise in Harlem, where a generation earlier, up and coming black stars like Francine Everett had performed.

She shortened her name in honor of the Lola character from *Damn Yankees* (who sings the memorable song "Whatever Lola Wants, Lola Gets...," which became Falana's signature song). In 1958, blues singer Dinah Washington appeared in Philadelphia and needed a dancer. Falana, 16 and still in high school at that time, asked for the job. In the middle of her act, her swimsuit strap broke, but she continued to perform superbly.

Falana released her first single ("My Baby") for Mercury Records in 1965. She later recorded for Frank Sinatra's Reprise Records. It was in the mid-sixties that Sammy Davis, Jr. became her mentor and lover. She toured with Davis as a singer and dancer and appeared with him in the Broadway show *Golden Boy* (1964), then later reprised her role on the London stage. She made her film debut in *A Man Called Adam* (1966), in the supporting role of Theo. It was a melodrama starring Davis as a jazz trumpeter.

Falana left the U.S. for Europe, settled in Italy, and performed her way to stardom. She learned to speak and read Italian and was twice voted Number One Performer of the Year, largely due to her impressive appearances on TV variety shows. She was able to translate her success to England, and ultimately to the United States, where she broke down barriers against what a female black entertainer could do. She was the spokeswoman for L'eggs hosiery and, most memorably,

America's Josephine Baker: Lola Falana in *Doctor Jazz* (1975). (Photograph by Martha Swope.)

for Faberge's Tigress perfume (her 1967 Italian-German Western, *Lola Colt*, was also known as *Black Tigress*).

Falana was everywhere during this period. She performed with Bob Hope on his U.S.O. South East Asia Tour in 1972. She earned a reported $2 million for a five-month performance in Las Vegas. But her show business peak was relatively brief, and her entire film career spans only a decade.

Lola Colt (aka *Lola Baby*; 1967) is the most well known of her Italian films (and the most seen in the U.S., although it remains rather obscure). It is a very average Western filled with all the predictable clichés of the genre, but Falana's presence makes it unusual, and even a bit memorable. She is a traveling showgirl who headlines at saloons, periodically bursting into variations on her contemporary lounge act, complete with stereophonic vocals and 1970s dance moves. She looks spectacular, but the film is best placed in the high camp category. Variant prints of this film exist, but no matter which version you see, it is a curio. She accepted a role in the Broadway show *Dr. Jazz* (1975); it ran only four nights, but Falana was brilliant and buzz from the cognescenti helped make her a star in the U.S. She was nominated for a Tony in for *Dr. Jazz.*

The blaxploitation era in Hollywood coincided with the peak of Falana's popularity. She had prominent roles in two big budget mainstream films, *The Liberation of L.B. Jones* (1970) and *The Klansman* (aka *The Burning Cross*, 1973). *The Klansman*, despite a cast headlined by Richard Burton and Lee Marvin, who were both big stars at the time, is a by-the-numbers exploitation of Southern racial politics, made strictly for a dollar, with no interest in genuine social issues. It was a deserved box office flop, and Falana's presence is negligible. *The Liberation of L.B. Jones*—featuring Falana's only effective screen performance — is another story altogether. Literally one of the most racially explosive films ever made, it is painful to watch even now, if you can locate a print; it was the last film directed by Hollywood giant William Wyler. It was not a critical or financial success, and it is a very uneven film, but it is undeniably powerful. Falana is the slutty wife of an older man, the decent but weak funeral director L.B. Jones (Roscoe Lee Browne in a touching performance). Emma Jones is having an affair with a white cop (Anthony Zerbe). Zerbe is excellent as the sleazy, racist cop. Emma is her own worst enemy, and Falana conveys the pathetic nature of the character.

Lady Cocoa (aka *Pop Goes the Weasel*, 1975) was her final film. It is essentially a low-budget vanity production, with Falana overacting as an endangered witness sprung from jail to testify against her ex-boyfriend. This is a well-worn story, invigorated only by the acting of Millie Perkins as a hit woman with a transgender iden-

Lola Falana at age 24.

tity secret. Falana was married to Feliciano Tavares (of the popular disco group Tavares) from 1971 to 1975. She was diagnosed with multiple sclerosis in December 1987 and had a relapse in 1996. Her last performance of record was in 1997 at Wayne Newton's theater in the music mecca of Branson, Missouri.

Feature Films including TV Movies: *A Man Called Adam* (1966), *Stasera mi butto* (1967), *Lola Colt* (aka *Black Tigress, Lola Baby*, 1967), *Quando dico che ti amo* (1968), *The Liberation of L.B. Jones* (1970), *The Klansman* (1974), *Lady Cocoa* (aka *Pop Goes the Weasel*; 1975).

TV: *Hullabaloo* (2 segments; 1965), *The Hollywood Palace* (3 segments; 1966–69), *The Ed Sullivan Show* (1967), *Gira, gira* (1968), *Sammy Davis, Jr.* (1969), *The F.B.I.* ("The Sanctuary," 1969), *The Flip Wilson Show* (2 segments; 1970), *The Mod Squad* ("The Song of Willie," 1970), *The Tonight Show Starring Johnny Carson* (16 segments; 1970–78), *The 43rd Annual Academy Awards* (1971), *The Bob Hope Vietnam Christmas Show* (1971), *The New Bill Cosby Show* (series regular; 1972), *Hai visto mai?* (1973), *Soul Train* (2 segments; 1973 and 1974), *The Streets of San Francisco* ("A String of Puppets," 1974), *Sammy and Company* (1975), *Ben Vereen ... Comin' at Ya!* (series regular; 1975), *The 28th Annual Primetime Emmy*

Awards (1976), *Dinah!* (1976), *Cos* (series regular; 1976), *Celebrity Challenge of the Sexes* (1977), *The Mike Douglas Show* (1977), *The Merv Griffin Show* (1977), *Happy Birthday, Las Vegas* (1977), *Circus of the Stars 2* (1977), *The Love Boat* (2 episodes; "Marooned," Parts I and II, 1978), *The Television Annual 1978/79* (1979), *The Muppet Show* (1979), *Vega$* ("Red Handed," 1979), *Fantasy Island* (1979), *Liberace: A Valentine Special* (1979), *Circus of the Stars 4* (1979), *Bob Hope's Overseas Christmas Tours: Around the World with the Troops 1941–1972* (1980), *The Big Show* (1980), *Omnibus* (1980), *Lola, Lola y Lollo* (1982), *Capitol* (recurring role as Charity Blake; 1982), *Hotel* ("Changes of Heart," 1986), *Motown Merry Christmas* (1987), *Sammy Davis, Jr. 60th Anniversary Celebration* (1990), *Mad About You* (1990), *Reading Rainbow* (voice; "Sophie and Lou," 1992), *La Tele de tu vida* (archival; 2007).

Video/DVD: *The Original Leads of the Temptations* (1992).

Fantasia (aka Barrino, Fantasia) Born in High Point, North Carolina, June 30, 1984.

Fantasia Monique Barrino — best known simply as Fantasia — was the winning singer in the third season of TV's top-rated series *American Idol* and, it is fair to say, one of the best singers ever to emerge from the series. She also starred, very winningly, in the autobiographical Lifetime TV movie *Life Is Not a Fairy Tale: The Fantasia Barrino Story* (2006). The film, based on her 2005 memoir, is refreshingly honest about the tribulations of Fantasia's life, showing how an unwed mother and illiterate high school dropout can make something of her life.

Her most effective acting was seen on Broadway in April 2007 when she stepped into the starring role of Celie in *The Color Purple*, the musical version of Alice Walker's classic novel. Fantasia added new box office power to the show, and the *New York Post* critic wrote that she had "some elemental quality ... that is either greatness or something close to it." Originally signed for a six-month run, she stayed with the production until January 2008. It has been announced that a musical film version of *The Color Purple* starring Fantasia as Celie will be produced by Oprah Winfrey.

Fantasia played Aretha Franklin (singing "Respect") on an episode of NBC's *American Dreams* (2004) and was the voice of Clarissa in a scene with Krusty the Clown on *The Simpsons* (2005). Since the *American Idol* win, she has also kept busy touring and released the albums *Free Yourself* (2004) and *Fantasia* (2006). She is winner of the 2005 NAACP Image Award for Outstanding Female Artist (in addition to being nominated for two other Image Awards in 2007), and has been nominated for three American Music Awards (2005/07), seven Grammy Awards (2006/08), and two BET Awards (2005).

Feature Films including TV Movies: *Life Is Not a Fairytale: The Fantasia Barrino Story* (TV; 2006), *The Color Purple* (2010).

TV: *American Idol* (winner; 2004), *4th Annual BET Awards* (2004), *Macy's 4th of July Fireworks Spectacular* (2004), *On-Air with Ryan Seacrest* (3 segments; 2004), *Good Day Live* (2004), *2004 MLB All-Star Game*, *The 32nd Annual American Music Awards* (2004), *The 2nd Annual Vibe Awards* (2004), *U-Pick Live* (2004), *Kelly, Ruben & Fantasia: Home for Christmas* (2004), *Macy's Thanksgiving Day Parade* (2004), *The 2004 Billboard Music Awards*, *The Kennedy Center Honors: A Celebration of the Performing Arts* (2004), *American Dreams* ("One in a Million," 2004), *20/20* (2 segments; 2004 and 2005), *The Early Show* (2 segments; 2004 and 2005), *E! True Hollywood Story* (2 segments; "American Idol," 2004 and 2005), *The Tonight Show with Jay Leno* (5 segments; 2004–06), *Today* (2 segments; 2004 and 2006), *The View* (4 segments; 2004–06), *Ellen* (4 segments; 2004–07), *Larry King Live* (2 segments; 2004 and 2007), *Good Morning America* (5 segments; 2004–07), *Live with Regis and Kathie Lee* (4 segments; 2004–07), *Behind the Scenes at the Michael Jackson Trial* (2005), *All That* (2005), *Soul Train* (2005), *All of Us* ("So I Creep," 2005), *The Simpsons* (voice of Clarissa; "A Star Is Torn," 2005), *BET Awards 2005*, *The 19th Annual Soul Train Music Awards* (2005), *36th NAACP Image Awards* (2005), *The Tony Danza Show* (2005), *The 700 Club* (2005), *Access Granted* ("Fantasia: Hood Boy Video," 2006), *An Evening of Stars: Tribute to Stevie Wonder* (2006), *The 48th Annual Grammy Awards* (2006), *Jimmy Kimmel Live!* (2006), *Good Day L.A.* (2006), *The Tyra Banks Show* (2006), *The Megan Mullally Show* (2006), *106 & Park Top 10 Live* (3 segments; 2006–07), *The Late Late Show with Craig Ferguson* (2 segments; 2007), *An Evening of Stars: Tribute to Aretha Franklin* (2007), *The Oprah Winfrey Show* (2007), *The 61st Annual Tony Awards* (2007),

American Idol (2008), *Jimmy Kimmel Live!* (2008), *Extra* (2008), *Grammy Awards Pre-Show* (2008), *An Evening of Stars: Tribute to Patti LaBelle* (2009).

Ferrell, Tyra Born in Houston, Texas, January 28, 1962.

Tyra Ferrell's memorable film roles include *Jungle Fever* (as Orin Goode; 1991), *Boyz N the Hood* (as Mrs. Baxter; 1991), *White Men Can't Jump* (as Rhonda Deane; 1992), *Poetic Justice* (as Jessie; 1993). She had a recurring role on *ER* in 1994 as Dr. Sarah Langworthy; she was Roberta on *The Bronx Zoo* (1987–88); Ricky Bianca on *thirtysomething* (1989–90); and Tamara St. James on *The Cape* (1996–97).

Ferrell was in the national tour of *Dreamgirls* in 1983.

She was nominated for an NAACP Image Award for Outstanding Actress in a Television Movie for *NTSB: The Crash of Flight 323* (2004). Ferrell teaches in her own Actors Studio, covering everything from Acting 101 to advanced class. Her husband is Don Carlos Jackson; they married in 1992.

Feature Films including Video and TV Movies: *So Fine* (1981), *Gimme an "F"* (1984), *Lady Beware* (1987), *Nuts* (1987), *School Daze* (1988), *Side by Side* (TV; 1988), *Tapeheads* (1988), *The Neon Empire* (TV; 1989), *The Mighty Quinn* (1989), *The Exorcist III* (1990), *Jungle Fever* (1991), *Boyz n the Hood* (1991), *Ulterior Motives* (1992), *White Men Can't Jump* (1992), *Equinox* (1992), *Better Off Dead* (TV; 1993), *Poetic Justice* (1993), *The Perfect Score* (2004), *NTSB: The Crash of Flight 323* (2004).

TV: *Hill Street Blues* ("Somewhere Over the Rambo," 1985), *Reaching for the Stars* (1985), *Moonlighting* ("Knowing Her," 1985), *The Twilight Zone* ("Dead Woman's Shoes," 1985), *ABC Afterschool Specials* ("Are You My Mother," 1986), *Hunter* ("Love, Hate and Sporty James," 1986), *Mathnet* ("The Problem of the Missing Baseball," 1987), *The Bronx Zoo* (recurring role of Roberta; 1987–88), *Mr. Belvedere* ("Hooky," 1988), *Quantum Leap* ("So Help Me God," 1989), *City* (recurring role as Wanda Jenkins; 1990), *Full House* ("Bye, Bye Birdie," 1990), *thirtysomething* (recurring role as Ricky Bianca; "Michael's Campaign," "The Burning Bush," "Pulling Away," "Three Year Itch," 1989–90), *The Trials of Rosie O'Neill* ("An Act of Love," 1990), *Wonderworks* ("You Must Remember This," 1992), *ER* (recurring role of Dr. Sarah Langworthy; 1994); *Early Edition* ("Faith," 1997), *The Cape* (recurring role of Tamara St. James; 1996–97), *The Corner* (miniseries; 2000), *Soul Food* ("Truth Be Told," 2000), *The Shield* ("Two Days of Blood," 2002), *Law & Order: Special Victims Unit* ("Futility," 2003).

Tyra Ferrell in ***Boyz N the Hood*** (1991).

Short: *Coochie* (2004).

Fields, Kim (aka Fields-Morgan, Kim) Born in New York, New York, May 12, 1969.

Fields started playing the 12-year-old character "Tootie" Ramsay on NBC's long running hit *The Facts of Life* (1979–88) when she was only nine years old. *The Facts of Life* was a spin-off of the hit series *Diff'rent Strokes*. Mrs. Garrett (Charlotte Rae), the housekeeper on that show, became a housemother to a diverse group of girls at Eastland, a private all-girls school. The original group was Dorothy "Tootie" Ramsay, the gossipy cute one; Blair Warner (Lisa Whelchel), the spoiled, rich one; overweight, naïve, but appealing Natalie Green (Mindy Cohn); and streetwise, pugnacious Jo Polniaczek (Nancy McKeon). Their misadventures carried them through a decade of popularity with the American viewing public.

Fields was discovered after appearing in a commercial for Mrs. Butterworth's pancake syrup. Before appearing on *Facts of Life*, she starred on a short-lived sitcom called *Baby, I'm Back* (1978), and also appeared on *Good Times* (1978–79) as a friend of the Penny Woods character (Janet Jackson).

Kim Fields' parents divorced when she was still a baby. She is part of an acting family. Her real-life mother would eventually play her onscreen mother in both of Fields' popular series

(*Facts of Life*, *Living Single*). Her sister is actress Alexis Fields, who was a cast member on *Sister, Sister*. Her father lives in San Bernadino, California, and remains in close contact with his daughter. Fields discovered later in life that she is of Jamaican heritage, and this has broadened her awareness. She attended Burbank High School and graduated from Pepperdine University in 1990 with a bachelor's degree in communications (broadcast journalism and TV production). While still at Pepperdine, she started her own production company, called Victory Entertainment, Inc.

Lightning struck twice for Kim Fields. She became one of the rare child stars who went on to success as an adult performer. Her second hit series was the FOX sitcom *Living Single* (starting in 1993), in which she played Regine Hunter, a trendy man-hunting buyer for a boutique who lives in a brownstone with the other characters in the series: Kadijah James (Queen Latifah), editor and publisher of *Flavor* magazine; Kadijah's sweet but naïve cousin Synclaire (Kim Coles); and Maxine "Max" Shaw, a gritty, sharped-tongued attorney (Erika Alexander). *Living Single* had a nice feel for urban reality, and the strong cast of varied characters led to an endless variety of interesting storylines. Fields was perfectly cast as Regine and gave a smooth, appealing spin to the character. After the cancellation of *Living Single*, Fields performed spoken word and smooth jazz with the group Imprompt2.

Fields, who has directed episodes of *Living Single* (1996–97), *Kenan & Kel* (1997–99), and the series *Teen Talk* (also associate producer; 2002), has become increasingly more involved in the production and writing end of the industry. She also co-wrote, directed and executive produced *The Silent Bomb* (1994) about a young woman cop with AIDS, shown on HBO. Other credits include a documentary about Grammy-nominated jazz saxophonist Najee (*Najee: Sax in South Africa*; 2006), which Fields produced and directed, and which was shown on the BET J network; the documentary *Discovering Monk and Trane: One Night at Carnegie Hall* (director; 2005); the feature *Tall, Dark and Handsome* (executive producer; 2004); the miniseries *A Royal Birthday* (director, executive producer, writer; 2006); the *2007 Anguilla Tranquility Fest* (director, producer, writer); and the "Krumpshakers" episode of the series *Just Jordan* (director; 2007). Theatre credits include *Fight the Good Fight*, for which she won a 1985 NAACP Image Award, *The Vagina Monologues* (2001), *Pandora's Box* (2003), and *Issues: We Got 'Em All* (2007).

In 1995, she married executive Johnathan Franklin Freeman, and they were divorced in 1998. In July 2007 she married Broadway actor Christopher Morgan, and they have a son named Sebastian Alexander (born 2007).

Feature Films including Video and TV Movies: *The Comeback Kid* (TV; 1980), *Children of Divorce* (TV; 1980), *The Kid with the Broken Halo* (TV; 1984), *Glow* (2000), *Hidden Blessings* (TV; 2000), *Me and Mrs. Jones* (2001), *Bow* (TV; 2005).

TV: *Hallmark Hall of Fame* ("Have I Got a Christmas for You," 1977), *Baby, I'm Back* (recurring role as Angie Ellis; 1978), *Good Times* (2 episodes in the role of Kim; "The Snow Storm," "The Physical," 1978 and 1979), *Roots: The Next Generations* (miniseries; 1979), *Mork & Mindy* ("Mork's Health Hints," 1979), *The Facts of Life* (recurring role of Dorothy "Tootie" Ramsey; 1979–81), *Diff'rent Strokes* (6 episodes as Dorothy "Tootie" Ramsey; 1979–88), *Good Evening, Captain* (1981), *One to Grow On* (1982), *An Evening at the Improv* (1982), *The Facts of Life Goes to Paris* (1982), *Family Feud* (1984), *The 5th Annual Black Achievement Awards* (1984), *Pryor's Place* ("Cousin Rita," 1984), *Battle of the Network Stars XVI* (1984), *Body Language* (3 segments; 1984), *Battle of the Network Stars XVII* (1984), *Disneyland's 30th Anniversary Celebration* (1985), *NBC 60th Anniversary Celebration* (1986), *The 7th Annual Black Achievement Awards* (1986), *Disneyland's Summer Vacation Party* (1986), *The New Hollywood Squares* (1987), *The Facts of Life Down Under* (1987), *Walt Disney World Celebrity Circus* (1987), *20th NAACP Image Awards* (1988), *227* ("The Roommate," 1988), *The 10th Annual Black Achievement Awards* (1989), *The Golden Palace* ("Can't Stand Losing You," 1992), *Martin* ("Radio Days," 1992), *Roc* ("Second Time Around," 1993), *The 1993 Billboard Music Awards*, *The Fresh Prince of Bel-Air* ("The Best-Laid Plans," 1993), *Living Single* (recurring role of Regine Hunter; 1993–97), *The Crew* ("The Mating Season," 1995), *The Fresh Prince of Bel-Air* ("For Whom the Wedding Bells Toll," 1995), *C-Bear and Jamal* (voice; 1996), *Kenan & Kel* (2 episodes in the role of Miss Horn; "The Crush," "The Graduates," 1997 and 1999), *Cupid* ("Hung Jury," 1998), *An Invited Guest* (aka *Uninvited Guest*; 1999), *Strong Medicine* ("Side Effects," 2000), *The Drew Carey Show* ("What's Wrong with This Episodes IV," 2001), *The Facts of Life Reunion* (2001), *Hollywood Squares* (1998), *Child Stars: Their Story* (2000), *Who Wants to Be a Millionaire* (2 segments; 2001), *The Steve Harvey Show* ("Dissin' Cousins," 2001), *Biography* ("Kim Fields: A Little Somethin' Somethin'," 2001), *Me and Mrs. Jones* (2001), *Intimate Portrait* (2 segments; "Kim Fields," "Gladys Knight," 2001 and 2003), *Inside TV Land: African Americans in Television* (2002), *NBC 75th Anniversary Special* (2002), *I Love the '80s* (2002), *Miss Match* ("Matchmaker, Matchmaker," 2003), *Star Dates* (2003), *Cedric the Entertainer Presents* (2003), *9th Annual Soul Train Lady of Soul Awards* (2003), *Good Day Live* (2004), *Def Poetry Jam* (2004), *One on One* (2 episodes in the role of Ms. Swain; "No More Wire Hangers," "You Don't Have to Go Home," 2004), *The Division* (2 episodes in the role of Principal Ogden; "Zero Tolerance," Parts I and II, 2004), *50 Cutest Child Stars: All Grown Up* (archival; 2005), *My Nappy Roots: A Journey Through Black Hair-itage* (2005), *The Comeback* (pilot; 2005), *Eve* ("Banishing Acts," 2006).

Gail Fisher.

Fisher, Gail Born August 18, 1935, Orange, New Jersey; died December 2, 2000.

The contribution of Gail Fisher to the role of black women in television hasn't been sufficiently acknowledged. Fisher was the first African American to win an Emmy Award. It was for her role as Peggy Fair on *Mannix*, and she garnered four additional Emmy nominations for the role. Fisher played a "girl Friday" to Mike Connors' detective Joe Mannix. The fact that she happened to be black was of no import whatsoever. This was a series that predated *Julia*, at a time when few African Americans appeared regularly on any series.

Her long-running role on the detective adventure *Mannix* (1968–75; while the show started in 1967, she joined the cast in the second season) is only part of Fisher's legacy, although it is surely the keystone of her career. In 1961, she was the first black performer to do a national television commercial with spoken lines (for "All" detergent). Fisher's first TV appearance was at age 25 in the syndicated program *Play of the Week* (1959). She was also a beauty pageant winner (Miss Black New Jersey) and a model. One 1950s assignment involved modeling swimsuits for *Hue* (later *Jet*) magazine.

Early on, Fisher was also active in theater: She appeared in *The Rocks Cried Out* (San Francisco Actors' Workshop; 1959); was understudy to Ruby Dee in *Purlie Victorious* (1961); and was in the touring company of *A Raisin in the Sun* (1961–62). Fisher used her earnings as a model to take acting lessons in New York. She studied with Lee Strasberg and was later a member of the Lincoln Center Repertory, where she worked with Elia Kazan and Herbert Blau, among others. It was Blau who gave Fisher her first significant stage credit, a major role in the production of *Danton's Death* (1965) at the Vivian Beaumont Theatre. James Earl Jones, Stacy Keach, Roscoe Lee Browne and Lincoln Kilpatrick were also in the cast.

Once she landed the role on *Mannix*, the course of Fisher's career was essentially set. She debuted in the episode "The Silent Cry." Peggy was a widowed secretary with a young son named Tobey (just as *Julia*'s Diahann Carroll was a widowed working mom with a young son named Corey). Peggy was a distinctive character — earnest, lovely, supportive — loyal to the point that you knew (especially from the look in her eyes) that she loved Joe Mannix. But the show was not quite willing to come right out and say it (although most viewers knew it).

Gail Fisher was one of five children. She was married twice, with two daughters from her first marriage. Her stormy personal life was marred by problems with substance abuse. In her more idyllic moments, Fisher was a painter, a lyricist, and a billiards player (she showed off her skills in a virtually wordless appearance in the "Love and the Hustler" episode of *Love, American Style*; 1969).

Fisher died of kidney failure and emphysema complicated by heavy smoking in 2000 at age 65. Those fans who cared enough to watch her in the obscure "B" film *Mankillers* (1987) saw an overweight, puffy woman who bore little resemblance to their beloved Peggy of yore.

Feature Films including Video and TV Movies: *Every Man Needs One* (1972), *Donor* (TV; 1990), *Mankillers* (1987).

TV: *Play of the Week* ("Simply Heavenly," 1960), *He & She* ("One of Our Firemen Is Missing," 1967), *Mannix* (recurring role of Peggy Fair; 1968–75), *My Three Sons* ("Gossip Incorporated," 1968), *Room 222* (1968), *Love, American Style* (2 segments, "Love and the Baby," and "Love and the Hustler," 1969–71), *Insight* ("Incident on Danker Street," 1970), *It Takes Two* (1970), *The Art Linkletter Show* (1970), *The Tonight Show* (1971), *Soul Train* (1972), *Match Game '73*, *Medical Center* ("Street Girl," 1975), *Fantasy Island* ("Hit Man/The Swimmer," 1979), *The White Shadow* ("The Russians Are Coming," 1980), *General Hospital* (recurring role of Judge Heller; 1983), *Knight Rider* ("Short Notice," 1983), *Hotel* ("Hearts and Minds," 1985), *He's the Major* ("Take My Father, Please," 1986).

Fitzgerald, Ella Born in Newport News, Virginia, on April 25, 1917; died June 15, 1996, Beverly Hills, California.

If you were about to be stranded on the proverbial desert island, and you could only take one record with you, your best bet would probably be one by Frank Sinatra or Ella Fitzgerald. Sinatra, of course, also had a significant acting career, but Fitzgerald cannot make that claim. Even so, she appeared in five features during the course of her career.

Ella Jane Fitzgerald, "The First Lady of Song," was arguably America's finest female jazz singer ever. Her father William and her mother Temperance separated shortly after her birth. In 1934, Fitzgerald won a weekly drawing which allowed her to perform on amateur night at the Apollo Theater. Jazz saxophonist and arranger Benny Carter heard her sing. He knew that this was a rare talent, and he became her mentor and lifelong friend. The following year she met drummer Chick Webb and became the vocalist with his band. She made her first recording in 1936 ("Love and Kisses" for Decca) and experimented with improvisational scat with songs like "You Have to Swing It." Fitzgerald became *the* scat singer, and second place remains vacant.

Her film debut was in Abbott and Costello's *Ride 'Em Cowboy* (1942). Dressed as a cowgirl, she sang her hit "A-Tisket, A-Tasket," with that impossibly mellifluous voice sounding perfect even at that early age. She didn't appear in another feature film for 13 years, when she undertook her first dramatic role as Maggie Jackson in the Jack Webb production *Pete Kelly's Blues* (1955), followed by strictly a singing role in *St. Louis Blues* (1958) and *Let No Man Write My Epitaph* (as Flora; 1960). After the death of Chick Webb, she toured with Dizzy Gillespie, and in the 1950s and 1960s appeared on every major television variety program. She continued to tour the world and to appear at the country's top jazz venues until she succumbed to the effects of diabetes and a heart ailment.

Feature Films including TV Movies: *Ride 'Em Cowboy* (1942), *Pete Kelly's Blues* (1955), *St. Louis Blues* (1958), *Let No Man Write My Epitaph* (1960), *All My Life* (1966).

TV: *Adventures in Jazz* (1949), *Floor Show* (2 segments; 1949), *Calvacade of Stars* (1950), *Chrysler Bandstand* (1951), *Saturday Night Dance Party* (1952), *Four Star Revue* (1952), *The Colgate Comedy Hour* (1955), *Music 55* (1955), *Ford Star Jubilee* ("I Hear America Singing," 1955), *Stage Show* (1956), *Frankie Laine Time* (1956), *The Nat King Cole Show* (2 segments; 1957), *The Ed Sullivan Show* (9 segments; 1957–69), *The Frank Sinatra Show* (1958), *The Milton Berle Show* (1958), *Swing Into Spring!* (1959), *Playboy's Penthouse* (1959), *The Pat Boone Chevy Showroom* (1959), *Sunday Showcase* ("The 1st Annual Grammy Awards," 1959), *The Garry Moore Show* (3 segments; 1959–60), *The Bell Telephone Hour* (3 segments; "American Festival," "The Music of George Gershwin," "Salute to Jerome Kern," 1959–65), *The Dinah Shore Chevy Show* (2 segments; 1960 and 1963), *The Jo Stafford Show* (1961), *President Kennedy's Birthday Salute* (1962), *What's My Line?* (1962), *The Lively Ones* (2 segments; 1962), *The Steve Allen Playhouse* (1963), *The Andy Williams Show* (4 segments; 1965–70), *The Dean Martin Show* (3 segments; 1965–67), *Noche del sábado* (1966), *The Kraft Summer Music Hall* (1966), *The Danny Kaye Show* (1966), *Frank Sinatra: A Man and His Music + Ella + Jobim* (1967), *The Carol Burnett Show* (3 segments; 1967–1969), *The Hollywood Palace* (3 segments; 1967–1970), *The Pat Boone Show* (1968), *Die drehscheibe* (1969), *The Flip Wilson Show* (1970), *This Is Tom Jones* (1970), *Timex All Star Swing Festival* (1972), *Duke Ellington ... We Love You Madly* (1973), *The Tonight Show Starring Johnny Carson* (2 segments; 1973 and 1976), *Bing Crosby: His Life and Legend* (1978), *All-Star Salute to Pearl Bailey* (1979), *Arthur Fiedler: Just Call Me Maestro* (1979), *The Captain and Tennille Songbook* (1979), *The Kennedy Center Honors: A Celebration of the Performing Arts* (1979), *The Carpenters: Music, Music, Music* (1980), *The 33rd Annual Primetime Emmy Awards* (1981), *American Bandstand's 30th Anniversary Special* (1981), *The Kennedy Center Honors: A Celebration of the Performing Arts* (1981), *The American Music Awards* (1982), *Lou Rawls Parade of Stars* (1984), *The White Shadow* ("A Day in the Life," 1985), *20th NAACP Image Awards* (1988), *Sammy Davis, Jr. 60th Anniversary Celebration* (1988), *The 32nd Annual Grammy Awards* (1990), *Aspel & Company* (1990), *Listen Up: The Lives of Quincy Jones* (1990), *Sinatra 75: The Best Is Yet to Come* (1990), *Fuzzy's vaerksted* (1992), *Muhammad Ali's 50th Birthday Celebration* (1992), *Apollo Theatre Hall of Fame* (1993), *Victor Borge's Tivoli 150 år* (archival; 1993), *The Carol Burnett Show: A Reunion* (archival; 1993), *American Masters* (archival; 3 segments; "Adventures in the Kingdom of Swing," "Yours for a Song; The Women of Tin Pan Alley," "The World of Nat King Cole," 1993–2006), *Carnegie Hall Salutes the Jazz Masters: Verve Records at 50* (archival; 1994), *Close to You: Remembering the Carpenters* (archival; 1997), *A Celebration of America's Music* (archival; 1998), *Frank Sinatra: The Very Good Years* (archival; 1998), *A Really Big Show: Ed Sullivan's 50th Anniversary* (archival; 1998), *Sinatra: The Classic Duets* (archival; 1999), *Rhapsody in Black* (archival; 2002), *It's Black Entertainment* (archival; 2002), *Mwah! The Best of the Dinah Shore Show* (archival; 2003), *When I Fall in Love: The One and Only Nat King Cole* (archival; 2003), *Strangers in the Night: The Bert Kaempfert Story* (archival; 2003), *Beyond Tomorrow* (archival; 2006), *Protagonistas del requerdo* (archival; 2006).

Video/DVD: *Ella Fitzgerald: Something to Live For* (archival; 1999), *Oscar Peterson: Music in the Key of Oscar* (1995), *Monterey Jazz Festival: 40 Legendary Years* (1998).

Shorts: *All My Life* (1966).

Foster, Gloria Born in Chicago, Illinois, November 15, 1933; died September 29, 2001, New York, New York.

Gloria Foster studied at Chicago's Goodman Theater. She had a long career in theatre before moving into films. She won Obie Awards for *In White America* (1963) and *A Raisin in the Sun,* and was in the Broadway production of *Having Our Say* (1995).

She made her film debut in Shirley Clarke's unrelenting study of drug addition, *The Cool World* (as Mrs. Custis; 1964). She was also in *Nothing but a Man* (1964), *The Comedians* (as Mrs. Philipot; 1967), *The Angel Levine* (1970), two Bill Cosby misfires, *Man and Boy* (as Ivy Revers; 1972), and *Leonard Part 6* (as Medusa; 1987), and *City of Hope* (as Jeanette; 1991).

Gloria Foster in *Leonard Part 6* (1987).

Her character in both her appearances on *Law & Order* (1992–97) was based on Betty Shabazz, the widow of Malcolm X. Foster appeared on *I Spy*, *The Mod Squad*, *The Atlanta Child Murders* miniseries (as Camille Bell; 1985), *The Cosby Show* and *Soul Food*. She also appeared in the acclaimed TV movies *To All My Friends on Shore* (as Serena; 1972) and *Separate but Equal* (as Buster; 1991). Foster is best known to contemporary audiences for her role as the Oracle in *The Matrix* (1999), and *The Matrix Reloaded* (2007). She was replaced by Mary Alice in *The Matrix Revolutions* (2007).

She was married to and divorced actor Clarence Williams III of TV's *Mod Squad* fame. Foster died during the filming of *The Matrix Reloaded* (she had almost completed her scenes; 2007) from complications of diabetes.

Feature Films including TV Movies: *The Cool World* (1964), *Nothing but a Man* (1964), *The Comedians* (1967), *The Angel Levine* (1970), *To All My Friends on Shore* (TV; 1972), *Man and Boy* (1972), *Top Secret* (TV; 1978), *The Files on Jill Hatch* (TV; 1983), *House of Dies Drear* (TV; 1984), *Leonard Part 6* (1987), *Separate But Equal* (TV; 1991), *City of Hope* (1991), *Percy & Thunder* (TV; 1993), *The Matrix* (1999), *The Matrix Reloaded* (2007).

TV: *Eternal Light* (1964), *I Spy* ("Shana," 1968), *The Outcasts* ("Take Your Lover in the Ring," 1968), *The Mod Squad* (2 episodes in the role of Jenny Wills; "A Hint of Darkness, A Hint of Light," "Return to Darkness, Return to Light," 1969 and 1970), *The White Shadow* ("Artist," 1980), *The Atlanta Child Murders* (miniseries; 1985), *12th Annual People's Choice Awards* (1986), *The Cosby Show* ("Hillman," 1987), *Law & Order* (2 episodes in the role of Satima Tate; "Conspiracy," "Entrapment," 1992–97), *The 49th Annual Tony Awards* (1995), *Soul Food* ("Heart of the Matter," 2000), *Christianity: The First 2000 Years* (miniseries; 2001).

Fox, Crystal R. Born in Tryon, North Carolina, January 16, 1979; died August 25, 2002.

Crystal Fox is best known for her role on *In the Heat of the Night* (1988–94). She played Luann Corbin, an officer with the Sparta, Mississippi, police department, and she later appeared in several made-for-TV movies based on the series. She also played Katie Bell, Boolie's cook, in *Driving Miss Daisy* (1989) and was Miss Doll in *Once Upon a Time ... When We Were Colored* (1995). She also appeared in *Drop Squad* (as Alva; 1994).

Her varied stage credits include *Everybody's Ruby* (Marie; waitress; receptionist; New York Shakespeare Festival, Public Theater, New York, 1999); *Three Sistahs* (Marsha; Metro Stage, Alexandria, Virginia, 2002); *Home* (Patti Mae and other roles; Round House Theatre, Silver Springs, Maryland, 2002); *Antony and Cleopatra* (Charmian; Oregon Shakespeare Festival, Ashland, Oregon, 2003); *The Comedy of Errors* (Adriana; Oregon Shakespeare Festival, 2004); *A Raisin in the Sun* (Ruth Younger; Oregon Shakespeare Festival, Angus Bowmer Theatre, Ashland, Oregon, 2004). She was also Lala Lamazing Grace in *The Colored Museum*, and appeared in productions of *The Amen Corner*; *The Boys from Syracuse*; *From the Mississippi Delta*; and *Seven Guitars* (all at the Alliance Theatre Company, Atlanta, Georgia). Other stage roles are *Bessie's Blues*, *She'll Find Her Way Home* (Jomandi Theatre Productions, Atlanta, Georgia) and *Little Shop of Horrors*, *The Rocky Horror Picture Show* (Theatrical Outfit, Atlanta, Georgia).

Feature Films including TV Movies: *Driving Miss Daisy* (1989), *Drop Squad* (1994), *Once Upon a Time ... When We Were Colored* (1995),

TV: *In the Heat of the Night* (recurring role of Officer Luann Corbin; 1988–94), *In the Heat of the Night: Give Me Your Life* (1994), *In the Heat of the Night: A Matter of Justice* (1994), *In the Heat of the Night: By Duty Bound* (1995), *In the Heat of the Night: Grow Old Along with Me* (1995), *Law & Order* ("White Lie," 2001), PBS *Hollywood Presents* "The Old Settler," 2001), *The Sopranos* ("Pine Barrens," 2001), *Third Watch* ("And Zeus Wept," 2001).

Fox, Vivica A. Born in Indianapolis, Indiana, July 30, 1964.

Perhaps the most underrated of the black actresses of her generation, Vivica Anjanetta Fox is a 5'7" blend of African American and Native American descent. She is the daughter of Everleyna Fox, a pharmaceutical technician, and private school administrator William Fox. This graduate of Arlington High School in Indianapolis moved to California, where she attended Golden West College, graduating with an associate of arts degree in social sciences.

She began her acting career with appearances on such daytime soaps as *Generations*, *The Young and the Restless* and *Days of Our Lives*. Another early credit is a recurring role as Charisse Chamberlain, the fashion designer daughter of Patti LaBelle in *Out All Night* (1992). At age 25 she appeared in the pilot for *Living Dolls* (1989), spun off from an episode of *Who's the Boss*? When it was picked up as an ongoing series, her role was recast, rewritten and given to 21-year-old Halle Berry. Her big film breakthrough was as Will Smith's exotic dancer girlfriend in the giant box office hit about an alien invasion of Earth, the ambitious *Independence Day* (1996). She was equally impressive in the underrated *Set It Off* (1996), the story of four desperate black women who rob a bank. Fox was quite good as the "buppie" insider at the bank who crashes and burns when the plan goes seriously awry.

She earned even greater critical attention for her role as Maxine in the original film version of *Soul Food* (1997), later a successful Showtime series. Her work garnered her MTV Movie Award and NAACP Image Award nominations. She was the best thing about *Why Do Fools Fall in Love* (1998), an ineffective character study of the much-married rock 'n' roll singer Frankie Lymon. She had a starring role as Shant Smith in the witty *Two Can Play That Game* (2001), one of the best of the black romantic comedies. She portrayed a successful business executive who outplays a lascivious Lothario who cheats on her with archrival Conny (Gabrielle Union). Shant institutes her "Ten Day Plan" to whip her man into shape and keep her pride intact. After a string of films unworthy of her ability, she returned to prominence as hired assassin turned suburban mom Vernite Green in Quentin Tarantino's *Kill Bill, Vol. 1* (2003). Her kick-ass, to-the-death duel with Uma Thurman is the best part of the film. She turns up in flashback footage in *Kill Bill, Vol. 2* (2004).

Her television work is quite varied and almost as impressive as her film work. She was a regular on the medical drama *City of Angels* (2000) as Dr. Lillian Price. She replaced Gloria Reuben on the cable series *1-800-Missing* (2004–06), giving the series a grittier, more urban feel. She's also been on *The Fresh Prince of Bel-Air*, *Martin*, *Cosby* and *Curb Your Enthusiasm* as the mother of a family displaced by a disastrous hurricane and taken in by Larry David. She received an NAACP Image Award nomination for her work on the fox-tv sitcom *Getting Personal* (1998).

Recent years have seen Fox biding her time

Top: **Vivica A. Fox.** ***Bottom:*** **Fox with Morris Chestnut in *Two Can Play That Game* (2001).**

as a contestant on *Dancing with the Stars* (2006), dating rapper 50 Cent, and posing for black pin-up magazines such as *King*. She was married to singer Christopher Harvest from 1998 to 2002.

Feature Films including Video and TV Movies: *Born on the Fourth of July* (1989), *The Tuskegee Airmen* (TV; 1995), *Don't Be a Menace to South Central While Drinking Your Juice in the Hood* (1996), *Independence Day* (1996), *Set It Off* (1996), *Booty Call* (1997), *Batman & Robin* (1997), *Soul Food* (1997), *Solomon* (TV; 1997), *Why Do Fools Fall in Love* (1998), *A Saintly Switch* (TV; 1999), *Idle Hands* (1999), *Teaching Mrs. Tingle* (1999), *Hendrix* (TV; 2000), *Double Take* (2001), *Kingdom Come* (2001), *Two Can Play That Game* (2001), *Little Secrets* (2001), *Juwanna Mann* (2003), *Boat Trip* (2002), *Kill Bill: Vol. 1* (2003), *Ride or Die* (2003), *Motives* (2004), *Kill Bill: Vol. 2* (archival; 2004), *Hair Show* (2004), *Ella Enchanted* (2004), *Blast!* (2004), *The Salon* (2005), *Getting Played* (2005), *The Hard Corps: Call to Action* (2006), *Citizen Duane* (2006), *Natural Born Komics* (2007), *Kickin' It Old School* (2007), *Motives 2: Retribution* (2007), *Cover* (2007), *Fa-*

thers of Lies (2008), *San Saba* (2008), *Three Can Play That Game* (2008), *Major Movie Star* (2008), *Caught on Tape* (2008), *Street* (2008), *Miss Nobody* (2008), *Shark City* (2008), *Private Valentine: Blonde and Dangerous* (2009), *Hacking Hollywood* (2009), *Hollywood & Wine* (2009), *Unstable Fables: Tortoise vs. Hare* (2009).

TV: *China Beach* ("Lost and Found," Parts I and II, 1988), *Days of Our Lives* (recurring role as Carmen Silva; 1988), *Generations* (recurring role as Maia; 1989), *Who's the Boss?* ("Living Dolls," 1989), *The Fresh Prince of Bel-Air* ("It Had to Be You," 1991), *Beverly Hills, 90210* ("Ashes to Ashes," 1991), *Family Matters* ("Jailhouse Blues," 1992), *Out All Night* (recurring role as Charisse Chamberlain; 1992), *Matlock* ("The Obsession," 1993), *Martin* ("The Ex-Files," 1995), *The Watcher* ("Second Chances," 1995), *The Young and the Restless* (recurring role as Stephanie Simmons; 1995), *The Bill Bellamy Show* (1996), *Living Single* ("Do You Take This Man's Wallet," 1996), *Arsenio* (recurring role as Vicki Atwood; 1997), *The Chris Rock Show* (1997), *The Rosie O'Donnell Show* (3 segments; 1997–2001), *Late Night with Conan O'Brien* (4 segments; 1997–2004), *Rock 'N' Jock Super Bowl II* (1998), *Getting Personal* ("Sam I Am," 1998), *Essence Awards* (1998), *MADtv* (2 episodes; 1998 and 2002), *Walking After Midnight* (1999), *Happy Hour* (1999), *Cosby* ("War Stories," 1999), *The Hughleys* (3 episodes in the role of Regina; "I Do, I Do Again," Parts I and II, "Milsap Moves Up," 1999), *Hollywood Squares* (22 segments; 1999–2004), *City of Angels* (recurring role of Dr. Lillian Price; 2000), *ESPY Awards* (2000), *Who Wants to Be a Millionaire* (2000), *An Evening of Stars: A Celebration of Educational Excellence* (2001), *The Source Hip Hop Music Awards* (2001), *Howard Stern* (2001), *2001 alma Awards, The Ananda Lewis Show* (2001), *Headliners & Legends: Will Smith* (2001), *The Proud Family* (voice; "Seven Days of Kwanzaa," 2001), *The Late Late Show with Craig Kilborn* (3 segments; 2001–04), *Intimate Portrait* (2 episodes; "Lela Rochon," "Tisha Campbell-Martin," 2000 and 2002), *2nd Annual BET Awards* (2002), *My Wife and Kids* ("Sister Story," 2002), *The View* (2 segments; 2002 and 2005), *America's Most Talented Kid* (2003), *3rd Annual BET Awards* (2003), *MTV Video Music Awards 2003, 9th Annual Soul Train Lady of Soul Awards* (2003), *The Daily Show* (2003), *The Making of Kill Bill* (2003), *VH1 Big in '03* (2003), *Ozzy & Drix* (2 episodes; voice; "An Out of Body Experience," Parts I and II, 2003), *The Twilight Zone* ("Memphis," 2003), *Tremors* ("The Key," 2003), *The Parkers* ("Kimmie Has Two Moms," 2003), *Kim Possible: A Stitch in Time* (voice; 2003), *The Sharon Osbourne Show* (2 segments; 2003 and 2004), *The Magical World of Ella Enchanted* (2004), *Alias* (2 episodes in the role of Toni Cummings; "After Six," "Legacy," 2004), *On-Air with Ryan Seacrest* (2004), *2004 MTV Movie Awards, Punk'd* (2004), *Apollo at 70: A Hot Night in Harlem* (2004), *4th Annual BET Awards* (2004), *Hip-Hop Honors* (2004), *The 2004 Source Hip-Hop Music Awards, The 5th Annual Women Rock* (2004), *Last Call with Carson Daly* (2 segments; 2004 and 2005), *1-800-Missing* (recurring role as FBI Agent Nicole Scott; 2004–06), *My Nappy Roots: A Journey Through Black Hair-itage* (2005), *Eve* ("Kung Fu Divas," 2005), *My Music: Funky Soul Superstars* (2005), *Steve Harvey's Big Time* (2005), *Live with Regis and Kathie Lee* (2005), *The Starlet* (4 segments; judge; 2005), *36th NAACP Image Awards* (2005), *The Greatest: The 40 Hottest Rock Star Girlfriends ... and Wives* (2005), *The 32nd Annual Daytime Emmy Awards* (2005), *Ultimate Superheroes, Vixens and Villains* (2005), *The Late Late Show with Craig Ferguson* (2005), *BET Awards 2005, Hi-Jinks* (2005), *Jimmy Kimmel Live!* (2005), *The Tyra Banks Show* (2005), *The Black Movie Awards* (2005), *Loonatics Unleashed* (voice; "The Cloak of Black Velvet," 2005), *BET Awards* (2006), *An Evening of Stars: Tribute to Stevie Wonder* (2006), *2006 Asian Excellence Awards, All of Us* (2 episodes in the role of Beverly Hunter; "Surprise, Surprise," Parts I and II, 2006), *The 20th Annual Soul Train Music Awards* (2006), *2006 Trumpet Awards, Icons* ("Jamie Kennedy," 2006), *In the Mix* (2 segments; 2006), *Keith Barry: Extraordinary* (2006), *TV Land's Top Ten* ("Top Ten Musical Moments," 2006), *The Wendy Williams Experience* (2006), *Dancing with the Stars* (contestant; 2006), *Quite Frankly with Stephen A. Smith* (2006), *Entertainment Tonight* (4 segments; 2006–07), *Curb Your Enthusiasm* (recurring role as Loretta Black; 2007), *The Game* ("When the Chickens Come Home to Roost," 2007), *Glam God with Vivica A. Fox* (host and judge; 2008).

Frazier, Sheila Born in the Bronx, New York, November 13, 1948.

Sheila Frazier went from the Bronx to Manhattan's Lower East Side to Englewood, New Jersey. She wanted to be an actress since she was a little girl, but first she had to overcome a pronounced stutter. Richard Roundtree (of *Shaft* fame) convinced her to study acting at the Negro Ensemble Company. She also studied at HB Studios in New York with Bill Hickey, and with Dick Anthony Williams at the New Federal Theatre. She was at the Negro Ensemble Company only a few months when Roundtree got her an interview with *Shaft* director Gordon Parks, Jr.

Frazier is best known for her role of Georgia, the love of the drug dealer named Priest (Ron O'Neal) in *Super Fly* (1972) and its sequel *Super Fly T.N.T.* (1973). *Super Fly* was one of the biggest financial successes of its day, played for months, and was reissued several times to appreciative inner city audiences. Priest and Georgia were the black power couple of the seventies, but many social critics complained that the film glorified drug dealers. Frazier disagrees, and notes that Priest was trying to get out of his situation. She also appeared in the famous blaxploitation film *Three the Hard Way* (1974) starring three black action icons: Jim Brown, Fred Williamson and Jim Kelly. That same year she was in the rambunctious *The Super Cops* (1974), another box office success. Frazier went mainstream in the Richard Pryor–Bill Cosby segment of Neil Simon's *California Suite* (1978).

She became a story editor at Pryor's production company when her acting career started to slow down, and started a public relations company called Sheila Frazier & Associates. But she missed show business, so she became the West Coast producer for the *Essence* TV program and helped produce a talk show for Black Entertainment Television. She stayed with BET for almost 13 years as a producer and later as head of their talent department. About a year before leaving BET in 2003, she started Frazier MultiMedia Group, a television, talent acquisition, and special events company, which also trains and coaches people for TV and public appearances. Her first marriage produced a son, Derek McKeith. Her second husband is John Atchinson (married in 2008).

Feature Films including TV Movies: *Super Fly* (1972), *Firehouse* (TV; 1973), *Super Fly T.N.T.* (1973), *The Super Cops* (1974), *Three the Hard Way* (1974), *California Suite* (1978), *The Hitter* (1979), *Two of a Kind* (1983), *All About You* (2001), *The Last Stand* (2006).

TV: *Starsky and Hutch* ("Manchild on the Streets," 1977), *King* (miniseries; 1978), *The Lazarus Syndrome* (recurring role as Gloria Sinclair, 1979), *ABC Afterschool Specials* ("Run, Don't Walk," 1981), *Lou Grant* ("Execution," 1981), *The Phoenix* ("One of Them," 1982), *Dallas* ("Changing of the Guard," 1982), *The Love Boat* (1982), *Gimme a Break!* ("Friendship," 1985), *Magnum P.I.* ("Round and Around," 1985), *Cagney & Lacey* ("Capitalism," 1986), *227* ("The Roommate," 1988), *1st & Ten* ("The Squeeze," 1990), *The West Wing* ("Five Votes Down," 1999), *The District* ("The Jackal," 2000), *Jim Brown: All American* (2002), *E! True Hollywood Story* ("Superfly: The Ron O'Neal Story," 2002), *NCIS* ("Reveille," 2004).

Sheila Frazier.

Freeman, Bee Born in Brooklyn, New York, January 16, 1899; died August 25, 2002.

Bee Freeman was a famed contralto, dancer and actress who was in several Oscar Micheaux films in the 1930s. Her breakthrough was in *Shuffle Along* (1921), the acclaimed Sissle and Black Broadway success. Her signature song was "If You've Never Been Vamped by a Brown Skin, You've Never Been Vamped at All" (and she would prove it every night with her uninhibited dancing). She had a featured role in Micheaux's *Murder in Harlem* (1935). In a risqué production number, Freeman, decked out in a fishnet costume, sings "Harlem Rhythm" before dancing a frenzied tap and shimmy.

Her final film appearance was in Micheaux's *Underworld* (1937). It was her biggest and best screen role as the hostess of a road house in Chicago called "The Red Lily." Freeman is a vamp who is juggling two men, a racketeer (Alfred Chester) and an abusive husband (Oscar Polk). She also attracts a young man (Sol Johnson) who has been invited to Chicago by the racketeer. She shows sincere affection for him, but when they have a falling out over another woman, she conspires with the racketeer to rob him. But the robbery goes awry and the young man is drugged into a stupor. The vamp's jealous husband — guided by detective who has been paid to trail her — shows up unannounced, threatening retaliation. The racketeer shoots the husband. When the young man wakes up, Freeman tells him that *he* shot the husband. The police arrest him, but Freeman's maid knows the truth, a situation she rectifies by strangling the maid. She has a burst of guilt and her head fills with accusing voices. Insane with paranoia, she drives her car into a speeding train.

Feature Films: *A Son of Satan* (1924), *Harlem After Midnight* (1934), *Temptation* (1935), *Murder in Harlem* (aka *Lem Hawkins' Confession*; 1935), *Underworld* (1937).

Gaye, Nona Born in Washington, D.C., September 4, 1974.

Nona Marvisa Gaye is the daughter of storied soul singer Marvin Gaye and his wife Janis (née Hunter). She is also the granddaughter of jazz legend Slim Gaillard, and has a brother named Marvin. Gaye first signed a record contract at age 14. She released the Atlantic Records album *Love for the Future* (1992) and singles like "I'm Overjoyed." She had a relationship with singer, songwriter and showman Prince in the 1990s and contributed to his albums, including several duets. She starred in a Prince-produced TV special shown in Europe called *The Beautiful Experience*, which was basically designed to promote new and upcoming Prince material. In 1993, she signed with the Ford Modeling Agency, beginning a career on the runway.

She also has made her mark as an actress. She played Khalilah Ali in the Will Smith bio pic *Ali* (2001). With no acting experience or any training, she was comfortable and believable in the role of Muhammad Ali's wife. She replaced Aaliyah in the second and third films in the *Matrix* series in the role of Zee (2003) when Aaliyah perished in a plane crash. She was nominated for an NAACP Image Award as Best Supporting Actress for her work in *The Matrix Revolutions*. She did effective voice work in the Christmas film *The Polar Express* (2004), filmed in the "motion capture" technique, a digital variation on rotoscoping. She had a rather meaningless and fairly brief role in Academy Award winning Best Picture *Crash* (2005), as Karen, assistant to the district attorney played by Brendan Frazier. She was Lola Jackson, a former car thief turned businesswoman, in the overwrought spy thriller *xXx: State of the Union* (2005). She was in *The Gospel* (2005) as the wife of an egotistical preacher (Idris Elba).

While she does not intend to abandon her musical career, Gaye's polished acting has been a real outlet for her creative energy. She has a son, Nolan, born in 1997, with former boyfriend Justin Martinez.

Feature Films including TV Movies: *Harlem Nights* (1989), *Ali* (2001), *The Matrix Reloaded* (2003), *The Matrix Revolution* (2003), *Crash* (2004), *The Polar Express* (voice; 2004), *xXx: State of the Union* (2005), *Gospel* (2005), *Blood and Bone* (2008).

TV: *The Making of Ali* (2001), *33rd NAACP Image Awards* (2003), *HBO First Look* (2 segments, *Ali* and *The Matrix Revolution*, 2001 and 2003), *Tavis Smiley* (2004), *Motown 45* (2004).

Gentry, Minnie Born in Norfolk, Virginia, December 2, 1915; died May 6, 1993, New York, New York.

Born Minnie Lee Watson, Minnie Gentry began her acting career with the African American Karamu Theater in Cleveland, Ohio, where she grew up. She returned to Karamu from time to time for 60 years, appearing there for the final time in 1990. She was the daughter of Mincie and Taylor Watson and the grandmother of popular actor Terrence Howard. He credits her with providing the inspiration for his becoming an actor. She studied piano beginning at age nine at the Phyllis Wheatley School of Music. Gentry had a recurring role as Aunt Bess on the daytime drama *All My Children* (1975), and was Miriam George on another soap, *Ryan's Hope* (1979). She guest starred on *The Cosby Show* and *Law & Order.*

Broadway credits include *Lysistrata* (Young Woman's Chorus; October 17–19, 1946); *Ain't Supposed to Die a Natural Death* (October 1971–July 1972); *The Sunshine Boys* (registered nurse; December 1972–April 1974); and *All God's Chillun Got Wings* (Mrs. Harris; March 20–May 4, 1975). She married Lloyd Gentry in 1932; they had one child.

Feature Films including Video and TV Movies: *Georgia, Georgia* (1972), *Come Back, Charleston Blue* (1972), *Black Caesar* (1973), *Claudine* (1974), *Just an Old Sweet Song* (TV; 1976), *Greased Lightning* (1977), *Hollow Image* (TV; 1979), *The Brother from Another Planet* (1984), *America* (1986), *Apprentice to Murder* (1988), *Def by Temptation* (1990), *Bad Lieutenant* (1992).

TV: *All My Children* (recurring role of Aunt Bess; 1975), *Ryan's Hope* (recurring role of Miriam George; 1975), *The Cosby Show* ("The Storyteller," 1990), *Law & Order* ("Poison Ivy," 1990).

Gibbs, Marla Born in Chicago, Illinois, June 14, 1931.

Gibbs married at age 13, and she had three children before she was 20. Her sister is the late actress Susie Garrett. Gibbs is a graduate of Wendell Phillips High School in Chicago. Gibbs is best known for her role as Isabel Sanford and Sherman Helmsley's sarcastic maid Florence Johnston on *The Jeffersons* (and its short-lived spin-off *Checking In*), as well as for the starring role of Mary Jenkins on *227*, for which she co-wrote the theme song. Gibbs worked for United Airlines. She continued working there even after she landed the role on *The Jeffersons* and did not quit until the show was a hit.

The Jeffersons first aired in January of 1975 as a midseason replacement; the series was a spin-off of *All in the Family*, on which the Jeffersons were Archie and Edith Bunker's next door neighbors. George's success with his dry cleaning business leads to his moving the family to a better apartment in Manhattan. Florence Johnson is hired in the first episode, but it quickly becomes obvious that she doesn't get along with George, and that she doesn't plan to do one more iota of work than is necessary. The sitcom *227* co-starred Jackée Harry and was a substantial hit in its own right. Gibbs was a housewife living with her contractor husband Lester Jenkins (Hal Williams).

Marla Gibbs and Robert Guillaume in *The Meteor Man* (1993).

She was a five-time Emmy Award nominee for Outstanding Supporting Actress in a Series for *The Jeffersons* (1981–85). She also received a 1985 Golden Globe for *The Jeffersons* and won an NAACP Image Award in 1982. She was also nominated for NAACP Image Awards for Outstanding Supporting Actress in a Comedy Series for *Martin* (1992), Outstanding Supporting Actress in a Motion Picture for *The Visit* (2000); Outstanding Actress in a Drama Series for *Touched by an Angel* (1994); and had two nominations for Outstanding Actress in a Daytime Drama Series for *Passions* (1998–99). She was Eve Russell's (Tracey Ross) cranky old Aunt Irma on the soap *Passions* (1998–99) and Hattie Mae Hughley on *The Hughleys* (1998–2002).

Since 1990, Gibbs has been operating the Vision Theater Complex (which closed in 1997) and Marla's Memory Lane Jazz and Supper Club (1981–99), both in Los Angeles. She recorded a CD of songs in 2006 called *It's Never Too Late!*

Feature Films including Video and TV Movies: *Sweet Jesus, Preacher Man* (1973), *Black Belt Jones* (1974), *The Missing Are Deadly* (TV; 1975), *Passing Through* (1977), *You Can't Take It with You* (TV; 1979), *Menu for Murder* (TV; 1990), *Last Breeze of Summer* (1991), *Up Against the Wall* (1991), *The Meteor Man* (1993), *Lily in Winter* (TV; 1994), *Border to Border* (1998), *Foolish* (1999), *Lost & Found* (1999), *The Visit* (2000), *Stanley's Gig* (2000), *The Brothers* (2001), *The Ties That Bind* (2006), *Hollywood Desperado: Rebel or Royalty* (documentary; 2007), *Two for Paula* (2007).

TV: *Barney Miller* ("Vigilante," 1975), *The Jeffersons* (recurring role of Florence Johnston; 1975–85), *The Moneychangers* (miniseries; 1976), *Checking In* (as Florence Johnston; 1981), *The Love Boat* (1981), *CBS All American Thanksgiving Day Parade* (1982), *Star Search* (1983), *Pryor's Place* (3 episodes as Miss Stern; "Voyage to the Planet of the Dumb," "Sax Education," "The Show-off," 1984), *Night of 100 Stars II* (1985), *227* (recurring role of Mary Jenkins; "Honesty," "Mary's Brother," "The Refrigerator," "Double Your Pleasure," 1985–88), *Amos 'n' Andy: Anatomy of a Controversy* (1986), *NBC 60th Anniversary Celebration* (1986), *Super Password* (1986), *19th Annual NAACP Image Awards* (1987), *The 13th Annual People's Choice Awards* (1987), *Circus of the Stars 12* (1987), *Living the Dream: A Tribute to Dr. Martin Luther King* (1988), *20th NAACP Image Awards* (1988), *The 9th Annual American Black Achievement Awards* (1988), *The More You Know* (1989), *The Arsenio Hall Show* (1990), *The 4th Annual Soul Train Music Awards* (1990), *Math, Who Needs It?* (1991), *A Different World* ("To Whit, with Love," 1993), *In the Heat of the Night* ("A Baby Called Rocket," 1993), *Empty Nest* ("Mother Dearest," 1993), *50 Years of Funny Females* (archival; 1995), *Burke's Law* ("Who Killed the Hollywood Headshrinker," 1995), *Martin* ("Housekeeper from Hell," 1995), *The Fresh Prince of Bel-Air* ("I, Done," Part II, 1996), *101 Dalmatians* (recurring role as the voice of Duchess; 1997), *The Hughleys* (recurring role of Hattie Mae Hughley; 1998–2002), *Martial Law* (2 episodes in the role of Delores Samuels; "Wild Life," "Big Trouble," 1999), *Happily Ever After: Fairy Tales for Every Child* ("Ali Baba and the Forty Thieves," 1999), *Dawson's Creek* ("First Encounters of the Close Kind," 1999), *Passions* (recurring role as Aunt Irma; 1998–99), *Hollywood Squares* (3 segments; 1999–2004), *Touched by an Angel* ("The Invitation," 2000), *Judging Amy* ("Between the Wanting and the Getting," 2001), *Weakest Link* (2001), *The King of Queens* ("Patrons Ain't," 2002), *The Rerun Show* (2002), *Arli$$* ("Profiles in Agenting," 2002), *I Love the '80s* (2002), *Inside TV Land: African Americans in Television* (2002), *Comedy Central Presents: The Commies* (2003), *Passions* (2004), *Listen Up* ("Thanksgiving," 2004), *SoapTalk* (2004), *BET Comedy Awards* (2004), *TV's Greatest Sidekicks* (2004), *ER* ("Only Connect," 2005), *Cold Case* ("Best Friends," 2005), *The 4th Annual TV Land Awards: A Celebration of Classic TV* (2006), *The Surreal Life* (2006), *Living in TV Land* ("Sherman Helmsley," 2006), *Chappelle's Show* (2006), *The John Kerwin Show* (2006), *In the Mix* (2006), *The 100 Greatest TV Quotes and Catchphrases* (2006), *TV Land Confidential* ("Oddballs & Original Characters," 2007), *Back to the Grind* (2007), *Entertainment Tonight* (2007), *Lincoln Heights* ("The Day Before Tomorrow," 2008), *Hollywood Desperado: Rebel or Royalty* (2008), *Why We Laugh: Black Comedians on Black Comedy* (2008).

Video/DVD: *Drug Free Kids: A Parent's Guide* (1986), *Your Alcohol I.Q.* (1988), *TV in Black: The First Fifty Years* (2004), *5 Keys to a Healthy Heart* (2005).

Gibson, Althea Born in Silver, South Carolina, August 25, 1927; died September 28, 2003, East Orange, New Jersey.

Long before the Williams sisters began their domination of women's tennis, Althea Gibson was blazing a trail for black women on the courts. She won 56 singles and doubles titles during her amateur career before winning 11 major titles as a pro, among them the singles title at the French Open (1956), Wimbledon (1957, 1958), and the U.S. Open (1957, 1958), as well as three straight doubles titles at the French Open (1956–1958). Gibson was New Jersey State Commissioner of Athletics for a decade beginning in 1975. She was the first African American to be voted Female Athlete of the Year by the Associated Press (1957, 1958), and she was sometimes referred to as "the Jackie Robinson of Tennis." Gibson was inducted into the International Tennis Hall of Fame in 1971.

Few are aware that she flirted with an acting career, appearing in John Ford's *The Horse Soldiers* (1958) with John Wayne and William Holden. Although it will never be mistaken for one of the great Ford films, *The Horse Soldiers* was a major production of its era, and the unusual teaming of Wayne and Holden is of interest. Gibson plays Lukey, the maid of the Hannah Hunter character (Constance Towers). She also appeared many years later in 1992's *The Player*, directed by Robert Altman. She has an unaccredited bit as herself. She acted in the "Play to Win" episode of *Thirty-Minute Theatre* (1966), a British Broadcasting Corporation telecast.

Although born in South Carolina, she grew up in Harlem and had somewhat of a troubled youth. Although her family was poor, she attracted the attention of Dr. Walter Johnson, a physician from Lynchburg, Virginia, who was active in the tennis community. Johnson saw to it that she received good training and paved the way for her to appear in higher level competitive matches. The title of her autobiography, written in 1958, was *I Always Wanted to Be Somebody.*

Feature Films: *The Horse Soldiers* (1959), *The Player* (1992).

TV: *What's My Line?* (1958), *Toast of the Town* (3 segments; 1958–59), *This Is Your Life* (1959), *Thirty-Minute Theatre* ("Play to Win," 1966), *The Journey of the African American Athlete* (archival; 1996).

Gilbert, Mercedes Born in Jacksonville, Florida, July 26, 1894; died March 1, 1952, New York, New York.

This novelist, poet, actress and songwriter grew up in Jacksonville and Tampa, Florida, and was the daughter of business owners. She attended Edward Waters College in Jacksonville and later trained as a nurse. While completing her nursing instruction she wrote plays as well as an unpublished book of poems titled *Looking Backward,* many of them in dialect. Gilbert moved to New York in 1916 to work as a nurse. She met and began to collaborate with songwriter Chris Smith, who put her poems to music. She wrote a number of blues songs, including "I've Got the World in a Jug" (1924). As her music career accelerated, she began to act in films and on stage (sometimes concurrently).

Gilbert's most important literary work consisted of three plays, of which only *Environment* survives. *Environment* can be found in *Lost Plays of the Harlem Renaissance: 1920–40* (Detroit: Wayne State University Press, 1996). She also wrote the novel *Aunt Sora's Wooden God* (Boston: The Christopher Publishing House, 1938).

Gilbert appeared in four films and one TV role. She was in the silent *Body and Soul* (1925) with Paul Robeson, directed by Oscar Micheaux. She is Martha Jane, the devout mother of Isabelle (Julia Theresa Russell, a schoolteacher turned actress for Micheaux), who stays by her daughter's bedside as she dies of an unspecified illness. Most of the movie (including Isabelle's death) turns out to be a dream sequence. In Michaeux's original cut, her death was presented as real, but he had to re-edit the film to appease the censor board, mostly because of the venality of Robeson's preacher character, who then became two characters: the preacher and a twin posing as the preacher, to keep the preacher from appearing as the villain.

She was also in *The Call of His People* (1921), Micheaux's *The Exile* (sandwiching in a small role while appearing on Broadway in *Green Pastures*; 1931), director Edgar G. Ulmer's *Moon Over Harlem* (1939), and in "The Green Dress" episode of the Arch Oboler TV series *Lights Out* (1950), based on his radio program.

Her major acting career was in theater. She made her Broadway debut in *Lace Petticoat* as Mammy Dinah (January 1927). Two months later she was Honoria in *Lost.* In June–July 1929 she was Rhodendra Frost in the all black cast comedy *Bomboola.* Her key theatrical role was as Zipporah in *The Green Pastures* (1930–31 and again in 1935). She was in *Play, Genius, Play!* (as Ambrosia; October–November 1935); *How Come, Lawd?* (Mother; September–October 1937); *The Searching Wind* (as Sophronia; 1944–45); *Carib Song* (as The Tall Woman; 1945); *Lysistrata* (as Lampito; October 1946); and *Tobacco Road* (as Sister Bessie Rice; March 1950). She was also the female lead in Langston Hughes' *Mullato* (1936). During the forties, she toured the U.S. and Canada with a one-woman show of original material.

Feature Films: *The Call of His People* (1921), *Body and Soul* (1925), *The Exile* (1931), *Moon Over Harlem* (1939).

TV: *Lights Out* ("The Green Dress," 1950).

Givens, Robin Born in New York, New York, November 27, 1964.

Robin Givens is a skilled, sometimes subtle actress, but her skills have inevitably been overshadowed by her personal life, most specifically her marriage to heavyweight boxing champion Mike Tyson (1988–89) and an affair with Brad Pitt.

Robin Simone Givens is the daughter of Ruth and Reuben Givens. She was raised with her younger sister Stephanie by their mother in suburban Westchester County in New York. She showed an interest in music and studied violin, but that interest soon gave way to an emphasis on acting. At age 10 she began studying drama at Manhattan's American Academy of Dramatic Arts. At only 15, she enrolled in a pre-med program at Sarah Lawrence College, but left in her junior year, again to fulfill her desire to act.

She made appearances on *The Cosby Show* and *Diff'rent Strokes* before landing the role that made her famous: Darlene Merriman on *Head of the Class*, a teen-oriented slice of high school life. She stayed with the show from 1986 to 1989. Already both her acting skills and the template for her career were apparent. Givens would specialize in roles as pretty, ego-driven characters, often with some redeeming values, but also a bit manipulative. But her career shows that she has more range than that: She's vulnerable and appealing as the servant who finds herself in an interracial relationship in the little-seen *Foreign Student* (1994).

The quintessential Givens' role is probably in *A Rage in Harlem* (1991), where she is very much the femme fatale, giving a new meaning to the "noir" in film noir. She's also at the top of her game in Eddie Murphy's *Boomerang* (1992), playing Jacqueline Broyer, the cold, manipulative businesswoman who becomes the new boss of the film's womanizing central character. Her big screen career continued with a role in Tyler Perry's *The Family That Preys* (2008). She is Abigail Dexter, the woman hired instead of the owner's arrogant son to run a construction company. She is seen to good advantage in the 1989 Oprah Winfrey miniseries *The Women of Brewster Place* as Kiswana, a militant young woman seeking to organize her neighbors, and in the TV movies *A Face to Die For* (1996), and *The Penthouse* (1989), a suspense thriller that was one of the early stalker movies.

Robin Givens.

Her most unusual TV assignment was replacing hostess Mother Love in 2000 on the *Forgive or Forget* show. The strange format involved real people seeking to reconcile with friends or family members they had wronged (tearful singer-actress Melba Moore turned up on the show). Givens did a really nice job amid all the pathos and the angst, and it gave audiences a chance to see a more measured and charitable side of her. But it did not catch on with audiences and was soon cancelled.

Givens has done some theatre work in recent years. She turned up off–Broadway in *The Vagina Monologues* (1999), and took over the role of Roxy Hart on Broadway in *Chicago* (1996). Critical reaction to both performances was positive. In 2007, she toured the country in Tyler Perry's play *Men, Money and Golddiggers*. The year 2007 also saw the publication of her well-received book *Grace Will Lead Me Home*, published by Miramar. It is a treatise on the power of faith and the strength it provides. She also discusses how domestic violence stalked her family for three generations, and sets the record straight on a more spiritual side of her persona not often reflected in the media.

She remarried in 1997 to tennis instructor Svetozar Marinkovic, but the marriage set a record for brevity, since the two apparently separated on the day of the marriage. She has two sons: Buddy; born 1992; and William, born 1999. William is the son of professional tennis player Murphy Jensen.

Feature Films including Video and TV Movies: *Beverly Hills Madam* (TV; 1986), *The Penthouse* (TV; 1989), *A Rage in Harlem* (1991), *Boomerang* (1992), *Foreign Student* (1994), *Blankman* (1994), *Dangerous Intentions* (1995), *A Face to Die For* (1996), *Secrets* (1998), *Michael Jordan: An American Hero* (TV; 1999), *Everything's Jake* (2000), *The Expendables* (TV; 2000), *Spinning Out of Control* (TV; 2001), *The Elite* (2001), *Book of Love* (2002), *Antibody* (2002), *Head of State* (2003), *A Good Night to Die* (2003), *Love Chronicles* (2003), *Hollywood Wives: The New Generation* (TV; 2003), *Flip the Script* (2005), *Captive Hearts* (TV; 2005), *Restraining Order*

(2006), *Little Hercules* (2008), *Queen of Media* (2008), *The Family That Preys* (2008), *The Verdict* (TV; 2008), *4-Bidden* (2009).

TV: *The Cosby Show* ("Theo and the Older Woman," 1985), *Diff'rent Strokes* ("The Big Bribe," 1986), *Soul Train* (1986), *Philip Marlowe, Private Eye* ("Pickup on Noon Street," 1986), *Head of the Class* (recurring role of Darlene Merriman; 1986–89), *The 9th Annual American Black Achievement Awards* (1988), *The Women of Brewster Place* (miniseries; 1989), *Angel Street* (recurring role as Detective Anita King; 1992), *HBO First Look* (2 episodes; "The Making of Blankman," "Head of State," 1994 and 2003), *Me and the Boys* (2 episodes in the role of Rita; "Goldilocks," "The B Word," 1995), *The Fresh Prince of Bel-Air* ("Cold Feet, Hot Body," 1995), *Court House* (recurring role as Suzanne Graham; 1995), *Sparks* (recurring role as Wilma Cuthbert; 1996), *In the House* (3 episodes in the role of Alex; "Love on a One-Way Street," "My Crazy Valentine," "Three the Hard Way," 1996), *Moesha* ("Strike a Pose," 1997), *The Love Boat: The Next Wave* ("Don't Judge a Book By Its Lover," 1999), *Cosby* (2 episodes as Ms. Malone; "Afterschool Delight," "The Vesey Method," 1999), *The Howard Stern Radio Show* (2 segments; 1999–2000), *Howard Stern* (4 segments; 1999–2000), *Intimate Portrait* (2000), *Talk Soup* (2000), *Chicken Soup for the Soul* ("The Right Thing," 2000), *DAG* ("Jennifer Returns," 2000), *Forgive or Forget* (host; 2000), *ESPN Sports Century* (archival; 2002), *One on One* (2 episodes in the role of Sheila; "Spy Games," "Spy Games Reloaded," 2003 and 2004), *Driven* (2004), *The Oprah Winfrey Show* (2004), *The View* (2 segments; 2006), *Howard Stern on Demand* (2007), *House of Payne* (recurring role as Tanya; "Unexpected Results," "Sex, Lies and Videotapes," "It's Getting Hot in Here," 2008), *Burn Notice* ("Scatter Point," 2008).

Music Videos: *He Wasn't Man Enough* (2000).

Goldberg, Whoopi Born in New York, New York, November 13, 1955 (some sources say 1949, 1950).

This quintessential black actress was born in the Chelsea section of Manhattan. Her mother was a nurse and teacher who raised her son Clyde and daughter Caryn Elaine Johnson on her own after their preacher father abandoned the family. The family lived in a public housing project. At the peak of her career, Caryn — better known as Whoopi Goldberg — was America's biggest African American female star ever. She was the second black female to win an Academy Award (after Hattie McDaniel). She also has won an Emmy, Grammy, and Tony Award, and two Golden Globes. She is renowned as an actress, a comedienne, a radio and TV talk show host, and an author. Her achievements as an activist and fund raiser have been most prominently through the Comic Relief specials on HBO, which began in 1980, and as a unicef Goodwill Ambassador.

Whoopi Goldberg and Sam Elliott in *Fatal Beauty* (1987).

Her Academy Award was for Best Supporting Actress for *Ghost* (1991). Her performance as fake psychic Oda Mae Brown — who reluctantly comes to realize she's the real thing when she's contacted by the ghost of Sam Wheat (Patrick Swayze) — is a wonderful blend of humor and drama. We come to know and love this character through the course of this touching film. She also received an Academy Award nomination for her performance as Celie in *The Color Purple* (1985). Goldberg's Celie is a poignant, subtle realization of Alice Walker's immortal character, a poor, abused young black woman who eventually becomes a successful businesswoman and reunites with her missionary sister who had gone to Africa.

Her Emmy Award was for her talk show hosting on daytime TV and for Outstanding Special, *Beyond Tara: The Extraordinary Life of Hat-*

tie McDaniel (2001) (she has four other daytime Emmy nominations). The Tony Award was for her work as producer of *Thoroughly Modern Millie*, which enjoyed a long run on Broadway; the Grammys were for producer of the cast recording of the show, and for *Whoopi Goldberg Original Broadway Show Recording*. She was also the recipient of three People's Choice Awards, and was awarded the prestigious Mark Twain Prize for American Humor in a ceremony at the Kennedy Center. She has two Golden Globe Awards, for Best Actress in a Motion Picture Drama for *The Color Purple* and Best Actress in a Supporting Role in a Motion Picture for *Ghost*.

Infatuated with performing from an early age, she made her debut at age eight with the Helena Rubinstein Children's Theatre at the Hudson Guild. Later, she sang in the choruses of Broadway shows like *Hair* and *Pippin*. She left her first husband and moved with her daughter to California in 1974. Goldberg began her career in character-driven avant-garde comedy, performing with the San Diego Repertory Theatre and the improvisational theatre group Spontaneous Combustion. She can first be seen on screen in *Citizen* (subtitled *I'm Not Losing My Mind, I'm Giving It Away;* 1982). Then she created a one-woman collection of character studies called *The Spook Show* (1983). Director Mike Nichols saw her work, loved it, and brought her to Broadway. *Whoopi Goldberg* ran from October 24, 1984, to March 10, 1985, establishing her as an "overnight" comedy star. Steven Spielberg saw the show, and noticed the poignancy beneath the humor in her various characters. This led him to cast her in *The Color Purple*, the beginning of a long and storied film career.

Goldberg was now able to handpick starring projects, appearing in a rapid succession of films, but although she never failed to add deft comedic touches and interesting character quirks to her performances, too many of the films were simply genre programmers, and eventually her star began to wane. There were action films *Jumpin' Jack Flash* (1986), *Burglar* (1987), and *Fatal Beauty* (1987), which essentially emulated *Beverly Hills Cop* and the other Eddie Murphy action comedies of the era. There were well-intentioned soap operas like *Clara's Heart* (1988), *Homer and Eddie* (1989) and *The Long Walk Home* (1990). But the time stretch between *The Color Purple* and *Ghost* is relatively devoid of quality.

Goldberg is nothing if not a survivor, however, and just as her career started to flag again after *Ghost*, along came the immensely successful *Sister Act* (1992) and its sequel *Sister Act 2: Back in the Habit* (1993). Goldberg gives assured, relaxed comic performances in both films as a gangster's moll who is forced to go into hiding as a nun.

Worthy films were still to come—*Corrina, Corrina* (1994), *Girl Interrupted* (1999)—but by and large her career eventually began to consist of voiceover work in animated films (most memorably *The Lion King*, 1994), and smaller roles in obscure films. When *Theodore Rex* (1995) went directly to video without benefit of a theatrical release, it was clear the wheels had fallen off the Whoopi express.

But not for very long. Goldberg exchanged her acting career for hosting duties on the popular Barbara Walters–produced ensemble talk show *The View*, beginning in 2007. Here she has the ideal forum for expressing her often controversial but always thoughtful sociopolitical beliefs, and gets to interview presidential candidates and other top newsmakers of the day.

Other television work has included starring for two seasons in *Bagdad Café* (1990), based on the Rainer Werner Fassbinder film. She was in 28 episodes of *Star Trek: The Next Generation* in the role of the acerbic bartender Guinan, and reprised her role in two *Star Trek* films (1988 and 1993). She was also the host of *The Whoopi Goldberg Show*, a daytime talk show (1992), but she reached a career low with *Whoopi* (2003–04), an unfunny sitcom that struggled through a single season. On

Whoopi Goldberg.

the other hand, she has been an able host on the Academy Awards.

Her books are *Alice*, a children's book that gives a contemporary urban spin to a tale with touches of *Alice in Wonderland* (Bantam; 1992); *Book*, a collection of her thoughts on a variety of topics (Bantam; 1996); and *Whoopi's Big Book of Manners*, another children's book, a lighthearted look at etiquette for kids (Hyperion; 2006). The indefatigable Goldberg even tried her hand at a nationally syndicated radio program (*Waking Up with Whoopi*, 2006–08). Goldberg has been married three times, with a daughter, Alexandrea, from the first marriage (born in 1973). Her husbands were Alvin Martin (1973–79), David Claessen (1986–88), and Lyle Trachtenberg (1994–95). She has also had well-publicized relationships with Frank Langella and Ted Danson.

Feature Films including Video and TV Movies: *Citizen* (1982), *The Color Purple* (1985), *Jumpin' Jack Flash* (1986), *Burglar* (1987), *Fatal Beauty* (1987), *The Telephone* (1988), *Clara's Heart* (1988), *Comicitis* (1989), *Beverly Hills Brats* (1989), *The Trouble with Teachers* (1989), *Kiss Shot* (TV; 1989), *Homer and Eddie* (1989), *Ghost* (1990), *The Long Walk Home* (1990), *Blackbird Fly* (1991), *Soapdish* (1991), *The Player* (1992), *Sister Act* (1992), *Sarafina!* (1992), *Defenders of Dynatron City* (TV; voice; 1992), *Loaded Weapon 1* (1993), *Made in America* (1993), *Sister Act 2: Back in the Habit* (1993), *Yuletide in the 'Hood* (TV; voice; 1993), *Naked in New York* (1993), *The Lion King* (voice; 1994), *A Cool Like That Christmas* (voice; 1994), *The Little Rascals* (1994), *Corrina, Corrina* (1994), *The Pagemaster* (voice; 1994), *The Sunshine Boys* (TV; 1995), *Boys on the Side* (1995), *Moonlight and Valentino* (TV; 1995), *Theodore Rex* (1995), *Eddie* (1996), *Bordello of Blood* (1996), *Bogus* (1996), *The Associate* (1996), *Ghosts of Mississippi* (1996), *A Christmas Carol* (voice; 1997), *Pitch* (1997), *In the Gloaming* (TV; 1997), *Destination Anywhere* (1997), *Cinderella* (TV; 1997), *Alegria* (1998), *Titey* (1998), *An Alan Smithee Film: Burn, Hollywood, Burn* (1998), *How Stella Got Her Groove Back* (1998), *Rudolph the Red-Nosed Reindeer* (voice; 1998), *A Knight in Camelot* (TV; 1998), *The Rugrats Movie* (voice; 1998), *Junket Whore* (1998), *Our Friend, Martin* (voice; 1999), *Alice in Wonderland* (TV; 1999), *The Deep End of the Ocean* (1999), *Jackie's Back!* (TV; 1999), *The Magical Legend of the Leprechauns* (TV; 1999), *Girl, Interrupted* (1999), *The Adventures of Rocky & Bullwinkle* (2000), *A Second Chance at Life* (2000), *More Dogs Than Bones* (2000), *Golden Dreams* (voice; 2001), *What Makes a Family* (TV; 2001), *Kingdom Come* (2001), *Monkeybone* (2001), *Rat Race* (2001), *The Hollywood Sign* (2001), *Call Me Claus* (TV; 2001), *Madeline: My Fair Madeline* (TV; voice; 2002), *Searching for Debra Winger* (documentary; 2002), *It's a Very Merry Muppet Christmas Movie* (TV; 2002), *Star Trek: Nemesis* (2002), *Good Fences* (TV; 2003), *Harry for the Holidays* (TV; 2003), *Blizzard* (voice; 2003), *Pinocchio 3000* (voice; 2004), *SuperBabies: Baby Geniuses 2* (2004), *Jiminy Glick in Lalawood* (2004), *Racing Stripes* (voice; 2005), *The Aristocrats* (documentary; 2005), *Mississippi Rising* (TV; 2005), *The Magic Roundabout* (voice; 2005), *Farce of the Penguins* (voice; 2006), *Doogal* (voice; 2006), *Everyone's Hero* (voice; 2006), *If I Had Known I Was a Genius* (2007), *Mr. Warmth: The Don Rickles Project* (documentary; 2007), *Homie Spumoni* (2007), *Stream* (2007), *Snow Buddies* (voice; 2008).

TV: *Whoopi Goldberg: Direct from Broadway* (1985), *Night of 100 Stars II* (1985), *Moonlighting* ("Camille," 1986), *Comic Relief* (1986), *The 12th Annual People's Choice Awards* (1986), *The American Film Institute Salute to Billy Wilder* (1986), *The 43rd Annual Golden Globe Awards* (1986), *The 58th Annual Academy Awards* (1986), *Saturday Night Live* (2 segments; 1986 and 1998), *The Importance of Being Funny in America* (1987), *Dolly* (1987), *Happy 100th Birthday, Hollywood* (1987), *Funny, You Don't Look 200: A Constitutional Vaudeville* (1987), *The Pointer Sisters: Up All Nite* (1987), *Comic Relief '87, 19th NAACP Image Awards* (1987), *The 29th Annual Grammy Awards* (1987), *The 1st Annual American Comedy Awards* (1987), *Carol, Carl, Whoopi and Robin* (1987), *The Tonight Show Starring Johnny Carson* (1987), *Nelson Mandela 70th Birthday Tribute* (1988), *Christmas at Pee Wee's Playhouse* (1988), *Whoopi Goldberg: Fontaine ... Why Am I Straight?* (1988), *Star Trek: The Next Generation* (recurring role of Guinan; 1988–93), *Whoopi Goldberg Presents Billy Connolly* (1989), *The Debbie Allen Special* (1989), *CBS Schoolbreak Special* ("My Past Is My Own," 1989), *Comic Relief III* (1989), *Circus of the Stars 15* (1990), *Help Save Planet Earth* (1990), *Motown 30: What's Goin' On!* (1990), *Smokey Robinson: The Quiet Legend* (1990), *Tales from the Whoop: Hot Rod Brown Class Clown* (1990), *Happy Birthday, Bugs! 50 Looney Years* (1990), *Red Hot and Blue*

(1990), *Bagdad Café* (recurring role as Brenda; 1990), *A Different World* ("If I Should Die Before I Wake," 1991), *Star Trek 25th Anniversary Special* (1991), *Wisecracks* (1991), *Tales from the Crypt* ("Dead Wait," 1991), *Big Bird's Birthday or Let Me Eat Cake* (1991), *Captain Planet and the Planeteers* (voice; "Mind Pollution," 1991), *Voices That Care* (1991), *Comic Relief IV* (1991), *The 63rd Annual Academy Awards* (1991), *The 45th Annual Tony Awards* (1991), *Walt Disney World's 20th Anniversary Celebration* (1991), *The Whoopi Goldberg Show* (host; 1992), *The 64th Annual Academy Awards* (1992), *The Comedy Store's 20th Birthday* (1992), *Comic Relief V* (1992), *Hurricane Relief* (1992), *The Magical World of Chuck Jones* (1992), *The 34th Annual Grammy Awards* (1992), *The 65th Annual Academy Awards* (1993), *Mo Funny: Black Comedy in America* (archival; 1993), *Late Show with David Letterman* (2 segments; 1993–2003), *Carol Burnett: The Special Years* (archival; 1994), *The 66th Annual Academy Awards* (1994), *All-Star 25th Birthday: Stars and Street Forever!* (archival; 1994), *But ... Seriously* (archival; 1994), *The Arsenio Hall Show* (1994), *20 Years of Comedy on HBO* (archival; 1995), *50 Years of Funny Females* (archival; 1995), *ABC Afterschool Specials* ("Bonnie Raitt Has Something to Talk About," 1995), *In the Wild* ("Zoo Babies with Whoopi Goldberg," 1995), *The American Film Institute Salute to Steven Spielberg* (1995), *The Celluloid Closet* (1995), *Happily Ever After: Fairy Tales for Every Child* (1995), *Comic Relief VII* (1995), *Rolling Stones: Voodoo Lounge* (1995), *Classic Stand-Up Comedy of Television* (archival; 1996), *The Good, the Bad and the Beautiful* (archival; 1996), *Comic Relief's American Comedy Special* (1996), *MADtv* (1996), *The 66th Annual Academy Awards* (1996), *Muppets Tonight* (1996), *The Rosie O'Donnell Show* (12 segments; 1996–2002), *The Tonight Show with Jay Leno* (3 segments; 1996–2001), *Mary Pickford: A Life on Film* (1997), *Tracey Takes On...* ("Supernatural," 1997), *The 53rd Presidential American Gala: An American Journey* (1997), *The Rodman World Tour* (1997), *Sports on the Silver Screen* (1997), *The 51st Annual Tony Awards* (1997), *Mother Goose: A Rappin' and Rhymin' Special* (1997), *In & Out* (1997), *The Chris Rock Show* (1997), *Smap x Smap* (1998), *30 Years of Billy Connolly* (1998), *The 70th Annual Academy Awards* (1998), *The Roseanne Show* (1998), *TFI Friday* (1998), *Late Lunch* (1998), *Bob Hope: The Road to the Top* (1998), *Comic Relief VIII* (1998), *AFI's 100 Years ... 100 Movies* (1998), *Penn & Teller's Sin City Spectacular* (19??), *L.A. Doctors* ("A Prayer for the Living," 1998), *Inside the Actor's Studio* (1998), *The Nanny* (2 episodes; "Making Whoopi," "The Pre-Nup," 1998), *A Very Special Christmas from Washington, D.C.* (1998), *E! True Hollywood Story* (archival; 2 segments; "Elizabeth Taylor," "Liza Minnelli," 1998 and 2002; 2 segments with new footage: "Richard Pryor," "Hollywood Squares," 2003), *Great Performances* (2 episodes; "Creating Ragtime," "Chuck Jones: Extremes and In-Betweens: A Life in Animation," 1998 and 2000), *Hollywood Squares* (panelist; 1998–2002), *Pulp Comics: Caroline Rhea* (1999), *AFI's 100 Years ... 100 Stars* (1999), *Celebrity Profile* ("Janine Turner," 1999), *HBO First Look* ("The Making of 'Girl Interrupted,'" 1999), *Foxbusters* (voice; 1999), *Thursday Night with Oscar* (1999), *Get Bruce* (1999), *The 71st Annual Academy Awards* (1999), *The Martin Short Show* (1999), *Our World: Zoo Babies with Whoopi Goldberg* (2000), *6th Annual Screen Actors Guild Awards* (2000), *Here's to You, Charlie Brown: 50 Great Years* (2000), *Biography* ("George Reeves: The Perils of a Superhero," 2000), *Movie Stars* (2000), *Celebrity Dish* (2000), *MonsterFest 2000: The Classics Come Alive, Strong Medicine* (4 episodes in the role of Dr. Lydia Emerson; 2000), *Cursed* (2001), *Celebrity Profile* (archival; "Brooke Shields," 2001), *Talking to Americans* (2001), *The Making of a "Charlie Brown Christmas"* (2001), *Howard Stern* (2001), *The Mark Twain Prize: Whoopi Goldberg* (2001), *I Love Lucy's 50th Anniversary Special* (2001), *Express Yourself* (2001), *Beyond Tara: The Extraordinary Life of Hattie McDaniel* (2001), *America: A Tribute to Heroes* (2001), *Whose Line Is It Anyway?* (2 episodes; 2001 and 2002), *The 56th Annual Tony Awards* (2002), *Showboy* (2002), *The 74th Annual Academy Awards* (2002), *Cool Women* (2002), *Leute heute* (2002), *Liberty's Kids: Est. 1776* (2002), *Absolutely Fabulous* ("Gay," 2002), *V Graham Norton* (2003), *Heroes of Black Comedy* (2003), *Unchained Memories: Readings from the Slave Narratives* (2003), *Freedom: A History of Us* (5 episodes; "Working for Freedom," "What is Freedom," "Wake Up America," "Let Freedom Ring," "A Fatal Contradiction," 2003), *The Disco Ball ... A 30-Year Celebration* (2003), *Daytona 500: The Great American Race Pre-Race Show* (2003), *Bitter Jester* (2003), *Pauly Shore Is Dead* (2003), *The Desilu Story* (2003), *Beyond the Skyline* (2003), *Richard Pryor: I Ain't Dead Yet* (2003), *Willie Nel-*

son and Friends: Live and Kickin' (2003), *Intimate Portrait* ("Penny Marshall," 2003), *Late Night with Conan O'Brien* (2 segments; 2003 and 2004), *Whoopi* (recurring role of Mavis Rae; 2003–04), *The Tony Danza Show* (2004), *The N-Word* (2004), *Sesame Street Presents: The Street We Live On* (2004), *When Stand-Up Comics Ruled the World* (archival; 2004), *Whoopi's Littleburg* (recurring role as Mayor Whoopi; 2004), *2004 Hispanic Heritage Awards*, *Live with Regis and Kelly* (4 segments; 2004–05), *Movies That Shook the World* ("Shaft," 2005), *An Evening of Stars: Tribute to Quincy Jones* (2005), *The 77th Annual Academy Awards* (2005), *Whoopi: Back to Broadway, The 20th Anniversary* (2005), *Real Time with Bill Maher* (2 segments; 2005), *Bear in the Big Blue House* ("The Great Bandini," 2005), *Christmas in Rockefeller Center* (2005), *Corazon de...* (archival; 2 segments; 2005–06), *Ellen* (2 segments; 2005–06), *Cinema tres* (archival; 2006), *The 78th Annual Academy Awards* (2006), *African American Lives* (4 episodes; "The Promise of Freedom," "Listening to Our Past," "Searching for Our Names," "Beyond the Middle Passage," 2006), *Sunday Morning Shootout* (2006), *AFI's 100 Years ... 100 Cheers: America's Most Inspiring Movies* (2006), *Girls Who Do: Comedy* (2006), *American Masters* (2 episodes; "The World of Nat King Cole," "Annie Leibovitz: Life Through a Lens," 2006), *It's Showtime at the Apollo* (2006), *Comic Relief 2006*, *So NoTORIous* ("Cursed," 2006), *Law & Order: Criminal Intent* ("To the Bone," 2006), *Everybody Hates Chris* (2 episodes in the role of Louise; "Everybody Hates Rejection," "Everybody Hates a Liar," 2006), *30 Rock* ("The Rural Juror," 2007), *Happy Birthday, Elton!* (2007), *The Word According to Whoopi* (2007), *18th Annual glaad Media Awards* (2007), *The Sophisticated Misfit* (2007), *Entertainment Tonight* (2007), *The View* (co-host; 2007–08), *Letters to Santa: A Muppet Christmas* (2008).

Video/DVD: *Doctor Duck's Super Secret All-Purpose Sauce* (1986), *Celebrity Guide to Wine* (1990), *Oscars Greatest Moments* (archival; 1992), *The Directors: Norman Jewison* (1997), *Michael Jackson: HIStory on Film, Vol. II* (1997), *Jackie Chan: My Story* (1998), *Rescued from the Closet* (2001), *Declaration of Independence* (2003), *Inside the Industry* (2003), *TV in Black: The First Fifty Years* (archival; 2004), *Late Night with Conan O'Brien: The Best of Triumph the Insult Comic Dog* (2004), *Our Country USA to Z* (2007).

Shorts: *Descendants* (voice; 2008), *Stream* (voice; 2008).

Gomez-Preston, Reagan Born in Detroit, Michigan, April 24, 1980.

Reagan Gomez-Preston was born to an African American mother and Puerto Rican father. She married producer DeWayne Tunentine in 2003. Preston-Gomez attended the famous Freedom Theatre in Philadelphia. She starred with Robert Townsend as his daughter Zaria Petersen on *The Parent 'Hood*. She also played Francine opposite Holly Robinson-Peete on the short-lived UPN sitcom *Love, Inc.* (2005–06).

After small roles in *Jerry Maguire* (1996) and *Love Don't Cost a Thing* (2003), her breakout film role was in the crime thriller *Never Die Alone* (2004). She also appeared with Mo'Nique, Vivica A. Fox and Taraji P. Henson in *Beauty Shop* (2005).

Feature Films including TV Movies: *Freaky Friday* (1995), *Jerry Maguire* (1996), *Carmen: A Hip-Hopera* (TV; 2001), *Dead Above Ground* (2002), *Love Don't Cost a Thing* (2003), *Never Die Alone* (2004), *Doing Hard Time* (2004), *Hair Show* (2004), *Trois 3: The Escort* (2004), *Beauty Shop* (2005).

TV: *Moesha* ("Hakeem's New Flame," 1996), *Smart Guy* ("Love Letters," 1997), *The Parent 'Hood* (recurring role of Zaria Peterson; 1995–99), *Felicity* ("Ancient History," 1999), *Undressed* (1999), *Martial Law* ("Scorpio Rising," 2000), *That '70s Show* ("Hyde Gets the Girl," 2001), *Oh Drama* (2001), *Strong Medicine* ("Trauma," 2002), *Off Centre* ("The Deflower Half-Hour," 2002), *One On One* ("Daddy's Other Girl," 2003), *ER* ("No Strings Attached," 2003), *JAG* ("Pulse Rate," 2003), *She Spies* ("The Gift," 2004), *Love, Inc.* (5 episodes in the role of Francine; "Family Ties," "Hope and Faith," "One on One," "Three's Company," "Fired Up," 2005–06), *'Til Death* ("Performance Anxiety," 2007).

Music Videos: *Sorry 2004* (2004), *No Better Love* (2003).

Good, Meagan Born in Panorama, California, August 8, 1981.

Meagan Monique Good has successfully made the transition from child actress to adult actress. She began by appearing in commercials at the age of four and moved on to sitcoms such as *The Parent Hood*, *Moesha*, *The Steve Harvey Show* and *Raising Dad.* While still a child, she had a breakthrough film role as Jurnee Smollett's sister in the evocative, haunting *Eve's Bayou* (1997). Later, she had recurring roles on the TV series *My Wife and Kids* (2003) and *Kevin Hill* (2005). Other memorable feature films include *D.E.B.S.* (2004), about a group of female teen assassins who dress like Catholic schoolgirls, and the retro roller disco teen musical *Roll Bounce* (2005). In 2006, she produced and starred in *Miles from Home* (2006). Her second production was scheduled to be *Sundays in Fort Greene* (a neighborhood in Brooklyn). She appeared in the music video *Single for the Rest of My Life* with her older sister, La'Myia, who is a member of the R&B group Isyss.

Award nominations include Teen Choice Awards for Choice Female Breakout (*Waist Deep*) and Choice Movie Actress (*Stomp the Yard*); two Black Movie Award nominations for Outstanding Performance by an Actress in a Leading Role (*D.E.B.S.*, *Waist Deep*); and two NAACP Image Award nominations for Outstanding Youth Actress (*Eve's Bayou*) and Outstanding Supporting Actress in a Motion Picture (*Stomp the Yard*).

Of Cherokee and Puerto Rican descent, Good is the daughter of a Los Angeles police officer. She has another sister named Lexus, and also a brother.

Feature Films including Video and TV Movies: *House Party 3* (1994), *Friday* (1995), *Make a Wish, Molly* (1995), *Eve's Bayou* (1997), *The Secret Life of Girls* (1999), *3 Strikes* (2000), *House Party 4: Down to the Last Minute* (2001), *Biker Boyz* (2003), *Deliver Us from Eva* (2003), *Ride or Die* (2003), *D.E.B.S.* (2004), *You Got Served* (2004), *The Cookout* (2004), *Brick* (2005), *Venom* (2005), *Roll Bounce* (2005), *Miles from Home* (2006), *Waist Deep* (2006), *Stomp the Yard* (2007), *One Missed Call* (2008), *The Love Guru* (2008), *Saw V* (2008), *Sundays in Fort Greene* (2009), *The Unborn* (2009).

TV: *Gabriel's Fire* ("Birds Gotta Fly," 1991), *On Our Own* ("Swiss Family Jerricos," 1994), *ABC Afterschool Specials* ("Me and My Hormones," 1996), *Just One of the Girls* (1997), *Figure It Out* (panelist; 1997), *Pacific Blue* ("Blood for Blood," 1997), *Touched by an Angel* ("The Pact," 1997), *The Gregory Hines Show* ("Three's Not Company," 1997), *The Parent 'Hood* (2 episodes; "No Soul on Ice," "Flaked Out," 1997 and 1998), *Cousin Skeeter* (2 episodes; "The Candidate," "Sugar Daddy," 1999), *Moesha* ("He Doth Protest Too Much," 2000), *The Steve Harvey Show* ("Don't Stand Too Close to Me," 2000), *The Division* ("The Parent Trap," 2001), *The Famous Jett Jackson* ("Awakenings," Parts I and II, 2001), *Raising Dad* ("Sex Ed," "Losing It," 2001–02), *The Jersey* ("The Playbook," 2002), *My Wife and Kids* (5 episodes in the recurring role of Vanessa; "Jr.'s Risky Business," Parts I and II, "Here Comes Da Judge," "Graduation," Parts I and II, 2003), *9th Annual Soul Train Lady of Soul Awards* (2003), *Kevin Hill* (4 episodes in the recurring role of Melanie; "Occupational Hazard," "Cardiac Episode," "Sacrificial Lambs," "Losing Isn't Everything," 2005), *The Kelly Slater Celebrity Turf Invitational* (2006), *2006 Black Movie Awards, Bring That Year Back 2006: Laugh Now, Cry Later, Angels Can't Help But Laugh* (2007), *House* ("Words and Deeds," 2007), *All of Us* (2 episodes; "Sins of the Father," "She Blinded Me with Science," 2007).

Music Videos: *I Got You* (2002), *Get wit Me* (2002), *Single for the Rest of My Life* (2002), *21 Questions* (2003), *No Doubt* (2003), *Black Suits Comin' (Nod Ya Head)* (2002), *Do My* (2001), *One* (2006), *This Very Moment* (2007).

Meagan Good in *Eve's Bayou* (1997).

Graves, Teresa Born in Houston, Texas, January 10, 1948; died October 10, 2002, Los Angeles, California.

When Teresa Graves perished in a house fire started by a faulty space heater in 2002, she had, by choice, been out of the limelight for some time. In fact, few of her neighbors had any idea that the middle-aged woman caring for her sick mother had been, a generation before, a TV star. Her religious beliefs had caused her to abandon her acting career and to live a life of quiet solitude. But to the generation who grew up in the 1970s, she was known as the first African American actress to star in her own one-hour drama series, *Get Christie Love!* (1974), for which she was nominated for a Golden Globe Award for Best Actress—Drama in 1975. Energetic, cocky, and full of good humor, the Christie Love character was something very new in the TV landscape.

There is no doubt that *Get Christie Love!* was inspired by the blaxploitation films of the era, especially the Pam Grier action hits. But Graves brought a quirky sense of humor to the project that didn't resemble the Pam Grier persona. She was her own woman and she was a cop, so the formula fit nicely into the plethora of cop shows on the air at the time. Originally a 90-minute TV movie (essentially a long-form pilot), *Get Christie Love!* was shown on ABC in the spring of 1974 and was converted quickly into a fall TV series. Graves became very involved in the Jehovah's Witnesses religion by the time the series went into production. She had very strong ideas of what the character couldn't do, which precluded romantic involvement and killing the bad guys. The series was dropped after a single season, the victim of low ratings and constant tinkering with the format (including the addition of Jack Kelly as Christie's new commanding officer). It has been rumored that Quentin Tarantino was considering a big screen remake of *Get Christie Love!*, but nothing seems to have come of that. It would be great fun to hear the catchphrase "You're under arrest, sugah," one more time. The line can be heard in Tarantino's *Reservoir Dogs* (1992).

Graves began her career as a singer with the feel-good folk-pop group The Doodletown Pipers. They were featured on a summer replacement variety series (filling the Smothers Brothers' slot) in the summer of 1967. Then she appeared on *Rowan & Martin's Laugh-In* (in 1969–70), at that time the most popular show on television. Despite her success on television, Graves' film career was negligible. The brevity of her career really didn't give her much of a chance to build a big screen portfolio. *That Man Bolt* (1973) and *Black Eye* (1974) are typical Fred Williamson entries, and when Fred Williamson is on screen, no one else in the cast seems to matter much. *Vampira* (1974) is truly awful, the worst film of David Niven's career. The sight of an aging Niven as a vampire in blackface is horrible beyond belief. However, Graves is at her most beautiful as his vampire lover, even with fangs. She married William D. Reddick in 1977, and they were later divorced.

Teresa Graves.

Feature Films including TV Movies: *That Man Bolt* (1973), *Vampira* (aka *Old Dracula*, 1974), *Black Eye* (1974).

TV: *Our Place* (1967), *Turn-On* (1970), *Ed Sullivan's Armed Forces Tour* (1970), *The Mike Douglas Show* (1970), *The Merv Griffin Show* (1970), *The Bob Hope Show* ("Bob Hope Looks at Women's Lib," 1970), *The Ed Sullivan Show* (1971), *Rowan & Martin's Laugh-In* (series regular; 1969–71), *The Funny Side* (1971), *The Tonight Show Starring Johnny Carson* (1972), *Soul Train* (1972), *Keeping Up with the Joneses* (1972), *The New Dick Van Dyke Show* (1972), *The Rookies* ("Easy

Money," 1973), *Get Christie Love!* (90-minute pilot and recurring title role in series; 1974), *Bob Hope's Women I Love* (1982).

Video: *TV in Black: The First Fifty Years* (2004).

Gray, Macy Born in Canton, Ohio, September 6, 1967.

Macy Gray (born Natalie Renee McIntyre) is an old school singer who carries the heritage of black jazz and pop music in her voice. Her quirky, idiosyncratic style has enthralled fans since the release of her debut album *On How Life Is* (1999), which yielded the hit single "I Try" and went on to double platinum sales. "I Try" won the Grammy Award for Best Female Pop Vocal Performance (2001), and she was nominated for Song of the Year and Record of the Year. In all, she has been nominated for five Grammy Awards, winning one. The remainder of her discography consists of *The Id* (2001), *The Trouble with Being Myself* (2003), *The Very Best of Macy Gray* (2004), *Live in Las Vegas* (2005) and *Big* (2007). While none have achieved the massive success of *On How Life Is*, *Big* qualified as a valid comeback album, and she continues to make potent music and attract substantial audiences.

Gray decided to try for a music career after being expelled from Western Reserve Academy in Hudson, Ohio. She graduated from the University of Southern California in 1990 and started writing songs and making demos. She met writer-producer Joe Solo while she was working as a cashier, and together they put together a large song collection which they recorded in Solo's studio.

Gray began singing at small jazz clubs in Los Angeles. Atlantic Records signed her to a contract, but that partnership didn't work out. Gray was carrying her third child at that time and watching her marriage dissolve (she was married to Tracy Hinds from 1996 to 1998), so she decided to move back to Canton and collect her thoughts. But the demo tape was still circulating, and it led to a record deal with Epic in 1998, and the substantive career that followed.

Gray has also managed to carve out an impressive acting career, appearing in *Training Day* (2001), *Domino* (2005), *Idlewild* (2006), and contributing a cameo to the original *Spider-Man* film (2002). TV acting appearances include *MDs* (2002), *American Dreams* (as soul singer Carla Thomas; 2002), *That's So Raven* (2004) and *1-800-Missing* (2005). In 2005, she opened the Macy Gray Music Academy, which gives needy but talented children and teenagers an opportunity to perform and show their skills.

Feature Films including Video and TV Movies: *Training Day* (2001), *Spider-Man* (2002), *Scary Movie 3* (2003), *Gang of Roses* (2003), *Lightning in a Bottle* (2004), *Motown 45* (TV; 2004), *Around the World in 80 Days* (2004), *All We Are Saying* (TV; 2005), *Mississippi Rising* (TV; 2005), *Lackawanna Blues* (TV; 2005), *The Crow: Wicked Prayer* (2005), *Shadowboxer* (2005), *Domino* (2005), *Idlewild* (2006), *Mama Black Widow* (2009).

TV: *Sessions at West 54th* (1999), *TFI Friday* (1999), *Late Show with David Letterman* (4 segments; 1999–2007), *A Very Special Christmas from Washington, D.C.* (2000), *MTV Video Music Awards* (2000), *Saturday Night Live* (2000), *Late Night with Conan O'Brien* (2000), *MTV Backstage at the Grammys* (2000), *Ally McBeal* ("Hope and Glory," 2000), *2000 MTV Movie Awards*, *Soul Train* (2 segments; 2000–01), *The Rosie O'-Donnell Show* (5 segments; 2000–01), *My VH1 Music Awards* (2001), *The 43rd Annual Grammy Awards* (2001), *MTV Icon: Janet Jackson* (2001), *All Access: Front Row, Backstage, Live!* (2001), *MTV Video Music Awards 2001*, *The Concert for New York City* (2001), *HermanSIC* (2001), *HBO First Look* (3 episodes; "Training Day: Crossing the Line," "Behind the Ultimate Spin: The Making of 'Spider-Man,'" "Idlewild," 2001–06), *One-Hit Wonders* (2002), *MDs* ("Wing and a Prayer," 2002), *The National Lottery Wright Ticket* (2003), *V Graham Norton* (2003), *The New Tom Green Show* (2003), *The Sharon Osbourne Show* (2003), *When I Was a Girl* (2003), *Cribs* (2003), *Macy Gray: Custom Concert* (2003), *MTV2: The Shortlist 2003*, *The Tonight Show with Jay Leno* (3 episodes; 2003–07), *Blue's Clues* ("Bluestock," 2004), *On-Air with Ryan Seacrest* (2004), *I Love the '90s* (2004), *American Dreams* ("Real-to-Reel," 2004), *Simply the Best* (2004), *That's So Raven* ("Taken to the Cleaners," 2004), *The Late Late Show with Craig Ferguson* (2005), *2005 American Music Awards*, *Punk'd* (2005), *Duck Dodgers in the 24th Century* (voice; "Diva Delivery/Castle High," 2005), *American Dragon: Jake Long* (2 episodes as Trixie's Grandmother; "Act 4, Scene 15," "Professor Rotwood's Thesis," 2005), *1-800-Missing* ("A Death in the Family," 2005), *Tavis*

Smiley (2 segments; 2005 and 2006), *Top of the Pops* (2006), *2006 Independent Spirit Awards*, *In the Mix* ("From Soul Train to Tony Orlando," 2006), *Celebrity Poker Showdown* (2006), *Amazon Fishbowl with Bill Maher* (2006), *George Clinton: Tales of Dr. Funkenstein* (2006), *Karaoke Superstars* (2006), *Macy Gray's Big Special* (2007), *Loose Women* (2007), *Dancing with the Stars* (2007), *Jimmy Kimmel Live!* (2 segments; 2007–08).

Video/DVD: *Fatboy Slim and Macy Gray: Demons* (2000), *Macy Gray: Live in Las Vegas* (2005).

Grier, Pam Born in Winston-Salem, North Carolina, May 26, 1949.

From the late sixties through the mid-seventies, there was an explosion of black action films referred to in the pages of *Variety* and elsewhere as "blaxploitation" films. Pam Grier reigned supreme as the queen of blaxploitation. However, this does not begin to hint at the influence and complexity of her career. She is one of the most seminal of African American actresses. Her career means many things to many people.

To feminists, she is not just a strong black woman, but a strong woman *per se*. (It's no surprise that, in 1975, she was the first black woman to appear on the cover of *MS.* magazine.) You'd have to look to Chinese action films of the era to find a handful of women as strong as Pam Grier. Grier wrote the book on how fierce a woman could be. To fans of the blaxploitation genre, she was the sexiest, boldest exponent of black power out there. The young Grier had no problem doing nude scenes, and she posed in a tight-fitting swimsuit for a *New York* magazine in the mid-seventies, which featured a cover line wondering if she was the next Marilyn Monroe. The scene where she displays the jar containing the testicles of the white mobster in *Foxy Brown* (1974), or the one where she guns down her unfaithful black lover in *Coffy* (1973), remain ultra-violent reminders that this lady was not playing and that she was no incarna-

Pam Grier in *Coffy* (1973).

tion of the soft, breathy Monroe. To those who take a historic viewpoint, and who can appreciate the struggles of the black actress to find a foothold in Hollywood, Grier is an example of someone who made the most of her opportunities.

Pamela Suzette Grier was one of four children born to Air Force mechanic Clarence Grier and nurse Gwendolyn Samuels. Due to her father's military career, the family moved frequently during her childhood, as far away as England, but eventually they settled in Denver, Colorado, where Grier Attended East High School. While there, she appeared in stage productions and competed in beauty contests (including the Miss Colorado Universe) in an effort to raise money for college tuition to Metropolitan State College in Denver. Grier moved to Los Angeles in 1967, where she lived with her cousin, football player Roosevelt (Rosey) Grier. She began attending UCLA.

She was hired as a receptionist at American International Pictures and took acting classes at Jack Baumgarten's Agency of the Performing Arts. She caught the eye of director-producer Roger Corman, who cast her in the films *The Big Doll House* (1971) and *The Big Bird Cage* (1972), both shot in the Philippines. These audacious, over-the-top films helped define the women-in-prison genre, made great money at the drive-ins, and garnered Grier lots of attention.

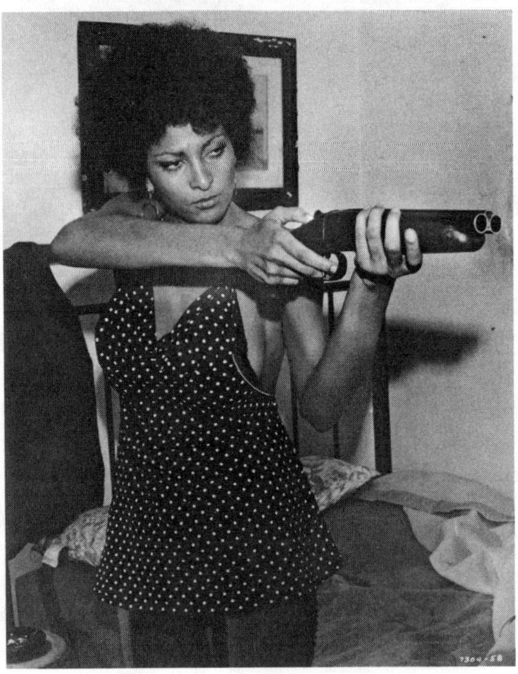

Pam Grier in *Coffy* (1973).

But it was Jack Hill's *Coffy* (1973) which shot her to the top of the blaxploitation world. *Coffy* is by far her best film of this era, and it is one of the great B-movies of any era. It has a resonance and visceral power usually lacking in the action genre and it is — given the script's web of betrayal and conceit — a close cousin to film noir, right down to the existential, unhappy, moody ending.

Foxy Brown and *Sheba, Baby* (both 1974) tried to duplicate the appeal of *Coffy* but not surprisingly fell a bit short, although Grier is at her most iconic and at the height of her screen powers in *Foxy Brown*. By *Friday Foster* (1975), her screen image was already softening, as the blaxploitation era wound rapidly to a close. *Bucktown* (1975) is a very interesting Fred Williamson vehicle about a man who returns to his hometown to confront a former friend who is now the town boss. The film deals with the gray area between good and evil and is all the better for it, but Grier is simply along for the ride.

The Arena (1974) was an Italian-made sword and sandal epic with Grier at her best as a kidnapped African princess who is sold into slavery. She becomes a gladiator and fights her way to freedom. It paired Grier with blonde actress Margaret Markov (wife of producer-director-actor Mark Damon). They had already appeared together in *Black Mama, White Mama* (1972), a somewhat listless women-in-prison film that was a reworking of the Sidney Poitier–Tony Curtis film *The Defiant Ones* (1958).

Grier didn't make another strong impact on screen until she played an out-of-her-mind junkie in a small but fabulous role in the Paul Newman vehicle *Fort Apache the Bronx* (1981). You remember Grier's short but potent scene long after you've forgotten the rest of the film. She was a witch in the Disney production *Something Wicked This Way Comes* (1983), a big budget box office flop that captured none of the grace and texture of the great Ray Bradbury novel on which it was based. She was back at the top of her game again in John Carpenter's *Escape from L.A.* (1995), a dystopian science fiction epic that featured Kurt Russell as the Clint Eastwood–like Snake Plissken. Grier made the best of her limited screen time. She was also in John Carpenter's *Ghosts of Mars* (2001), to lesser effect.

She was nominated for a Golden Globe and an NAACP Image Award for her performance in *Jackie Brown* (1997), her "comeback" film. (Interestingly, it was co-star Robert Forster who received the most positive notice for his work in the film, and who was nominated for a Best Supporting Actor Oscar.) *Jackie Brown* was a labor of love for director Quentin Tarantino, who conceived the project strictly as a tribute to Pam Grier. Here she is a more mature, thoughtful character than she was in her earlier incarnations in black action films. She gives a subtle, occasionally tender performance. *Jackie Brown* is among her best acting work, as a flight attendant who smuggles illegal arms sales money.

Her television appearances have been relatively limited, although she has done more TV in recent years, most notably her role of Kit Porter on *The L Word* (2004–07), the refreshingly unapologetic soap opera about the Los Angeles lesbian world. She was nominated for two NAACP Image Awards (2005–06) for her work on the series. She appeared in three episodes of *Miami Vice* in the recurrent role of Valerie Gordon (1984). She was a regular on *Linc's* (1999), a sitcom set in a bar. For this she received two more NAACP Award nominations for Outstanding Supporting Actress in a comedy series (1999–2000).

Grier has never married, but she had a close, long-term relationship with basketball star Kareem Abdul-Jabbar of the L.A. Lakers and with comic Richard Pryor, with whom she appeared in the racing car film *Greased Lightning* (1977).

Feature Films including Video and TV Movies: *Beyond the Valley of the Dolls* (1970), *The Big Doll House* (1971), *Women in Cages* (1971), *Black Mama, White Mama* (1972), *Cool Breeze* (1972), *The Big Bird Cage* (1972), *Hit Man* (1972), *The Twilight People* (1973), *Coffy* (1973), *Scream Blacula Scream* (1973), *The Arena* (aka *Naked Warriors*, 1974), *Foxy Brown* (1974), *Sheba, Baby* (1974), *Bucktown* (1975), *Friday Foster* (1975), *Drum* (1976), *La notte dell'alta marea* (aka *Twilight of Love*, 1977), *Greased Lightning* (1977), *Fort Apache the Bronx* (1981), *Something Wicked This Way Comes* (1983), *Tough Enough* (1983), *On the Edge* (1985), *Stand Alone* (1985), *Badge of the Assassin* (TV; 1985), *The Vindicator* (1986), *The All-nighter* (1987), *Above the Law* (1988), *The Package* (1989), *Class of 1999* (1990), *Bill & Ted's Bogus Journey* (1991), *A Mother's Right: The Elizabeth Morgan Story* (TV; 1991), *Posse* (1993), *Serial Killer*

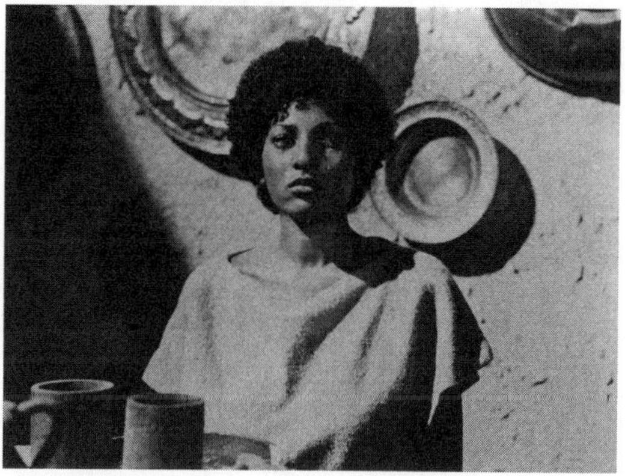

Pam Grier in *The Arena* (1974).

(1995), *Original Gangstas* (1995), *Escape from L.A.* (1995), *Family Blessings* (TV; 1996), *Mars Attacks!* (1996), *Fakin' Da Funk* (1997), *Strip Search* (1997), *Jackie Brown* (1997), *Hayley Wagner, Star* (TV; 1999), *Fortress 2* (1999), *Jawbreaker* (1999), *No Tomorrow* (1999), *In Too Deep* (1999), *Holy Smoke* (1999), *Snow Day* (2000), *Wilder* (2000), *3 A.M.* (2001), *Love the Hard Way* (2001), *Ghosts of Mars* (2001), *Bones* (2001), *Feast of All Saints* (TV; 2001), *Baby of the Family* (2002), *The Adventures of Pluto Nash* (2002), *Undercover Brother* (archival; 2002), *1st to Die* (TV; 2003), *Back in the Day* (2005), *The Conjuring* (2007), *Ladies of the House* (TV; 2008), *Identity* (2009), *The Invited* (2009), *Co-op of the Damned* (in development, 2011).

TV: *The Tonight Show Starring Johnny Carson* (3 segments; 1973), *Soul Train* (3 episodes; 1973–77), *Roots: The Next Generations* (miniseries; 1979), *The Love Boat* (2 episodes in the role of Cynthia Williams; 1980), *The Making of "Something Wicked This Way Comes"* (1983), *Miami Vice* (3 episodes in the role of Valerie Gordon; "Rites of Passage," "Prodigal Son," "Too Much, Too Late," 1985–90), *Night Court* (2 episodes in the role of Benet Collins; "Hurricane," Parts I and II, 1986), *Crime Story* (5 episodes in the role of Suzanne Terry; "Abrams for the Defense," "Pursuit of a Wanted Felon," "Justice Hits the Skids," "Seize the Time," "Going Home," 1986–88), *The Cosby Show* ("Planning Parenthood," 1987), *Frank's Place* ("Frank's Place: The Movie," 1988), *Midnight Caller* ("Blood Red," 1989), *Knot's Landing* (2 episodes in the role of Lieutenant Guthrie; "Dead But Not Buried," Part I, "What If," 1990), *Monsters* ("Hostile Takeover," 1991), *Pacific Sta-*

tion ("My Favorite Dad," 1992), *The Sinbad Show* ("The Telethon," 1994), *The Fresh Prince of Bel-Air* ("M Is for the Many Things She Gave Me," 1994), *The Marshall* ("Rainbow Comix," 1995), *Martin* ("All the Players Came," 1995), *Sparks* ("Pillow Talk," 1996), *The Wayans Bros.* ("Goin' to the Net," 1996), *The Rosie O'Donnell Show* (1998), *Pinky and the Brain* (voice; "Inherit the Wheeze," 1998), *The 4th Annual Screen Actors Guild Awards* (1998), *Mundo VIP* (1998), *Mad TV* (1998), *Intimate Portrait* ("Pam Grier," 1999), *The 1999 Source Hip-Hop Music Awards*, *Hollywood Squares* (1999), *The Wild Thornberrys* (voice; "Stick Your Neck Out," 1999), *Happily Ever After: Fairy Tales for Every Child* (voice; "The Empress' Nightingale," 1999), *For Your Love* ("The Sins of the Mother ... and the Boyfriend," 1999), *Linc's* ("What I Did for Love," 1999), *Strange Frequency* ("Time Is on My Side," 2001), *It Conquered Hollywood! The Story of American-International Pictures* (2001), *The Late Late Show with Craig Kilborn* (2001), *HBO First Look* ("Ghosts of Mars," 2001), *E! True Hollywood Story* (2 episodes; "Miami Vice," "Snoop Dogg," 2001 and 2005), *Night Visions* ("Switch," 2002), *Baadasssss Cinema* (2002), *Justice League* (voice; 2 episodes in the role of My'ri-a'h; "A Knight of Shadows," Parts I and II, 2002), *A Decade Under the Influence* (2003), *2003 Trumpet Awards*, *Law & Order: Special Victims Unit* (2 episodes in the role of Claudia Williams; "Disappearing Acts," "Pandora," 2002 and 2003), *The Wayne Brady Show* (2004), *Totally Gayer* (2004), *The 100 Most Memorable TV Moments* (2004), *The L Word* (recurring role of Kit Porter; 2004–08), *Legends Ball* (2006), *Sexo en serie* (archival; 2008).

Video/DVD: *Doggy Dogg World* (1994), *Sex at 24 Frames Per Second* (archival; 2003).

Groves, Napiera Danielle Born in Cincinnati, Ohio, December 17, 1979.

Napiera Danielle Groves received a bachelor of fine arts from Howard University in Washington, D.C. At first she was interested in journalism, but then decided to pursue acting. While attending college, she won the Miss District of Columbia USA pageant and was honored with the Miss Congeniality award in the 1997 Miss USA competition. She joined the cast of *As the World Turns* in 2001 in the role of Bonnie McKechnie, the stuck-up offspring of Jessica Griffin and Duncan McKechnie. The character was the first bi-racial child born on a television series. Groves stepped into the role as the grown-up incarnation of the character. (In real time, the character would have been eight years old, not a young woman.) She stayed with the show until 2003, then returned for a week in 2004.

Groves was a member of a national tour of *Dreamgirls* and has been in regional theater productions of *Jelly's Last Jam*, *As You Like It* and *Oliver*! She was in *Bright Lights, Big City* (1999) at the New York Theatre Workshop. Film credits include *Airborne* (1993), the TV bio *Don King: Only in America* (1997) and *Sacred Is the Flesh* (2001).

Feature Films including TV Movies: *Airborne* (1993), *Don King: Only in America* (TV; 1997), *Killjoy* (2000), *Sacred Is the Flesh* (2001), *Redrum* (2007).

TV: *As the World Turns* (recurring role of Bonnie McKechnie; 2003–04), *SoapTalk* (2003), *Eve* ("They've Come Undone," Part I, 2004), *Without a Trace* ("Showdown," 2005), *One on One* ("Venice Boulevard of Broken Dreams," 2005), *How I Met Your Mother* (2 episodes; "The Wedding," "Drum Roll, Please," 2006), *Zoey 101* (2 episodes; "Spring Break-Up," Parts I and II, 2006), *All of Us* (2 episodes; "Surprise, Surprise," Parts I and II, 2006).

Guy, Jasmine Born in Boston, Massachusetts, March 10, 1962.

Self-centered, manipulative, conniving and an utter delight: that was Jasmine Guy in her signature role of Whitney Gilbert on *A Different World*. A student at fictional Hillman College (although real-life Spelman College was used to film scenes), Whitley was always in conflict with the other female students, always flirting with every guy in sight, and constantly devising one or another scheme to get over (and usually seeing it backfire).

In 1981, at age 17, Guy studied at Alvin Ailey American Dance Center. Her father is the African American Reverend William Guy, pastor of the Friendship Baptist Church in Atlanta; her mother is Jaye Rudolph, who is Portuguese. Guy married Terrence Duckette in 1998; they divorced in 2008. She gave birth to a baby girl, Imani, in 1999.

Guy had roles in such popular sitcoms as *The Fresh Prince of Bel-Air*; *Living Single*, playing a psychiatrist who advised the Kadijah character (Queen Latifah), who had begun exhibiting signs of bipolar disorder; *Malcolm & Eddie*; and *Ladies Man*. She was equally at home in dramatic series, including *Melrose Place* (as a love interest for the Jack Wagner character), *NYPD Blue*, *The Equalizer* and *Touched by an Angel*. She hosted *America's Ballroom Challenge* on PBS, which was appropriate considering her roots in dance. She was Roxy Harvey on *Dead Like Me* (2003–04), a clever and darkly funny series about dead people moving invisibly through the world of the living, but encountering very much the same turmoil and personality conflicts in the spirit world as in the real world.

Guy's film career has not been as stellar as her TV work, but she has been in some interesting films. Her most prominent role was Dominique La Rue in *Harlem Nights* (1989), with what was then a dream pairing of Eddie Murphy and Richard Pryor, the two top black comedic stars of their respective generations. Murphy got most of the footage (Pryor was already ill from multiple sclerosis), and Guy was relegated to a bad girl role that exhibited little of the charm of her work as Whitley; her character was killed off in shockingly short order. Nor was her role in Spike Lee's *School Daze* (1988) equal to her talents. This is surprising, considering the film was set in a college milieu.

Guy was Dina, a member of the light-skinned students of the Gamma Ray fraternity. Lee deserves considerable credit for addressing the black-on-black color problem, and the film is on the whole quite good. Some of her best big screen work is in an effective independent film about traveling salesmen called *Diamond Men* (2000). Like Henry Winkler on *Happy Days* and Carroll O'Connor on *All in the Family*, Guy's association with a role on a long-running, popular series made it difficult for her to break through in her subsequent career.

Guy toured in the musical *Grease!* in the role of Betty Rizzo (1996–97). She also toured with *Chicago* in the starring role of Velma Kelly (1999), including a stint at the Schubert Theater on Broadway. She appeared in *The Wiz* on Broadway (1984) in several roles, and was Mickey in *Leader of the Pack* (1985). She released a self-titled album in 1990. The album resulted in three singles that charted on the *Billboard* Top 100: "Try Me," "Just Want to Hold You," and "Another Like My Lover." She wrote *Afeni Shakur: Evolution of a Revolutionary* (Atria Books; 2005), a biography of the mother of her close friend, slain actor and hip-hop artist Tupac Shakur.

Jasmine Guy and Eddie Murphy in *Harlem Nights* (1989).

Feature Films including Video and TV Movies: *At Mother's Request* (TV; 1987), *School Daze* (1988), *Runaway* (TV; 1989), *Biao Cheng* (aka *Runaway*, 1989), *Harlem Nights* (1989), *A Killer Among Us* (TV; 1990), *Stompin' at the Savoy* (TV; 1992), *Boy Meets Girl* (1993), *Klash* (aka *Kla$h*, 1993), *America's Dream* (TV; 1996), *Cats Don't Dance* (voice; 1997), *Perfect Crime* (TV; 1997), *Madeline* (1998), *Guinevere* (1998), *Lillie* (1999), *The Law of Enclosures* (2000), *Diamond Men* (2000), *Dying on the Edge* (2001), *Feast of All Saints* (TV; 2001), *Carrie* (TV; 2002), *I Was a Network Star* (TV; 2006), *Tru Loved* (2007).

TV: *Fame* (as a dancer; 1982), *The Equalizer* ("Out of the Past," 1986), *Uptown Comedy Express* (1987), *A Different World* (recurring role of Whitley; 1987–93), *The More You Know* (1989), *The 3rd Annual American Comedy Awards* (1989), *21st NAACP Image Awards* (1989), *The 3rd Annual Soul Train Music Awards* (1989), *Funny Women of Television* (1991), *The Fresh Prince of Bel-Air* ("Love at First Fight," 1991), *Soul Train Comedy Awards* (1993), *25th NAACP Image Awards* (1993), *Queen* (miniseries; 1993), *26th NAACP Image Awards* (1994), *A Century of Women* (1994), *Going, Going, Almost Gone! Animals in Danger* (narrator; 1995), *Melrose Place* (3 episodes in the role of Caitlin Mills; "Bye, Bye, Baby," "They Shoot Mothers, Don't They," Parts I and II, 1995), *NYPD Blue* ("Heavin' Can Wait," 1995), *Touched by an Angel* (3 episodes in the role of Kathleen; "Sympathy for the Devil," "Lost and Found," "Clipped Wings," 1995–97), *Living Single* ("Shrink to Fit," 1996), *America's Dream* ("The Boy Who Painted Christ Black," 1996), *The Outer Limits* ("The Heist," 1996), *Lois & Clark: The New Adventures of Superman* ("The People vs.

Lois Lane," 1996), *The Rosie O'Donnell Show* (1997), *Malcolm & Eddie* ("Two Men and the Baby," 1997), *Celebrity Profile* ("Diahann Carroll," 1998), *Partners* ("A Beautiful Day," 1999), *Any Day Now* ("Blue," 1999), *Ladies Man* (3 episodes in the role of Allegra; "Boys Can't Help It," "Jimmy's Song," "Neutered Jimmy," 1999), *Happily Ever After: Fairy Tales for Every Child* ("The Frog Princess," 2000), *Broadway on Broadway* (2000), *Linc's* ("The Music in Me," 2000), *Between the Lions* ("Humph! Humph! Humph!," 2001), *It's Black Entertainment* (2002), *Cyberchase* (voice; "Secrets of Symmetria," 2002), *The Parkers* ("Lights, Camera, Action," 2002), *Inside TV Land: Taboo TV* (2002), *Cyberchase* (voice of Ava and Ms. Fileshare; 2002), *Intimate Portrait* (4 episodes; "Queen Latifah," "Jasmine Guy," "Tisha Campbell-Martin," "Isabel Sanford," 2002–2003), *Unchained Memories: Readings from the Slave Narratives* (2003), *Dorothy Dandridge: An American Beauty* (2003), *Tupac: Resurrection* (archival; 2003), *Dead Like Me* (recurring role of Roxie Harvey; 2003–04), *50 Most Wicked Women of Primetime* (archival; 2004), *The Wayne Brady Show* (2004), *Tavis Smiley* (2004), *The 56th Annual Primetime Emmy Awards* (2004), *Dennis Miller* (2005), *2005 Trumpet Awards*, *TV Land Confidential* (2 episodes; "Network Notes," "Being Bad Behind the Scenes," 2005), *That's So Raven* ("Checkin' Out," 2006), *In the Mix* (2006), *Rwanda Rising* (narrator; 2007), *Angels Can't Help But Laugh* (2007), *2007 Trumpet Awards*, *11th Annual Ribbon of Hope Celebration* (2008), *The People Speak* (documentary; 2009).

Video/DVD: *Time Out: The Truth About HIV, AIDS, and You* (1992), *Michael Jackson: HIStory on Film, Vol. II* (1997), *TV in Black: The First Fifty Years* (2004).

Guyse, Sheila Born in Detroit, Michigan, 1925.

Sheila Guyse appeared in four all-black cast films: *Boy! What a Girl!*, *Sepia Cinderella* (both 1947), *Miracle in Harlem* (1948), and *Harlem Follies of 1949* (1950). She also released recordings showing her expertise in jazz, pop and gospel, such as *This Is Sheila* (1958).

Miracle in Harlem was directed by Jack Kemp. Aunt Hattie declares she is ill and afraid she is dying. Her niece Julie Weston (Guyse) is set to take over her candy business along with Hattie's adopted son Bert. But Hattie falls victim to a swindle and appears to have lost her company. She fakes her own death and lies in a coffin to trap swindler. The cast included Juanita Hall and Stepin Fetchit (doing his typical stereotype of the lazy "darkie"—even in this, an all-black film!).

Sepia Cinderella is Guyse's signature film. She is the good girl in a guy, good girl, bad girl triangle, as a struggling bandleader tries to find his way in romance as well as in love. *Boy! What a Girl!* is a musical revue about two producers trying to raise money to finance a show. Drummer Gene Krupa has a cameo. Guyse appeared in stage productions such as *Lost in the Stars* (as Linda; October 1949–July 1950); *Finian's Rainbow* (sharecropper; January 1947–October 1948); and *Memphis Bound!* (as Lily Valentine; May–June 1945).

Feature Films: *Boy! What a Girl!* (1947), *Sepia Cinderella* (1947), *Miracle in Harlem* (1948), *Harlem Follies of 1949* (1950).

TV: *Hallmark Hall of Fame* ("The Green Pastures," 1957).

Hall, Irma P. Born in Beaumont, Texas, June 16, 1935.

Irma P. Hall is best known for playing matriarchal figures in such films as *A Family Thing* (1996), *Soul Food* (1997), and *The Ladykillers* (2004). She had her first acting role at age 38 as a character named Georgia Brown in an independent film called *Book of Numbers* (1973). Hall was a language teacher in Dallas, Texas, for almost 20 years when actor-director Raymond St. Jacques (who directed *Book of Numbers* and appeared in the film as Blueboy Harris) saw her performing at a poetry reading. He liked her so much he offered her a role in the film on the spot. This late bloomer discovered that she had a love of acting and not long after founded a repertory theater in Dallas, and she appeared in films and TV from that point on.

Her role as the compassionate, blind Aunt T. in *A Family Thing* (1996) caused audiences and critics to take notice of her. Hall won the Chicago Film Critics Association Award and the Kansas City Film Critics Circle Award for Best Supporting Actress. *Soul Food* was such a box office hit that it spawned a TV series, in which Hall reprised her role as Mama Joe. An extended family is obliged to put their many differences aside when Mama is hospitalized with complications from diabetes. She was cast in the Coen brothers' remake

Dixie Litho Co., Inc. P.O. Box 882
Atlanta I, Ga.

YOUR THEATRE
YOUR TOWN, U.S.A.
1,000—$6.50
Additional 1,000's—$5.00
(PLUS POSTAGE--1,000 HERALDS WEIGH 11 LBS.)
(EXTRA COPY BILLED AT 3¢ PER WORD.)

INCLUDE MONEY WITH FIRST ORDER UNLESS HAVE ESTABLISHED CREDIT.

Name
Town
Quantity
Picture
Playdate
Copy

A KAY EXCHANGES RELEASE

New Movie Shows Why "Brown Dots" Are Hailed As Hottest Rhythmeers

Romance Set To Rhythm !
Jive Like You Never Heard Before . . . Romance That Warms Your Heart With Melody

The HERALD PICTURE
Sepia CINDERELLA

Guest Star FREDDIE BARTHOLOMEW
8 SMASHING SONG HITS
Played and Sung by DEEK WATSON'S BROWN DOTS
JOHN KIRBY'S ALL-STAR BAND
WALTER FULLER ORCHESTRA
and
SHEILA GUYSE
BILLY DANIELS
TON DALEYO
and RUBLE BLAKEY

You'll Not Forget Her

This Nite Club Princess Looking For Romance Set To The Beat Of Jive

Directed by ARTHUR LEONARD

Rivals In Battle Of Romance!

JOHN KIRBY'S ALL-STAR BAND

Music and Romance Combine to Make "Sepia Cinderella" a Hit

DIXIE LITHO CO., INC. P.O. BOX 882 ATLANTA 1, GA.

Promotional flyer for *Sepia Cinderella* (1947) with Sheila Guyse.

of *The Ladykillers* (2004) with Tom Hanks. She won a special Jury Prize at the Cannes Film Festival and an NAACP Image Award for her role as Marva Munson, a canny old landlady who is more than a match for a confidence man (Tom Hanks) and his band of thieves.

Hall's TV films include *Miss Lettie and Me* (2002)—yet another feisty mama role.

She was born Irma Dolores Player Hall in Beaumont, Texas, and raised on the South Side of Chicago. Her father was a jazz saxophonist. Hall attended Briar Cliff College in Sioux City,

Iowa. She is the mother of two and a grandmother numerous times over.

Feature Films including Video and TV Movies: *Book of Numbers* (1973), *Dallas Cowboys Cheerleaders II* (TV; 1979), *Dallas Cowboys Cheerleaders* (TV; 1980), *Crisis at Central High* (TV; 1981), *Broken Promise* (TV; 1981), *Split Image* (1982), *He's Not Your Son* (TV; 1984), *The Long Hot Summer* (TV; 1985), *The George McKenna Story* (TV; 1986), *On Valentine's Day* (1986), *Square Dance* (1987), *They Still Call Me Bruce* (1987), *Uncle Tom's Cabin* (TV; 1987), *The Kid Who Loved Christmas* (TV; 1990), *Backdraft* (1991), *Straight Talk* (1992), *The Babe* (1992), *In the Shadow of a Killer* (TV; 1992), *Mo' Money* (1992), *In the Company of Darkness* (TV; 1993), *A Family Thing* (1996), *To Sir, with Love II* (TV; 1996), *Buddy* (1997), *Nothing to Lose* (1997), *Steel* (1997), *Soul Food* (1997), *Midnight in the Garden of Evil* (1997), *The Love Letter* (TV; 1998), *Beloved* (1998), *Patch Adams* (1998), *A Slipping-Down Life* (1999), *A Lesson Before Dying* (TV; 1999), *Something to Sing About* (TV; 2000), *A Girl Thing* (TV; 2001), *Our America* (TV; 2002), *Don't Let Go* (2002), *Bad Company* (2002), *Miss Lettie and Me* (TV; 2002), *An Unexpected Love* (TV; 2003), *The Ladykillers* (2004), *Collateral* (2004), *P.N.O.K.* (2005), *Gift for the Living* (2005), *Hollywood on Fire* (documentary; 2007), *Rain* (2007), *Vacuuming the Cat* (2008), *Meet the Browns* (2008).

TV: *Dallas* ("Bar-B-Que," 1978), *Touched by an Angel* ("Seek and Ye Shall Find," 1998), *Getting Personal* ("Guess Who Else Is Coming to Dinner?" 1998), *Judging Amy* ("An Impartial Bias," 1999), *7th Heaven* ("All By Myself," 2000), *A Rugrats Kwanzaa Special* (2001), *All Souls* (recurring role as Nurse Glory St. Claire; 2001), *The Bernie Mac Show* (2 episodes; "Sweet Home Chicago," Parts I and II, 2002), *Soul Food* (recurring role of Mama Joe (2002–04).

Hall, Regina Born in Washington, D.C., December 12, 1970.

This adept comedienne is of Native American and African American descent. Her father was a contractor; her mother was a teacher. She earned a master's degree in journalism in 1997 from New York University before starting a movie career. Hall began appearing in TV commercials, and then broke through into feature films. She is known for her role in the *Scary Movie* (2001–2006) horror film spoofs, parts I through IV, as the feisty but inept Brenda Meeks. Her first film was a small role as Candy in the effective ensemble drama *The Best Man* (1999), followed by the second lead in *Love & Basketball* (2000), starring real-life friend Sanaa Lathan, who was also in *The Best Man* and the TV movie *Disappearing Acts* (2000) with Hall. Hall returned to comedy in *The Other Brother* (2002) in the role of Vicki. She had a change of pace with the action drama *Paid in Full* (2002). This was followed by a string of comedies, most notably the character-driven Ice Cube comedy *First Sunday* (2008), and the ill-advised black cast remake of *The Honeymooners* (2005), which opened to withering reviews and bad box office. But Hall gave her usual well-shaded, amusing performance as Trixie Norton, wife of Ed (Mike Epps).

Her television work includes a recurring role as the strait-laced attorney Coretta Lipp on *Ally McBeal* (2001–02). She was nominated for an NAACP Image Award for Outstanding Supporting Actress in a Comedy Series for her work on the show. She also appeared in a recurring role on the soap opera *Loving* (1992) and guest starred on the police dramas *New York Undercover* (1997) and *NYPD Blue* (2000).

Feature Films including Video and TV Movies: *The Best Man* (1999), *Love & Basketball* (2000), *Scary Movie* (2000), *Disappearing Acts* (TV; 2000), *Scary Movie II* (2001), *The Other Brother* (2002), *Paid in Full* (2002), *Malibu's Most Wanted* (2003), *Scary Movie III* (2003), *King's Ransom* (2005), *The Honeymooners* (2005), *Six Months Later* (2005), *Scary Movie 4* (2006), *Danika* (2006), *The Elder Son* (2006), *First Sunday* (2008), *Superhero Movie* (2008), *Scary Movie 5* (2009), *Mardi Gras* (2009).

TV: *Loving* (1992), *New York Undercover* ("No Place Like Hell," 1997), *NYPD Blue* ("Little Abner," 2000), *Ally McBeal* (22 episodes in the role of Coretta Lipp; 2001 and 2002), *Total Request Live* (2003), *The Sharon Osbourne Show* (2003), *106 & Park Top Ten Live* (2005), *The Early Show* (2005), *The Tyra Banks Show* (2006), *Late Night with Conan O'Brien* (4 segments; 2003–06), *Fuse Fangoria Chainsaw Awards* (2006), *Late Night with Conan O'Brien* (2008).

Hamilton, Lisa Gay Born in Los Angeles, California, March 25, 1964.

The most admirable aspect of Lisa Gay Hamilton's life has been her crusade against physical violence directed at women. She became active in the fight against violence after performing in Eve Ensler's *The Vagina Monologues*, which addresses issue of vital interest to and impact on today's woman. Hamilton was responsible for bringing V-Day (an ongoing series of events initiated by Ensler) to the Apollo Theater in Harlem. Hamilton is the daughter of a social worker; her father is a realtor. She holds a degree in theatre from New York University and earned a master's degree from The Juilliard School. Hamilton also has an admirable desire to educate the public about pioneering black actresses who have paved the way for others. This was the genesis of her documentary *Beah: A Black Woman Speaks* (2003), a documentary about the remarkable African American actress Beah Richards.

Her theatrical breakthrough came when she played Isabella opposite Kevin Kline in *Measure for Measure* in 1993 at the New York Shakespeare Festival. Hamilton's career-defining role was as attorney Rebecca Washington on ABC's *The Practice*, a role she played from 1997 to 2003. Film roles include *Reversal of Fortune* (1990), *Twelve Monkeys* (1995), *Jackie Brown* (1997), *Beloved* (1998) and *Honeydripper* (2007), which gave Hamilton one of her best roles, as Delilah, wife of Tyrone "Pinetop" Purvis (Danny Glover). Purvis is struggling to keep his little juke joint open in 1950s Alabama in this film directed by John Sayles.

Feature Films including Video and TV Movies: *Krush Groove* (1985), *Reversal of Fortune* (1990), *Naked in New York* (1993), *Drunks* (1995), *Clarissa, Now* (TV; 1995), *Palookaville* (1995), *Twelve Monkeys* (1995), *The Defenders: Choice of Evils*; 1996), *Nick and Jane* (1997), *Lifebreath* (1997), *Jackie Brown* (1997), *Beloved* (1998), *Halloween H_2O: 20 Years Later* (voice; 1998), *Swing Vote* (TV; 1999), *True Crime* (1999), *A House Divided* (TV; 2000), *Hamlet* (TV; 2000), *Women Remember Men* (2001), *The Sum of All Fears* (2002), *The Truth About Charlie* (2002), *Beah: A Black Woman Speaks* (documentary; 2003), *The N Word* (documentary; 2004), *Conviction* (TV; 2005), *Nine Lives* (2005), *Honeydripper* (2007), *Deception* (2008).

TV: *Way Cool* (1991), *Homicide: Life on the Street* ("Dog and Pony Show," 1993), *New York Undercover* ("To Serve and Protect," 1994), *All My Children* (recurring role as Celia Wilson; 1994), *Law & Order* ("Purple Heart," 1995), *One Life to Live* (recurring role as Dr. Laura Reed; 1996), *The Practice* (recurring role of Rebecca Washington; 1997–2003), *Ally McBeal* ("The Inmates," 1998), *The L Word* ("Losing It," 2004), *Politically Incorrect* (2000), *Intimate Portrait* (2002), *Hollywood Squares* (3 segments; 2002), *Sex and the City* ("Critical Condition," 2002), *Until the Violence Stops* (2003), *Tribeca Film Festival Presents* (2003), *ER* ("All About Christmas Eve," 2005), *Without a Trace* ("The Calm Before," 2006), *Numb3rs* ("Money for Nothing," 2007), *Law & Order: Special Victims Unit* (2 episodes in the role of Theresa Randall; "Venom," "Screwed," 2006 and 2007).

Hamilton, Lynn Born in Yazoo City, Mississippi, April 25, 1930.

Hamilton is best known as Donna Harris, Fred Sanford's girlfriend, an intermittent role she played on the hit sitcom *Sanford and Son* from 1972 to 1977. She also had a recurring role as Verdie Foster on the long-running *The Waltons* (1973–81). She made her film debut in a small role as a girl at a party in director John Cassavetes' first film *Shadows* (1959), a murky drama about an interracial woman (Lelia Goldini) and her relationships. This remains an important film because it launched Cassavetes' directing career, it was an early example of an independent film (Cassavetes helped define independent films), and the subject matter was quite controversial and unusual for its time. Hamilton didn't appear in another feature until she had a small role in Sidney Poitier's quasi-religious fantasy *Brother John* (1971), one of his few box office misfires.

She was also in the revisionist Western *Buck and the Preacher* (1972) with Poitier and Harry Belafonte — as well as *Lady Sings the Blues* (as Aunt Ida; 1972); the forgotten but memorable *Leadbelly* (as Sally Ledbetter; 1976), a bio pic of blues singer Huddie Ledbetter; and the TV movie that served as a pilot film for the acclaimed *Kojak* series with Telly Savalas, *The Marcus-Nelson Murders* (as Arless Humes; 1973). She also appeared in the miniseries *Roots: The Next Generations* (as Cousin Georgia; 1979), the sequel to one of the most acclaimed programs in television history. Hamilton's later career has consisted largely of short-lived or semi-regular roles on a variety of TV shows. She was Mae Dawson on the soap *The Young and the Restless* (1997); Selita Jones on *Sunset Beach* (1997–98); Judge Fulton on *The Practice* (1997–2002); and Alice Morgan on another soap,

Port Charles (1999). Her most recent acting role was on an episode of *Judging Amy* in 2004.

Feature Films including Video and TV Movies: *Shadows* (1959), *Brother John* (1971), *The Seven Minutes* (1971), *Buck and the Preacher* (1972), *Lady Sings the Blues* (1972), *The Marcus-Nelson Murders* (TV; 1973), *A Dream for Christmas* (TV; 1973), *Hangup* (1974), *Leadbelly* (1976), *The Jesse Owens Story* (TV; 1984), *Legal Eagles* (1986), *Elvis and Me* (TV; 1988), *The Vanishing* (1993), *Baby's Breath* (2003).

TV: *Room 222* ("Triple Date," 1969), *Then Came Bronson* ("All the World and God," 1969), *Mannix* ("Tooth of the Serpent," 1969), *Gunsmoke* (2 episodes; "The Good Samaritans," "The Sisters," 1969), *The Bill Cosby Show* ("The Runaways," 1970), *The Psychiatrist* (pilot; "God Bless the Children," 1970), *Insight* ("The King of the Penny Arcade," 1971), *Ironside* (2 episodes; "A World of Jackals," "Gentle Oaks," 1969 and 1971), *Hawaii Five-O* ("Nine, Ten, You're Dead," 1971), *Ghost Story* ("Time of Terror," 1972), *Sanford and Son* (recurring role of Donna Harris; 1972–77), *Barnaby Jones* ("Sunday; Doomsday," 1973), *The Waltons* (recurring role of Verdie Foster; 1973–81), *Good Times* ("The Gang," Part II, 1974), *Starsky and Hutch* ("Captain Dobey, You're Dead," 1975), *The Rockford Files* ("The Hammer of C Block," 1976), *Roots: The Next Generations* (miniseries; 1979), *The Powers of Matthew Star* ("The Accused," 1982), *Knight Rider* ("Not a Drop to Drink," 1982), *Quincy, M.E.* (2 episodes; "Baby Rattlesnakes," "Women of Valor," 1982 and 1983), *ABC Afterschool Specials* ("The Hero Who Couldn't Read," 1984), *Riptide* ("Fuzzy Vision," 1985), *Highway to Heaven* ("Popcorn, Peanuts, and Cracker Jacks," 1985), *Rituals* (1985), *Amen* ("The Twleve Songs of Christmas," 1987), *Hunter* ("Naked Justice," Part I, 1988), *The Golden Girls* ("Mixed Blessings," 1988), *227* (2 episodes in the role of Emma Johnson; "Country Cousins," "A Class Act," 1988 and 1989), *Generations* (recurring role of Vivian Potter; 1989), *Dangerous Women* (1991), *A Walton Thanksgiving Reunion* (1993), *Sister, Sister* ("Wedding Bells and Box Boys," 1994), *Murphy Brown* ("Be Careful What You Wish For," 1994), *Sisters* ("Guess Who's Coming to Seder," 1996), *Life's Work* ("Harassment," 1997), *Dangerous Minds* ("A Different Light," 1997), *A Walton Easter* (1997), *The Young and the Restless* (recurring role as Mae Dawson; 1997), *Sunset Beach* (5 episodes in the role of Selita Jones; 1997–98), *The Practice* (7 episodes in the role of Judge Fulton; 1997–2002), *Moesha* ("Homecoming," 1998), *Port Charles* (recurring role as Alice Morgan; 1999), *NYPD Blue* ("Oh, Mama!" 2002), *Curb Your Enthusiasm* ("Krazee-Eyez Killa," 2002), *Beah: A Black Woman Speaks* (2003), *Judging Amy* ("Sins of the Father," 2004).

Lynn Hamilton and Hari Rhodes in *A Dream for Christmas* (1973).

Harbin, Suzette Born in Ledbetter, Texas, July 4, 1911; died September 5, 1994, Texas.

Suzette Harbin was an attractive, personable actress who was prominently featured on the cover of *Jet* and other popular black-oriented magazines, and who would have had a more prominent career if mainstream opportunities for black actresses hadn't been so limited during her era. Harbin segued from beauty contestant to actress in a career that endured from 1942 to 1957. She has an uncredited role as a slave, Belle, in *The Foxes of Harrow* (1947).

Her best known "race movie" (a film intended for black audiences and shown in black theaters) is *Look-Out Sister* (1947). This musical Western satire is short on plot and long on musical numbers. The film, named after star Louis Jordan's hit record, is set at a modern dude ranch. Jordan dreams that he's in charge of the ranch. As a suave gunslinger, he saves comely Betty Scott (Harbin) from the evil Mack Gordon (Monty Hawley), who wants to get his hands on her ranch (and on her). Harbin played a jungle chieftain's daughter who is accidentally killed in the seventh film in the Bomba the Jungle Boy series, *Bomba and the Jungle Girl* (1952). Her final screen appearance came five years later in another uncredited role in the negligible low-budget juvenile delinquent melodrama *The Green-Eyed Blonde* (1957).

Feature Films including TV Movies: *Up Jumped the Devil* (1941), *To Have and Have Not* (1944), *Look-Out Sister* (1947), *The Foxes of Harrow* (1947), *The Pirate* (1948), *The Sky Dragon* (1949), *Destination Murder* (1950), *Skirts Ahoy!* (1952), *Lydia Bailey* (1952), *Bomba and the Jungle Girl* (1952), *The Green-Eyed Blonde* (1957).

TV: *Wagon Train* ("The Charles Maury Story," 1958), *That's Black Entertainment: Westerns* (archival; 2002).

Harris, Edna Mae Born in Harlem, New York, September 29, 1910; died September 15, 1997.

Edna Mae Harris was born into a well-known Harlem family. Her mother ran a boardinghouse for performers near the famous Lafayette Players Theatre founded by Anita Bush. While still a student at Manhattan Wadleigh High School, she worked at the Alhambra Theatre doing stock company dramatic sketches. Harris was also an excellent swimmer, and in 1928 competed in the *New York Daily News'* swimming meet and won the event. Her first major film break came as Zeba in *Green Pastures* (1936), where she recreated her 1935 performance in the Broadway production. Stories from the Old Testament are recounted from a black perspective in this painfully dated adaptation of the Broadway play, featuring Rex Ingram as Da Lawd, and also starring Eddie "Rochester" Anderson.

Harris was the leading lady in *The Spirit of Youth* (1938), the thinly disguised biographical film about heavyweight champion Joe Louis (here referred to as Joe Thomas); Louis starred as himself in his solo film appearance. Harris also had a lead in the Oscar Micheaux film *The Notorious Elinor Lee* (1940), an attempt to do a Chicago-set boxing film that basically retold the Louis story with crime film elements added. There's even a German fighter named Max Wagner (for Max Schmeling). Harris plays a light-skinned character named Fredi (clearly an attempt to pay tribute to Fredi Washington's considerable fame at the time in *Imitation of Life*, which was released in 1934). *Paradise in Harlem* (1939) was the story of a comedian (Norman Astwood) whose plans to be a dramatic actor run into a roadblock after he witnesses a mob murder and is forced to flee for his life. Harris appears in the role of Doll Davis.

During this era, Harris was singing, dancing and performing patter at the famed Harlem nightspot Connie's Inn. One of her more significant roles came in Oscar Micheaux's *Lying Lips* (1939). Elsie Bellwood (Harris), a young nightclub singer, is convicted and sent to prison for the murder of her aunt. Benjamin, who loves Elsie, and a detective named Danzer set out to prove her innocence. She had much smaller roles, usually uncredited, in mainstream Hollywood films, including *Bullets or Ballots* (featuring Edward G. Robinson and an early appearance by Humphrey Bogart), *Private Number* and *The Garden of Allah,* a Marlene Dietrich vehicle in an early Technicolor process (all 1936). She was also in the crime drama programmer *X Marks the Spot* (1942), wherein a private detective brings black market racketeers to justice after they kill his policeman father. She was billed as Edna Harris. She appeared in the race picture *The Girl in Room 20* (1946), a cautionary tale about a young black girl's (Geraldine Brock) misadventures in the big city.

Between films Harris toured with the famous Noble Sissle orchestra as a featured vocalist; Lena Horne and Bill Banks also sang vocals with Sissle's orchestra. In 1942, she did 14 weeks at the Elks' Rendezvous as the mistress of ceremonies, and was the announcer on a weekly radio show over station WMCA in New York (which exists to this day, now as a Christian station). She also did character dialect parts on many broadcasts for the Columbia Workshop Program. Harris discussed the role of the pioneer black filmmakers in the documentary *Midnight Ramble* (1994), the fascinating story of independently produced race films.

Feature Films: *Fury* (1936), *Private Number* (1936), *Bullets or Ballots* (1936), *The Green Pastures* (1936), *The Garden of Allah* (1936), *Spirit of Youth* (1938), *Paradise in Harlem* (1939), *Lying Lips* (1939), *Sunday Sinners* (1940), *The Notorious*

Elinor Lee (1940), *Murder on Lenox Avenue* (1941), *X Marks the Spot* (1942), *First Aid* (1943), *A Night for Crime* (1943), *So's Your Uncle* (1943), *Mystery Broadcast* (1943), *Night & Day* (1946), *The Razor's Edge* (1946), *The Girl in Room 20* (1946), *Fall Guy* (1947), *Smart Girls Don't Talk* (1948), *Take Me Out to the Ball Game* (1949).

TV: *The American Experience* ("Midnight Ramble," 1994).

Shorts: *First Aid* (1943).

Harris, Theresa (aka Harris, Teresa)

Born in Houston, Texas, December 31, 1909; died October 8, 1985, Inglewood, California.

The beautiful Theresa Harris alternated between roles in mainstream Hollywood productions with roles in black-cast race films. She was often confined to maid roles, but performed with grace and distinction. Black America knew her as an articulate, candid woman who often bemoaned the lack of decent roles for African Americans in Hollywood.

She sang "Daddy, Won't You Please Come Home" in a black nightclub in Josef von Sternberg's *Thunderbolt* (1929), her film debut. Stunningly gowned and glamorous, this was a Harris mainstream audiences would not see again. Her second screen appearance was an unbilled role in von Sternberg's *Morocco* (1930). She's uncredited as Vera, Ginger Rogers' maid, in *Professional Sweetheart* (1933). She also had showy roles in *Hold Your Man* and *Baby Face* that same year, as well as standard maid roles in films like *Jezebel* and *The Toy Wife* (both 1938). Harris had a nice role as Josephine, Eddie "Rochester" Anderson's girlfriend, in the hilarious Jack Benny vehicle *Buck Benny Rides Again* (1940). She teamed with Anderson in *Love Thy Neighbor* in 1940.

Harris' sexy side emerged again in the black cast production *Gangsters on the Loose* (aka *Bargain with Bullets*; 1937). The genesis of this film is a fascinating story. It was produced by Million Dollar Productions, a company co-founded and co-owned by black actor Ralph Cooper, who co-starred with Harris in this film. The company also produced such key race films as *Life Goes On* (1938), *The Duke Is Tops* (Lena Horne's film debut; 1938), *Gang Smashers* (1938), *Reform School* (1939), *One Dark Night* (1939), and *Four Shall Die* (with 17-year-old Dorothy Dandridge; 1940). The company continued until 1942, when it was done in by financial and distribution problems. Unfortunately, *Gangsters on the Loose* was the only film Harris starred in for the company.

Harris was a favorite of RKO horror film producer Val Lewton and was prominently cast in several of his low-budget genre classics. (Lewton was one of the few producers to integrate blacks into his films in non-stereotyped roles.) She was a sarcastic waitress in *Cat People* (1943) and Alma the maid in *I Walked with a Zombie* (1943). She also appeared in two superb B-films, Robert Siodmak's *Phantom Lady* (another maid role; 1944) and Edgar G. Ulmer's *Strange Illusion* (an uncredited maid role; 1945).

She continued to act in features throughout the 1950s, most notably in *The File on Thelma Jordan* (as Esther; 1950), *Angel Face* (an uncredited role as a nurse; 1952) and *Back from Eternity* (uncredited role of Mamie; 1956). Harris did very little television, but a highlight is an appearance on the *Alfred Hitchcock Presents* episode "Back for Christmas" (1956).

Feature Films: *Thunderbolt* (1929), *Morocco* (1930), *The Road to Reno* (1931), *Arrowsmith* (1931), *Merrily We Go to Hell* (1932), *Weekends Only* (1932), *Horse Feathers* (1932), *Night After Night* (1932), *The Half Naked Truth* (1932), *Grand Slam* (1933), *Gold Diggers of 1933* (1933), *Professional Sweetheart* (1933), *Private Detective 62* (1933), *Hold Your Man* (1933), *Baby Face* (1933), *Mary Stevens, M.D.* (1933), *Morning Glory* (1933), *Penthouse* (1933), *Broadway Thru a Keyhole* (1933), *Blood Money* (1933), *Roman Scandals* (1933), *Success at Any Price* (1934), *A Modern Hero* (1934), *Finishing School* (1934), *Drums o' Voodoo* (1934), *Black Moon* (1934), *Desirable* (1934), *Go Into Your Dance* (1935), *Broadway Melody of 1936* (1935), *Fifteen Maiden Lane* (1936), *Banjo on My Knee* (1936), *Gangsters on the Loose* (1937), *Charlie Chan at the Olympics* (1937), *The Lady Escapes* (1937), *Big Town Girl* (1937), *Jezebel* (1938), *The Toy Wife* (1938), *A Hundred to One* (1939), *The Women* (1939), *One Hour to Live* (1939), *City of Chance* (1940), *Buck Benny Rides Again* (1940), *Santa Fe Trail* (1940), *Love Thy Neighbor* (1940), *The Flame of New Orleans* (1941), *Blossoms in the Dust* (1941), *Our Wife* (1941), *Sing Your Worries Away* (1942), *Tough As They Come* (1942), *Cat People* (1942), *I Walked with a Zombie* (1943), *What's Buzzin' Cousin?* (1943), *Phantom Lady* (1944), *Strange Illusion* (1945), *The Dolly Sisters* (1945), *Smooth as Silk* (1946), *Three Little Girls in Blue* (1946), *Hit Parade of 1947* (1947), *Miracle on 34th Street*

(1947), *Out of the Past* (1947), *The Big Clock* (1948), *The Velvet Touch* (1948), *Alias Nick Beal* (1949), *Neptune's Daughter* (1949), *Tension* (1949), *And Baby Makes Three* (1949), *The File on Thelma Jordan* (1950), *Grounds for Marriage* (1951), *Al Jennings of Oklahoma* (1951), *The Company She Keeps* (1951), *Angel Face* (1952), *Here Come the Girls* (1953), *The French Line* (1954), *Back from Eternity* (1956), *Spoilers of the Forest* (1957), *The Gift of Love* (1958), *Val Lewton: The Man in the Shadows* (archival; documentary; 2007).

TV: *Lux Video Theatre* ("A Place in the Sun," 1954), *The Loretta Young Show* ("The New York Story," 1954), *Alfred Hitchcock Presents* ("Back for Christmas," 1956).

Shorts: *Free Wheeling* (1932).

Harris, Zelda Born in New York, New York, February 17, 1985.

Zelda Harris was born to Karen and Philip Harris; her sister is named Kenya. Her acting career was launched well before she graduated from Princeton University in 2007. She began appearing in commercials as an infant; then she became a regular on *Sesame Street.* In 1991 she appeared in her series debut in *I'll Fly Away* (as Adlaine; 1991). Other series guest star work was on *Law & Order* (1994), *NYPD Blue* (1998), and *Cosby* (2002). Harris made her feature film debut as Troy, Alfre Woodard's daughter, in Spike Lee's bittersweet *Crooklyn* (1994). She was nine years old. She was next seen as Jessi in *The Baby-Sitter's Club* (1995). In 1998, she appeared in another Spike Lee film, *He Got Game* with Denzel Washington. She played Mary, the young sister of basketball prospect Jesus Shuttleworth (Ray Allen).

In 2005 Harris played the Queen in a performance of Shakespeare's *Cymbeline* for Princeton's Theatre Intime. She was nominated for an NAACP Image Award for Outstanding Youth Actress for *He Got Game,* as well as the Young Artist Award for Best Performance by a Young Actress in a Motion Picture for *Crooklyn,* and the Best Performance in a TV Series, Youth Ensemble, for *Second Noah* (1996).

Feature Films including TV Movies: *Crooklyn* (1994), *The Piano Lesson* (TV; 1995), *The Baby-Sitters Club* (1995), *Clover* (TV; 1997), *He Got Game* (1998).

TV: *I'll Fly Away* ("The Hat," 1991), *Law & Order* ("Nurture," 1994), *Second Noah* (pilot; 1996), *413 Hope St.* ("Falling," 1998), *Cosby* ("A Team of His Own," 1998), *NYPD Blue* ("Below the Belt," 2002).

Hartley, Pat Birth date unavailable.

Pat Hartley was fresh out of high school when she met Chuck Wein, a member of Andy Warhol's inner circle, in the West Village. Wein took her to the Factory, Warhol's inner sanctum of art and the nexus of the numerous avant-garde films Warhol made during the sixties and seventies. Hartley became part of the Warhol filmmaking scene — she loved the idea of being an actress — and appeared in two documentaries about rock legend Jimi Hendrix. Although she appeared in five Warhol films, her only appearance in a mainstream film was in the 1986 British musical *Absolute Beginners* (1986).

Hartley is married to Dick Fontaine, British experimental and documentary filmmaker. Their son is writer, music critic and editor Smokey Fontaine. Fontaine and Hartley co-directed the documentary *Art Blakey: The Jazz Messenger* (1988). Hartley directed the six-minute short *Hung Up* (1994) and acts in it.

Feature Films: *Screen Test* (1965), *Prison* (aka *Girls in Prison*; 1965), *My Hustler II* (1965), *Double Pisces, Scorpio Rising* (1970), *Jimi Hendrix Rainbow Bridge* (1971), *Rainbow Bridge* (1971), *Ciao! Manhattan* (1972), *Jimi Hendrix* (aka *A Film About Jimi Hendrix* (1973), *Absolute Beginners* (1986).

Shorts: *Hung Up* (1994).

Hartman, Ena Birth date unavailable.

Ena Hartman deserved more and better roles. She is probably best remembered today for the B-film *Terminal Island* (1973), which was her last acting credit. *Terminal Island* provided an early, humble role for Tom Selleck, who would go on to much bigger and better things soon after. Hartman plays Carmen, a political activist transported to the prison island of the title, after being told that she is now considered legally dead. Carmen's fellow prisoners include B-film favorites Phyllis Davis and Barbara Leigh. Carmen is physically abused as part of her initiation into the camp, and she joins the other female prisoners, who are essentially field slaves forced into sexual servitude at night. Although directed by a woman (Stephanie Rothman) and a production of Roger Corman's New World Pictures (which did the Pam Grier women-in-prison films like *Women in*

Cages), *Terminal Island* is a listless, meandering affair. The women eventually team up with a group of rebellious male prisoners, gain control of the prison environment, and start a free society.

Her most prominent mainstream film role was in *Airport* (1970), the huge box office success in which she played Ruth, a stewardess. Hartman appeared uncredited as a crew member in the first episode of the original *Star Trek* series, "The Corbomite Maneuver" (1966). She appeared as Katy Grant, police dispatcher, on the ABC cop drama *Dan August*, starring Burt Reynolds (1970–71). She also played Laneen in three episodes of NBC's pleasant update of *Tarzan* starring Ron Ely (1967).

Feature Films including TV Movies: *Our Man Flint* (1966), *Fame Is the Name of the Game* (TV; 1966), *Games* (1967), *Prescription: Murder* (TV; 1968), *Double Jeopardy* (TV; 1970), *Airport* (1970), *Terminal Island* (1973).

TV: *Bonanza* ("Enter Thomas Bowers," 1964), *The Jean Arthur Show* (2 episodes; "Blackstone, Italian Style," "The Lady or the Tiger," 1966), *Star Trek* ("The Corbomite Maneuver," 1966), *Tarzan* (3 episodes in the role of Laneen; "The Prisoner," "The Three Faces of Death," "The Blue Stone of Heaven," Part I, 1967), *Dragnet 1967* ("The Missing Realtor"), *Adam-12* ("The Impossible Mission," 1968), *The Name of the Game* ("The Taker," 1968), *It Takes a Thief* ("Get Me to the Revolution on Time," 1968), *The Outsider* ("I Can't Hear You Scream," 1968), *Ironside* (3 episodes; "Let My Brother Go," "Memory of an Ice Cream Stick," "A World of Jackals," 1967–69), *Dan August* (recurring role of Katy Grant; "The King Is Dead," "The Meal Ticket," 1970 and 1971).

Hayman, Lillian Born in Baltimore, Maryland, July 17, 1922; died October 25, 1994, Hollis, New York.

Lillian Irene Hayman received a bachelor of arts degree from Wilberforce University in Ohio. She studied music in New York and became the director of several church choirs. Her Broadway debut was in *Shinbone Alley* (1957), followed by

Ena Hartman in *Terminal Island* (1973).

Kwamina (as Mammy Trader) in 1961. Her career making role came when she won the 1968 Tony Award for Best Supporting Actress for her role of Leslie Uggam's mother in *Hallelujah, Baby!* at the Martin Beck Theatre (1967). Uggams won a Tony for Best Actress; Jule Styne, Betty Comden and Adolph Green won for Best Composer and Lyricists; and the show was acknowledged as Best Musical of the Year. *Hallelujah, Baby!* also received Tony Award nominations for Best Book, Best Actor (Robert Hooks), Best Costume Design, Best Direction, and Best Choreography. After this Hayman was in *70, Girls, 70* (as Melba; 1971) and the short-lived *Dr. Jazz* (as Georgia Sheridan; 1975).

Hallelujah, Baby! led to her being cast in the ongoing role of Sadie Gray in the popular daytime soap opera *One Life to Live* (1968–1986)—a remarkable run of 17 years—until she was fired and unceremoniously replaced by Esther Rolle. Then she became part of the ensemble supporting cast of the short-lived variety series *The Leslie Uggams Show* (1969), which had the misfortune to air in the same time slot as the ratings powerhouse *Bonanza*. Hayman also distinguished herself off–Broadway in *Dream About Tomorrow* and *Along Came a Spider* (as Mrs. Franklin; 1963). She made very few films, but can be seen in *Gone Are the Days* (the film version of Ossie Davis' play *Pulie Victorious*, 1963). She had the dubious honor of being one of the last black actresses to play mammy roles (as the slave Lucrezia Borgia) in the mind-numbingly racist epic *Mandingo* (1975) and its little-seen sequel *Drum* (1976). Hayman died of a heart attack and was survived by her sister Coreania.

Feature Films: *Gone Are the Days* (aka *Purlie Victorious*, 1963), *The Night They Raided Minsky's* (1968), *Mandingo* (1975), *Drum* (1976).

TV: *The 22nd Annual Tony Awards* (1968), *One Life to Live* (recurring role as Sadie Gray; 1968–1986), *The Leslie Uggams Show* (cast member; 1969), *Barefoot in the Park* ("Something Fishy," 1970), *The Mod Squad* ("A Faraway Place So Near," 1970), *Love, American Style* ("Love and the Newscasters," 1972), *The Corner Bar* ("Cook's Night Out," 1972).

Headley, Heather Born in Barataria, Trinidad and Tobago, October 5, 1974.

Lovely Trinidadian Heather Headley sprang to prominence as the originator of the title role in Disney's long-running Broadway production of *Aida*, with music and lyrics by Tim Rice and Elton John, which earned her the Tony Award for Best Actress in 2000. At age four, Headley sang at the Barataria Church of God in Trinidad. In 1989, the family (her father Iric, mother Hannah, and brother Junior) moved to Fort Wayne, Indiana, when her father was offered the job as pastor at McKee Street Church of God (both her parents are ministers). After graduating from Northrop High School, Headley attended Northwestern University to study communications and musical theater; after she completed her junior year, she made the difficult decision to drop out of school and become part of the Broadway musical *Ragtime* (as Audra McDonald's understudy). *Ragtime* was not the hit everyone expected it to be, but in 1997 she played Nala in *The Lion King*, one of the all-time Broadway hits. After *Aida* she starred in a concert version of *Dreamgirls* (2001) with Audra McDonald.

Her debut album, *This Is Who I Am*, was released by RCA Records in 2002. It earned her a Grammy Award nomination for Best Female R&B Vocal Performance and for Best New Artist. She was also nominated for a *Billboard* Music Award for R&B/Hip-Hop New Artist of the Year (2003), and NAACP Image Awards for Outstanding New Artist and Outstanding Female Artist (2003). Her second album, *In My Mind*, was released in 2006.

She appeared in two films in 2004, *Breakin' All the Rules* and *Dirty Dancing: Havana Nights*, both of which took advantage of her musical talents. In 2003, she married Brian Musso, formerly of the New York Jets.

Feature Films: *Breakin' All the Rules* (2004), *Dirty Dancing: Havana Nights* (2004).

TV: *The Rosie O'Donnell Show* (2 segments; 2000), *The 55th Annual Tony Awards* (2001), *Great Performances* (2 segments; "My Favorite Broadway: The Love Songs," "Andrea Bocelli: Amore Under the Desert Sky," 2001 and 2006), *Walt Disney World Christmas Day Parade* (2002), *Sidewalks Entertainment* (2003), *9th Annual Soul Train Lady of Soul Awards* (2003), *An Evening of Stars: Tribute to Stevie Wonder* (2006), *The Tonight Show with Jay Leno* (2006), *Today* (2006), *Ellen* (2006), *Tavis Smiley* (2006), *Soul Train* (2006), *Showtime at the Apollo* (2006), *An American Celebration at Ford's Theater* (2006), *The Mark Twain Prize: Neil Simon* (2006).

Video/DVD: *Elmo's Magic Cookbook* (2001).

Headley, Shari Born in Queens, New York, July 15, 1964.

The youngest of four children, Shari Headley began her college education studying pre-med, but when she was offered a Ford Modeling Agency contract, she passed on medicine and concentrated on modeling and acting. She achieved fame in both feature films — with her appealing role of Lisa McDowell, love interest of Eddie Murphy in 1988's *Coming to America*— and on television with her role as policewoman Mimi Reed Frye Williams on the popular soap opera *All My Children* (1991–95, and again in 2005). She also was featured in the role of Felicia Boudreau in another soap, *Guiding Light* (2001–02), and was on yet another soap, *The Bold and the Beautiful,* as Heather Engle (2004–05). In 1997, she co-starred on the short-lived TV drama *413 Hope St.* in the role of Juanita Barnes. Other key film roles are in *The Preacher's Wife* (as Arlene Chattan; 1996) with Whitney Houston and Denzel Washington and *Johnson Family Vacation* (as Jacqueline; 2004).

She has an extensive résumé as a guest star on popular TV shows, including *The Cosby Show* (1985), *Miami Vice* (1986), *Quantum Leap* (1990), *Matlock* (1990–93), *New York Undercover* (1995), *Walker, Texas Ranger* (1996), *Cosby* (1996), *Malcolm & Eddie* (1998), *The Wayans Bros.* (1999), *Veronica Mars* (2005) and *House* (2005). Headley was married to rapper-actor Christopher "Play" Martin, star of the immensely popular *House Party* series (which started in 1990). They were married from 1993 to 1995, and have a son, Skyler Martin.

Shari Headley.

Feature Films including TV Movies: *Coming to America* (1988), *Paris Is Burning* (documentary; 1990), *The Preacher's Wife* (1996), *A Woman Like That* (1997), *Johnson Family Vacation* (2004), *Nothing Is Private* (2007), *Millionaire Boyz Club* (2007), *Towelhead* (2008).

TV: *The Cosby Show* ("Denise's Friend," 1985), *Miami Vice* ("French Twist," 1986), *Kojak* (2 episodes; "Ariana," "None So Blind," 1989 and 1990), *Gideon Oliver* (3 episodes in the role of Zina Oliver; "Sleep Well, Professor Oliver," "Tongs," "By the Waters of Babylon," 1989), *Quantum Leap* ("Pool Hall Blues," 1990), *Matlock* (2 episodes: "The Cover Girl," "The Revenge," 1990 and 1993), *New York Undercover* ("Brotherhood," 1995), *Walker, Texas Ranger* ("Behind the Badge," 1996), *Cosby* ("No Nudes Is Good News," 1996), *413 Hope Street* (recurring role of Juanita Barnes; 1997), *The Love Boat: The Next Wave* ("Smooth Sailing," 1998), *Getting Personal* ("Bring in 'da Milo, Bring in 'da Robyn," 1998), *Malcolm & Eddie* ("Twisted Sisters," 1998), *For Your Love* ("The Sister Act," 1998), *The Wayans Bros.* (2 episodes in the role of Dawn; "Crazy 4 U," "Three on a Couch," 1999), *The Guiding Light* (2001), *Half & Half* ("The Big Bitter Shower Episode," 2003), *One on One* ("Sleepless in Baltimore," 2004), *The Bold and the Beautiful* (recurring role of Heather Engle; 2004–05), *Veronica Mars* ("Lord of the Bling," 2005), *House* ("Kids," 2005), *All My Children* (recurring role of Officer Mimi Reed Frye; 2005), *The 32nd Annual Daytime Emmy Awards* (2005).

Video/DVD: *Daytime's Greatest Weddings* (archival; 2004).

Music Video: *Wild Wild West* (1999).

Hemphill, Shirley Born in Asheville, North Carolina, July 1, 1947; died December 10, 1999, West Covina, California.

Born into a poor family in North Carolina, Shirley Ann Hemphill was determined to be a stand-up comic, but wasn't having much luck until she sent a tape of her routine to Flip Wilson,

Left to right: Fred Berry, Ernest Thomas, Haywood Nelson and Shirley Hemphill in *What's Happening!!*

then a major TV star. Wilson liked her comedy, invited her to a taping of his show, and gave her some much needed encouragement. Meanwhile, Hemphill, who had attended Hill Street High, was working in a fast food restaurant and beginning to appear in local comedy clubs at night. She proved that perseverance and talent could take the place of connections and that a determined individual could overcome meager beginnings.

By 1976, her routines got her enough attention for some series TV work, and landed her the breakthrough role as the sharp-tongued waitress Shirley Wilson on ABC's sitcom *What's Happening!!* (1976–79), a spin-off of the hit movie *Cooley High* (1975). It ran for three highly successful seasons and, in a rarely seen situation (other examples include *Baywatch* and *Hee Haw*), it returned in an all-new syndicated version, again with Hemphill in her signature role of Shirley Wilson. *What's Happening Now!* (one exclamation point) ran from 1985 to 1988, equaling the success of the original show.

In between that show and its revival, Hemphill starred in her own series, *One in a Million* (1980), as an L.A. cab driver who strikes it rich. The show did not catch on and only aired 13 episodes before it was cancelled. After the *What's Happening!!* phenomenon ran its course, Hemphill returned to working comedy clubs and turned up as a guest star on various sitcoms (*Martin, The Sinbad Show, The Wayans Bros., Linc's*). After she was found dead of kidney failure in her home by a gardener at age 52, television fans remembered her gruff, authoritative, yet oddly lovable Shirley character and were grateful for the years of unpretentious, escapist entertainment she had given them.

Feature Films: *CB4* (1993), *Shoot the Moon* (1996).

TV: *Good Times* ("Rich Is Better Than Poor," 1976), *What's Happening!!* (recurring role of Shirley Wilson; 1976–79), *The Richard Pryor Special* (1977), *One in a Million* (recurring role as Shirley Simmons; 1980), *The Love Boat* (1982), *Trapper John, M.D.* ("Fat Chance," 1983), *Pryor's Place* ("Sax Education," 1984), *What's Happening Now!* (recurring role of Shirley Wilson; 1985–88), *The Sinbad Show* ("I Coulda' Been the Man,"

1993), *Martin* ("Go Tell It on the Martin," 1994), *The Wayans Bros.* ("Hearts and Flowers," 1996), *Linc's* ("Speaking in Tongues," 1999).

Hemsley, Estelle Born in Boston, Massachusetts, May 5, 1887; died November 5, 1968, Hollywood, California.

Estelle Hemsley was in *Edge of the City* (1957) as the mother of Lucy Tyler (Ruby Dee), wife of a New York City longshoreman who loses his life when he befriends a white coworker (John Cassavetes). She is best known for co-starring in *Take a Giant Step* (1959), directed by Philip Leacock and produced by Burt Lancaster via his Hecht-Hill-Lancaster company. *Take a Giant Step* is *A Raisin in the Sun*–inspired domestic drama about the travails of a young black man named Spencer Scott (Johnny Nash) in a predominantly white middle class community; the film also starred a young Ruby Dee as the housemaid for the Scott family. Hemsley was nominated for a Golden Globe Award for her work in the film as Grandma "Gram" Martin, Spencer's grandmother. But *The New York Times* called the film "a cross between a social justice brochure and a Negro Andy Hardy film." Of Hemsley's role, *The Times* critic wrote, "as a wise old grandmother, she does everything cranky and cozy but suck on a corncob pipe."

Her film debut was in the race movie *The Return of Mandy's Husband* (1948), a Mantan Mooreland comedy. Hemsley was Mandy. In the "B" horror film *The Leech Woman* (1960) — which is much better than its title or low budget would suggest — there is an effective scene where Hemsley, as an old African woman about to be given restored youth, delivers a rather proto-feminist message about how an aging man gains wisdom and respect, while for an aging woman there is no respect or recognition.

Hemsley was Cla Cla in the exquisite *Green Mansions* (1959), with Audrey Hepburn as the mysterious rain forest beauty Rima the Bird Girl. She was an old Greek named Grandmother Topouzoglou in *America, America* (1963), Elia Kazan's paean to his Greek youth. She was Catherine, a housekeeper, in her final film, the pretentious *Baby the Rain Must Fall* (1965).

Feature Films: *The Return of Mandy's Husband* (1948), *Edge of the City* (1957), *Take a Giant Step* (1959), *Green Mansions* (1959), *The Leech Woman* (1960), *America, America* (1963), *Baby the Rain Must Fall* (1965).

TV: *The Philco Television Playhouse* ("The Mother," 1954), *Hallmark Hall of Fame* ("The Green Pastures," 1957).

Hendry, Gloria Born in Winter Haven, Florida, March 3, 1949.

Gloria Hendry effortlessly alternated between blaxploitation films (a term she rightfully hates) to a significant role as history's second black Bond girl (after Trina Parks), including a daring at the time love scene with Roger Moore in *Live and Let Die* (1973). With the perfect look for the "black is beautiful" era — which also saw the rise of darker-skinned actresses like Judy Pace and Brenda Sykes — Hendry parlayed style and sexuality into a healthy run in films and an occasional foray on television. She is a mixture of Creek and Seminole Indian, Chinese and Irish, as well as African blood.

Born in Florida, the eldest of two daughters, she moved with her mother and sister to their grandparents' home in Newark, New Jersey, living there until she was seven. She continued to live with her mother in Newark until she was 18. While in elementary school, she played violin with the All-City Orchestra, performing on the radio and at a number of academic events. She sharpened her secretarial skills with shorthand and typing classes and attended the Essex College of Business after high school. She was also skilled in a number of sports and physical activities beginning in her school days, which held her in good stead as an action heroine. These included swimming, gymnastics, skating, tennis, karate, running and rollerblading. Although acting was not on her radar screen at the time, she was ambitious and hard working. She juggled a job as the assistant to the legal secretary at the New York office of the NAACP with work as a model and a Playboy bunny.

In November 1972, after small roles in a Sidney Poitier film and a foray into blaxploitation with *Across 110th Street* (1972), she was informed by Harry Saltzman's office through her manager that they wanted to interview her for a role in *Live and Let Die*, the first of the Roger Moore Bond films. Saltzman arranged a meeting with Moore and director Guy Hamilton, and Hendry was informed soon after that she had gotten the role of Rosie Carver. Ostensibly a CIA agent, Rosie is actually working with the bad guy Mr. Big — but her lust for James Bond is real. A spate of black action roles followed in the wake of *Live and Let Die*: *Slaughter's Big Rip-Off* (1973), *Hell Up in Harlem* (1973), *Savage Sisters* (1974), and *Bare Knuckles* (1977).

Her standout black era action film — along with Pam Grier's *Coffy*, which probably represents the best of the entire genre — is director Larry Cohen's *Black Caesar* (1973) starring Fred Williamson. Essentially a remake of the gangster classic *Little Caesar*, *Black Caesar* is a paranoid, white-hot vision of power gained and lost. It is dark, uncompromising, and nothing like the other facile, feel-good blaxploitation films of the era. Hendry stands out as the wife of mob kingpin Tommy Gibbs, who eventually becomes attracted to Tommy's more sensitive friend Joe (Philip Roye).

Feature Films including Video and TV Movies: *For Love of Ivy* (1968), *The Landlord* (1970), *Across 110th Street* (1972), *Black Caesar* (1973), *Live and Let Die* (1973), *Slaughter's Big Rip-Off* (1973), *Hell Up in Harlem* (1973), *Come Back, Charleston Blue* (1974), *Black Belt Jones* (1974), *Savage Sisters* (1974), *Bare Knuckles* (1977), *Doin' Time on Planet Earth* (1988), *Seeds of Tragedy* (TV; 1991), *Pumpkinhead II: Blood Wings* (1994), *South Bureau Homicide* (1996), *Lookin' Italian* (aka *Showdown*, 1998), *Seven Swans* (2005), *Black Kissinger* (2009).

TV: *Love, American Style* ("Love and the Flunky," 1973), *The Blue Knight* ("The Candy Man," 1976), *The Brady Brides* ("Cool Hand Phil," 1981), *Emerald Point N.A.S.* ("The Assignment," 1984), *Falcon Crest* ("Opening Moves," 1987), *Small Steps, Big Strides* (documentary; 1998), *Hunter* ("The Incident," *E! True Hollywood Story* ("Superfly: The Ron O'Neal Story," 2000), *Baadasssss Cinema* (2002), *Macked, Hammered, Slaughtered and Shafted* (2004).

Shorts: *Seven Swans* (2005).

Henson, Taraji P.

Born in Washington, D.C., September 11, 1970.

Taraji Penda Henson gives vivid, memorable performances that stay in the mind. Her three most accomplished roles are as the pregnant prostitute Shug in John Singleton's *Hustle & Flow* (2005); the bombastic ghetto diva girlfriend of Don Cheadle in *Talk to Me*, directed by Kasi Lemmons (2007); and Queenie, the caregiver and surrogate mother of an old man who grows younger instead of aging, eventually becoming a helpless baby, in *The Curious Case of Benjamin Button* (2008). Henson made her singing debut in *Hustle & Flow*. She provided the vocals for the Three 6 Mafia track "It's Hard Out Here for a Pimp," which won the Academy Award for Best Original Song (2006). Henson performed the song with the group on the Oscar telecast.

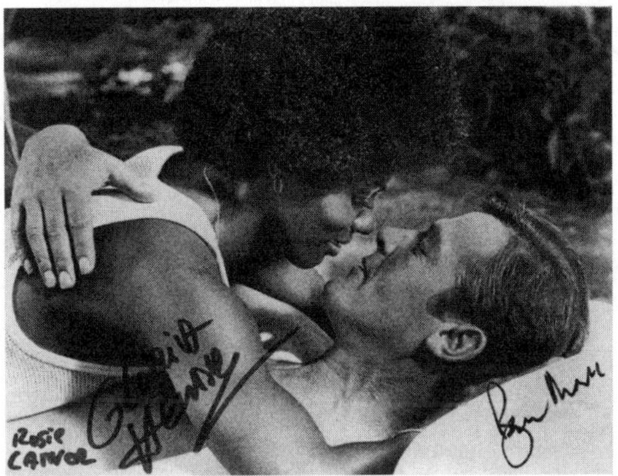

Gloria Hendry and Roger Moore in *Live and Let Die* (1973).

Born and raised in the District of Columbia, she attended Oxon Hill High School in Oxon Hill, Maryland. She attempted to study electrical engineering at North Carolina Agricultural and Technical State University, but when she failed pre-calculus, she transferred to Howard University in D.C., graduating in 1995. She also worked two jobs — as a secretary at the Pentagon by day and as an entertainer and waitress on a cruise ship by night. In addition to her work and studies, she was supporting her son Marcel, whose father had died in 1997. Henson's own father died in 2007. After graduation, she took her baby and headed to Los Angeles in search of film work.

She got her first break when she was cast in an episode of the sitcom *Smart Guy* (1997) and landed a role in the film *Streetwise* (1998), about crack dealers in Washington, D.C. Other, more substantial films followed: John Singleton's *Baby Boy* (2001), as Yvette, who makes the mistake of having a baby with the title character; and a "best friend" role in *Something New* (2006), the touching drama of an interracial love affair, starring Sanaa Lathan. Henson appeared as Inspector Raina Washington in *The Division* (2003–04). Most recently, she has been featured in the role of Whitney Rome on ABC's *Boston Legal* (2007–08), and as Angela on another lawyer series, *Eli Stone* (2008).

Henson has received many awards and award nominations in her career. She has won a Black Movie Award for Best Actress (*Hustle & Flow*); a BET Award for Best Actress (*Hustle & Flow*); a Gotham Award for Best Ensemble Performance (*Talk to Me*); and a Black Reel Award for Best Supporting Actress (*Hustle & Flow*). She garnered NAACP Image Award nominations for Outstanding Supporting Actress in a Motion Picture (*Hustle & Flow*) and Outstanding Actress in a Motion Picture (*Talk to Me*); an MTV Movie Award nomination for Best Breakthrough Performance (*Hustle & Flow*); a Satellite Award nomination for Best Supporting Actress in a Motion Picture (*Talk to Me*); three Black Reel Award nominations (for *Baby Boy*, *Four Brothers*, and *Hustle & Flow*); and two Screen Actors Guild award nominations for Outstanding Cast in a Motion Picture (*Hustle & Flow*) and Outstanding Cast in a Television Drama (*Boston Legal*).

Feature Films including Video and TV Movies: *Streetwise* (1998), *Satan's School for Girls* (TV; 2000), *The Adventures of Rocky & Bullwinkle* (2000), *All or Nothing* (2001), *Baby Boy* (2001), *Hair Show* (2004), *Hustle & Flow* (2005), *Four Brothers* (2005), *Animal* (2005), *Something New* (2006), *Smokin' Aces* (2006), *Talk to Me* (2007), *The Family That Preys* (2008), *The Curious Case of Benjamin Button* (2008), *Once Fallen* (2009), *Not Easily Broken* (2009), *Hurricane Season* (2009).

TV: *Smart Guy* ("Big Picture," 1997), *Sister, Sister* ("Two's Company," 1997), *ER* (2 episodes; "Of Past Regret and Future Fear," "Split Second," 1998), *Felicity* (2 episodes; "Drawing the Line," Part I, "Todd Mulcahy," Part II, 1998 and 1999), *Pacific Blue* ("The Right Thing," 1999), *Strong Medicine* ("Drug Interactions," 2000), *Murder, She Wrote* ("The Last Free Man," 2001), *Holla* (2002), *The Division* (recurring role of Inspector Raina Washington; 2003–04), *All of Us* ("In Through the Out Door," 2004), *The 18th Annual Soul Train Music Awards* (2004), *Half & Half* ("The Big How to Do It and Undo It Episode," 2005), *House* ("Spin," 2005), *C.S.I.* ("I Like to Watch," 2006), *Boston Legal* (recurring role as Whitney Rome; 2007–08), *Eli Stone* (recurring role as Angela; "Help," "Happy Birthday, Nate," "The Humanitarian," 2008).

Music Video: *Testify* (2005).

Hill, Lauryn Born in South Orange, New Jersey, May 25, 1975.

Lauryn Noelle Hill attracted major national attention with The Fugees (with Wyclef Jean and Pras Michel). Their breakthrough album, *The Score* (1996), featuring the hit single "Killing Me Softly," a remake of the Roberta Flack classic, made the group international superstars, and their album the biggest worldwide-selling rap album ever, with in excess of 17 million copies sold. The album won two Grammys: Best Rap Album and Best R&B Performance by a Group or Duo.

Hill achieved huge solo fame with the multiple–Grammy winning *The Education of Lauryn Hill* (1998), which she also produced, and for which she earned a remarkable 10 Grammy nominations, and won five Grammys — a record for a female solo artist—including Album of the Year and Best R&B Album. Her second solo album, *MTV Unplugged 2.0* (2002), featured just Hill's vocals while accompanying herself on acoustic guitar and was a relative sales failure. Her career in music (and as an actress) has been quiet in recent years, although she appeared with The Fugees in several concerts in 2004–05. They also did a European tour in 2005 and a Hollywood reunion concert in 2006.

Her acting career pales in relation to her music career, but she was in Whoopi Goldberg's *Sister Act 2: Back in the Habit* (1993), playing problem student Rita Watson. She was also in the documentary *Rhyme & Reason* (1997), had a small role in the comedy *Hav Plenty* (1997), and appeared in *Restaurant* (as Leslie; 1998), *Turn It Up* and *Dave's Chappelle's Block Party* (which features a Fugees reunion; 2005). On TV, she did voice work on *King of the Hill* (1993) and acted in the *ABC Afterschool Special* "Daddy's Girl" (1996). She also appeared and performed on the soap opera *As the World Turns* (1991) in the role of Kira Johnson.

Hill graduated from Columbia High School in Maplewood, New Jersey, and attended Columbia University for a year. Hill's father, Mal, had once been a professional vocalist, but became a computer analyst; her mother, Valerie, was a teacher in Newark, New Jersey. Her husband is Rohan Marley, son of reggae legend Bob Marley. There are four children from the marriage: Zion David Marley (1997), Selah Louise (1998), Joshua (2002) and John (2003).

Feature Films including TV Movies: *Sister Act 2: Back in the Habit* (1993), *Rhyme & Reason* (documentary; 1997), *Hav Plenty* (1997), *Restaurant* (1998), *Dave Chappelle's Block Party* (2005).

TV: *As the World Turns* (1991), *Here and Now* ("Lovers and Other Dangers," 1992), *King of the Hill* (voice; 1993), *MTV Video Music Awards 1996*, *It's Showtime at the Apollo* (1996), *Emporio Armani: A Private Party* (1996), *ABC Afterschool Specials* ("Daddy's Girl," 1996), *The Rosie O'Donnell Show* (2 segments; 1996 and 1999), *The 39th Annual Grammy Awards* (1997), *The 1998 Billboard Music Awards*, *MTV Review with Lauryn Hill* (1998), *MTV Review with Everclear* (1998), *Saturday Night Live* (1998), *Top of the Pops* (1999), *All That* (1999), *The 1999 Source Hip-Hop Music Awards*, *MTV Music Video Awards 1999*, *Lauryn Hill Live* (1999), *A Supernatural Evening with Carlos Santana* (2000), *Essence Awards* (2001), *Unplugged* (2002), *And You Don't Stop: 30 Years of Hip-Hop* (archival; 2004), *Russell Simmons Presents Def Poetry* (2005), *BET Awards 2005*, *Live 8* (2005), *MOBO Awards 2005*, *Boulevard of Broken Dreams* (2007), *This Is the N* (2007), *Africa Unite* (2007).

Video/DVD: *Hip Hop Uncensored, Vol. 2: The Real Hip Hop* (2000), *Hip Hop Uncensored, Vol. 1: Newrock Stars* (2003), *Nas: Video Anthology, Vol. 1* (2004).

Hill, Nellie (aka Hill, Nelle)

Born in Detroit, Michigan, June, 1922.

Nellie Hill was a nightclub performer who appeared in two black cast films. *Murder with Music* (1941), which also features famed composer Noble Sissle, is the story of a reporter who tries to get the goods on a gangster. *Killer Diller* (1948) is essentially a musical revue, reminiscent of a night at the Apollo, featuring Hill, Nat King Cole, Jackie "Moms" Mabley, Butterfly McQueen, Dusty Fletcher, and Sid Easton.

Feature Films: *Murder with Music* (1941), *Killer Diller* (1948).

Holly, Ellen

Born in New York, New York, January 16, 1931.

Ellen Holly's underrated career spans more than 40 years, and she is best known for pioneering inroads for African American actresses in the soap opera genre. She graduated from Hunter College with a fine arts degree. She was one of the first black actresses to gain entry into the prestigious Actors Studio, which led to roles on Broadway and at the New York Shakespeare Festival.

Ellen Holly in *Take a Giant Step* (1959).

She was in productions of *Tiger, Tiger, Burning Bright*, *Taming of the Shrew*, *Macbeth* and *The Cherry Orchard*. She also appeared on Broadway in *A Hand Is on the Gate* (1966). In 1959 she was cast in her first film in the role of Carol in *Take a Giant Step*. It was a small role as a bar girl, but her striking looks made moviegoers remember her.

Holly wrote a letter to the editor of *The New York Times* about the challenges of being a light-skinned African American actress. Agnes Nixon, creator of the soap opera *One Life to Live*, saw the letter, and wrote a role into the show which she offered to Holly in 1968. It was not the part of an African American woman, but rather an Italian American character (ethnic enough by the standards of the day) named Carla Benari. She fell in love with an all–American white character named Dr. Jim Craig. Then Carla fell in love with a black doctor and a romance began. The on-air kiss between the two caused quite a controversy until it was revealed that Carla was "passing" for white, and viewers had not actually seen a black man kissing a white woman. Carla eventually confessed her true heritage, and the role that was originally contracted to last one year lasted until 1983. Holly helped devise much of the storyline for her character on *One Life to Live* and wrote a book about her experiences on the show called *One Life*.

Feature Films including TV Movies: *Take a Giant Step* (1959), *Cops and Robbers* (1973), *Sergeant Matlovich vs. the U.S. Air Force* (TV; 1978), *School Daze* (1988), *10,000 Black Men Named George* (TV; 2002).

TV: *The Defenders* ("Man Against Himself," 1963), *Sam Benedict* ("Accomplice," 1963), *Dr.*

Kildare ("The Middle of Ernie Mann," 1964), *The Doctors and the Nurses* (2 episodes; "The Unwanted," "The Skill in These Hands," 1963 and 1964), *One Life to Live* (recurring role as Assistant District Attorney Clara "Carla" Grey Hall Scott (Benari); 1969–80; 1983–85), *The Mike Douglas Show* (1973), *King Lear* (1974), *Family Feud* (1978), *ABC Afterschool Specials* ("High School Narc," 1985), *Spenser for Hire* ("A Madness Most Discreet," 1986), *In the Heat of the Night* (4 episodes in the role of Ruth Peterson; "Intruders," "Brotherly Love," Parts I and II, "Lessons Learned," 1989–90), *Guiding Light* (recurring role as Judge Collier; 1991–93), *Intimate Portrait* ("Agnes Nixon," 1999).

Hopkins, Linda Born in New Orleans, Louisiana, December 14, 1924.

Melinda Helen Mathews was a child prodigy discovered at age 11 by gospel legend Mahalia Jackson. Professionally known as Linda Hopkins, she embraced not only gospel but blues, jazz, rhythm and blues, Broadway show tunes and pop with her soaring, passionate voice. She was the second youngest of six children, and like many African American performers, she made her first public appearances singing in church.

Hopkins was deeply influenced by seminal blues singer Bessie Smith (she had met Smith briefly at a concert at the New Orleans Palace Theatre when she was 12 years old), and eventually portrayed Smith in the production *Jazz Train* (1959) and, even more notably, in the self-written one-woman show *Bessie and Me*, which premiered in Los Angeles in 1974 and was taken to the Edison Theatre on Broadway the following year. She also played Bessie Smith in the TV production *Mitzi: Roarin' in the '20s* (1976). Other musical revues included *Black and Blue*, which premiered in Paris in 1985 and journeyed to Broadway, where it netted Hopkins a Tony Award nomination in 1989; and *Wild Woman Blues*, which debuted in Berlin in 1997.

At age 27, Hopkins was performing at the Slim Jenkins Night Club and was seen by R&B singer Little Esther, who got her a recording gig with the Johnny Otis Orchestra on Savoy Records. Hopkins continued recording and touring throughout the 1950s. A career highlight was recording duets with Jackie Wilson on the Brunswick label (including "Shake a Hand," the only hit single of her career). Given her dramatic singing technique, it was predictable that Hopkins would segue into acting. She attended the famous Stella Adler Acting School in New York City. This led to a role in the Broadway musical *Purlie* in 1970. Hopkins won the Tony Award for Best Featured Actress in a Musical and followed this with a Drama Desk Award for *Inner City* (1972).

Film roles followed: as Lil' Boy's mother in *The Education of Sonny Carson* (1974), the story of a real-life activist in Brooklyn, New York; and Flossie King in Clint Eastwood's *Honkytonk Man* (1982). She appeared in a TV production of *Purlie* (1981) and the miniseries *King* (1978); she was a blues singer in the miniseries sequel *Roots: The Next Generations* (1979) and was featured as Sister McCandless in *Go Tell It on the Mountain*, a 1985 TV movie about black family life and the integral role of the church. In 2005, Linda Hopkins was honored with a star on the Hollywood Walk of Fame.

Feature Films including Video and TV Movies: *The Education of Sonny Carson* (1974), *Mitzi: Roarin' in the '20s* (TV; 1976), *Honkytonk Man* (1982), *Go Tell It on the Mountain* (TV; 1985), *Disorderlies* (1987), *Black and Blue* (TV; 1993), *Leprechaun 2* (1994), *The Survivors Club* (TV; 2004), *Cries in the Dark* (TV; 2006).

TV: *The Tonight Show Starring Johnny Carson* (7 segments; 1972–81), *King* (miniseries; 1978), *Roots: The Next Generations* (miniseries; 1979), *Purlie* (1981), *Ad Lib* (1981), *SCTV Network* (1982), *Living the Dream: A Tribute to Dr. Martin Luther King, Jr.* (1988), *The 9th Annual Black Achievement Awards* (1988), *Great Performances* ("The Colored Museum," 1991), *Something Wilder* ("Holy Water," 1994), *33rd NAACP Image Awards* (2002), *Golden Globes* (2006).

Hopkins, Telma Born in Louisville, Kentucky, October 28, 1948.

When Telma Hopkins experienced huge success as a vocalist with the 1970s pop group Tony Orlando and Dawn, no one could have predicted that this was just the beginning of a long career in show business. She would go on to roles in the sitcoms *Bosom Buddies, Gimme a Break!, Family Matters, Getting By* and *Half & Half.* Prior to her involvement with Tony Orlando and Dawn, Hopkins had been a backup singer for the Jackson Five, Diana Ross and the Supremes, Dionne Warwick and the Four Tops. It is Hopkins' voice

Telma Hopkins, TV sons Merlin Santana and Deon Richmond, Cindy Williams, and TV daughters Nicki Vannice and Ashleigh Blair Sterling in *Getting By*.

saying "Shut your mouth!" on the recording of Isaac Hayes' Academy Award winning song "Shaft!" That alone is a guarantee of immortality.

Her debut series was a variety show called *Tony Orlando and Dawn* (aka *The Tony Orlando and Dawn Rainbow Hour*; 1974). The group, which consisted of Orlando, Hopkins and Joyce Vincent Wilson, was joined by other top acts of the era, and sang their catalogue of hits, including "Candida," "Knock Three Times," "Tie a Yellow Ribbon Round the Old Oak Tree," "Say Has Anybody Seen My Sweet Gypsy Rose?" and "He Don't Love You (Like I Love You)."

After Tony Orlando and Dawn finally cooled off, Hopkins did not skip a beat in maintaining a solo career. She has had such a prolific TV career that her résumé constitutes virtually a mini-history of the sitcom genre. She was a regular on *Bosom Buddies* 1980–81— the series that launched the career of Tom Hanks — in the role of Isabelle Hammond, resident of— and starting in the second season, manager of— the all-girls hotel where two guys dress in drag and pose as women to take advantage of the cheap rent.

On *Gimme a Break!* (1984–87), Hopkins made several noteworthy appearances as Nell Carter's best friend and occasional nemesis Addy Wilson. On *Family Matters*, she was restaurant owner and single parent Rachel Crawford (perhaps the character closest to her own persona), who becomes part of her sister's family when she moves in following the death of her husband. Hopkins stayed with the popular show from 1989 to 1997. She did take a brief hiatus to co-star with Cindy Williams on *Getting By* (1993), but returned to *Family Matters* when that show failed. In later years, she has been a semi-regular on *The Hughleys* (as Mrs. Williams; 1999–2001); *Any Day Now* (Judge Wilma Evers; 2000–01); and a regular on *Half & Half* (14 episodes in the role of Phyllis Thorne; 2002–06), the mother of Mona, the Rachel True character.

In 1996, Hopkins was scheduled to play Bill Cosby's wife Ruth on the CBS comedy *Cosby*, but was replaced at the last minute by Phylicia Rashad, replicating the leads of *The Cosby Show* (1984–92). She appeared in the sci-fi trilogy *Trancers* (as Commander Ruth Raines; 1985–91), *Count on Me* (as Beverly English; 1994) and the sensitive coming of age drama *The Wood* (as Slim's mother; 1999). Hopkins was married to and is divorced from Donald B. Allen; they have a son.

Feature Films including Video and TV Movies: *The Kid with the Broken Halo* (TV; 1982), *Trancers* (1985), *Rock 'n' Roll Mom* (TV; 1988), *Vital Signs* (1990), *How to Murder a Millionaire* (TV; 1990), *Trancers II* (1991), *Trancers III* (1992), *Count on Me* (TV; 1994), *The Wood* (1999), *The Love Guru* (2008).

TV: *Tony Orlando and Dawn* (aka *The Tony Orlando and Dawn Rainbow Hour*; 1974), *The Carol Burnett Show* (1975), *Roots: The Next Generations* (miniseries; 1979), *A New Kind of Family* (2 episodes in the role of Jess Ashton; "Thank You for a Lovely Evening," "Is There a Gun in the House?" 1979), *The Love Boat* (4 episodes; 1979–85), *Bosom Buddies* (recurring role of Isabelle Hammond; 1980–81), *Fridays* (1981), *Battle of the Network Stars XI* (1981), *Battle of the Network Stars XII* (1982), *Fantasy Island* (1984), *Gimme a Break!* (2 episodes in the role of Addie Wilson; "Julie's Birthday," "Joey's Train," 1984 and 1987), *Circus of the Stars 10* (1985), *The 1st Annual Soul Train Music Awards* (1987), *American Film Institute Comedy Special* (1987), *Sex Symbols: Past, Present and Future* (1987), *Amen* ("Wedding Bell Blues," 1988), *The 16th Annual American Music Awards* (1989), *Circus of the Stars 14* (1989), *Family Matters* (recurring role of Rachel Crawford; 1989–97), *ABC TGIF* (1990), *Getting By* (recurring role of Dolores Dixon; 1993), *Soul Train Comedy Awards* (1993), *25th NAACP Image Awards* (1993), *Woman of the House* ("The Conjugal Cottage," 1995), *Spider-Man* (voice; "Sins of the Fathers: The Rocket Racer," 1996), *The Nanny* ("Fran's Roots," 1997), *Behind the Music* (archival; "Tony Orlando," 1998), *ER* ("Think Warm Thoughts," 1998), *Batman Beyond* (voice; "Hooked Up," 1999), *The Hughleys* (5 episodes in the role of Mrs. Williams; "I Do, I Do, Again," Parts I and II, "Body Double," "Oh Thank Heaven for Seven-Eleven," "Mother's Day," 1999–2001), *Suddenly Susan* ("The Reversal," 2000), *Any Day Now* (4 episodes in the role of Judge Wilma Evers; "Nope," "It's a Good Thing I'm Not Black," "Children Are the Most Important Thing," "Peace of Mind," 2000–01), *Good vs. Evil* ("Portrait of Evil," 2000), *Static Shock* (voice; "The Breed," 2000), *For Your Love* ("The Next Best Thing," 2001), *Pulse Pounders* (archival; 2002), *Half & Half* (recurring role of Phyllis Thorne; 2002–06), *E! True Hollywood Story* ("Gimme a Break!" 2003), *ABC's 50th Anniversary Celebration* (2003), *Hollywood Squares* (2004), *The 2nd Annual TV Land Awards: A Celebration of Classic TV* (2004), *Straight from the Heart: Timeless Music of the '60s & '70s* (2004), *Entertainment Tonight* (2005), *Jimmy Kimmel Live!* (2006), *Dancing with the Stars* (2007), *Psych* ("There's Something About Mira," 2008).

Shorts: *Rain* (2001).

Horne, Lena Born in Brooklyn, New York, June 17, 1917.

Lena Mary Calhoun Horne was born in the Bedford-Stuyvesant section of Brooklyn to Edna and Teddy Horne. Teddy was a "numbers" banker and Edna was a struggling actress. The family moved into Teddy's parents' home because they were unable to maintain a household of their own. The marriage ended after four years when Teddy left his wife. Lena Horne attended Brooklyn's public schools until she was 14. She was raised by her grandparents, since her mother had spent several years traveling as an entertainer and returned from a Cuban tour with a new husband, Miguel Rodriguez. The poverty continued for the family, with a move to the Bronx, New York. Rodriguez was mostly unemployed and Edna continued to struggle as an actress. At age 16, the beautiful Lena was able to find work as a chorus girl at Harlem's famed Cotton Club. The choreographer, Elida Webb, was a friend of Lena's mother. A portion of her salary was set aside for the teenager to take music lessons.

In 1934, Horne was discovered by producer Lawrence Schwab and became a singer with Noble Sissle's Society Orchestra, beginning in Philadelphia and then touring with the band. Horne's father Teddy reappeared in her life and remained there until his death in 1970. He operated the Belmont Hotel in Pittsburgh. Horne's first husband was a friend of her father, Louis Jones, a man who was nine years her senior. Their four-year marriage produced two children, Gail and Teddy. Gail would go on as an author to chronicle her mother's legacy.

Horne broke out into crossover stardom when Charlie Barnett made her the lead vocalist with his all-white band in 1940. She recorded under the Bluebird label with his band and became a successful pop singer. She began dating heavyweight champion Lou Louis and was making a name for herself as a cabaret star. It seemed like a natural evolution of events when Horne moved to Hollywood in early 1942. If any black woman could break the color line that others before her — most notably Fredi Washington — had failed to break, surely it would be the exquisite, supremely talented Horne. Or would it? Hollywood ultimately decided that Horne would stay in the back of the bus.

She had made one modest race picture in 1938 (*The Duke Is Tops*, later retitled and reissued as *The Bronze Venus*) when she auditioned for producer Athur Freed of Metro-Goldwyn-Mayer.

Lena Horne in *Meet Me in Las Vegas* (1956).

The result was that she became the second black woman, after Jeni LeGon in 1935, to sign an extended contract with MGM. It was a seven-year contract for an initial salary of $200 per week, specifically stipulating that Horne would not play stereotypical maid roles. And she didn't. Except for her flashy role as home wrecker Georgia Brown in *Cabin in the Sky* (1943), with its strange message that black people were better off dead, Horne really didn't play any meaningful roles at all. In film after film, she merely functioned as eye candy — the beautiful black woman who would come on camera, lean against a pillar or prop, and then disappear. MGM did lend her to 20th Century–Fox for her signature film *Stormy Weather* (1943), but even here she was eye candy, although her singing was other-worldly and classic.

Other big MGM musicals in which she appeared were *Till the Clouds Roll By* (1946), *Ziegfeld Follies* (1946), and *Words and Music* (1948), but it wasn't until 1956's *Meet Me in Las Vegas* that Horne actually had a functioning speaking part, and by then the day of the great Hollywood musicals was ending — and, for all intents and purposes, so was Lena Horne's screen career. The ultimate insult was losing the role of Julie in the remake of *Show Boat* (1951)—which would have been perfect for her—to Ava Gardner.

During the filming of *Stormy Weather* she met her second husband, Lenny Hayton—like her first husband, nine years her senior. They were married for 24 years until his death in 1971. Lena's father, who had moved out to Hollywood, died in the summer of 1970. Within months, her son Teddy died of kidney disease. Horne, who was living in Santa Barbara at the time, recovered emotionally from the three tragedies and found new life on Broadway, first in 1974 in concert with Tony Bennett, and then in her own one-woman show (*Lena Horne: The Lady and Her Music*), in which she sang and recounted her days in Hollywood (often with sarcasm, but always with grace). She was given a special Tony Award in 1981 for the show. She also received a Grammy Lifetime Achievement Award in 1989.

Her last film appearance was in *The Wiz* (1978).

Feature Films including TV Movies: *The Duke Is Tops* (aka *The Bronze Venus*, 1938), *Panama Hattie* (1942), *Cabin in the Sky* (1943), *Stormy Weather* (1943), *Thousands Cheer* (1943), *I Dood It* (1943), *Swing Fever* (1943), *Broadway Rhythm* (1944), *Boogie-Woogie Dream* (1944), *Two Girls and a Sailor* (1944), *Harlem Hotshots* (1942), *Studio Visit* (1946), *Mantan Messes Up* (1946), *Till the Clouds Roll By* (1946), *Ziegfeld Follies* (1946), *Words and Music* (1948), *Some of the Best* (1949), *Duchess of Idaho* (1950), *Meet Me in Las Vegas* (1956), *The Heart of Show Business* (1957), *Death of a Gunfighter* (1969), *That's Entertainment* (archival; 1974), *That's Entertainment, Part II* (archival; 1976), *The Wiz* (1978), *That's Entertainment III* (1994), *Strange Frame: Love & Sax* (digitally altered archival footage; 2008).

TV: *The Colgate Comedy Hour* (1951), *Your Show of Shows* (2 segments; 1951–53), *The Ed Sullivan Show* (aka *Toast of the Town*; 3 segments; 1951–57), *What's My Line?* (2 segments; 1953–58), *A.N.T.A. Album of 1955*, *Music 55* (1955), *The Steve Allen Show* (1958), *The Perry Como Show* (6 segments; 1958–66), *Sunday Night at the London Palladium* (1959), *The DuPont Show of the Week* ("USO, Wherever They Go!" 1961), *At This Very Moment* (1962), *Password* (2 segments; 1963), *The Jack Paar Program* (1963), *The Judy Garland Show* (1963), *The Twentieth Century* ("The Songs of Harold Arlen," 1964), *Now* (voice; 1965), *The Bell Telephone Hour* (2 segments; "The Sound of Music," "Music in Manhattan," 1965), *The Andy Williams Show* (1966), *The Merv Griffin Show* (1967), *The Dean Martin Show* (3 segments; 1967–69), *Rowan & Martin's Laugh-In* (4 segments; 1968–69), *The Kraft Music Hall* ("Things Ain't What They Used to Be," 1970), *The Flip Wilson Show* (4 segments; 1970–74), *Film Night* ("The Black Man in the Cinema," 1971), *Sanford and Son* ("A Visit from Lena Horne," 1973), *Keep U.S. Beautiful* (1973), *The Bruce Forsyth Show* (1973), *Sesame Street* (1973), *The Muppet Show* (1976), *America Salutes Richard Rodgers: The Sound of His Music* (1976), *The 35th Annual Tony Awards* (1981), *Night of 100 Stars* (1982), *The 36th Annual Tony Awards* (1982), *The Tonight Show Starring Johnny Carson* (1982), *The 37th Annual Tony Awards* (1983), *The Cosby Show* ("Cliff's Birthday," 1985), *Brown Sugar* (miniseries; 1986), *Carnegie Hall: The Grand Reopening* (1987), *That's Black Entertainment* (archival; 1990), *Reading Rainbow* ("Snowy Day: Stories and Poems," 1991), *60 Minutes: The Entertainers* (archival; 1991), *Liberators: Fighting on Two Fronts in World War II* (archival; 1992), *The 65th Annual Academy Awards* (1993), *A Different World* ("A Rock, a River, a Lena," 1993), *Aretha Franklin: Duets* (1993), *American Justice: Target Mafia* (archival; 1993), *One on One: Classic Television Interviews* (archival;

Lena Horne.

1993), *An Evening with Lena Horne* (1994), *Sinatra Duets* (1994), *A Century of Women* (miniseries; 1994), *All-Star 25th Birthday: Stars and Street Forever* (archival; 1994), *Entertaining the Troops* (archival; 1994), *American Masters* (two segments: first is archival; "Judy Garland: By Myself," 1994; "Lena Horne: In Her Own Words," 1996), *The Rosie O'Donnell Show* (2 segments; 1997 and 1998), *Small Steps, Big Strides: The Black Experience in Hollywood* (archival; 1998), *The Nightclub Years* (archival; 2001), *Walk on By: The Story of Popular Song* (archival; 2001), *Sinatra: The Classic Duets* (archival; 2002), *It's Black Entertainment* (archival; 2002), *Great Performances* (archival; "The Great American Songbook," 2003), *Andy Williams: My Favorite Duets* (archival; 2004), *War Stories with Oliver North* (archival; "Hollywood Goes to War," 2006).

Video/DVD: *Muppet Moments* (archival; 1985), *Somewhere Over the Rainbow: Harold Arlen* (archival; 1999), *Then I'll Be Free to Travel Home* (2001), *The Masters Behind the Music* (2004), *TV in Black: The First Fifty Years* (archival; 2004).

Shorts: *Boogie Woogie Dream* (1941).

Horsford, Anna Maria Born in Harlem, New York, March 6, 1948.

Anna Maria Horsford's parents emigrated from the island nation of Antigua and Barbuda in the 1940s. Her mother is Lillian Agatha (née Richardson) and her father is Victor, an investment real estate broker. Horsford had an urge to travel and vacationed in the Caribbean as a way of maintaining her island roots. The travel urge also led her to attend college in Stockholm, Sweden, after she had graduated from the New York High School of Performing Arts, the alma mater of so many who went on to show business acclaim. She auditioned for the New York Shakespeare Festival, but her first major achievement in the entertainment industry was not as an actress but as a producer. She produced the well-remembered PBS series *Soul!* (1967–73), hosted by Ellis Haizlip. *Soul!* was one of the first television venues to present the black perspective on a regular basis.

There is little question that Horsford remains best known for her role as Thelma Frye, daughter of Deacon Ernest Frye (Sherman Helmsley) on the popular sitcom *Amen*, which settled in for a long run on NBC from 1986 to 1991. She also played Dee Baxter on *The Wayans Bros.* from 1996 to 1999.

Horsford has an extensive filmography, having appeared to date in over 50 theatrical and TV movies. TV movie highlights include *Bill* (1981), the Mickey Rooney film about a mentally challenged man; the jury drama *A Killer Among Us* (1990); and *Murder Without Motive: The Edmund Perry Story* (as Veronica Perry; 1992). Theatrical films of note include the "brat pack" time capsule *St. Elmo's Fire,* in which she played a prostitute (1985); *Heartburn* (1986), with Meryl Streep and Jack Nicholson; *Once Upon a Time ... When We Were Colored* (1995); the comedic character study *Friday* (1995) and its sequel *Friday After Next* (2002); *Nutty Professor II: The Klumps* with Eddie Murphy (2000); and *Minority Report* (as Casey; 2002), director Steven Spielberg's melding of the sci-fi and crime genres. Her creative interests are many: she has maintained an art institute in upstate New York and has an active interest in international black culture.

Feature Films including Video and TV Movies: *An Almost Perfect Affair* (1979), *Hollow Image* (TV; 1979), *Times Square* (1980), *The Fan* (1981), *Bill* (TV; 1981), *Muggable Mary, Street Cop* (TV; 1982), *Benny's Place* (TV; 1982), *Love Child* (1982), *Class* (1983), *Crackers* (1984), *A Doctor's Story* (TV; 1984), *Charlotte Forten's Mission: Experiment in Freedom* (TV; 1985), *St. Elmo's Fire* (1985), *Stone Pillow* (TV; 1985), *Nobody's Child* (TV; 1986), *A Case of Deadly Force* (TV; 1986), *Permanent Wave* (1986), *Heartburn* (1986), *C.A.T. Squad* (TV; 1986), *Street Smart* (1987), *If It's Tuesday, It Still Must Be Belgium* (TV; 1987), *Who Gets the Friends?* (TV; 1988), *Taken Away* (TV; 1989), *Presumed Innocent* (1990), *A Killer Among Us* (TV; 1990), *Murder Without Motive: The Edmund Perry Story* (TV; 1992), *Mr. Jones* (1993), *Baby Brokers* (TV; 1994), *Once Upon a Time ... When We Were Colored* (1995), *Friday* (1995), *Circle of Pain* (TV; 1996), *Widow's Kiss* (TV; 1996), *Dear God* (1996), *Set It Off* (1996), *One Fine Day* (1996), *Kiss the Girls* (1997), *At Face Value* (1999), *Dancing in September* (2000), *Nutty Professor II: The Klumps* (2000), *Lockdown* (2000), *Along Came a Spider* (2001), *Jacked* (2001), *How High* (2001), *Minority Report* (2002), *Friday After Next* (2002), *Justice* (2004), *Guarding Eddy* (2004), *My Big Phat Hip Hop Family* (2005), *Ganked* (TV; 2005), *Broken Bridges* (2006), *Gridiron Gang* (2006), *I Tried* (2007), *Trade* (2007), *Pretty Ugly People* (2007).

TV: *NBC Special Treat* ("The Tap Dance Kid," 1978), *ABC Afterschool Specials* (2 episodes;

"Starstruck," "Summer Switch," 1981 and 1984), *Nurse* ("The Store," 1982), *Amen* (recurring role of Thelma Frye; 1986–91), *The Bronx Zoo* ("It's Hard to Be a Saint in the City," 1987), *21st NAACP Image Awards* (1989), *Baby Talk* ("Womb with a View," 1991), *L.A. Law* ("Do the Spike Thing," 1991), *The Fresh Prince of Bel-Air* ("Geoffrey Cleans Up," 1992), *Rhythm & Blues* (recurring role as Veronica Washington; 1992), *Tall Hopes* (1993), *Sparks* ("How Poppa Got His Groove Back," 1996), *The Wayans Bros.* (76 episodes in the role of Dee Baxter; 1996–99), *The Good News* (pilot; 1997), *L.A. Doctors* (2 episodes in the role of Angela Daly; pilot; "Under the Radar," 1998), *7th Heaven* ("Here Comes Santa Claus," 1998), *The Wild Thornberrys* (voice; "Chump Off the Old Block," 1999), *Judging Amy* ("Crowded House," 1999), *Essence Awards* (2001), *Moesha* ("The Candidate"), *The Chronicle* ("Touched by an Angel," 2002), *The Bernie Mac Show* ("Family Reunion," 2004), *The District* (3 episodes in the role of Bobbi Yates; "Breath of Life," "Family Values," "Passing Time," 2004), *Method & Red* ("Something About Brenda," 2004), *The Shield* (recurring role of Assistant District Attorney Encardi; "The Cure," "Grave," "Bang," "The Doghouse," 2005–08), *Entourage* (2 episodes in the role of Saigon's Mother; "Good Morning, Saigon," "I Want to Be Sedated," 2005 and 2006), *Grey's Anatomy* (2 episodes in the role of Liz Fallon; "No Man's Land," "Some Kind of Miracle," 2005 and 2007), *Heist* ("How Billy Got His Groove Back," 2006), *Living in TV Land* ("Sherman Helmsley," 2006).

Houston, Whitney Born in Newark, New Jersey, August 9, 1963.

Like Diana Ross, Whitney Houston seemed to be on the brink of a major movie career, but for a variety of reasons — voluntary and otherwise — that was not to be. She did appear in a succession of major Hollywood films, starting with the immensely successful *The Bodyguard* (1992). *The Bodyguard* is the story of Frank Farmer, a bodyguard hired to protect superstar singer Rachel Marron (Houston). Houston's version of Dolly Parton's "I Will Always Love You" was a huge hit single and is now considered one of the seminal pop songs. The film grossed $400 million worldwide and the soundtrack spent 20 weeks at the top of the *Billboard* chart in the U.S., and also went to number 1 in the United Kingdom and other countries. Except for the interracial love story angle — which is handled with sensitivity — this is a fairly conventional film noir, although leading man Kevin Costner strives to make it more than that, and Houston does not embarrass herself in her movie debut.

Her follow-up film, *Waiting to Exhale* (1995), is the ultimate chick-flick movie for African American women, and it broke through to the mass audience, with a $66.2 million gross in the U.S. Here Houston is in a fairly passive (although lead) role and takes a back seat to Angela Bassett's impassioned performance as a wife scorned (she received an NAACP Image Award for her work). Savannah (Houston), Bernadine (Bassett), Robin (Lela Rochon) and Gloria (Loretta Devine) are four friends who provide a support system for each other despite their ups and downs with men. Well directed by actor Forest Whittaker, *Exhale* (based on the Terry McMillan novel) is several notches above conventional soap opera. It benefits from good acting by Devine and Gregory Hines, as well as the incandescent Bassett. Houston, although not bad in her role, is basically along for the ride. She gained another massive hit with "The Shoop Shoop Song" from the film's soundtrack, *Exhale*, and was nominated for an NAACP Image Award for Outstanding Lead Actress in a Motion Picture (as were Hines, Rochon and Devine for their supporting roles).

Her third film (and last major theatrical release to date) was *The Preacher's Wife* (1996). While not a major box office hit (with an okay $48 million domestic gross), this movie won Houston an NAACP Image Award for Outstanding Actress in a Motion Picture (Loretta Devine won for Supporting Actress). This is a sweet, sentimental film, benefiting by the presence of the always dependable Denzel Washington as an angel sent to Earth to patch up trouble in a preacher's (Courtney B. Vance) troubled marriage. The angel attracts the preacher's wife (Houston) and causes more complications. While a bit syrupy for today's audiences, the film shows that Houston had become even more comfortable as an actress.

Save for the TV movie *Cinderella* (1997) and a guest cameo in the low-budget *Nora's Hair Salon* (2004), which featured her then-husband Bobby Brown, Houston's acting career basically came to a full stop. *Rodgers and Hammerstein's Cinderella* was the official title of the film, which aired as a "Wonderful World of Disney" production. Sixty million viewers tuned in to see Houston as the

Whitney Houston in *The Preacher's Wife* (1996).

Fairy Godmother, Brandy as Cinderella, and Whoopi Goldberg as The Queen. A radiant Brandy, then at the peak of her career, was the major attraction. The film was produced by Houston's BrownHouse Productions and received seven Emmy nominations, including Outstanding Variety Musical or Comedy Program, and won an Emmy for its lush art direction. It became the best-selling video ever for a made-for-television movie.

Whitney Elizabeth Houston is one of the most successful singers in R&B and pop music history. She is the most awarded female recording artist of all time, according to the *Guinness Book of Records*. After her marriage to singer Bobby Brown in 1992, her career eventually took a downturn; she divorced Brown in 2006 and took custody of their daughter, Bobbi Kristina (the ups and downs of that marriage were recorded for posterity on the popular cable reality show *Being Bobby Brown* in 2005, on which an erratic Houston frequently appeared).

She is the third and youngest child of John and Cissy Houston. Cissy is a well-known back-up singer (having sung with Elvis Presley) and gospel singer, and well regarded as an artist in her own right. The family moved to middle class East Orange, New Jersey, after the Newark riots of 1976. At age 11, Houston became a soloist in the junior gospel choir of the New Hope Baptist Church in Newark. She attended the all-girl Roman Catholic Mount Saint Dominic Academy. In her teen years, she modeled, toured with her mother, and sang back-up on recordings until she signed a contract with Clive Davis' Arista Records in 1983 (Davis remains a mentor to this day). Her self-titled 1985 debut album took awhile to build, but once hits like "Saving All My Love for You" began to top the *Billboard* charts, the album exploded and spent 14 weeks at number 1. More smash singles followed — "How Will I Know," "You Give Good Love" — and the album became the best-selling debut album by a female singer ever, eventually selling over 25 million copies worldwide.

More albums — *Whitney* (1987), *I'm Your Baby Tonight* (1990), *My Love Is Your Love* (1998) — and more hits — "I Wanna Dance with Somebody

(Who Loves Me)," "So Emotional," and "The Star Spangled Banner" (in the wake of the 9/11 attacks) — followed in rapid succession. Her subsequent albums have not done well compared to the earlier releases; these include *Just Whitney* (2002) and *One Wish: The Holiday Album* (2003). Her long-awaited comeback album, *I Look to You*, reuniting her with Clive Davis, was released in 2009.

Feature Films including TV Movies: *The Bodyguard* (1992), *Waiting to Exhale* (1995), *The Preacher's Wife* (1996), *Cinderella* (TV; 1997), *Nora's Hair Salon* (2004).

TV: *Gimme a Break!* ("Katie's College," 1984), *Top of the Pops* (archival; 3 segments; 1985; 6 new segments, 1987–2000), *Show vann der maand* (1985), *Soul Train* (1985), *The Merv Griffin Show* (1985), *Late Night with David Letterman* (1985), *Silver Spoons* ("Head Over Heels," 1985), *The Tonight Show Starring Johnny Carson* (2 segments; 1985–1990), *The 13th Annual American Music Awards* (1986), *The 3rd Annual Black Gold Awards* (1986), *Liberty Weekend* (1986), *MTV Video Music Awards 1986, Brit Awards 1987, The 29th Annual Grammy Awards* (1987), *The 1st Annual Soul Train Music Awards* (1987), *Aretha Franklin: The Queen of Soul* (1988), *20th NAACP Image Awards* (1988), *The 15th Annual American Music Awards* (1988), *The 30th Annual Grammy Awards* (1988), *Nelson Mandela 70th Birthday Tribute* (1988), *That's What Friends Are For: Arista's 15th Anniversary Concert* (1989), *The 21st NAACP Image Awards* (1989), *The 31st Annual Grammy Awards* (1989), *The Songwriter's Hall of Fame 20th Anniversary ... The Magic of Music* (1989), *The Word* (1990), *Welcome Home Heroes with Whitney Houston* (1990), *7th Annual American Cinema Awards* (1990), *Sammy Davis, Jr. 60th Anniversary Celebration* (1990), *Super Bowl XXV* (1991), *The Simple Truth: A Concert for Kurdish Refugees* (1991), *Coca Cola Pop Music Backstage Pass to Summer* (1991), *1991 Billboard Music Awards, Saturday Night Live* (2 segments; 1991–96), *The 19th Annual American Music Awards* (1992), *Muhammad Ali's 50th Birthday Celebration* (1992), *1993 MTV Movie Awards, The 1993 World Music Awards, 1993 Billboard Music Awards, The 8th Annual Soul Train Music Awards* (1994), *The 36th Annual Grammy Awards* (1994), *26th NAACP Image Awards* (1994), *The 21st Annual American Music Awards* (1994), *The 66th Annual Academy Awards* (1994), *Whitney Houston: The Concert for a New South Africa* (1994), *The History of Rock 'N' Roll, Vol. 5* (1995), *Soul Train's 25th Anniversary* (1995), *Television's Greatest Performances I & II* (archival; 1995), *27th NAACP Image Awards* (1996), *1996 MTV Movie Awards, The 38th Annual Grammy Awards* (1996), *Celebrate the Dream: 50 Years of Ebony Magazine* (1996), *The Rosie O'Donnell Show* (2 segments; 1996–98), *Whitney Houston: Classic Whitney* (1997), *Dolly Parton: She Ain't No Dumb Blonde* (archival; 1997), *Scratch the Surface* (1997), *The 39th Annual Grammy Awards* (1997), *Macy's 21st Annual Fourth of July Fireworks Spectacular* (1997), *Essence Awards* (1998), *Mundo VIP* (1998), *MTV Video Music Awards 1998, When You Believe: Music From the "Prince of Egypt"* (1998), *Warner Bros. 75th Anniversary: No Guts, No Glory* (archival; 1998), *The 26th Annual American Music Awards* (1998), *The 1998 Billboard Music Awards, The Great Christmas Movies* (1998), *VH1 Divas Live 2* (1999), *Arista Records' 25th Anniversary Celebration* (1999), *Sen kvall med luuk* (1999), *Brit Awards 1999, ABC 2000: The Millennium* (archival; 1999), *The 71st Annual Academy Awards* (1999), *All Access: Whitney Houston* (1999), *Making the Video* (1999), *MTV Europe Music Awards 1999, MTV Video Music Awards 2000, 106 & Park Top 10 Live* (2000), *Whitney TV* (2000), *100 Greatest Dance Songs of Rock & Roll* (archival; 2000), *1st Annual BET Awards* (2001), *Michael Jackson: 30th Anniversary Celebration* (2001), *MTV Europe Music Awards 2002, It's Black Entertainment* (2002), *American Bandstand's 50th Anniversary Celebration* (2002), *VH1 Divas Las Vegas* (2002), *Whitney Houston: The True Story* (2002), *Primetime Live* (2002), *Top of the Pops 2* (archival; 2003), *101 Most Shocking Moments in Entertainment* (archival; 2003), *Boston Public* ("Chapter 66," 2003), *VH1 Divas Duets* (2003), *Les 40 ans de la 2* (archival; 2004), *The Most Shocking Celebrity Moments of 2004* (archival; 2004), *World Music Awards 2004, Being Bobby Brown* (recurring appearances as herself; 2005), *25 Strong: The BET Silver Anniversary Special* (2005), *Vivement Dimanche* (archival; 2006), *Exclusiv: Das Star-magazin* (archival; 2006), *The Tyra Banks Show* (archival; 2006), *Biography* (archival; 2006), *20 to 1* (archival; 2006), *Video on Trial: '80s Superstars* (archival; 2006), *Entertainment Tonight* (2 segments; 2006–08), *The Best of the Doves Marathon* (archival; 2007), *Extra* (2008).

Video/DVD: *Whitney Houston: Live in Con-*

cert (1991), *Whitney Houston: The Greatest Hits* (2000), *Whitney Houston: Fine* (2000).

Howard, Gertrude Born in Hot Springs, Alabama, October 13, 1892; died September 30, 1934, Los Angeles, California.

Gertrude Howard was one of the early group of black actresses and actors who were able to storm fortress Hollywood and get cast in mainstream films with varying degrees of success.

She appeared in the chorus of *The Wife Hunters* on Broadway in November–December 1911, then moved to Los Angeles in 1919 and was able to get small roles in silent films, including *Uncle Tom's Cabin* (1927). She had roles in the first all-talking black cast film *Hearts in Dixie* and the lavish musical *Show Boat* (both 1929). Her most sizable and well-remembered role was as Mae West's maid in *I'm No Angel* (1932). West always had a black maid to bounce double entendres off of. Hattie McDaniel also had a bit role in that film (again, strictly to feed West a line).

Howard was a religiously devout, beloved figure in the African American community. Heavyset and dark-skinned like Hattie McDaniel and Louise Beavers, she was the image of the way Hollywood envisioned black people at the time.

Feature Films: *The Circus Cyclone* (1925), *Easy Pickings* (1927), *Uncle Tom's Cabin* (1927), *On Your Toes* (1927), *South Sea Love* (1927), *Synthetic Sin* (1929), *His Captive Woman* (1929), *Hearts in Dixie* (1929), *Show Boat* (1929), *Guilty?* (1930), *Conspiracy* (1930), *The Prodigal* (1931), *Father's Son* (1931), *Sporting Blood* (1931), *Penrod and Sam* (aka *The Adventures of Penrod and Sam*, 1931), *Secret Service* (1931), *Consolation Marriage* (1931), *Strangers in Love* (1932), *The Wet Parade* (1932), *I'm No Angel* (1932), *The Fighting Code* (1933), *Carolina* (1934), *Peck's Bad Boy* (1934).

Howard, Shingzie (aka Howard McClane, Shingzie) Born in Steelton, Pennsylvania.

Intelligent, exquisite Elcora "Shingzie" Howard replaced Evelyn Preer as the leading lady in the films of legendary black director Oscar Micheaux. How she did so is an interesting story.

Oscar Micheaux was a film director but he was also a door-to-door book salesman who went into middle-class black homes to sell his latest novel. One evening he found himself in the Howard household. Mr. Howard was a high school principal and his wife was a professional elocutionist. The older daughter was a teacher and the younger daughter was a recent high school graduate. Micheaux noticed her photo on the mantle, liked her looks, and felt that she might have a place in his films. He returned to the home to meet the daughter and discovered that she could type and take shorthand — so instead of asking her to act, he asked her to come to New York and become his secretary. Howard could live with her sister, who was already in New York. She proved adept at office work, and even helped Michaeux to edit his films.

Evelyn Preer, Michaeux's erstwhile leading lady, was by now sought after for other stage and screen projects. At any rate, it wasn't likely that Micheaux could have afforded her steadily rising salary. Filming on Micheaux's *The Dungeon* (1922) with Shingzie Howard got underway in Roanoke, Virginia. It was a strange, *Jane Eyre*–like story about a beautiful young woman who breaks off her engagement to an upstanding young man after she has a terrible dream. Instead, Myrtle Downing (Howard) marries a notorious crook and bigamist who takes his wives off to a strange and lonely house, the dungeon of the title. Howard took to the stage to introduce herself and *The Dungeon* before sold-out crowds at the New Douglas and Lenox Theaters in Harlem, and she traveled with the film to other East Coast cities.

Howard and William E. Fountaine, her costar in *The Dungeon,* were reunited in *The Virgin of Seminole* (1923), the story of a black man who receives a substantial reward for helping to capture a bandit and is able to buy a ranch. The film was effectively done and quite light-hearted for a Micheaux production. Originally planned as a vehicle for Evelyn Preer, *The House Behind the Cedars* (1927) turned into another role for Shingzie Howard, who was cast as Rena, a mulatto encouraged by her brother to "pass." Micheaux was running into serious financial problems — a periodic dilemma throughout his career — and it would be two years before *The House Behind the Cedars* was released.

A Son of Satan (aka *The Ghost of Tolston's Manor*, 1923) was Howard's last film for Micheaux, a haunted house comedy featuring song and dance numbers with the cast of Broadway's *Shuffle Along.* It was the closest Micheaux would come to making a horror film. Unfortunately, it too is one of the many "lost" Micheaux films. Howard made a couple of other "race pictures" (*The Prince of His Race* in 1926 and *Children of Fate* in 1928) before retiring from films and following in her older sister's footsteps to become a school teacher. Howard was interviewed onscreen in the documentary *Midnight Ramble* (1994), shown on the PBS series *The American Experience.* The first-person testimony of these pioneering black filmmakers provides the best record we will ever have of those epochal days.

Feature Films: *Uncle Jasper's Will* (aka *Jasper Landry's Will,* 1922), *The Dungeon* (1922), *The Ghost of Tolston's Manor* (1923), *The Virgin of Seminole* (1923), *The Prince of His Race* (1926), *The House Behind the Cedars* (1927), *Children of Fate* (1928).

TV: *The American Experience* (*Midnight Ramble,* 1994).

Hubert, Janet (aka Hubert-Whitten, Janet)

Born in Chicago, Illinois, January 13, 1956.

Janet Louise Hubert, raised on Chicago's South Side, attended Juilliard Elementary as a child and then graduated from Momence High School in Illinois. She is best known for her featured role as Vivian Banks on *The Fresh Prince of Bel-Air* (1990–93). The birth of her character's child, Nicky Banks, was worked into the storyline to accommodate her real-life pregnancy. She subsequently left the show (after much duress with star Will Smith), and her character was played by Daphne Maxwell Reid.

Hubert came to New York and signed on with the Alvin Ailey Dance Company. Her theatrical debut was in the national tour of *Bob Fosse's Dancin'* (1981). She made her

Broadway debut in *The First* (1981), based on the life of baseball's Jackie Robinson. She is best known for her role of Tantomile in the original Broadway cast of *Cats* (1982). She also served as lead Betty Buckley's understudy in the production. She later performed a one-woman show at the Sports Club in Monte Carlo, a tribute to Josephine Baker. She also appeared in the original off–Broadway productions of *Anteroom* (1985) and *The Vagina Monologues* (1999).

She was Alice Dawson on the soap *All My Children* (1990). In 2005, she played Lisa Williamson, mother of attorney Evangeline Williamson, on the soap *One Life to Live.* Her husbands are James Whitten (married 1990 and divorced later in the decade), with one child, Elijah (born 1993); and Larry Kraft (2005–present). Hubert is ambassador of the National Osteoporosis Foundation, a condition from which she suffers.

Feature Films including Video and TV Movies: *A Piece of the Action* (1977), *Agent on Ice* (1986), *New Eden* (TV; 1994), *White Man's Burden* (1995), *California Myth* (1999), *30 Years to Life* (2001), *Neurotica* (2004), *Proud* (2004), *Christmas at Water's Edge* (TV; 2004).

TV: *All My Children* (recurring role as Alice Dawson; 1970), *Hunter* ("The Fourth Man," 1988), *21 Jump Street* ("Fun with Animals," 1988), *Hooperman* ("Look Homeward, Dirtbag," 1989), *A Man Called Hawk* ("Poison," 1989), *The More You Know* (1989), *Tales from the Crypt* ("'Til Death," 1990), *The Fresh Prince of Bel-Air* (recurring role of Vivian Banks; 1990–93), *Reasonable Doubts* ("Brother's Keeper," 1992), *Dave's World* ("Shel in Love," 1994), *Coach* ("Blue Chip Blues," 1994), *CBS Schoolbreak Special* ("What About Your Friends?" 1995), *The Faculty* ("Somewhere There's Music," 1996), *The Pretender* ("The Paper Clock," 1996), *The Jamie Foxx Show* ("Act Like You Love Me," 1997), *Goode Behavior* ("Goode Lovin'," 1997), *NYPD Blue* ("Weaver of Hate," 1998), *The Job* (4 episodes in the role of Adina Phillips; "Elizabeth," "Massage," "Gina," "Barbeque," 2001–02), *Gilmore Girls* ("Back in the Saddle Again," 2002), *Friends* ("The One Where Emma Cries," 2002), *Weakest Link* (2002), *The Bernie Mac Show* (2 episodes; "Meet the Grandparents," "Make Room for Caddy," 2003 and 2004), *One Life to Live* (recurring role as Lisa Williamson; 2005).

Hudson, Jennifer

Born in Chicago, Illinois, September 12, 1981.

Jennifer Kate Hudson lived the ultimate show business Cinderella story until the tragic shooting of her mother, brother and nephew in October 2008. Her estranged brother-in-law was charged with the crimes. Hudson went from *American Idol* also-ran (sixth runner-up; 2002) to Academy Award winner for Best Supporting Actress for her role in *Dreamgirls* (2006). She is the third African American to win a Best Supporting Actress Award (Halle Berry is the only Best Actress winner). Fourteen black actresses have been nominated for the supporting award (Hattie McDaniel, Ethel Waters, Juanita Moore, Beah Richards, Alfre Woodard, Margaret Avery, Oprah

Winfrey, Marianne Jean-Baptiste, Whoopi Goldberg [also nominated for Best Actress], Queen Latifah, Sophie Okonedo, Ruby Dee and Viola Davis).

Hudson grew up singing in church choirs, doing community theater, and touring for Disney in *Hercules: The Musical* (2002). She decided to give *American Idol* a try to see if it would jumpstart her career. Three African American females were among the 12 finalists: Hudson, Fantasia Barrino and LaToya London. All three were quite talented, so perhaps it was the luck of the ethnic draw or her plus-size image that caused Hudson to leave the show so prematurely. After her stirring version of "The Circle of Life" from *The Lion King*, it came as quite a shock when she was voted off the show.

She went on the *Idols* summer tour with the rest of the finalists, and then spent two years working on cruise ships and playing small concert venues. Then Hudson heard of the casting call for Effie White in the long-awaited movie version of Broadway's *Dreamgirls*. Every young black actress who bore a passing resemblance to Broadway's original 1981 Tony-winning Effie, Jennifer Holliday, vied for the role. Hudson reportedly beat out nearly 800 actresses for the role, including *American Idol* winner Fantasia Barrino.

Effie, the magnificent but weight-challenged singer who does not fit the glamour girl image of the Supremes-like singing group and is cast aside, is a powerful role highlighted by the song "And I'm Telling You I'm Not Going." Many felt Hudson had a lock on the Oscar based on advanced screenings of the film. In addition to the Oscar, she won the National Board of Review Award for Best Newcomer, the New York Film Critics Award, the Golden Globe, the Screen Actors Guild Award, the British Film Award, and the Golden Satellite Award.

Her role in *Sex in the City* (2008) seemed to smack of tokenism and didn't give her much to do — but the film itself was well received and did potent box office. Her third film, *The Secret Life of Bees* (2008), was an all-star showcase for black actresses; in addition to Hudson, the cast included Queen Latifah, Alicia Keys and Sophie Okonedo. Reviews were tepid, but the warm-hearted film did decent box office. Hudson played Rosaleen Daise, caregiver and friend of a lonely 14-year-old (Dakota Fanning) who escapes from her repressive father and moves in with a family of nurturing

Jennifer Hudson.

black sisters. In 2006, Hudson signed a contract with Arista Records. Her self-titled debut album was released in the fall of 2008 and opened at number 2 on the *Billboard* chart with first week sales of a healthy 217,000 copies.

Feature Films: *Dreamgirls* (2006), *Sex and the City* (2008), *The Secret Life of Bees* (2008), *Winged Creatures* (2009).

TV: *On Air with Ryan Seacrest* (2 segments; 2004), *E! True Hollywood Story* (2004), *The Oprah Winfrey Show* (2006), *HBO First Look* ("The Making of *Dreamgirls*," 2006), *The Tonight Show with Jay Leno* (3 segments; 2006–08), *Entertainment Tonight* (6 segments; 2006–08), *Dreamgirls: T4 Movie Special* (2007), *The View* (2 segments; 2007 and 2008), *Late Show with David Letterman* (2007), *The 64th Annual Golden Globe Awards* (2007), *The 2007 Screen Actors Guild Awards, An Evening of Stars: A Tribute to Aretha Franklin* (2007), *The Film Programme* (2007), *Larry King Live* (2007), *The 49th Annual Grammy Awards* (2007), *The Ellen DeGeneres Show* (2007), *The Oprah Winfrey Oscar Special* (2007), *Sunday*

Morning Shootout (2007), *The 79th Annual Academy Awards* (2007), *38th NAACP Image Awards* (2007), *The Late Late Show with Craig Ferguson* (2007), *18th Annual glaad Media Awards* (2007), *BET Awards 2007, Live with Regis and Kathie Lee* (2007), *Elmo's Christmas Countdown* (2007), *Jimmy Kimmel Live!* (2008).

Video/DVD: *Building the Dream* (2007).

Hyson, Roberta Born in Dallas, Texas, March 27, 1905.

Actress, dancer and singer Roberta Hyson starred in the historically important all-black talkie comedy shorts released by the Christie Film Company featuring a character called Florian Slappey. These shorts made Hyson the first black actress to appear in talkies. Hyson is charming and relaxed on screen and does not overact the way so many performers did in early sound films. In fact, she seems incredibly contemporary.

Florian Slappey was a bumbling black detective created by a Jewish writer from Charleston, South Carolina, named Octavus Roy Cohen. Cohen may have written the screenplays for the Slappey two-reelers as well, under the pen name Alfred A. Cohn. Slappey's adventures were recounted in a long-running series of short stories in the "Darktown Birmingham" column in *The Saturday Evening Post* from 1919 to 1938. In addition to the comedy shorts, the stories resulted in a play, *Come Seven*, presented in 1920 at the Broadhurst Theatre. It ran for 72 performances and was advertised as a "blackface play in three acts." The Florian Slappey tales were collected in four volumes: *Come Seven* (1920), *Florian Slappey Goes Abroad* (1928), *Carbon Copies* (1932) and *Florian Slappey* (1938).

The film series started with *Melancholy Dame,* followed by *Music Hath Harms* and *The Framing of the Shrew* (all 1929). Hyson was in all of them — two feature Oscar Micheaux and leading lady Evelyn Preer — as well as in the non–Slappey short *Oft in the Silly Night* (1929). All of these ultra-rare shorts are preserved and collected on a DVD called *Birmingham Black Bottom,* issued in 2003. The two comedy shorts with which Hyson ended her brief career are *The Lady Fare* (1929) and *Georgia Rose* (1930), and are not included on the DVD.

Evelyn Preer was Jonquil Williams and Hyson was Sapho Dill in the 21-minute *Melancholy Dame.* A store owner's wife (Preer) is disturbed with her husband's flirtation with a comely waitress (Hyson). Spencer Williams, who would go on to direct a number of key race pictures, is, like Hyson, in the cast of all three of the Slappey shorts. Florian Slappey is played by Harry Tracy in *Music Hath Charms*, while Charles Olden plays the role in *Melancholy Dame* and *The Framing of the Shrew*, in which a henpecked husband unwisely seeks advice from Slappey. Evelyn Preer is also in *Shrew* as Clarry Robson, wife of Privacy Robson (Edward Thompson).

Shorts: *Melancholy Dame* (1929), *Music Hath Harms* (1929), *The Framing of the Shrew* (1929), *Oft in the Silly Night* (1929), *The Lady Fare* (1929), *Georgia Rose* (1930).

DVD: *Birmingham Black Bottom* (2003).

Jackée (aka Harry, Jackée) Born in Winston-Salem, North Carolina, August 14, 1956.

Jacqueline Yvonne Harry, much better known as Jackée, has been an exuberant, scene-stealing sitcom star for several generations. Her main claim to fame is her role as Sandra Clark on NBC'S *227*, a Saturday night staple of 1985–89, as next-door neighbor and confidant to series star Marla Gibbs. She won an Emmy Award and two NAACP Image Awards for the role. Hers' was the first Emmy ever won by a black woman for supporting actress in a comedy (Gail Fisher having been the first-ever black woman to win, for supporting actress in a drama for *Mannix*).

She was the youngest of five children of parents Flossie and Warren Harry. Although born in North Carolina, she grew up in New York City. She graduated from the C.W. Post campus of Long Island University. Her first marriage lasted from 1980 to 1984. She was married to her second husband, hair salon owner Elgin Charles Williams, from 1996 to 2003. Jackée had originally tried teaching history at Brooklyn Tech High School — she says she was too sexy for the classroom, and getting too much attention from her male students — and gave that up to study acting at the Henry Street Settlement on New York's Lower East Side.

She made her professional debut in *A Broadway Musical* (actually an off–Broadway production that moved to Broadway; 1978) as a chorus girl. She also appeared on Broadway in *Eubie!* (1975), *One Mo' Time* (1980), *Child of the Sun* (1981), *Diamonds* (1984) and *The Boys from Syracuse* (2002). Jackée began her TV career as Lily

Mason on the daytime soap *Another World* (1983–86). One of the actors she worked with was then little-known Morgan Freeman. In 2003, she was a guest on the soapnet *Another World Reunion*.

She made a series of failed pilot projects in the wake of her *227* success. *Jackée* was a direct spin-off of the series (aired 1989), and there was *The Cheech Show* and *Friday Night Surprise* (both 1988) and *We'll Take Manhattan* (1990). She also joined the cast of the ill-fated *The Royal Family* (1991) after the sudden death of star Redd Foxx. She was Etta Mae, denizen of a Chicago housing project, in Oprah Winfrey's *The Women of Brewster Place*, the 1989 ABC miniseries. She is also known for playing Lisa Landry on the sitcom *Sister, Sister* (1994–99). In 2008, she joined the national touring company of *Wicked* in the role of Madame Morrible.

Feature Films including Video and TV Movies: *The Incredible Ida Early* (TV; 1987), *Crash Course* (TV; 1988), *Double Your Pleasure* (TV; 1989), *We'll Take Manhattan* (TV; 1990), *Ladybugs* (1992), *It's Lonely at the Top* (TV; 1992), *Living and Working in Space: The Countdown Has Begun* (1993), *You Got Served* (2004), *All You've Got* (2006), *The Last Day of Summer* (TV; 2007), *G.E.D.* (2009), *Man of Her Dreams* (2009).

TV: *Another World* (recurring role as Lily Mason; 1983–86), *227* (recurring role of Sandra Clark; 1986–89), *Super Password* (2 segments; 1986), *Soul Train* (1986), *19th Annual NAACP Image Awards* (1987), *Dolly* (1987), *The 9th Annual American Black Achievement Awards* (1988), *Late Night with David Letterman* (1988), *Amen* (3 episodes; "A Slight Case of Murder," Parts I and II, "Don't Rain on My Shower," 1988 and 1989), *The Cheech Show* (1988), *Friday Night Surprise* (1988) and *We'll Take Manhattan* (1990), *The 10th Annual American Black Achievement Awards* (1989), *The Women of Brewster Place* (miniseries; 1989), *Jackée* (pilot; 1989), *ABC TGIF* (1990), *The Royal Family* (6 episodes in the role of CoCo Royal; 1991–92), *Designing Women* ("Shades of Vanessa," 1992), *Dave's World* ("Saved by Estelle," 1994), *Sister, Sister* (recurring role of Lisa Landry; 1994–99), *Happily Ever After: Fairy Tales for Every Child* (1995), *50 Years of Funny Females* (archival; 1995), *Unhappily Ever After* ("Girls Who Wear Glasses," 1996), *Hollywood Squares* (13 segments; 1998–2004), *The Rosie O'Donnell Show* (1996), *To Tell the Truth* (panelist; 2000), *Twice in a Lifetime* ("Used Hearts," 2000), *The Another World Reunion* (2003), *Ask Rita* (2003), *7th Heaven* ("It's Not Always About You," 2003), *The Nick at Nite Holiday Special* (2003), *Retrosexual: The '80s* (archival; 2004), *TV's Greatest Sidekicks* (2004), *Celebrity Fit Club* (2005), *That's So Raven!* ("Goin' Hollywood," 2005), *One on One* ("Waiting for Huffman," 2005), *Everybody Hates Chris* (recurring role of Vanessa; 2006–08), *TV Land Confidential* ("Oddballs & Original Characters," 2007).

Jackée in *Sister, Sister.*

Jackson, Ernestine Born in Corpus Christie, Texas.

Ernestine Jackson grew up in Corpus Christie, Texas, was accepted by the prestigious Juilliard School in New York, and found theater work soon after graduation. Primarily a theater actress, she has been nominated for the Tony Award twice: in 1974, as Best Supporting or Featured Actress in a Musical for *Raisin* (as Ruth Younger; 1973–75), and in 1977 as Best Actress in a Musical for *Guys and Dolls* (as Sarah Brown; 1976–77). She won the Theatre World Award and Black Theatre Alliance Award for playing the blues legend Alberta Hunter in *Cookin' at the Cookery* (the New York jazz club where Hunter sang regularly for many years).

Other theater credits include *Hello, Dolly!* (as Irene Molloy; 1964–70); *Applause* (Singer;

1970–72); *Tricks* (Ernestina; January 8–13, 1973); *The Bacchae* (Chorus of Bacchae; October–November 1980); and *Joe Turner's Come and Gone* (as standby for Bertha Holly, Martha Pentecost, Mattie Campbell, and Molly Cunningham; March–June 1988). She played Billie Holliday in *Lady Day at Emerson's Bar and Grill* by Lanie Robertson in Cincinnati in 1987 and at the Long Wharf Theatre in New Haven, Connecticut. Her TV work includes roles on *Law & Order* and *The West Wing*. Jackson has been married three times.

Feature Films including TV Movies: *Aaron Loves Angela* (1975), *Homework* (1982), *The Bonfire of the Vanities* (1990), *Girls' Town* (1996), *10,000 Black Men Named George* (TV; 2002), *Freedomland* (2006), *Steam* (2008).

TV: *Musical Chairs* (1975), *Roots: The Next Generations* (miniseries; 1979), *A Man Called Hawk* ("Choice of Chance," 1989), *Law & Order* ("Wager," 1996), *Swift Justice* ("Takin' Back the Street," 1996), *D.C.* ("Justice," 2000), *The West Wing* ("20 Hours in America," Part I, 2002), *Law & Order: Criminal Intent* ("Stray," 2003), *Character Studies* (2005).

Video: *Mystery Disc: Many Roads to Murder* (1983).

Jackson, Janet Born in Gary, Indiana, May 16, 1966.

It comes as a surprise when you realize that Janet Jackson has to date only appeared in three feature films (not counting an appearance as herself at the end of Spike Lee's *Malcolm X*). Part of this is because she has been attached to or proposed for so many projects (most famously the biographical film based on the life of Lena Horne). It is also because most of her acting work has been on the small screen. She began her on-screen career with *The Jacksons* (1976) variety show (doing a mean Mae West impersonation). She appeared as a regular on *Good Times* (1977–79), hired at age 10 by producer Norman Lear, *A New Kind of Family* (1979–80), *Diff'rent Strokes* (1981–82) and *Fame* (1984–85).

In her feature film career, Tupac Shakur, making his film debut, stole the show in John Singleton's *Poetic Justice* (1993), but Jackson had the loveliest braids in screen history as the poetic heroine Justice. She was on much more assured acting footing in *The Nutty Professor II: The Klumps* (2000), the big box office sequel starring Eddie Murphy. And she won the NAACP Image Award for Outstanding Supporting Actress in a Motion Picture for her work as the psychotherapist Patricia in Tyler Perry's *Why Did I Get Married?* (2007).

Of course, Janet Jackson will always be best known as a singer. She began her recording career in 1982. Her self-titled debut album (1982) and *Dream Street* (1984) were only modest successes. Her big success came from the collaboration with producers Jimmy Jam and Terry Lewis, and the release of five number-one selling studio albums: *Control* (1986), *Rhythm Nation 1814* (1989), *janet* (1993), *The Velvet Rope* (1997), and *All for You* (2001). Subsequent albums have not met with equal success: *Damita Jo* (2004), *20 Y.O.* (2006), and *Discipline* (2008). *Rhythm Nation* was the number-one selling album of the year. This album alone earned Jackson three Grammy nominations, three MTV Video Music Awards, six *Billboard* Music Awards, and 12 American Music Award nominations (the most ever). Half the songs on the album scored as hit singles: "What Have You Done for Me Lately?" "Control," "Let's Wait Awhile," "When I Think of You," and "The Pleasure Principle." All these songs are considered R&B classics, and the *Rhythm Nation* tour was the most financially successful tour ever by a new artist.

She is the daughter of Katherine Esther (née Scruse) and Joseph Walter Jackson, the youngest of the nine show business Jackson children. When Janet was a small child, her brothers Michael, Marlon, Jermaine, Tito and Jackie were already enjoying great success as The Jackson 5 (sisters Rebbie and LaToya also had recording careers). The hitherto lower middle class family moved to the upscale Encino section of Los Angeles. By 1974, seven-year-old Janet was already appearing onstage in Las Vegas with her brothers. She attended Portola Middle School in Tarzana, California, and Valley Professional School, class of 1984. Her first marriage was to singer James Debarge (1984), but the marriage was annulled in 1985. In 1991, Jackson secretly entered into her second marriage with dancer Ren Elizondo; the fact that they were married did not become public knowledge until Elizondo filed for divorce in 2000. Her current relationship is with Jermaine Dupri.

It is unfortunate that no biographical entry on the career of Janet Jackson can fail to include the incident at the halftime show of Super Bowl XXXVIII (38), when a famously described "wardrobe malfunction" during a duet with Justin Timberlake resulted in the exposure of Jackson's right breast (2004). This became the most replayed moment in TiVo history, and earned Jackson a dubious place in the *Guinness Book of World Records* as the most searched topic in Internet history. Fortunately, her career has gotten beyond that — if just barely, no pun intended — and she continues to tour, record albums, appear on TV, and make the occasional feature film acting appearance.

Feature Films including TV Movies: *Malcolm X* (1992), *Poetic Justice* (1993), *Nutty Professor II: The Klumps* (2000), *Why Did I Get Married?* (2007).

TV: *The Jacksons* (variety show cast member; 1976), *Good Times* (recurring role of Millicent "Penny" Gordon; 1977–79), *A New Kind of Family* (2 episodes in the role of Jojo Ashton; "Thank You for a Lovely Evening," "Is There a Gun in the House?" 1979), *Diff'rent Strokes* (recurring role of Charlene DuPrey; 1980–84), *Musikladen* (1983), *Fame* (recurring role as Cleo Hewitt; 1984–85), *Fame* (2 episodes; "The Heart of Rock 'N' Roll," Parts I and II, 1984 and 1985), *Soul Train* (2 segments; 1984–86), *American Bandstand* (1984), *The Love Boat* (2 episodes; 1985), *The 12th Annual American Music Awards* (1985), *The 13th Annual American Music Awards* (1986), *The 29th Annual Grammy Awards* (1987), *The 1st Annual Soul Train Music Awards* (1987), *The 4th Annual Black Gold Awards* (1987), *Top of the Pops* (14 segments; 1987–2004), *Rhythm Nation 1814* (1989), *America's Top 10* (1989), *The Royal Variety Performance 1989*, *Pero esto que es?* (1990), *MTV Video Music Awards 1990*, *Great Performances* (archival; "Everybody Dance Now," 1991), *The 6th Annual Soul Train Music Awards* (1992), *MTV Video Music Awards 1993*, *American Bandstand's Teen Idol* (archival; 1994), *The Jackson Family Honors* (1994), *24 Hours in Rock and Roll* (1994), *Saturday Night Live* (2 segments; 1994 and 2004), *The 66th Annual Academy Awards* (1994), *Elvis: The Tribute* (1994), *Michael & Janet Jackson: Scream — History in the Making* (1995), *MTV Video Music Awards 1995*, *Smash Hits Poll Winners Party 1997*, *Dreamworlds II: Desire, Sex, Power in Music Video* (archival; 1997), *3rd Annual Soul Train Lady of Soul Awards* (1997), *MTV Europe Music Awards* 1997, *Des O'Connor Tonight* (1997), *Janet Jackson* (1998), *TFI Friday* (1998), *Janet: The Velvet Rope* (1998), *Hollywood Aids* (1998), *The Rosie O'Donnell Show* (3 segments; 1998–2002),

Janet Jackson in ***Poetic Justice*** (1993).

The 1999 Source Hip-Hop Music Awards (1999), *MTV Video Music Awards 1999*, *100 Greatest Dance Songs of Rock & Roll* (archival; 2000), *The 2000 World Music Awards*, *MTV Video Music Awards 2000*, *2000 Blockbuster Entertainment Awards*, *Making the Video* ("Janet Jackson: Doesn't Really Matter," 2000), *2000 MTV Movie Awards*, *The 2001 Billboard Music Awards*, The *28th Annual American Music Awards* (2001), *Sen kvall med Luuk* (2001), *MTV Icon: Janet Jackson* (2001), *Wetten, dass...?* (2001), *VH1 Divas Live: The One and Only Aretha Franklin* (2001), *CNN World Beat* (2001), *MTV Video Music Awards 2001*, *The Concert for New York City* (2001), *Late Show with David Letterman* (2 segments; 2001–04), *The Tonight Show with Jay Leno* (2 segments; 2001–04), *AFI's 100 Years ... 100 Passions* (2002), *MTV Icon: Arrowsmith* (2002), *Exclusif* (2002), *Janet Jackson: Live in Hawaii* (2002), *The 44th Annual Grammy Awards* (2002), *Star Boulevard* (2002), *American Bandstand's 50th Anniversary Celebration* (2002), *8th Annual Screen Actors Guild Awards* (archival; 2002), *Essence Awards* (2002), *50 Sexiest Video Moments* (2003), *Tupac: Resurrection* (archival; 2003), *Cher: The Farewell Tour* (archival; 2003), *Michael Jackson's Private Home Movies* (archival; 2003), *E! True Hollywood Story* (archival; "Michael Jackson," 2003), *Super Bowl XXXVIII* (2004), *Retrosexual: The '80s* (archival; 2004), *Last Laugh '04* (archival; 2004), *Intimate Portrait* ("Missy 'Misdemeanor' Elliot," 2004), *The Most Shocking Celebrity Moments of 2004* (archival; 2004), *T4* (2004), *The 18th Annual Soul Train Music Awards* (2004), *Good Morning America* (2004), *On-Air with Ryan Seacrest* (2004), *Ant*

& Dec's Saturday Night Takeaway (2004), *Late Night with Conan O'Brien* (2004), *Rove Live* (2004), *Friday Night with Jonathan Ross* (2004), *TV Total* (2004), *Anke Late Night* (2004), *20h10 petantes* (2004), *4th Annual BET Awards* (2004), *Maxim Hot 100* (2004), *A galicia vente xa* (2004), *The Teen Choice Awards 2004, Will & Grace* ("Back Up, Dancer," 2004), *MOBO Awards 2004, 2004 Radio Music Awards, CD:UK* (2 new segments; 2004; archival; 2006), *Michael Jackson's Boys* (archival; 2005), *Beyond the Glory* (archival; "Sex and Sports," 2005), *New Year's Rockin' Eve 2005, BET Awards 2006, Video on Trial: '80s Superstars* (2 episodes; archival; 2006), *Legends Ball* (2006), *The Oprah Winfrey Show* (2006), *In the Cutz* (2006), *The Ellen DeGeneres Show* (3 segments; 2006–08), *The 2006 Billboard Music Awards, Entertainment Tonight* (3 segments; 2006–08), *La tele de tu vida* (archival; 2007), *Forbes' 20 Richest Women in Entertainment* (2004), *Extreme Hollywood* (2007), *50 Most Shocking Celebrity Scandals* (2007), *America United: In Support of Our Troops* (2008), *19th Annual GLAAD Media Awards* (2008), *Larry King Live* (2008), *Jimmy Kimmel Live!* (2008), *39th Annual NAACP Image Awards* (2008), *What Perez Sez* (2008), *Extra* (2008).

Video/DVD: *Michael Jackson: The Legend Continues* (archival; 1988), *Janet Jackson: The Rhythm Nation Compilation* (1990), *Dangerous: The Short Films* (archival; 1993), *Janet Jackson: Design of a Decade 1986–1996* (1996), *Michael Jackson: HIStory on Film, Vol. II* (1997), *The Westside* (archival; 2002), *Michael Jackson: Number Ones* (archival; 2003), *From Janet to Damita Jo* (2004), *Saturday Night Live: The Best of Jimmy Fallon* (archival; 2005).

Jackson, Mahalia Born in New Orleans, Louisiana, October 26, 1911; died January 27, 1972, Evergreen Park, Illinois.

Mahalia Jackson the actress was certainly no threat to Mahalia Jackson the quintessential, Grammy-winning gospel singer, whose signature song was "Take My Hand, Precious Lord," but she did appear in several feature films: *St. Louis Blues* (1958), *Imitation of Life* (1959), and *The Best Man* (1964). Although she had no dialogue in *Imitation of Life*, her rendition of "Trouble of the World" at the funeral of the tragic Annie (Academy Award nominee Juanita Moore) provided a powerful dramatic moment in the film. Beginning in 1954, she hosted a Sunday night radio show on CBS. She also appeared on television in the drama series *The DuPont Show of the Month* (1957) and on the religious anthology series *Lamp Unto My Feet* (1963).

She was the third child of John A. Jackson, a preacher and barber, and Charity Clark, who died when Mahalia was six years old. Her father sent her to live with her aunt Mahalia Paul. She attended McDonough School in New Orleans and began to express her Baptist faith by singing at the Plymouth Rock Church. Influenced by blues legends Bessie Smith, Ida James, and others, Jackson soon began to find her own impassioned style. She signed with Decca Record in 1937 and continued to record and tour until she collapsed while performing in Munich, Germany.

Jackson was married to Isaac Hockenhull (1936–1965), and after her divorce she married Sigmond Galloway, to whom she stayed married until her death from heart disease and complications from diabetes. Upon her death, she was honored with a Grammy Lifetime Achievement Award.

Jackson was deeply involved in the Civil Rights Movement, dating from the 1955 Montgomery Bus Boycott. In 1963 she sang at the March on Washington, and in 1968 she sang at the funeral of Dr. Martin Luther King.

Feature Films: *St. Louis Blues* (1958), *Imitation of Life* (1959), *Jazz on a Summer's Day* (documentary; 1960), *The Best Man* (1964), *4 Little Girls* (documentary; archival; 1997).

TV: *The Ed Sullivan Show* (6 segments; 1952–62), *Look Up and Live* (2 episodes; 1956), *The DuPont Show of the Month* ("Crescendo," 1957), *The Nat King Cole Show* (1957), *The Steve Allen Show* (1958), *Person to Person* (1958), *The Dinah Shore Chevy Show* (1958), *The Bell Telephone Hour* ("One Nation Indivisible," 1960), *What's My Line?* (1961), *Westinghouse Presents: The Sound of the Sixties* (1961), *The Bell Telephone Hour* ("Portals of Music," 1962), *Lamp Unto My Feet* ("And Joy Is My Witness," Part I, 1963), *The Hollywood Palace* (1964), *The Dean Martin Show* (2 segments; 1966), *Girl Talk* (1967), *The Tonight Show Starring Johnny Carson* (1970), *The Flip Wilson Show* (1971), *Aretha Franklin: Mahalia Jackson: The Power and the Glory* (archival; 1987), *The Queen of Soul* (archival; 1988), *American Roots Music* ("The Times They Are A-Changin'," 2001), *Mwah! The Best of the Dinah Shore Show* (2003).

James, Ida Birth date unavailable.

The beautiful Ida James' signature song was "Shoo Shoo Baby," and James was known as the Shoo Shoo Baby and the Shoo Shoo Girl. She is best known today for her duet with Nat King Cole, "Is You Is, or Is You Ain't My Baby?" They sang the duet in a "soundie" together. Soundies were short musical films, the forerunner to music videos, shown on jukeboxes and featuring the hit songs of the day.

She had feature roles in the Nina Mae McKinney vehicle *The Devil's Daughter* (1939) and was Cab Calloway's manager Nettie in *Hi-De-Ho* (1947). James sang with many of the foremost musicians and bandleaders of her day, including Earl "Fatha" Hines, Erskine Hawkins, "Hot Lips" Page and John Kirby.

Feature Films: *The Devil's Daughter* (aka *Pocomania*; 1939), *Trocadero* (1944), *Hi-De-Ho* (1947).

Shorts: *Is You Is, or Is You Ain't My Baby?* (1944).

Jean-Baptiste, Marianne Born in London, England, April 26, 1967.

Marianne Raigipcien Jean-Baptiste graduated from the Royal Academy of Dramatic Arts and performed at the Royal National Theatre. She appeared in the films *Once Upon a Time* and *London Kills Me* (both 1991), but director Mike Leigh's *Secrets & Lies* (1996) is the film that made her an international star. Her role as Hortense, a woman who seeks out her birth mother and discovers that the mother is a white woman, earned her a Golden Globe and an Academy Award Best Supporting Actress nomination in 1997. She was the first black British actress nominated for an Oscar. *Secrets & Lies* is a lovely, touching character study with a subtle, naturalistic performance by Jean-Baptiste that ranks among the best of its era. It is not a film that bowls you over, but rather one that draws you in slowly, gingerly casting a spell that stays in the viewer's mind.

Jean-Baptiste has achieved considerable fame and recognition for her starring role as FBI agent Vivian Johnson of the missing persons division in the popular CBS series *Without a Trace* (2002–08). She is also a singer and a composer. She wrote the music for the Mike Leigh film *Career Girls* (1997) and has released an album of blues songs. In 1993, she appeared in Mike Leigh's musical stage production *It's a Great Big Shame*. She is married to ballet dancer Evan Williams and they have a daughter.

Feature Films including Video and TV Movies: *Once Upon a Time* (1991), *London Kills Me* (1991), *Secrets & Lies* (1996), *Mr. Jealousy* (1997), *How to Make the Cruelest Month* (1998), *The Wedding* (TV; 1998), *Nowhere to Go* (1998), *The 24-Hour Woman* (1999), *The Murder of Steven Lawrence* (TV; 1999), *A Murder of Crows* (1999), *The Man* (TV; 1999), *28 Days* (2000), *The Cell* (2000), *Women in Film* (2001), *Men Only* (TV; 2001), *New Year's Day* (2001), *Spy Game* (2001), *Don't Explain* (2002), *Loving You* (TV; 2003), *Welcome to California* (2005), *Jam* (2006), *City of Ember* (2008), *Bone Deep* (2010).

TV: *Cracker* ("Men Should Weep," 1994), *Sharman* ("A Good Year for the Roses," 1996), *The 69th Annual Academy Awards* (1997), *The Rosie O'Donnell Show* (1997), *Masterchef* (1999), *HBO: First Look* ("28 Days," 2000), *Without a Trace* (recurring role of Vivian Johnson; 2002–08), *The Late Late Show with Craig Ferguson* (2005), *50 Films to See Before You Die* (2006).

Johari, Azizi Born in New York, New York, August 24, 1948.

Stunning Azizi Johari turned an appearance in *Playboy* magazine as the June 1975 Playmate of the Month into an acting and modeling career. She was touring as a dancer with Sammy Davis, Jr., when she appeared in *Playboy* (the fourth African American to do so). Johari spent her childhood living in many different countries since her stepfather was in the military. The family settled in Seattle when she was a teenager; she attended high school and college there and has lived much of her life there.

Her only acting appearance on TV was in an episode of *The Six Million Dollar Man*, but you can see her in four feature films. Her film debut was in director John Cassavetes' *The Killing of a Chinese Bookie* (1976), an intense, character-driven crime drama starring Cassavetes. She was also in *Dreamer* (1979), *Seed of Innocence* (aka *Teen Mothers*; 1980), and *Body and Soul* (1981).

Feature Films including TV Movies: *The Killing of a Chinese Bookie* (1976), *Dreamer* (1979), *Seed of Innocence* (aka *Teen Mothers*; 1980), *Body and Soul* (1981).

TV: *The Six Million Dollar Man* ("Clark Templeton O'Flaherty," 1975).

Video: *Playboy Playmates: The Early Years* (1992).

Johns, Tracy Camilla Born in Queens, New York, April 12, 1963.

Tracy Camilla Johns will always be remembered as Nola Darling, the "she" of *She's Gotta Have It* in Spike Lee's 1986 debut film. This low-budget, Woody Allen–like comedy centers around three diverse men who lust after the self-assured Nola. There's the sweet but vaguely ineffectual Jamie Overstreet — the "nice guy" — played by Tommy Redmond Hicks; the vain, attractive model (John Canada Terrell); and Mars Blackmon (the fast-talking bike messenger with transparent bravado, well played by Lee himself).

But Lee is doing much more than a Woody Allen knock-off here: the film has an urban Brooklyn feel and a sharp, trenchant character byplay that's pure Spike Lee. Nola is not the most sympathetic character ever to grace the screen — she's at times cold, distant, cynical and manipulative — but her obsessed lovers have no one to blame but themselves for their obsession with her.

Tracy Camila Johns in *She's Gotta Have It* (1986).

She's Gotta Have It is at heart a feminist treatise. This was the first time we saw a black woman on screen who had multiple sex partners and was okay (and in charge) with it. Johns was nominated for an Independent Spirit Award in 1987 for her work in the film, which was shot in 12 days for a budget of $18,000.

Sometimes it seems that if it wasn't for Spike Lee (and later, for Tyler Perry) black women wouldn't get many film leads at all. While that's not quite true, Johns was not able to generate much film work after her star turn in *She's Gotta Have It.* She had a lesser role in Lee's rather anemic jazz drama *Mo' Better Blues* (1990), and had a small role as a drug-addled mob prostitute in the excellent *New Jack City* (1991), looking beautiful and delivering a sharp performance despite her limited screen time. Johns was in an Air Jordan commercial with Michael Jordan and with basketball fan supreme Spike Lee. She also had a recurring role as Yolanda in the ABC comedy-mystery-adventure series about a girl detective agency called *Snoops* (1989).

Feature Films including TV Movies: *She's Gotta Have It* (1986), *Mo' Better Blues* (1990), *New Jack City* (1991).

TV: *Family Ties* ("Mister Sister," 1987), *Snoops* (recurring role as Yolanda; 1989).

Music Video: *Wild Things* (1986).

Johnson, A.J. Born in Newark, New Jersey, September 3, 1963.

Adrienne-Joi Johnson has been acting since 1988, dividing her time between feature work and television. She graduated from Rumson-Fair Haven Regional High School in 1981,and magna cum laude from Spelman College in Atlanta, Georgia, with a degree in psychology.

She made her film debut in Spike Lee's *School Daze* (1988) and made quite a splash as the female lead in the immensely popular Kid 'N Play comedy *House Party* (1990) — she played Sharane and did choreography for the film. She was also in *Sister Act* (as Lawanda; 1992) and *The Inkwell* (billed as Adrienne-Joi Johnson; 1994), as Heather Lee, a married woman who befriends Drew, the film's teenage protagonist. Perhaps her best role was as the mother of a directionless twenty-something in John Singleton's *Baby Boy* (2001).

Her TV work is just as varied and extensive. She was one of the leads on the female cop show *Sirens* (1993–95) and made guest star appearances on *In the Heat of the Night*, *A Different World*, *The Fresh Prince of Bel-Air*, *Chicago Hope*, *Touched by an Angel*, and *The Jamie Foxx Show*. Johnson is also a dancer and a fitness instructor, and was host of the fitness competition show *From Flab to Fab* (2004).

Feature Films including Video and TV Movies: *School Daze* (1988), *A Mother's Courage: The Mary Thomas Story* (TV: 1989), *House Party* (1990), *Clippers* (TV; 1991), *Dying Young* (1991), *Murder Without Motive: The Edmund Perry Story* (TV; 1991), *Double Trouble* (1992), *Sister Act* (1992), *Love, Lies & Lullabies* (TV; 1993), *The Inkwell* (1994), *Peter Benchley's The Beast* (TV; 1996), *High Freakquency* (1998), *Two Shades of Blue* (2000), *Tara* (2001), *Baby Boy* (2001), *Skin Deep* (2003).

TV: *A Different World* ("Mr. Hillman," 1988), *In the Heat of the Night* ("These Things Take Time," 1989), *CBS Summer Playhouse* ("Coming to America," 1989), *The Fresh Prince of Bel-Air* ("Def Poet's Society," 1990), *Amen* ("My Fair Homeboy," 1991), *Sirens* (recurring role of Officer Lynn Stanton; 1993–95), *Chicago Hope* ("Liver Let Die," 1996), *The Jamie Foxx Show* ("I Do, I Didn't," 1997), *Touched By an Angel* ("Angels Anonymous," 2001), *It's Black Entertainment* (archival; 2002), *From Flab to Fab* (series host; 2004).

Johnson, Anne-Marie Born in Los Angeles, California, January 18, 1960.

With her patrician beauty and dignified mien, Anne-Marie Johnson has graced both films and television. She was elected first national vice president of the Screen Actors Guild in 2005. Johnson has been one of the busiest African American actresses of her generation, primarily on series TV and in TV movies, although she was also in the theatrical features *Hollywood Shuffle* (1987), *I'm Gonna Git You Sucka* (1988), *The Five Heartbeats* (1991), and *Down in the Delta* (1998).

Her first notable role was as Aileen Lewis on the 1984 NBC comedy series *Double Trouble*. After the 1985 syndicated series *What's Happening Now!* (as Raj's wife Nadine Hudson Thomas), she became well known for portraying Althea Tibbs on the NBC (and later CBS) series *In the Heat of the Night* (1988–93), where she eventually wound up marrying the Carroll O'Connor character.

Johnson joined the cast of the FOX Network series *In Living Color* in its final season (1993–94).

Anne-Marie Johnson with Regina King and Ernest Thomas in *What's Happening Now!*

She also played Alycia Barnett on one season of the Fox series *Melrose Place* (1995–96), had a recurring role on *JAG* as Representative Bobbi Latham (1997–2002), and another recurring role as Donna Cabonna on *That's So Raven* (2006). She graduated from UCLA with a degree in theater. Her husband is Martin Grey (1996–present).

Feature Films including Video and TV Movies: *His Mistress* (TV; 1984), *Hollywood Shuffle* (1987), *I'm Gonna Git You Sucka* (1988), *Dream Date* (TV; 1989), *Robot Jox* (aka *Robojox*, 1990), *The Five Heartbeats* (1991), *True Identity* (1991), *Strictly Business* (1991), *Why Colors?* (1992), *Asteroid* (TV; 1997), *Down in the Delta* (1998), *Pursuit of Happiness* (2001), *Life/Drawing* (aka *Apartment 12*, *Low Rent*, 2001), *Through the Fire* (TV; 2002).

TV: *Solo One* ("My Bonnie," 1976), *Diff'rent Strokes* ("Undercover Lover," 1984), *Double Trouble* ("Do You Believe in Magic?" 1984), *Hill Street Blues* (4 episodes in the role of Lynn Williams; "Fowl Play," "Bangladesh Slowly," "Blues for Mr. Green" "You're in Alice's," 1984–85), *What's Happening Now!* (recurring role of Nadine Hudson Thomas; 1985–88), *Hunter* ("Saturday Night Special," 1986), *The 9th Annual American Black Achievement Awards* (1988), *Houston Knights* ("Vigilante," 1988), *In the Heat of the Night* (recurring role of Althea Tibbs; 1988–93), *Singer & Sons* ("Once Bitten," 1990), *Jackie Collins' Lucky/Chances* (miniseries; 1990), *The Best of Robert Townsend and His Partners in Crime* (1991), *The Larry Sanders Show* ("The Guest Host," 1992), *In Living Color* (3 segments; 1993–94), *Living Single* ("What's Next?" 1994), *Babylon 5* ("The Long Dark," 1994), *Sirens* ("Color Blind," 1995),

Murder, She Wrote ("Big Easy Murder," 1995), *Melrose Place* (recurring role of Alycia Barnett; 1995–96), *ER* ("Ask Me No Questions, I'll Tell You No Lies," 1996), *Spider-Man* (voice; 3 episodes; 1996–97), *JAG* (recurring role of Rep. Bobbi Latham; 1997–2002), *Any Day Now* ("Making Music with the Wrong Man," 1998), *The Pretender* ("Once in a Blue Moon," 1998), *Chicago Hope* ("Vanishing Acts," 1999), *It's Like, You Know...* ("Two Days in the Valley," 1999), *Ally McBeal* ("Love's Illusions," 1999), *Hope Island* ("You Can't Look at the Sea Without Wishing for Wings," 1999), *Happily Ever After: Fairy Tales for Every Child* ("The Frog Princess," 2000), *Family Law* ("Are You My Father?" 2000), *Chicken Soup for the Soul* ("A Pearl of Great Value," 2000), *Pajama Party* (2000), *For Your Love* ("The Shrink Gets Shrunk," 2000), *The X Files* ("Redrum," 2000), *Strong Medicine* ("Gray Matter," 2001), *The Parkers* ("Nobody's Fool," 2001), *The District* (2 episodes; "Rage Against the Machine," "Criminally Insane," 2001 and 2003), *Dharma & Greg* ("The Mamas and the Papas," Part I, 2002), *What I Like About You* ("Loose Lips," 2003), *The Division* ("Castaways," 2003), *Girlfriends* (6 episodes in the role of Sharon Upton Farley; 2003–04), *Rock Me, Baby* ("I Love You, You Don't Love Me," 2004), *That's So Raven* (recurring role as Donna Cabonna; 2006), *CSI* ("Leaving Las Vegas," 2007), *NCIS* (2007), *Bones* (2007), *Tyler Perry's House of Payne* (2007).

Video/DVD: *That's So Raven: Raven's Makeover Madness* (2006).

Johnson, Ariyan A.

Born in Brooklyn, New York, 1976.

Ariyan Johnson garnered a good deal of attention with the starring role in the independent film *Just Another Girl on the IRT* (1992), the first feature film produced, directed and written by an African American woman (Leslie Harris). It was Harris' only film, and the role of Chantel Mitchell proved to be Ariyan Johnson's first and only lead. She was wonderfully natural in this slice of life tale of a black teenager starting to discover who she is. The film did not do well at the box office. Nonetheless, it's a time capsule of an era, and a film ripe for rediscovery. Johnson was nominated for an Independent Spirit Award in 1994 as Best Female Lead for her sensitive work.

Johnson followed this with smaller roles in *Bulworth*, *The General's Daughter* and the TV movie *Something to Sing About*. Her only recurring role on a series was as Aisha on *The Steve Harvey Show* (1997–98). She continued acting on television until 2004, but has not been heard from since. Her last work was on episodes of *JAG* and *Strong Medicine*.

Feature Films including TV Movies: *Just Another Girl on the IRT* (1992), *Bulworth* (1998), *The General's Daughter* (1999), *Something to Sing About* (TV; 2000).

TV: *Law & Order* ("Hot Pursuit," 1995), *The Steve Harvey Show* (recurring role of Aisha; "Whatever You Want," "Big Daddy Meets the Man of Steel," "You're Driving Me Crazy," 1997–98), *L.A. Doctors* ("A Prayer for the Lying," 1998), *For the People* ("The Double Standard," 2002), *Static Shock* (voice; "The Usual Suspect," 2003), *JAG* ("Hard Time," 2004), *Strong Medicine* ("Positive Results," 2004).

Johnson, Beverly

Born in Buffalo, New York, October 13, 1952.

Beverly Johnson was raised in a middle class section of Buffalo in upstate New York. She was a swimming champion in her teens. She studied criminal justice at Northwest University, but her outstanding looks led to a modeling assignment with *Glamour* magazine, and from that point on her career on the runway was virtually assured.

Iconic model and sometime actress Johnson is more known for her 500-plus magazine cover appearances than for her films, but she began acting in 1976 and was in *Deadly Hero* (1976), *Ashanti* (1979), *The Meteor Man* (1993), *54* (1998), and *Crossroads* (2002), and series TV such as *Emergency!* (1976), *Law & Order* (1992–93), *Arli$$* (1996) and *Girlfriends* (2004). Her *Vogue*

Ariyan Johnson in *Just Another Girl on the I.R.T.* (1992).

cover in August 1974 was groundbreaking; she was the first black model to appear on *Vogue* and it had a dramatic effect on opportunities for African American models.

She is the author of the best seller *Beverly Johnson's Guide to a Life of Health and Beauty* (Times Books; 1981). In 2008, Johnson became a celebrity judge on the reality show *She's Got the Look*, a variant of *America's Next Top Model* for women over 35.

Feature Films including Video and TV Movies: *Deadly Hero* (1976), *The Baron* (1977), *Crisis in Sun Valley* (TV; 1978), *Ashanti* (1979), *The Sky Is Gray* (TV; 1980), *The Cover Girl Murders* (TV; 1993), *Loaded Weapon 1* (1993), *The Meteor Man* (1993), *A Brilliant Disguise* (1994), *Ray Alexander: A Menu for Murder* (TV; 1995), *Crossworlds* (1996), *True Vengeance* (1997), *How to Be a Player* (1997), *54* (1998), *Down 'n Dirty* (2000), *Crossroads* (2002).

TV: *Emergency!* ("Rules of Order," 1976), *Hunter* ("This Is My Gun," 1990), *Saturday Night Live* (1989), *Martin* ("Blackboard Jungle Fever," 1990), *The Jane Whitney Show* (1993), *Law & Order* (2 episodes; "Consultation," "Black Tie," 1992 and 1993), *A Perry Mason Mystery: The Case of the Wicked Wives* (1993), *The Mommies* ("A Day in the Life," 1994), *Lois & Clark: The New Adventures of Superman* ("Barbarians at the Planet," "The House of Luthor," 1994), *MADtv* (1995), *The Wayans Bros.* ("I'm Too Sexy for My Brother," 1995), *Arli$$* ("The Client's Best Interest," 1996), *Red Shoe Diaries* ("The Forbidden Zone," 1996), *The Parent 'Hood* ("I'm O'Tay, You're O'Tay," 1996), *E! True Hollywood Story* ("Margaux Hemingway," 1997), *Ed's Night Party* (1997), *Sabrina, The Teenage Witch* ("As Westbridge Turns," 1997), *3rd Rock from the Sun* (2 episodes; "36! 24! 36! Dick!," Parts I and II, 1998), *Girlfriends* ("Leggo My Ego," 2004), *Retrosexual: The '80s* (2004), *The Tyra Banks Show* (4 segments: three with new footage, "Secrets of the Supermodels," "Full-Figured Top Model," "Model Madness;" one archival, "Tyra's Favorite Model Search Moments," 2005–06), *America's Next Top Model* (2 segments; 2005 and 2007), *Legends Ball* (2006), *Ebony Fashion Fair: 50 Years of Style* (2008), *The 6th Annual TV Land Awards* (2008), *She's Got the Look* (judge, various episodes; 2008).

Video/DVD: *Michael Jackson: HIStory on Film, Vol. II* (1997), *Red Shoe Diaries 15: Forbidden Zone* (2002).

Johnson, Penny (aka Johnson Jerald, Penny)

Born in Baltimore, Maryland, March 14, 1961.

Johnson studied acting at the Juilliard School for the Arts. Her first professional acting role was in the TV movie *The Files on Jill Hatch* (1983), followed by appearances on *T.J. Hooker* and *Hill Street Blues* (both 1984), and a recurring role on *Boston Legal* as Vivian Elizabeth Conway (1984–86). She was also a regular on the soap *General Hospital* in 1986. Guest spots on *The Jeffersons* (1986) and *The Cosby Show* (1988) followed. She played Condoleeza Rice in two TV movies: *DC 9/11: Time of Crisis* (2003) and *The Path to 9/11* (2006).

Johnson's defining role is without question that of Sheri Palmer, the all-but-Satanic wife of ill-fated President David Palmer (Dennis Haysbert) on *24* (2001–04). First lady Sheri is one of great mean characters in TV history. Other outstanding television work is her character Beverly Barnes on *The Larry Sanders Show* (1992–98), for which she was nominated in 1998 for an NAACP Image Award for Outstanding Supporting Actress in a Comedy Series. Sci-fi genre fans revere her most for her role of Kasidy Yates on *Star Trek: Deep Space Nine* (1995–99) and her stint on *The 4400* (2007). She has also had recurring roles on *ER* (1998–99) and *October Road* (2007–08).

She has been married to musician Gralin Jerald since 1982; they have a daughter, Danyel, born in 1983. Johnson teaches acting workshops and produces and directs for the Outreach Christian Theater Company, which she founded with her husband in 1994.

Feature Films including TV Movies: *The Files on Jill Hatch* (TV; 1983), *Swing Shift* (1984), *The Imposter* (TV; 1984), *The Hills Have Eyes Part II* (1985), *The Grand Baby* (TV; 1985), *Kaleidoscope* (TV; 1990), *Chameleon Blue* (TV; 1990), *Goin' to Chicago* (1991), *What's Love Got to Do with It* (1993), *Class of '61* (TV; 1993), *Empty Cradle* (TV; 1993), *Automatic* (1994), *Molly & Gina* (1994), *Fear of a Black Hat* (1994), *The Road to Galveston* (TV; 1996), *Death Benefit* (TV; 1996), *The Writing's on the Wall* (TV; 1996), *Absolute Power* (1997), *A Secret Life* (TV; 1999), *The Test of Love* (TV; 1999), *The Color of Friendship* (TV; 2000), *Deliberate Intent* (TV; 2000), *DC 9/11: Time of Crisis* (TV; 2003), *Secrets of the International Spy Museum* (TV; 2004), *Rent* (2005), *The Path to 9/11* (TV; 2006), *October Road* (2008).

TV: *T.J. Hooker* ("Anatomy of a Killing," 1984), *Hill Street Blues* ("Blues for Mr. Green," 1984), *The Paper Chase: The Third Year* (recurring role of Vivian Elizabeth Conway; 1984–86), *The Jeffersons* ("Last Dance," 1985), *General Hospital* (recurring role as Debbie; 1986), *The Cosby Show* ("The Visit," 1988), *Simon & Simon* (2 episodes; "Out-of-Town Brown," "Zen and the Art of the Split-Finger Fastball," 1985 and 1986), *Tour of Duty* ("For What It's Worth," 1989), *Homeroom* (1989), *Freddy's Nightmares* ("Life Sentence," 1990), *Coach* ("The Day That Moses Came to Town," 1990), *Parker Lewis* ("Teacher, Teacher," 1990), *Columbo: Caution Murder Can Be Hazardous to Your Health* (1991), *The Larry Sanders Show* (recurring role of Beverly Barnes; 1992–98), *Star Trek: The Next Generation* ("Homeward," 1994), *Star Trek: Deep Space Nine* (recurring role of Kasidy Yates; 1995–99), *Grace Under Fire* (2 episodes as Bailey Alford; "Love Thy Neighbor," "Pregnant Pause," 1996), *Cosby* ("Brave New Hilton," 1997), *The Gregory Hines Show* (pilot; 1997), *ER* (recurring role of nurse practitioner Lynette Evans; 1998–99), *Family Law* ("Family Values," 2000), *The X-Files* ("Medusa," 2001), *The Practice* ("Awakenings," 2001), *Citizen Baines* ("A Day Like No Other," 2001), *24* (recurring role of Sherry Palmer; 2001–04), *Touched By An Angel* ("The Impossible Dream," 2002), *24 Heaven* (2002), *24: The Postmortem* (2002), *The Wayne Brady Show* (2002), *Frasier* ("Maris Returns," 2003), *Hollywood Squares* (2003), *24: Access All Areas* (2003), *Pure 24* (2 segments; 2003), *The View* (2003), *Pyramid* (2003), *24Inside* (2004), *Journeys Below the Line: 24—The Editing Process* (2004), *The 100 Most Unexpected TV Moments* (2005), *Eve* (4 episodes in the role of Beverly Williams; "Shelly & ?," "All About Eve," "Daughter Don't Preach," "Daddy's Home," 2005–06), *Law & Order* ("Choice of Evils," 2006), *E! True Hollywood Story* ("24," 2007), *Angels Can't Help But Laugh* (2007), *The 4400* (recurring role of Rebecca Parrish; "One of Us," "Tiny Machines," "The Great Leap Forward," 2007), *October Road* (recurring role of Dean Etwood; 2007–08).

Penny Johnson in *Homeroom.*

Joi, Marilyn (aka King, Tracy; King, Tracy Ann; King, T.A.; King, Ineda)

Born May 22, 1945.

Marilyn Joi's first film appearance was a wordless cameo as a sexy dancer in *Hammer* (1972), starring Fred Williamson and directed by Al Adamson, who discovered her performing in an exotic dance club. Much of her career was in Adamson films. However, her most famous role and her biggest box office success was as Cleopatra Schwartz in *The Kentucky Fried Movie* (1977), a collection of comedy sketches that connected well with young audiences of the day, helping to popularize outrageous satirical comedies.

Another famous role was in *The Naughty Stewardesses* and its sequel, the less financially successful but very interesting and underrated retro comedy *Blazing Stewardesses* (both 1975). Although she has a great role in *The Naughty Stewardesses* and delivers her dialogue with crisp authority, she unfortunately has little to do in the sequel other than to stand around in scene after scene. She is billed here as Tracy King.

Joi brought variety and a measure of depth to her big and small screen performances. She never walked through a role and she knew the meaning of nuance. She could be a bad girl, a traditional action film heroine, or a light comedienne of considerable charm. Observe the delightfully humorous touches she adds to the graveyard scene in *Nurse Sherri* (1978). Also check out her outrageous team-up with Tanya Boyd (who went on to mainstream fame in daytime soaps) in the misogynistic, ultra-violent *Ilsa, Harem Keeper of the Oil Sheiks* (1976). Joi plays Velvet, a sadistic lesbian "enforcer" to Boyd's Satin. Joi has a ball with this role. They are two of the most ruthless women you will ever see on screen.

She is further seen to excellent advantage—

Left to right: Connie Hoffman, Tracy King (Marilyn Joi), Yvonne De Carlo and Bob Livingston in *Blazing Stewardesses* (1975).

stealing every scene she's in — in *Mean Mother* (1974) and *Black Heat* (1976), two black action films from Adamson. *Black Samurai* is a lesser entry in the Adamson oeuvre, and Jim Kelly is a bland hero to say the least, but Joi has fun with a villainous role. One of her last screen roles was in low budget sci-fi film *Galaxina* (1988). This is a hapless film, and relentlessly unfunny, but it's great to see Joi pop up as a winged batgirl. Although her big screen career was limited to exploitation films, her TV work in the '70s and '80s includes mainstream hits such as *Hill Street Blues, Charlie's Angels, Starsky and Hutch*, and *Hunter*.

Feature Films: *Hammer* (1972), *Hit Man* (1972), *Wonder Women* (1973), *Coffy* (1973), *Detroit 9000* (1973), *The Student Teachers* (1973), *Black Samson* (1974), *Mean Mother* (1974), *Tender Loving Care* (1974), *Black Starlet* (1974), *The Naughty Stewardesses* (1975), *Candy Tangerine Man* (1975), *Blazing Stewardesses* (1975), *Uncle Tom's Cabin* (1976), *Ilsa, Harem Keeper of the Oil Sheiks* (1976), *Mansion of the Doomed* (1976), *Black Samurai* (1976), *The Happy Hooker Goes to Washington* (1977), *The Kentucky Fried Movie* (1977), *Nurse Sherri* (aka *The Possession of Nurse Sherri, Black Voodoo*; 1978), *The Great American Girl Robbery* (aka *Cheerleaders' Wild Weekend*; 1979), *Galaxina* (1980), *C.O.D.* (1981), *Satan's Princess* (1990).

TV: *Starsky and Hutch* (2 episodes; "Omaha Tiger," "Gillian," 1976), *Good Times* ("J.J. in Business," 1977), *Charlie's Angels* ("The Blue Angels," 1977), *Hunter* ("The Beautiful and the Dead," Part I, 1986), *Hill Street Blues* ("A Case of the Klapp," 1986).

Jones, Grace Born in Spanish Town, Jamaica, May 19, 1948.

Quirky disco queen Grace Jones encapsulated the Studio 54 era and managed to have a fairly substantial film career in addition to a significant musical career. But no screen role she ever played could match her outre real life persona. Born Grace Mendoza Jones, she was the daughter of Marjorie and Robert W. Jones, a clergyman and politician. Her parents moved with

Grace and her brother, Christian, to Syracuse, New York, in 1965. She studied theater at Syracuse University and then became a successful model in New York and Paris. The 5'10½" Grace had a killer body as well as height, so she acclimated herself to the runway very well, and moved with assurance and authority when it came time to take her act to the big screen.

She began recording for Island Records in 1977, and although she had a fine, powerful contralto voice, her showmanship was her main appeal. Her three disco albums—*Portfolio* (1977), *Fame* (1978) and *Muse* (1979)—resounded especially with the gay community. Given her gorgeous but androgynous look and her tenure as queen of the New York disco scene, it was not too surprising that she appealed to the artist Andy Warhol. Warhol is now rightly recognized as the great artist of his generation. He took many photographs of Jones that have become iconic with the passing years. Warhol and Jones were regulars at the legendary disco Studio 54, and Jones performed her disco hits in outrageous stage shows clad in equally outrageous costumes at this and other venues.

Jones was a living legend by the time she released the albums *Warm Leatherette* (1980), *Nightclubbing* (1981), and her classic *Slave to the Rhythm* (1985). She also had quite a string of hit singles, including "La Vie en Rose" and "I'm Not Perfect (But I'm Perfect for You)."

Amazingly, Jones did manage to transfer her aura to the big screen, whether as a barbarian warrior in *Conan the Destroyer* (1984); the deadly May Day in the James Bond film *A View to a Kill* (1985); or the Kabuki-faced vampire in *Vamp* (1986). In the 1980s, she had relationships with bodybuilder Sven-Ole Thorsen and bodybuilder and actor Dolph Lundgren (and did a *Playboy* pictorial with him). She has a son named Paulo from a relationship with singer Jean-Paul Goude. In 1996, she married bodyguard Atila Altaunbay, although they later divorced. In 2006, she was engaged to music producer Ivor Guest.

Her intense look and her angular face, her cubist-nightmare haircut, and her bizarre, padded, uniform-like clothing have long been a creative statement. Jones' greatest role has always been herself. She continues to be revered by the avant-garde, but it's almost as if the times have grown too

Christopher Walken, Grace Jones and Patrick Bauchau in *A View to a Kill* (1985).

small for Grace Jones, rather than vice versa. Fans were glad to discover that in 2008 she released her first album in 19 years, the distinctive *Hurricane*, which the *Village Voice* called "a massive tsunami of sonic detail matched to an equally finessed and poetic sense of self."

Feature Films including Video and TV Movies: *Gordon's War* (1973), *Attention les yeux!* (1976), *Quelli della calibro 38* (1976), *Armee der liebenden oder revolte der perversen* (1979), *Deadly Vengeance* (1981), *Scandals* (TV; 1984), *Mode in France* (1984), *Conan the Destroyer* (1984), *A View to a Kill* (1985), *Vamp* (1986), *Straight to Hell* (1987), *Siesta* (1987), *Superstar: The Life and Times of Andy Warhol* (documentary; 1990), *Boomerang* (1992), *Pret-a-Porter* (1994), *Cyber Bandits* (1995), *McCinsey's Island* (1998), *Palmer's Pick Up* (1999), *Wolf Girl* (aka *Blood Moon*; TV; 1999), *Shaka Zulu: The Citadel* (TV; 2001), *No Place Like Home* (2006), *Chelsea on the Rocks* (documentary; 2008).

TV: *Musikladen* (1978), *American Bandstand* (1979), *Soul Train* (2 segments; 1979–87), *Top of the Pops* (1980), *Aplauso* (1983), *The 25th Annual Grammy Awards* (1983), *Nojesmassakern* (1985), *The Tube* (1986), *The 1st Annual Soul Train Music Awards* (1987), *Marvin Gaye* (archival; 1987), *Pee-Wee Herman's Christmas Special* (1988), *A Reggae Session* (1988), *Wetten, dass...?* (1990), *The Full Wax* (1991), *De mar a mar* (1991), *Bellezas al agua* (1993), *In Search of Dracula with Jonathan Ross* (1996), *In and Out of Fashion* (archival; 1998), *Behind the Music* ("Studio 54," 1998), *So Graham Norton* (1998), *Beast Master* ("The Umpatra," 1999), *100 Greatest Dance Songs of Rock & Roll* (2000), *I Love the '80s* ("I Love 1985," 2001), *Pavarotti and Friends 2002 for Angola*, *VH1: Where Are They Now* ("Girls' Night Out," 2002), *V Graham Norton* (2 segments; 2002 and 2003), *Tout le monde en parle* (2004), *Retrosexual: The '80s* (archival; 2004), *Favouritism* (archival; 2005), *La tele de tu vida* (archival; 2007), *Les grands du rire* (archival; 2007), *FalcoVerdammt wir leben noch!* (2008).

Video/DVD: *Playboy Video Magazine, Vol. 8* (1985).

Jones, Jill Marie

Born in Dallas, Texas, January 4, 1975.

Jones was a Dallas Cowboys cheerleader and a Dallas Mavericks dancer who toured with the United Service Organization (USO) and the Department of Defense, traveling to Asia and the Middle East. After attending Duncanville High School and Texas Woman's University, she started modeling, then moved to Los Angeles to pursue acting full time. Jones' portrayal of the self-centered and materialistic real estate broker Toni Childs for six seasons in *Girlfriends* marked her series debut, she left the show in May 2006 when her contract ended. Other acting credits include the Saturday morning series *City Guys* (2000).

Her most prominent film appearance was in *The Perfect Holiday* (2007), a sweetly sentimental Christmas romance with Gabrielle Union. She was also in the independent horror film *Redrum* (2007) as a housewife turned serial killer. In *The Longshots* (2008), she's a teacher who takes a mentoring interest in a female member of the school's football team. The film starred Ice Cube and Keke Palmer, and was not a financial success. In the all-but-shelved *Major Movie Star* (2008) with Jessica Simpson, she's a single mom who joins the army in search of opportunity.

Feature Films including Video/DVD and TV Movies: *Redrum* (2007), *Universal Remote* (2007), *The Perfect Holiday* (2007), *Major Movie Star* (2008), *The Longshots* (2008), *Drool* (2009).

TV: *City Guys* ("Shock Treatment," 2000), *Girlfriends* (recurring role of Toni Childs; 2000–06), *35th NAACP Image Awards* (2004), *The Sharon Osbourne Show* (2004), *BET Comedy Awards* (2004), *106 & Park Top 10 Live* (2005), *All Shades of Fine: 25 Hottest Women of the Past 25 Years* (2005).

Jones, Krysten Leigh

Birth date unavailable.

Krysten Leigh Jones was nominated for an NAACP Image Award for Outstanding Youth Actress for *Remember the Titans* (2000) for her role as Denzel Washington's daughter. Her mother, Leigh Dupree, is also her manager. Dupree also acts, owns a production company, and teaches children's acting classes. The family moved from Los Angeles to Georgia in the '90s, which is where Jones got her role in *Titans*, but after no other work turned up, it was back to L.A. TV viewers remember Leigh as Tasha on *The Bernie Mac Show* (2006).

Feature Films including Video and TV Movies: *Don't Be a Menace to South Central While Drinking Your Juice in the Hood* (1996), *Remember the Titans* (2000), *Akeelah and the Bee* (2006), *The Neighbor* (2007).

TV: *North Hollywood* (pilot; 2001), *Even Stevens* (2 episodes; "Almost Perfect," Quest for Coolness," 2001), *The Parkers* ("Take the Cookies and Run," 2001), *The Guardian* ("Where Are You?" 2003), *The District* ("The Devil You Know," 2003), *Joan of Arcadia* ("Double Dutch," 2004), *Listen Up* ("Grandmaster of the Wolfhunt," 2004), *Strong Medicine* ("Cutting the Cord," 2005), *Fatherhood* (recurring role of Carmel; 2004–05), *Unfabulous* ("The Pink Guitar," "The Partner," 2004–05), *Judging Amy* ("The Long Run," "Dream a Little Dream," 2005), *Over There* ("It's Alright Ma, I'm Only Bleeding," 2005), *The Bernie Mac Show* (3 episodes in the recurring role of Tasha; "Sweet Home Chicago," Parts I and II, "Fumes of Détente," 2006), *Without a Trace* ("Two of Us," 2007).

Jones, Rashida Born in Los Angeles, California, February 25, 1976.

Rashida Leah Jones went to the Buckley School in Sherman Oaks, California, and graduated from Harvard University in 1997. She is the daughter of composer-musician Qunicy Jones and actress Peggy Lipton, the younger sister of Kidada Jones, and the half-sister of Quincy Jones III, and Jolie, Martina, Kenya and Rachel Jones. She became interested in acting in 1997 and played Laura Fenn on Fox's *Boston Public* (2000–02), for which she received an NAACP Image Award nomination. Later she appeared in the seven episode series *ny-lon* (2004) and appeared as government agent Carmen Merced on TNT's *Wanted* (2005).

She joined the cast of NBC's *The Office* in the role of Karen Filippelli in September 2006 at the start of its third season. She was also in the Farrelly brothers' short-lived Fox series *Unhitched* (2008). She had a small role in director Steven Soderbergh's *Full Frontal* (2002). Jones was at one time engaged to actor Tobey Maguire. Her other interests include singing and songwriting (she is an accomplished pianist), and she has modeled, notably for The Gap.

Feature Films including Video and TV Movies: *Myth America* (1998), *East of A* (2000), *If These Walls Could Talk 2* (TV; 2001), *Roadside Assistance* (2001), *Full Frontal* (2002), *Now You Know* (2002), *Death of a Dynasty* (2003), *Little Black Book* (2004), *Our Thirties* (TV; 2006), *Brief Interviews with Hideous Men* (2008), *I Love You, Man* (2009), *Chilled in Miami* (2009).

TV: *The Last Don* (miniseries; 1997), *Rocky Horror 25: Anniversary Special* (2000), *Freaks and Geeks* ("Kim Kelly Is My Friend," 2000), *Boston Public* (recurring role of Louisa Fenn; 2000–02), *Tupac Shakur: Thug Angel* (2002), *Chappelle's Show* (2 episodes; 2003 and 2004), *ny-lon* (recurring role of Edie Miller; 2004), *Wanted* (recurring role of Detective Carla Merced; 2005), *Stella* (pilot; 2005), *The Late Late Show with Craig Ferguson* (2005), *Late Night with Conan O'Brien* (2006), *Paul Reiser* (pilot; 2006), *The Rules for Starting Over* (pilot; 2006), *The Office* (recurring role of Karen Filippelli; 2006–08), *Last Call with Carson Daly* (2007), *Guys' Choice* (archival; 2007), *Saturday Night Live* (2007), *Unhitched* (recurring role as Kate; 2008).

Music Video: *Long Road to Ruin* (2007).

Jones, Renée Born in Opa-Locka, Florida, October 15, 1958.

Renée Jones was born in Florida into a family of five siblings and grew up in Georgia and New York. At age 19, she signed a contract with the renowned Ford Models. After several TV movies, she did her first theatrical feature, *Jason Lives: Friday the 13th, Part VI* (1986). Her best big screen work is found in *Talkin' Dirty After Dark* (1991), the story of a struggling stand-up comic starring Martin Lawrence.

Her main claim to fame has been her work as Dr. Lexie Carver on the daytime soap *Days of Our Lives* (1993–2008), for which she was nominated for five NAACP Image Awards for Outstanding Actress in a Daytime Drama Series. She had originally played another role on the show, Nikki Wade, in the early 1980s. She also appeared briefly in another daytime soap, *Santa Barbara*, and in the nighttime soap *Knots Landing* (both 1984). Other prominent TV work includes two episodes of *The White Shadow* (her acting debut, 1979–81), and a recurring role as Diana Moses on *L.A. Law* (1989–90). Jones is a skilled tennis player and a pianist.

Feature Films including Video and TV Movies: *Forbidden Love* (TV; 1982), *Deadly Lessons* (TV; 1983), *Jason Lives: Friday the 13th, Part VI* (1986), *The Liberators* (TV; 1987), *Heart and Soul* (TV; 1989), *The Terror Within II* (1990), *Talkin' Dirty after Dark* (1991), *Tracks of Glory* (TV; 1992).

TV: *The White Shadow* (2 episodes; "Globetrotters," "Psyched Out," 1979 and 1981), *Tenspeed and Brown Shoe* (pilot; 1980), *The Jeffersons*

("A Night to Remember," 1980), *Diff'rent Strokes* (2 episodes; "First Day Blues," "The Houseguest," 1981 and 1984), *Days of Our Lives* (recurring role as Nikki Wade; recurring role as Lexie Carver, 1993–2008), *WKRP in Cincinnati* ("You Can't Go Out of Town Again," 1982), *Quincy M.E.* ("Beyond the Open Door," 1983), *Jessie* (recurring role as Ellie Mack's secretary; 1984), *Santa Barbara* (recurring role of Toni Carlin; 1984), *Hotel* ("Encores," 1984), *ABC Afterschool Specials* ("The Hero Who Couldn't Read," 1984), *Knots Landing* (4 episodes in the role of Robin; 1984), *Trapper John, M.D.* ("A False Start," 1985), *T.J. Hooker* ("Return of a Cop," 1985), *What's Happening Now!* ("Thy Boss's Daughter," 1986), *Isabel's Honeymoon Hotel* (1987), *Marblehead Manor* ("I Led Three Wives," 1987), *21 Jump Street* (3 episodes; "Besieged," Parts I and II, "Crossfire," 1987–91), *Highway to Heaven* ("Country Doctor," 1988), *Night Court* ("The Last Temptation of Mac," 1988), *L.A. Law* (11 episodes in the role of Diana Moses; 1989–90), *In the Heat of the Night* (2 episodes; "Stranger in Town," "Legacy," 1989 and 1993), *Bodies of Evidence* ("Afternoon Delights," 1992), *Star Trek: The Next Generation* ("Aquiel," 1993), *The Fresh Prince of Bel-Air* ("Father Knows Best," 1994), *Murder, She Wrote* ("Deadly Bidding," 1995), *Days of Our Lives' 35th Anniversary* (archival; 2000), *Days of Our Lives' Christmas* (archival; 2001), *Soap Talk* (2 segments; 2006).

Music Video: *On Bended Knee* (1994).

Jones, Tamala Born in Pasadena, California, November 12, 1974.

Tamala Jones began her career as a model in print ads and TV commercials; today she is best known as an actress, alternating television and feature film work. Her acting aspirations go back to childhood: she staged backyard shows with her cousin and started studying drama in the sixth grade. Her extensive feature filmography goes back to 1995, often in black cast comedies like *Booty Call* (1997), *Next Friday* (2000), *Two Can Play That Game* (2001), *Head of State* (2003), *Nora's Hair Salon* (2004), and *Daddy Day Camp* (2007). She has been equally adept in dramas, such as *The Wood* (1999) and *The Brothers* (2001).

On television, she was a student on *Dangerous Minds* (1996); she appeared in three episodes of *ER* (1995–2001) in the role of Joanie Robbins; appeared as Tina in eight episodes of *Veronica's Closet* (1998); was Bobbi Seawright in *For Your Love* (1998–2002); Tonya on *One on One* (2001–05); and Alicia Mitchell on *The Tracy Morgan Show* (2003).

Feature Films including Video and TV Movies: *How to Make an American Quilt* (1995), *Booty Call* (1997), *Can't Hardly Wait* (1998), *The Wood* (1999), *Blue Streak* (1999), *Next Friday* (2000), *Little Richard* (TV; 2000), *Turn It Up* (2000), *How to Kill Your Neighbor's Dog* (2000), *The Ladies' Man* (2000), *Cedric the Coach* (TV; 2001), *Kingdom Come* (2001), *The Brothers* (2001), *Two Can Play That Game* (2001), *On the Line* (2001), *Couples* (TV; 2002), *Head of State* (2003), *Nora's Hair Salon* (2004), *Long Distance* (2005), *Nadine in Date Land* (TV; 2005), *Flirt* (TV; 2006), *Confessions* (2006), *What Love Is* (2007), *Who's Your Caddy?* (2007), *Daddy Day Camp* (2007), *Thug Passion* (2007), *Protect and Serve* (TV; 2007), *Show Stoppers* (2008), *American Dream* (2008), *The Black Man's Guide to Understanding Black Women* (2008), *Who's Deal?* (2008), *The Hustle* (2008), *Janky Promoters* (2009), *Busted* (2009).

TV: *California Dreams* (1992), *The Parent 'Hood* ("The Bully Pulpit," 1995), *The Fresh Prince of Bel-Air* ("Not I, Barbeque," 1995), *The Wayans Bros.* (2 episodes; "Shawn Takes a New Stand," "Scared Straight," 1995), *ER* (3 episodes in the role of Joanie Robbins; "The Birthday Party," "Motherhood," "Four Corners," 1995–2001), *Dangerous Minds* (recurring role as Callie Timmons; 1996), *JAG* ("The Brotherhood," 1996), *Duckman* (voice; "Das Sub," 1997), *Malcolm & Eddie* ("Two Men and a Baby," 1997), *Veronica's Closet* (recurring role of Tina; 1998), *For Your Love* (recurring role of Bobbi Seawright; 1998–2002), *City of Angels* ("Dress for Success," 2000), *Weakest Link* (2001), *One on One* (recurring role of Tonya; 2001–05), *Rendez-View* ("Surfs' Up, Thumbs Down," 2002), *HBO First Look* ("Head of State," 2003), *9th Annual Soul Train Lady of Soul Awards* (2003), *The Tracy Morgan Show* (recurring role as Alicia Mitchell; 2003), *The Sharon Osbourne Show* (2004), *The Wayne Brady Show* (2004), *The 18th Annual Soul Train Music Awards* (2004), *Jimmy Kimmel Live!* (2004), *Love, Inc.* ("Bosom Buddies," 2005), *Ghost Whisperer* ("Drowned Lives," 2006), *CSI: Miami* ("Going, Going, Gone," 2006), *Angels Can't Help But Laugh* (2007), *Studio 60 on the Sunset Strip* (2007), *Short Circuitz* (2007), *My Name Is Earl* ("Blow," 2007), *Castle* (pilot; 2009).

Joyce, Ella Born in Chicago, Illinois, June 12, 1954.

Ella Joyce was born Cherron Hoye. She took her professional name from her grandmother (Ella) and from her mother (Joyce). She graduated in 1972 from the Performing Arts Curriculum of Detroit's Cass Technical High School, and then attended the Dramatic Arts program at Eastern Michigan University. Although she has done feature films and was a regular on the FOX series *Roc* as Eleanor Emerson (1991–94), appeared in the pilot for *NewsRadio* (1995), and had a recurring role on *My Wife and Kids* (2003–04), Joyce has tended to concentrate on regional theater.

Her theater credits include *Fences* at the National Black Theater Festival, as well as *Medea and the Doll* and *Steppin' into Tomorrow*. She was the first to play the role of Risa at the Yale world premiere production of August Wilson's *Two Trains Running;* Tonya in the world premiere of August Wilson's *King Hedley II*; and Lily Ann Green in *Crumbs from the Table of Joy* (presented at the Goodman Theatre in Chicago). Other plays in which she has appeared include *Last Street Play (The Mighty Gents)*; *Checkmates*; *Brothers, Sisters, Husbands and Wives*; *Don't Get God Started!*; *Louis and Ophelia*; *Split Second*; *Home*; *Not a Single Blade of Grass*; *Odessa*; and *Anna Lucasta*. She has also appeared in *The Vagina Monologues* at the Millennium Theater in Detroit, joining an all-star cast which included Mo'Nique, Vanessa Bell Calloway, and Wendy Raquel Robinson. The highlight of her varied theatrical career is *A Rose Among Thorns*—a tribute to Rosa Parks — her acclaimed one-woman show, which she presented at the Alabama Shakespeare Festival.

Joyce is a professional acting coach and consultant (clients have included Toni Braxton). She is the author of the book *Kink Phobia: Journey Through a Black Woman's Hair*, and she appeared in the documentary *My Nappy Roots: A Journey Through Black Hair-itage* (2005), an exploration of how black women celebrate the beauty of their hair. She is married to Dan Martin.

Feature Films including Video and TV Movies: *Stop! Or My Mom Will Shoot* (1992), *Reality Bites* (1994), *Set It Off* (1996), *Her Married Lover* (1999), *Selma, Lord, Selma* (TV; 1999), *Frozen Hot* (1999), *Clockin' Green* (2000), *Stranger Inside* (TV; 2001), *What About Your Friends?: Weekend Getaway* (TV; 2002), *Bubba Ho-tep* (2002), *Salvation* (2003), *My Nappy Roots: A Journey Through Black Hair-itage* (2005), *Forbidden Fruits* (2006), *Who Made the Potatoe Salad?* (2006), *City Teacher* (2007), *A Simple Promise* (2008), *Lost Signal* (2008), *Busted* (2009).

TV: *Katts and Dog* ("Officer Down," 1989), *Roc* (recurring role of Eleanor Emerson; 1991–94), *Choices* (1992), *NewsRadio* (pilot; 1995), *The Client* ("Them That Has," 1995), *Dangerous Minds* (pilot; 1996), *Sabrina, the Teenage Witch* ("Bundt Friday," 1996), *Seinfeld* ("The Voice," 1997), *The Jamie Foxx Show* ("Convent-ional Gifts," 1998), *In the House* ("My Pest Friend's Wedding," 1998), *PBS Hollywood Presents* ("The Old Settler," 2001), *My Wife and Kids* (5 episodes in the role of Jasmine; "Meet the Parents," "Ultrasound," "What Do You Know?" "Childcare Class," "The Wedding," 2003–04), *Eve* ("Dateless in Miami," 2004), *Bid Whist Party Throwdown* (2005).

Video/DVD: *Waterfalls* (1994).

Katon, Rosanne Born in New York, New York, February 5, 1952.

Rosanne Katon had already made a foray into acting before she appeared as the *Playboy* Playmate of the Month in September 1978. She began attending New York City's High School of the Performing Arts at the precocious age of 13. After getting work in TV commercials, Katon made her theatrical film debut in director Jack Hill's *The Swinging Cheerleaders* (1974). She is also known for the blaxploitation film *Ebony, Ivory and Jade* (1975), and for other B-films such as *The Muthers* (1976) and *Lunch Wagon* (1981). In the 1970s, she was on episodes of *That's My Mama*, *Good Times*, *Sanford and Son*, *Starsky and Hutch*, *The White Shadow* and *The Facts of Life*.

Her husband is Richard Walden; they married in 1984 and have two children. Walden is president and CEO of Operation USA, an international organization that aids Third World countries. Katon is a political activist, appearing as a guest on Bill Maher's *Politically Incorrect* in 2001. She is of Jamaican heritage (her father was born in Jamaica). She also has had a career as a stand-up comic.

Feature Films including TV Movies: *The Swinging Cheerleaders* (1974), *Let's Do It Again* (1975), *Ebony, Ivory and Jade* (aka *American Beauty Hostages*; 1976), *Chesty Anderson, USN* (1976), *The Muthers* (1976), *American Raspberry* (1977), *The Night They Took Miss Beautiful* (TV; 1977), *Coach*

(1978), *The Comeback Kid* (TV; 1980), *Motel Hell* (1980), *Lunch Wagon* (1981), *Body and Soul* (1981), *Illusions* (1982), *Zapped!* (1982), *Rich* (1983), *City Girl* (1984), *Bachelor Party* (1984), *Harem* (1985), *Peter Gunn* (TV; 1989).

TV: *Chopper One* ("Strain of Innocence," 1974), *That's My Mama* ("Song and Dance Man," 1974), *Good Times* ("The Debutante Ball," 1975), *Sanford and Son* ("The Family Man," 1975), *Joe Forrester* ("Stake Out," 1975), *Starsky and Hutch* ("Death Notice," 1975), *Grady* (recurring role as Clarissa Robinson; 1975), *What's Happening!* ("Saturday's Hero," 1976), *Logan's Run* ("Carousel," 1978), *Jason of Star Command* (3 episodes in the role of Allegra; "A Cry for Help," "Wiki to the Rescue," "Planet of the Lost," 1978), *Chips* ("High Explosive," 1978), *The White Shadow* (2 episodes in the role of Diana; "Me?" "Salami's Affair," 1979 and 1980), *The Facts of Life* ("Brian and Sylvia," 1981), *Pink Lady* (1981), *Dallas* ("And the Winner Is...," 1984), *St. Elsewhere* (5 episodes in the role of Amanda Taylor; "Drama Center," "Attack," "After Dark," "Vanity," "Equinox," 1984), *Full House* (2 episodes in the role of Mrs. Manning; "A Pinch for a Pinch," "The Graduates," 1990 and 1991), *Miller & Mueller* (1991), *Playboy: The Party Continues* (2000), *E! True Hollywood Story* (2000), *Politically Incorrect* (2001), *Macked, Hammered, Slaughtered and Shafted* (documentary; 2004), *Autism: The Musical* (documentary; 2007).

Video/DVD: *Playboy Playmates: The Early Years* (1992).

Kelly, Paula Born in Jacksonville, Florida, October 21, 1943; died August 25, 2002.

Paula Kelly was a musician's daughter who, though born in Florida, was raised in Harlem. She was a music major at the Fiorello Laguardia High School of Music and Art. She continued her studies at the Juilliard School of Music, majoring in dance under Martha Graham (the stately Graham influence is strikingly evident in her work). She was a dance soloist for Graham, Alvin Ailey and Donald MacKayle.

The highlight of Paula Kelly's film career comes in her debut film, the "Hey, Big Spender" dance number with Shirley MacLaine and Chita Rivera in *Sweet Charity* (1969). Paula Kelly was only a child during the golden age of Hollywood musicals and wouldn't have had much of an opportunity to flourish in the genre, considering the racism of the day. But she only came truly alive when she was dancing, and it's a shame she didn't have more of an opportunity to preserve her dance skills on film. But we can be grateful for what we do have (archival footage of the *Sweet Charity* sequence is shown in the 1985 compilation documentary *That's Dancing!*).

Paula Kelly and Robert Hooks in *Trouble Man* (1972).

Since musicals were not much in vogue during Kelly's film career, her films fall primarily into the blaxploitation genre. She did, however, follow *Charity* with a nice role in the science fiction doomsday thriller *The Andromeda Strain* (1971) directed by Robert Wise. Then she made the black crime thriller *Cool Breeze* (1972), a remake of John Huston's *The Asphalt Jungle*. This was followed by an unusual film that seems to have vanished from sight, the surrealistic *Top of the Heap* (1972), about the racially troubled fantasies of a black man, including being the first man on the moon. Then she co-starred with Robert Hooks in the black private eye film *Trouble Man* (1972). She had a fairly small role in the sci-fi cult film *Soylent Green* (1973), an ahead of its time doomsday ecological thriller with Charlton Heston. A box office flop at the time, its reputation has grown over the years.

Her next film was perhaps even stranger than *Top of the Heap*. It was *The Spook Who Sat by the Door* (1973), about a former black CIA agent who starts a violent revolution in the United States. Only in the blaxploitation era could a film like this have been made. Fortunately, it has finally become available on DVD, after being impossible to see for many years. Kelly played a prostitute who becomes involved with the revolution, and then becomes the mistress of a racist senator. She lent her talents to the American Film Theater version of Kurt Weill's *Lost in the Stars* (1974). She went back to big budget films with the amiable Sidney Poitier, Bill Cosby and Harry Belafonte comedy *Uptown Saturday Night* (1974). This one was big box office, but another two years went by before Kelly turned up onscreen in *Drum* (1976), the ill-fated sequel to *Mandingo*, which had been a financial success. *Drum* was obviously badly cut before its release — what's left has very little footage of Kelly, and her presence barely makes any sense. Set in the Old South, this racially offensive film climaxes in a violent slave revolt.

A BBC-TV version of *Peter Pan* (1976) is another Kelly film little seen these days; she plays Tiger-Lily and was co-choreographer. Neil Simon's *The Cheap Detective* (1980) is an all-star mess better left unseen, and Richard Pryor's self-indulgent *Jo Jo Dancer, Your Life Is Calling* (1986) is an *All That Jazz*–inspired fiasco. Her last film of any note is *Once Upon a Time ... When We Were Colored* (1995).

Television also provided Kelly with a steady stream of work. The highlight is her sensitive work in the Oprah Winfrey miniseries *The Women of Brewster Place* (1989), as an inner city woman who tries to make a life with her partner (Lonette McKee), but who encounters prejudice that can only lead to tragedy. She had a regular role on *Night Court* (1984) and was in the series *Room for Two* (1992). Kelly also made the circuit of variety shows popular at the time: *The Carol Burnett Show*, *The Dean Martin Show*, and *This Is Tom Jones*.

Paula Kelly in *The Andromeda Strain* (1971).

Much of her Broadway work suffered from short runs. *The Dozens* ran for three days during March of 1969. *Paul Sills' Story Theatre* was an ensemble piece (1970–71), and she was in a production of Ovid's *Metamorphosis* that ran from April to July of 1971. She was Mrs. Veloz in *Something More!*, a musical that closed in 1978 before it reached Broadway. She won the London Variety Award for Best Supporting Actress in the British play *Helen* and starred in the London production of *Sweet Charity* (1967). She was in the West Coast premiere of *Don't Bother Me, I Can't Cope* at the Mark Taper Forum, winning the Los Angeles Drama Critics Circle Award and an NAACP Image Award. She was a member of the national tour of *Sophisticated Ladies* (1982).

Kelly's work as a choreographer must also be mentioned. She was assistant choreographer for the TV special *Sammy and Friends* (starring Sammy Davis, Jr.) and Quincy Jones' *We Love You Madly* (a tribute to Duke Ellington). She received an Emmy nomination for her choreography on *The Richard Pryor Show* (and danced on the show). And she choreographed and danced a duet with Gene Kelly on the special *New York, New York*.

Feature Films including TV Movies: *Sweet Charity* (1969), *The Andromeda Strain* (1971), *Cool Breeze* (1972), *Top of the Heap* (1972), *Trouble Man* (1972), *Soylent Green* (1973), *The Spook Who Sat by the Door* (1973), *Three Tough Guys* (1974), *Lost in the Stars* (1974), *Uptown Saturday Night* (1974), *Drum* (1976), *Peter Pan* (TV; 1976), *The Cheap Detective* (1980), *That's Dancing!* (archival; 1985), *Jo Jo Dancer, Your Life Is Calling* (1986), *Uncle Tom's Cabin* (TV; 1987), *Bank Robber* (1993), *Drop Squad* (1994), *Once Upon a Time ... When We Were Colored* (1995), *Run for the Dream: The Gail Devers Story* (TV; 1996).

TV: *The Carol Burnett Show* (2 segments; 1968–73), *The 41st Annual Academy Awards* (1969), *The Dean Martin Show* (1969), *This Is Tom Jones* (1970), *The Young Lawyers* ("A Busload of Bishops," 1970), *Medical Center* (2 episodes; "The Rebel in White," "Saturday's Child," 1970 and 1974), *The 27th Annual Tony Awards* (1973), *San-*

ford and Son ("Lamont Goes African," 1973), *Cannon* ("The Wedding March," 1975), *The Streets of San Francisco* (2 episodes; "Men Will Die," "The Thrill Killers," Part I, 1975 and 1976), *Police Woman* (3 episodes in the role of Linda Summers; "The Company," "Wednesday's Child," "Once a Snitch," 1975–77), *Insight* (2 episodes; "Jesus B.C.," "A Step Too Slow," 1976 and 1981), *The Richard Pryor Show* (1977), *Kojak* ("The Queen of Hearts Is Wild," 1977), *Good Times* ("Where Have All the Doctors Gone?" 1979), *Trapper John, M.D.* ("Straight and Narrow," 1981), *Feel the Heat* (1983), *Chiefs* (miniseries; 1983), *Night Court* (12 episodes in the role of Public Defender Liz Williams; 1984), *Hot Pursuit* ("Portrait of a Lady Killer," 1984), *Santa Barbara* (recurring role of Ginger Jones; 1984–85), *Hill Street Blues* ("Davenport in a Storm," 1985), *Finder of Lost Loves* ("Aftershocks," 1985), *St. Elsewhere* ("Cheek to Cheek," 1986), *Amen* ("Rolly Falls in Love," 1986), *CBS Summer Playhouse* ("Kung Fu: The Next Generation," 1987), *The Golden Girls* ("The Housekeeper," 1987), *The Women of Brewster Place* (miniseries; 1989), *Mission: Impossible* ("Bayou," 1989), *American Playhouse* ("Zora Is My Name!" 1990), *Baby Talk* (3 episodes in the role of Claire; "Give a Sucker an Even Break," "Whiz Kid," "Tooth and Nail," 1991), *Room for Two* (recurring role as Diahnn Boudreau; 1992), *South Central* (recurring role as Sweets; 1994), *University Hospital* ("Shadow of a Doubt," 1995), *Any Day Now* ("Family Is Family," 1999).

Kennedy, Jayne Born in Washington, D.C., October 27, 1951.

Born Jane Harrison, Jayne Kennedy has excelled as a sportscaster, model, beauty contestant and actress. Her greatest achievement was becoming the first woman to break through in sports announcing as one of the hosts of *The NFL Today* in 1975. She was Miss Ohio USA in 1970 and one of 10 semi-finalists in the Miss USA pageant that year. While her film career consists largely of B-movies (*Group Marriage*, *Body and Soul*), her TV work is varied, and she has been a guest star on many top-rated shows, including *Kojak* (1974), *Sanford and Son* (1974), *The Rockford Files* (1976), *Wonder Woman* (1977), *The Love Boat* (1981–83), and *Diff'rent Strokes* (1983).

For many years Kennedy has done charity work for the Children's Miracle Network, and she appears on various Christian Television Network shows. She was married to actor Leon Isaac Kennedy from 1970 to 1982. She married actor Bill Overton in 1985. They have three daughters: Savannah Re (born 1985), Kopper Joi (born 1989) and Zaire Ollie (born 1995).

Feature Films including Video and TV Movies: *Lady Sings the Blues* (1972), *Group Marriage* (1973), *Let's Do It Again* (1975), *The Muthers* (1976), *Cover Girls* (TV; 1977), *Big Time* (1977), *Death Force* (1978), *Mysterious Island of Beautiful Women* (TV; 1979), *The Dorothy Dandridge Story* (unreleased; 1980), *Ms. 45* (1981), *Body and Soul* (1981), *Mardi Gras for the Devil* (aka *Night Trap*; 1993).

TV: *The Dean Martin Show* (series regular as a member of The Golddiggers; 1965), *Dean Martin Presents the Golddiggers* (series regular; 1968), *Rowan & Martin's Laugh-In* (regular; 1968), *Shaft* ("The Kidnapping," 1973), *Ironside* ("The Last Payment," 1973), *Kojak* ("Die Before They Wake," 1974), *Banacek* ("Rocket to Oblivion," 1974), *Sanford and Son* ("There'll Be Some Changes Made," 1974), *The NFL Today* (host; 1975), *That's My Mama* ("The Hero," 1975), *The Six Million Dollar Man* ("The Song and Dance Spy," 1975), *The Rockford Files* ("Foul on the First Play," 1976), *Starsky and Hutch* ("The Las Vegas Strangler," 1976), *Police Story* ("Pressure Point," 1977), *Wonder Woman* ("Knockout," 1977), *Police Woman* ("The Inside Connection," 1977), *Trapper John, M.D.* ("Deadly Exposure," 1979), *Speak Up, America* (1980), *The 32nd Annual Primetime Emmy Awards* (1980), *Bob Hope for President* (1980), *Circus of the Stars 5* (1980), *CHips* (2 episodes; "Kidnap," "Mitchell & Woods," 1980 and 1981), *All-American Ultra Quiz* (1981), *The Love Boat* (3 episodes; 1981–83), *Diff'rent Strokes* ("The Moonlighter," 1983), *Greatest Sports Legends* (series hostess; 1983), *Benson* (2 episodes in the role of Elizabeth Burnett; "Let's Get Physical," "Three on a Mismatch," 1984 and 1986), *Passion and Memory* (1986), *227* ("Washington Affair," 1986), *Happy 100th Birthday, Hollywood* (1987), *20th NAACP Image Awards* (1988), *Family Reunion: A Gospel Music Celebration* (1988), *Jackie Robinson: An American Journey* (1988).

Video/DVD: *Breastfeeding Your Baby: A Mother's Guide* (1987).

Keymàh, T'Keyah Crystal Born in Chicago, Illinois, October 13, 1962.

Her birth name is Crystal Walker, but fans

know her as T'Keyah Crystal Keymàh (pronounced Tah-kee-ah Crystal Kee-Mah). This born entertainer was enchanting her family with sketches and song and dance routines since age three. She joined a comedy troupe in high school before going on to A&M University's School of Business and Industry. She was Miss Black America from Illinois and runner-up in the national Miss Black America contest.

She has been a regular on several series, most prominently *Cosby* (1996–2000) as daughter Erica Lucas to stars Bill Cosby and Phylicia Rashad. She was Tanya Baxter on Disney's *That's So Raven* (2003–05) for three seasons. She was a cast member of the comedy ensemble show *In Living Color* from 1990 to 1994. She was Scotti Decker in *On Our Own* (1995) and Denise Everett on *The Show* (1996).

Theater has long been her passion. She was in *A Christmas Carol* at the Goodman Theatre in Chicago (1987–89); performed *Playboy of the West Indies* at the International Theatre Festival in 1988; starred as Melissa Gardner in *Love Letters* (1991); was in *The Five Heartbeats Live* (1994); and was in *A Raisin in the Sun* at Chicago's Goodman Theatre (2000). She has toured extensively with several productions: *Some of My Best Friends: A Collection of Characters Speaking in Verse and Prose* (a solo show; 1991); *T'Keyah Live!* (2001), and *The Old Settler*, performed at the Napokrovki Theatre in Moscow, among other Russian venues. She has taught acting, dance and pantomime.

Feature Films including Video and TV Movies: *Big Shots* (1987), *Tales from the Hood* (1995), *One Last Time* (1996), *Circle of Pain* (TV; 1996), *Jackie Brown* (1997), *Tweety's High-Flying Adventure* (voice; 2000), *The Gilded Six Bits* (2001), *The Creature of the Sunny Side Up Trailer Park* (2004).

TV: *Miss Black America Pageant* (1985), *Channel One News* (1990), *In Living Color* (cast member; 1990–94), *A.M. Los Angeles* (1991), *Live with Regis and Kathie Lee* (1991), *The Home Show* (1991), *Quantum Leap* ("A Song for the Soul: April 7, 1963," 1992), *'Mo Funny: Black Comedy in America* (archival; 1993), *Soul Train* (2 segments; 1993 and 1997), *Soul Train Comedy Awards* (1993), *Roc* ("Ebony and Ivory," 1993), *Fox Live at the Taste: The Fireworks!* (1993), *Comic Relief: Baseball Relief 1993*, *The 8th Annual Soul Train Music Awards* (1994), *The Commish* ("Born in the USA," 1994), *A Cool Like That Christmas* (voice; 1994), *The John Larroquette Show* (2 episodes in the role of Sara; "Good News/Bad News," "The Wedding," 1994 and 1995), *Soul Train's 25th Anniversary* (1995), *On Our Own* (recurring role of Scotti Decker; 1995), *The Show* (recurring role of Denise Everett; 1996), *Waynehead* (recurring role of Roz; 1996–97), *Histeria!* (voice; "Queen Nzinga," 1996), *Cosby* (recurring role of Erica Lucas; 1996–2000), *KTLA Morning Show* (1997), *Crook & Chase* (1997), *Fox After Breakfast* (1997), *3rd Annual Soul Train Lady of Soul Awards* (1997), *Orange Bowl Parade* (1997), *69th Annual Bud Billiken Back-to-School Parade* (1997), *The Keenan Ivory Wayans Show* (2 segments; 1997 and 1998), *CBS This Morning* (1998), *Pinky and the Brain* ("Inherit the Wheeze," 1998), *NAACP act-so Awards* (1998), *The O'Reilly Factor* (1998), *Aloha Parade* (1998), *Politically Incorrect* (1999), *Happy Hour* (1999), *Happily Ever After: Fairy Tales for Every Child* ("The Snow Queen," 2000), *Batman Beyond* (voice; 3 episodes; "Babel," "Untouchable," "Countdown," 2000–01), *5th Annual Prism Awards* (2001), *Static Shock* (voice; 2 episodes; "Power Play," "Hard as Nails," 2002 and 2003), *My Wife and Kids* ("Moving on Out," 2004), *Teen Titans* (4 episodes as the voice of Bumblebee; "Wavelength," "Titans East," Parts I and II, "For Real," 2004–05), *Comedy Gold* (2005), *American Dragon: Jake Long* (voice; 3 episodes; "Professor Rotwood's Thesis," "Half Baked," "Hairy Christmas," 2005–06), *10th Annual Prism Awards* (2006), *That's So Raven* (recurring role as Tanya Baxter; 2003–05), *Jury Duty* (2007), *Celebrity Family Feud* (2008).

Video/DVD: *That's So Raven: Supernaturally Stylish* (2004).

King, Regina Born in Los Angeles, California, January 15, 1971.

Regina King went from appearing as Marla Gibbs' daughter Brenda Jenkins on the sitcom *227* (in the pilot film and intermittently from 1985 to 1987) to major roles in mainstream Hollywood features. She was the wife of Rod Tidwell (Cuba Gooding, Jr.) in *Jerry Maguire* (1996); Robert Clayton Dean's (Will Smith) wife in *Enemy of the State* (1998); and Marge Hendricks, the backup singer Ray Charles has an affair with and drops in *Ray* (2004). Certainly by the time *Ray* saw release, it was clear that King had emerged as a serious actress. She won an NAACP Image Award for Outstanding Supporting Actress in 2005 for this performance, as well as a BET Best Actress Award.

Other honors include a Screen Actors Guild Award for Outstanding Cast in a Motion Picture (also for *Ray*), and NAACP Image Awards for Outstanding Actress for *Enemy of the State* (1998) and *Down to Earth* (2001).

She is a graduate of Westchester High School and the University of Southern California. Her mother, Gloria, was a special education teacher; her father, Thomas, an electrician. Her sister is actress Reina King. She was married to recording executive Ian Alexander from 1997 to 2007, and they have one child.

She began her film career with appearances in a trilogy of John Singleton films: *Boyz n the Hood* (nominated for the Academy Award for Best Picture; 1991), *Poetic Justice* (1993), and *Higher Learning* (1995). King has seemingly effortlessly alternated between comedy and drama roles. Her best comedic roles include *Friday* (1995), *Daddy Day Care with Eddie Murphy* (2003), *Legally Blonde 2: Red, White & Blonde* (2003), and *Miss Congeniality 2: Armed and Fabulous* (2005). She's superb in a "best friend" role (one of many such) in the little-seen but emotionally gripping *Year of the Dog* (2007).

In 2007 she appeared in nine episodes of *24* in the role of Sandra Palmer. King did the voices for the characters of Huey and Riley Freeman in the animated series *The Boondocks* (2005–07), based on the iconoclastic comic strip.

Feature Films including Video and TV Movies: *Boyz N the Hood* (1991), *Poetic Justice* (1993), *Higher Learning* (1995), *Friday* (1995), *A Thin Line Between Love and Hate* (1996), *Don't Be a Menace to South Central While Drinking Your Juice in the Hood* (1996), *Jerry Maguire* (1996), *How Stella Got Her Groove Back* (1998), *Enemy of the State* (1998), *Mighty Joe Young* (1998), *Where the Truth Lies* (TV; 1999), *Love and Action in Chicago* (1999), *If These Walls Could Talk 2* (TV; 2000), *The Acting Class* (2000), *Down to Earth* (2001), *Final Breakdown* (2002), *Damaged Care* (TV; 2002), *Daddy Day Care* (2003), *Legally Blonde 2: Red, White & Blonde* (2003), *A Cinderella Story* (2004), *Ray* (2004), *The N-Word* (documentary; 2004), *Miss Congeniality 2: Armed and Fabulous* (2005), *The Ant Bully* (voice; 2006), *Year of the Dog* (2007), *Grindin'* (2007), *This Christmas* (2007), *Living Proof* (TV; 2008), *Sit Down, Shut Up* (2009), *LAPD* (TV; 2009).

Regina King.

TV: *227* (recurring role of Brenda Jenkins; pilot, "Honesty," "Guess Who's Not Coming to Christmas," 1985–89), *Backstage at Masterpiece Theatre* (1991), *Northern Exposure* ("Baby Blues," 1994), *New York Undercover* ("Tasha," 1994), *Living Single* ("The Shake-Up," 1995), *Headliners & Legends: Chris Rock* (2001), *Leap of Faith* (6 episodes in the role of Cynthia; 2002), *Tupac: Resurrection* (archival; 2003), *Biography* ("Will Smith: Hollywood's Fresh Prince," 2003), *Last Call with Carson Daly* (2 segments; 2003 and 2005), *Jimmy Kimmel Live!* (2004), *Good Day Live* (2004), *The 10th Annual Critics' Choice Awards* (2005), *Late Show with David Letterman* (2005), *The 20th IFP Independent Spirit Awards* (2005), *106 & Park Top 10 Live* (2005), *The Today Show* (2005), *36th NAACP Image Awards* (2005), *Tavis Smiley* (2005), *The Late Late Show with Craig Ferguson* (2005), *Ellen* (2005), *Weekends at the DL* (2005), *The Teen Choice Awards 2005*, *2nd Annual VH1 Hip-Hop Honors* (2005), *The 2nd Annual BET Comedy Awards* (2005), *The Black Movie Awards* (2005), *The Boondocks* (recurring role as the voice of Riley Freeman; 2005–08), *An Evening of Stars: Tribute to Stevie Wonder* (2006), *Women in Law* (pilot; 2006), *Keith Barry: Extraordinary* (2006), *3rd Annual VH1 Hip-Hop Award Honors* (2006), *Angels Can't Help But Laugh* (2007), *The View* (2007), *Entertainment Tonight* (2007), *24* (recurring role of Sandra Palmer; 2007).

Shorts: *Rituals* (1998).

Kitt, Eartha Born in St. Matthews, South Carolina, January 17, 1927; died December 25, 2008, New York, New York.

Eartha Mae Keith was born to a white father (reportedly the son of the owner of the plantation on which Kitt was born) and a black–Cherokee mother named Mamie, a sharecropper in the northern part of South Carolina. Kitt was the eldest of two sisters. Eartha's father abandoned the family when she was a toddler, and her mother in turn abandoned the children for a man with eight children of his own. She was then raised by a woman named Anna Mae Riley, who the child believed to be her mother. Eventually, Mamie Kitt, supposedly Riley's sister, but in Kitt's estimation Eartha's biological mother, sent for the children to live with her in New York's Harlem when Eartha was nine years old.

Kitt became interested in entertaining, forging her unique style of singing and dancing that doesn't seem to owe much to anyone else. She excelled as a student at the New York School of Performing Arts, but it was necessary to leave school at 14 and work in a factory. Even so, she used some of her money to pay for piano lessons. Her career break came at 16 when she met Katherine Dunham, the great dancer, choreographer and ethnologist. She toured with Dunham's troupe throughout the United States, Mexico and South America. Her film debut was with Dunham in 1948's *Casbah* (they both danced in the film). In 1948, the Dunham dancers toured London and Paris, and Kitt remained in Paris to sing at the nightclub Carroll's. This was the beginning of her stardom as a singer.

Eartha Kitt and Rex Ingram in *Anna Lucasta* (1959).

Recording artist, Broadway star and chanteuse Kitt broke out in a big way in the 1950s. Orson Welles, who adored her, gave her the starring role in Helen of Troy in his production of *Dr. Faustus* (1950). The Broadway revue *New Faces of 1954* became her launching point in America, and a filmed version was released in theaters (as *New Faces*), with Kitt prominently displayed on the poster. Her purring "sex kitten" image was on full display — audiences had never seen a black woman transcend all racial barriers to become the first equal opportunity sex symbol. Her stage persona was cynical, worldly, been-there, done-that, and incredibly sophisticated by the standards of any era.

She is best known today for her recording of "Santa Baby" (1953), an antidote to the sugary sweetness of most Christmas songs, and a salute to sugar daddies everywhere. Her other signature hit was "C'est si Bon" (Kitt had learned French during the era of her nightclub work in Paris). Her many other hits include "Let's Do It," "Monotonous," "Uska Dara," "Just an Old-Fashioned Girl," "Love for Sale," and the unbelievable "I Want to Be Evil." Albums include *RCA Victor Presents Eartha Kitt* (1953), *That Bad Eartha* (1954), *Down to Eartha* (1955), *Thursday's Child* (1956), *St. Louis Blues* (1958), *The Fabulous Eartha Kitt* (1959), and *Eartha Kitt in Person at the Plaza* (1965).

She made her feature film debut with Sidney Poitier in *Mark of the Hawk* (1958) and appeared in *St. Louis Blues* that same year, then starred in *Anna Lucasta* the following year. Kitt's brilliance didn't quite translate to the big screen, especially when she wasn't given much to do, as in *Mark of the Hawk*. In the 1960s she became famous to a whole new audience with her excellent performance as Catwoman on the campy *Batman* series with Adam West (1967–68). She was one of the best villains on the show, having followed the equally excellent Julie Newmar on the series. The role also played in feature films by Lee Meriweather, Michele Pfeiffer and Halle Berry.

In 1968 she created a huge stir when, after having been invited to a White House luncheon with Lady Bird Johnson, she used the opportunity to lambaste President Lyndon Johnson's handling of the Vietnam War. Recent books have taken a revisionist, kinder look at LBJ, especially in terms of his great contribution to the civil rights movement. All was forgiven when Jimmy Carter welcomed her back to the White House in 1974. She was twice nominated for Broadway Tony Awards: in 1978 for Best Actress in a Musical for *Timbuktu!* and in 2000 for Best Actress in a Featured Role for *The Wild Party*.

Kitt was the author of the books *Thursday's Child* (Duell, Sloane and Pearce; 1956); *Alone with Me* (Regnery; 1976); *I'm Still Here* (Sedgwick and Jackson; 1989), also known as *Confessions of a Sex Kitten* (Barricade; 1989); and *Rejuvenate!: It's Never Too Late* (Scribner; 2001). She was married to Bill McDonald from 1960 to 1965. Her daughter Kitt became her mother's manager and was at her bedside when she passed away of colon cancer on Christmas Day in 2008.

Feature Films including Video and TV Movies: *Casbah* (1948), *New Faces* (1954), *The Mark of the Hawk* (1957), *St. Louis Blues* (1958), *Anna Lucasta* (1959), *Seventy Times Seven* (aka *Saint of Devil's Island*, 1961), *Onkel Toms Hütte* (*Uncle Tom's Cabin*, 1965), *Synanon* (1965), *All About People* (narrator; 1967), *Up the Chastity Belt* (1971), *Lieutenant Schuster's Wife* (TV; 1972), *Friday Foster* (1975), *To Kill a Cop* (TV; 1978), *A Night on the Town* (TV; 1983), *The Serpent Warriors* (1985), *Dragonard* (1987), *The Pink Chiquitas* (1987), *Master of Dragonard Hill* (1989), *Erik the Viking* (1989), *Living Doll* (1990), *Ernest Scared Stupid* (1991), *Desperately Seeking Roger* (TV; 1991), *Boomerang* (1992), *Fatal Instinct* (1993), *Unzipped* (1995), *James Dean and Me* (TV; 1995), *Harriet the Spy* (1996), *Ill Gotten Gains* (voice; 1997), *I Woke Up Early the Day I Died* (1998), *The Jungle Book: Mowgli's Story* (voice; 1998), *The Emperor's New Groove* (voice; 2000), *The Feast of All Saints* (TV; 2001), *The Sweatbox* (2002), *Holes* (2003), *One the One* (aka *Preaching to the Choir*, 2005), *The

Eartha Kitt.

Emperor's New Groove 2: Kronk's New Groove* (voice; 2005), *And Then Came Love* (2007).

TV: *Toast of the Town/The Ed Sullivan Show* (15 appearances, 1952–63; archival; 1962), *The Colgate Comedy Hour* (1954), *Person to Person* (1954), *Your Show of Shows* (1954), *What's My Line?* (3 segments; 1954–61), *Omnibus* ("Salome," 1955), *The Nat King Cole Show* (1956), *Playhouse 90* ("Heart of Darkness," 1958), *Sunday Night at the London Palladium* (2 segments; 1960–62), *Play of the Week* ("The Wingless Victory," 1961), *Drei Manner Spinnen* (1962), *Stump the Stars* (2 segments; 1963), *The Celebrity Game* (7 segments; 1964–65), *Not So Much a Programme, More a Way of Life* (1965), *Blackpool Night Out* (1965), *Burke's Law* ("Who Killed the Rest?" 1965), *Ben Casey* ("A Horse Named Stravinsky," 1965), *I Spy* ("The Loser," 1965), *Hollywood Squares* (4 segments, 1966–67; 5 segments, 2003), *Mission: Impossible* ("The Traitor," 1967), *Batman* (3 episodes in the role of Catwoman; "Catwoman's Dressed to Kill," "The Funny Feline Felonies," "The Joke's on Catwoman," 1967–68), *The Pat Boone Show* (1968), *The Other Americans* (1969), *Romeo und Julia '70* (1969), *The Barbara McNair Show* (1970), *Frost on Sunday* (1970), *The Tonight Show Starring Johnny Carson* (3 segments; 1972–73), *The Protectors* ("A Pocketful of Posies," 1974), *Police

Woman ("Tigress," 1978), *All By Myself: The Eartha Kitt Story* (1982), *Musikladen* (1983), *Miami Vice* ("Whatever Works," 1985), *Brown Sugar* (miniseries; 1986), *Entre Amigos* (1986), *Que Noche la de Aquel Ano!* (archival; 1987), *Forty Minutes* ("Adventures in the Skin Trade," 1990), *It's Showtime at the Apollo* (1992), *Reading Rainbow* ("Is This a House for Hermit Crab?" 1993), *Victor Borge's Tivoli 150 år* (archival; 1993), *Matrix* ("Moths to a Flame," 1993), *Space Ghost Coast to Coast* ("Batmantis," 1994), *The Magic School Bus* ("Going Batty," 1995), *New York Undercover* ("Student Affairs," 1995), *Living Single* ("He Works Hard for the Money," 1995), *Lauren Hutton and ...* (1996), *The Real Las Vegas* (archival; 1996), *The Nanny* (2 episodes; "A Pup in Paris," "The Tart with Heart," 1996), *The Rosie O'Donnell Show* (2 segments; 1997–2000), *Nat King Cole: Loved in Return* (1998), *The Roseanne Show* (1998), *The Wild Thornberrys* (voice; "Flood Warning," 1998), *VH1: Where Are They Now?* ("Superheroes," 1999), *The Famous Jett Jackson* ("Field of Dweebs," 1999), *The 54th Annual Tony Awards* (2000), *Happily Ever After: Fairy Tales for Every Child* ("The Snow Queen," 2000), *Welcome to New York* (2 episodes in the role of June; "Jim Gets an Apartment," "The Car," 2000), *Oz* ("Medium Rare," 2001), *Michael Jackson: 30th Anniversary Celebration* (2001), *Santa Baby!* (voice; 2001), *We Are Family* (2002), *It's Black Entertainment* (archival; 2002), *Anything But Love* (2002), *Inside TV Land: African Americans in Television* (2003), *My Life as a Teenage Robot* (voice; "Hostile Takeover," 2003), *The 2nd Annual TV Land Awards: A Celebration of Classic TV* (2004), *Biography* ("Catwoman: Her Many Lives," 2004), *The American Experience* (archival; "Las Vegas: An Unconventional History," Part I, 2005), *Larry King Live* (2 segments; 2005), *American Masters* (2 episodes; "James Dean: Sense Memories," "The World of Nat King Cole," 2005 and 2006), *The Emperor's New School* (recurring role as the voice of Yzma; 2006–07), *Loose Women* (2007), *Breakfast* (2008), *PBS Special* (2009).

Shorts: *Behind the Director's Son's Cuts* (2007).

Eartha Kitt.

Knight Pulliam, Keisha Born in Newark, New Jersey, April 9, 1979.

"Child star": these are often deadly words when the individual seeks to extend their fame into an adult acting career—especially when the child star is one as cute and charming as Keisha Knight Pulliam. Her childhood performances are infused with an almost adult sensibility and insight, but the better known you are for your precocious early work, the more difficult it is to make the transition to adult star.

At age six, she became the youngest actress ever to be nominated for an Emmy for her exceptional work as Rudy Huxtable on *The Cosby Show.* She appeared in 164 episodes of the show from 1984 to 1992. Rudith Lillian "Rudy" Huxtable was the cutest, most personable kid on TV, and the character and the actress who played her was clearly a favorite of Bill Cosby both on and off camera. *The Cosby Show* wasn't even her show business debut; she was already a regular on *Sesame Street* at age three.

Other highlights of her TV career are the two Polly films: *Polly* (1989) and *Polly: Comin' Home!* (1990). The Polly films were musical adaptations of *Pollyanna* set in the 1950s, about an orphan who spreads cheer in a small Southern town.

Knight Pulliam is of Jamaican extraction. She attended Rutgers Preparatory School in Somerset, New Jersey, and the Potomac School in McLean, Virginia, and graduated from the Foxcroft School in Middleburg, Virginia. She graduated from prestigious Spelman College in 2001 with a degree in sociology. She appeared in an episode of Tyler Perry's sitcom *House of Payne* in 2007.

Feature Films including Video and TV Movies: *The Last Dragon* (1985), *The Little Match Girl* (TV; 1987), *Polly* (TV; 1989), *A Connecticut Yankee in King Arthur's Court* (TV; 1989), *Polly: Comin' Home!* (TV; 1990), *What About Your Friends?: Weekend Getaway* (TV; 1990), *Motives* (2004), *Christmas at Water's Edge* (TV; 2004), *Beauty Shop* (2005), *The Gospel* (2005), *Cuttin Da Mustard* (2006), *Death Toll* (2008), *Cuttin Da Mustard* (2008), *Madea Goes to Jail* (2009).

TV: *Sesame Street* (various episodes; 1969), *The Tonight Show Starring Johnny Carson* (2 segments; 1984 and 1985), *The Cosby Show* (recurring role of Rudy Huxtable; 1984–92), *Night of 100 Stars II* (1985), *Motown Returns to the Apollo* (1985), *Andy Williams and the NBC Kids Search for Santa* (1985), *NBC 60th Anniversary Celebration* (1986), *A Different World* (3 episodes as Rudy Huxtable; pilot; "Rudy and the Snow Queen," "My Dinner with Theo," 1987–88), *The 3rd Annual American Comedy Awards* (1989), *The Oprah Winfrey Show* (2 segments; 1989–2008), *Reading Rainbow* ("The Magic School Bus Inside the Earth," 1990), *The Last Laugh: Memories of the Cosby Show* (archival; 1992), *Cosby* ("The Return of the Charlites," 1997), *E! True Hollywood Story* (archival; "The Cosby Kids," 2001), *Weakest Link* (2001), *NBC 75th Anniversary Special* (2002), *The Cosby Show: A Look Back* (2002), *Celebrity Fear Factor 3* (2002), *TV Land Awards: A Celebration of Classic TV* (2003), *Celebrity Mole: Yucatan* (2004), *Good Day Live* (2004), *Jimmy Kimmel Live!* (2005), *100 Greatest Kid Stars* (2005), *50 Cutest Child Stars: All Grown Up* (2005), *I Was a Network Star* (archival; 2006), *Gylne tider* (2 segments; 2006 and 2007), *La tele de tu vida* (archival; 2007), *House of Payne* ("Sad, Sad Leroy Brown," Part I, 2007).

Music Videos: *One Call Away* (2004).

Kravitz, Ze

Born in Los Angeles, California, December 1, 1988.

Ze Kravitz, the daughter of musician Lenny Kravitz and actress Lisa Bonet, made her big screen debut in two 2007 films: *No Reservations*, the old fashioned Catherine Zeta Jones–Aaron Eckhart comedy, and *The Brave One*, Jodie Fos-

Keisha Knight Pulliam.

ter's reworking of the vigilante theme of the old Charles Bronson series *Death Wish*.

Kravitz attended Miami Country Day School in Florida and Rudolf Steiner High School in New York. She began attending State University of New York Purchase's Performing Arts program in 2007.

Feature Films: *No Reservations* (2007), *The Brave One* (2007), *Sophomore* (2008).

Music Videos: *Savior Self* (2007), *I Know* (2007).

Lathan, Sanaa

Born in New York, New York, September 19, 1971.

Sanaa (pronounced like the "*sina*" in Frank Sinatra) McCoy Lathan comes from a show business family. Her mother was a Broadway performer and dancer who appeared with Alvin Ailey, and her father worked as a behind the scenes executive for the Public Broadcasting System (PBS). She has four siblings: an older brother named Tendaji, and three younger sisters — Arielle, Colette, and Liliane. When her parents divorced, she had to adapt to a bicoastal lifestyle, shuttling back and forth between Los Angeles and New York, and between the public schools of New York and

Beverly Hills High. Lathan went on to attend the University of California at Berkeley with a concentration on English. As an undergrad, she began to perform with the Black Theatre Workshop, and decided to apply for the master's program at the Yale School of Drama. Performing Shakespeare and beginning to realize the depth of what a career in acting could mean, Lathan began to forge the mature perspective that has infused her acting skills.

She came back to New York and started to perform off–Broadway. With some encouragement from her father, she eventually decided to go back to the West Coast to take advantage of opportunities in the film and television industries. She started doing series TV (*Moesha*, *Family Matters*, *NYPD Blue*) and landed a part in her first TV movie, *Miracle in the Woods* (1979). Her first theatrical feature was *Drive* (1997), as Malik Brody's (Kadeem Hardison) estranged wife. Then she was the love interest for Claude Banks (Martin Lawrence) in *Life* (1999) and Mike's (Omar Epps) girlfriend in *The Wood* (1999). Then came her best and most critically acknowledged role up to that point in the fine ensemble drama *The Best Man* (1999). Audiences were starting to notice her. In *Love & Basketball* (2000), a cogent romantic drama, she was again cast opposite then real-life boyfriend Omar Epps. In 2003 she co-starred with Denzel Washington in director Carl Franklin's twisty crime drama *Out of Time*. She was nominated for an Independent Spirit Award for her work.

Sanaa Lathan and Omar Epps in *Love & Basketball* (2000).

Lathan was then given the lead in a choice TV movie, *Disappearing Acts* (2000), the story of two unlikely lovers, co-starring Wesley Snipes and based on the best seller by Terry McMillan. She returned to romantic comedy in *Brown Sugar* (2002) and had a major lead in the big box office science fiction film *Alien vs. Predator* (2004), handling an uncharacteristic action role very well.

In many ways, the tender interracial love story *Something New* (2006) is Lathan's signature role. Playing a self-centered businesswoman who finds herself— slowly and reluctantly — falling in love with a white landscaper, Lathan gives a multi-layered, quite touching performance as a woman who finds herself as she finds love. She received a 2007 NAACP Image Award nomination for Best Actress. (This was her sixth Image Award nomination, with one win for *Love & Basketball.*) The other nominations were for *The Best Man*, *Brown Sugar*, *Out of Time*, and the TV series *Nip/Tuck* for her role as Michelle Landau.

Theater has continued to be a part of her professional life. She was nominated for a 2004 Tony Award as Best Actress for her role of Beneatha in the revival of *A Raisin in the Sun*. She reprised that role in the 2008 TV movie version of *Raisin*.

Feature Films including TV Movies: *Drive* (1997), *Miracle in the Woods* (TV; 1997), *Blade* (1998), *Life* (1999), *Catfish in Black Bean Sauce* (1999), *The Wood* (1999), *The Best Man* (1999), *Love & Basketball* (2000), *The Smoker* (2000), *Disappearing Acts* (TV; 2000), *Brown Sugar* (2002), *Out of Time* (2003), *Alien vs. Predator* (2004), *The Golden Blaze* (voice; 2005), *Something New* (2006), *A Raisin in the Sun* (TV; 2008), *The Family That Preys* (2008), *Wonderful World* (2009), *Macbett (The Caribbean Macbeth)* (2009), *The Middle of Nowhere* (2009).

TV: *In the House* ("The Curse of Hill House," 1996), *Moesha* ("A Concerned Effort," Parts I and II, 1996), *Family Matters* ("Revenge of the Nerd," 1997), *Built to Last* (pilot; 1997), *NYPD Blue* ("You're Under a Rasta," 1998), *Late-Line* (recurring role of Briana Gilliam; 1998–99), *The 2001 IFP/West Independent Spirit Awards* (2001), *The Sharon Osbourne Show* (2003), *The 58th Annual Tony Awards* (2004), *HBO: First Look* (*Alien vs. Predator*, 2004), *Tavis Smiley* (2004), *The Directors* ("The Films of Carl Franklin," 2005), *The 3rd Annual Vibe Awards* (2005), *Nip/Tuck* (recurring role of Michelle Landau), *The 11th Annual Critics' Choice Awards* (2006), *Late Night with Conan O'Brien* (2006), *The Late Late Show with Craig Ferguson* (2006), *The Tyra Banks Show* (2006), *The Oprah Winfrey Show* (2006), *38th NAACP Image Awards* (2007), *Entertainment Tonight* (2008), *Baisden After Dark* (2008) *39th Annual NAACP Image Awards* (2008).

Video/DVD: *Out of Time: Crime Scene* (2004).

Shorts: *The Smoker* (2000).

Lawson, Bianca Born in Los Angeles, California, March 20, 1979.

Bianca Lawson is the daughter of Denise (née Gordy) and Richard Lawson. Her father is a soap opera actor (*All My Children*). She began acting at age nine and did commercials for Barbie dolls, and later for Levi's and Revlon. Her series break came with the role of Megan Jones on *Saved by the Bell: The New Class* (1993–94); this was not as popular as the original *Saved by the Bell*, but it did put Lawson's career in orbit.

Lawson has had a long and interesting history with the cult series *Buffy the Vampire Slayer*. She was originally chosen for the role of Cordelia Chase in 2007, but she passed on the role to take a part on UPN's *Goode Behavior*. This proved to be a bad move, as *Goode Behavior* barely lasted a month before it was cancelled. But there was a reprieve when the producers of *Buffy* called her back to play Kendra the Slayer in 1997–98. This was a sexy role for which Lawson is well known to this day.

Memorable film roles include the TV movie *The Temptations* (TV; 1998), her film debut, where she played Diana Ross; *Feast of All Saints* (2001), the popular cable film based on the Anne Rice novel; and the very popular theatrical feature *Save the Last Dance* (2001), where she had a knock-down, drag-out catfight with lead Julia Stiles.

Feature Films including Video and TV Movies: *The Temptations* (TV; 1998), *Twice the Fear* (1998), *Primary Colors* (1998), *The Pavilion* (1999), *Big Monster on Campus* (2000), *Feast of All Saints* (TV; 2001), *Save the Last Dance* (2001), *Bones* (2001), *Dead & Breakfast* (2004), *Fearless* (TV; 2004), *The Big House* (TV; 2004), *Breakin' All the Rules* (2004), *Flip the Script* (2005), *Broken* (2006), *Pledge This!* (2006), *Supergator* (2007), *Killing of Wendy* (2008).

TV: *Saved by the Bell: The New Class* (recurring role of Megan Jones; 1993–94), *What'z Up?* (series co-host; 1994), *My So-Called Life* (pilot; 1994), *The Late Late Show with Craig Kilborn* (2001), *Loose Lips* (2003), *Me and the Boys* ("The Age of Reason," 1995), *In the House* ("The Final Cut," 1995), *Sister, Sister* (recurring role of Rhonda Coley; 1995–96), *Goode Behavior* (recurring role of Bianca Goode; 1996), *The Parent 'Hood* (2 episodes as Jasmine; "Zaria Peterson's Day Off," "Bad Rap," 1997), *Silk Stalkings* ("Rage," 1998), *The Steve Harvey Show* (3 episodes in the role of Rosalind; "Breakfast with Tiffany," "White Men Can Funk," "That's a Bunch of Bull, Ced," 1998), *Buffy the Vampire Slayer* (3 episodes in the role of Kendra; "What's My Line?" Parts I and II, "Becoming," Part I, 1997–98), *Smart Guy* (2 episodes in the role of Shirley; "Baby, It's You and You and You," "It Takes Two," 1997 and 1999), *Dawson's Creek* (4 episodes in the role of Nikki Green; "First Encounters of the Close Kind," "Barefoot at Capefest," "Northern Lights," "To Green, with Love," 1999–2000), *Strong Medicine* ("Control Group," 2001), *For the People* ("Textbook Perfect," 2002), *Haunted* ("Blind Witness," 2002), *The Division* ("Play Ball," 2004), *Living in TV Land* (2006), *The Cleaner* ("Meet the Joneses," 2008).

Leal, Sharon Born in Tucson, Arizona, October 17, 1972.

Sharon Leal's career highlights include her role as Michele Morris in *Dreamgirls* (2006), Effie White's replacement in the singing trio. It's a significant role — considering she plays "the other girl" — and Leal makes the most of it. Another highlight is her role on *Boston Public* as music teacher Marilyn Sudor (2003–05). She joined the ensemble cast of *Rent* in 1998 and played the role of Mimi in the San Francisco run of the musical's first national tour in 1999. She had a lead in the feature *Face the Music* (2000); she was in the holiday romance *This Christmas* and Tyler Perry's

Why Did I Get Married? (both 2007). Leal also had a role on the much-hyped but short-lived *LAX* (2004–05) as the wife of airport director Roger de Souza.

Leal was born to an African American father and a Filipino mother. Her adoptive father, Jesse Leal, was a master sergeant in the U.S. Air Force. He married Leal's mother in 1972. She later married again (to Elmer Manakil, the father of Leal's step-sister Katrina). She graduated from Roosevelt High School of the Arts in Fresno, California, and attended Diablo Valley Junior College, where she studied acting. She began doing community theater productions as a teenager. She won a vocal scholarship at the Santa Cruz Jazz Festival, which enabled her to study with famed voice teacher Seth Riggs. She has sung cabaret at top New York nightspots like B. Smith's and Steve McGraw's.

Theater credits include *Bright Lights, Big City* (New York Theatre Workshop); *Little Shop of Horrors* (Arizona Theatre Company); *Into the Woods* (Theatreworks, California); and regional productions of *Ain't Misbehavin', West Side Story, Me and My Girl* and *Nunsense*. She is in the film *Soul Men* (2008) with Samuel L. Jackson (Leal plays his daughter) and Bernie Mac, in his last film role (Isaac Hayes, who died around the same time as Mac, has a cameo).

Feature Films including Video and TV Movies: *Face the Music* (2000), *What Are the Odds* (2004), *Dreamgirls* (2006), *Motives 2* (2007), *Why Did I Get Married?* (2007), *This Christmas* (2007), *Soul Men* (2008), *Linewatch* (2008).

TV: *Guiding Light* (recurring role as Dahlia Crede; 1998), *Legacy* (recurring role as Marita; 1998), *Boston Public* (recurring role of Marilyn Sudor; 2003–05), *LAX* (3 episodes; "The Longest Moment," "Thanksgiving," "Senator's Daughter," 2004–05), *Las Vegas* ("Sperm Whales and Spearmint Rhinos," 2005), *2006 Asian Excellence Awards, CSI: Miami* ("Internal Affairs," 2007), *Baisden After Dark* (2007), *2008 Asian Excellence Awards.*

Video/DVD: *Building the Dream* (2007).

Lee, Joie

Born in Brooklyn, New York, June 22, 1962.

Joie Lee got her first taste of fame in brother Spike Lee's 1986 film *She's Gotta Have It.* She also appeared in Spike Lee's *Mo' Better Blues* (1990) playing Indigo Downes, girlfriend of the jazz musician played by Denzel Washington. This was probably her best screen performance, and she looked lovely in this romantic role. Joie's father, Bill, was a jazz musician and composer (he wrote the score for *Mo' Better Blues*). Her mother was a private school teacher. The Lee children — four boys and one girl — were exposed to the arts and black culture at an early age.

Joie once noted that she'd like to do work in every film genre, because that's the best way to break down the barriers erected against black actresses. She has her own production comedy and has expressed a desire to obtain a multimedia ensemble company.

Feature Films including Video and TV Movies: *She's Gotta Have It* (1986), *School Daze* (1988), *Do the Right Thing* (1989), *Bail Jumper* (1990), *Mo' Better Blues* (1990), *A Kiss Before Dying* (1991), *Fathers & Sons* (1992), *Crooklyn* (1994), *Losing Isaiah* (1995), *Girl 6* (1996), *Get on the Bus* (1996), *Nowhere Fast* (1997), *Personals* (aka *Hook'd Up*, 1999), *Summer of Sam* (1999), *Coffee and Cigarettes* (2003), *She Hate Me* (2004), *Full Grown Men* (2006), *Starting Out in the Evening* (2007).

TV: *Making Do the Right Thing* (1989), *The Cosby Show* ("The Lost Weekend," 1989), *100 Centre Street* ("Zero Tolerance," 2002), *Law & Order: Special Victims Unit* ("Rotten," 2003).

Lee, Mabel

Birth date unavailable.

Singer–tap dancer Mabel Lee was one of the original chorus line Apollo Girls at the famed Harlem theater. She toured with Cab Calloway's band and was one of Eubie's Girls on the record of that name, and appeared in the revival of Blake and Sissel's *Shuffle Along* (1952). Lee was the honoree at the 2005 Tapology Festival and 2001 recipient of the New York Tap Committee's Positive Role Model Award.

William Forest Crouch, a producer and director of "soundies" (short films featuring song hits of the 1940s, serving the same function as today's music videos), "discovered" the beautiful Lee (already a star chorus girl) and gave her star billing over Noble Sissle for her dance routine in *Sizzling with Sissle* (1946). She's also in the soundie *Brother Bill* (1945), appearing in a brief pre-music segment in an acting bit with Eddie "Rochester" Anderson. She can also be glimpsed briefly in the Louis Jordan soundie *Old Man Mose* (1942). Lee also has a red hot dance in the Jordan feature *Reet, Petite and Gone* (1946) and fulfilled all three adjectives in the film's title.

Her most unusual soundie—no contest here—is *The Chicken Shack Shuffle* (1943), a salute to the famed Harlem restaurant in Sugar Hill known for its fried chicken and sweet potato pie. An uncharacteristically demurely dressed Lee sings with a boogie-woogie quartet in *The Cat Can't Dance* (1945). Of her features, the most widely distributed was *Ebony Parade* (1947), an all-star musical revue that also showcases a young Dorothy Dandridge (whose name is misspelled on the film's poster).

Feature Films: *Swanee Showboat* (1940), *Reet, Petite, and Gone* (1947), *O'Voutie O'Rooney* (1947), *Ebony Parade* (1947), *The Dreamer* (1948).

Shorts: *Old Man Mose* (1942), *The Chicken Shack Shuffle* (1943), *Brother Bill* (1945), *Pigmeat Throws the Bull* (1945), *Sizzling with Sissle* (1946), *Baby Don't Go Away From Me* (1946).

Lee, Robinne Born in Mount Vernon, New York, July 16, 1974.

Of Jamaican and Chinese ancestry, Robinne Lee began her career with a role in the romantic comedy *Hav Plenty* (1997), and was also in the *Taming of the Shrew* comedy *Deliver Us from Eva* (2003). She was in *National Security* (2003) with Martin Lawrence and the Will Smith box office hit *Hitch* (2005). Recent big screen projects include the morose *Seven Pounds* (2008), again with Will Smith, and *Hotel for Dogs* with Don Cheadle (2009). Her television work includes appearances on *Buffy the Vampire Slayer* (2002) and Tyler Perry's *House of Payne* (2007). She holds a law degree from New York's Columbia University and a bachelor of arts in psychology from Yale.

Feature Films including Video and TV Movies: *Hav Plenty* (1997), *Cupid & Cate* (TV; 2000), *The Runaway* (TV; 2000), *Almost a Woman* (TV; 2001), *National Security* (2003), *Deliver Us From Eva* (2003), *Shook* (2004), *13 Going on 30* (2004), *Hitch* (2005), *This Is Not a Test* (2008), *Seven Pounds* (2008), *Hotel for Dogs* (2009).

TV: *Buffy the Vampire Slayer* ("Sleeper," 2002), *The Big House* ("Hart Transplant," 2004), *Numb3rs* (2 episodes; "Uncertainty Principle," "Sabotage," 2005), *House of Payne* (3 episodes; "The Perfect Storm," "Sad, Sad Leroy Brown," "The Big Test," 2007).

Video/DVD: *Radio City Volume One: Caught Up* (2005).

LeGon, Jeni Born in Chicago, Illinois, August 14, 1916.

Dancer, dance instructor and actress Jennie LeGon (the original spelling of her name) grew up in what was known as Chicago's teeming Black Belt. She was the fifth child of Hector and Harriet LeGon. Hector was a Gullah creole from the Georgia Sea Islands ("Geechie" country). Lee received her first formal training from Mary Bruce's School of Dance and graduated from Sexton Elementary School in 1928.

LeGon was only 13 in 1930 when she auditioned successfully for the Count Basie Orchestra's chorus line. Her burgeoning dance career caused her to leave Englewood High School the following year. In 1931, she became a member of the Whitman Sisters troupe. In 1933, she formed the tap dance duo LeGon and Lane with her half-sister Willa Mae Lane.

In 1935, she was discovered by Earl Dancer, the former manager of Ethel Waters. This led to her being the first black woman to sign an extended contract with MGM, then the biggest studio in Hollywood (although it was cancelled a short time later). In her first screen role, *Hooray for Love* (1935), she danced with Bill "Bojangles" Robinson, the only black woman ever to do so in a film. Many dancing and acting roles in musicals and dramas followed: *Broadway Melody of 1936* (1935), *While Thousands Cheer* (1940), *Sundown* (1941), *Birth of the Blues* (1941), and *Easter Parade* (1948). She appeared on TV's *Amos 'n' Andy* in the 1950s. Later films included a role as a teacher in *Bright Road* (1953) and, after an absence of many years from the screen, an appearance in the campy 2001 horror film *Bones*.

LeGon married composer Phil Moore in 1943. In later years, she settled in Vancouver, British Columbia, teaching tap; she worked with the youth dance group Troupe One in the 1970s and toured with the Pelican Players in the 1980s.

In 1999, the National Film Board of Canada released Grant Greshuk's documentary *Jeni LeGon: Living in a Great Big Way*. She has been honored by the Black Filmmakers Hall of Fame and the National Congress of Black Women.

Feature Films: *Hooray for Love* (1935), *Broadway Melody of 1936* (1935), *Dishonour Bright* (1936), *Ali Baba Goes to Town* (1937), *Fools for Scandal* (1938), *Double Deal* (1939), *I Can't Give You Anything But Love, Baby* (1940), *While Thousands Cheer* (1940), *Glamour for Sale* (1940), *Sun-*

down (1941), *Birth of the Blues* (1941), *Bahama Passage* (1941), *Take My Life* (1942), *Arabian Nights* (1942), *Stormy Weather* (1943), *My Son, the Hero* (1943), *I Walked with a Zombie* (1943), *Hi-De-Ho* (1947), *Easter Parade* (1948), *I Shot Jesse James* (1949), *Somebody Loves Me* (1952) *Bright Road* (1953), *Home Is Where the Hart Is* (1987), *Bones* (2001), *In the Shadow of Hollywood: Race Movies and the Birth of Black Cinema* (documentary; 2007).

TV: *The Amos 'n' Andy Show* (5 episodes; "The Lodge Brothers Complain," "The Happy Stevenses," "Kingfish's Secretary," "Call Lehigh 4-9900," "Andy Falls in Love with an Actress," 1953–55).

Lemmons, Kasi Born in St. Louis, Missouri, February 24, 1961.

Kasi Lemmons is the foremost female African American film director. Her most important films are *Eve's Bayou* (1997) and *Talk to Me* (2007). Lemmons had a career as an actress before she turned to directing. Kasi (pronounced "Casey") was born Karen Lemmons. She has been married to actor-director Vondie Curtis-Hall since 1995; they have two children, Henry Hunter and Zora. Her mother is a psychotherapist and poetess and her father is a biology teacher.

Lemmons was Ardelia Mapp, Jodie Foster's FBI agent cohort in the Academy Award winning Best Picture *The Silence of the Lambs* (1991); she had a cameo in Spike Lee's *School Daze* (1988); and she was Jackie, the attractive woman Peter Loew (Nicholas Cage) picks up and takes to his apartment in *Vampire's Kiss* (1989). Lemmons was also Cookie in *The Five Heartbeats* (1991); Bernadette Walsh in the horror film *Candyman* (1992); a tough Louisiana cop in John Woo's *Hard Target* (1993); and Nina Blackburn in the funny pseudo-documentary *Fear of a Black Hat* (1994).

Lemmons' desire to direct took over when she appeared in the drug drama *Gridlock'd* (1995), directed by her husband, Vondie Curtis-Hall. Although Lemmons had gone to film school (at UCLA and NYU), her husband taught her many things, including how to set up a shot. She rewarded his training by directing the evocative time-and-memory masterpiece *Eve's Bayou*, the finest feature ever directed by a black woman and the most financially successful independent film of its year.

Feature Films including Video and TV Movies: *11th Victim* (TV; 1979), *Adam's Apple* (TV; 1986), *School Daze* (1988), *Vampire's Kiss* (1989), *The Court Martial of Jackie Robinson* (TV; 1990), *The Big One: The Great Los Angeles Earthquake* (TV; 1990), *Before the Storm* (TV; 1991), *The Silence of the Lambs* (1991), *The Five Heartbeats* (1991), *Afterburn* (TV; 1992), *Candyman* (1992), *Hard Target* (1993), *Fear of a Black Hat* (1994), *Override* (TV; 1994), *Drop Squad* (1994), *Zooman* (TV; 1995), *Gridlock'd* (1995), *'Til There Was You* (1997), *Liars' Dice* (1998), *Waist Deep* (2006).

TV: *Spenser: For Hire* ("Resurrection," 1985), *ABC Afterschool Specials* ("The Gift of Amazing Grace," 1986), *As the World Turns* (recurring role as Nella Franklin; 1986–89), *The Cosby Show* ("The Birth," Parts I and II, 1988), *The Equalizer* ("The Day of the Covenant," 1988), *A Man Called Hawk* ("Life After Death," 1989), *Another World* (recurring role as Tess Parker; 1989–90), *Under Cover* ("Sacrifices," 1991), *Murder, She Wrote* ("The Survivor," 1993), *Walker, Texas Ranger* ("Night of the Gladiator," 1993), *The 2001 IFP/West Independent Spirit Awards, ER* ("It's All in Your Head," 2002), *Sisters in Cinema* (2003).

Lenoir, Noémie Born in Les Ulis, France, September 19, 1979.

This French model (well known for her appearances in the swimsuit issues of *Sports Illustrated*) has also had an acting career, in France as well as in several American productions. She is of Madagascan descent, the daughter of a French father and mother from the island of La Runion.

Her silent role as the model Karine in *Le Doublure* (2006), a warm, old-fashioned comedy, is tribute to her overwhelming beauty and to her screen presence. She had more to do as Carter's (Chris Tucker) girlfriend in the box office hit *Rush Hour 3* (2007). She also had a small role in *After the Sunset* (2007), a listless robbery thriller.

Lenoir's TV appearances have all been as herself, and she hosted a show on France's Trace TV for two years. Her husband is soccer star Claude Makélélé. Their son Kelyan was born in 2005.

Feature Films including TV Movies: *Astérix & Obélix: Mission Cléopatra* (2002), *Gomez & Tavares* (aka *Payoff*, 2003), *After the Sunset* (2004), *Le Doublure* (aka *The Valet*, 2004), *Rush Hour 3* (2007).

TV: *Tout le monde en parle* (5 segments; 2000–03), *20h10 pétantes* (2004), *Le grand journal* *de canal+* (2005), *French Beauty* (2005), *On n'est pas couché* (2007), *The Victoria's Secret Fashion Show* (2007).

Lester, Ketty Born in Hope, Arkansas, August 16, 1934.

Ketty Lester, birth name Revoyda Frierson, remains best known for her huge 1962 hit single "Love Letters (Straight from the Heart)." It was a top-five *Billboard* hit in the U.S., and an equally big hit in England. Lester studied music at San Francisco State College and performed at that city's famous Purple Onion nightclub in the 1950s. The Purple Onion was later home to acts like the Smothers Brothers. Later in the decade she toured with Cab Calloway's orchestra. She appeared off–Broadway in a revival of *Cabin in the Sky* in the early sixties, and then signed a contract with Era Records, which released "Love Letters." She also joined R&B singer Betty Everett for a collaborative album appropriately titled *Betty Everett & Ketty Lester.*

Lester had a career turnover in the 1970s and 1980s when she became a TV (and sometime film) actress. She is best remembered for her role as Hester-Sue Terhune on the top-rated Michael Landon vehicle *Little House on the Prairie* (1978–83). Prior to that, she had tested her acting wings on the venerable daytime soap *Days of Our Lives* in the role of Helen Grant (1975–77). She was in the film version of Neil Simon's *The Prisoner of Second Avenue* (1975), but like fellow singer Emily Yancy, she is best remembered for her role in *Blacula* (1972), one of the best of the blaxploitation films. She was the cabbie who makes the mistake of taking Blacula as a fare, later winding up coming to vampiric life in the morgue, where she kills attendant Elisha Cook, Jr. It's the creepiest scene in the film — and a far cry from "Love Letters."

Feature Films including Video and TV Movies: *Just for Fun* (1963), *Up Tight!* (1968), *Blacula* (1972), *It's Good to Be Alive* (TV; 1974), *Uptown Saturday Night* (1974), *The Prisoner of Second Avenue* (1975), *Louis Armstrong Chicago Style* (TV; 1976), *Adventurizing with Chopper* (TV; 1976), *Cops and Robin* (TV; 1978), *Battered* (TV; 1978), *The Night the City Screamed* (TV; 1980), *Street Knight* (1993), *Percy & Thunder* (TV; 1993), *House Party 3* (1994), *Jack Reed: A Search for Justice* (TV; 1994), *Runaway Car* (aka *Out of Control,* TV; 1997).

Ketty Lester.

TV: *American Bandstand* (5 segments; 1962–68), *Shindig!* (1964), *Shivaree* (1965), *Where the Action Is* (3 segments; 1965–66), *The Woody Woodbury Show* (1968), *The F.B.I.* ("Eye of the Storm," 1969), *Green Acres* (2 episodes; "The Birthday Gift," "Retreat from Washington," 1969), *That Girl* ("The Defiant One," 1969), *Julia* ("The Undergraduate," 1969), *Love, American Style* (2 episodes; 1970 and 1973), *Temperatures Rising* (3 episodes; "Operation Fastball," "Witchcraft, Washington Style," "Panic in the Sheets," 1972–73), *Marcus Welby, M.D.* ("A Joyful Song," 1973), *Sanford and Son* ("The Infernal Triangle," 1973), *The Streets of San Francisco* ("Endgame," 1975), *Harry O* ("Street Games," 1975), *Days of Our Lives* (recurring role as Helen Grant; 1975–77), *Sugar Time!* (1977), *The Waltons* ("The Stray," 1977), *Little House on the Prairie* (recurring role of Hester-Sue Terhune; 1977–83), *Lou Grant* ("Murder," 1978), *The White Shadow* ("Mainstream," 1979), *Happy Days* ("Southern Crossing," 1982), *Hill Street Blues* (2 episodes; "Life in the Minors," "Eugene's Comedy Empire Strikes Back," 1983), *Webster* ("San Francisco," 1983), *This Is the Life* ("Reprise for the Lord," 1984), *G.I. Joe* (voice; 3 episodes in the role of Satin; 1985), *Scarecrow and Mrs. King* ("The Eyes Have It,"

1986), *Morningstar/Eveningstar* (recurring role as Nora Blake; 1986), *Hotel* ("Separations," 1986), *Trying Times* ("Moving Day," 1987), *St. Elsewhere* ("Curtains," 1988), *In the Heat of the Night* ("Gunshots," 1989), *Alien Nation* (1989), *Quantum Leap* ("So Help Me God: July 29, 1957," 1989), *Gabriel's Fire* ("To Catch a Con," Parts I and II, 1990), *L.A. Law* ("Monkey on My Back Lot," 1991), *Courthouse* ("Fair-Weathered Friends," 1995), *Getting Personal* ("Guess Who Else Is Coming to Dinner?" 1998).

Video/DVD: *Shindig! Presents Groovy Gals* (archival; 1991).

Lewis, Dawnn Born in Brooklyn, New York, August 13, 1961.

Dawnn Lewis is fondly recalled for her portrayal of Jaleesa Vinson Taylor on *A Different World* (1987–92). She followed *World* with the role of Robin Dumars on *Hangin' with Mr. Cooper* (1962). Later she joined the cast of *Any Day Now* as Gail Williams (2000–02). She has done a good deal of voice work for animated productions throughout her career (*Spider-Man*, Storm of the X-Men in *Marvel: Ultimate Alliance*, and *Futurama*). She was Melba Early in *Dreamgirls* (2006) and has appeared in the TV movies *Stompin' at the Savoy* (1992) and *Race to Freedom: The Underground Railroad* (1994).

Lewis appears on the innovative PBS series *Endgame: Ethics and Values in America* with Roma Maffia. The show incorporates an interactive web site and challenges viewers as to where they stand on difficult moral issues. In 2000, she won the NAACP Image Award for her role in the play *The Marriage*. She also appeared in the Washington, D.C., production *Whatever Happened to Black Love?* (2005); she was featured in *Sister Act: The Musical* at the Pasadena Playhouse (2006); and her other appearances include *Black Woman's Blues*, *Let the Church Roll On!* and *Celebrating the Negro Spirituals*. She was also in the musical *Fat Girls* at Stage 52 Theatre in Los Angeles.

She released her debut CD of songs, *Worth Waiting For*, in 2006. She hosted and performed in the *Sisters in the Spirit Tour* with Yolanda Adams, Shirley Caesar and the duo Mary, Mary. Her parents are Joyce and Carl Lewis (the former NBA player). She was married to Johnny Newman from 2004 to 2006.

Feature Films including TV and Video Movies: *I'm Gonna Git You Sucka* (1988), *Stompin' at the Savoy* (TV; 1992), *Race to Freedom: The Underground Railroad* (TV; 1994), *The Cherokee Kid* (TV; 1996), *Spiderman: Sins of the Fathers* (voice; 1996), *Bruno the Kid* (voice; 1996), *Bad Day on the Block* (aka *Under Pressure*, 1997), *The Wood* (1999), *Before Now* (2002), *Charlotte's Web 2: Wilbur's Big Adventure* (voice; 2003), *I Was a Network Star* (TV; 2006), *The Adventures of Brer Rabbit* (voice; 2006), *Hollie Hobbie and Friends: Christmas Wishes* (voice; 2006), *Dreamgirls* (2006), *The Last Sentinel* (voice; 2007), *Hell on Earth* (voice; 2008), *Futurama: Bender's Big Score* (voice; 2008). *Futurama: Into the Wild Green Yonder* (voice; 2009).

TV: *A Different World* (recurring role of Jaleesa Vinson Taylor; 1987–92), *The Magical World of Disney* (1988), *The Second Annual Soul Train Music Awards* (1988), *The 10th Annual Black Achievement Awards* (1989), *The More You Know* (1989), *Hangin' with Mr. Cooper* (recurring role of Robin Dumars; "Miracle in Oaktown," "Boyz in the Woodz," 1992–93), *Yuletide in the 'Hood* (voice; 1993), *A Cool Like That Christmas* (voice; 1994), *Happily Ever After: Fairy Tales for Every Child* (1995), *ABC Weekend Specials* (voice; "Jirimpimbira: An African Folk Tale," 1995), *Spider-Man* (voice; 7 episodes in the recurring role of Lt. Terri Lee; 1995–97), *C-Bear and Jamal* (voice; 1996), *The Faculty* ("Daisy's Secret," 1996), *The Steve Harvey Show* ("Coming to Chicago," 1997), *Sliders* ("The Breeder," 1997), *The Burning Zone* ("Elegy for a Dream," 1997), *The Parent 'Hood* ("Father Wendell," 1997), *The Incredible Hulk* (voice; "Mission: Incredible," 1997), *King of the Hill* (2 episodes; "Plastic White Female," "Wings of the Dope," 1997 and 1999), *The Secret Files of the SpyDogs* (voices, various episodes; 1998), *The Jamie Foxx Show* ("Scareder Than a Mug," 1999), *Nash Bridges* ("Resurrection," 1999), *Early Edition* ("Number One with a Bullet," 1999), *Futurama* (7 episodes as the voice of LaBarbara Conrad; 1999–2003), *The 10th Kingdom* (miniseries; 2000), *Buzz Lightyear of Star Command* (voice; "Panic on Bathyos," 2000), *Any Day Now* (7 episodes in the role of Gail Williams; 2000–02), *Scene Smoking: Cigarettes, Cinema and the Myth of Cool* (2001), *Andy Richter Controls the Universe* ("We're All the Same, Only Different," 2002), *Endgame: Ethics and Values in America* (2002–present), *Grim & Evil* (voice; recurring role of Grim's Granny; 2002–07), *Strong Medicine* ("Risk," 2003), *Girlfriends* (2 episodes in the role of Linda

Dent; "And Baby Makes Four," "Viva Las Vegas," 2003), *Medical Investigation* ("Little Girl," 2004), *NYPD Blue* ("The 3-H Club," 2004), *Black in the '80s* (2005), *The Boondocks* (voice; "The Garden Party," 2005), *Black Theater Today: 2005, In the Cutz* (2006), *14th Annual Inner City Destiny Awards* (2006), *Angels Can't Help But Laugh* (2007), *Handy Manny* (2007), *One Tree Hill* (2 episodes; "Bridge Over Troubled Water," "Get Cape, Wear Cape, Fly," 2008).

Lewis, Jenifer Born in Kinloch, Missouri, January 25, 1957.

Jenifer Lewis began her show business career as a singer and went from her church choir to roles on Broadway in *Eubie!* (her Broadway debut in 1979), *Ain't Misbehavin'* and *Dreamgirls*. She was also one of The Harlettes, Bette Midler's back-up singers. But it was her one-woman, character-driven comedy shows that really put her on the map. No one in the audience would have guessed that Lewis was suffering from bipolar disorder. She has subsequently spoken out articulately and courageously about the disease. She even had a one-woman stage show titled *Bipolar, Bath and Beyond*. From that title, you know she's not letting her disorder get the best of her.

In addition to theater, she began doing series TV (*Roc, A Different World, Murphy Brown, Touched by an Angel*) and feature films, notably *What's Love Got to Do with It* (1993). She was also in Spike Lee's *Girl 6* (1996), *The Preacher's Wife* (1996), and the underrated black power treatise *Panther* (1995). She has shown equal facility with comedy and drama. Jenifer Jeannette Lewis was the youngest of seven children. She attended Webster University in Webster Groves, Missouri. She has an adopted daughter named Charmaine.

Feature Films including Video and TV Movies: *Star Tours* (1987), *Red Heat* (1988), *Beaches* (1988), *Sister Act* (1992), *Frozen Assets* (1992), *What's Love Got to Do with It* (1993), *Poetic Justice* (1993), *The Meteor Man* (1993), *Undercover Blues* (1993), *Sister Act 2: Back in the Habit* (1993), *Renaissance Man* (1994), *Deconstructing Sarah* (TV; 1994), *Corrina, Corrina* (1994), *Shake, Rattle and Rock!* (TV; 1994), *Panther* (1995), *Deadline for Murder: From the Files of Edna Buchanan* (TV; 1995), *Dead Presidents* (1995), *Girl 6* (1996), *The Preacher's Wife* (1996), *Rituals* (1998), *The Mighty* (1998), *An Unexpected War* (TV; 1998), *The Temptations* (TV; 1998), *Blast from the Past* (1999), *Jackie's Back: Portrait of a Diva* (TV; 1999), *Mystery Men* (1999), *Partners*

Jenifer Lewis and Kadeem Hardison in *Panther* (1995).

(TV; 2000), *Little Richard* (TV; 2000), *Dancing in September* (2000), *Cast Away* (2000), *The Brothers* (2001), *The Ponder Heart* (TV; 2001), *Juwanna Mann* (2002), *Antwone Fisher* (2004), *The Sunday Morning Stripper* (2004), *Nora's Hair Salon* (2004), *The Cookout* (2004), *Shark Tale* (voice; 2004), *Madea's Family Reunion* (2006), *Cars* (voice; 2006), *Dirty Laundry* (2006), *Who's Your Caddy?* (2007), *Redrum* (2007), *Meet the Browns* (2008), *The Princess and the Frog* (voice; 2009), *Not Easily Broken* (2009).

TV: *Murphy Brown* (2 episodes; "Jingle Hell, Jingle Hell, Jingle All the Way," "Uh-Oh," Part II, 1990 and 1991), *A Different World* (recurring role of Dean Dorothy Dandridge Davenport; 1990–93), *Sunday in Paris* (pilot; 1991), *Stat* ("Psychosomatic," 1991), *The Fresh Prince of Bel-Air* (recurring role of Aunt Helen; 1991–96), *Roc* ("Joey the Bartender," 1993), *Moon Over Miami* ("If You Only Knew," 1993), *Hangin' with Mr. Cooper* ("Father Fairest," "Double Cheeseburger, Hold the Diploma," 1993–94), *Lois & Clark: The New Adventures of Superman* ("All Shook Up," 1994), *Friends* ("The One with the Thumb," 1994), *New York Undercover* ("Private Enemy No. 1," 1995), *Living Single* ("Talk Showdown," 1995), *Courthouse* (recurring role as Judge Rosetta Reide; 1995), *Cosby* ("Basketball Story," 1996), *The Rosie O'Donnell Show* (2 segments; 1996 and 1999), *Touched by an Angel* (2 episodes; "Amazing Grace," Parts I and II, 1997), *The Parent 'Hood* ("Hurricane Linda," 1998), *The Chris Rock Show* (1998), *For Your Love* (2 episodes; "The Brother's Day," "Father Fixture," 1998 and 2000), *Get Bruce* (1999), *The Jamie Foxx Show* ("Always Follow Your Heart," 1999), *Happily Ever After: Fairy Tales for Every Child* ("The Bremen Town Musicians," 1999), *Moesha* ("A Den Is a Terrible Thing to Waste," 1999), *Grown Ups* ("Family Circus," 1999), *Time of Your Life* ("The Time They Had Not," 1999), *The PJs* (recurring role as the voice of Bebe Ho; 1999–2008), *Strong Medicine* (recurring role of Lana Hawkins; 2000–06), *Bette* ("The Grammy Pre-Show," (2000), *Hollywood Squares* (2001–04), *Pyramid* (2002), *Family Affair* (pilot; 2002), *Girlfriends* (recurring role of Veretta Childs; 2002–06), *The Proud Family* (voice; "Penny Potter," 2003), *26th NAACP Image Awards* (2004), *The Wayne Brady Show* (2004), *CMT: 40 Greatest Done Me Wrong Songs* (2004), *That's So Raven* ("To See or Not to See," 2004), *Earth to America* (2005), *21st Annual Stellar Gospel Music Awards* (2006), *The Road to "Cars"* (2006), *Day Break* ("What If She's Lying?" 2007), *Shark* ("Backfire," 2007).

Lifford, Tina Birth date N/A.

Tina Lifford is an acclaimed actress, but many consider her work as a motivational speaker and facilitator to be her crowning achievement. A certified life coach and spiritual practitioner (she is a graduate of the master's degree program in spiritual psychology from the University of Santa Monica), she has shown many women how to empower themselves and reclaim their lives. She is the author of *30 Days to a More Fabulous You* and the founder of Totally Fabulous Woman. Her ultimate vision is of "women as a global healing force, standing in our magnificence, lighting up the world."

Prominent film roles include *Blood Work* (2002) with Clint Eastwood; the Golden Globe–nominated TV movie about the superstar Motown group *The Temptations* (1998), which won director Allan Arkush an Emmy for his work; voice work as one of the beloved sheep in the Academy Award–nominated Best Picture *Babe* (1998); and a strong role as a recovering addict in the electrifying crime drama *New Jack City* (1991).

Lifford is currently best known for her role of Paulette Hawkins on NBC's *Heroes* (2006), but her TV work has been multi-faceted, from the sci-fi of *Star Trek: Deep Space Nine* to police dramas (*Hill Street Blues*, *CSI*), to courtroom dramas (*Family Law*), and nighttime soaps (*Knots Landing*, *Beverly Hills 90210*).

Feature Films including Video and TV Movies: *The Ladies Club* (1986), *Nuts* (1987), *Colors* (1988), *Moe's World* (TV; 1990), *New Jack City* (1991), *Paris Trout* (1991), *Wedlock* (aka *Deadlock*, 1991), *The Rape of Doctor Willis* (TV; 1991), *Grand Canyon* (1991), *Bebe's Kids* (voice; 1992), *The Ernest Green Story* (TV; 1993), *Born Too Soon* (TV; 1993), *Country Estates* (TV; 1993), *In the Line of Duty: The Price of Vengeance* (TV; 1994), *Babe* (voice; 1995), *Divas* (TV; 1995), *A Streetcar Named Desire* (TV; 1995), *America's Dream* (TV; 1996), *Run for the Dream: The Gail Devers Story* (TV; 1996), *After Jimmy* (TV; 1996), *Mandela and de Klerk* (TV; 1997), *Cloned* (TV; 1997), *Letters from a Killer* (1998), *Secrets* (1998), *The Temptations* (TV; 1998), *The Loretta Claiborne Story* (TV; 2000), *Panic* (2000), *The '70s* (TV; 2000), *Pay It Forward* (2000), *A Girl Thing* (TV; 2001), *Amy's*

Left to right: **Tasha Scott, Keith Mbulo, Tina Lifford, Larenz Tate in *South Central.***

Orgasm (2001), *Joe Somebody* (2001), *Blood Work* (2002), *The Law and Mr. Lee* (TV; 2003), *Mystery Woman: Sing Me a Murder* (TV; 2005), *Hostage* (2005), *Urban Legends 3: Bloody Mary* (2005), *Mystery Woman: Redemption* (TV; 2006), *Catch and Release* (2006).

TV: *Hill Street Blues* ("Death by Kiki," 1983), *Knots Landing* (4 episodes in the role of Tina; 1 additional appearance; "Celebration," "Friendly Enemies," "Slow Burn," "For Appearance's Sake," "With a Heavy Heart," 1983–88), *Cagney & Lacey* ("The Bounty Hunter," 1984), *T.J. Hooker* (2 episodes; "Hooker's Run," "The Assassin," 1984 and 85), *Murder, She Wrote* ("Tough Guys Don't Die," 1985), *Amen* ("Maitre D'eacon," 1986), *Perfect Strangers* ("Dog Gone Blues," 1987), *Jake and the Fatman* (2 episodes; "Fatal Attraction," Parts I and II, 1987), *Simon & Simon* (2 episodes; "Shadows," "Love Song of Abigail Marsh," 1988), *Tour of Duty* ("Doc Hock," 1989), *Hunter* ("Unacceptable Losses," 1990), *The Fresh Prince of Bel-Air* ("The Mother of All Battles," 1991), *Beverly Hills, 90210* ("Ashes to Ashes," 1991), *Life Goes On* ("Five to Midnight," 1993), *L.A. Law* (2 episodes in the role of Faith Glassman; "Safe Sex," "Pacific Rimshot," 1993), *South Central* (recurring role as Joan Mosley; 1994), *Star Trek: Deep Space Nine* (2 episodes; "Past Tense," Parts I and II, 1995), *Court House* ("Conflict of Interest," 1995), *American Gothic* (4 episodes in the role of Loris Holt; "Eye of the Beholder," "Resurrector," "Dr. Death Takes a Holiday," "Potato Boy," 1995–96), *Crisis Center* (recurring role as Tess Robinson; 1997), *Gun* ("All the President's Women," 1997), *Touched by an Angel* ("Doodlebugs," 1998), *The Practice* ("Trees in the Forest," 1998), *Matrial Law* ("How Sammo Got His Groove Back," 1998), *Family Law* (recurring role of Judge Alice Kingston; 1999–2001), *Any Day Now* ("Homegirl," 2000), *NYPD Blue* ("Brothers Under Arms," 2000), *That's Life* (pilot; 2000), *JAG* (2 episodes in the role of Juanita Ressler; "Act of Terror," "JAG TV," 1998 and 2000), *Strong Medicine* ("Bloodwork," 2001), *Judging Amy* ("Darkness for Light," 2003), *For the People* ("Power Play," 2003), *Karen Cisco* ("Blown Away," 2003), *The Lyon's Den* ("Hubris," 2003), *Threat Matrix* ("PPX," 2004), *NCIS* ("Witness," 2005), *ER* (2 episodes in the role of Evelyn Pratt; "Nobody's Baby," "Dream House," 2005), *CSI* (3 episodes in the role of Judge Witherspoon; "Mea Culpa," "Compulsion," "Secrets & Files," 2004–05), *Heroes* (recurring role as Paulette Hawkins; 2006).

Lil' Kim (aka Jones, Kimberly) Born in Brooklyn, New York, July 11, 1975.

Multiple-platinum rapper Kimberly Denise Jones won a Grammy Award for her contribution to the ensemble remake of Labelle's classic "Lady Marmelade" in 2002. Kim's parents, Linwood and Ruby Mae, separated when she was nine years old. She and her brother Christopher remained with their father. Kim attended Brooklyn College Academy High School. In 1994, she met her life's mentor, Christopher "B.I.G." Wallace, aka the Notorious B.I.G. He made her part of the inner circle at Bad Boy Records, encouraging her to join the group Junior M.A.F.I.A., with whom she released the album *Conspiracy* and several hit singles.

Jones began her solo career with the album *Hard Core* (1996), which debuted at an impressive number 11 on the *Billboard* chart. The single "No Time," a duet with Puff Daddy, was number one for nine weeks on the rap charts.

In 1997, Notorious B.I.G., who had become Lil' Kim's lover, was shot to death in Los Angeles. Despite this tragedy, Lil' Kim continued to hold her career together, touring with P. Diddy and releasing a second album, *The Notorious K.I.M.* (2000). It went to number 4 on *Billboard* and sold one million copies in the U.S. alone. Her third album, *La Bella Mafia* (2003), yielded the *Billboard* Hot 100 hit single "Magic Stick," a duet with Fifty 50 that crested at number 2. The album received two Grammy nominations (Best Female Rap Solo Performance and Best Rap Collaboration). She received a third nomination for Best Pop Collaboration (with Christina Aguilera for "Can't Hold Us Down").

On May 17, 2005, Lil' Kim was found guilty of conspiracy and perjury. She had lied to a grand jury about a friend's role in a 2001 shooting which had taken place outside the Hot 97 radio studios in Manhattan. She was sentenced to one year and a day, to be served at the Philadelphia Detention Center. She then began filming a bizarre reality show called *Lil' Kim: Countdown to Lockdown* (2006) about the waning days before her incarceration. Her fourth album, *The Naked Truth* (2005), was released while she was in prison.

Upon her release on July 3, 2006, Lil' Kim began recording with Keyshia Cole and Missy Elliot (their song "Let It Go" was nominated for a Grammy in 2008 for Best Rap/Sung Collaboration). She also appeared as a celebrity judge on the CW Network's *Pussycat Dolls Present: Search for the Next Doll* and *The Pussycat Dolls: Girlicious* (2007–08).

Lil' Kim's acting career consists of a spate of feature films and a smattering of roles on TV. She played pop singer — one could say early rapper — Shirley "The Name Game" Ellis on *American Dreams*, and played a character named Diamond on a *Moesha* episode. Her film debut was in *She's All That* (1999); she was a character named Alex Sawyer in this variation on *Pygmalion*. She had cameos in *Zoolander* (2001), *Juwanna Mann* (2002), *Nora's Hair Salon* (2004) and *Superhero Movie* (2008; billed as Kimberly Jones, she played the daughter of Professor X of the X-Men). She had a full-length role in *Gang of Roses* (2003) as a gun-slinging cowgirl, but even though the film was fun, it went directly to DVD (and to broadcast TV). Not only is Lil' Kim *in* movies, a movie was made about her. In *Notorious* (2009), the story of rap mogul Notorious B.I.G., Naturi Naughton plays Lil' Kim, although Lil' Kim herself would have been a good choice for the role.

Feature Films including Video and TV Movies: *She's All That* (1999), *Zoolander* (2001), *Juwanna Mann* (2002), *Those Who Walk in Darkness* (2003), *Gang of Roses* (2003), *You Got Served* (2004), *Nora's Hair Salon* (2004), *Lil' Pimp* (voice; 2005), *Life After Death: The Movie* (2007).

TV: *The 1995 Source Hip-Hop Music Awards*, *The 1999 Source Hip-Hop Music Awards*, *MTV Video Music Awards 1999*, *The Howard Stern Radio Show* (1999), *VH1/Vogue Fashion Awards* (1999), *V.I.P.* ("Mao Better Blues," 1999), *Howard Stern* (2 segments; 1999–2000), *The Chris Rock Show* (2000), *100 Greatest Dance Songs of Rock & Roll* (2000), *The Cindy Margolis Show* (2000), *Making the Video* ("Lady Marmelade," 2001), *2001 MTV Movie Awards*, *1st Annual BET Awards* (2001), *MTV Video Music Awards 2001*, *VH1/Vogue Fashion Awards* (2001), *The Parkers* ("Take the Cookies and Run," 2001), *Michael Jackson: 30th Anniversary Celebration* (2001), *DAG* ("Guns and Roses," 2001), *Moesha* ("Paying the Piper," 2001), The 44th Annual Grammy Awards (2002), *100 Greatest Videos* (2003), *3rd Annual BET Awards* (2003), *E! Entertainment Special: Christina Aguilera* (2003), *Tinseltown TV* (2003), *Fuse's Summer*

Jam X (2003), *MOBO Awards 2003, 2003 Radio Music Awards, Spike TV VGA Video Game Awards* (2003), *Fromage 2003, American Dreams* ("Another Saturday Night," 2003), *40 Most Awesomely Dirty Songs ... Ever* (2004), *And You Don't Stop: 30 Years of Hip-Hop* (archival; 2004), *MTV Video Music Awards 2004, The 2004 Source Hip-Hop Music Awards, The Apprentice* (2 episodes; "Crimes of Fashion," "Bling It On," 2004 and 2005), *There's a God on the Mic* (2005), *MTV Video Music Awards 2005, 2nd Annual VH1 Hip-Hop Honors* (2005), *All Shades of Fine: 25 Hottest Women of the Past 25 Years* (2005), *Video on Trial* (archival; 2006), *The Tyra Banks Show* (archival; 2006), *106 & Park Top 10 Live* ("It's All About the Benjamins," archival; 2006), *BET Awards 2006, Lil' Kim: Countdown to Lockdown* (reality series; 2006), *MTV Video Music Awards 2006, 3rd Annual VH1 Hip-Hop Honors* (2006), *Boulevard of Broken Dreams* (2007), *The Pussycat Dolls Present: The Search for the Next Doll* (judge; 2007), The Game ("Media Blitz," 2007), *The Pussycat Dolls Present: Girlicious* (judge; 2008), *BET Awards 2008.*

Video/DVD: *Missy "Misdemeanor" Elliot: Hits of Miss E.: Vol. 1* (2001), *Hardware: Uncensored Music Videos: Hip-Hop, Vol. 1* (2003), *Chronicles of Junior Mafia* (2004), *Hip Hop Uncensored: Vol. 4, Miami Vice* (2004), *Bad Boy's 10th Anniversary: The Hits* (2004), *Mobb Deep: Life of the Infamous* (2006).

Lincoln, Abbey Born in Chicago, Illinois, August 6, 1930.

One of America's foremost jazz singers, Abbey Lincoln was born Anna Marie Woolridge. Her legacy as a singer is more celebrated with the passing years, but her acting legacy needs to be rediscovered. While Lincoln has only appeared in a handful of films, they were all choice projects. She sings "Spread the Word" in director Frank Tashlin's historic early rock 'n' roll musical *The Girl Can't Help It* (1956). She co-starred in a straight dramatic role with Ivan Dixon in *Nothing but a Man* (1964). Lincoln was Josie, a preacher's daughter in a relationship with Duff (Ivan Dixon), who is unsure about being committed to a relationship. *Nothing but a Man* works on many levels: a love story beyond color consideration — thus, the phrase "nothing but a man"; a time capsule look at black life in the South during the mid–Civil Rights era; and an almost documentary film look similar to the effect of the Italian neorealism films of the 1940s.

Nothing but a Man helped launch the independent film movement in America. Unlike many singers who attempt to act, Lincoln gave a fully shaded performance, as rich and subtle as that of any veteran actress. She was nominated for a Golden Globe Award for Best Actress — Drama for her performance opposite Sidney Poitier in the simple, touching romance *For Love of Ivy* (1969). Again, it was a perfectly modulated, fully realized performance from Lincoln, this time as Ivy Moore, a maid who decides to quit her job with the Austin family and go to secretarial school. The Austins don't want her to go, and the teenagers in the family set her up with Jack Parks (Poitier), a trucking company executive, hoping a romance will persuade her to stay. Another love story that transcends race, *Ivy* may be a bit patronizing, but it is also delightful light entertainment.

Lincoln was wasted in Spike Lee's *Mo' Better Blues* (1990) in a brief role as the domineering mother of Bleek, the boy who grows up to be the Denzel Washington character. Bleek's mother nags him into playing the trumpet in a "look, it's Abbey Lincoln!" moment rather than a real performance.

Her albums include *Abbey Is Blue* (1959), *Straight Ahead* (1961), *Abbey Sings Billie, Vols. 1 & 2* (1987), *Devil's Got Your Tongue* (1992), *Over the Years* (2000), and *Abbey Sings Abbey* (2007). Lincoln has been with Verve Records since 1989. She was married to jazz drummer Max Roach from 1962 to 1970.

Feature Films including TV Movies: *The Girl Can't Help It* (1956), *Nothing but a Man* (1964), *For Love of Ivy* (1968), *Short Walk to Daylight* (TV; 1972), *Mo' Better Blues* (1990).

TV: *The Steve Allen Show* (1957), *The Hollywood Palace* (1968), *The Name of the Game* ("The Black Answer," 1968), *The 41st Annual Academy Awards* (1969), *Mission: Impossible* ("Cat's Paw," 1971), *On Being Black* ("Wine in the Wilderness," 1971), *All in the Family* ("What'll We Do with Stephanie?" *1978), Abbey Lincoln: You Gotta Pay the Band* (TV; 1993), *Carnegie Hall Salutes the Jazz Masters: Verve Records at 50* (1994), *Jazzwomen* (2000), *Strange Fruit* (2002).

Video/DVD: *Great Women Singers of the 20th Century: Abbey Lincoln* (2005).

LisaRaye (aka McCoy, LisaRaye; McCoy-Misick, LisaRaye) Born in Chicago, Illinois, September 23, 1967.

LisaRaye attended Eastern Illinois University. She is a model and singer as well as an actress. She appeared in Tupac Shakur's final video, "Toss It Up." Her film roles include the lead in *The Players Club* (1998), about a young woman whose financial problems cause her to try exotic dancing; the women-in-prison melodrama *Civil Brand* (2002); the black cowgirl western *Gang of Roses* (2003); *Beauty Shop* (2005) with Queen Latifah; and — what is perhaps her best film — the evocative male bonding character study *The Wood* (1999). In this ensemble film, a young writer begins to reminisce about his friends when one of them fails to show up for his own wedding.

She was Neesee James on TV's *All of Us*, the Duane Martin character's ex-wife and the mother of their son (2003–07). She also hosted the shows *Live in L.A.* and *The Source: All Access*, and was on the reality series *The It Factor*.

She is the half-sister of rap singer Da Brat, via her father. LisaRaye is of African American and Native American ancestry. Her father is a businessman in the hospitality and banking industries, and her mother was a model. She has a daughter, Kai, from her first marriage. In April 2006 she married Michael Misick, the premier of the Turks and Caicos Islands.

Feature Films including Video and TV Movies: *Reasons* (1996), *The Players Club* (1998), *The Wood* (1999), *The Cheapest Movie Ever Made* (2000), *Rhapsody* (TV; 2000), *Date from Hell* (2001), *All About You* (2001), *Civil Brand* (2002), *Go for Broke* (2002), *Love Chronicles* (2003), *Gang of Roses* (2003), *Super Spy* (2004), *Beauty Shop* (2005), *Envy* (2005), *The Proud Family Movie* (voice; TV; 2005), *The Black Man's Guide to Understanding Black Women* (2008).

TV: *In the House* (2 episodes; "Saint Marion," "Abstinence Makes the Heart Grow Fonder," 1997), *The Parent 'Hood* ("An Affair to Forget," 1998), *The 1999 Source Hip-Hop Music Awards*, *Source: All Access* (series host; 2000), *Acapulco Black Film Festival* (2000), *Teen Summit* ("Video Girls," 2002), *The It Factor* (2003), *Faking It* (2003), *All of Us* (recurring role of Neesee James; 2003–07), *The Sharon Osbourne Show* (2004), *BET Comedy Awards* (2004), *Diamond Life* (2005), *Steve Harvey's Big Time* (2005), *106 & Park Top 10 Live* (2005), *BET Awards 2005*, *All Shades of Fine: 25 Hottest Women of the Past 25 Years* (2005), *Turn Up the Heat with G. Garvin* (2005), *2006 Trumpet Awards*, *38th NAACP Image Awards* (2007), *Entertainment Tonight* (2008), *6th Annual TV Land Awards* (2008), *Hollywood Trials* (2008), *An Evening of Stars: Tribute to Patti LaBelle* (2009).

Long, Nia Born in Brooklyn, New York, October 30, 1970.

Nitara Carlynn Long (her real name) has specialized in charming, fresh-faced good girl roles, but her versatility goes far beyond that. Looking a bit deeper, she is one of the better actresses of her generation — even though she so often makes it seem easy. She was born to Doc and Talita Long, who divorced when she was just past the age of two. She moved with her mother to Iowa and then to South Central Los Angeles when she was seven. As a Catholic schoolgirl, she was eager to develop as many creative skills as possible — acting and dance in particular. Even though Talita had two master's degrees, she and her daughter were having rough financial times, and this was the emphasis that drove Long to excel at her goals.

Like so many burgeoning actresses, she got her foot in the door with an ongoing role on a daytime soap (*Guiding Light*, 1991). Work on sitcoms followed, capped by a career-making role as Will Smith's girlfriend on *The Fresh Prince of Bel-Air* (1991–95). Around this same time, Long landed a role in director John Singleton's Academy Award–nominated Best Picture *Boyz n the Hood*.

The talent for getting linked to quality projects is one of the cornerstones of Long's career. Her excellent track record includes the hit film *Friday* (1995), a day-in-the-life drama, as the girlfriend of the main character Craig (Ice Cube); as Bird, the youngest daughter in the tightly knit Joseph family in the seminal *Soul Food* (1997), which went on to become a cable TV series; as photographer Nina Mosley, who becomes involved in a relationship with Darius Lovehall (Larenz Tate) in 1997's *Love Jones*, which helped cement her position in leading roles; and as the secretary Aby in the Wall Street drama *Boiler Room* (2000). Long has also had recurring roles on *Judging Amy* and *Third Watch*, for which she received an NAACP Image Award for Best Actress in a Series. Long joined *Third Watch* in 2003 as Officer Sasha Monroe.

Long ended her relationship with boyfriend Massai Dorsey, but they have a son, also named

Massai; he was born in 2000. Her current relationship is with Kevin Phillips.

Feature Films including Video and TV Movies: *The B.R.A.T. Patrol* (TV; 1986), *Buried Alive* (1990), *Boyz n the Hood* (1991), *Made in America* (1993), *Friday* (1995), *Love Jones* (1997), *Hav Plenty* (1997), *Soul Food* (1997), *Butter* (1998), *Black Jaq* (TV; 1998), *In Too Deep* (1999), *The Best Man* (1999), *Stigmata* (1999), *Held Up* (1999), *The Secret Laughter of Women* (1999), *The Broken Hearts Club* (2000), *Boiler Room* (2000), *If These Walls Could Talk 2* (2000), *Big Momma's House* (2000), *Sightings: Heartland Ghost* (TV; 2002), *Baadasssss!* (2003), *Alfie* (2004), *The N-Word* (documentary; 2004), *Are We There Yet?* (2005), *Big Momma's House 2* (2006), *Premonition* (2007), *Are We Done Yet?* (2007).

TV: *227* ("Slam Dunk," 1987), *The Guiding Light* (recurring role as Katherine "Kat" Speakes; 1991–93), *The Fresh Prince of Bel-Air* (recurring role of Lisa Wilkes; 1991–95), *Living Single* ("Love Takes a Holiday," 1993), *The Jon Stewart Show* (1995), *Live Shot* (recurring role as Ramona Greer; 1995), *ER* ("Baby Shower," 1996), *Moesha* (2 episodes; "A Concerted Effort," Parts I and II, 1996), *2000 Blockbuster Entertainment Awards*, *32nd NAACP Image Awards* (2001), *Judging Amy* (recurring role of Andrea Solomon; 2001–02), *America Beyond the Color Line* (2002), *Third Watch* (recurring role of Officer Sasha Monroe; 2003–05), *2004 Hispanic Heritage Awards*, *Late Night with Conan O'Brien* (3 segments; 2004–06), *The Tony Danza Show* (2005), *50 Cent's BBQ Pool Party* (2005), *2nd Annual VH1 Hip-Hop Honors* (2005), *The Black Movie Awards* (2005), *25 Strong: The BET Silver Anniversary Special* (2005), *The 3rd Annual Vibe Awards* (2005), *Martha* (2006), *Last Call with Carson Daly* (2006), *That's What I'm Talking About* ("Riches, Pitches and Britches," 2006), *Everwood* ("Truth," 2006), *38th NAACP Image Awards* (2007), *Boston Legal* (3 episodes in the role of Vanessa Walker; "Angel of Death," "Nuts," "Dumping Bella," 2007), *The Late Late Show with Craig Ferguson* (3 segments; 2007), *Big Shots* (recurring role as Katie Graham; 2007–08).

Nia Long in *Friday* (1995).

Mabley, Jackie "Moms"

Born in Brevard, North Carolina, March 19, 1894; died May 23, 1975, White Plains, New York.

Loretta Mary Aiken, better known as Jackie "Moms" Mabley, had essentially two careers. There was her early career as an "adult" comic on the so-called Chitlin' Circuit, and her later, more mainstream career, when she started appearing in feature films and on popular TV programs (*The Ed Sullivan Show*, *ABC Stage 67*, *The Smothers Brothers Comedy Hour*, *The Bill Cosby Show*), and appeared at Carnegie Hall in 1962. In this respect, her career paralleled that of Redd Foxx, another entertainer who went from "party records" (X-rated material), to mass acceptance; Foxx landed on the situation comedy *Sanford and Son*.

Mabley will always be known for her comedy albums, stretching from *Moms Mabley on Stage* (1961) to the retrospective *Comedy Ain't Pretty* (2004). Other album highlights include *I Got Something to Tell You!* (1963), *The Funny Sides of Moms Mabley* (1964), *Now Hear This* (1965), *Live at Sing Sing* (1970), and *I Like 'Em Young* (1972). Mabley rarely went outside of the "Moms" character in public, and for most of her many fans she *was* Moms Mabley. Even as a young woman, she played the part of an aged, toothless crone (she had the look of what would later be referred to as a "bag lady").

Born into a large family, Mabley was forced by her stepfather to marry a much older man; not so ironically, her stage persona revolved around the search of the older black woman for some "young stuff." It was a form of revenge. Her biological father died in a car accident when she was

11; shortly after, her mother was hit by a truck and died on Christmas day. By age 15 she had borne two children (both the product of rape, and both given up for adoption).

Life became kinder as she grew into adulthood and was able to take control of her own destiny. She made a name for herself in vaudeville and collaborated on a play with the famed writer Zora Neale Hurston titled *Fast and Furious: A Colored Review in 37 Scenes.* Mabley starred in a short run of the play. She appeared on Broadway in *Blackberries of 1932* and met Pigmeat Markham, who was also in the show. This was the beginning of a comedy collaboration that would endure until the 1960s. In 1939, she joined an all-star black cast (Louis Armstrong, Butterfly McQueen, the Dandridge Sisters) in a "hep" Broadway jazz version of *A Midsummer Night's Dream* called *Swingin' the Dream.* It was clearly ahead of its time, closing after only 13 performances.

In the mid–1940s, Mabley started appearing in race films, which were intended for black audiences, fulfilling a need that Hollywood was not going to fulfill. She is credited with being in *The Big Timers* (1945), but does not show up in any extant prints, nor is her name in the credits. Mabley passed away only a year after she starred in the feature film *Amazing Grace* (1974). Although she had starred in a couple of black audience films — such as *Boarding House Blues* (1948), where she was the landlord to a group of down on their luck vaudevillians, and *Killer Diller* (also 1948; she performed along with other stars in a vaudeville-type format)—*Amazing Grace* was her first and only starring role in a mainstream feature. Unfortunately, *Amazing Grace* is not a fitting tribute to Moms Mabley. It's a tepid, almost child-like film (not too surprising, since the script was written by Matt Robinson, the original "Gordon" on *Sesame Street*).

Jackie "Moms" Mabley and Nipsey Russell in *Amazing Grace* (1974).

Another Mabley appearance was in the concert film *It's Your Thing* (1970), a hard film to track down these days. It also featured Ike and Tina Turner. Mabley suffered a heart attack about midway through the filming of *Amazing Grace*. She had a pacemaker installed and was able to complete the film, but you can see how debilitated she was in the scenes filmed after the heart attack. The film is priceless as a historical record.

Feature Films: *The Emperor Jones* (1933), *Big Timers* (unconfirmed; 1945), *Boarding House Blues* (1948), *Killer Diller* (1948), *The Cincinnati Kid* (1965), *Amazing Grace* (1974).

TV: *The Smothers Brothers Comedy Hour* (3 segments; 1967–68), *The Merv Griffin Show* (4 segments; 1967–70), *The Ed Sullivan Show* (3 segments; 1969–70), *It's Your Thing* (1970), *The Flip Wilson Show* (1970), *The Pearl Bailey Show* (1971), *The Tonight Show Starring Johnny Carson* (1972), *Mo' Funny: Black Comedy in America* (archival; 1993), *Who Makes You Laugh?* (archival; 1995), *50 Years of Funny Females* (archival; 1995), *American Masters* ("Vaudeville," archival; 1997), *Playboy: The Party Continues* (archival; 2000), *The "N" Word* (archival; 2004), *BET Comedy Awards* (archival; 2004).

MacLachlan, Janet Born in New York, NY, August 8, 1933.

Janet MacLachlan is the daughter of actress Samantha MacLachlan. She began appearing in films in 1968. She went on to co-star as Jackie Bruce in the sitcom *Love Thy Neighbor*, then was seen on *Friends* in 1979 as Mrs. Jane Summerfield. Her best known TV role is perhaps caustic housekeeper Polly Swanson in 1980–81 episodes of *Archie Bunker's Place*. She played Lieutenant Charlene Masters in the original *Star Trek* series episode "The Alternative Factor" (1967), and she played Dr. Montclair on the soap *Santa Barbara* in 1985.

Feature films she appeared in include *Sounder* (as Camille; 1972), *Heart and Souls* (as Agnes Miller; 1993) with Alfre Woodard, *Murphy's Law* (as Dr. Lovell) and *The Boy Who Could Fly* (as Mrs. D'Gregario; both 1986). Other films include *Up Tight!* (as Jeannie; 1968), *Halls of Anger* (as Lorraine Nash), and *Darker Than Amber* (as Noreen; both 1970). She was in the made-for-cable movie *The Tuskegee Airmen* (1995), as the mother of Hannibel Lee, leader of a black squadron of World War II fighter pilots.

Janet MacLachlan.

Her TV credits constitute a virtual history of the medium in the 1970s and 1980s: *Cagney & Lacey*; *Punky Brewster*; *Murder, She Wrote*; *Hill Street Blues*; *The Mary Tyler Moore Show*; *Quincy*; *Wonder Woman*; *The Bill Cosby Show*; *Golden Girls*; *Good Times*; *Trapper John, M.D.*; *Love Thy Neighbor*; *Six Million Dollar Man*; *Baretta*; *Mod Squad*; *Fantasy Island*; *All in the Family*; *The Rockford Files*; *swat*; *Police Story*; *I Spy*; *Beauty and the Beast*; *Barney Miller*; *Friends*. She also starred in the Emmy-winning PBS special *Voices of Our People: In Celebration of Black Poetry* (1982).

Feature Films including TV Movies: *Up Tight!* (1968), *Change of Mind* (1969), *...tick ...tick ...tick* (1969), *Halls of Anger* (1970), *Darker Than Amber* (1970), *Cutter* (TV; 1972), *The Man* (1972), *Sounder* (1972), *Trouble Comes to Town* (TV; 1973), *Maurie* (1973), *Louis Armstrong Chicago Style* (TV; 1976), *Dark Victory* (TV; 1976), *Roll of Thunder, Hear My Cry* (TV; 1978), *She's in the Army Now* (TV; 1981), *The Sophisticated Gents* (TV; 1981), *Valley of the Dolls* (TV; 1981), *The Other Victim* (TV; 1981), *The Kid from Nowhere* (TV; 1982), *Voices of Our People: In Celebration of Black Poetry* (1982), *For Us the Living: The Medgar Evers Story* (TV; 1983), *Thursday's Child* (TV; 1983), *Tightrope* (1984), *Toughlove*

(TV; 1985), *Murphy's Law* (1986), *The Boy Who Could Fly* (1986), *Baby Girl Scott* (TV; 1987), *Big Shots* (1987), *For Keeps?* (1988), *Killer Instinct* (TV; 1988), *A Family for Joe* (TV; 1990), *Runaway Father* (TV; 1991), *Something to Live For: The Alison Gertz Story* (TV; 1992), *Tracks of Glory* (TV; 1992), *Heart and Souls* (1993), *Criminal Passion* (1994), *There Goes My Baby* (1994), *Covenant* (1995), *The Tuskegee Airmen* (TV; 1995), *Pinocchio's Revenge* (1996), *The Big Squeeze* (1996), *My Last Love* (TV; 1999), *The Thirteenth Floor* (1999), *A Private Affair* (TV; 2000), *Black Listed* (2003).

TV: *The Alfred Hitchcock Hour* ("Completely Foolproof," "The Monkey's Paw: A Retelling," 1965), *Bob Hope Presents the Chrysler Theatre* ("Kicks," 1965), *The Fugitive* ("Second Sight," 1966), *Run for Your Life* ("A Game of Violence," 1966), *The F.B.I.* (3 episodes; "The Defector," Part II, "The Camel's Nose," "The Intermediary," 1966–68), *The Girl from U.N.C.L.E.* ("The U.F.O. Affair," 1967), *Star Trek* ("The Alternative Factor," 1967), *I Spy* ("Laya," 1967), *The Invaders* ("The Vise," 1968), *Ironside* ("Rundown on a Bum Rap," 1969), *My Friend Tony* ("Casino," 1969), *The Mod Squad* ("To Linc, with Love," 1969), *The Name of the Game* (3 episodes; "The Third Choice," "I Love You, Billy Baker," Parts I and II, 1969–70), *Insight* ("The Immigrant," 1971), *Longstreet* ("Elegy in Brass," 1971), *The Mary Tyler Moore Show* ("His Two Right Arms," 1972), *Ghost Story* ("Alter-Ego," 1972), *Love Thy Neighbor* (recurring role as Jackie Bruce; 1973), *Love Story* ("A Glow of Dying Embers," 1973), *Griff* ("Fugitive from Fear," 1974), *Police Story* ("Chain of Command," 1974), *The Streets of San Francisco* ("Rampage," 1974), *Medical Center* ("The Hostile Heart," 1974), *The Manhunter* ("To Kill a Tiger," 1975), *S.W.A.T.* ("Jungle War," 1975), *The Rockford Files* ("The Deep Blue Sleep," 1975), *The Six Million Dollar Man* ("The Blue Flash," 1975), *The Blue Knight* ("Triple Threat," 1975), *Ellery Queen* ("The Adventure of the Sunday Punch," 1976), *Barney Miller* ("Werewolf," 1976), *Baretta* ("Nuthin' for Nuthin'," 1976), *What's Happening!!* ("Shirley's Date," 1976), *Wonder Woman* (2 episodes in the role of Sakri; "Judgment from Outer Space," Parts I and II, 1977), *Most Wanted* ("The Hit Men," 1977), *Rafferty* ("The Narrow Thread," 1977), *Good Times* ("Florida Gets a Job," 1978), *All in the Family* ("The Family Next Door," 1979), *Friends* (recurring role as Jane Summerfield; 1979), *Archie Bunker's Place* (3 episodes in the role of Polly Swanson; "Archie Alone," Parts I and II, "Hiring the Housekeeper," 1980), *ABC Weekend Specials* ("Zack & The Magic Factory," 1981), *Voices of Our People: In Celebration of Black Poetry* (1982), *Cagney & Lacey* (6 episodes in the role of Lynne Sutter; 1982–87), *Quincy, M.E.* ("A Loss for Words," 1983), *Fantasy Island* ("Edward/The Extraordinary Miss Jones," 1983), *Hill Street Blues* ("Ewe and Me, Babe," 1984), *Trapper John, M.D.* ("Buckaroo Bob Rides Again," 1985), *Santa Barbara* (4 episodes in the role of Dr. Montclair; 1985), *Punky Brewster* ("The Search," 1985), *Murder, She Wrote* ("Jessica Behind Bars," "Time to Die," 1985–94), *L.A. Law* ("Raiders of the Lost Bark," 1986), *Our House* ("The Best Intentions," 1987), *Who's the Boss?* ("Raging Housekeeper," 1987), *The Golden Girls* ("Old Friends," 1987), *Moonlighting* ("Fetal Attraction," 1988), *Beauty and the Beast* ("Chamber Music," 1988), *Amen* (2 episodes; "Wedding Bell Blues," "Who's Sorry Now?" 1988 and 1990), *Wild Jack* (miniseries; 1989), *Murphy Brown* ("The Unspeakable Murphy Brown," 1989), *Free Spirit* ("The New Secretary," 1989), *Knots Landing* (2 episodes in the role of Susan Barbiza; "Never Judge a Book by Its Cover," "Twice Victim," 1989), *Midnight Caller* ("The Reverend Soundbite," 1990), *Father Dowling Mysteries* ("The Reasonable Doubt Mystery," 1990), *Gabriel's Fire* ("Tis the Season," 1990), *Reasonable Doubts* ("Dicky's Got the Blues," 1991), *In the Heat of the Night* ("Who was Geli Bendi?" 1994), *ER* ("Love Among the Ruins," 1995), *NYPD Blue* ("The Bank Dick," 1995), *Home Improvement* ("Doctor in the House," 1995), *Murder One* (3 episodes in the role of Mrs. Latrell; 1996–97), *Family Law* (2 episodes in the role of Judge Anne Taft; "Affairs of the State," "The Gay Divorcee," 2000–01), *Alias* ("Cipher," 2002).

MC Lyte Born in Queens, New York, October 11, 1971.

One of the architects of hip-hop, Lana Michelle Moorer, better known as MC Lyte, began rapping at age 12, started a professional career at age 15, and released an album at age 17 (*Lyte as a Rock*, 1988). That was the beginning. Her second album, *Eyes on This*, was out the following year, and the third release, *Act Like You Know*, was released in 1991. By 1993, she had a fourth album (*Ain't No Other*) and her first Grammy nomination for Best Rap Single, "Ruffneck," which was also the first gold single by a solo female rap artist. *Bad as I Wanna B.* (1996) and *The Underground Heat, Vol. 1* (2001) kept her on the charts, and she started an independent label.

While her career as a rapper set many precedents, it was only one side of the story. MC Lyte has also had an active and varied career as an actress. She did comic turns on *In Living Color, Half & Half, In the House* and *Moesha*, and tried police drama on *New York Undercover* and *The District*. In 2007, she became a celebrity coach on MTV's *Celebrity Rap Superstar*. She made her film debut in *Fly by Night* (as Akusa; 1993) and followed with roles in the prison drama *Civil Brand* (as Sgt. Cervantes; 2002) and the hip-hop comedy *Playas Ball* (as La Quinta; 2003). Her father is music executive Nat Robinson. Her two brothers are also musicians.

Feature Films including Video and TV Movies: *Sisters in the Name of Rap* (TV; 1992), *Fly by Night* (1993), *An Alan Smithee Film: Burn Hollywood Burn* (1998), *A Luv Tale* (1999), *Train Ride* (2000), *Civil Brand* (2002), *Playas Ball* (2003).

TV: *MTV Unplugged* (1991), *In Living Color* (2 episodes; 1992), *Late Night with Conan O'Brien* (1993), *The 9th Annual Soul Train Music Awards* (1995), *New York Undercover* (2 episodes; "You Get No Respect," "Kill the Noise," 1995 and 1996), *Moesha* ("A Concerted Effort," Part II, 1996), *The Rosie O'Donnell Show* (1997), *In the House* ("Working Overtime," Part II, 1998), *For Your Love* (4 episodes in the role of Lana; "The Cuckoo's Nest," "Accidental Doctor," "Pre-Nuptial Disagreement," "The Reunion," 1998–2002), *Get Real* ("Denial," 1999), *42nd Annual L.A. County Arts Commission Holiday Celebration* (2001), *Essence Awards* (2003), *Hip Hop Babylon 2* (2003), *I Love the '80s Strikes Back* (2003), *Apollo at 70: A Hot Night in Harlem* (2004), *4th Annual BET Awards* (2004), *Russell Simmons Presents Def Poetry* (2004), *And You Don't Stop: 30 Years of Hip-Hop* (2004), *Hip-Hop Honors* (2004), *My Wife and Kids* ("The Return of Bobby Shaw," 2004), *My Coolest Years* (2004), *Star Search* (judge; 2004), *There's a God on the Mic* (2005), *The District* ("Russian Winter," 2002), *Holla* (2002), *Platinum*

("Loyalty," 2003), *Strong Medicine* ("Prescriptions," 2003), *Half & Half* (recurring role of Kai Owens; 2004–06), *Black in the '80s* (2005), *Ego Trip's Race-O-Rama* (2005), *Love Lounge* ("Office Antics," "Getting It On-Line," 2005),

MC Lyte.

Live 8 (2005), *Kathy Griffin: My Life on the D-List* ("Adjusted Gross," 2005), *Made You Look: Top 25 Moments of BET History* (2005), *3rd Annual VH1 Hip-Hop Honors* (2006), *Ali Rap* (2006), *Bring That Year Back 2006: Laugh Now, Cry Later* (2006), *Parallel Paths* (2007), *Celebrity Rap Superstar* (2007), *Just In with Laura Ingraham* (2008), *Hip Hop vs. America II; Where Did Our Love Go?* (2008), *The Boot* (host; 2008), *Life on the Road Mr. and Mrs. Brown* (2008), *Whatever Happened to Hip-Hop?* (2008).

Shorts: *Da Jammies* (voice; 2006).

Video/DVD: *Female American Rap Stars* (2004), *From Janet, To Damita Jo: The Videos* (2004), *The Art of 16 Bars: Get Ya' Bars Up* (2005), *Letter to the President* (2005), *Hip Hop Life* (2007).

McBroom, Marcia (aka McBroom-Small, Marsha) Born in New York, New York, August 6, 1947.

Dancer, actress and fashion model Marcia McBroom comes from a politically active family and was very much a part of the revolutionary sixties. She is known for her role as Pet in Russ Meyer's *Beyond the Valley of the Dolls* (1970), with a script by film critic Roger Ebert. Pet and her friends Kelly (Dolly Read) and Casey (Cynthia Myers) form the group The Carrie Nations, who worm their way in to the Los Angeles party scene and meet bizarre music producer Ronnie "Z-Man" Barzell, who turns them into superstars. But in true *Valley of the Dolls* fashion (which this tongue-in-cheek film parodies hilariously), the ladies in the group fall prey to the evils of the show business world. Pet, the drummer, sleeps around with her lawyer boyfriend and pays dearly for her sexual freedom; Kelly, the lead singer, gets used and abused by a male gigolo; and Casey, the bass guitarist, succumbs to pills, booze and lesbianism. *Beyond the Valley of the Dolls* is one of the great oddball films, it defines the term "cult classic," and it was a substantial box office hit. It was also Marcia McBroom's first and only leading role.

Feature Films: *Beyond the Valley of the Dolls* (1970), *The Legend of Nigger Charley* (1972), *Come Back, Charleston Blue* (1972), *Jesus Christ Superstar* (1973), *Willie Dynamite* (1974), *The Bingo Long Traveling All-Stars and Motor Kings* (1976), *New York Nights* (1984).

McDaniel, Hattie Born in Wichita, Kansas, June 10, 1893.

Hattie McDaniel was the thirteenth child of Susan and Rev. Henry McDaniel. Soon after she was born, the family moved to Denver, Colorado. Children of a former slave, the McDaniel siblings rebelled against the societal restraints that forced them into menial labor. For example, McDaniel's older brother Otis drew cartoons and could sing and dance. In the early 1900s, he wrote, constructed the scenery for, and cast the play *The Isles of Pingapoo*, which received very favorable reviews. He later took eight-year-old Hattie to a carnival where she sang and danced. The spectators tossed coins, and by the end of the week she had earned five dollars, which she gave to her parents. McDaniel continued to perform, often with her siblings, until she was old enough to travel by herself to engagements at out-of-town tent shows.

Martha O'Driscoll and Hattie McDaniel in *Hi, Beautiful* (1944).

At age 17 she met and fell in love with Howard Hickman, a talented pianist with connections in the black entertainment community. He was the first black person in Denver to play accompaniment at silent films. The couple married in 1911. They worked at menial jobs during the day and pursued their show business careers at night. But only a few years later Hickman became ill and died of pneumonia. He was 26 and McDaniel was only 21. McDaniel was devastated and moved back home with her parents, temporarily withdrawing from the entertainment world. She gradually overcame her grief, and in 1931 she moved to Hollywood and made her movie debut in *The Golden West*. Over the next 20 years, she purportedly appeared in more than 300 films in bits and walk-ons without receiving screen credit. She also landed a role on the radio show *The Optimistic Do-Nut Hour*.

In 1939 she achieved perhaps the single greatest achievement by an African American performer by becoming the first ever black person to win an Academy Award for her role as Mammy in *Gone with the Wind* (1939). In 1941 she eloped with real estate dealer James Lloyd Crawford. Even in the racial climate of the times, McDaniel gave a subtle, non-stereotyped performance in *In This Our Life* (1942). But the movie roles eventually started to dry up, and it was a maid role that resurrected her latter day career.

In 1947 she signed a contract to star in *Beulah* on the radio. Her contract stipulated that she would not use dialect and that she could demand the right to alter any script that did not meet with her approval. When *The Beulah Show* premiered on television in 1950, Ethel Waters was cast at the lead, but quickly had her own problems with the character and the scripts. McDaniels took over the role (and was wonderful in it), but she suffered a heart attack and was replaced by Louise Beavers. She recovered, but in 1952 she had a stroke. Later that year she was diagnosed with breast cancer and passed away.

Feature Films: *Love Bound* (1932), *Impatient Maiden* (1932), *Are You Listening?* (1932), *The Washington Masquerade* (1932), *The Boiling Point* (1932), *Crooner* (1932), *Blonde Venus* (1932), *The Golden West* (1932), *Hypnotized* (1932), *Hello, Sister* (1933), *I'm No Angel* (1933), *Goodbye Love* (1933), *Mickey's Rescue* (1934), *Merry Wives of Reno* (1934), *Operator 13* (1934), *King Kelly of the U.S.A.* (1934), *Judge Priest* (1934), *Flirtation* (1934), *Lost in the Stratosphere* (1934), *Fate's Fathead* (1934), *Babbitt* (1934), *Little Men* (1934), *The Chases of Pimple Street* (1934), *Anniversary Trouble* (1935), *Okay Toots!* (1935), *The Little Colonel* (1935), *Transient Lady* (1935), *Traveling Saleslady* (1935), *Wig-Wag* (1935), *The Four Star Boarder* (1935), *China Seas* (1935), *Alice Adams* (1935), *Murder by Television* (1935), *Harmony Lane* (1935), *Music Is Magic* (1935), *Another Face* (1935), *We're Only Human* (1935), *Can This Be Dixie?* (1936), *High Tension* (1936), *Next Time We Love* (1936), *The First Baby* (1936), *The Singing Kid* (1936), *Gentle Julia* (1936), *Arbor Day* (1936), *Show Boat* (1936), *The Bride Walks Out* (1936), *Postal Inspector* (1936), *Star for a Night* (1936), *Valiant Is the Word for Carrie* (1936), *Libeled Lady* (1936), *Reunion* (1937), *Mississippi Moods* (1937), *Racing Lady* (1937), *Don't Tell the Wife* (1937), *The Crime Nobody Saw* (1937), *The Wildcatter* (1937), *Saratoga* (1937), *Stella Dallas* (1937), *Sky Racket* (1937), *Over the Goal* (1937), *Merry Go Round of 1938* (1937), *Nothing Sacred* (1937), *45 Fathers* (1937), *Quick Money* (1937), *True Confession* (1937), *Battle of Broadway* (1938), *Vivacious Lady* (1938), *The Shopworn Angel* (1938), *Carefree* (1938), *The Mad Miss Manton* (1938), *The Shining Hour* (1938), *Everybody's Baby* (1939), *Zenobia* (1939), *Gone with the Wind* (1939), *Maryland* (1940), *The Great Lie* (1941), *Affectionately Yours* (1941), *They Died with Their Boots On* (1941), *The Male Animal* (1942), *In This Our Life* (1942), *George Washington Slept Here* (1942), *Johnny Come Lately* (1943), *Thank Your Lucky Stars* (1943), *Since You Went Away* (1944), *Janie* (1944), *Three Is a Family* (1944), *Hi, Beautiful* (1944), *Janie Gets Married* (1946), *Margie* (1946), *Never Say Goodbye* (1946), *Song of the South* (1946), *The Flame* (1947), *Mickey* (1948), *Family Honeymoon* (1949), *The Big Wheel* (1949).

TV: *The Ed Wynn Show* (1949), *The Beulah Show* (aka *Beulah*, 1952), *Black History: Lost, Stolen or Strayed* (archival; 1968), *The Making of a Legend: Gone with the Wind* (archival; 1988), *John Ford* (archival; 1990), *Mo' Funny: Black Comedy in America* (archival; 1993), *The Young and the Dead* (archival; 2000), *Beyond Tara: The Extraordinary Life of Hattie McDaniel* (archival; 2001), *Corazon de....* (archival; 2006).

Video/DVD: *TV in Black: The First Fifty Years* (archival; 2004).

McDonald, Audra

Born in Berlin, Germany, July 3, 1970.

Although best known as a multi–Tony winning Broadway star, Audra McDonald has been doing an increasing amount of television and feature film work in recent years. Born in Berlin, she was raised in Fresno, California, the older of two daughters. She graduated from the Roosevelt School of the Arts program of Roosevelt High School in Fresno. Then she studied classical voice at Juilliard, graduating in 1993. McDonald had already won three Tony Awards by age 28 — for *Carousel* (1994), *Master Class* (1995) and *Ragtime* (1998). She was then nominated for a Tony for her performance in *Marie Christine* (1999), before winning a fourth Tony in 2004 for the revival of *A Raisin in the Sun*, and she won the Drama League Award and the Outer Critics Circle Award. (She reprised her role in the 2008 ABC TV movie.) She last appeared on Broadway as the "plain Jane" dustbowl girl Lizzie, who blossoms when a handsome, charismatic preacher comes to town in the revival of *110 in the Shade* (2007), based on the film *The Rainmaker*). This brought her a sixth Tony nomination, and she won the Drama Desk Award for Best Actress in a Musical. McDonald performed as an opera singer in *The Seven Deadly Sins: A Song Cycle* (2005), *La Voix Humane* (2006) and Kurt Weill's *Rise and Fall of the City of Mahagonny* (2007).

She was awarded an Emmy for Outstanding Supporting Actress for the HBO film *Wit* (2001), directed by Mike Nichols. In 1999's TV remake of Broadway's *Annie*, she was cast as Daddy Warbucks' secretary, Miss Farrell, who accepts his marriage proposal in the final scene. Many preferred this TV version to the John Huston film (1982), and McDonald's charming performance had much to do with that. Another memorable TV movie is *Having Our Say: The Delany Sisters' First 100 Years* (1999), in flashbacks as the young Bessie Delany in her twenties. Guest star series work includes *Homicide: Life on the Street* and *Law & Order: Special Victims Unit*. McDonald appears as Naomi Bennett, ex-wife of the Sam character (Taye Diggs) in *Private Practice* (2007–08), a spin-off of *Grey's Anatomy*.

Her feature films include *Seven Servants* (1996), *The Object of My Affection* (1998), *Cradle Will Rock* (1999), *It Runs in the Family* (2003), and *Best Thief in the World* (2004). She recorded four albums for Nonesuch Records: *Way Back to Paradise* (1998), *How Glory Goes* (2000), *Happy Songs* (2002), and *Build a Bridge* (2006). McDonald is married to bassist Peter Donovan (2000–present); they have a daughter, Zöe Madeline. In 2007, McDonald's father was killed when an experimental plane he was flying crashed.

Feature Films including TV Movies: *Seven Servants* (1996), *The Object of My Affection* (1998), *Having Our Say: The Delany Sisters' First 100 Years* (TV; 1999), *Cradle Will Rock* (1999), *Annie* (TV; 1999), *The Last Debate* (TV; 2000), *Wit* (TV; 2001), *Partners and Crime* (TV; 2003), *It Runs in the Family* (2003), *Tea Time with Roy and Sylvia* (2003), *The Best Thief in the World* (2004), *A Raisin in the Sun* (TV; 2008).

TV: *The 48th Annual Tony Awards* (1994), *Some Enchanted Evening: Celebrating Oscar Hammerstein II* (1995), *The 49th Annual Tony Awards* (1995), *Leonard Bernstein's New York* (1997), *Christmas in Washington* (1998), *The 52nd Annual Tony Awards* (1998), *Great Performances* (2 segments; "Carnegie Hall Opening Night 1998," "My Favorite Broadway: The Leading Ladies," 1999), *The Rosie O'Donnell Show* (3 segments; 1998–99), *The 53rd Annual Tony Awards* (1999), *Homicide: Life on the Street* ("Forgive Us Our Trespasses," 1999), *Law & Order: Special Victims Unit* (2 episodes in the role of Audrey Jackson; "Contact," "Slaves," 2000), *The 55th Annual Tony Awards* (2001), *Divas on Ice* (2001), *The Kennedy Center Honors: A Celebration of the Performing Arts* (2001), *Mister Sterling* (recurring role as Jackie Brock; 2003), *The 58th Annual Tony Awards* (2004), *Broadway: The American Musical* (6 episodes; 2004), *Character Studies* (2005), *The 60th Annual Tony Awards* (2006), *The Megan Mullally Show* (2006), *Great Performances: Live from Lincoln Center* (3 segments; "American Songbook: Audra McDonald and Friends Build a Bridge," "Audra McDonald Sings the Movies for New Year's Eve with Members of the New York Philharmonic," "Passion," 2006), *The Bedford Diaries* (recurring role of Prof. Carla Bonatelle; 2006), *Kidnapped* (3 episodes in the role of Jackie Hayes; pilot, "Number One with a Bullet," "Front Page," 2006–07), *Tavis Smiley* (2 segments; 2007), *The View* (2 segments; 2007), *Entertainment Tonight* (2007), *Private Practice* (recurring role of Dr. Naomi Bennett; 2007–08), *Broadway: The Next Generation* (2009).

McGee, Vonetta Born in San Francisco, California, January 14, 1940.

World-class beauty Vonetta McGee — arguably one of the most beautiful women in film history — amassed a filmography of mainstream Hollywood fare and blaxploitation films, including some of the best black cult films of her era.

She attended Polytechnic High School and San Francisco State University in the sixties and joined a socially aware black theater group called The Aldridge Players West. Then she went to Italy and immediately landed starring roles in some interesting films, including what was her first film: *Faustina* (1968). Faustina (McGee) is the offspring of a black soldier and a Roman woman who met during World War II. She has to choose between two Italian lovers in this romantic comedy. Her second film, director Sergio Corbucci's *Il grande silenzio* (*The Great Silence*; 1968) is considered a classic by many fans of the Italian western. McGee pays Pauline, a townswoman who becomes romantically involved with the hero, who is named Silence (Jean-Louis Trintignant). Klaus Kinski dominates the film as the heartless, sadistic villain Tigrero (better known as Loco). Extremely atmospheric and well made on all counts, this remains one very depressing film (don't expect a happy ending).

Her next Italian film was *Io monaca ... per*

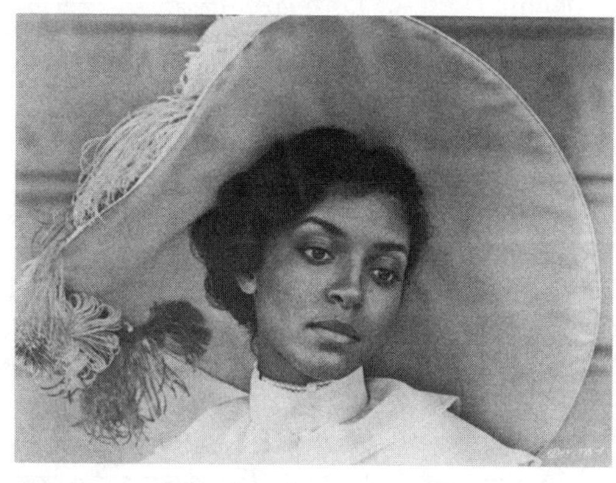

Vonetta McGee in *Thomasine and Bushrod* (1974).

Vonetta McGee, lobby card for *Detroit 9000* (1972).

tre carogne e sette peccatrici (1972), widely released in the U.S. in 1974 by New World Pictures as *The Big Bust Out.* It was directed by Sergio Garrone, and even though McGee is top billed she is brutally whipped and dies from her wounds about halfway through the film. She is one of seven women who escape from a maximum security prison dressed as nuns. She began her career in American films with a small role in the Sidney Poitier vehicle *The Lost Man* (1969), a downbeat tale about a militant black man who commits a robbery and falls in love with a white woman (Poitier's real life wife, Joanna Shimkus).

McGee was front and center for the era of blaxploitation films, including rarely seen (these days) films like *Melinda* (1972) and *Thomasine & Bushrod* (1974). Directed by Gordon Parks, Jr., *Thomasine & Bushrod* was obviously inspired by Bonnie and Clyde. A male-female black outlaw team from the early 20th century (McGee and Max Julien, with whom she had a long live-in relationship) rob from the rich and redistribute the wealth among the poor. The script was a perfect reflection of the militant black power era — which is one reason why the film is so difficult to see today. *Melinda* is, if anything, an even more rare film. A charismatic DJ (Calvin Lockhart) falls in love with the mysterious Melinda (McGee). When she is found dead in his apartment, the mob tries to frame him for the murder.

In *Blacula* (1972) — *the* black horror movie — McGee is Tina, the reincarnation of the vampire Prince Mamuwalde's long-lost wife, Luva. The film is a fast-paced mélange of horror, tongue-in-cheek humor, police detective thriller — and Vonetta McGee at her loveliest. By 1973, McGee was everywhere: on the cover of *Jet* magazine, and on movie screens throughout America in the second Shaft sequel, *Shaft in Africa*, and in the excellent police thriller *Detroit 9000*, which contains perhaps McGee's best performance, as an ill-fated police informer.

The Eiger Sanction (1975) looked to be McGee's breakthrough movie — here was a black actress cast in a leading role with a white male co-star — but it was more like her swan song. Not one of the big Eastwood hits, he also directed this misfire about Jonathan Hemlock, an art teacher and collector who moonlights as an assassin for a government bureau. McGee was his confrere,

Jemima Brown. The hope was that this would be a Bond-like series for Eastwood — since it was based on a best-selling series of novels — but it went nowhere.

In the 1980s, as opportunities for black women in films began to wane quickly, McGee started showing up on television, including in a recurring role on *Cagney & Lacey*, on an episode of *L.A. Law*, and in TV movies like *Superdome* (1978) and *Scruples* (1981). In 1987 she married actor Carl Lumbly; they had one child.

Feature Films including TV Movies: *Faustina* (1968), *Il grande silenzio* (aka *The Great Silence*, 1968), *The Lost Man* (1969), *The Kremlin Letter* (1970), *Io monaca ... per tre carogne e sette peccatrici* (aka *The Big Bust Out*, 1972), *Melinda* (1972), *Blacula* (1972), *Hammer* (1972), *The Norliss Tapes* (TV; 1973), *Shaft in Africa* (1973), *Detroit 9000* (1972), *Thomasine & Bushrod* (1974), *The Eiger Sanction* (1975), *Woo Fook* (aka *Foxbat*, 1977), *Brothers* (1977), *Superdome* (TV; 1978), *Scruples* (TV; 1981), *Repo Man* (1984), *To Sleep with Anger* (1990), *Stormy Weathers* (TV; 1992), *The Man Next Door* (TV; 1996), *Johnny B Good* (1998).

TV: *Western, Italian Style* (1968), *Soul Train* (1973), *Police Woman* ("Don't Feed the Pigeons," 1975), *Starsky and Hutch* ("Black and Blue," 1978), *A Man Called Sloane* ("Architect of Evil," 1979), *Diff'rent Strokes* ("Friendly-Mate," 1980), *Whiz Kids* ("Candidate for Murder," 1983), *Magnum, P.I.* ("The Case of the Red-Faced Thespian," 1984), *The Yellow Rose* ("Sport of Kings," 1984), *Cagney & Lacey* (4 episodes as Claudia Petrie; "Child Witness," "Entrapment," "Role Call," "Revenge," 1984–86), *Hell Town* (series regular in the role of Sister Indigo; 1985), *Bustin' Loose* (series regular in the role of Mimi Shaw; 1987), *The 7th Annual Black Achievement Awards* (1987), *Amen* ("The Divorce Lawyer," 1987), *20th NAACP Image Awards* (1988), *L.A. Law* (7 episodes in the role of Jackie Williams; 1989–90), *Wonderworks* (2 episodes; "Brother Future," "You Must Remember This," 1991–92), *Perry Mason: The Case of the Reckless Romeo* (1992), *Cagney & Lacey: The Return* (1994).

McKee, Lonette Born in Detroit, Michigan, July 22, 1954.

Lonette McKee has excelled in theater, on records and in clubs, and in films and on television. She was a child prodigy who played piano at age seven and recorded her first record at age fourteen. Her father is of African American and her mother is of European descent. She has a sister named Kathrine. She appeared in the soap opera *As the World Turns* for two years (1997–98), guest starred on such series as *Amen*, *The Equalizer*, and *Law & Order: Special Victims Unit*, and she had a recurring role as Maggie Davis on *Third Watch* (1999–2003).

She initially appeared on Broadway in the musical *The First* (1981), playing the wife of baseball's Jackie Robinson. McKee was nominated for a Tony for her role as Julie LaVerne in the revival of *Show Boat* (the first black woman to play Julie in a major stage production; 1994) and Received a Drama Desk Award for her impressive turn as Billie Holliday in the one-woman drama *Lady Day at Emerson's Bar and Grill* (1986).

She made her feature film debut in *Sparkle* (1974), about the trials and tribulations of a musical girl group. She was also in the Richard Pryor comedy *Which Way Is Up?* (1977), Francis Ford

Vonetta McGee, lobby card for *Detroit 9000* (1972).

Lonette McKee and Dexter Gordon in *Round Midnight* (1986).

Coppola's big budget *The Cotton Club* (1984), and Spike Lee's *Jungle Fever* (1991), *Malcolm X* (1992) and *He Got Game* (1998). *The Cotton Club*, Coppola's film in the wake of *The Godfather*, was purportedly the story of the legendary Harlem nightclub, and looked likely to propel McKee into stardom, but the black characters got amazingly short shrift, and most of the film focused on the romance between the Richard Gere and Diane Lane characters. It was not a box office success.

She appeared in the acclaimed film *Lift* (2001), co-starring Kerry Washington, which was shown on Showtime and premiered at the Sundance Film Festival. Another key role is in director Bertrand Tavenier's *Round Midnight* (1986), where she sings while accompanied by the great saxophonist Dexter Gordon. It is perhaps her most memorable big screen moment.

She was nominated for two NAACP Image Awards for her roles on *As the World Turns* and in the TV movie murder mystery *To Dance with Olivia* (as Olivia "Libby" Stewart; 1997). Her record albums include *Natural Love* (1992). McKee studied film direction at the New School in Manhattan and was an adjunct professor at Centenary College, where she taught an acting workshop.

Feature Films including TV Movies: *Sparkle* (1976), *Which Way Is Up?* (1977), *Cuba* (1979), *Illusions* (1982), *The Cotton Club* (1984), *Brewster's Millions* (1985), *'Round Midnight* (1986), *Gardens of Stone* (1987), *Dangerous Passion* (TV; 1990), *Jungle Fever* (1991), *Malcolm X* (1992), *To Dance with Olivia* (TV; 1997), *Blind Faith* (1998), *He Got Game* (1998), *A Day in Black and White* (1999), *Having Our Say: The Delany Sisters' First 100 Years* (TV; 1999), *Fast Food Fast Women* (2000), *Men of Honor* (2000), *Lift* (2001), *For Love of Olivia* (TV; 2001), *The Paper Mache Chase* (2003), *Honey* (2003), *She Hate Me* (2004), *Dream Street* (2005), *ATL* (2006).

TV: *Soul Train* (1975), *The Equalizer* ("Reign of Terror," 1985), *The 57th Annual Academy Awards* (1985), *Miami Vice* ("Stone's War," 1986), *Amen* ("The Psychic," Parts I and II, 1989), *The Women of Brewster Place* (miniseries; 1989), *L.A. Law* ("There Goes the Judge," 1991), *Alex Haley's Queen* (miniseries; 1993), *Some Enchanted Evening: Celebrating Oscar Hammerstein II* (1995), *The 49th Annual Tony Awards* (1995), *As the World Turns* (1997–98), *Third Watch* (recurring role of Maggie Davis; 1999–2003), *Law & Order: Special Victim's Unit* ("Chameleon," 2002), *Half & Half* ("The Big Thanks for Nothing Episode," 2004), *1-800-Missing* ("Exposure," 2006), *The Game* ("It's Hard Being Kelly Pitts," 2007).

McKinney, Nina Mae Born in Lancaster, South Carolina, June 12, 1913; died May 3, 1967.

This seminal black actress deserves rediscovery in the way that icons such as Anna Mae Wong and Josephine Baker have been reassessed and rediscovered. Although Nina Mae McKinney didn't have the opportunity to develop a formidable filmography, her role in King Vidor's *Hallelujah!* (1929) and surviving footage of her song and dance routines shows that she was a major talent.

Christened Nannie Mayme, she grew up with her great aunt. She displayed a talent for dance at a very young age. As her dance style evolved, it became gangly, athletic, knowingly sexy. She performed her dance routines on the local level and in school productions until she moved to New York at age 13 to join her mother, Georgia Crawford McKinney. Her big breakthrough came in the 1928 Broadway musical Lew Leslie's *Blackbirds of 1928*. It was here that she was

Nina Mae McKinney.

seen by director King Vidor and chosen for a role in the landmark early talkie *Hallelujah!*

Although MGM was impressed enough to sign McKinney to a five-year contract, little came of it — there was a role in the film *Safe in Hell* (1931) and an assignment dubbing Jean Harlow's singing voice in *Reckless* (1935). And the poor box office response to *Hallelujah!* certainly did nothing for her career. The amazing thing about *Hallelujah!*— and the factor that ultimately killed its chances — is that it was a mainstream production featuring black actors and an almost documentary-like black story. If the film had done well, the course of black film history might have been radically altered. McKinney had nowhere to go in the racial climate of the day. She quickly wound up where she "belonged"— in "race films," with occasional small roles in mainstream films. Even in the memorable *Pinky* (1949), much later in her career, her brief and rather thankless role is little more than a stereotype.

Her stunning performance, at age 16, as the pathetic con woman Chick in *Hallelujah!* should have been good enough to guarantee her an Academy Award nomination. *Hallelujah!* was a showcase for McKinney; the film took advantage of her acting as well as her dancing and singing talents. Although her performance suggests a darker (as in evil) Clara Bow — McKinney channels Bow's unsteady grace and extravagant sexuality pretty closely — the role is distinctive for its quintessential blackness. Chick takes her place in the gallery of great film characters. McKinney's dance in the film, the Swanee Shuffle, proved quite popular, striking a chord with young black girls across America. There is more than a bit of Chick in Dorothy Dandridge's performance in *Carmen Jones*.

Lesser McKinney films worth noting include *The Devil's Daughter* (aka *Pocomania*; 1939), a horror film aimed at black audiences. She gives this campy, threadbare production whatever value it has. In *Gun Smashers* (aka *Gun Moll*; 1938), another race movie, we get to see McKinney in a film noir–crime film context. The poster for the film is especially striking, and the prominent billing shows what a major star McKinney was with black audiences.

Like so many black performers before and after her — from Josephine Baker to Nina Simone — McKinney took her act to Europe, traveling to Paris, London, Dublin and Budapest. World War II led her to return to New York, where she married jazz musician Jimmy Monroe and toured the country with his band. McKinney lived in Athens, Greece, in the 1950s and 1960s, where she continued to perform on the nightclub scene. She moved to New York shortly before passing away in 1967. There are unconfirmed rumors that she worked as a maid in her later years, and that she was having problems with drugs and alcohol. Although her death was little remarked upon, indeed barely noticed, McKinney's renown has continued to grow in the intervening years.

Feature Films: *Hallelujah!* (1929), *They Learned About Women* (uncredited; 1930), *Passing the Buck* (1932), *Safe in Hell* (aka *The Lost Lady*) (1931), *Pie, Pie Blackbird* (1932), *Kentucky Minstrels* (uncredited; 1934), *Sanders of the River* (1935), *Reckless* (1935), *The Black Network* (1936), *The Lonely Trail* (uncredited; 1936), *On Velvet* (1938), *Gun Smashers* (aka *Gun Moll*) (1938), *The Devil's Daughter* (aka *Pocomania*; 1939), *Straight to Heaven* (1939), *Swanee Showboat* (1940), *Dark Waters* (1944), *Together Again* (uncredited; 1944), *The Power of the Whistler* (uncredited; 1945), *Mantan Messes Up* (1946), *Night Train to Memphis* (1946), *Danger Street* (1947), *Pinky* (1949), *Copper Canyon* (uncredited; 1950), *Bessie Smith and Friends: 1929–1942* (archival; 1986).

McNair, Barbara Born in Racine, Wisconsin, March 4, 1934; died February 4, 2007, Los Angeles, California.

A Las Vegas headliner who starred in her own TV variety show and had a brief but impressive film career, Barbara Joan McNair opened far more doors for black women than she is generally given credit for. Her father, Horace McNair, was a factory foreman. She studied at the Racine Conservatory and the American Conservatory of Music in Chicago, and was a student at ucla for one year in the 1950s before heading to New York City, where she did secretarial work, hoping to score as an entertainer.

Her first top-level booking was at the Village Vanguard in 1957, which led to her Broadway debut in the short-lived musical *The Body Beautiful* (a two-month run in 1958), and a week's stint on *Arthur Godfrey's Talent Scouts*, then one of the top-rated TV programs. Then she co-hosted her own variety series, the virtually forgotten half-hour local ABC-TV show *Schaeffer Circle* on Sat-

Barbara McNair and Raymond St. Jacques in *If He Hollers, Let Him Go* (1968).

urday night in the early sixties. She also performed in stage revues with Nat King Cole (*I'm with You*, *The Merry World of Nat King Cole*). She is best known on the Great White Way as Diahann Carroll's replacement in the hit *No Strings* in 1963. Ten years later she starred with Hal Linden in an interracial revival of *The Pajama Game* and toured with *Sophisticated Ladies* in Berlin, Germany.

McNair gained increasing fame as a nightclub singer in the 1960s (prime bookings included the Persian Room at New York's Plaza Hotel and The Coconut Grove in L.A.), and took advantage of the opportunities in TV that opened up for black women as the decade continued. Her biggest single was "You Could Never Love Him," although McNair's forte was as an overall entertainer rather than as a hit maker. This and many of her best sixties recordings can be heard on the 2004 British import CD *Barbara McNair: The Ultimate Motown Collection*.

McNair did well in films for a time in the late 1960s and early 1970s. Her film debut in 1968's *If He Hollers, Let Him Go* saw her cast as a nightclub singer — not a big stretch, of course — and she garnered publicity for her explicit nude scene, which was featured in men's magazines like *Playboy* and *Knight*. She began getting roles opposite major stars, such as Elvis Presley in *Change of Habit* (1969). McNair played a nun in what turned out to be Presley's last non-documentary film appearance. Her most prominent film role was as Virgil Tibbs' (Sidney Poitier) wife in *They Call Me Mister Tibbs!* (1970), an unexceptional sequel to *In the Heat of the Night* (1967), and *The Organization* (1971), the third and thankfully the last of the increasingly tepid Tibbs series. One of her best-acted roles was in director Jesus Franco's *Venus in Furs* (1970), a hallucinogenic supernatural thriller. McNair, in one of her most shaded performances, was Rita, a nightclub singer who falls in love with a white musician (James Darren) obsessed with the spirit of a dead woman (Maria Rohm).

In the 1960s she appeared on *Dr. Kildare*, *I*

Spy, and *Hogan's Heroes*. The 1970s saw her making the TV variety show circuit: *The Flip Wilson Show*, *The Sonny and Cher Comedy Hour*, and appearing on police dramas like *Police Woman* and *McMillan & Wife*. In the 1980s she guest starred on sitcoms like *The Redd Foxx Show* and *The Jeffersons*, and had a recurring role on the daytime drama *General Hospital* as Aunt Bettina in 1984. She wrote the book *The Complete Book of Beauty for Black Women*, coauthored with Stephen Lewis (Prentice-Hall, 1972).

After two previous marriages, McNair married Rick Manzie, a shadowy figure with probable Mafia attachments who was shot to death in 1976. In 1972 she and Manzie were charged with heroin possession; although she was later cleared of the charges, her career suffered as a result. At the time of her death she was married to Charles Blecka.

She died of throat cancer at age 72.

Feature Films including TV Movies: *Spencer's Mountain* (1963), *The Unkissed Bride* (aka *Mother Goose a Go-Go*, 1966), *If He Hollers, Let Him Go!* (1968), *Stiletto* (1969), *Venus in Furs* (1969), *The Lonely Profession* (TV; 1969), *Change of Habit* (1969), *They Call Me Mister Tibbs!* (1970), *The Organization* (1971), *Fatal Charm* (TV; 1990), *Neon Signs* (1996).

TV: *The Ed Sullivan Show* (7 segments; 1957–1970), *The Jack Paar Tonight Show* (1958), *The Arlene Francis Show* (2 segments; 1958), *The Steve Allen Show* (1958), *Sing Along with Mitch* (1961), *The New Steve Allen Show* (1961), *The Eleventh Hour* ("Who Is to Say the Battle Is to Be Fought?" 1964), *Dr. Kildare* ("The Elusive Dik-Dik," 1964), *The Bell Telephone Hour* (3 episodes; episode #6.11, "Lyrics by Oscar Hammerstein," "Valentine's Day," 1964–66), *You Don't Say* (2 segments; 1964–75), *Hullabaloo* (1965), *Art Linkletter's Hollywood Talent Scouts* (1966), *The Hollywood Palace* (2 segments; 1965–67), *The 38th Annual Academy Awards* (1966), *Mickie Finn's* (1966), *The Dean Martin Show* (2 segments; 1966), *Tienerklanken* (1967), *I Spy* ("Night Train to Madrid," 1967), Hogan's Heroes ("Is General Hammerschlag Burning?" 1967), *Rowan & Martin at the Movies* (1968), *The Jonathan Winters Show* (1968), *Playboy After Dark* (1969), *The Barbara McNair Show* (1969), *This Is Tom Jones* (1970), *The 42nd Annual Academy Awards* (1970), *To Rome with Love* ("Live from Heaven," 1970), *The Gordon McCrea Variety Special* (1971), *Password* (1971), *Rollin' on the River* (1971), *The Tonight Show Starring Johnny Carson* (2 segments; 1971–73), *The 26th Annual Tony Awards* (1972), *The Sonny and Cher Comedy Hour* (1972), *McMillan & Wife* ("An Elementary Case of Murder," 1972), *The Mod Squad* ("The Connection," 1972), *The Flip Wilson Show* (2 segments; 1972–73), *Jack Paar Tonite* (1973), *Mission: Impossible* ("Imitation," 1973), *Celebrity Sweepstakes* (1974), *Police Woman* ("Sixth Sense," 1978), *Vega$* (2 episodes in the role of Beverly; "Yes, My Darling Daughter," "Lady Ice," 1978), *The Jeffersons* ("George's Old Girlfriend," 1984), *General Hospital* (recurring role as Aunt Bettina; 1984), *Hell Town* ("One Ball," 1985), *The Redd Foxx Show* ("Al's First Date," 1986).

McNeil, Claudia Born in Baltimore, Maryland, August 13, 1917; died November 25, 1993, Englewood, New Jersey.

Claudia McNeil was a former librarian who came to acting late in life, and also became a singer. McNeil was the new generation and the new breed of black actress. She played archetypal "strong black women" roles — a refreshing change from all those years when black women were offered little but domestic servant roles. She is best known for her starring role as matriarch Lena Younger in the stage and screen versions of *A Raisin in the Sun*, and was twice nominated for a Tony Award as Best Dramatic Actress for *A Raisin in the Sun* (1959) and *Tiger, Tiger Burning Bright* (1962). She was nominated for a Golden Globe Award for the screen version of the play (1961). She appeared in a 1981 production of the musical version of the play called simply *Raisin*, presented by the Equity Library Theater.

Her parents were Marvin Spencer and Annie Mae Anderson McNeil; her mother was an Apache Indian. She was raised by her mother after her father left the family. She was adopted by a Jewish family she first met at age 12 when she was working for the Hecksher Foundation, but was raised as a Catholic. She was married when she was 18 to a man who died in World War II. Her second marriage ended in divorce after two years; the marriage produced one son (who was killed in the Korean War).

McNeil sang with the Katherine Dunham Dance Troupe on its South American Tour. She made her stage debut as Tituba in Arthur Miller's *The Crucible* at the Martin Beck Theater. Four

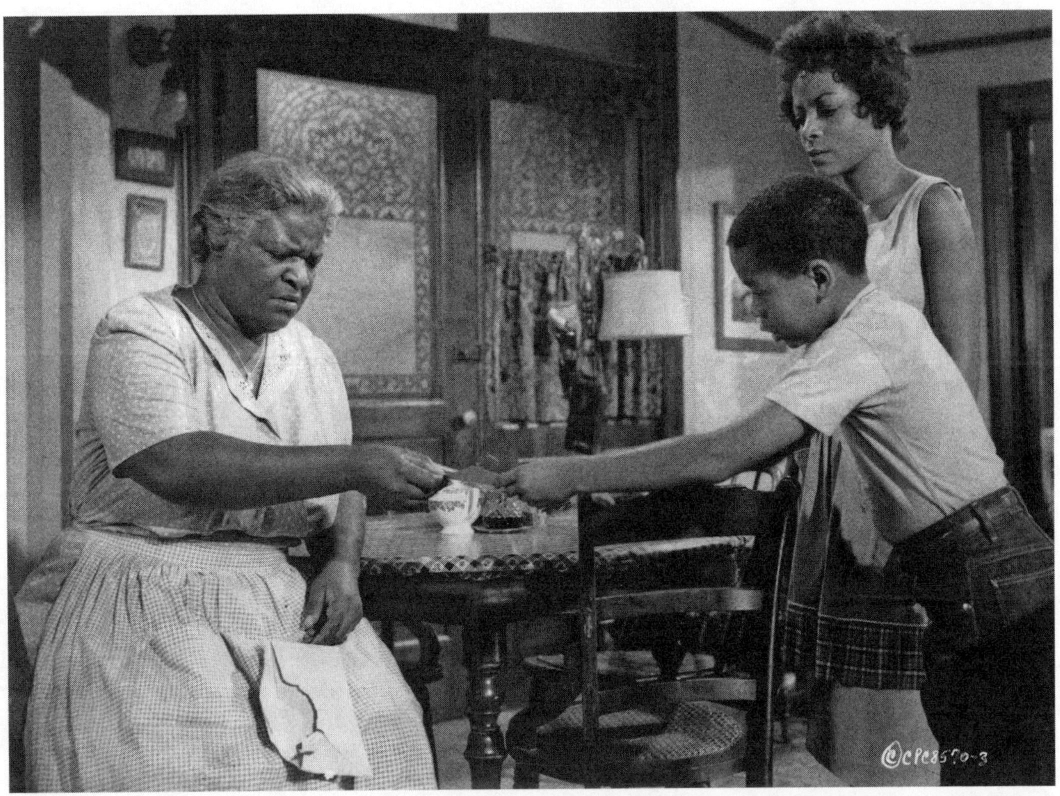

Claudia McNeil, Ruby Dee and Stephen Perry in *A Raisin in the Sun* (1959).

years later, Langston Hughes gave her a chance to sing in his musical *Simply Heavenly* (1957). Other theater roles included James Baldwin's *The Amen Corner* (1965), *Something Different* (1967), *Her First Roman*, with Leslie Uggams (1968), as Mrs. Devereaux in *Wrong Way Light-Bulb* (1969), and *Contributions* (1970).

McNeil made her share of TV appearances, including *The Dupont Show of the Month* (1957), *The Nurses* (1962), *Profiles in Courage* (1965), the miniseries *Roots: The Next Generations* (1979), and the TV movie *Roll of Thunder, Hear My Cry* (1978). Her film appearances included *The Last Angry Man* (as Mrs. Quincy; 1959), *There Was a Crooked Man...* (as Madam; 1970) and *Black Girl* (as Mu' Dear; 1972). She died at the Actors' Fund Nursing Home from complications of diabetes.

Feature Films including TV Movies: *The Last Angry Man* (1959), *A Raisin in the Sun* (1961), *There Was a Crooked Man...* (1970), *Incident in San Francisco* (TV; 1971), *To Be Young, Gifted and Black* (TV; 1972), *Moon of the Wolf* (TV; 1972), *Black Girl* (1972), *The Migrants* (TV; 1974), *Cry Panic* (TV; 1974), *Roll of Thunder, Hear My Cry* (TV; 1978).

TV: *The DuPont Show of the Month* ("The Member of the Wedding," 1958), Play of the Week ("Simply Heavenly," 1959), *The Nurses* ("Express Stop from Lenox Avenue," 1963), *Profiles in Courage* (2 episodes; "Frederick Douglass," "Woodrow Wilson," 1965), *CBS Playhouse* ("Do Not Go Gentle into That Good Night," 1967), *Storefront Lawyers Girl Talk* (1968), ("The Emancipation of Bessie Gray," 1970), *The Mod Squad* ("The Connection," 1972), *Lorraine Hansberry: The Black Experience in the Creation of Drama* (1975), *The American Woman: Portraits of Courage* (1976), *Roots: the Next Generations* (miniseries; 1979).

McQueen, Thelma "Butterfly" Born in Tampa, Florida, January 11, 1911; died 1995, Augusta, Georgia.

Thelma McQueen's father was a stevedore and her mother was a maid. In 1916 her father left the family and Thelma's mother eventually found work in Babylon, New York, and Thelma was able to finish high school there. After high school she became a dancer in a Negro youth group. She began to seriously study dramatic dancing, music and ballet. Her dance instructors included such eventual icons as Katherine Dunham, Geoffrey Holder and Venezuela Jones. In 1935 she made her stage debut in the New York City College production of *A Midsummer Night's Dream* as a butterfly. She was given the nickname "Butterfly," and it stayed with her for the rest of her life.

In the late 1930s, McQueen auditioned for and won the role of Prissy in the film version of Margaret Mitchell's novel *Gone with the Wind*, released in 1939 after much hype and publicity. It was quickly considered a cinematic landmark. During the filming, McQueen — who was an intellectual — rebelled against Mitchell's conception of Prissy as unintelligent, but despite reservations she played the part with all the conviction she could muster. There were some stereotyped images she absolutely refused to participate in, such as eating watermelon and spitting out the seeds; and she requested that the phrase "simple-minded wench" be changed to "simple-minded darkie."

The role of Prissy bought McQueen a lifetime of fame — fame that she did not always welcome with open arms. In 1941 she again appeared with Hattie McDaniel, this time in *Affectionately Yours*, playing a maid. In 1943 she was featured, albeit rather fleetingly, in *Cabin in the Sky*. She was Annette the maid opposite Red Skelton in *I Dood It* that same year. McQueen never married and worked for the betterment of her race instead of seeking wealth or taking advantage of her uneasy fame. The real Thelma McQueen was light years away from her Butterfly persona.

Thelma "Butterfly" McQueen.

McQueen tired of being typecast as servants and refused to accept any more roles as such. As a result, she did not work very much in films for the next 20 years — instead she concentrated on the theater. She made guest appearances on many popular television talk shows, including *The Mike Wallace Show*, *The Virginia Graham Show*, *The Mike Douglas Show* and *The Today Show*.

Feature Films including TV Movies: *The Women* (1939), *Gone with the Wind* (1939), *Affectionately Yours* (1941), *Cabin in the Sky* (1943), *I Dood It* (1943), *Flame of Barbary Coast* (1945), *Mildred Pierce* (1945), *Duel in the Sun* (1946), *Killer Diller* (1948), *The Phynx* (1970), *Amazing Grace* (1974), *The Adventures of Huckleberry Finn* (TV; 1981), *The Mosquito Coast* (1986), *Polly* (TV; 1989).

TV: *Studio One* ("Give Us Our Dream," 1950), *The Beulah Show* (aka *Beulah*; recurring role of Oriole (1950–53), *Lux Video Theatre* ("Weather for Today," 1951), *Hallmark Hall of Fame: The Green Pastures* (1957), *Black History: Lost, Stolen or Strayed* (archival; 1968), *ABC Weekend Specials* ("The Seven Wishes of Joanna Peabody," 1978), *ABC Afterschool Specials* ("Seven Wishes for a Rich Kid," 1979), *Good Morning America* (1983), *The Making of a Legend: Gone with the Wind* (1988), *Wogan* (1989).

Merkerson, S. Epatha Born in Saginaw, Michigan, November 28, 1952.

Sharon Epatha Merkerson much preferred the name Epatha to Sharon, so she legally changed her first name to "S." Her multi-award career has reached the point where she has begun to receive the recognition she deserves as one of the most skilled actresses of her day. She may have begun her career with an appearance on *The Cosby Show* and a recurring role on *Pee Wee's Playhouse* (as the charming Reba the Mail Lady; 1987), but she has moved on to more dramatic fare. She was nominated for a Tony Award for Best Actress in a Play for her role of Berneice in August Wilson's *The Piano Lesson* (1990), and was an Obie Award winner for her acting in *I'm Not Stupid* (1992). She earned her second Tony nomination in 2008 for her starring role as Lola Delaney in the revival of William Inge's *Come Back, Little Sheba* (she had played the role in Los Angeles before taking it to Broadway). She was also nominated for the Outer Critics Circle Award.

The HBO movie *Lackawanna Blues* (2005) provided her breakthrough role, and this was the first time she had starred in a film. For this she won the Golden Globe, the Emmy, and the Screen Actors Guild Award. She played Rachel "Nanny" Crosby, who runs a little boarding house and is guardian to a half-black, half–Hispanic child. Set in the 1950s and '60s, this rich character study deals with serious issues like spousal abuse. She joined the cast of *Law & Order* during the fourth season of the show as the authoritative Lieutenant Anita Van Buren (beginning in 1993).

She is a graduate of Wayne State University in Detroit, Michigan, with a bachelor of fine arts in theater. Before studying acting she majored in dance at Wayne State. Merkerson has been nominated for seven NAACP Image Awards, winning two in 2006, for *Lackawanna Blues* and *Law & Order*. She is the youngest of five children. She was married to Toussaint L. Jones, Jr., from 1994 to 2006.

S. Epatha Merkerson.

Feature Films including TV Movies: *She's Gotta Have It* (1986), *Moe's World* (TV; 1990), *Loose Cannons* (1990), *Equal Justice* (TV; 1990), *Navy Seals* (1990), *Jacob's Ladder* (1990), *Terminator 2: Judgment Day* (1991), *It's Nothing Personal* (TV; 1993), *A Place for Annie* (TV; 1994), *A Mother's Prayer* (TV; 1995), *Breaking Through* (TV; 1996), *An Unexpected Life* (TV; 1998), *Random Hearts* (1999), *A Girl Thing* (TV; 2001), *The Rising Place* (2001), *Radio* (2003), *Jersey Girl* (2004), *Lackawanna Blues* (TV; 2005), *Black Snake Moan* (2006), *Girl, Positive* (TV; 2007), *Slipstream Dream* (2007), *The Six Wives of Henry Lefay* (2008).

TV: *Pee Wee's Playhouse* (recurring role as Reba, the Mail Lady; 1987), *Pee Wee Herman's Christmas Special* (1988), *The Cosby Show* ("Bookworm," 1988), *The More You Know* (1989), *CBS Summer Playhouse* ("Elysian Fields," 1989), *The 44th Annual Tony Awards* (1990), *Law & Order* (328 recurring role of Lt. Anita Van Buren; 1991–2009), *ABC Afterschool Specials* ("Summer Stories: The Mall," Part II, 1992), *Mann & Machine* (recurring role of CaPart Margaret Claghorne; 1992), *Here and Now* (recurring role as Ms. St. Marth; 1992), *South Beach* ("I Witness," 1993), *Exiled: Law & Order* (1998), *5th Annual Screen Actors Guild Awards* (1999), *Late Night with Conan O'Brien* (1999–2000), *Larry King Live* (2000), *Frasier* ("Dark Side of the Moon," 2000), *Hollywood Squares* (2001), *Inside TV Land: Cops on Camera* (2002), *Law & Order: Criminal Intent* ("Badge," 2002), *Life & Style* (2005), *The WIN Awards* (2005), *Ellen* (2 segments; 2005 and 2006), *Corazon de...* (2 segments; 2005 and 2006), *Tavis Smiley* (2 segments; 2005 and 2007), *Law & Order: Trial by Jury* ("Skeleton," 2005), *The 63rd Annual Golden Globe Awards* (2006), *Live with Regis and Kelly* (2006), *2006 Independent Spirit Awards, Inside the Actors Studio* (2006), *The 60th Annual Tony Awards* (2006), *Comic Relief 2006, The Closer* (3 episodes in the role of Dr. Rebecca Dioli; "Four to Eight," "Manhunt,"

"Culture Shock," 2007), *The View* (2 segments; co-host; 2007–08), *The Late Late Show with Craig Ferguson* (2007), *American Masters* ("Zora Neale Hurston: Jump at the Sun," 2008), *Live with Regis and Kelly* (2008), *Martha* (2008).

Merritt, Theresa Born in Emporia, Virginia, September 24, 1924; died 1998, the Bronx, New York.

Theresa Merritt was nominated for the 1985 Tony Award as Best Actress in a Play for August Wilson's *Ma Rainey's Black Bottom.* In the 1950s she was a member of the Helen Way Singers and was a session singer for recording artists like Buddy Holly and a backup singer for Harry Belafonte. She played Aunt Em to Diana Ross' Dorothy in *The Wiz* (1979), the film version of the musical *Wizard of Oz.* (She had replaced Mabel King as Evillene in the Broadway version of the musical in 1975–79.) She was also in Bob Fosse's *All That Jazz* (1979) and *The Best Little Whorehouse in Texas* (1982), with Burt Reynolds and Dolly Parton.

But it is her Broadway career, which stretched from 1943 to 1991, for which she will be best remembered. Her Broadway debut was as a member of the ensemble in *Carmen Jones* (1943–54), then she took over the role of Frankie in that musical in 1945–46. She was Patsy Ross in *Our Lan'* (which had a brief run from September to November 1947). She didn't turn up on Broadway again until she was a member of the choir, and various other characters, in *Tambourines to Glory* (November 2–23, 1963). She was Theresa in *Golden Boy* with Sammy Davis, Jr. (1964–66); Sister Henrietta Pinkston in *Trumpets of the Lord* (April–May, 1969); Tituba in *The Crucible* (April–June 1972); Mrs. Brichinski in *Division Street* (October 8–25, 1980); and Katie Pitts in *Mule Bone*, her final Broadway appearance (February–April, 1991).

Many fans knew her best for her recurring role as Mama Eloise on the TV sitcom *That's My Mama* (1974). She was married to Benjamin Hines from 1945 until the time of her death; they had four children, including a set of twins.

Feature Films including TV Movies: *J.T.* (1969), *They Might Be Giants* (1971), *The Furst Family of Washington* (TV; 1973), *Ningen no shomei* (1977), *The Goodbye Girl* (1977), *The Wiz* (1978), *The Great Santini* (1979), *All That Jazz* (1979), *The Best Little Whorehouse in Texas* (1982), *Concealed Enemies* (TV; 1984), *Astonished* (1988), *The Serpent and the Rainbow* (1988), *Miracle at Beekman's Place* (TV; 1984), *Zwei Frauen* (1989), *Voodoo Dawn* (1990), *Driving Miss Daisy* (TV; 1992), *Billy Madison* (1995), *Dangerous Proposition* (1998), *Home Fries* (1998).

TV: *That's My Mama* (recurring role of "Mama" Eloise Curtis; 1974), *Police Story* ("Face for a Shadow," 1975), *NBC Special Treat* ("Sunshine's on the Way," 1980), *The Love Boat* (1983), *Law & Order* ("Double Down," 1997), *NYPD Blue* ("Weaver of Hate," 1998), *Cosby* ("Mud," 1998).

Michele, Michael Born in Evansville, Indiana, August 30, 1966.

The eldest of two daughters, Michael Michele is the offspring of a white father and an African American mother. Her father was an entrepreneur and her mother was a corporate manager. She got her unusual first name from one of her mother's close friends, a woman who was also named Michael. She was a star forward on Benjamin Boose High School's basketball team (Michele is 5'9").

After high school she relocated to New York, where she began to get work in commercials and landed a role in the Eddie Murphy–Richard Pryor vehicle *Harlem Nights* (1989); although the film wasn't very good, Michele got noticed. She had a role in the crime thriller *New Jack City* (as Selina Thomas; 1991). Her most prominent film role to date was as Veronica Porsche Ali in the Will Smith biographical film *Ali* (2001).

She had a recurring role in the blink-and-you-missed-it run of the TV series *Dangerous Curves* (1993). She also had brief ongoing roles in *New York Undercover* (1994–95), the much-hyped *Central Park West* (1995–96), and *Kevin Hill* (2004–05), the fine Taye Diggs series that deserved a much better fate than quick cancellation. Her star-making TV series role was as Detective Rene Sheppard on *Homicide: Life on the Street* (1998). This was followed by a run on *ER* as Dr. Cleo Finch (1999–2001), which she stayed with for three seasons. At that time, the medical drama was at or near the top of the ratings charts. She had her first child, Brandon, with New York restaurant owner Jimmy Rodriguez in December 2004.

Feature Films including Video and TV Movies: *Def by Temptation* (1990), *Private Times* (TV; 1991), *New Jack City* (1991), *The Sixth Man*

(1997), *The Substitute 2: School's Out* (TV; 1991), *Creature* (TV; 1998), *Ali* (2001), *Dark Blue* (2002), *How to Lose a Guy in 10 Days* (2003), *The Hunt for the BTK Killer* (TV; 2005), *Company Town* (TV; 2006), *Judy's Got a Gun* (TV; 2007), *Relative Stranger* (TV; 2008).

TV: *1st & Ten* (1988), *Dangerous Curves* ("The French Defection," 1993), *Trade Winds* (miniseries; 1993), *New York Undercover* (3 episodes in the role of Sandra; "After Shakespeare," "Private Enemy No. 1," "Downtown Girl," 1994–95), *Central Park West* (recurring role of Nikki Sheridan; 1995–96), *Oddville, MTV* (1997), *Players* ("Con-tinental," 1998), *Law & Order* ("Sideshow," 1999), *Homicide: Life on the Street* (recurring role of Detective Rene Sheppard; 1998–99), *ER* (recurring role of Dr. Cleo Finch; 1999–2002), *Homicide* (2000), *The Rosie O'Donnell Show* (3 segments; 2000), *Won't Anybody Listen?* (2001), *My VH1 Music Awards* (2001), *MADtv* (2001), *HBO First Look* (*Ali*, 2001), *The Making of Ali* (2001), *Oprah* (2003), *The Late Late Show with Craig Kilborn* (2003–04), *Dennis Miller* (2004), *Tavis Smiley* (2004), *Last Call with Carson Daly* (2004), *Kevin Hill* (recurring role of Jessie Grey; 2004–05), *Law & Order: Special Victims Unit* ("Burned," 2007), *House* (2 episodes as Dr. Samira Terzi; "Ugly," "Whatever It Takes," 2007).

Michelle, Janee

Birth date unavailable.

Janee Michelle is best known for her role in the mild but atmospheric horror film *The House on Skull Mountain* (1974). Once an obscure film that had little theatrical release and was very difficult to track down, it is now a DVD staple. The last act of a dying black heiress is to give her priest a box containing letters to beckon her family members to a reading of her will. This is a setup that has been used in countless "old dark house" movies, and you know in advance that family members will begin to get killed off in short order. One of the victims is played by Mike Evans (well known for his role as Lionel on *All in the Family* and *The Jeffersons*). Victor French, a white actor who sometimes played bad guys and was a regular on *Little House on the Prairie,* plays a character that is supposed to be a descendant of the black woman, in what is an example of ridiculous casting. He becomes attracted to the woman's niece, played by Michele. Michele is quite pretty and gives a charming performance in her undemanding role. It seems that the old woman was a devotee of voodoo and of raising the dead, but all ends well for the characters of French and Michelle.

Feature Films: *Clarence, The Cross-Eyed Lion* (1965), *The Love-Ins* (1967), *Soul Soldier* (1970), *The Mephisto Waltz* (1970), *Scream Blacula Scream* (1973), *The House on Skull Mountain* (1974).

TV: *Ironside* ("Due Process of the Law," 1968), *Love, American Style* ("Love and the Uncoupled Couple," 1970), *The F.B.I.* ("The Architect," 1970), *Bewitched* ("Sisters at Heart," 1970), *Sanford and Son* ("Tower Power," 1974), *In the Heat of the Night* ("A Necessary Evil," 1988).

Miles, Rosalind

Birth date unavailable.

Rosalind Miles was a commanding actress who appeared in cult director Al Adamson's crime drama *Girls for Rent* (1974), released on video with the highly unappealing title of *I Spit on Your Corpse* (so called to cash in on the considerable success at that time of a feminist revenge film called *I Spit on Your Grave*). Miles plays a woman who tries to set up her partner in crime, played by erstwhile porn star Georgina (*The Devil in Miss Jones*) Spelvin.

Feature Films including TV Movies: *How's Your Love Life?* (1971), *Shaft's Big Score!* (1972), *The Black Six* (1974), *Girls for Rent* (aka *I Spit on Your Corpse*, 1974), *Attack on Terror: The FBI vs. the Ku Klux Klan* (TV; 1975), *Gibbsville: The Turning Point of Jim Malloy* (TV; 1975), *The Manhandlers* (1975), *Friday Foster* (1975), *Benny and Barney: Las Vegas Undercover* (TV; 1977), *To Kill a Cop* (TV; 1978).

TV: *Columbo: Short Fuse* (1972), *Here's Lucy* (2 episodes; "Lucy Helps David Frost Go Night-Night," "The Case of the Reckless Wheelchair Driver," 1971 and 1972), *Starsky and Hutch* ("Bounty Hunter," 1976), *Baretta* ("Can't Win for Losin'," 1976).

Milian, Christina

Born in Jersey City, New Jersey, September 26, 1981.

Christine Marie Flores (Christina Milian is her stage name) is an actress, but also an accomplished singer, songwriter, record producer, dancer, and an erstwhile MTV VJ. Her first solo single, "AM to PM," was a hit in 2001, leading to her self-titled debut album. Her music is popular throughout Europe (especially the United Kingdom) as well as in North America.

She was originally billed as Tina Flores as a reporter on the Disney Channel's *Movie Surfers* in 1998. Her breakthrough theatrical film was *Love Don't Cost a Thing* (2003) in a starring role opposite Nick Cannon, which she handled with considerable aplomb. One of her best roles to date (she also got to sing) was as Linda Moon in *Be Cool* (2005), the fun sequel to *Get Shorty*. She was also in the popular horror film *Pulse* (2006).

Milian is of Cuban heritage (her parents are named Don and Carmen). She has two younger sisters, Dannielle and Elizabeth. As a child, she shot commercials for Wendy's restaurants and Honeycombs cereal. The family moved to Los Angeles when she was 13, better to pursue her acting career. Her parents divorced soon after this. The family then relocated to Maryland, where she graduated from Matthew Henson Middle School in Indian Head and Westlake High School in Waldorf.

TV guest star work includes *Smart Guy, Clueless, Charmed, The Steve Harvey Show, Smallville* and *Sister, Sister*. She had a starring role in the ABC Family Movie *Snowglobe*, shown at Christmas time in 2007. She has been nominated for four Teen Choice Awards and two Grammy Awards (for Best R&B Album and Best Rap/Sung Collaboration in 2005).

Feature Films including Video and TV Movies: *Clips' Place* (TV; 1998), *A Bug's Life* (voice; 1998), *Durango Kids* (1999), *American Pie* (1999), *The Wood* (1999), *Love Don't Cost a Thing* (2003), *Torque* (2004), *Man of the House* (2005), *Be Cool* (2005), *Pulse* (2006), *Snowglobe* (TV; 2007), *The Ghosts of Girlfriends Past* (2009).

TV: *Sister, Sister* ("Kid-Napped," 1996), *Movie Surfers* (1998), *The Steve Harvey Show* ("Working Homegirl," 1999), *Get Real* (3 episodes in the role of Tennisha; "Sexual Healing," "Passages," "Prey," 1999), *Charmed* ("The Wendigo," 1999), *The Wild Thornberrys* (voice; "Rumble in the Jungle," 1999), *Clueless* (2 episodes in the role of Megan; "Graduation," "All Night Senior Party," 1999), *Wannabe* (host; 2001), *The Teen Choice Awards 2001, TMF Awards 2002, TRL Italy* (2002), *The Big Breakfast* (2002), *SM:TV Live* (2002), *ri:se* (2002), *Top of the Pops* (2 segments; 2002–03), *TV Total* (2 segments; 2002–05), *2003 MTV Movie Awards, Tinseltown TV* (2003), *The Sharon Osbourne Show* (2003), *20 Most Awesomely Bad Songs of 2004* (archival; 2004), *40 Most Awesomely Bad Dirty Songs ... Ever* (2004), *Best Hit USA* (2004), *The Teen Choice Awards 2004, Mad TV* (2004), *The 10th Annual Walk of Fame Honoring Smokey Robinson* (2004), *Cribs* (2004), *Live with Regis and Kelly* (2 segments; 2004 and 2006), *Reel Comedy: Be Cool* (2005), *Video on Trial* (archival; 2005), *The 31st Annual People's Choice Awards* (2005), *The 47th Annual Grammy Awards* (2005), *Diary* (2005), *The 19th Annual Soul Train Music Awards* (2005), *Ellen* (2005), *Richard & Judy* (2005), *The Paul O'Grady Show* (2005), *Late Night with Conan O' Brien* (2 segments; 2005–06), *The Tony Danza Show* (2006), *106 & Park Top 10 Live* (2006), *The VIP* (2006), *Jimmy Kimmel Live!* (2006), *Making the Video* ("A Public Affair," 2006), *The Tonight Show with Jay Leno* (2006), *The Late Late Show with Craig Ferguson* (2006), *Eight Days a Week* (recurring role as Olivia; 2007), *The Jace Hall Show* (2008).

Miller, Tangi Born in Miami, Florida, February 28, 1970.

Tangi Miller, born and raised in Miami, Florida, is the eldest of six children. At first, acting took a back burner to a more practical academic approach: she attended Alabama State University, majoring in marketing. After graduation, Miller realized that she was spending most of her time pursuing acting, so she made that her focus. She earned a master of fine arts degree at the University of Irvine, California, and studied at the Alabama Shakespeare Festival, where she appeared in *The Crucible* (Dancer) and *The Tempest* (as Ariel), and at London's Royal National Theatre Studio and the Chautauqua Summer Conservatory Company in New York, New York. She also attended the University of Legon in Accron, Ghana, West Africa, and the Kingo Institute in Yaounde, Cameroon, Africa.

Miller has been quite active in television, most prominently as Elena Tyler on *Felicity* (1998–2002), the popular series on the former WB. She was nominated for a 2002 NAACP Image Award for Best Actress in a Dramatic Series for her role. She has done guest star work on *Half & Half, The Shield, The District, Cold Case, The Division, Fastlane, Arli$$*, and *Shacking Up*. TV movies include *Too Legit: The MC Hammer Story* (2001), the Sci-Fi channel movie *Phantom Force* (nominated for a 2005 NAACP Image Award for Outstanding Actress in a Television Movie), and the BET movie *Playing with Fire* (2000).

Films include *Love ... & Other Four Letter*

Words (which she produced and starred in, as a Chicago talk show host who fakes her own marriage to please her dying grandmother); Tyler Perry's *Madea's Family Reunion* (2006), the box office hit based on Perry's stage play; *Hurricane in the Rose Garden* (2006), a culture clash comedy about a Nigerian man who marries an African American (Miller) and then has to cope with his imperious mother when she visits the U.S.; *After School* (2008), which she also co-produced; the horror movie spoof *Leprechaun: Back 2 tha Hood* (2003); the independent film *The Other Brother* (2002) with Mekhi Phifer; and *Rhinos* (1998), an independent comedy that won Best Feature Film at the New York International Independent Film & Video Festival. Theater credits include *Great Woman of Color* (as Phyliss Wheatley; White Fire Theatre) and *Anokye's Golden Stool* (as Agatha; West Angeles Theatre). Miller's many other interests include dance (African-Caribbean, hip-hop, period and modern), modeling, radio announcing, and directing.

Feature Films including Video and TV Movies: *Rhinos* (1998), *Actress* (documentary; 1999), *Playing with Fire* (TV; 2000), *Too Legit: The MC Hammer Story* (TV; 2001), *The Other Brother* (2002), *Leprechaun Back 2 tha Hood* (2003), *Phantom Force* (TV; 2004), *Class Actions* (TV; 2004), *Hurricane in the Rose Garden* (2006), *Madea's Family Reunion* (2006), *Love ... & Other Four-Letter Words* (2007), *Saravia* (documentary; 2008), *Drones* (2008), *My Girlfriend's Back* (2009), *The Misguided Adventures of Three Brothers Dating in Hollywood* (2009).

TV: *Arli$$* ("His Name Is Arliss Michaels," 1998), *Felicity* (recurring role of Elena Tyler; 1998–2002), *The Amanda Show* (2000), *The Enforcers* (miniseries; 2001), *The Shield* ("Throwaway," 2002), *Fastlane* ("Girl's Own Juice," 2002), *The Twilight Zone* ("Harsh Mistress," 2002), *Hollywood Squares* (2002), *Kim Possible* (voice; "All the News," 2002), *The District* (2 episodes in the role of Dyanne; "Blind Eye," "In God We Trust," 2003), *The Division* ("Hail, Hail, the Gang's All Here," 2004), *Cold Case* ("The Badlands," 2004), *Living with Fran* ("The Reunion," 2005), *Half & Half* ("The Big Sexism in the City Episode," 2005), *14th Annual Inner City Destiny Awards* (2006).

Tangi Miller.

Monica (aka Arnold, Monica) Born in Atlanta, Georgia, October 24, 1980.

The 1996 *Billboard* Music Award winner for R&B Artist of the Year, Monica Denise Arnold is best known for her 1998 duet with Brandy, the outstanding number one hit "The Boy Is Mine," which exploited the "rivalry" between the two singers, who both had big careers at the time. It was nominated for the Grammy for Record of the Year in 1999 and won the Grammy for Best R&B Vocal Performance by a Duo or Group. As a solo artist, she has been nominated for four American Music Awards, two MTV Video Music Awards, and seven Soul Train Music Awards. Her albums are *Miss Thang* (1995), *The Boy Is Mine* (1998), *All Eyez on Me* (2002), *After the Storm* (2003), *The Makings of Me* (2006) and *Lessons Learned* (2008).

She also has a fair number of acting credits, but like Brandy, she has had only middling success with her acting career. Monica has been in a couple of features—*Boys and Girls* (2000) and *ATL* (2006), and the TV movie *Love Song* in 2000—and has done TV guest star work since 1996, including *Living Single*, *New York Under-*

cover, *Beverly Hills 90210*, *Felicity* and *American Dreams*, where she played legendary soul singer Mary Wells. As her music videos demonstrate, she has a smooth, laid-back style in front of the camera, with an expressive face and an appealing demeanor.

Monica grew up in a single parent home after her parents' separation in 1984 and their eventual divorce in 1987. She was the youngest member of the gospel choir she traveled with at age 12, and soon started making her name in local talent competitions, leading to her debut album in 1995. She signed with Arista Records in 1997. She gave birth to her first child, Rodney Ramone Hill III, in 2005, and a second son, Romello Montez, in 2008.

Feature Films including Video and TV Movies: *Boys and Girls* (2000), *Love Song* (TV; 2000), *ATL* (2006), *Pastor Brown* (2009).

TV: *Living Single* ("Kiss of the Spider Man," 1996), *New York Undercover* ("If This World Were Mine," 1996), *BET Hip-Hop Awards* (1996), *The Rosie O'Donnell Show* (2 segments; 1996 and 1998), *Beverly Hills 90210* (2 episodes; "Mother's Day," "The End of the World as We Know It," 1997 and 1999), *The 26th Annual American Music Awards* (1998), *1998 MTV Video Music Awards*, *The 41st Annual Grammy Awards* (1999), *Brak Presents The Brak Show Starring Brak* (2000), *'Twas the Night Before Christmas* (2000), *Felicity* ("Miss Conception," 2001), *Michael Jackson: 30th Anniversary Celebration* (2001), *The Early Show* (2002), *I Love the '80s* (2002), *American Dreams* ("R-E-S-P-E-C-T," 2003), *The Tonight Show with Jay Leno* (2003), *Essence Awards* (2003), *American Juniors* (2 segments; 2003), *The New Tom Green Show* (2003), *The Wayne Brady Show* (2003), *AMA Red Carpet Party* (2003), *The Sharon Osbourne Show* (2004), *Faking the Video* (2004), *E! True Hollywood Story* (2004), *106 & Park Top 10 Live* (2006), *Late Show with David Letterman* (2006), *Ellen* (2006), *The Late Late Show with Craig Ferguson* (2006), *Live with Regis and Kathie Lee* (2 segments; 2006 and 2007), *Battleground Earth: Ludacris vs. Tommy Lee* ("You've Got Junk Mail," 2008).

Video/DVD: *MTV 20: Jams* (2001), *Ciara Goodies: The Videos and More* (2005).

Mo'Nique

Mo'Nique Born in Woodlawn, Maryland, December 11, 1967.

Mo'Nique is showing that oversized black women can be just as attractive and appealing as their slimmer sisters. That's not an insignificant contribution to the popular culture. Although her roots are in stand-up comedy, she has smoothly segued into sitcom success and has had an active big screen career. She was consistently funny as Nicole "Nikki" Parker on *The Parkers* (1999–2004). The show did receive its share of barbs for presenting what some considered a stereotypical, one-dimensional view of black women, but *The Parkers* was unabashed low comedy and should be judged on its own entertaining terms. Her 2007 documentary *Mo'Nique Behind Bars*, consisting of many one-on-one interviews with incarcerated women, shows that there is another, more relevant side to Mo'Nique, and that she is capable of digging deeper.

She has done mostly character work in feature films, often in "best friend" supporting roles such as in *Two Can Play That Game* (2001), *Hair Show* (2004), and in free-wheeling ensemble comedies like *Soul Plane* (2004). She was also in John Singleton's acclaimed *Baby Boy* (2001). She had a starring role in *Phat Girlz* (2006), which was loaded with her "fat is beautiful" manifesto. She co-starred in *Welcome Home, Roscoe Jenkins* (2008) with Martin Lawrence, giving a typically rambunctious performance. Many fans were first introduced to her in the documentary concert film *Queens of Comedy* (2001). Mo'Nique is also known for hosting the BET Awards, and for the reality shows *Mo'Nique's Fat Chance* (2005) and *Flavor of Love Girls: Charm School* (2007). She co-hosted a local show on whur radio in Washington until 2002. She is the author of *Skinny Women Are Evil* (2003) and *Skinny Cooks Can't Be Trusted* (2006).

She is the daughter of Steven and Alice Imes, with two brothers (Steven and Gerald) and a sister (Millicent). She gave birth to twins Jonathan and David in 2005 with husband Sidney Hicks. She has one child (Shalon) from her first marriage to Mark Jackson (1997–2001), and she adopted his son Mark, Jr.

Feature Films including Video and TV Movies: *3 Strikes* (2000), *Baby Boy* (2001), *Two Can Play That Game* (2001), *Half Past Dead* (2002), *Good Fences* (TV; 2003), *Soul Plane* (2004), *Hair Show* (2004), *Shadowboxer* (2005), *Domino* (2005), *Farce of the Penguins* (voice; 2006), *Phat Girlz* (2006), *Beerfest* (2006), *The Better Man* (2008), *Welcome Home, Roscoe Jenkins* (2008), *Push* (2008), *Steppin': The Movie* (2009).

TV: *Penn & Teller's Sin City Spectacular* (1998), *Moesha* (3 episodes in the role of Nikki Parker; "It Takes Two," "I Studied Twelve Years for This?" "The Candidate," 1999–2000), *The Parkers* (recurring role of Nicole "Nikki" Parker; 1999–2004), *You Lie Like a Dog* (panelist; 2 segments; 2000), *Late Night with Conan O'Brien* (2000), *The Rosie O'Donnell Show* (2001), *Weakest Link* (2001), *The Hughleys* ("Forty Acres and a Fool," 2001), *Hollywood Squares* (2 segments; 2001–03), *Platinum Comedy Series: Roasting Shaquille O'Neal* (2002), *It's Showtime at the Apollo* (hostess; 2002), *Intimate Portrait* (2 episodes; "Isabel Sanford," "Mo'Nique," 2003), *Heroes of Comedy: Women on Top* (2003), *3rd Annual BET Awards* (2003), *The Sharon Osbourne Show* (4 segments; 2003–04), *Ellen* (2 segments; 2003–05), *Pryor Offenses* (2004), *TV's Greatest Sidekicks* (archival; 2004), *35th NAACP Image Awards* (2004), *Pyramid* (2004), *Last Comic Standing* (series regular; 2004), *Apollo at 70: A Hot Night in Harlem* (2004), *4th Annual BET Awards* (2004), *Steve Harvey's Big Time* (2004), *The 100 Most Memorable TV Moments* (2004), *The Bernie Mac Show* ("Who's That Lady?" 2004), *Tavis Smiley* (3 segments; 2004–07), *An Evening of Stars: Tribute to Quincy Jones* (2005), *Girlfriends* ("See J-Spot Run," 2005), *36th NAACP Image Awards* (2005), *The Tony Danza Show* (2005), *Mo'Nique's Fat Chance* (host; 2005), *Made You Look: Top 25 Moments of BET History* (2005), *The 100 Most Unexpected TV Moments* (2005), *Richard Pryor: The Funniest Man Dead or Alive* (2005), *106 & Park Top 10 Live* (3 segments; 2005–07), *The Late Late Show with Craig Ferguson* (3 segments; 2005–07), *BET Awards 2006*, *Fox and Friends* (2006), *The View* (2 segments; 2006), *Nip/Tuck* ("Conor McNamara," 2006), *Entertainment Tonight* (4 episodes; 2006–07), *Thank God You're Here* (2 episodes; 2007), *Flavor of Love Girls: Charm School* (5 episodes; "No Mo' Nicknames," "Dirty Drawers Done Dirt Cheap," "Big Girl No-No," "Master Debaters," "It's Mo's Birthday and I'll Cry If I Want To," 2007), *7th Annual BET Awards* (2007), *Mo'Nique: Behind Bars* (2007), *Mo'Nique's Fat Chance: The Road to Paris* (2007), *Celebrity Family Feud* (2008), *Entertainment Tonight* (2008), *Hollywood Trials* (2008), *The Late Late Show with Craig Ferguson* (2008), *The Ellen DeGeneres Show* (2008), *Why We Laugh: Black Comedians on Black Comedy* (2008), *An Evening of Stars: Tribute to Patti LaBelle* (2009).

Video/DVD: *The Queens of Comedy* (2001), *Shaq's All Star Comedy Roast 2* (2003), *TV in Black: The First Fifty Years* (2004), *The Big Black Comedy Show, Vol. 2* (2005).

Moody, Lynne Born in Detroit, Michigan, 1950.

As a lovely and talented young actress, Lynne Moody started her career in B-movies, but soon graduated to appealing girl-next-door roles on TV and had a long, rewarding and incredibly varied career. She was born in Detroit but raised in Evanston, Illinois, and studied at the Pasadena Playhouse in California and the Goodman Theatre in Chicago.

Once a Playboy bunny at the Los Angeles' Sunset Boulevard club, she made her film debut as a vampire in *Scream, Blacula, Scream* (1973); she was in the awful B-movie *Las Vegas Lady* (1975) starring Stella Stevens and Stuart Whitman, two name actors who were down on their luck at the time; she did another horror film, *The Evil* (1978), with Richard Crenna; she appeared with Richard Pryor, who was then at the height of his career, in *Some Kind of Hero* (1982); and she had a prominent role in director Samuel Fuller's controversial *White Dog* (1982), about a dog trained to attack black people — little seen for many years but now getting its due on DVD.

Television became Moody's salvation, and her low-key, fresh-faced persona was perfect for the medium. She played Tracy Curtis Taylor on the first season of *That's My Mama* (1974–75), but was replaced in the second season by Joan Pringle. A succession of plum roles followed, including several of the all-time great miniseries. Moody was Alex Haley's great-grandmother in the epochal *Roots* miniseries (1977) and repeated the role in *Roots: The Next Generations* (1979). She starred in the award-winning miniseries *The Atlanta Child Murders* (1985) as Selina Cobb.

Moody must have set a record for the number of recurring roles in series: Polly Dawson in the outrageous *Soap* (1979–80), which introduced Billy Crystal to the world; Patricia Williams in the superior nighttime soap *Knot's Landing* (1988–90); and she also had recurring roles on *Hill Street Blues*, *Lou Grant*, *Love and War*, *Clueless* and *Chicago Hope*. Moody's last recurring role to date was as Florence Campbell on the endlessly running daytime soap *General Hospital* (2000).

She was the first actress to play Jenny Willis

in what amounted to a prototype for *The Jeffersons* on *All in the Family* ("Lionel's Engagement"). When the official pilot film was cast, Berlinda Tolbert replaced her in the role. Her guest star work is a "Who's Who" of nighttime TV: *Quincy*; *Trapper John, M.D.*; *The Love Boat*; *Walker, Texas Ranger*; *Amen*; *MacGyver*; *Tenspeed and Brownshoe*; *Beverly Hills, 90210*; *The Trials of Rosie O'Neill*; *T.J. Hooker*; *21 Jump Street*; and *Arli$$*.

Moody also starred with Deborah Raffin in an infamous TV movie. *Nightmare in Badham County* (1974) is a good candidate for the sleaziest TV movie ever made. It's incredible that this racist piece of softcore pornography was shown on national TV (it was later issued on video in an even sleazier version). A rip-off of the popular theatrical feature *Jackson County Jail*, it tells the story of two young college students arrested on false charges. The scene where the deputy played by Chuck Connors rapes the student played by Moody is still disturbing to watch.

Feature Films including TV Movies: *Scream, Blacula, Scream* (1973), *Las Vegas Lady* (1975), *Nightmare in Badham County* (TV; 1976), *The Evil* (1978), *Charleston* (TV; 1979), *Willow B: Women in Prison* (TV; 1980), *A Matter of Life and Death* (TV; 1981), *The Oklahoma City Dolls* (TV; 1981), *Goldie and the Boxer Go to Hollywood* (TV; 1981), *Fly Away Home* (TV; 1981), *Some Kind of Hero* (1982), *White Dog* (1982), *Wait Till Your Mother Gets Home!* (TV; 1983), *A Caribbean Mystery* (TV; 1983), *The Toughest Man in the World* (TV; 1984), *Lost in London* (TV; 1985), *A Fight for Jenny* (TV; 1986), *Last Light* (TV; 1993), *Ray Alexander: A Taste for Justice* (TV; 1994), *Ray Alexander: A Menu for Murder* (TV; 1995), *Escape to Witch Mountain* (TV; 1995), *Trials of Life* (TV; 1997), *The Ditchdigger's Daughters* (TV; 1997), *Ellen Foster* (TV; 1997), *The Reading Room* (TV; 2005).

TV: *The F.B.I.* ("The Confession," 1973), *All in the Family* ("Lionel's Engagement," 1974), *That's My Mama* (recurring role of Tracy Curtis Taylor; 1974–75), *S.W.A.T.* ("Any Second Now," 1975), *Roots* (miniseries; 1977), *Quincy, M.E.* ("A Blow to the Head ... A Blow to the Heart," 1977), *Roots: The Next Generations* (miniseries; 1979), *Soap* (recurring role of Polly Dawson; 1979–80), *Tenspeed and Brown Shoe* ("The Sixteen Byte Data Chip and the Brown-Eyed Fox," 1980), *The White Shadow* ("Burnout," 1980), *Strike Force* ("The Victims," 1981), *Lou Grant* (2 episodes in the role of Sharon McNeil; "Rape," "Risk," 1981), *Trapper John, M.D.* ("Tis the Season," 1981), *The Love Boat* (1982), *The Jeffersons* ("A Small Victory," 1982), *Magnum, P.I.* ("Black on White," 1982), *Hill Street Blues* (recurring role of Marty Nichols; 1982–84), *T.J. Hooker* (pilot and 3 episodes; "The Protectors," "Death on the Line," "The Chicago Connection," 1982–85), *Benson* ("Love in a Funny Phase," 1983), *Just Our Luck* ("Wedding Bell Shablues," 1983), *ER* ("A Cold Night in Chicago," 1984), *The Atlanta Child Murders* (miniseries; 1985), *Foofur* (voice; 4 episodes; "Nothing to Sneeze At," "A Royal Pain," "This Little Piggy's on TV," "Russian Through New York," 1986), *Amen* (2 episodes; "Reuben's Romance," "Three's a Crowd," 1986 and 1991), *Houston Knights* ("Scarecrow," 1987), *Outlaws* ("Orleans," 1987), *Murder, She Wrote* ("Death Takes a Dive," 1987), *21 Jump Street* ("Two for the Road," 1987), *Living the Dream: A Tribute to Dr. Martin Luther King* (1988), *A Pup Named Scooby-Doo* (voices; 1988), *Knot's Landing* (recurring role of Patricia Williams; 1988–90), *MacGyver* ("Lesson in Evil," 1990), *Civil Wars* ("His Honor's Offer," 1992), *Chicago Hope* (3 episodes; "Over the Rainbow," "Every Day a Little Death," "And Baby Makes 10," 1994–99), *Walker, Texas Ranger* ("Patriot," 1996), *Beverly Hills, 90210* ("Aloha, Beverly Hills," Parts I and II, 1997), *Arli$$* ("Comings and Goings," 2000), *General Hospital* (recurring role as Florence Campbell; 2000), *Alias* ("The Index," 2005), *Crossing Jordan* ("Faith," 2007), *Roots Remembered* (2007).

Moore, Juanita Born in Los Angeles, California, October 19, 1922.

Juanita Moore received an Academy Award nomination in 1959 for her performance in the remake of *Imitation of Life*, the Fredi Washington vehicle of 1934. She played Annie Johnson, the black servant whose daughter is "passing" (pretending to be white because of her fair skin). Susan Kohner (a white actress who was half Mexican and half Czech) played Sarah Jane, the daughter who breaks tragic Annie's heart. Kohner also received a Best Supporting Actress nomination for the film. Moore was the third African American to be nominated for an Academy Award in the Best Supporting Actress category, along with Hattie McDaniel and Ethel Waters, and the fourth overall; Dorothy Dandridge had been nominated for Best Actress. In the 1934 version,

Left to right: **Lana Turner, Juanita Moore and Terry Burnham in *Imitation of Life* (1959).**

Claudette Colbert and Louise Beavers were friends and business partners, but in the 1959 version, Moore was merely Lana Turner's housekeeper. Pearl Bailey was the first choice for Annie, but producer Ross Martin really wanted Moore. Moore remembers that director Douglas Sirk (the king of gorgeous-looking soap operas) was patient with her. This was a demanding, major role in one of the key films of its time. By the end of the film, when a contrite Sarah Jane (Kohner) is weeping bitterly alongside her mother's coffin, the film was going full blast for the audience's tear ducts. On the other hand, it was a reminder that Hollywood was still playing the same old racial tune.

Moore's film debut was a small role in *Pinky* (1949), the film for which Ethel Waters had received her Oscar nomination. Moore had graduated from roles in B+ films like *Lydia Bailey* (1952), *Affair in Trinidad* (1952), *Queen Bee* (1955) and *Ransom!* (1956) to the plum role of Annie. Post-*Imitation* roles — never anywhere near as significant — included *Walk on the Wild Side* (1962) and *The Singing Nun* (1966). By the blaxploitation era of the 1970s, Moore was a presence (and not much else) in films like *The Mack* (1973), *Thomasine & Bushrod* (1973) and *Abby* (1974). After a 25-year absence from the screen, Moore returned with a role in Disney's negligible *The Kid* (2000).

Feature Films including TV Movies: *Pinky* (1949), *No Questions Asked* (1951), *Skirts Ahoy!* (1952), *Lydia Bailey* (1952), *Affair in Trinidad* (1952), *Witness to Murder* (1954), *The Gambler from Natchez* (1954), *Women's Prison* (1955), *Lord of the Jungle* (1955), *Not as a Stranger* (1955), *Queen Bee* (1955), *Ransom!* (1956), *The Opposite Sex* (1956), *The Girl Can't Help It* (1956), *Something of Value* (1957), *Band of Angels* (1957), *The Helen Morgan Story* (1957), *Bombers B-52* (1957), *The Green-Eyed Blonde* (1957), *Imitation of Life* (1959), *Tammy Tell Me True* (1961), *Walk on the Wild Side* (1962), *Papa's Delicate Condition* (1963), *The*

Singing Nun (1966), *Rosie!* (1967), *Up Tight!* (1968), *The Whole World Is Watching* (TV; 1969), *Angelitos Negros* (1970), *Skin Game* (1971), *The Mack* (1973), *Fox Style* (1973), *A Dream for Christmas* (TV; 1973), *Thomasine & Bushrod* (1973), *The Zebra Killer* (1974), *Abby* (1974), *Everybody Rides the Carousel* (voice; 1975), *Fugitive Lovers* (1975), *Joey* (aka *Deliver Us from Evil*, 1977), *Paternity* (1981), *O'Hara's Wife* (1982), *Two Moon Junction* (1988), *The Sterling Chase* (voice; aka *Graduation Week*, 1999), *The Kid* (2000), *8 Mile* (archival: *Imitation of Life*; 2002).

TV: *Ramar of the Jungle* ("Savage Challenge," 1953), *Soldiers of Fortune* ("Walk Wide of Lions," 1955), *The Thin Man* ("The Screaming Doll," 1958), *The 31st Annual Academy Awards* (1959), *The June Allyson Show* ("Dark Fear," 1960), *Alfred Hitchcock Presents* ("Bang! You're Dead," 1961), *Going My Way* ("Run, Robin, Run," 1961), *Here's Hollywood* (1961), *Wagon Train* ("The Blane Wessels Story," 1963), *77 Sunset Strip* ("White Lie," 1963), *The Alfred Hitchcock Hour* (3 episodes; "The Lonely Hours," "The Gentleman Caller," "Where the Woodbine Twineth," 1963–65), *Ben Casey* ("August Is the Month Before Christmas," 1964), *Mr. Novak* ("Boy Under Glass," 1964), *Slattery's People* ("Of Damon, Pythias and Sleeping Dogs," 1965), *Dragnet 1967* ("The Missing Realtor"), *Gentle Ben* ("Mama Jolie," 1968), *The Bold Ones: The Lawyers* ("The Crowd Pleasers," 1969), *Mannix* ("Time Out of Mind," 1970), *Ironside* ("Accident," 1971), *Marcus Welby, M.D.* (2 episodes; "Once There Was a Bantu Prince," "Nguyen," 1972 and 1973), *Adam-12* ("Clear with a Civilian," Parts I and II, 1973), *Ellery Queen* ("The Adventure of the Sunday Punch," 1976), *The Richard Pryor Show* (1977), *ABC Weekend Specials* ("The Notorious Jumping Frog of Calaveras County," 1981), *ER* ("Flight of Fancy," 2000), *Lana Turner ... A Daughter's Memoir* (2001), *Judging Amy* ("One for the Road," 2001), *Rita* (2003), *Hollywood Legenden* (2004).

Video: *Spencer Williams: Remembrances of an Early Black Film Pioneer* (1996).

Moore, Kenya Born in Detroit, Michigan, January 24, 1971.

Kenya Summer Moore's accessible, unpretentious personality complements her beauty. She was raised by her grandmother. She attended Cass Technical High School, and then Wayne State University, where she was a psychology major. Like many a future actresses, Moore went the beauty pageant route beginning in 1993, but she had far more success than most. She became Miss Michigan USA and went on to become Miss USA 1993 (the second African American to win the title), and finished fifth in the Miss Universe contest.

Many fans remember her from the direct-to-DVD sleeper *Trois* (2000), a romantic triangle co-starring Gretchen Palmer and Gary Dourdan, which was especially popular with black women. She had smaller roles in *Waiting to Exhale* (1995) and *Deliver Us from Eva* (2003), and guest starred in sitcoms like *The Fresh Prince of Bel-Air*, *Living Single*, *Girlfriends* and *The Steve Harvey Show*. She was a guest hostess on *BET's Video Soul*.

She is the founder of the Kenya Moore Foundation, awarding scholarships to underprivileged girls from her high school alma mater. In 2007, she released her first book, *Game, Get Some!*, a guide for men seeking the ideal mate, discussing the things women really desire from men.

Feature Films including Video and TV Movies: *Waiting to Exhale* (1995), *Senseless* (1998), *Trois* (2000), *No Turning Back* (2001), *Deliver Us from Eva* (2003), *Resurrection: The J.R. Richard Story* (2005), *Brothers in Arms* (2005), Cloud 9 (2006), *I Know Who Killed Me* (2007), *Haitian Nights* (2009).

TV: *The Fresh Prince of Bel-Air* ("Mother's Day," 1994), *Homeboys in Outer Space* ("Super Bad Foxy Lady Killer, or Ty and Morris Get the Shaft," 1996), *Martin* ("You're All I Need," 1996), *Sparks* ("I, Spy," 1997), *Smart Guy* ("Brother, Brother," 1997), *Living Single* ("One Degree of Separation," 1997), *Damon* ("The Designer," 1998), *The Steve Harvey Show* ("Educating Peggy," 1998), *The Jamie Foxx Show* ("Change of Heart," 1999), *The Parent 'Hood* (2 episodes in the role of Celeste; "A Sister Scorned," "Wedding Bell Blues," 1998 and 1999), *In the House* (2 episodes in the role of Valerie Bridgeforth; "Not as Good as It Gets," "How Nana Got Her Groove Back," 1999), *Nubian Goddess* (host; 1999), *Men, Women & Dogs* ("Sick as a Dog," 2001), *The Parkers* ("It's Showtime," 2002), *Girlfriends* (2 episodes in the role of Kara; "New York Bound," "Maybe Baby," 2004), *Made You Look: Top 25 Moments of BET History* (2005), *BET's Video Soul* (2006), *Parallel Paths* (2007), *Baisden After Dark* (2008).

Video/DVD: *Hot Parts* (2003), *Nas: Video Anthology, Vol. I* (2004).

Moore, Melba Born in New York, New York, October 29, 1945.

Charming Melba Moore has had her share of personal and professional ups and downs, but her talents as a singer, actress, jazz pianist and consummate entertainer have made her an audience favorite for over 40 years. Melba Hill (her birth name) had a father who played saxophone and owned the popular Harlem jazz club Mitten's Playhouse. She studied piano and voice at the High School for Performing Arts and received a bachelor's degree in music education from Montclair (New Jersey) State College. For a time she was a teacher. Moore was married to Charles Higgins (1975–91) and they have a daughter.

She made her debut in the epochal hippie musical *Hair* (1967), but her personal triumph (and her Tony Award) came for her role as Lutiebelle Gussiemae Jenkins when she loosed her four-octave voice in *Purlie* (1970), the musical version of Ossie Davis' *Purlie Victorious*. Moore was the proverbial "toast of Broadway" during this era, combining dynamism and sweetness in a way few actresses have done in any medium before or since. She was the first black actress to win the Best Supporting Actress in a Musical Tony.

At the dawn of the 1970s, Moore traded the role of Broadway diva for that of pop star. Her first album was *I Got Love* (1970). Her second album, which featured a tasteful but somewhat controversial semi-nude photo cover, was one of her best, *Look What You're Doing to the Man* (1971). In 1972, she was nominated for the Grammy for Best New Artist. Other albums were *Peach Melba* (1977) and *The Other Side of the Rainbow* (1982). Her hit singles have included "Lean on Me" (Grammy nominated for Best Rhythm and Blues Vocal Performance), "You Stepped into My Life," "Love's Comin' at Ya," and "Read My Lips."

In 1978, she starred as Marsinah in *Timbuktu!* Despite the fine cast, which included Eartha Kitt, the reviews were far from kind, and the show closed quickly. She also starred in *Inacent Black*, in which she played the title character and contributed music and lyrics, but it closed after 12 days in May 1981. In 1995 she took over the role of Fantine in *Les Miserables*. After she fell on hard times and went on welfare in 1998, she rebounded with a one-woman show, *Sweet Songs: A Journey in One Life*.

Moore's film and TV work has always been secondary to her careers in theater and music, but

Melba Moore.

she can be seen in *Cotton Comes to Harlem* (1970) and the film version of Kurt Weill's *Lost in the Stars* (1974), and she had an electrifying couple of minutes in the screen version of *Hair* (1979) over 20 years after she kicked off her career with Joseph Papp's Shakespeare in the Park version. In 2003, fans were delighted to see her turn up in *The Fighting Temptations* with Beyoncé and Cuba Gooding, Jr.

She had her own television variety show, *The Melba Moore–Clifton Davis Show* (1972), and who can forget her cute-as-a-button Afro wig and sexy outfits in her appearances on *The Flip Wilson Show*? She had another show of her own (*Melba*, 1986); a recurring role as Francine Hope on *Falcon Crest* (1987); and was a guest star on *The Cosby Show* (1988).

Feature Films including Video and TV Movies: *The Sidelong Glances of a Pigeon Kicker* (aka *Pigeons*, 1970), *Cotton Comes to Harlem* (1970), *Opryland* (TV; 1973), *Lost in the Stars* (1974), *Hair* (1979), *Flamingo Road* (TV; 1980), *Charlotte Forten's Mission: Experiment in Freedom* (TV; 1980), *Mother's Day* (TV; 1989), *All Dogs Go to Heaven* (voice; 1989), *Def by Temptation* (1990), *The Fighting Temptations* (2003).

TV: *The 24th Annual Tony Awards* (1970), *The Ed Sullivan Show* (1970), *The Tonight Show*

Starring Johnny Carson (13 segments; 1970–72), *The Mike Douglas Show* (2 segments; 1970–73), *The Flip Wilson Show* (5 segments; 1971–73), *The Melba Moore–Clifton Davis Show* (1972), *Soul Train* (3 segments; 1972–88), *The American Woman: Portraits of Courage* (1976), *The Love Boat* (1979), *The Tim Conway Show* (1980), *The Beatrice Arthur Special* (1980), *Purlie* (1981), *Broadway Plays Washington on Kennedy Center Tonight* (1982), *Top of the Pops* (1982–83), *Ellis Island* (TV; 1984), *Night of 100 Stars II* (1985), *ABC Weekend Specials* ("The Two-Minute Werewolf," 1985), *Hotel* ("Passports," 1985), *Melba* (1986), *The 3rd Annual Black Gold Awards* (1986), *The 59th Annual Academy Awards* (1987), *The 4th Annual Black Gold Awards* (1987), *Falcon Crest* (4 episodes in the role of Francine Hope; "Battle Lines," "Nowhere to Run," "Cold Hands," "Body & Soul," 1987), *It's Showtime at the Apollo* (2 segments; 1987), *ABC Afterschool Specials* ("Seasonal Differences," 1987), *The Cosby Show* ("Twinkle, Twinkle Little Star," 1988), *The 10th Annual Black Achievement Awards* (1989), *Great Performances* ("Christmas with Flicka," 1989), *Monsters* ("The Mandrake Root," 1989), *Mathnet* ("The Case: Off the Record," 1992), *Square One TV* (1992), *Loving* (recurring role as Dr. Burkhart; 1992), *Behind the Music* ("Hair," 2001), *2002 Trumpet Awards*, *Legends Ball* (2006), *Ear of the Heart: The Music of Gail McDermott* (2007), *Hair: Let the Sun Shine In* (2007), *Broadway: Beyond the Golden Age* (2009), *Raspberry & Lavender: Diaries of a Lavender Girl* (2009).

Moorefield, Olive Born in Pittsburgh, Pennsylvania, August 23, 1932.

Here is an African American star that very few Americans even know exists. Olive Moorefield was one of a handful of entertainers (in this case an opera star) who performed on tour with European companies and decided not to return to the United States. Instead she became a star soprano at Vienna's Volksoper.

Moorefield was already beginning to develop an impressive career in the U.S. before she opted for Europe. She was Lolly in *My Darlin' Aida* on Broadway in 1952. Marcel Prawy, a Vienna-born American citizen, had a great inspiration to popularize American musical comedy in Vienna—and he did. His vehicle of choice was *Kiss Me Kate* (originally staged in 1949). In Vienna in 1956 it was carefully translated into colloquial German and presented as *Do Kiss Me Kate*, starring Olive Moorefield as the shrewish Bianca, opposite Hubert Dilworth, who was also black, as Paul. Against all reasonable odds, it worked beautifully, and it opened to excellent reviews. A cast recording is still sought after by collectors. Moorefield was also Bess in the mid-fifties German revival of *Porgy and Bess*, opposite William Warfield, Broadway's definitive Porgy. In 1958 she was in producer Arthur Brauner's theatrical review *Rollen und ihre darstellen*.

German theatergoers were in love with Moorefield, who combined sexy good looks with a distinctive, opera-trained voice. She also became a popular German film actress, although few of her films were widely distributed in the U.S. There were, however, a handful of U.S. theaters that specialized in showing German films, usually without subtitles, to German-American audiences (such as the Wagner Theater in Brooklyn, New York).

She was in *Monpti* (1957) with Romy Schneider, playing, according to *The New York Times*, "a gaudy seductress in the role of a chambermaid." American audiences did get to see her in the big-budget 70mm German production *Onkel Toms hutte* (*Uncle Tom's Cabin*, 1965), recently rediscovered and released here on DVD. Moorefield plays Herbert Lom's sexual obsession, in a role that would have been impossible to imagine in an American film even in the mid-sixties. Moorefield is really gorgeous in this.

She released some singles in the U.S., including the catchy "Mr. Bum Bum" (pronounced "Boom Boom") and "Chico Cha-Cha." Campy material to be sure, but Moorefield's vibrant voice and charismatic delivery is undeniable. She married Dr. Kurt Mach; they have one son, Oliver Kurt Fidelio, born in 1970.

Feature Films including TV Movies: *Das licht der liebe* (1954), *Liebe, die den kopf verliert* (1956), *Das alte forsterhaus* (1956), *Scherben bringen glück* (1957), *Die liebe familie* (1957), *Einmal eine grosse dame sein* (1957), *Monpti* (1957), *Die beine von Dolores* (1957), *Skandal um Dodo* (1958), *Der schwarze blitz* (1958), *Scala: Total verruckt* (1958), *Riviera Story* (1961), *Straße der verheißung* (1962), *Onkel Toms Hütte* (*Uncle Tom's Cabin*, 1965), *Requiem fur eine nonne* (TV; 1965), *Rosemarie* (TV; 1966), *Porgy in wein* (TV; 1966).

TV: *Vergißmeinnicht* (1969), *Fritz Muliar Schau* (1971).

Morgan, Debbi Born in Dunn, North Carolina, September 20, 1956.

Debbi Morgan is the daughter of Lora, a teacher, and George, a butcher. When she was three months old, the family moved to New York City. Morgan's father died of leukemia when she was eight; she was raised by her mother, who was then a typing instructor at Junior High School 80 in the Bronx. Morgan attended Catholic school. Even though she didn't receive a Best Supporting Actress Oscar nomination for the role of clairvoyant Mozelle Batiste Delacroix in *Eve's Bayou* (1997), she did receive a Chicago Film Critics Association Award, an Independent Spirit Award, and an NAACP Image Award nomination for her work.

In *She's All That* (1999), she has a bit role as an eccentric art teacher; in *Coach Carter* (2005), she's the coach's wife; she has a small role in the inner city crime and romance film *Back in the Day* (2005). In *Woman Thou Art Loosed* (2004), she's the matchmaking friend of the young heroine who overcomes abuse and addiction, and in *Love & Basketball* (2000) she is the mother of leading man Quincy McCall (Omar Epps).

Morgan is best known for her succession of roles on daytime soaps, often playing a doctor. On *All My Children* she was Dr. Angie Baxter Hubbard (1982–90, returning to the role in 2008); she won a daytime Emmy for the role in 1989. She reprised the part on *Loving* and *The City*. She was Chantal Marshall on *Generations* and Dr. Ellen Burgess on *Port Charles* (1997–98). On the prime time TV front, she had a recurring role as Diane Harris in *What's Happening!!* (1976–77); she was Laura Gibson on the Lifetime series *For the People*; and The Seer during the fourth season of *Charmed* (a role that was an echo of her part in *Eve's Bayou*). She received some of the best critical notices of her career for her portrayal of Alex Haley's great-aunt Elizabeth Harvey in *Roots: The Next Generations* (1979). Morgan was also a celebrity judge on *I Wanna Be a Soap Star* (2004–06). She is the ex-wife of actor Charles S. Dutton.

Feature Films including Video and TV Movies: *Cry Uncle* (1971), *Amazing Grace* (1974), *Mandingo* (1975), *Taxi Driver* (1976), *The Monkey Hu$tle* (1976), *Love's Savage Fury* (TV; 1979), *Thornwell* (TV; 1981), *The Jesse Owens Story* (TV; 1984), *Guilty of Innocence: The Lenell Geter Story* (TV; 1987), *Eve's Bayou* (1997), *Asunder* (1998), *She's All That* (1999), *Spawn 3: Ultimate Battle*

Debbi Morgan.

(1999), *The Hurricane* (1999), *Love & Basketball* (2000), *The Runaway* (TV; 2000), *Woman Thou Art Loosed* (2004), *Back in the Day* (2005), *Coach Carter* (2005), *Relative Strangers* (2006), *Color of the Cross* (2006), *The Black Man's Guide to Understanding Black Women* (2008).

TV: *Good Times* (2 episodes; "The Break Up," "A Friend in Need," 1976 and 1977), *What's Happening!!* (recurring role of Diane; 1976–77), *The Love Boat* (1979), *Roots: The Next Generations* (miniseries; 1979), *The White Shadow* ("Delores, of Course," 1979, *The Incredible Hulk* ("Falling Angels," 1980), *Trapper John, M.D.* (2 episodes; "Hot Line," "Ladies in Waiting," 1980 and 1982), *Sanford* ("Love Is Blind," 1981), *Behind the Screen* (recurring role as Lynette Porter; 1981–82), *Loving* (pilot; 1983), *ABC Afterschool Specials* ("The Celebrity and the Arcade Kid," "The Less Than Perfect Daughter," 1983 and 1991), *Family Feud* (1985), *Miss Black America Pageant* (1985), *All My Children* (1986–2008), *Generations* (recurring role as Chantal Marshall; 1990–91), *A Different World* ("To Tell the Truth," 1991), *The Cosby Show* ("Eat, Drink and Be Wary," 1992), *Perry Mason: The Case of the Fatal Framing* (1992), *Herman's Head* ("Brackenhooker," 1992), *Roc* (2 episodes in the role of Linda; "The Hand That Rocs the Cradle,"

"Crazy George in Love," 1992 and 1993), *50 Years of Soaps: An All-Star Celebration* (1994), *The City* (recurring role as Dr. Angie Baxter Hubbard Harrison Foster; 1995), *The Rosie O'Donnell Show* (1996), *Port Charles* (recurring role as Dr. Ellen Burgess; 1997–98), *General Hospital* (recurring role as Dr. Ellen Burgess; 1997–98), *Any Day Now* (2 episodes; "Elephants in the Room," "You Think I Am Lying to You?" 1999 and 2000), *City of Angels* ("Smoochas Gracias," 2000), *Strong Medicine* (2 episodes in the role of Chloe Simons; pilot; "Mortality," 2000 and 2001), *Boston Public* (4 episodes in the role of Marsha Shinn; 2000–01), *The Practice* ("The Day After," 2001), *Providence* ("Home Sweet Home," 2001), *Soul Food* (3 episodes in the role of Lynette Van Adams; "God Bless the Child," "Lovers and Other Strangers," "Child Safety," 2001–02), *For the People* (recurring role as District Attorney Lora Gibson; 2002), *Pyramid* (2 segments; 2002 and 2003), *Charmed* (recurring role of The Seer; 2002–03), *Touching Evil* (pilot; 2004), *SoapTalk* (2 segments; 2005 and 2006), *I Wanna Be a Soap Star* (12 segments as a judge; 2005–06), *Forbidden Pages: Voices of Black Erotic Fiction* (narrator; 2006), *Ghost Whisperer* ("Melinda's First Ghost," 2006), *Close to Home* ("Prodigal Son," 2006), *The Bold and the Beautiful* (recurring role of District Attorney Jennifer Tartaro; 2006–07), *The View* (2008).

Video/DVD: *Daytime's Greatest Weddings* (archival; 2004).

Morrow, Mari (aka Morrow, Mary)

Born in Miami, Florida, February 18, 1974.

Mari Morrow is of Barbadian and African American extraction. She was Wendy Mallow on *Baywatch Hawaii* (1992). She also had a recurring role as Eddie's girlfriend, Oneisha, on *Family Matters* (1992–97). She has guest starred on *Soul Food* as Nyla, *The Parkers*, and *The Fresh Prince of Bel-Air*. Morrow has mostly been in action, horror, and black cast films: *Children of the Corn III* (1995), the series derived from a Stephen King story; *Def Jam's How to Be a Player* (1997), with Morrow as Katrina, the best friend of a woman determined to teach her playboy brother a lesson; *Uninvited Guest* (1999), as a woman celebrating her wedding anniversary who experiences terror when her husband lets a stranger into the house; *Today You Die* (2005), with Morrow as the girlfriend of thief Harlan Banks (Steven Seagal); and *Restraining Order* (2006), the tale of a troubled marriage.

She is involved in charity work, especially Project Angel Food, which distributes food to aids patients. Morrow is also a Los Angeles real estate agent. She noted in an interview that a Picasso painting titled "Woman in the Mirror" best describes her: the wild side co-existing with the quiet side.

Feature Films including Video and TV Movies: *Children of the Corn III* (1995), *Undercover Heat* (1995), *Virtuosity* (1995), *Bodily Harm* (1995), *One Last Time* (1996), *How to Be a Player* (1997), *Dead Man on Campus* (1998), *Uninvited Guest* (1999), *Nikita Blues* (2001), *House Party 4: Down to the Last Minute* (2001), *Wanted: Soulful Energy Xchange* (2002), *Book of Love* (2002), *Straight Out* (2003), *National Security* (2003), *Malibooty!* (2003), *Choices 2* (2004), *Hair Show* (2004), *Traci Townsend* (2005), *Flip the Script* (2005), *Today You Die* (2005), *Restraining Order* (2006), *Pastor Brown* (2009).

TV: *Baywatch Hawaii* (recurring role of Wendy Mallow; "The Lost Treasure of Tower 12," "Dead of Summer," 1992), *Family Matters* (recurring role of Oneisha; "Jailhouse Blues," "Dudes," "Higher Anxiety," "Le Jour d'Amour," "Who's Afraid of the Big Black Book?" 1992–97), *The Fresh Prince of Bel-Air* ("Just Say Yo," 1993), *The Jackie Thomas Show* ("Guys and Balls," 1993), *The Sinbad Show* ("Shades of Acceptance," 1993), *Red Shoe Diaries* ("Emily's Dance," 1994), *M.A.N.T.I.S.* ("Cease Fire," 1994), *One Life to Live* (recurring role as Rachel "Ricki" Gannon; 1995–96), *Living Single* ("Dear John," 1996), *Lush Life* ("Lush Beginning," 1996), *Sliders* ("Double Cross," 1996), *Malcolm & Eddie* ("Jugglin'," 1997), *In the House* (3 episodes in the role of Amber; "Love Wars," "Marion Strikes Back," "Return of the Stiletto," 1997), *The Jamie Foxx Show* ("Is She Is, or Is She Ain't?" 1997), *Sparks* ("Brotherly Love," 1997), *Conan* ("Homecoming," 1998), *Sister, Sister* ("Prom Night," 1998), *The Parkers* (recurring role of Desiree Littlejohn; 1999), *Oh Drama!* (various episodes; 2000), *Men, Women & Dogs* (pilot; 2001), *The Tick* ("The License," 2001), *The Twilight Zone* ("Shades of Guilt," 2002), *The District* ("Old Wounds," 2002), *Soul Food* (recurring role of Nyla; "Successful Failure," "Love Me or Leave Me," "Take It to the Limit," "Fear Eats the Soul," 2004).

Shorts: *At Face Value* (1999).

Moses, Ethel Born in Virginia, 1908.

Ethel Moses was a chorus girl and popular stage dancer who appeared in several key Oscar Micheaux films. She came from a big family: three boys and three girls. She grew up in Philadelphia, but when she was a teenager her family moved to New York. All of the Moses sisters — Ethel, Lucia and Julia — were beautiful and talented and went into show business, becoming chorus girls and actresses despite the wishes of their conservative preacher father, Minister W.H. Moses of the New York National Baptist Church.

Composer, performer and musical director Will Marion Cook gave Ethel and Lucia their start and taught them the dance steps that landed them in *Dixie to Broadway* (1924) starring Florence Mills. All three Moses sisters danced at Harlem's world-famous Cotton Club. Ethel also danced at Connie's Inn and the Ubangi Club, two other top-notch Harlem showcases of the era.

Ethel toured and performed with the Cab Calloway and Lucky Milander bands in major European venues — in Monte Carlo, Nice, Cannes, Naples and Paris. She was featured in some of the best stage shows of the era: *Keep Shuffling* (1928), *Show Boat* (1932), and *Blackbirds of 1935*. This led to her appearance in musical shorts which featured her dance skills. These shorts include *Cab Calloway's Hi De Ho* (1934), *Cab Calloway's Jitterbug Party* 1935), *HarlemMania* and *Policy Man* (both 1938).

In a 1936 interview with the *Amsterdam News*, Moses said that she wanted to become a serious actress. She did come of age in the Micheaux films. *Temptation* (1936) made her a full-fledged race film star. She played a naïve, impressionable model who poses nude, inadvertently gets enmeshed with gangsters and smugglers, and winds up falsely accused of murder. In *Underworld* (1937), she is a college girl who unwittingly becomes the "other woman." Again, her naïveté gets her in trouble.

Her next film, *God's Step Children* (1937), is one of Micheaux's most famous productions, and it continues to be controversial and topical to this day. *God's Step Children* includes variations on themes from *Imitation of Life* (1934) and *These Three* (1936), but it has its own dramatic power. Moses appears in the dual roles of Mrs. Cushinberry and her daughter. The film seems to be alleging that an interracial child will look down on darker-skinned blacks as being naturally inferior. Naomi, the light-skinned black woman, dies at the end of the film in "Bad Seed" fashion — ostensibly as an act of nature. Her last film roles were in *Gone Harlem* and *Birthright* (both 1939). As Sissy in *Birthright*, another Micheaux film, she's involved with two men, a ne'er-do-well and an educated but "green" fellow. This sets up a classic Micheaux morality lesson.

Unlike many of her contemporaries, Moses did not appear in mainstream Hollywood films — which explains the absence of gratuitous bit parts and maid roles in her filmography. Moses was a woman of strong, liberal-leaning principles. She made news when she protested a German Bund Meeting in Madison Square Garden in 1939 and was escorted out of the building by the police. This was at a time when pro–German feelings in the U.S. were quite high in some quarters.

Moses was married to Benny Payne, a pianist with Cab Calloway's band. She left show business in the early 1940s and lived a quiet life in New Jersey out of the spotlight for the remainder of her life.

Feature Films: *Birthright* (1924), *Temptation* (1935), *Underworld* (1937), *God's Step Children* (1938), *Gone Harlem* (1939), *Birthright* (1939).

Shorts: *Cab Calloway's Hi De Ho* (1934), *Cab Calloway's Jitterbug Party* (1935), *Harlemania* (1938), *Policy Man* (1938).

Moses, Lucia Lynn Born in Virginia, 1906.

Although predominantly known as a popular dancer and showgirl, Lucia Lynn Moses also appeared in a key race film, her only film appearance. She was one of three Moses sisters in show business; Ethel and Julia were also entertainers. Lucia was well known as a popular dancer at the Plantation Club and the Cotton Club in Harlem, and toured Europe in the twenties, including a famous stint in Paris.

In *The Scar of Shame* (1927) she stars as Louise Howard, a woman from the lower socioeconomic class who marries Harry Henderson (Alvin Hillyard), an educated young musician. He wants to get her away from the bad influence of her stepfather. However, he is ashamed to introduce her to his mother because of her lower caste. The title of the film refers to the scar the Louise receives as a result of being wounded in the neck from a crossfire bullet in a gun battle between the hero and an unscrupulous saloon owner named Eddie. Louise becomes involved in Eddie's machinations and tries to dupe the young musician.

One of four films produced by The Colored Film Players Corporation of Philadelphia, this well-executed melodrama benefits from decent production values and its timeless themes of race and class. While filming *The Scar of Shame*, Moses was commuting back and forth between the studio in Philadelphia and her chorus line job at the Cotton Club.

Feature Films: *The Scar of Shame* (1927).

Moten, Etta (aka Moten Barnett, Etta)

Born in Weimar, Texas, November 5, 1901; died in Chicago, Illinois, January 2, 2004.

Etta Moten was the daughter of Ida and Freeman Moten. Her father was a Methodist minister. At the age of ten, she received an educational scholarship and was already exhibiting a fine singing voice, which led to her becoming a member of the choral club in Paul Quinn College, the theological college where her father taught. When the family was transferred to Los Angeles, she became a member of the chorus at Western University. She abandoned college after her first marriage (to one of her high school teachers), becoming the mother of three children. But the marriage didn't last, and she returned to college. Her first professional job was with the Jackson Jubilee Singers. The money she made paid for her education at Western and at the University of Kansas. In 1931, Moten graduated with a bachelor's degree in fine arts and, at the urging of her professors, relocated to the Mecca known as New York as a member of the Eva Jessye Choir. She began getting some work on Broadway and began flirting with the idea of acting in films, but only her voice was used in *Ladies of the Big House* (1931), dubbing vocals for Barbara Stanwyck.

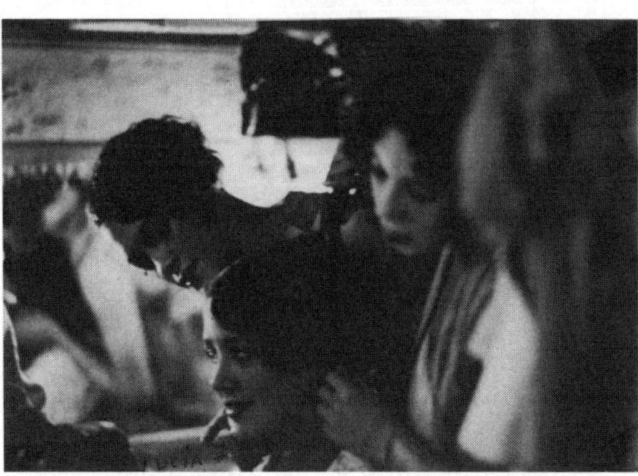

Lucia Lynn Moses in Paris in the 1920s. (Photograph by Germaine Krull. Ada "Bricktop" Smith Photograph Collection, Photographs and Prints Division, Schomburg Center for Research in Black Culture, The New York Public Library, Astor, Lenox and Tilden Foundations.)

Her two Broadway shows were *Fast and Furious* (1931), which was not a hit, and *Zombie* (1932), which was. When the Los Angeles production of *Zombie* was staged, Moten went along with the show to get closer to Hollywood in order to audition for films. Moten knew she had the skills to score strongly in musicals — but even Moten could not quite pierce the Iron Curtain of racism, although she came surprisingly close.

Her singing voice was used in several other films (such as for Theresa Harris in 1933's *Professional Sweetheart*), but it wasn't until *Gold Diggers of 1933* that she actually appeared on screen, as a war-widowed housewife, singing "My Forgotten Man." She was one of the first black women to appear as something other than a maid in a Hollywood film and was heralded as "the New Negro Woman" by the black press. She would have appeared onscreen in the Jean Harlow vehicle *Bombshell* (1933), but her scenes were cut. She did wind up on screen again one more memorable time, singing "The Carioca" (which was nominated for an Academy Award for Best Song) in *Flying Down to Rio* (1933) with Fred Astaire and Ginger Rogers. Moten had fruit in her hair, predating Carmen Miranda (who made a career of that look).

Composer George Gershwin saw Moten on screen and heard her radio show "Etta Moten Sings," which was broadcast from San Francisco, and was deeply struck by her musical ability. He was so impressed that he asked her to star in a new folk opera he was working on, by the name of *Porgy and Bess* (which opened on Broadway in 1935). Moten agreed to star, but wanted to alter the songs, which were written for a soprano, to fit her contralto voice, and Gershwin had a problem with that. The role of Bess went to Ann Brown, although Moten took over the role on Broadway in 1942 and toured with it, including in Los Angeles, until 1945. Moten was the definitive Bess, and that became her signature role. An aspiring young singer and actress named Lena Horne saw Moten in *Porgy and Bess*, and she became Horne's inspiration and role model.

In 1934, Moten was the first black woman

ever to sing at the White House, on Franklin Delano Roosevelt's birthday. Despite strains and increasing limitations on her voice, Moten continued to sing professionally until the 1952. Her last Broadway appearance was in an all-black version of Aristophanes' *Lysistrata* (1946) with Fredi Washington and a young, unknown Sidney Poitier in a small role. Moten married Claude Barnett, her second husband, in 1934. Barnett was the head of the Associated Negro Press.

In her later years, Moten became deeply involved with a number of key civic organizations, including the National Council of Negro Women. She represented the United States at various independence ceremonies of African nations at the request of the federal government. She also hosted a local radio show in Chicago on WMAQ/NBC.

Moten was inducted into the Black Filmmakers Hall of Fame in 1979. Her 100th birthday celebration was held in Chicago in 2001. The festivities included an award presented by Halle Berry at the Chicago International Film Festival for the retrospective "Black Women in Film—From Etta to Halle."

Etta Moten died of pancreatic cancer at the age of 102.

Feature Films: *Gold Diggers of 1933* (1933), *Flying Down to Rio* (1933).

Etta Moten (Photographs and Prints Division, Schomburg Center for Research in Black Culture, The New York Public Library, Astor, Lenox and Tilden Foundations).

Mowry, Tamera Born in Gelhausen, West Germany, July 6, 1978.

Tamera Darvette Mowry is the twin sister of Tia Mowry. Together they starred on the hit sitcom *Sister, Sister* (1994–99). Her parents are Timothy and Darlene (née Flowers); her father is an Italian American who was a sergeant in the armed services and later became a police officer; her mother was also in the armed services and has managed her daughters' careers. The pair met in high school in Miami, Florida.

The twins were raised in Honolulu, Hawaii, and then moved to Los Angeles. Tamera attended Birmingham High School in Van Nuys, California, along with her sister. She is older than Tia by two minutes and can be identified from Tia by a mole on her cheek. Her brothers are Tavior and Tahj, who had quite a success with his own series, *Full House* (1992) and *Smart Guy* (1997).

When *Sister, Sister* ended its long run, both sisters studied psychology at California's Pepperdine University. After graduation they alternated working together and having individual careers. They were in the Disney Channel movies *Twitches* (2006) and *Twitches Too* (2007). Tamera starred solo as Dr. Kayla Thornton in the Lifetime series *Strong Medicine* (2004–05).

She won two NAACP Image Awards in 1999 and 2000 for Outstanding Role in a Comedy Series for *Sister, Sister* (shared with Tia).

Feature Films including Video and TV Movies: *Something to Sing About* (TV; 2000), *Seventeen Again* (2000), *The Hot Chick* (2002), *Twitches* (TV; 2005), *Twitches Too* (TV; 2008), *Hollywood Horror* (2008).

TV: *ABC TGIF* (1990), *Flesh 'n' Blood* ("Bebe's Wedding," 1992), *Full House* ("The Devil Made Me Do It," 1992), *Sister, Sister* (recurring role of Tamera Ann Campbell; 1994–99), *Sidewalks Entertainment* (1995), *Are You Afraid of the Dark?* ("The Tale of the Chameleons," 1995), *The Adventures of Hyperman* (recurring role as the voice of Emma C. Squared; 1995–96), *The Rosie O'Donnell Show* (1996), *Smart Guy* ("Brother, Brother,"

1997), *All-Star TGIF Magic* (1997), *Blue's Clues* ("Blue's Birthday," 1998), *The 26th Annual American Music Awards* (1998), *Detention* (recurring role as Orangejella LaBelle; 1999), *Hollywood Squares* (1999), *Express Yourself* (various episodes; 2001), *Tavis Smiley* (2004), *Strong Medicine* (recurring role of Dr. Kayla Thorton; 2004–06), *Hope Rocks: The Concert with a Cause* (2005), *50 Cutest Child Stars: All Grown Up* (2005), *Stranded with a Star* (2006), *101 Guiltiest Guilty Pleasures* (2006), *Child Star Confidential* (2006), *Family Guy* (4 episodes; voice; "Peterotica," "Mother Tucker," "Barely Legal," "Peter's Two Dads," 2006–07), *America's Next Top Model* (2007), *Roommates* (recurring role of Hope Daniels; 2008).

Video/DVD: *TV in Black: The First Fifty Years* (2004).

Mowry, Tia Born in Gelhausen, West Germany, July 6, 1978.

Tia Dashon Mowry is the twin sister of Tamera Mowry. Together they starred on the hit sitcom *Sister, Sister* (1994–99). The premise of *Sister, Sister* is that two twins separated at birth, one raised by her mother and the other by her father, are reunited after 15 years. They hit it off immediately after meeting and persuade their parents to try living together for their sake. This is a variant on the basic situation of Disney's old film *The Parent Trap* (1960), and it was a sturdy format that yielded many laughs as the twins discovered that their personalities were actually quite different. The series settled in for a popular five-year run. Tia won two NAACP Image Awards in 1999 and 2000 for Outstanding Role in a Comedy Series for *Sister, Sister* (shared with Tamera).

Tia's parents, Timothy and Darlene, were both in the armed services and had met in high school. The twins were raised in Honolulu, Hawaii; they began competing in pageants and talent shows when their parents were stationed in Texas. They convinced their parents to move to Los Angeles so the girls could pursue acting. Both girls attended Birmingham High School in Van Nuys, California, and later Pepperdine University, where they both majored in psychology.

In their post–*Sister, Sister* careers, the twins have alternated working together and having individual careers. They were both in the Disney Channel movies *Twitches* (2006) and *Twitches Too* (2007), and Tia has done solo voice work as Sasha on the animated series *Bratz* (2006). She is Melanie Barnett in the CW series *The Game* (2006–08) and also played the character on two episodes of *Girlfriends* (2006–07). Tia is showing new acting maturity in the role, adding dramatic shading and complexity to her character Melanie. She married Cory Hardrict in 2008.

Feature Films including Video and TV Movies: *Seventeen Again* (2000), *The Hot Chick* (2002), *Twitches* (TV; 2005), *Twitches Too* (TV; 2008), *Hollywood Horror* (2008), *Four to the Floor* (2009).

TV: *ABC TGIF* (1990), *Dangerous Women* (1991), *Full House* ("The Devil Made Me Do It," 1992), *Sister, Sister* (recurring role of Tia Landry; 1994–99), *Sidewalks Entertainment* (1995), *Are You Afraid of the Dark?* ("The Tale of the Chameleons," 1995), *The Adventures of Hyperman* (voice; 1995), *Smart Guy* ("Brother, Brother," 1997), *The Rosie O'Donnell Show* (1996), *All-Star TGIF Magic* (1997), *Blue's Clues* ("Blue's Birthday," 1998), *The 26th Annual American Music Awards* (1998), *Praise the Lord* (1998), *Hollywood Squares* (1999), *Detention* (recurring role as Lemonjella LaBelle; 1999), *Express Yourself* (various episodes; 2001), *50 Cutest Child Stars: All Grown Up* (2005), *Hope Rocks: The Concert with a Cause* (2005), *Love, Inc.* (2 episodes in the role of Kim; "Hope & Faith," "The Honeymooners," 2005), *Stranded with a Star* (2006), *The 20th Annual Soul Train Music Awards* (2006), *101 Guiltiest Guilty Pleasures* (2006), *Child Star Confidential* (2006), *The Tyra Banks Show* (2006), *Strong Medicine* ("My Sister, My Doctor, Myself," 2006), *Bratz* (voice; "Survivor," 2006), *Girlfriends* (2 episodes in the role of Melanie Barnett; "The Game," "It's Been Determined," 2006 and 2007), *The Game* (recurring role of Melanie Barnett; 2006–08), *America's Next Top Model* (2 segments; 2007), *The American Standards* (2007).

Video/DVD: *TV in Black: The First Fifty Years* (2004).

Mumba, Samantha Born in Dublin, Ireland, January 18, 1983.

Samantha Tamania Anne Cecilia Mumba is an Irish pop star who has seen success in Europe and the United States, mixing a recording career with a sometime acting career. Half Irish and half Zambian, her father Peter is an aircraft engineer; her mother Barbara is a cabin crew member with Aer Lingus; she has a sister named Omero.

She attended Billy Barry's Stage School from

Samantha Mumba and Guy Pearce in *The Time Machine* (2002).

age three to 15. She was the lead in *The Hot Mikado*, a jazz version of the Gilbert and Sullivan opera. She was discovered and signed to Polydor Records at age 15, releasing her first album, *Gotta Tell You*, which yielded a hit single of the same name, and which went Platinum.

She took a break from music when her sales started to slow, appearing on the British daytime TV show *Loose Women* (2008). After *Women* was cancelled, she concentrated on looking for film work. Mumba had the Yvette Mimieux role in the remake of George Pal's *The Time Machine* (2002). The film did fairly well internationally, and she did other features in quick succession, but none was outstanding or successful.

Feature Films including Video Movies: *The Time Machine* (2002), *Spin the Bottle* (2003), *Boy Eats Girl* (2005), *Nailed* (2006), *Johnny Was* (2006), *3 Crosses* (2008), *Shifter* (2009).

TV: *The 2000 Billboard Music Awards* (2000), *Top of the Pops* (2 segments; 2000), *Samantha Mumba and Aaron Carter in Concert* (2001), *Top of the Pops Plus* (2 segments; 2001–02), *GMTV* (2001), *CD:UK* (2001), *The Royal Variety Performance 2001*, *Friday Night with Jonathan Ross* (2001), *SM:TV Live* (2001), *Richard & Judy* (2001), *The Big Breakfast* (2001), *HBO First Look* (*The Time Machine*, 2002), *Brit Awards 2002*, *V Graham Norton* (2002), *Smile* (2002), *The Elle Style Awards* (2002), *This Morning* (2002), *The Kumars at No. 42* (2002), *Close Encounters with Keith Barry* (2002), *Irish Film and Television Awards* (2003), *Astounding Celebrities* (2003), *The Late Late Show* (2004), *Off the Rails* (2004), *The 2nd Meteor Irish Music Awards* (2005), *The Afternoon Show* (2005), *The Panel* (2005), *Anonymous* (2005), *Harvey Goldsmith: Get Your Act Together* (2007), *Xpose* (2007), *Saturday Night with Miriam* (2007), *Loose Women* (2008), *This Morning* (2008).

Mya (aka Harrison, Mya)

Born in Greenbelt, Maryland, October 10, 1978.

R&B singer Mya had a conspicuous cameo in the Academy Award–winning Best Picture *Chicago* (2002), in which she got to sing and dance in the great "He Had It Coming" sequence, and roles in *Dirty Dancing: Havana Nights* (2004) and *How She Move* (2007); she has also done guest star work on *Sister, Sister*, *1-800-Missing* and *NCIS*. Mya

Marie Harrison is of Italian American and Jamaican American extraction. Her parents are Sherman (a singer and musician) and Theresa (an accountant), and she has two younger brothers, Chaz and Nijel.

Mya began her show business career as a tap dancer, having studied tap with Savion Glover, the contemporary master of that art form. She has performed tap routines at Lincoln Center, the Smithsonian Institution and the Shakespeare Theater. She is the winner of two MTV Video Music Awards and a Grammy for her ensemble performance of *Lady Marmelade*, heard on the *Moulin Rouge* soundtrack in 2001. Other hit singles include "The Best of Me," "Ghetto Supastar," (with Pras and Dirty Ol' Bastard), and "My Love Is Like ... Wo!" Her albums are *Mya* (1998), *Fear of Flying* (2000), *Moodring* (2004) and *Liberation* (2008). She was scheduled to star as Velma Kelly on Broadway in *Chicago* in 2008, but broke her foot just days before the opening.

Her philanthropic work is admirable. She is a committed animal rights activist who frequently does charity work in that area; she is a spokesperson for the North Shore Animal League. She was also spokesperson for Secret to Self Esteem (1998–2001) and founded the Mya Arts and Tech Foundation in 2005.

Feature Films including Video and TV Movies: *In Too Deep* (1999), *WaSanGo* (2001), *Chicago* (2002), *Dirty Dancing: Havana Nights* (2004), *Shall We Dance* (2004), *Cursed* (2005), *Swap Meet* (2006), *The Heart Specialist* (aka *Ways of the Flesh*, 2006), *How She Move* (2007), *The Metrosexual* (2007), *Cover* (2007), *Bottleworld* (2008), *Love for Sale* (2008), *Penthouse* (2008).

TV: *Sister, Sister* ("FreakNik," 1999), *All That* (1999), *The 28th Annual American Music Awards* (2001), *The Rosie O'Donnell Show* (2001), *2gether: The Series* ("Lyrics," 2001), *MTV Icon: Janet Jackson* (2001), *Making the Video* ("Lady Marmelade," 2001), *2001 MTV Movie Awards*, *1st Annual BET Awards* (2001), *MTV Video Music Awards 2001*, *Michael Jackson: 30th Anniversary Celebration* (2001), *The 44th Annual Grammy Awards* (2002), *VH1 Behind the Movie* ("Chicago," 2002), *Haunted* ("Abby," 2002), *I Love the '80s* (2002), *The 30th Annual American Music Awards* (2003), *The Disco Ball ... a 30-Year Celebration* (2003), *The Late Late Show with Craig Kilborn* (2003), *2003 MTV Movie Awards*, *2003 Much Music Video Music Awards*, *3rd Annual BET Awards* (2003), *MTV Bash: Carson Daly* (2003), *Passions* (2003), *MTV Video Music Awards 2003*, *The Blues* (2003), *The GQ Men of the Year Awards* (2003), *Punk'd* (2003), *MADtv* (2 episodes; 2003), *40 Most Awesomely Bad Dirty Songs ... Ever* (2003), *The Tonight Show with Jay Leno* (2004), *Freestyle with Brian Friedman* (2004), *1-800-Missing* ("Pop Star," 2004), *Maxim Hot 100* (2004), *Forever in Our Hearts: The "Making of" Documentary* (2005), *The 19th Annual Soul Train Music Awards* (2005), *The 3rd Annual TV Land Awards* (2005), *It's Showtime at the Apollo* (2005), *NCIS* ("Pop Life," 2005), *Soul Train* (2005), *Video on Trial* (archival; 2006), *Love Monkey* ("Coming Out," 2006), *TV Land's Top Ten* ("Top Ten Musical Moments," 2006), *Secret Talents of the Stars* (2008).

Video/DVD: *Now That's What I Call Music!: The Best Videos of 2003* (2003).

Nash, Niecy Born in Los Angeles, California, February 23, 1970.

Niecy Nash's breakout role was as deputy Raineesha Williams on the freewheeling, frequently hilarious improvisational Comedy Central hit *Reno 911!* (2003–08). She was also in the not quite equally amusing spin-off movie *Reno 911!: Miami* (2007). She was Bernie Mac's sister Bonita on *The Bernie Mac Show* (2003–05), and Miss Cassandra, the dubious psychic on *That's So Raven* (2003). She is the voice of Mrs. Boots on the animated ABC Family cartoon *Slacker Cats* (2007). Style Network viewers know her as the host of *Clean House* (2004–08), and she has been a regular correspondent on *The Tonight Show with Jay Leno* (since 2006). She has also had a recurring role on *City of Angels* (as Eveline Walker; 2000).

Nash made her film debut with Whoopi Goldberg and Drew Barrymore in *Boys on the Side* (1995) and was in *Guess Who* (2005), a loose remake of *Guess Who's Coming to Dinner?* with Bernie Mac and Ashton Kutcher.

Although she was born in Los Angeles, her family lived in St. Louis until Niecy was eight, at which time they moved back to L.A. She is a graduate of California State University, Dominguez Hills. Nash is a spokesperson for M.A.V.I.S. (Mothers Against Violence in Schools). She has three children. She was married for 16 years, divorcing in 2007. She has her own production company, Next in Line, and is considering a variety of TV and feature film projects.

Feature Films including Video and TV Movies: *Boys on the Side* (1995), *Cookie's Fortune* (1999), *The Bachelor* (1999), *Malibu's Most Wanted* (2003), *Hair Show* (2004), *Guess Who* (2005), *Here's Comes Peter Cottontail* (voice; 2005), *Cook-Off!* (2006), *Reno 911!: Miami* (2007), *Horton Hears a Who* (voice; 2008), *Pretty/Handsome* (TV; 2008), *Not Easily Broken* (2009), *G-Force* (2009), *The Proposal* (2009).

TV: *Party of Five* ("Spring Breaks," Part I, 1996), *Malcolm & Eddie* ("B.S. I Love You," 1999), *City of Angels* (4 episodes in the role of Eveline Walker; "Prototype," "The High Cost of Living," "Unhand Me," "When Worlds Collide," 2000), *Popular* ("Hard on the Outside, Soft in the Middle," 2000), *Kate Brasher* ("Tracy," 2001), *One on One* ("15 Candles," 2001), *NYPD Blue* ("Baby Love," 2001), *Judging Amy* ("Beating the Bounds," 2001), *Reba* ("He's Having a Baby," 2002), *Girlfriends* ("Just Dessert," 2002), *For Your Love* ("The Blast from the Past," 2002), *Presidio Med* ("Milagros," 2002), *CSI* ("Snuff," 2002), *That's So Raven* ("Psychics Wanted," 2003), *Kid Notorious* (voice of Tollie Mae; 2003), *Comedy Central Presents: The Commies* (2003), *ER* ("Missing," 2003), *The Bernie Mac Show* (3 episodes; "The Other Sister," "Family Reunion," "Who Gives This Bride," 2003–05), *Reno 911!* (recurring role of Deputy Raineesha Williams; 2003–08), *Half & Half* ("The Big Mother of a Mother's Day Rides Again Episode," 2004), *E! 101 Most Awesome Moments in Entertainment* (2004), *Monk* (Mr. Monk and the Girl Who Cried Wolf," 2004), *Clean House* (series host; 2004–08), *VH1 Big in '05* (2005), *My Name Is Earl* ("Cost Dad the Election," 2005), *Weekends at the DL* (2005), *The 2nd Annual BET Comedy Awards* (2005), *101 Craziest TV Moments* (2005), *Minoriteam* (voice of Fausto's Mama, Meka; 2005), *Celebrity Autobiography: In Their Own Words* (2005), *In the Cutz* (2006), *Holidays with Style* (2006), *The Boondocks* ("Wingmen," 2006), *The Megan Mullally Show* (2006), *Minoriteam* (voice of Fasto's Mama; "His Story," "Illegal Aliens," "Evilfellas," "Balactus," Parts I and II, 2006), *The Morning Show with Mike and Juliet* (2007), *Kathy Griffin: My Life on the D-List* (2007), *Slacker Cats* (voice of Mrs. Boots; 2007), *American Dad* (voice; 2 episodes; "American Dream Factory," "Haylias," 2007), *MADtv* (2008), *Baisden After Dark* (2 segments; 2008), *Entertainment Tonight* (4 segments; 2008), *BET Awards 2008*, *Do Not Disturb* (recurring role as Rhonda; 2008), *Chocolate News* (2008).

Shorts: *Jepardee* (2005).

Nelson, Novella Born in Brooklyn, New York, December 17, 1939.

Perhaps more fans know Novella Nelson as an outstanding jazz singer and cabaret artist, but Nelson has had an extensive theatrical, film and television career. Her Broadway career began as an understudy and replacement in *Hello, Dolly!* (1964–70). She was Missy in *Purlie* (1970–71); Ftatateeta in *Caesar and Cleopatra* (1977); Addie in *The Little Foxes* (1981), with which she also toured; and was a standby for the starring role of Bessie Delany in *Having Our Say* (1995). In 2007 she performed at London's Young Vic Theatre and was in Theodore Ward's *Big White Fog* at the Almeida Theatre; it is the story of a black family in Chicago during the Depression.

Roles in regional theater include *The Resistable Rise of Arturo Ui* (National Actors' Theater), *Boesman and Lena* (Yale Repertory Theater), and *Oedipus* (Harvard's American Repertory Theater). Nelson has directed productions at the Lincoln Center Theater and the Public Theater, and for the Negro Ensemble Company. In 2008 she taught a class in voice-over craft and practice at Philadelphia's Scribe Video Center.

Her television credits include *The West Wing* (2004) and the recurring role of Judge Fitzwater on the daytime drama *One Life to Live* (1997). Nelson has worked with major directors such as Francis Ford Coppola (*The Cotton Club*; 1984), Peter Weir (*Green Card*; 1990), actor-director Denzel Washington (*Antwone Fisher*; 2002), and Lars van Trier (*Dear Wendy*; 2005). Her parents are James Nelson and Evelyn Hines. She has a daughter, Alesa Novella Blanchard-Nelson.

Feature Films including Video and TV Movies: *An Unmarried Woman* (1978), *The Seduction of Joe Tynan* (1979), *The Cotton Club* (1984), *A Doctor's Story* (TV; 1984), *He's Fired, She's Hired* (TV; 1984), *The Flamingo Kid* (1984), *Orphans* (1987), *The Littlest Victims* (TV; 1989), *Privilege* (1990), *The Bonfire of the Vanities* (1990), *Green Card* (1990), *Strictly Business* (1991), *Citizen Cohn* (TV; 1992), *Daybreak* (TV; 1993), *Weekend at Bernie's II* (1993), *Dead Funny* (1994), *The Keeper* (1995), *Mercy* (1995), White Lies (1996), *The Summer of Ben Tyler* (TV; 1996), *Harambee* (TV; 1996), *Girl 6* (1996), *Manny &*

Lo (1996), *The Devil's Advocate* (1997), *1999* (1998), *Mama Flora's Family* (TV; 1998), *A Perfect Murder* (1998), *Judy Berlin* (1999), *Antwone Fisher* (2002), *Head of State* (2003), *Birth* (2004), *Dear Wendy* (2005), *Preaching to the Choir* (2005), *Stephanie Daley* (2006), *Premium* (2006), *Griffin & Phoenix* (2006), *The Ten* (2007), *The Toe Tactic* (2008), *Sweet Kandy* (2009).

TV: *Chiefs* (miniseries; 1983), *Kojak: The Price of Justice* (1987), *A Man Called Hawk* ("Never My Love," 1989), *The Days and Nights of Molly Dodd* ("Here's Why You Should Always Make Your Bed in the Morning," 1989), *Law & Order* (2 episodes; "Out of the Half-Light," "Humiliation," 1990 and 1995), *New York News* (1995), *New York Undercover* (2 episodes; "Olde Tyme Religion," "Capital Punishment," 1995 and 1998), *Oz* ("Plan B," 1997), *One Life to Live* (recurring role of Judge Fitzwater; 1997), *Sex in the City* ("Oh Come All Ye Faithful," 1998), *Law & Order: Special Victims Unit* (3 episodes; "Sophomore Jinx," "Conscience," "Unorthodox," 1999–2008), *100 Centre Street* ("Things Change," 2001), *Taboo* (narrator; 5 segments; "Tests of Faith," "Death," "Rites of Passage," "Marriage," "Sexuality," 2002), *Third Watch* ("In Confidence," 2003), *Whoopi* ("Once Bitten," 2003), *The West Wing* (2 episodes in the role of Gail Fitzwallace; "Gaza," "N.S.F. Thurmont," 2004), *The Starter Wife* (miniseries; 2007), *The Ten* (2007), *Law & Order: Special Victims Unit* ("Unorthodox," 2008).

Shorts: *The Gilded Six Bits* (2001), *Conversations with Id* (2003), *King* (2007).

Newkirk, Toy Born in Brooklyn, New York, January 16, 1979.

Toy Newkirk was a competitive ice skater until age 13. Her first acting job was at age five in a Tide detergent commercial. She is known for her role in the popular horror series installment *A Nightmare on Elm Street 4: The Dream Master* (1988). She was also in the TV movie *The O.J. Simpson Story* (1995), which exploited the controversial life of the football star turned murder suspect. Her last known acting credit was in the film *Tapped Out* (2003).

Newkirk's series TV work is more substantial than her feature film output: *Diff'rent Strokes*, *227*, a recurring role as Bianca on *A Different World*, *Beverly Hills, 90210*, *The Commish*, *Living Single*, and the daytime soap *Days of Our Lives*.

Feature Films including Video and TV Movies: *Rafferty* (TV; 1977), *A Nightmare on Elm Street 4: The Dream Master* (1988), *What's Alan Watching?* (TV; 1989), *The O.J. Simpson Story* (TV; 1995), *Sammy the Screenplay* (voice; 1997), *Tapped Out* (2003).

TV: *ABC Weekend Specials* ("Little Lulu," 1978), *Diff'rent Strokes* ("So You Want to Be a Rock Star?" 1985), *227* ("A Funny Thing Happened on the Way to the Pageant," 1988), *A Different World* (recurring role of Bianca; "Everything Must Change," "How Bittersweet It Is," "Blues for Nobody's Child," 1990), *Beverly Hills, 90210* ("Hello Life, Goodbye Beverly Hills," 1995), *The Commish* (2 episodes; "Off Broadway," Parts I and II, 1995), *Living Single* ("Ride the Maverick," 1996), *Days of Our Lives* (1997).

Newton, Thandie Born in London, England, November 6, 1972.

Thandiwe Newton is the daughter of a Zimbabwean mother (Nyasha) and a British father (Nick). She is better known as Thandie (pronounced "Tandy"). She lived in Zambia until political strife caused her family to move back to England, where she lived in Cornwall until she was 11. She was enrolled in the London Art Educational School, where she began by studying dance but a back injury led her to switch to acting, and was later educated at Downing College, Cambridge (she has an anthropology degree)

Her film debut was as the Ugandan student who has an interracial affair with a white student in the Australian film *Flirting* (1991). Newton stole the film, and it was clear even at this point that she was an actress to be reckoned with. She became better known in America in the role of Sally Hemings, the slave President Thomas Jefferson had a relationship and children with in *Jefferson in Paris* (1995). She became well known from her role on TV's *ER* as Dr. Makemba "Lem" Likasu (2003–05).

Her film roles kept getting bigger, as illustrated by her work as Tom Cruise's love interest in *Mission Impossible II* (2000), a giant box office success, and by her fine work as the spoiled TV director's wife abused by a white cop in the Academy Award–winning Best Picture of 2004, *Crash*. She won the British Academy of Film and Television Arts Award for Best Supporting Actress for *Crash* and a Screen Actors Guild Award for her ensemble work in the film. She has also been nominated for five NAACP Image Awards. New-

Thandie Newton in *Loaded* (1994).

ton was nominated for Outstanding Supporting Actress in a Motion Picture for *Beloved* (1998), *Mission Impossible II*, *Crash*, and *The Pursuit of Happyness* (2006). She was nominated for Outstanding Actress in a Motion Picture for *The Truth About Charlie* (2002).

Newton is a delight even in bad films (*The Leading Man*, 1996; *The Truth About Charlie*), and has had her share of fine performances in "sleeper" films, even if the films themselves may not be well known (*Gridlock'd*, 1997; *Besieged*, 1998). She married British writer, director and producer Oliver Parker in 1998. Her daughter Ripley was born in 2000, and her son Nico was born in 2004.

Feature Films including Video and TV Movies: *Pirate Prince* (TV; 1991), *Flirting* (1991), *The Young Americans* (1993), *Loaded* (1994), *Interview with the Vampire* (1994), *Jefferson in Paris* (1995), *The Journey of August King* (1995), *The Leading Man* (1996), *In Your Dreams* (TV; 1997), *Gridlock'd* (1997), *Beseiged* (1998), *Beloved* (1998), *Mission: Impossible II* (2000), *It Was an Accident* (2000), *The Truth About Charlie* (2002), *Shade* (2003), *The Chronicles of Riddick* (2004), *Crash* (2004), *The Pursuit of Happyness* (2006), *Norbit* (2007), *Run, Fatboy, Run* (2007), *RocknRolla* (2008), *W.* (2008), *2012* (2009).

TV: *The Word* (1991), *The Directors* ("The Films of Jonathon Demme," 1999), *2000 Blockbuster Entertainment Awards*, *The Rosie O'Donnell Show* (2000), *The Orange British Academy Film Awards* (2001), *Brit Awards 2001*, *The Orange British Academy Film Awards* (2002), *The Orange British Academy Film Awards* (2003), *ER* (recurring role of Makemba "Kem" Likasu; 2003–05), *The Lowdown: The Chronicles of Riddick* (2004), *The Oprah Winfrey Show* (2005), *Tavis Smiley* (2 appearances; 2005 and 2006), *The Late, Late Show with Craig Ferguson* (3 appearances; 2005–08), *The Orange British Academy Film Awards* (2006), *Parkinson* (2006), *Screen Nation Television and Film Awards 2006*, *Jimmy Kimmel Live!* (2006), *2006 BET Awards Nominations Live* (2006), *American Dad!* (voice; "Camp Refoogee," 2006), *Weekend Sunrise* (2007), *This Morning* (2007), *HBO First Look: Norbit* (2007), *The Orange British Academy Film Awards* (2007), *Friday Night with Jonathan Ross* (2007), *Live Earth: The Concerts for a Climate in Crisis* (2007), *The Orange British Academy Film Awards* (2008), *The View*

(2008), *A Taste of My Life* (2008), *How to Lose Friends and Alienate People* (2008), *The Graham Norton Show* (2008), *Xpose* (2008).

Shorts: *Father and Son: Onscreen and Off* (documentary; 2007).

Nicholas, Denise Born in Detroit, Michigan, July 12, 1944.

When it comes to actresses who have had a significant influence on the image of black women on television, the name Denise Nicholas is too often undervalued. Her parents are Louise and Otto Nicholas. Her mother remarried and moved from Detroit to Milan, Michigan. Nicholas attended Milan High School (class of 1961) and studied at the University of Michigan for two years. She eventually received a bachelor of arts degree from the University of Southern California.

Nicholas was a founding member of the Free Southern Theater after leaving college. This was during the era of dramatic civil rights activity. After touring with the company, she relocated to New York and joined the legendary Negro Ensemble Company. She was seen by a producer while performing at the St. Marks Playhouse and was offered the role of school guidance counselor Liz McIntyre in the landmark, ahead-of-its-time ABC series *Room 222* (1969–74). She received two Golden Globe nominations for the role.

She is also known for her role as Harriet DeLong on *In the Heat of the Night* (1988–94). Nicholas became interested in writing at this time and scripted six episodes of the show. When *Heat* was cancelled, she enrolled in the Professional Writing Program at the University of Southern California, and had her first novel, *Freshwater Road*, published in 2005. It won the Zora Neale Hurston–Richard Wright Award for debut fiction in 2006. She was commissioned by Brown University to write a stage version of the novel. The University of Southern California had earlier staged her play *Buses*, in which she also took the lead role of Rosa Parks.

Feature Films including Video and TV Movies: *Five Desperate Women* (TV; 1971), *Blacula* (1972), *The Soul of Nigger Charley* (1973), *Mr. Ricco* (1975), *Let's Do It Again* (1975), *A Piece of the Action* (1977), *Ring of Passion* (TV; 1978), *Capricorn One* (1978), *The Big Stuffed Dog* (TV; 1981), *The Sophisticated Gents* (TV; 1981), *Valley of the Dolls* (TV; 1981), *Marvin & Tige* (1983), *Supercarrier* (TV; 1988), *Heart and Soul* (TV; 1989), *Mother's Day* (TV; 1989), *Ghost Dad* (1990), *On Thin Ice: The Tai Babilonia Story* (TV; 1991), *Color Adjustment* (documentary; 1992), *Ritual* (2000), *Proud* (aka *Proudly We Serve*, 2004).

TV: *NYPD* (4 episodes; "The Witness," "The Bombers," "Encounter on a Rooftop," "Three-Fifty-Two," 1967–69), *It Takes a Thief* ("To Catch a Roaring Lion," 1968), *Room 222* (recurring role of Liz McIntyre; "Richie's Story," "Naked Came Into the World," "Clothes Make the Boy," 1969), *The F.B.I.* ("Eye of the Storm," 1969), *The Flip Wilson Show* (1970), *The Tonight Show Starring Johnny Carson* (2 appearances; 1970 and 1973), *Night Gallery* ("Lagoda's Heads," 1971), *Soul Train* (1972), *Love, American Style* ("Love and the Split-Up," 1972), *Police Story* ("A Community of Victims," 1975), *Rhoda* ("The Party," 1975), *Marcus Welby, M.D.* ("The Strange Behavior of Paul Kelland," 1975), *Baby, I'm Back* (recurring role as Olivia Ellis; 1978), *Battle of the Network Stars IV* (1978), *The Paper Chase* ("Great Expectations," 1978), *Benson* ("Just Friends," 1980), *Diff'rent Strokes* ("Substitute Mother," 1980), *The Love Boat* (3 episodes; 1980–83), *Secrets of Midland Heights* ("The Race," 1981), *Aloha Paradise* (1981), *Masquerade* (pilot; 1983), *Wonderworks: And the Children Shall Lead* (1985), *Hotel* ("And

Denise Nicholas.

Baby Makes Two," 1987), *227* ("Shall We Dance?" 1988), *Amen* ("The Widow," 1988), *The Cosby Show* ("Birthday Blues," 1989), *A Different World* ("Here's to Old Friends," 1990), *B.L. Stryker* ("Plates," 1990), *Hangin' with Mr. Cooper* ("My Dinner with Mark," 1992), *In the Heat of the Night* (recurring role of Harriet DeLong; 1989–94), *In the Heat of the Night: Give Me Your Life* (1994), *In the Heat of the Night: A Matter of Justice* (1994), *In the Heat of the Night: Who Was Geli Bendl?* (1994), *In the Heat of the Night: By Duty Bound* (1995), *The Parent 'Hood* ("A Kiss Is Just a Kiss," 1995), *Living Single* (2 episodes in the role of Lilah James; "One Degree of Separation," "Never Can Say Goodbye," 1997), *The Rockford Files: Murders and Misdemeanors* (1997), *Biography* ("Carroll O'Connor: All in a Lifetime," 2001), *My Wife and Kids* ("Failure to Communicate," 2002), *Larry King Live* (2005), *TV Land Confidential* ("Changing Times and Trends," 2005).

Video/DVD: *TV in Black: The First Fifty Years* (2004).

Nichols, Nichelle Born in Robbins, Illinois, December 28, 1932.

Born Grace Nichols, she is synonymous with the role of communications officer Lieutenant Uhura of the USS *Enterprise* on the immensely influential and iconic *Star Trek* (1966–69) series, and in the first six theatrical films that followed the series: *Star Trek: The Motion Picture* (1979), *Star Trek II: The Wrath of Khan* (1982), *Star Trek III: The Search for Spock* (1984), *Star Trek IV: The Voyage Home* (1986), *Star Trek V: The Final Frontier* (1989) and *Star Trek VI: The Undiscovered Country* (1991). In 2006, she returned to the role of Uhura in the ambitious fan film *Star Trek: Of Gods and Men*. She also provided the voice of Uhura and other voices to *Star Trek: The Animated Series* (1973), and was the voice of Uhura in two *Star Trek* video games, *Star Trek: 25th Anniversary* (1992) and *Star Trek: Judgment Rights* (1994).

Uhura was one of the most important black female characters in television history: she was a sophisticated, professional woman who held her own with the male crew members. She was a role model and inspiration to a whole generation of young black women (and continues to be that). And she shared television's first interracial kiss with William Shatner in the "Plato's Stepchildren" episode of *Star Trek*.

For her help in spearheading their recruitment drive, she was named NASA's Woman of the Year in 1979. Many women and minorities were attracted by her efforts, which included appearing in recruitment and training films. She is the author of *Beyond Uhura: Star Trek and Other Memories* (Boulevard Books, 1995). And speaking of "beyond Uhura," there is much to the life and career of Nichelle Nichols that goes beyond that seminal role. She is the daughter of Lishia (née Parks) and Samuel Earl Nichols. She began her show business career as a singer and performed at top-notch Chicago nightspots like the Blue Angel and Playboy Club; she toured the U.S., Canada and Europe with the Duke Ellington and Lionel Hampton bands; and did theater in Los Angeles, including *Blues for Mister Charlie*, *For the People* and *The Roar of the Greasepaint—The Smell of the Crowd.*

When *Star Trek*—which was never a gigantic hit in its original incarnation—was cancelled in 1969, Nichols had typecasting problems to overcome, which is understandable after being so closely associated with a single role. Her contribution to the blaxploitation film cycle was *Truck Turner* (1974), in which she played a four-letter word spewing madam. It was basically a passive role, and she appeared in only a few scenes, but Nichols seemed to relish the change of pace. Many years later, she again played a madam in *Lady Magdalene's* (2006), which went directly to DVD. She was the executive producer and sang three songs in the film (two of which she composed).

In 1992 she appeared in the one-woman musical revue *Reflections*, in which she played tribute to a dozen song legends. Nichols was cast in a recurring role on the second season of NBC's sci-fi series *Heroes*, beginning with the episode "Kindred" in October 2007 as Nina Dawson, matriarch of a family devastated by hurricane Katrina. Nichols is the mother of Kyle Johnson, who starred, as a child actor, in the Gordon Parks film *The Learning Tree* (1969).

Feature Films including Video and TV Movies: *Porgy and Bess* (1959), *Great Gettin' Up Mornin'* (TV; 1964), *Made in Paris* (1966), *Mister Buddwing* (1966), *Doctor, You've Got to Be Kidding!* (1967), *Tarzan's Jungle Rebellion* (archival; 1967), *Truck Turner* (1974), *Star Trek: The Motion Picture* (1979), *Star Trek: The Wrath of Khan* (1982), *Antony and Cleopatra* (TV; 1983), *Star*

Trek III: The Search for Spock (1984), *The Supernaturals* (1986), *Star Trek IV: The Voyage Home* (1986), *Star Trek V: The Final Frontier* (1989), *Star Trek VI: The Undiscovered Country* (1991), *The Adventures of Captain Zoom in Outer Space* (TV; 1995), *Trekkies* (documentary; 1997), *Snow Dogs* (2002), *Surge of Power* (2004), *Are We There Yet?* (2005), *Lady Magdalene's* (2008), *Tru Loved* (2008), *The Torturer* (2008), *This Bitter Earth* (2009), *David* (2009), *Escape from Heaven* (2009).

TV: *The Lieutenant* ("To Set It Right," 1964), *Tarzan* (2 episodes in the role of Ruana; "The Deadly Silence," Parts I and II, 1966), *Star Trek* (recurring role of Lieutenant Uhura; 1966–69), *Dateline: Hollywood* (1967), *It Takes Two* (1969), *The D.A.* ("The People vs. Howard," 1971), *Ironside* ("The Deadly Gamesman," 1972), *Star Trek: The Animated Series* (voice of Uhura and other voices; 1973–74), *Leonard Nimoy: Star Trek Memories* (1983), *Head of the Class* ("For Better, For Worse," 1988), *The 11th Annual Black Achievement Awards* (1990), *Star Trek 25th Anniversary Special* (1991), *Showbiz Today* (1991), *Inside Space* (series host; 1992), *The Joan Rivers Show* (1993), *ABC Weekend Specials* (voice; "Commander Toad in Space," 1993), *Batman* (voice; "Avatar," 1994), *Star Trek: A Captain's Log* (1994), *Gargoyles* (4 episodes as the voice of Diane Maza; "Deadly Force," "Her Brother's Keeper," "The Cage," "Mark of the Panther," 1994–96), *Spider-Man* (2 episodes as the voice of Miriam the Vampire Queen, 1997), *Last Angel of History* (1995), *Star Trek: Deep Space Nine* (archival; "Trials and Tribble-lations," 1996), *Star Trek: 30 Years and Beyond* (1996), *Moonshot: The Spirit of '69* (1999), *Good vs. Evil* ("Renunciation," 2000), *Buzz Lightyear of Star Command* ("The Yukari Imprint," 2000), *Futurama* (voice; 2 episodes; "Anthology of Interest I," "Where No Fan Has Gone Before," 2000 and 2002), *Weakest Link* (2002), *Inside TV Land: African Americans in Television* (2002), *TV Land Awards: A Celebration of Classic TV* (2003), *After They Were Famous* ("Star Trek," 2003), *The Simpsons* (voice; "Simple Simpson," 2004), *The 100 Most Memorable TV Moments* (2004), *How William Shatner Changed the World* (2005), *Comedy Central Roast of William Shatner* (2006), *Star Trek: Beyond the Final Frontier* (2007), *Space Top 10 Countdown* (2007), *Heroes* (2007), *Heroes Unmasked* (2007), *11th Annual Ribbon of Hope Celebration* (2008), *Entertainment Tonight* (2008).

Video/DVD: *William Shatner's Star Trek Memories* (1995), *Gargoyles: Brothers Betrayed* (1998), *Star Trek: Of Gods and Men* (2007).

Nichelle Nichols.

Nicolet, Danielle Born in Ashtabula, Ohio, November 24, 1975.

Born Danielle Diggs in a small town in Ohio, Danielle Nicolet had two great loves: gymnastics and acting. At age eight, she attracted the attention of legendary gymnastics coach Bela Karoli, trainer of Olympic champions. She trained with him at his facility in Texas in preparation for the Olympic trials. She was doing well in gymnastics competitions when she sustained a substantial knee injury, thus ending her Olympic dreams, but not her acting dreams.

She has had outstanding results on television, starting with recurring roles on *Almost There!* (1990) and *Family Matters* (1991–92). Her keynote series role was as outspoken student Caryn on *3rd Rock from the Sun* (1996–2001), which became one of the most popular sitcoms of its era, keyed by a manic performance by John Lithgow as a fish-out-of-water alien from space. In 2005 Nicolet landed a starring role on UPN's *Second Time Around*, but it died after a season, and now the network itself is gone, submerged into the CW Network.

She had a recurring role as Nurse Mary Singletary on *Heartland* (2007) and is currently charming audiences with her role as Liz Marsh, the wife of baseball's highest paid relief pitcher Devon Marsh, on *The Starter Wife* (2008). Her first TV movie was a modern classic of sorts, *The Jacksons: An American Dream* (1992), a fair-minded look at the career of the famous (and infamous) show business family.

Feature Films including Video and TV Movies: *The Jacksons: An American Dream* (TV; 1992), *Loaded Weapon 1* (1993), *The Prince* (1996), *Fall into Darkness* (TV; 1996), *Where the Truth Lies* (1996), *Shadow of Doubt* (1998), *Race* (1998), *Ghost Soldier* (1999), *Child 2 Man* (2000), *A Light in the Forest* (2002), *A Wonderful Night in Split* (2004), *The Strange Case of Dr. Jekyll and Mr. Hyde* (2006), *Rocker* (2006), *The Weekend* (TV; 2007), *Knuckle Draggers* (2008).

TV: *Almost There!* (5 episodes in the role of Lisa Bartholomew; "A Matter of the Heart," Parts I and II, "The American Way," Parts I and II, "Freedom of Choice," 1990), *Family Matters* (3 episodes in the role of Vonda Mahoney; "The Love God," "Food, Lies and Videotape," "An Officer and a Waldo," 1991–92), *Step by Step* ("Head of the Class," 1995), *Diagnosis Murder* ("Murder by the Busload," 1996), *3rd Rock from the Sun* (recurring role of Caryn; 1996–2001), *Beyond Belief: Fact or Fiction* ("Number One with a Bullet," 1997), *In the House* ("Mr. Hill Goes to New York," 1998), *Brimstone* ("Slayer," 1998), *Moesha* ("Ohmigod, Fanatic," 1999), *Grown Ups* ("Bachelor Auction," 1999), *Undressed* (3 episodes in the role of Cory; "Surprize, Surprize," Parts I, II and III, 2000), *CSI* ("Chaos Theory," 2001), *Stargate SG-1* ("Menace," 2002), *For the People* ("Racing Form," 2002), *Half & Half* ("The Big Butting In Episode," 2003), *Angel* ("Harm's Way," 2004), *Good Day Live* (2004), *The 100 Scariest Movie Moments* (2004), *100 Cheesetastic Video Tricks Exposed* (2004), *Second Time Around* (recurring role of Paula; 2004–05), *The Bernie Mac Show* (3 episodes; "The Talk," "Big Brother," "Stone Nuts," 2004–05), *Crumbs* ("Sleeping with the Enemies," 2006), *So NoTORIous* (pilot; 2006), *All of Us* (3 episodes in the role of Jill; "It Was Fun While It Lasted," "The Boy Is Mine," "Everything Happens for a Reason," 2007), *Heartland* (9 episodes in the role of Nurse Mary Singletary; 2007), *The Starter Wife* (recurring role as Liz Marsh; 2008).

Noisette, Kathleen Died April 16, 1935, in Baltimore, Maryland.

Kathleen Noisette was born Catherine Hackett. She was an Oscar Micheaux leading lady in the late twenties and early thirties. She was in *Wages of Sin*, *When Men Betray* (both 1929), *A Daughter of the Congo* (a part talkie; 1930) and *The Exile* (1931). *Wages of Sin* was an adaptation of the story "Alias Jefferson Lee." It involves two brothers, one cowardly and unscrupulous, whose relationship comes to a head after the death of their mother. *When Men Betray* used most of the cast members from *Wages of Sin* and was Micheaux's last fully silent film. It raised the censors' wrath due to Noisette's semi-topless scene.

At three hours and 24 minutes, *The Betrayal* was at one point shown in three installments, but the critics were not impressed, although the film reportedly did good business in the South. It is another of Micheaux's many "lost" films. *A Daughter of the Congo* fared even worse with the critics, but audiences responded to its erotic and adventurous elements. After a painful and well publicized divorce, Noisette suffered a nervous breakdown and was institutionalized at Bellevue Hospital. She died at age 29.

Feature Films: *Wages of Sin* (1929), *When Men Betray* (1929), *A Daughter of the Congo* (1930), *The Exile* (1931).

Norman, Maidie Born in Villa Rica, Georgia, October 16, 1912; died May 2, 1998, San Josc, California.

Maidie Norman is another of those performers who combined a varied film and theater career with a laudable civil rights record and who waged an active campaign against the stereotyping of black actresses. Maidie Ruth Gamble was the daughter of Louis and Lila Gamble. She spent much of her childhood and teen years in Lima, Ohio. She attended Bennett College in North Carolina, receiving a bachelor of arts in 1934. She got her master of arts from New York's Columbia University in 1937. She trained at the Actors Laboratory in Hollywood from 1946 to 1949. She became active in radio (*The Jack Benny Show*, *Sears Mystery Theater*, *Amos 'n' Andy*) and in theater, making her stage debut as Honey in *Deep Are the Roots* at Los Angeles' Mayan Theatre.

Her film debut was in *The Burning Cross* (1948). Norman's first and only leading role was in *The Well* (1951), a critically-lauded film with refreshingly non-stereotypical black characters and a script with a cogent undercurrent about race relations. Her most famous film role was as Elvira, the outspoken, ill-fated housekeeper in *What Ever Happened to Baby Jane?* (1962), the Bette Davis–Joan Crawford scare fest that grows more admired with the passing years. Norman reportedly rewrote some of her lines to remove any trace of stereotyping.

Norman was also active in television, appearing on such shows as *The Man from U.N.C.L.E., Ironside* and *Dragnet.*

Norman was inducted into the Black Filmmakers Hall of Fame in 1977. She was a drama instructor at Texas State College in Tyler, Texas, and taught black theatre studies at the University of California Los Angeles. UCLA gives an annual Maidie Norman Research Award to the theater arts student who presents the best research paper on blacks in theater. She received an NAACP Award for Contribution to Education.

She was married in 1937 and divorced from McHenry Norman; the marriage produced one Son (McHenry "Skip" Norman III). Her second husband, from 1977 to the time of her death, was Weldon D. Canada. She died of lung cancer and was survived by a sister, her son, two stepchildren, five grandchildren and four great-grandchildren.

Maidie Norman and Mary Alice in *The Sty of the Blind Pig* (1974).

Feature Films including TV Movies: *The Burning Cross* (1947), *Manhandled* (1949), *The Well* (1951), *Bright Road* (1953), *Forever Female* (1953), *Torch Song* (1953), *Money from Home* (1953), *Executive Suite* (1954), *Susan Slept Here* (1954), *About Mrs. Leslie* (1954), *Mad at the World* (1955), *Tarzan's Hidden Jungle* (1955), *Man with the Gun* (1955), *The Opposite Sex* (1956), *Written on the Wind* (1956), *The Helen Morgan Story* (1957), *What Ever Happened to Baby Jane?* (1962), *4 for Texas* (1964), *The Final Comedown* (1972), *Another Part of the Forest* (TV; 1972), *Say Goodbye, Maggie Cole* (TV; 1972), *Maurie* (1973), *The Young Prey* (1973), *A Dream for Christmas* (TV; 1973), *A Star Is Born* (1976), *Airport '77* (1977), *Movie, Movie* (1978), *Thornwell* (TV; 1981), *Bare Essence* (TV; 1982), *Halloween III: Season of the Witch* (1983), *Secrets of a Mother and Daughter* (TV; 1983), *His Mistress* (TV; 1984), *Terrorist on Trial: The United States vs. Salim Ajami* (TV; 1988), *Side by Side* (TV; 1988).

TV: *Hallmark Hall of Fame* ("Martha Custis Washington," 1955), *Cavalcade of America* ("Toward Tomorrow," 1956), *Matinee Theatre* ("From the Desk of Margaret Tydings," 1956), *Four Star Playhouse* ("Autumn Carousel," 1956), *Celebrity Playhouse* ("I'll Make the Arrest," 1956), *Dragnet* ("The Big Missus," 1956), *The Loretta Young Show* ("Royal Partner," Parts I and II, "Mask of Evidence," 1957–59), *Alfred Hitchcock Presents* ("Mrs. Bixby and the Colonel's Coat," 1960), *Perry Mason* ("The Case of the Mystified Minor," 1962), *The Wide Country* ("Speckle Bird," 1963), *Ben Casey* ("Allie," 1963), *Twilight Zone* ("The Masks," 1964), *Dr. Kildare* ("A Marriage of Convenience," 1965), *The Long, Hot Summer* ("Home Is a Nameless Place," 1965), *Death Valley Days* ("No Place for a Lady," 1965), *The Man from U.N.C.L.E.* ("The Very Important Zombie Affair," 1965), *CBS Playhouse* ("The Final War of Olly Winter," 1967), *Dragnet 1967* (2 episodes; "The Big Dog," "The Big Problem," 1967 and 1968), *Ironside* (2 episodes; "Let My Brother Go," "Eden Is the Place We Leave," 1967 and 1970), *Daktari* ("Adam and Jenny," 1968), *Judd for the Defense* ("The Gates of Cerberus," 1968), *The Outcasts* ("Give Me Tomorrow," 1969), *Men* *at Law* ("Easy to Be Hard," 1970), *Barefoot in the Park* ("The Marriage Proposal," 1970), *The F.B.I.* ("The Innocents," 1970), *Mannix* (3 episodes; "The World Between," "The Glass Trap," "A Choice of Evils," 1970–71), *Adam-12* (2 episodes; "The Adoption," "Capture," 1972 and 1973), *Griff* ("Hammerlock," 1973), *Love Story* ("A Glow of Dying Embers," 1973), *The Sty of the Blind Pig* (1974), *Marcus Welby, M.D.* ("Every Day a Miracle," 1974), *Cannon* ("Triangle of Terror," 1974), *The Streets of San Francisco* ("Jacob's Boy," 1974), *Rhoda* ("I'm a Little Late, Folks," 1974), *Kolchak: The Night Stalker* ("Mr. R.I.N.G.," 1975), *Lucas Tanner* ("Those Who Cannot, Teach," 1975), *Kung Fu* ("Barbary House," 1975), *Good Times* ("The Enlistment," 1975), *Harry O* ("Shades," 1975), *The Jeffersons* ("Mother Jefferson's Fall," 1975), *Police Woman* (3 episodes; "Blast," "The Trick Book," "Screams," 1975–77), *Bronk* ("Death with Honor," 1976), *Baretta* ("Can't Win for Losin'," 1976), *Little House on the Prairie* ("The Wisdom of Solomon," 1977), The Incredible Hulk ("Like a Brother," 1979), *Roots: The Next Generations* (miniseries; 1979), *Barnaby Jones* ("Girl on the Road," 1979), *Enos* ("Once and Fur All," 1981), *Cagney & Lacey* ("Internal Affairs," 1982), *Bare Essence* ("Hour Four," 1983), *Hotel* ("Confrontations," 1983), *Matt Houston* ("Death Watch," 1985), *Amen* ("Man on a Ledge," 1988), *Simon & Simon* ("Little Boy Dead," 1988).

Odetta Born in Birmingham, Alabama, December 31, 1930; died December 2, 2008, New York, New York.

Born Odetta Holmes, folk singer, songwriter, civil rights activist and actress Odetta had a long and distinguished career. Born in Birmingham, she grew up in Los Angeles. She began her career in musical theater as a member of the Hollywood Turnabout Puppet Theatre. In 1949, she joined the touring company of *Finian's Rainbow*. Her folk singing career began in earnest starting in 1950, and she played all the top clubs during that folk-crazed era: the Blue Angel, the hungry i, and the Tin Angel. Albums followed: *Odetta Sings Ballads and Blues* (1956), *Odetta at the Gate of Horn* (1957), and *Odetta Sings Folk Songs* (1963), which was a best seller. In 1961, Martin Luther King, Jr. praised her contributions to folk music. Odetta's later albums — including *Odetta and the Blues* (1962) and *Odetta* (1967)— show a distinct jazz influence. Her most recent album was the Grammy-nominated *Goin' to Let It Shine* (2007).

Given her background in theater, it wasn't difficult for Odetta to contribute acting turns to the films *Sanctuary*, based on the William Faulkner novel (1961), and the memorable TV movie *The Autobiography of Miss Jane Pittman* (1974). On television, she acted on an episode of *Have Gun—Will Travel* in 1961, her only dramatic role on series TV. In 1999, President Bill Clinton presented her the National Endowment for the Arts' National Medal of the Arts and Humanities. In 2005, the Library of Congress presented her the Living Legend Award (only the third time this award was given).

Feature Films including TV Movies: *Cinerama Holiday* (1955), *Sanctuary* (1961), *Festival* (documentary; 1967), *The Autobiography of Miss Jane Pittman* (TV; 1974), *Chords of Fame* (documentary; 1984), *The Fire Next Time* (TV; 1993), *The Ballad of Ramblin' Jack* (documentary; 2000), *Lightning in a Bottle* (documentary; 2004), *Blues Divas* (documentary; 2005), *Bob Dylan: No Direction Home* (documentary; 2005).

TV: *The Ed Sullivan Show* (1960), *Have Gun—Will Travel* ("The Hanging of Aaron Gibbs," 1961), *The Les Crane Show* (1965), *Live from the Bitter End* (1967), *Clown Town* (1968), *The Johnny Cash Show* (1969), *The Dick Cavett Show* (1969), *The Virginia Graham Show* (1971), *Soundstage: Just Folks* (1980), *Ramblin' with Odetta* (1981), *Chords of Fame* (1984), *Boston Pops* (1991), *Tommy Makem and Friends* (1992), *Turnabout: The Story of the Yale Puppeteers* (1993), *Odetta: Woman in (E)motion* (1995), *Peter, Paul and Mary: Lifelines* (1996), *National Medal of Arts and Humanities Presentations* (1999), *CNN World Beat* (2000), *21st Annual W.C. Handy Blues Awards* (2000), *Songs for a Better World* (2000), *Later with Jools Holland* (2001), *Politically Incorrect* (2001), *Late Night with David Letterman* (2001), *Pure Oxygen* (2002), *Newport Folk Festival* (2002), *Janis Joplin: Pieces of My Heart* (2002), *Get Up, Stand Up* (2003), *Ralph Bunche: An American Odyssey* (2003), *Brother Outsider: The Life of Bayard Rustin* (2003), *Visionary Awards Presentation* (2004), *Talking Bob Dylan Blues* (2005), *Odetta: Blues Diva* (2005), *WoodSongs Old Time Radio Hour* (2006), *A Tribute to the Teacher of America* (2007), *The Tavis Smiley Show* (2008), *Mountain Stage HD* (2008).

Okonedo, Sophie Born in London, England, January 1, 1969.

Trained at the Royal Academy of Dramatic Art, and a graduate of Cambridge University, Sophie Okonedo is of half Nigerian and half European and Jewish descent. She was nominated for a Best Supporting Actress Oscar for her role as Don Cheadle's wife in *Hotel Rwanda* (2004), and was nominated for an NAACP Image Award for the role as well. *Hotel Rwanda* is the true story of a hotel manager who risks her life to save refugees during the course of the ethnic slaughter in the African nation of Rwanda. She was nominated for a Golden Globe as Lead Actress in a Miniseries for her powerful work in *Tsunami: The Aftermath* (2006), and was an Image Award winner for the role.

Okonedo considers herself essentially a character actress, and the diversity and depth of her roles affirms that. Most of Okonedo's television acting has been in British productions, most notably the 2003 miniseries *Doctor Who: Scream of the Shalka*. Her mother, Joan, was a pilates teacher, and her father Henry was a government worker. They separated when Okonedo was five and she was raised by her mother under tight financial circumstances. She has a daughter, Aoife, with film editor Eoin Martin. Their relationship has since ended.

Feature Films including Video and TV Movies: *Young Soul Rebels* (1991), *Maria's Child* (TV; 1992), *Age of Treason* (TV; 1993), *Go Now* (1995), *Ace Ventura: When Nature Calls* (1995), *Deep Secrets* (TV; 1996), *The Jackal* (1997), *This Year's Love* (1999), *Mad Cows* (1999), *Peaches* (2000), *Never Never* (TV; 2000), *Once Seen* (2001), *Sweet Revenge* (TV; 2001), *Dead Casual* (TV; 2002), *Dirty Pretty Things* (2002), *Cross My Heart* (2003), *Alibi* (TV; 2003), *Hotel Rwanda* (2004), *Whose Baby?* (TV; 2004), *Born with Two Mothers* (TV; 2005), *Blitz: London's Firestorm* (TV; 2005), *Aeon Flux* (2005), *Celebration* (TV; 2006), *The True Voice of Rape* (TV; 2006), *Alex Rider: Stormbreaker* (2006), *Flashing Frames* (2006), *Scenes of a Sexual Nature* (2006), *Tsunami: The Aftermath* (TV; 2006), *Martian Child* (2007), *Oliver Twist* (TV; 2007), *Skin* (2008), *The Secret Life of Bees* (2008), *Stringbean and Marcus* (2009).

TV: *Casualty* ("Judgment Day," 1991), *The Bill* ("Darkness Before Dawn," 1994), *The Governor* (recurring role as Moira Levitt; 1995), *Staying Alive* (recurring role as Kelley Booth; 1996), *Murder Most Horrid* ("Dead on Time," 1996), *In Defence* (2000), *Table 12* ("Opera Lovers," 2001), *Clocking Off* (recurring role as Jenny Wood; 2002), *The Inspector Lynley Mysteries* ("In the Presence of the Enemy," 2003), *Spooks* ("Blood and Money," 2003), *Doctor Who: Scream of the Shalka* (miniseries; 2003), *Stan Colleymore: Confessions of a Premiership Footballer* (2004), *The Late Late Show with Craig Ferguson* (2005), *11th Annual Screen Actors Guild Awards* (2005), *Tavis Smiley* (2005), *GMTV* (2005), *Sunday Morning Shootout* (2005), *The 77th Annual Academy Awards* (2005), *36th NAACP Image Awards* (2005), *Richard & Judy* (2005), *The Film Programme* (2006), *The 64th Annual Golden Globe Awards* (2007), *Jackanory Junior* (2007), *Racism: A History* (narrator; 2007).

Omilami, Elizabeth (aka Omilami-Williams, Elizabeth) Born in Atlanta, Georgia, February 18, 1951.

Elizabeth Omilami is the daughter of famous civil rights activist Hosea Williams and State Representative Juanita T. Williams. She worked for 15 years for her father's organization, Hosea Feed the Hungry and Homeless, and took over as CEO upon his passing in 2000. Omilami is a graduate of Hampton University and holds a bachelor of arts in theater. She founded Atlanta's People's Survival Theatre and has written several plays, including *There Is a River in My Soul*. She is a past member of the Georgia Council for the Arts and the Fulton County Arts Council.

She had a recurring role on *I'll Fly Away* (1991–92) and appeared in the PBS TV movie sequel *I'll Fly Away: Then and Now* (1993). She has also acted in a number of socially-conscious TV movies, including *Murder in Mississippi* (1990), *On Promised Land* (1994), *Selma, Lord, Selma* (1999), and *Boycott* (2001). She is the wife of actor Afemo Omilami, and has two children, Awodele and Juanita.

Feature Films including Video and TV Movies: *Murder in Mississippi* (TV; 1990), *Web of Deceit* (TV; 1990), *In the Line of Duty: Street War* (TV; 1992), *Silent Victim* (TV; 1993), *A Kiss to Die For* (TV; 1993), *On Promised Land* (TV; 1994), *Moment of Truth: Caught in the Crossfire* (TV; 1994), *Last Dance* (1996), *A Time to Kill* (1996), *Sudden Terror: The Hijacking of School Bus #17* (TV; 1996), *To Dance with Olivia* (TV; 1997),

Perfect Crime (TV; 1997), *Selma, Lord, Selma* (TV; 1999), *Funny Valentines* (TV; 1999), *The Color of Love: Jacey's Story* (TV; 2000), *Boycott* (TV; 2001), *Baby of the Family* (2002), *Nowhere Road* (2002), *Runaway Jury* (2003), *Bobby Jones: Stroke of Genius* (2004), *Ray* (2004), *Glory Road* (2006), *Madea's Family Reunion* (2006), *The Altar* (2006), *We Are Marshall* (2006), *The List* (2007).

TV: *In the Heat of the Night* (2 episodes; "Gunshots," "Citizen Trundel," Part I, 1989 and 1990), *I'll Fly Away* (5 episodes in the role of Joelyn; "I'll Fly Away," "Amazing Grace," "All God's Children," "On the Road," "Eighteen," 1991–92), *I'll Fly Away: Then and Now* (1993), *The Flash* (1997), *Second Noah* ("Desperately Seeking Mickey," 1997), *Rwanda Rising* (voice; 2007).

Pace, Judy Born in Los Angeles, California, June 15, 1942.

The last generation of truly pioneering black actresses was the Afro-wearing, black power ladies who brought the darkest of dark skin and the keenest of attitudes and political awareness to the screen. While the occasional individual black actress will still make a major difference — Halle Berry, for one — Brenda Sykes, Pam Grier, Rosalind Cash, Vonetta McGee, and dozens of others were the "Black is beautiful" generation. The image of the black woman on screen would never be the same again. This last generation of pioneers is also, as it turns out, the last to get credit. They were so modern, so intimately of their time, that they were soon outmoded and forgotten, vaguely ridiculous to a generation raised on affirmative action and a less militant perspective.

But in Judy Pace, we see the basic prototype of today's young black actress. Pace, as it turns out, had a rather schizophrenic career — by necessity, given the time of her work. On television, especially in earlier appearances, her characters had a bland, perky professionalism (on *I Dream of Jeannie, The Flying Nun, Tarzan*), to be replaced by a less accommodating, more sexualized image as the decade wore on (as the back-stabbing Judy Fletcher on the prime time soap *Peyton Place* [1968–69], or on *The New People*, or *Ironside*). For every good girl role — *Brian's Song* (TV; 1972), the touching TV movie about the death of football player Brian Piccolo — there was a more savvy, less stereotypical part, such as her recurring, landmark role as attorney Pat Walters on ABC's *The Young Lawyers* (1970–71), a career woman without apology.

Judy Pace.

She starred as Adelaide in a well-publicized (the cover story of *Jet* magazine) black production of *Guys and Dolls* in Las Vegas in 1973. In feature films, it was a whole different story. Pace played militant, overtly sexual, cocky, totally confident characters: *Three in the Attic* (as Eulice, one of three women being played by the same man who decide to take revenge; 1968); *Cotton Comes to Harlem* (as the seductive Iris, who seduces a dumb white cop by stripping naked and getting him to put a bag over his head; 1970); *Up in the Cellar* (the sequel to *Three in the Attic*; 1970); *Frogs* (a way ahead of its time ecological thriller; 1972); and *Cool Breeze* (a blaxploitation remake of *The Asphalt Jungle*; 1972).

Pace attended Los Angeles City College with a major in sociology. When she was laid up in the hospital for months with a recurring leg condition from childhood, Pace's thoughts turned seriously to acting, something she had considered for most of her life.

Her first husband was actor Don Mitchell of *Ironside*; that union produced two children but ended in divorce in 1986. She then married baseball icon Curt Flood, who passed away in 1997. Her sister is singer Jean Pace, wife of the late singer Oscar Brown, Jr.

In 2007, Pace kept her hand in by touring in the stage play *The Divorce* (Los Angeles, Miami, Richmond). Freda Payne, Dawnn Lewis and Vanessa Bell Calloway were also in the cast.

Feature Films including TV Movies: *13 Frightened Girls* (1963), *The Fortune Cookie* (1966), *The Thomas Crown Affair* (1968), *Three in the Attic* (1968), *Cotton Comes to Harlem* (1970), *Up in the Cellar* (aka *Three in the Cellar*, 1970), *Brian's Song* (TV; 1972), *Frogs* (1972), *Oh, Nurse!* (TV; 1972), *Cool Breeze* (1972), *The Slams* (1973), *Sucker Free City* (TV; 2004).

TV: *Bewitched* ("Follow That Witch," Part I, 1966), *Batman* ("Death in Slow Motion," 1966), *I Spy* ("One of Our Bombs Is Missing," 1966), *I Dream of Jeannie* ("Fly Me to the Moon," 1967), *The Flying Nun* ("The Fatal Hibiscus," 1967), *Days of Our Lives* (recurring role as Miss Kenneth; 1967), *Tarzan* ("King of the Dwsari," 1968), *The Mod Squad* ("Bad Man on Campus," 1968), *Peyton Place* (recurring role as Lillian Walters; 1968–69), *The New People* ("The Prisoner of Bomano," 1969), *The Young Lawyers* (pilot; 1969), *The Young Lawyers* (recurring role of Pat Walters; 1970–71), *O'Hara: U.S. Treasury* ("Operation: Hijack," 1971), *Soul Train* (1973), *Shaft* ("Hit-Run," 1973), *Medical Center* ("Trial by Knife," 1974), *Kung Fu* ("In Uncertain Bondage," 1974), *Sanford and Son* ("The Way to Lamont's Heart," 1974), *That's My Mama* ("Whose Child Is This?" 1974), *Ironside* ("Fall of an Angel," 1974), *Caribe* ("Lady Killer," 1975), *Good Times* ("The Weekend," 1975), *What's Happening!!* (2 episodes; "The Hospital Stay," "Shirley's Fired," 1977 and 1979), *Beyond Westworld* ("Take-Over," 1980), *What's Happening Now!* ("The New Kid," 1985), *E! True Hollywood Story* ("Christopher Jones," 1999), *ESPN Sports Century* (2 segments; 2000–04).

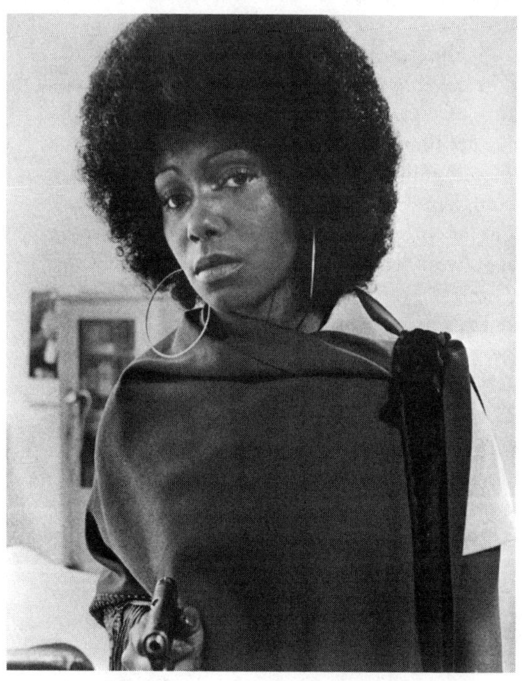

Judy Pace in *Cool Breeze* (1972).

Page, LaWanda Born in Cleveland, Ohio, October 19, 1920; died September 14, 2002, Hollywood, California.

Born Alberta Peal, LaWanda Page was best known for her portrayal of Aunt Esther on the hit seventies sitcom *Sanford and Son* (1973–77). Although born in Ohio, she was raised in St. Louis, Missouri, where she worked small burlesque clubs as an exotic dancer known as "The Bronze Goddess of Fire," purportedly lighting cigarettes with her fingertips. She later performed this routine on an episode of *Sanford and Son*. The Aunt Esther character was the sister of Fred Sanford's late wife. Fred was always criticizing Esther's looks, and getting back as good as he gave. Like Foxx, Page was a former "blue" stand-up comic (i.e., X-rated).

Page also guested on other popular sitcoms of the era: *Amen*, *227*, *Diff'rent Strokes* and *Martin*. She passed away from complications due to diabetes and was survived by a daughter, Clara Johnson.

Feature Films including Video and TV Movies: *The Legend of Dolemite* (1994), *Zapped!* (1982), *Good-bye Cruel World* (1983), *Mausoleum* (1983), *My Blue Heaven* (1990), *Shakes the Clown* (1992), *CB4* (1994), *The Meteor Man* (1993), *Friday* (1995), *Don't Be a Menace to South Central While Drinking Your Juice in the Hood* (1995), *West from North Goes South* (2004).

TV: *Sanford and Son* (recurring role of Aunt Esther Anderson; 1973–77), *The Dean Martin Celebrity Roast: Frank Sinatra* (1977), *The Richard Pryor Special* (1977), *Redd Foxx* (1977), *The Sanford Arms* (recurring role as Esther Anderson; 1977), *Stonestreet: Who Killed the Centerfold Model?* (1977), *The Love Boat* (1977), *Diff'rent Strokes*

("The Relative," 1979), *Starsky and Hutch* (3 episodes; "Huggy Bear and the Turkey," "Starsky and Hutch on Playboy Island," "Targets Without a Badge," 1977–79), *Detective School* (recurring role as Charlene Jenkins; 1979), *B.A.D Cats* (recurring role as Ma; 1980), *Good Evening, Captain* (1981), *Sanford* (recurring role of Aunt Esther Anderson; 1981), *Amazing Stories* ("Remote Control Man," 1985), *227* ("Pick Six," 1986), *Amen* (3 episodes in the role of Darla; "Ernie and the Sublimes," "Date with an Angel," "Deliverance," Part I, 1991), *Family Matters* ("Brown Bombshell," 1992), *CBS Schoolbreak Special* ("Words Up!" 1992), *Martin* (4 episodes in the role of Evelyn; "Boyz 'R Us," "The Great Payne Robbery," "Variety Show," "Baby You Can Drive My Car," 1992–93), *The Sinbad Show* ("Family Reunion," 1994), *The Parent 'Hood* ("Byte Me," 1995), *Biography* ("Redd Foxx: Say It Like It Is," 2000), *E! True Hollywood Story* (2 segments; "Richard Pryor," archival; "Redd Foxx," 2003).

Palmer, Keke Born in Harvey, Illinois, August 26, 1993.

Lauren Keyana "Keke" Palmer is Nickelodeon's new hope to emerge as the next "tween" superstar. In November 2008, *True Jackson, VP* premiered on the cable giant. When Max, the eccentric head of Mad Fashions, impetuously offers a vice president's position to a young girl selling sandwiches outside his company's building, she proves more than ready to take on the challenge. This gentle, family friendly satire of the fashion industry was being hyped as the next sensation for the young teen market, and it is essentially a variation on NBC's *Ugly Betty* without the "ugly." True is confident and in charge, but like Betty she does have her share of enemies and detractors. Palmer wrote and sings the title song, and since she released her debut pop–R&B album *So Uncool* in 2007, Nickelodeon's idea is to push her as a Miley Cyrus–like singer and actress. She appeared on the teenick Nickelodeon series *Just Jordan* in 2008.

Palmer has gone from singing in the church choir at age five to the brink of major stardom in her "tween" years. She is one of four children of Sharon, an elementary school teacher who works with mentally disabled children, and her father Laurence, who works for a polyurethane company. She has had the nickname "Keke" since a very young age.

The family moved to Los Angeles in 2004 to make it easier for her to pursue an acting career. The move soon paid off, on both the acting and singing fronts. Palmer made her acting debut in *Barbershop 2: Back in Business* (2004), worked on episodes of *Cold Case* and *Strong Medicine* that same year, and received her first serious critical attention later that year for her role of Lou in the TV movie *The Wool Cap*, the moving story of a mentally challenged man (William H. Macy) who excels as a salesman. This garnered Palmer a 2005 NAACP Image Award and Screen Actors Guild Award nomination for Outstanding Actress in a Mini-Series/TV Movie. She was the youngest actress ever to be nominated for the Guild Award for leading actress.

In 2007, she won an NAACP Image Award for Outstanding Actress in a Movie — one of the youngest actresses ever nominated for the award — for her work as Akeelah Anderson in *Akeelah and the Bee* (2006), the delightful, inspiring story of a young lady who takes on the challenge of a spelling bee. The Chicago Film Critics nominated her for Most Promising Newcomer for her work.

Other TV series work has included the premiere episode of Tyler Perry's *House of Payne*, *Law & Order: Special Victims Unit*, and *ER*. Palmer was prominently featured in the Disney Channel Original Movie *Jump In!* (2007), contributing two songs, "It's My Turn Now" and "Jumpin'," to the soundtrack album. Other feature films include *Madea's Family Reunion* (2006), *The Longshots* (2008), with Palmer as a young woman who joins a male football team, and *The Vapors* (2009), with Palmer portraying real-life hip-hop pioneer Roxanne Shanté.

Feature Films including TV Movies: *Barbershop 2: Back in Business* (2004), *The Wool Cap* (TV; 2004), *Keke & Jamal* (TV; 2005), *Knights of the South Bronx* (TV; 2005), *Akeelah and the Bee* (2006), *Madea's Family Reunion* (2006), *Jump In!* (TV; 2007), *Cleaner* (2008).

TV: *Cold Case* ("The Letter," 2004), *Strong Medicine* ("Race for a Cure," 2004), *Second Time Around* ("Big Bank, Little Bank," 2005), *ER* ("The Show Must Go On," 2005), *Law & Order: Special Victims Unit* ("Storm," 2005), *11th Annual Screen Actors Guild Awards* (2005), *36th NAACP Image Awards* (2005), *The 57th Annual Primetime Emmy Awards* (2005), *The Tonight Show with Jay Leno* (2006), *The Oprah Winfrey Show* (2006), *106 & Park Top 10 Live* (2006), *The Late Late Show with Craig Ferguson* (2006), *The Early Show*

(2006), *The 2006 Black Movie Awards, Sing-Along Bowl-Athon* (2006), *38th NAACP Image Awards* (2007), *House of Payne* ("Bully and the Beast," 2007).

Parker, Nicole Ari (aka Parker Kodjoe, Nicole Ari) Born in Baltimore, Maryland, October 7, 1970.

After she won a high school acting competition, Nicole Ari Parker found work at the Baltimore Actors Theatre and the Washington Ballet Company before graduating from New York University's Tisch School of the Arts with an acting degree in 1993. Parker was briefly a model before turning to acting. She brought the character of attorney Teri Joseph to vivid life on Showtime's *Soul Food,* based on the 1997 film. She has showcased her vibrant singing voice on several episodes of *Soul Food.* Her husband, Boris Kodjoe, was her co-star on *Soul Food,* and they also co-starred on the sitcom *Second Time Around* (2004). Parker has also guest starred on shows like *CSI* and *Law & Order.*

Although television has dominated her career, her filmography is quite interesting, consisting mainly of critically acknowledged independent films like *The Incredibly True Adventures of Two Girls in Love* (1995), *Boogie Nights* (1997), 1999 Sundance Film Festival winner *The Adventures of Sebastian Cole* (1998), and *200 Cigarettes* (1999). Parker's parents are Joanne (a health care professional) and Donald (a dentist). She and her husband have two children, Sophie Tei-Naaki Lee and Nicolas Neruda.

Feature Films including TV Movies: *The Incredibly True Adventures of Two Girls in Love* (1995), *Stonewall* (1995), *Divas* (TV; 1995), *Rebound: The Legend of Earl "The Goat" Manigault* (TV; 1996), *The End of Violence* (1997), *Boogie Nights* (1997), *Spark* (1998), *The Adventures of Sebastian Cole* (1998), *Exiled* (TV; 1998), *200 Cigarettes* (1999), *Mute Love* (1999), *Mind Prey* (TV; 1999), *Mirar Mirror* (1999), *Loving Jezebel* (aka *Chasing Beauties,* 1999), *Harlem Aria* (1999), *A Map of the World* (1999), *Blue Streak* (1999), *The Loretta Claiborne Story* (TV; 2000), *Dancing in September* (2000), *Remember the Titans* (2000), *Brown Sugar* (2002), *King's Ransom* (2005), *The Better Man* (2008), *Never Better* (TV; 2008), *Welcome Home, Roscoe Jenkins* (2008), *NowhereLand* (2008), *Pastor Brown* (2009).

TV: *Pyramid* (2 segments; 2004), *4th Annual BET Awards* (2004), *Tavis Smiley* (2004), *BET Comedy Awards* (2004), *Good Day Live* (2004), *Retrosexual: The '80s* (2004), *The Tyra Banks Show* (2006), *Subway Stories: Tales from the Underground* ("Honey-Getter," 1997), *Cosby* (3 episodes in the role of Rebecca; "Lucas Apocalypse," "The Hilton Hilton," "The Perfect Valentine," 1999–2000), *CSI: Crime Scene Investigation* ("Primum Non Nocere," 2002), *All of Us* ("Playdate," 2004), *Soul Food* (recurring role of Teri Joseph; 2000–04), *Second Time Around* (recurring role as Ryan Muse; 2004).

Parker, Paula Jai Born in Cleveland, Ohio, August 19, 1969.

Paula Jai Parker has been typecast — or she specializes, depending on how you look at it — in flashy, trashy parts, especially as hookers and loose women. Perfect examples of this can be found in *Phone Booth* (2002) and *Hustle & Flow* (2005). She has gotten her portrayals of gritty urban women down to a veritable science — see her get dressed as a chicken for no especially good reason before she has sex in *Sprung* (1997); watch her battle to steal a scene with Jada Pinkett Smith in *Woo*; or watch her turn on the funk as the raunchy Rolanda in *My Baby's Daddy*; or do her thing as Ice Cube's girlfriend Joi in *Friday.* No, it is not *Masterpiece Theatre*— but it stays with you. The bottom line is that she is a capable actress.

Cleveland-bred Parker moved to Washington, D.C., in 1987 to attend Howard University, from which she graduated with a bachelor of arts degree. She found her way to New York City — as everyone seems to do sooner or later — and started playing the comedy clubs to good effect.

As a result, she was on FOX's *The Apollo Comedy Hour* and won a Cable ACE Award for her work on the anthology program *Cosmic Slop* (for her role in the segment "Tang," based on a Chester Himes' short story), but Parker is perhaps best known these days as the voice of Trudy Proud in the animated series *The Proud Family* (2001–05).

In 1999, she joined the cast of the very short-lived ABC Saturday night series *Snoops* (in a sedate role for a change).

Others films for which she is remembered are the biography of doo-wop singer Frankie Lymon, *Why Do Fools Fall in Love* (1998), and Spike Lee's *She Hate Me* (2004), in which she plays a lesbian.

Feature Films including Video and TV

Movies: *Friday* (1995), *Tales from the Hood* (1995), *Don't Be a Menace to South Central While Drinking Your Juice in the Hood* (1996), *Get on the Bus* (1996), *Riot* (TV; 1997), *Sprung* (1997), *Always Outnumbered, Always Outgunned* (TV; 1998), *Woo* (1998), *Why Do Fools Fall in Love* (1998), *The Breaks* (1999), *30 Years to Life* (2001), *High Crimes* (2002), *Phone Booth* (2002), *Love Chronicles* (2003), *My Baby's Daddy* (2004), *She Hate Me* (2004), *Hustle & Flow* (2005), *The Proud Family Movie* (TV; 2005), *Animal* (2005), *Idlewild* (2006), *The Genius Club* (2006), *Cover* (2008), *So You Want Michael Madsen?* (TV; 2008).

TV: *The Apollo Comedy Hour* (regular; 1992–93), *Townsend Television* (1993), *Cosmic Slop* (1994), *Roc* ("No Place Like Home," 1994), *Pointman* ("Silent Auction," 1995), *The Wayans Bros.* ("Pulp Marion," Shawn Takes a New Stand," 1995–96), *The Parent 'Hood* ("Wendell and I Spy," 1997), *The Weird Al Show* (7 episodes in the role of Val Brentwood; 1997), *Cosby* ("The Two Hilton Lucases," 1997), *NYPD Blue* ("Speak for Yourself, Bruce Clayton," 1998), *Snoops* (recurring role of Roberta Young; 1999–2000), *Touched by an Angel* ("God Bless the Child," 2000), *Express Yourself* (2001), *The Proud Family* (recurring role as the voice of Trudy Proud; 2001–05), *I Love the '80s Strikes Back* (2003), *My Coolest Years* (2004), *The Shield* ("Cracking Ice," 2004), *CSI: Miami* ("Shattered," 2005), *Lilo & Stitch: The Series* (as the voice of Trudy Proud; "Spats: Experiment #397," 2005), *HBO First Look: Idlewild* (2006), *CSI* ("Toe Tags," 2006), *Angels Can't Help But Laugh* (2007), *Side Order of Life* (4 episodes as Stargell Grant; "Whose Sperm Is It Anyway?" "What Price Truth?" "Children and Art," "Try to Remember," 2007), *Baisden After Dark* (2007).

Parks, Trina Born in Brooklyn, New York, December 26, 1947.

Bambi and Thumper are the main characters in a classic 1942 Disney film, but to James Bond aficionados, Bambi and Thumper compose the two-woman bodyguard squad that almost spells curtains for 007 in *Diamonds Are Forever* (1972). Trina Parks was the Thumper half of the team; Lola Lawson was Bambi.

Parks is the daughter of Tennel and Charles Frazier. Her father was a tenor saxophonist with Cab Calloway's Orchestra. Parks is a graduate of the New York School of the Performing Arts with a major in modern dance (emphasizing Martha Graham technique), and is a dancer, dance instructor and singer as well as an actress. She also studied at Katherine Dunham's dance academy in Manhattan and has toured with major dance companies in the U.S., Europe and the Far East. These companies include Katherine Dunham, Alvin Ailey, Geoffrey Holder, Anna Sokolow and Rod Rogers. She has taught modern, jazz, African, Haitian and Broadway dance techniques in Los Angeles and New York. Teaching venues include the New Dance Group in New York City; the Los Angeles High School for the Arts; and the L.A. Music Center, Educational Dance Division.

Her Broadway appearances include *Her First Roman* with Leslie Uggams (as an Egyptian; October–November 1968), *The Selling of the President* (as Burgundy Moore; March 22–25, 1972), and off–Broadway's *In Dahomey* (as Mandisa; June 27–July 25, 1999). She arranged and produced the show *Trina's Tribute to Duke Ellington* and has performed it in New York and Los Angeles. She has been a featured dancer for the past five years in the *Fabulous Palm Spring Follies* in Palm Springs, California.

She was featured in "The Phantom Farmhouse" segment of Rod Serling's *Night Gallery*. She danced in *The Great White Hope* (1970) and *The Blues Brothers* (1980) films, and had a featured role in the B-movie *The Muthers* (1976), but there are two films for which Parks will be best remembered (or, in the case of one of those films, *should* be remembered, because it's a hard film to track down these days).

Diamonds Are Forever (1971) marked Sean Connery's return to the series after George Lazenby took over the role in the excellent *On Her Majesty's Secret Service* (1969). *Diamonds* was fast and amusing and loaded with lovely women (including Jill St. John and Lana Wood). It's a shame that the Thumper and Bambi roles were not well developed, and that the characters were given little screen time. However, Trina Parks was the screen's first African American Bond girl (followed by Gloria Hendry in *Live and Let Die*; 1973). Thumper and Bambi are guarding Willard Whyte (Jimmy Dean), a reclusive Howard Hughes–like billionaire who has been usurped and kept under house arrest by the villainous Ernst Stavro Blofeld. It's very sexy when Thumper tries to seduce Bond, but she and Bambi quickly go on the attack and try to kill him. They are defeated too easily and in too sexist a fashion. *Diamonds Are Forever* was un-

Trina Parks and Sean Connery in *Diamonds Are Forever* (1971).

derrated in its day (at least by the critics), mainly due to its very light tone — a harbinger of the Roger Moore films to come.

The second memorable Parks film appearance is in *Darktown Strutters* (aka *Get Down and Boogie*, 1975), a blaxploitation slapstick comedy and live action cartoon that is her only starring role. Parks is very funny, but the relentless and sometimes offensive slapstick humor is not for every taste (in fact, it's not for too many tastes). This is one of the weirdest movies of all time. The Darktown Strutters are an all-girl black motorcycle group dressed like the music group LaBelle (or the group Parliament Funkadelic, for that matter). The leader of the group is in search of her lost mother — and this is about as much coherent plot as you get. It's good to see Parks in a big role — this comedy can be refreshing after all the overly serious blaxploitation films of the era. *Darktown Strutters* was directed by veteran B-movie and action serial director William A. Witney.

Feature Films including TV Movies: *The Great White Hope* (1970), *Diamonds Are Forever* (1971), *The Big Rip-Off* (TV; 1975), *Darktown Strutters* (aka *Get Down and Boogie*, 1975), *The Muthers* (1976), *The Blues Brothers* (1980).

TV: *Night Gallery* ("The Phantom Farmhouse," 1971), *Bond Girls Are Forever* (archival; 2002).

Patton, Paula Born in Los Angeles, California, December 5, 1975.

Paula Patton is in the vanguard of the new generation of African American actresses. She knew she wanted an acting career from the time she was a little girl and began to prepare for it in high school (Alexander Hamilton High School Academy of Music). The Public Broadcasting System selected her as one of four young filmmakers to take part in a program titled *The Ride* (1994), in which each was given camera equipment and a small crew and told to film their experiences.

After this invaluable experience, Patton attended the University of California, Berkeley, but after a year she transferred to the University of Southern California (USC) Film School, from which she graduated magna cum laude. Her experience on *The Ride* helped her to get a job with the Discovery Channel as producer of the show *Medical Diaries* (2000).

From this behind-the-camera job she segued into acting, with a role in *Hitch* (2005) opposite Will Smith, and major roles in the thriller *Déjà Vu* (2006) opposite Denzel Washington and the light-hearted political allegory *Swing Vote* (2008) with Kevin Costner. She is married to singer Robin Thicke.

Feature Films including Video and TV Movies: *Hitch* (2005), *London* (2005), *Idlewild* (2006), *Murder Book* (TV; 2006), *Déjà Vu* (2006), *Swing Vote* (2008), *Push* (2008), *Mirrors* (2008), *This Wednesday* (2010).

TV: *The Ride* (1994), *OutKast Goes to Idlewild: The Rebirth of Cool* (2006), *HBO: First Look* ("Idlewild," 2006), *Entertainment Tonight* (3 segments; 2008), *The Late Late Show with Craig Ferguson* (2008).

Payne, Freda Born in Detroit, Michigan, September 19, 1942.

The exquisite Freda Payne remains best known for her 1970 hit song "Band of Gold" and her lesser hits "Bring the Boys Home" and "Deeper and Deeper," but she has also had an acting career of note.

Freda Charcelia Payne attended Detroit's Institute of Musical Arts in her teen years and won many local and regional talent shows. Berry Gordy, the guru of Motown Records, wanted to sign her to a contract and supervised her first recording sessions. She also attracted the attention of Duke Ellington and sang with his orchestra for two nights in Pittsburgh, and later performed with him for six months in Las Vegas. She made her national television debut on *Ted Mack's Original Amateur Hour* in 1956, finishing in second place behind an Italian tenor. But despite this early renown, her mother wanted her to complete her education before she embarked on a show business career.

She moved to Manhattan in 1963 and re-

Freda Payne.

leased several albums as a jazz artist (*After the Lights Go Down Low and Much More!* in 1963, followed by *And How Do You Say I Don't Love You Anymore?* in 1966). Subsequent albums took a more pop–R&B approach, including the big commercial breakthrough album *Band of Gold* (1970), *Contact* (1971), *Reaching Out* (1973), *Payne & Pleasure* (1974), *Out of Payne Comes Love* (1975), *Stares and Whispers* (1977), *Supernatural High* (1978) and *Hot* (1979). After a lull in her recording career, she released *An Evening with Freda Payne: Live in Concert* (1996) and *Come See About Me* (2001), among others.

She appeared at the Apollo Theater with the Quincy Jones band and toured throughout Europe with him. She was the understudy for Leslie Uggams in Broadway's *Hallelujah, Baby!* In 1967 she appeared with the Equity Theater in New York in a revival of *Lost in the Stars*. In 1970, Payne, Eartha Kitt and Jayne Kennedy were featured in a *Jet* magazine cover story, "The World's Most Beautiful Black Women."

Payne had the female lead in the light-hearted period film *Book of Numbers* (1973) as Kelly Simms, the "high yellow" love interest of numbers runner Philip Michael Thomas, who runs afoul of the local Mafia (along with his partner Raymond St. Jacques, who also directed). This nicely mounted film never found much of an audience and has fallen into obscurity.

Later roles have included *Ragdoll* (1999) and *The Nutty Professor II: The Klumps* (2000). Payne recently returned to acting with roles in the Sci-Fi Channel movie *Saurian* (2006) and the lead role in *Cordially Invited* (2007), a family comedy about a dream wedding that turns into a nightmare. She briefly hosted her own talk show in 1981 called *Today's Black Woman*. Payne was married to and divorced from singer Gregory Abbott; they have one child.

Feature Films including TV Movies: *Book of Numbers* (1973), *Private Obsession* (1995), *Sprung* (1997), *Ragdoll* (1999), *Nutty Professor II: The Klumps* (2000), *Deadly Rhapsody* (2001), *Fire & Ice* (TV; 2001), *Saurian* (TV; 2006), *Cordially Invited* (2008).

TV: *Ted Mack's Original Amateur Hour* (1956), *Get It Together* (1970), *The Ed Sullivan Show* (1970), *Top of the Pops* (1971), *The Tonight Show Starring Johnny Carson* (4 segments; 1970–73), *Soul Train* (2 segments; 1971–78), *Police Story* ("50 Cents — First Half-Hour, $1.75 All Day," 1976), *The Merv Griffin Show* (1977), *Today's Black Woman* (series host; 1981), *Ad Lib* (1981), *Solid Gold* (1981), *Legendary Ladies of Rock & Roll* (1988), *Living Single* ("I'll Take Your Man," 1993), *2002 Trumpet Awards*, *Pyramid* (2003), *I Love the '70s, Vol. 2* (2006).

Payton, JoMarie (aka Payton, Jo Marie) Born in Albany, Georgia, August 3, 1950.

The second oldest in a family of nine children, JoMarie Payton knew early on that she wanted a show business career, but her early emphasis was on singing. Her family moved to Opa-Locka, Florida, a suburb of Miami, before she was one year old. Her construction worker father and her mother, who was a maid, separated when Payton was around ten. Payton attended the University of Miami, where she studied drama.

She left Florida for California in the mid-seventies. She went to Los Angeles as part of the touring company of the show *Purlie* with Robert Guillaume. When the *Purlie* road company went to Paris, Payton decided to stay in L.A. These were lean times for the actress, and she supported herself with temp work until she found out that the Redd Foxx comedy hour was looking for a retro-style jazz singer. She was hired for the show and co-starred with Foxx in a recurring skit — a show within a show — called "Alfonse and Victoria." The Foxx program did not survive in the variety show glut of that era, and Payton found herself working as a full-time travel agent until she was able to jumpstart her show business career again.

She got a role as the sharp-tongued elevator operator on the buddy comedy *Perfect Strangers* (1987–89), and she proved such as popular cast member that it led to a spin-off sitcom, the long-running *Family Matters* (1989–97). Payton was Harriet Winslow, the sometimes harried but always quick with a quip wife and mother. *Family Matters* was the show that brought the character Steve Urkel (Jaleel White) to a waiting world. Urkel was the "boy next door" who had a crush on Harriet's daughter Laura. Like Henry Winkler's Fonzie on *Happy Days*, Urkel was a supporting character who eventually took over the show — which made ostensible series' star Payton the real supporting character. Payton left *Family Matters* in 1997 during the ninth season.

Her post–*Family Matters* life consists of appearances on a variety of popular series, including *Judging Amy*, *Desperate Housewives*, *Will & Grace* (she had a recurring role as the assistant of the Gregory Hines' character in the second season), and *Reba*. She was the voice of Suga Mama Proud on *The Proud Family* from 2001–05.

Payton is also a jazz singer. Her 1999 CD *Southern Shadows* reveals a side of her talent far removed from the sitcom world. She has been married three times (to Marc France, Rodney Noble and Landrus Clark) and is the mother of a daughter named Chantale.

Feature Films including TV Movies: *The Wiz* (1978), *The Hollywood Knights* (1980), *Deal of the Century* (1983), *Crossroads* (1986), *Disorderlies* (1987), *Colors* (1988), *Troop Beverly Hills* (1989), *Echoes of Enlightenment* (2001), *In the Eyes of Kyana* (TV; 2002), *Gas* (2004), *The Rev* (TV; 2005), *The Proud Family Movie* (TV; 2005), *Let's Ride* (2008).

TV: *Redd Foxx* (1977–78), *The New Odd Couple* (recurring role as Mona; 1982), *Deal of the Century* (1983), *Small Wonder* ("Vicki for the Defense," 1985), *227* ("The Handwriting on the Wall," 1987), *Perfect Strangers* (recurring role of Harriette Baines Winslow; "Your Cheatin' Heart," "Crimebusters," 1987–89), *Family Matters* (recurring role of Harriette Winslow; 1989–1997), *ABC*

TGIF (1990), *Moesha* ("A Concerted Effort," Part I, "Barking Up the Wrong Tree," "I Studied Twelve Years for This?" "Thanksgiving," 1996–99), *The Jamie Foxx Show* ("Just Don't Do It," 1998), *Will & Grace* (5 episodes in the role of Mrs. Freeman; "Terms of Employment," "Tea and a Total Lack of Sympathy," "Acting Out," "Advise and Resent," "Ben? Her?" 1999–2000), *City of Angels* ("Saving Faces," 2000), *7th Heaven* ("Liar, Liar," 2000), *Weakest Link* (2002), *The Hughleys* ("Bored of the Rings," 2002), *Lingo* (2002), *One on One* (voice; "It's Raining Women," 2002), *The Parkers* ("It's Showtime," 2002), *Judging Amy* ("Ex Parte of Five," 2003), *Wanda at Large* ("Hurricane Hawkins," 2003), *Girlfriends* (2 episodes as Annette Miles; "L.A. Bound," "Who's Your Daddy?" 2004), *The Proud Family* (recurring voice role of Suga Mama; 2001–05), *Lilo & Stitch* (voice of Suga Mama; "Spats: Experiment #397," 2005), *TV Land Confidential* ("Disappearing and Breakout Star," 2005), *Reba* ("No Good Deed," 2005), *Desperate Housewives* ("Thank You So Much," 2006).

Video/DVD: *Woof! Woof! Uncle Matty's Guide to Dog Training* (1997).

Pettiford, Valarie

Born in Queens, New York, July 8, 1960.

Valarie Pettiford is living proof that "Fosse girls rule!" Pettiford's storied career began with her training at the Bernice Johnson Theater of Performing Arts in Queens, New York. She then attended the Performing Arts High School. At age 14, she was in the chorus of the film version of *The Wiz*. Her off–Broadway appearances include productions of *The Balcony*, *Freefall*, *Tango Apasionado*, *The Naked Truth* and *Beehive*. She starred in regional productions of *Summer and Smoke* and *She Stoops to Conquer*.

But it was on Broadway that Pettiford achieved the "holy grail" all dancers dream of—she became part of the Bob Fosse dance troupe. As a "Fosse dancer" she appeared in Bob Fosse's *Dancin'* and was a key part of the ensemble in his last Broadway musical *Big Deal* in 1986. She was nominated for a Tony for Featured Role in a Musical for the posthumous tribute show *Fosse*, and she co-starred with Chita Rivera in the London production of Bob Fosse's *Chicago* (1999–2000).

Her performance as Julie in the Los Angeles production of *Show Boat* won her many awards, including an NAACP Image Award and L.A.'s Robby Award, in addition to a nomination for L.A.'s Ovation Award. She was also in the Broadway production *Grind*, a clear-eyed look at the world of burlesque, in 1985. Pettiford earned three NAACP Image Awards for her portrayal of Big Dee Dee Thorne on TV's *Half & Half*. She had a recurring role as Detective Courtney Walker on the soap *Another World*. Series on which she has guest-starred include *The Sentinel*, *Walker, Texas Ranger* and *Sliders*. Feature film appearances include *The Cotton Club*, *Another You* and *Street Hunter*.

She has performed her acclaimed one-woman show at venues ranging from the Gardenia and El Portal Theatres in Los Angeles to the Metropolitan Room in New York City. Her parents are Ralph and Blanche; she has a younger sister named Atonia and a husband named Tony.

Feature Films including Video and TV Movies: *The Cotton Club* (1984), *Robots* (1988), *Street Hunter* (1990), *Confidences* (2001), *Glitter* (2001), *Like Mike* (2002), *Paris* (2003), *Surviving in L.A.* (2005), *Stomp the Yard* (2007), *The Stolen Moments of September* (2007).

TV: *Another World* (recurring role as Detective Courtney Walker; 1986–90), *One Life to Live* (recurring role as Sheila Price Gannon; 1990–94), *The Sentinel* ("Out of the Past," 1996), *Silk Stalkings* ("Silent Witness," 1997), *Honey, I Shrunk the Kids* (2 episodes in the role of Bianca Fleisch; "Honey, You've Got Nine Lives," "Honey, I Got Duped," 1997), *Fame L.A.* (3 episodes in the role of Sylvia Williams; "Seize the Day," "Reality Check," "The Key to Success," 1997–98), *Walker, Texas Ranger* ("Angel," 1998), *Sliders* ("Asylum," 1998), *The X Files* ("Two Fathers," 1999), *Jack & Jill* ("Caution: Parents' Crossing," 1999), *Sabrina, The Teenage Witch* ("Sabrina, the Muse," 2001), *Frazier* ("Hooping Cranes," 2001), *Men, Women & Dogs* ("Top Dog," 200?), *The West Wing* ("Enemies Foreign and Domestic," 2002), *The District* (recurring role of Gayle Noland; 2002–04), *Black in the '80s* (2005), *Only in L.A.* (2005), *CSI: Miami* ("Open Water," 2006), *Half & Half* (recurring role of Big Dee Dee Thorne; 2002–06), *CSI: Crime Scene Investigation* ("Fallen Idols," 2007), *Bones* ("Bodies in the Book," 2007).

Pigford, Eva (aka Marcille, Eva)

Born in Los Angeles, California, October 30, 1984.

Eva Pigford was the winner on the third season of the popular Tyra Banks reality series *Amer-*

ica's Next Top Model. "Eva the Diva" is known for her natural green eyes, her honey-hued skin, and her stately body. Her prizes included a photo spread in *Elle* magazine, a CoverGirl cosmetics contract, and a modeling contract with Ford Models (she later switched to L.A. Models). One thing that was not part of the prize was acting roles in films and on TV, but Pigford has managed to snare her share of those as well.

She was on two episodes of *Kevin Hill* (2005), as well as guesting on *Everybody Hates Chris, Smallville,* and *The Game.* She has been featured in music videos by recording artists 50 Cent, Jamie Foxx and Angie Stone. She has had roles in the features *The Walk* (2005), *Crossover* (2006), and *I Think I Love My Wife* (2007). She has hosted two reality shows on BET, *My Model Looks Better Than Your Model* and *Rip the Runway.*

Feature Films: *The Walk* (2005), *The Wedding Album* (2006), *Premium* (2006), *Crossover* (2006), *I Think I Love My Wife* (2007), *Super Capers* (2008).

TV: *Live with Regis and Kathie Lee* (2004), *America's Next Top Model* (winning competitor; 2004–05), *The 19th Annual Soul Train Music Awards* (2005), *Kevin Hill* (2 episodes in the role of Sandra Clark; "Cardiac Episode," "Through the Looking Glass," 2005), *Best Week Ever* (2005), *The Tyra Banks Show* (2 segments; 2005), *106 & Park Top 10 Live* (2005), *2005 Trumpet Awards, BET Awards 2005, Life & Style* (2005), *Nick Cannon Presents Wild 'N Out* (2005), *E! True Hollywood Story* ("America's Next Top Model," 2006), *My Model Looks Better Than Your Model* (series host; 2006), *Beats Style and Flavor* (2006), *The Late Late Show with Craig Ferguson* (2006), *The Game* ("Out of Bounds," 2007), *House of Payne* (recurring role as Tracie; 2007), *The Young and the Restless* (recurring role as Tyra Hamilton; 2008), *Black Poker Invitational* (2008), *Rip the Runway* (2008).

Pilot, Bernice Birth date unavailable.

Bernice Pilot was the female lead in *Hearts in Dixie* (1929), the first all-talking big studio feature with a black cast. Billed as "the screen's first singing, dancing and talking comedy of the old South," it was a slice-of-life look at black America, with a cast that included Clarence Muse, Stepin Fetchit, and Pilot as Chloe, granddaughter to Muse's character and wife to Fetchit's, and mother of a young son (Ernest Jackson). After Chloe's death, the boy is sent North by his doting grandfather to escape the influence of his "shiftless" father and to get an education, so as not to not be influenced by the ignorance and superstition of the local community. "Forward thinking" in its day, hopelessly racist by today's standards, *Hearts of Dixie* is nevertheless a film of considerable historic importance, and it does deal with a theme — the empowerment of black youth — that is quite relevant today.

Feature Films: *Hearts in Dixie* (1929), *Carolina* (1934), *Diamond Jim* (1935), *Road Gang* (1936), *The Law in Her Hands* (1936), *Public Enemy's Wife* (1936), *Penrod and Sam* (1937), *White Bondage* (1937), *Dance Charlie Dance* (1937), *On Such a Night* (1937), *Back in Circulation* (1937), *Penrod and His Twin Brother* (1938), *Women Are Like That* (1938), *The Beloved Brat* (1938), *The Story of Doctor Carver* (1938), *My Bill* (1938), *Sky Giant* (1938), *Penrod's Double Trouble* (1938), *Secrets of an Actress* (1938), *Say It in French* (1938), *Kentucky* (1938), *Sweepstakes Winner* (1939), *No Place to Go* (1939), *Pride of the Blue Grass* (1939), *A Fugitive from Justice* (1939), *City for Conquest* (1940), *Santa Fe Trail* (1940), *Father's Son* (1941), *Three Sons o' Guns* (1941), *Criminals Within* (1943), *The Sea of Grass* (1947).

Pinkett Smith, Jada Born in Baltimore, Maryland, September 18, 1971.

Actress, clothing designer, director, vocalist for a metal band, philanthropist — she's even written a comic book! — Jada Pinkett Smith, born Jada Koren Pinkett, is a woman for all seasons. Her mother is Adrienne Banfield, head nurse of a clinic in Baltimore; her father is Robsol Pinkett, Jr., construction company owner. They were divorced after a brief marriage, and her mother has since remarried twice. Pinkett Smith graduated from the Baltimore School for the Arts, then she attended the North Carolina School of the Arts for a year.

Her breakthrough role was as student Lena James in 1991 on *A Different World.* Her motion picture debut came two years later in John Singleton's *Menace II Society.* She was Eddie Murphy's character's girlfriend in her first huge box office film *The Nutty Professor* (1996). In 2001 she had a featured role in *Ali*; she was quite good as the first wife of Muhammad Ali.

Pinkett Smith has given fine performances in a number of films. Her best work includes *The*

Inkwell and *Jason's Lyric* (both 1994), the former an evocative memory piece and the latter an erotically charged romance. *Set It Off* (1997) featured her in a starring role in a film about an ill-fated group of diverse young black women driven to rob a bank for a variety of personal reasons. *Collateral* (2004) was a superb crime thriller where she played a career woman whose life is jeopardized by getting in the wrong cab on the wrong night. Many know her best for her role as Niobe in the second and third films of the *Matrix* trilogy, and as the voice of Gloria the Hippo in the immensely popular *Madagascar* series.

Pinkett Smith has been nominated for six NAACP Image Awards: Outstanding Actress in a Mini-Series/Television Movie (*If These Walls Could Talk*, 1997); Outstanding Actress in a Motion Picture (*Set It Off* and *Bamboozled*, 2001); and Outstanding Supporting Actress in a Motion Picture (*Ali*, *The Matrix: Revolutions*, 2004, and *Collateral*, 2005). She is the wife of actor Will Smith (they married in 1997); they have a son, Jaden Christopher Syre, born in 1998, and a daughter, Willow Camille Reign, born in 2000.

She co-founded the Will and Jada Foundation with her husband. The foundation provides funding to youth educational projects.

Feature Films including TV Movies: *Moe's World* (TV; 1990), *Menace II Society* (1993), *The Inkwell* (aka *No Ordinary Summer*, 1994), *Jason's Lyric* (1994), *A Low Down Dirty Shame* (1994), *Tales from the Crypt: Demon Knight* (1995), *The Nutty Professor* (1996), *If These Walls Could Talk* (TV; 1996), *Set It Off* (1997), *Princess Mononoke* (voice; 1997), *Scream 2* (1997), *Woo* (1998), *Return to Paradise* (1998), *Blossoms and Veils* (1998), *Welcome to Hollywood* (2000), *Bamboozled* (2000), *Ali* (2001), *Tupac: Resurrection* (archival; 2003), *Maniac Magee* (narrator; TV; 2003), *The Matrix Reloaded* (2003), *The Matrix Revolutions* (2003), *Collateral* (2004), *Madagascar* (voice; 2005), *Reign Over Me* (2007), *Madagascar: Escape 2 Africa* (voice; 2008), *The Women* (2008), *The Human Contract* (2009).

TV: *True Colors* ("Life with Fathers," 1990), *21 Jump Street* ("Homegirls," 1991), *A Different World* (recurring role of Lena James; 1991–93), *The Rosie O'Donnell Show* (2 appearances; 1996–98), *Ellen* ("A Hollywood Tribute," Part I, 1998), *Essence Awards* (1998), *Ultra Sound* ("Will Smith," 1999), *The 55th Annual Golden Globe Awards* (1998), *The Tonight Show with Jay Leno* (4

Jada Pinkett Smith.

appearances; 2001–06), *Intimate Portrait* ("Jasmine Guy," 2002), *Total Request Live* (2002), *Player$* (2 segments; 2003), *Richard & Judy* (2003), *Biography* ("Will Smith: Hollywood's Fresh Prince," 2003), *Tinseltown TV* (2003), *It's Good to Be...* (archival; "It's Good to Be Will and Jada," 2003), *HBO First Look* (3 segments; "The Matrix Revolutions," "Collateral," "Madagascar: Welcome to the Jungle," 2003–05), *The View* (2 appearances; 2003–05), *The 76th Annual Academy Awards* (2004), *NY Graham Norton* (2004), *gmtv* (2004), *Late Night with Conan O'Brien* (2004), *Primetime Live* (2004), *Tavis Smiley* (2004), *This Morning* (2004), *Late Show with David Letterman* (3 segments; 2004–08), *Live with Regis and Kelly* (2 appearances; 2004–07), *The 10th Annual Critics' Choice Awards* (2005), *The Oprah Winfrey Show* (2005), *Today* (2005), *Ellen* (2005), *Corazon de...* (archival; 2005), *Nickelodeon Kids' Choice Awards 2005*, *BET Awards 2005*, *2005 American Music Awards*, *106 & Park Top 10 Live* (2 appearances; 2005–07), *Access Hollywood* (archival; 2006), *Last Call with Carson Daly* (2006), *Transmission with T-Mobile* (2006), *I Was a Network Star* (2006), *Entertainment Tonight* (2 segments; 2006–08), *Inside Edition* (2006), *The 64th Annual Golden Globe Awards* (2007), *Como consegiur* *un papel en Hollywood* (archival; 2007), *VH1 Rock Honors* (2007), *Larry King Live* (2008), *The Dog Whisperer* (2008), *46664: A Concert for Nelson Mandela* (2008), *The Big Give* (2008).

Video/DVD: *The Will Smith Music Video Collection* ("Just the Two of Us," 1999).

Poitier, Sydney Tamiia Born in Los Angeles, California, November 15, 1973.

Sydney Tamiia Poitier, the beautiful daughter of Academy Award–winning icon Sidney Poitier and actress Joanna Shimkus, has forged an increasingly impressive acting career of her own. She received a bachelor of fine arts degree in acting from New York University's Tisch School of the Arts.

Her performance as Jungle Julia in Quentin Tarantino's *Death Proof*, half of the two-part film *Grindhouse* (2007) (also released in a much expanded version as a single film on DVD), is a fan favorite. Leggy, arrogant Julia is a top local DJ who meets a bad end when the car she and her buddies are riding in is totaled by the evil Stuntman Mike (Kurt Russell) riding in his "death-proof" stunt car. Poitier is very funny in the role, with an abundance of that patented Tarantino "cool." Other features include *True Crime* (1999); the little-seen *Devil Cats* (2004), directed by her sister Anika; and *Hood of Horror* (2006), a spoofy horror film trilogy with Snoop Dogg.

On television, she had a recurring role as Rebecca Askew, girlfriend of Joan's brother Kevin, in the first season of the cancelled-too-soon *Joan of Arcadia* (2003–04). She had the lead in the series *Abby* (2003) as Abigail Walker. On *Veronica Mars* (2004), she was Mallory Dent, Veronica's journalism teacher. She was also seen in the recent series *Knight Rider* (2008), NBC's revival of its popular old action show, as FBI agent Carrie Rivai. Guest star roles include the revamped version of *The Twilight Zone* and *Grey's Anatomy*.

Poitier is capable of the light touch as well as deeper dramatics, and she should add an interesting variety of performances to her résumé in years to come.

Feature Films including TV Movies: *Park Day* (1998), *Free of Eden* (TV; 1999), *True Crime* (1999), *Noah's Ark* (TV; 1999), *MacArthur Park* (2001), *On the Edge* (TV; 2001), *Happy Birthday* (2001), *The Devil Cats* (2004), *Nine Lives* (2005), *The List* (2006), *Snoop Dogg's Hood of Horror* (2006), *Grindhouse* (two films consisting of *Planet Terror* and *Death Proof*; Poitier appeared in the *Death Proof* segment; 2007), *Death Proof* (expanded feature-length version; 2007).

TV: *First Years* ("No Place Like Homo," 2001), *Abby* (recurring role as Abby Walker; "The Breakup," "Abby Gets Her Groove Back," "Ted & Carol & Will & Abby," 2003), *The Twilight Zone* ("Placebo Effect," 2003), *Joan of Arcadia* (recurring role of Rebecca Askew; 2003–04), *Veronica Mars* (recurring role of Mallory Dent; 2004), *Grey's Anatomy* ("17 Seconds," 2006), *2006 BAFTA/LA Cunard Britannia Awards, Knight Rider* (recurring role as Carrie Rivai; 2008).

Pounder, CCH Born in Georgetown, Guyana, December 25, 1952.

The CCH (periods usually excluded) stands for Carol Christine Hilaria. Pounder was raised on a Guyanese sugar plantation, the daughter of Betsy Enid Arnella and Ronald Urlington Pounder. She was sent along with her sister to a convent boarding school in Sussex, England. The next phase of her life involved moving to New York and attending upstate Ithaca College, where she became formally involved in acting, and then got involved in regional and classic repertory theater. She appeared with Morgan Freeman in *The Mighty Gents* at the New York Shakespeare Festival and in *Open Admissions* (1984), her Broadway debut in an off–Broadway transplant, in the small role of Mrs. Brewster.

Pounder made little impression on audiences until the release of *Bagdad Café* (aka *Out of Rosenheim*, 1987), a West German art house film sleeper that captivated international audiences and jump-started Pounder's career. A fish-out-of-water Bavarian woman and her husband find their way to a desert hole-in-the-wall truck stop in America called the Bagdad Café. The proprietor is a perpetually infuriated black woman named Brenda (Pounder). We are introduced to the various eccentric local characters (including Jack Palance, in a refreshingly offbeat role). Slowly Brenda and the German woman, Jasmin, become friends. Quirky to a fault in the mind of some critics, *Bagdad Café* took off with the public and enjoyed a long, successful run. It continues to have a substantial cult following on DVD, and is now being discovered by a new generation.

Her *Bagdad Café* days long behind her, Pounder is much better known these days for her Emmy-nominated turn as Dr. Angela Hicks from

1994 to 1997 on the top-rated, long-running *ER*, and for a series of excellent TV movies that includes *Go Tell It on the Mountain* (1985), *Murder in Mississippi* (1990) and *Boycott* (2001). For current audiences, she is synonymous with her white-hot work as Detective Claudette Wyms on *The Shield* (2002–08), contributing some of the most impassioned acting seen on television. This garnered her an Emmy nomination in 2005 and two NAACP Image Award nominations for Best Actress in a Drama Series. She received a third Emmy nomination for her guest star work on an episode of *The X-Files*.

She is married to Senegalese anthropologist Boubacar Kone. Pounder is one of the founders of the activist group ANSA (Aritists for a New South Africa). In 1997, she was the recipient of an Excellence in the Arts award from the Institute of Caribbean Studies.

Feature Films including Video and TV Movies: *Coriolanus* (1979), *All That Jazz* (1979), *I'm Dancing as Fast as I Can* (1982), *Booker* (TV; 1984), *Go Tell It on the Mountain* (TV; 1985), *Prizzi's Honor* (1985), *Resting Place* (TV; 1986), *As Summers Die* (TV; 1986), *Bagdad Café* (1987), *Run Till You Fall* (TV; 1988), *Leap of Faith* (TV; 1988), *Third Degree Burn* (TV; 1989), *No Place Like Home* (TV; 1989), *Murder in Mississippi* (TV; 1990), *Common Ground* (TV; 1990), *Postcards from the Edge* (1990), *Psycho IV: The Beginning* (1990), *The Importance of Being Earnest* (1992), *The Ernest Green Story* (TV; 1993), *For Their Own Good* (TV; 1993), *Benny & Joon* (1993), *Sliver* (1993), *Lifepod* (1993), *RoboCop 3* (1993), *The Disappearance of Christina* (TV; 1993), *Aladdin and the King of Thieves* (voice; 1995), *Tales from the Crypt: Demon Knight* (1995), *White Dwarf* (TV; 1995), *Jack Reed: One of Our Own* (TV; 1995), *Things That Go Bump* (TV; 1996), *Face/Off* (1997), *House of Frankenstein* (TV; 1997), *Final Justice* (TV; 1998), *Melting Pot* (1998), *Blossoms and Veils* (1998), *Little Girl Fly Away* (TV; 1998), *NetForce* (TV; 1999), *To Serve and Protect* (TV; 1999), *Funny Valentines* (TV; 1999), *A Touch of Hope* (TV; 1999), *End of Days* (1999), *Batman Beyond: The Movie* (voice; TV; 1999), *Cora Unashamed* (TV; 2000), *Disappearing Acts* (TV; 2000), *Things Behind the Sun* (2001), *Boycott* (TV; 2001), *The Big Day* (2001), *Baby of the Family* (2002), *Tét grenné* (2002), *Redemption: The Stan "Tookie" Williams Story* (TV; 2004), *Warehouse 13* (TV; 2008), *Rain* (2008), *My Girlfriend's Back* (2009), *Avatar* (2009).

TV: *Hill Street Blues* (3 episodes; "The Second Oldest Profession," "Little Boil Blue," "Amazing Grace," 1981–86), *The Atlanta Child Murders* (miniseries; 1985), *If Tomorrow Comes* (miniseries; 1986), *Valerie* ("Full Moon," 1986), *Cagney & Lacey* ("Disenfranchised," 1986), *L.A. Law* (4 episodes as Judge Roseann Robin; "Those Lips, That Eye," "El Sid," "Lie Harder," "Back to the Suture," 1986–92), *Women in Prison* (1987), *CBS Schoolbreak Special* ("My Past Is My Own," 1989), *227* ("Babes in the Woods," 1989), *21st NAACP Image Awards* (1989), *Miami Vice* ("Too Much, Too Late," 1990), *Quantum Leap* ("Black on White on Fire: August 11, 1965," 1990), *Cop Rock* (3 episodes; "Oil of Ol'Lay," "Potts Don't Fail Me Now," "Marital Blitz," 1990), *Lifestories* ("Darryl Tevis," 1991), *The Cosby Show* ("Claire's Reunion," 1992), *Biker Mice from Mars* (1993), *Sisters* ("The Good Daughter," 1993), *Return to Lonesome Dove* (miniseries; 1993), *Birdland* (recurring role as Nurse Lucy; 1994), *South Central* ("Co-op," 1994), *The X-Files* ("Duane Barry," 1994), *Gargoyles* (2 episodes as the voice of Desdemona; "The Awakening," Part I, "City of Stone," Part I, 1994 and 1995), *ER* (24 episodes in the role of Angela Hicks; 1994–97), *Living Single* ("Mommy Not Dearest," 1995), *Millennium* (5 episodes in the role of Cheryl Andrews; "The Judge," "Weeds," "Force Majeure," "The Hand of Saint Sebastian," "Skull and Bones," 1996–98), *Batman Beyond* ("Rebirth," Part I, 1999), *Detention* ("The Contest," 1999), *The West Wing* ("Celestial Navigation," 2000), *Acapulco Black Film Festival* (2000), *Rude Awakening* ("Plastered," 2000), *The Outer Limits* ("Decompression," 2000), *Static Shock* (2 episodes as the voice of the mayor; "Aftershock," "Junior," 2000 and 2001), *The Practice* (2 episodes in the role of Helene Washington; "The Day After," "Awakenings," 2001), *Strong Medicine* ("Mortality," 2001), *The District* ("To Serve and Protect," 2001), *Law & Order: Special Victims Unit* (recurring role of Carolyn Maddox; 2001–08), *For the People* ("To DNA or Not to DNA," 2002), *The Shield* (recurring role as Detective Claudette Wyms; 2002–08), *Memories: Readings from the Slave Narratives* (2003), *Race: The Power of an Illusion* (3 episodes; "The Story We Tell," "The House We Live In," "The Difference Between Us," 2003), *Pyramid* (2003), *35th NAACP Image Awards* (2004), *The Wayne Brady Show* (2004), *Girlfriends* ("Prophet & Loss," 2004), *Justice League* (recurring role as the voice of Amanda

Waller; 2004–06), *Numb3rs* ("Vector," 2005), *9th Annual Prism Awards* (2005), *The Healing Passage: Voices from the Water* (2005), *10th Annual Prism Awards* (2006), *Square Off* (2006), *In the Mix* (2006), *W.I.T.C.H.* (3 episodes as the voice of Kadma; "S Is for Self," "P Is for Protectors," "Q Is for Quarry," 2006), *American Masters* ("Novel Reflections: The American Dream," 2007), *10th Annual Ribbon of Hope Celebration* (2007), *Breaking the Maya Code* (narrator; 2008).

Pratt, Kyla Born in Culver City, California, September 16, 1986.

The eldest of five children, Kyla Pratt has been acting since childhood. Her first role was as one of the kids on *Barney & Friends* and she was in a *Friends* episode, and later had a recurring role as Brianna Barnes on *One on One* from 2001 to 2006. She has done a remarkable amount of guest star work for one so young, with *Moesha, Living Single, Family Matters, Lizzie McGuire, The Parkers,* and *Sister, Sister* on her résumé, to name only a few. She is also the voice of Penny Proud on animated *The Proud Family* for the Disney Channel. Her latest show is *Hell on Earth* on the fledgling CW Network. In 1999, she was the winner of the Nickelodeon Kids' Choice Award for Favorite Rising Star.

She has settled into her own film franchise, the *Dr. Dolittle* series, as daughter Maya Dolittle. Even though Eddie Murphy has long since left the series, Pratt continues to star in a series of popular direct-to-DVD sequels. She made her film debut in *The Baby-Sitters Club* (1995), was Doris in the live-action film version of Bill Cosby's *Fat Albert* (2004), and played the childhood incarnation of the Sanaa Lathan character (Monica) in the warm-hearted romance *Love & Basketball* (2000). Pratt also sings and can be heard on *Disneymania 2* and *The Proud Family* album. She attended the renowned Hamilton Academy of Music in Los Angeles.

Feature Films including TV Movies: *The Baby-Sitters Club* (1995), *Riot* (1997), *Mad City* (1997), *Barney's Great Adventure* (1998), *Doctor Dolittle* (1998), *Jackie's Back!: Portrait of a Diva* (TV; 1999), *Love & Basketball* (2000), *Dr. Dolittle 2* (2001), *Maniac Magee* (TV; 2003), *The Seat Filler* (2004), *Fat Albert* (2004), *The Beach* (TV; 2005), *The Picnic* (TV; 2005), *The Proud Family Movie* (TV; 2005), *Dr. Dolittle 3* (2006), *Hell on Earth* (2007), *Dr. Dolittle: Tail to the Chief* (2008), *Dr. Dolittle: A Tinsel Town Tail* (2008), *Hotel for Dogs* (2009).

TV: *Barney & Friends* (recurring appearances; 1992), *Living Single* ("He Works Hard for the Money," 1995), *The Parent 'Hood* (2 episodes in the role of Monica; "A Kiss Is Just a Kiss," "To Kiss or Not to Kiss," 1995 and 1999), *In the House* (2 episodes in the role of Erica; "Love on a One-Way Street," "My Crazy Valentine," 1996), *Sisters* ("The Price," 1996), *Lois & Clark: The New Adventures of Superman* ("Through a Glass, Darkly," 1996), *ER* ("Take These Broken Wings," 1996), *Public Morals* ("The Cornflower Cover," 19??), *Touched by an Angel* ("The Journalist," 1996), *Friends* ("The One Where Rachel Quits," 1996), *Family Matters* ("Le Jour d'Amour," 1997), *A Walton Easter* (1997), *Walker, Texas Ranger* ("The Neighborhood," 1997), *Smart Guy* (3 episodes; "Baby, It's You and You and You," "Bad Boy," "She Got Game," 1997–98), *The Pretender* ("Gigolo Jarod," 1998), *The Rosie O'Donnell Show* (1998), *Any Day Now* ("You Shoulda Seen My Daddy," 1998), *Nickelodeon Kids' Choice Awards 1999, Sister, Sister* ("The Road Less Travelled," 1999), *Becker* ("Limits & Boundaries," 1999), *So Weird* ("Lost," 1999), *Moesha* (2 episodes; "The Crush," "Netcam," 1999 and 2000), *One on One* (pilot; 2000), *The Parkers* ("Bad to the Bone," 2000), *The Hughleys* ("The Thin Black Line," 2000), *Strong Medicine* ("Brainchild," 2000), *Lizzie Maguire* ("Gordo and the Girl," 2001), *One on One* (recurring role of Breanna Barnes; 2001–06), *HBO First Look: The Making of Dr. Dolittle 2* (2001), *Express Yourself* (2001), *The Proud Family* (as the voice of Penny Proud; 2001–05), *Super Short Show* (2002), *Veronica Mars* ("The Wrath of Con," 2004), *4th Annual BET Awards* (2004), *Dr. Phil* (2005), *Lilo & Stitch: The Series* (as the voice of Penny Proud; "Spats: Experiment #397," 2005).

Preer, Evelyn Born in Vicksburg, Mississippi, July 16, 1896; died Los Angeles, California, November 19, 1932.

Following her father's death, Evelyn Preer, born Evelyn Jarvis, and her mother moved to Chicago when she was two years old. She made her acting debut in high school in *Lady American Minstrels* and after graduation she became the leading lady with Charley Johnson's vaudeville troupe, touring the Orpheum theater circuit. She was also a street corner preacher accompanied by her mother as a youth, expounding her Pentecostal faith and seeking to raise money to build a church.

In 1918 she pioneered a career in feature films. She was the lead in great black director Oscar Micheaux's first film, *The Homesteader* (1919), and starred in a number of other Micheaux films, including *Within Our Gates* (1920), *The Gunsaulus Mystery* (1921; remade in 1935 by Micheaux as *Lem Hawkins' Confession,* aka known as *Murder in Harlem*), *The Brute* (1920), *Birthright* (1924), and *The Devil's Disciple* (1926). Micheaux had reportedly first seen her street preaching in Harlem and was deeply impressed by her magnetism, which amply transferred to the screen, such as in her riveting performance as the shantytown girl Cissie in *Birthright.*

Although many of the Micheaux films of this era are lost, *Within Our Gates* (1920) exists, and provides ample testimony not only to Micheaux's sweeping talent as a director, but to Preer's charisma and skill as an actress. She plays Sylvia Landry, an African American teacher who allies with a wealthy older white woman who finances a school for black children (based on an actual school in Mississippi called Piney Woods). In a parallel story, it turns out that Sylvia is the daughter of a white plantation owner who raped her mother. Micheaux deals with epic themes that still concern today's black community: the importance of education; the venality in certain elements of the black church; and the hypocrisy of white racism versus the sexual exploitation of black women.

In 1920 Preer joined the legendary black theatrical group The Lafayette Players, the company founded by Anita Bush, "the Little Mother of Negro Drama." She toured with the troupe throughout the U.S. in between appearances in the Micheaux films. Preer did everything with the Lafayette Players from Shakespeare to Wilde's *Salome*, Somerset Maugham's *Rain*, the comic thriller *The Cat and the Canary*, and *Anna Christie.* Her 1928 starring role in *Rain* in Los Angeles was a major breakthrough for a black actress. Most white Americans were not aware that there was such diversity in the black theater, but Preer was even beginning to attract attention outside that insular, segregated world.

Even before this triumph, Preer had made it to Broadway in 1926 as a featured player as well as an understudy and replacement for the German star Lenore Ulrich in the lead role of *Lulu Belle*, the controversial study of a Harlem prostitute. She had gotten beyond working for Micheaux, and her presence in his films would be sorely missed. She was also an excellent vocalist and occasionally performed with legendary musicians like Duke Ellington and Red Nichols. Preer also made recordings, singing backup vocals and making blues records of her own as "Hotsy" Jarvis (her real last name). She made her talkie debut in the race musical *Georgia Rose* (1930). She also made low-budget comedy shorts for black audiences featuring the comic detective Florian Slappey at the Al Christie studios in 1928.

She married actor Edward Thompson, a fellow Lafayette Player, in 1924; they had one daughter, Edeve, born in 1932. Edeve joined the Sisters of Saint Francis and became a Roman Catholic nun, known as Sister M. Francesca Thompson. She taught at Marian College in Indianapolis and is an expert on African American film history. Preer died of double pneumonia brought on by post-delivery health complications. Thousands packed the Independent Church of Christ at her funeral. The black community was well aware that it had lost its shining star.

Feature Films: *The Homesteader* (1919), *Within Our Gates* (1920), *The Brute* (1920), *The Gunsaulus Mystery* (1921), *Deceit* (1923), *Birthright* (1924), *The Devil's Disciple* (1926), *The Conjure Woman* (1926), *The Spider's Web* (1927), *The Widow's Bite* (1929), *Melancholy Dame* (1929), *The Framing of the Shrew* (1929), *The Lady Fare* (1929), *Brown Gravy* (1929), *Georgia Rose* (1930), *Ladies of the Big House* (1931), *Blonde Venus* (1932).

Pringle, Joan Born in New York, New York, June 2, 1945.

Joan Pringle was principal Sybil Buchanan on the ahead-of-its-time series *The White Shadow*, about a white high school sports coach and his predominantly minority students. She also guest starred on top-rated shows like *The Waltons* and *Kojak.* Born in Harlem, Pringle was married — after a brief first marriage — to Teddy Wilson from 1980 until his death in 1991, and had twins (Nicole Naomi and Robert Kenyatta) with him. They met when he appeared in an episode of *The White Shadow*, and they became engaged when they worked together on *That's My Mama* in 1975 (she replaced Lynne Moody as Clifton Davis' sister Tracy). After Wilson's death, she married producer Vernon L. Bolling.

Her Jamaican-born father was a bank manager, and her mother a city government worker. Pringle went to St. Hilda's and St. Hugh's Episcopal Schools (she was the only African American in her class for eight years). She never considered acting until after she entered City College of New York (at the time she wanted to teach). But eventually she became involved in local theater and took acting classes with Uta Hagen. In 1972, she signed a contract with Universal Studios, which led to work on *Ironside* and *Marcus Welby, MD.*

Pringle was Dr. Patricia Mason on the soap *General Hospital* from 1982 to 1984 and Ruth Marshall on another soap, *Generations,* from 1989 to 1991, and was Joan Clayton's mother on *Girlfriends* (2004–07). She was Rianna Mayweather on the *Star Trek: Enterprise* episode "Horizon." She also had a recurring role on *One on One* (as Eunice Barnes; 2001–03).

Feature Films including TV Movies: *Double Indemnity* (TV; 1973), J.D.'s Revenge (1976), *Corey: For the People* (TV; 1977), *Best Friends* (1982), *Visions of Murder* (TV; 1992), *Percy & Thunder* (TV; 1993), *Eyes of Terror* (TV; 1994), *Greyhounds* (TV; 1994), *Gia* (TV; 1998), *Incognito* (TV; 1999), *Up, Up and Away!* (TV; 2000), *Original Sin* (2001), *For One Night* (TV; 2006), *Daddy's Little Girls* (2007).

TV: *Emergency* ("The Professor," 1973), *Banacek* ("The Two Million Clams of Cap'n Jack," 1973), *Toma* ("Blockhouse Breakdown," 1973), *Marcus Welby, M.D.* (2 episodes; "The Tall Tree," "Nguyen," 1973), *Love Story* ("Time for Love," 1974), *Sanford and Son* ("Fred's Cheating Heart," 1974), *Kojak* ("Therapy in Dynamite," 1974), *Lucas Tanner* ("Winners and Loser," 1974), *Ironside* (recurring role of Diana Sanger; 1974–75), *The Bob Crane Show* ("Acute Bussophobia," 1975), *That's My Mama* (recurring role as Tracy Curtis Taylor; 1974), *Most Wanted* ("The Ten-Percenter," 1976), *Rafferty* (recurring role as Nurse Beryl Keynes; 1977), *McMillan & Wife* ("Coffee, Tea or Cyanide?" 1977), *Barnaby Jones* ("The Deadly Valentine," 1977), *The Bionic Woman* ("African Connection," 1977), *Starsky and Hutch* ("Blindfold," 1978), *Fantasy Island* (1978), *The Waltons* ("The Illusion," 1978), *The White Shadow* (recurring role of Sybil Buchanan; 1978–81), *CBS All American Thanksgiving Day Parade* (1980), Shannon (2 episodes; "Beating the Prime," "Secret Rage," 1981), *Code Red* ("Revenge," 1982), *Quincy M.E.* ("To Clear the Air," 1982), *Trapper John, M.D.* ("The Ransom," 1982), *General Hospital* (recurring role of Dr. Patricia Mason; 1982–84), *This Is the Life* (1983), *L.A. Law* ("Rohner vs. Gradinger," 1987), *Simon & Simon* ("Little Boy Dead," 1988), *Moonlighting* ("Shirts and Skins," 1989), *Generations* (recurring role as Ruth Marshall; 1989–91), *The Trials of Rosie O'Neill* ("Double Bind," 1992), *Harry and the Hendersons* ("The Candidate," 1992), *The Sinbad Show* ("In the Beginning," 1993), *Where I Live* ("Miracle on 134th Street," 1993), *Roc* (3 episodes in the role of Matty; "Andrew Dates Matty," "1992 Presidential Election," "You Don't Send Me No Flowers," 1992–93), *Friends* ("The One with the Sonogram at the End," 1994), *Models Inc.* (3 episodes in the role of Roberta Williamson; "Strictly Business," "When Girls Collide," "Look Who's Stalking," 1994), *Burke's Law* ("Who Killed Cock-a-Doodle Dooley?" 1995), *Beverly Hills, 90210* ("Violated," 1995), *ER* (2 episodes; "And Baby Makes Two," "Four Corners," 1995 and 2001), *Moloney* ("All the King's Horses," 1996), *Party of Five* (2 episodes as Rose Wilcox; "Point of No Return," "You Win Some, You Lose Some," 1997), *The Gregory Hines Show* ("Love Thy Neighbor," 1998), *Timecop* ("Alternate World," 1998), *In the House* (4 episodes; "Mr. Hill Goes to New York," "There's Something About Tiffany," "How Nana Got Her Groove Back," "Cornbread, Marion and Me," 1998–99), *JAG* (3 episodes in the role of Agent Mary Holland; "Nobody's Child," "Goodbyes," "Mixed Messages," 1999–2001), *City of Angels* ("Ax and You Shall Receive," 2000), *NYPD Blue* ("In the Wind," 2001), *One on One* (recurring role of Eunice Barnes; 2001–03), *Any Day Now* ("Boys Will Be Boys," 2002), *Resurrection Blvd.* ("La Guerra di Bibi," 2002), *Enterprise* ("Horizon," 2003), *Girlfriends* (3 episodes in the role of Carol Hart; "The Mother of All Episode," "When Hearts Attack," "It's Been Determined," 2004–07).

Queen Latifah Born in Newark, New Jersey, March 18, 1970.

Dana Elaine Owens, stage name Queen Latifah, has had such a varied and successful career, it seems she's capable of excelling at anything she tries. She has won a Golden Globe Award, three Screen Actors Guild Awards, a Grammy (with six other nominations), earned an Emmy nomination, two NAACP Image Awards, and an Oscar nomination.

Her mother, Rita, was a teacher at Irvington High School in New Jersey, and her dad, Lancelot was — if not a knight in shining armor — at least a police officer, which is close enough. They divorced when Latifah was ten. (The name Latifah, given to her by a cousin when she was eight, is Arabic for "kind.") She started her career as a beatboxer and rapper, and released her first album, *All Hail the Queen* (1989), when she was 19. Then came the albums *Nature of a Sista* and *Black Reign*, which yielded the Grammy-winning single "U.N.I.T.Y." *Order in the Court* (1998) was her fourth rap–hip-hop album, and she surprised many fans with her album of jazz and pop standards, *The Dana Owens Album* (2004). The lady has an authentic voice — which, of course, comes as no surprise to the millions who saw her in her Academy Award–nominated turn in *Chicago* (2002). Her phrasing is quite beautiful. Her most recent album was *Travelin' Light* (2007), again in the jazz-pop vein.

Many singers have had a fling at an acting career. Few, however, have had the success of Queen Latifah. It all began with her starring role on the FOX sitcom *Living Single*, which enjoyed a healthy run from 1993 to 1998. Latifah played cool, collected, in-charge Khadijah James, magazine editor. Her interplay with the other cast members — Kim Fields, Kim Coles, Erika Alexander — made this one of the best showcases for black women in the history of TV. Latifah followed *Living Single* with her own daytime talk show (1999–2001), but it never quite caught fire.

That has not been the case with her film career. Outstanding film highlights include *Set It Off* (1996), a great crime thriller with strong sociological overtones, and brilliant work by an ensemble cast; Best Picture Oscar winner *Chicago*, with strong work from Latifah as the cagey, amoral prison matron "Mama" Morton; and *Hairspray* (2007), the surprisingly effective second film incarnation of the venerable John Waters film, which has enjoyed another life as a long-running Broadway musical, here incarnated with an all-star cast, featuring Latifah as civil rights activist Motormouth Maybelle, who helps integrate the local TV teen dance show. Her work as an AIDS-positive woman that same year in *Life Support* (2007) netted her a Golden Globe Award, an Emmy nomination, and a Screen Actors Guild Award. She continued to do authoritative, assured work as August Boatwright in the touching period drama set in South Carolina in 1964, *The Secret Life of Bees* (2008).

In her autobiography *Ladies First: Revelations of a Strong Woman* (1999), Latifah discusses the death of her brother in a motorcycle accident in 1992; her bouts with depression; and the fatuous "rumors" about her sexuality. As usual, Queen Latifah had the last word.

Feature Films including Video and TV Movies: *Jungle Fever* (1991), *House Party 2* (1991), *Juice* (1992), *Sisters in the Name of Rap* (TV; 1992), *Who's the Man?* (1993), *My Life* (1993), *Smart Kids* (TV; 1994), *Set It Off* (1996), *Hoodlum* (1997), *Sphere* (1998), *Living Out Loud* (1998), *Mama Flora's Family* (TV; 1998), *The Bone Collector* (1999), *Bringing Out the Dead* (voice; 1999), *Living with the Dead* (2002), *The Country Bears* (2002), *Brown Sugar* (2002), *Pinocchio* (2002), *Chicago* (2002), *Bringing Down the House* (2003), *Scary Movie 3* (2003), *Barbershop 2: Back in Business* (2004), *The Cookout* (2004), *Taxi* (2004), *Beauty Shop* (2005), *The Muppets' Wizard of Oz* (TV; 2005), *Last Holiday* (2006), *Ice Age: The Meltdown* (voice; 2006), *Stranger Than Fiction* (2006), *Life Support* (TV; 2007), *Arctic Tale* (narrator; documentary; 2007), *Hairspray* (2007), *The Perfect Holiday* (2007), *Mad Money* (2008), *What Happens in Vegas* (2008), *The Secret Life of Bees* (2008), *All of Me* (2009), *Welfare Queen* (2009), *Ice Age: Dawn of the Dinosaurs* (voice; 2009).

TV: *The Earth Day Special* (1990), *It's Showtime at the Apollo* (1990), *In Living Color* (1990), *MTV Video Music Awards 1990*, *The Fresh Prince of Bel-Air* ("Workin' It Out," "She Ain't Heavy," 1991), *The 1993 Billboard Music Awards*, *Living Single* (recurring role of Khadijah James; 1993–98), *Hangin' with Mr. Cooper* ("Wedding Bell Blues," 1994), *Roc* ("The Concert," 1994), *ABC Afterschool Specials* ("I Hate the Way I Look," 1994), *Apollo Theatre Hall of Fame* (1994), *The 9th Annual Soul Train Music Awards* (1995), *The Critic* ("Lady Hawke," 1995), *The Rosie O'Donnell Show* (9 segments; 1996–2000), *Ellen* ("Ellen Unplugged," 1997), *MADtv* (1997), *The 1998 Billboard Music Awards*, *The Queen Latifah Show* (hostess; 1999–2001), *One Love: The Bob Marley All-Star Tribute* (1999), *The 72nd Annual Academy Awards* (2000), *The Remarkable Journey* (2000), *Late Night with Conan O'Brien* (6 segments; 2000–07), *Intimate Portrait* (2 episodes; "Kim Fields," "Queen Latifah," 2000 and 2001), *Spin City* (2 episodes in the role of Robin Jones; "Yeah

Baby!" "Sleeping with the Enemy," 2001), *Platinum Comedy Series: Roasting Shaquille O'Neal* (2002), *VH1 Behind the Movie* (*Chicago*, 2002), *Hollywood Squares* (2002), *Essence Awards* (2003), *The 45th Annual Grammy Awards* (2003), *The 17th Annual Soul Train Music Awards* (2003), *Reel Comedy: Bringing Down the House* (2003), *Kung Faux* (2003), *The 75th Annual Academy Awards* (2003), *VH1 Divas Duets* (2003), *Richard & Judy* (2003), *V Graham Norton* (2003), *2003 MTV Movie Awards, The Teen Choice Awards 2003, Will on Will & Grace* (2003), *Hip Hop Babylon 2* (2003), *Inside the Industry* (2003), *200 Greatest Pop Culture Icons* (archival; 2003), *Saturday Night Live* (3 segments; 2003–08), *The View* (4 segments; 2003–07), *The 61st Annual Golden Globe Awards* (2004), *The 46th Annual Grammy Awards* (2004), *Tinseltown TV* (2 segments; 2004), *Nickelodeon Kids' Choice Awards 2004, 2004 MTV Movie Awards, MTV Video Music Awards 2004, Eve* ("Sister, Sister," 2004), *Premiere Women in Hollywood Awards* (2004), *101 Biggest Celebrity Oops* (archival; 2004), *Total Request with Carson Daly* (2004), *Sesame Street Presents: The Street We Live On* (archival; 2004), *Crash Nebula* (voice; "The Fairly Odd Parents," 2004), *Biography* (2 episodes; "Richard Gere," "Steve Martin," 2004 and 2006), *The Tonight Show with Jay Leno* (4 segments; 2004–07), *Late Show with David Letterman* (3 segments; 2004–07), *Live with Regis and Kelly* (5 segments; 2004–08), *The 47th Annual Grammy Awards* (2005), *36th NAACP Image Awards* (2005), *Nickelodeon Kids' Choice Awards 2005, Cinema Mil* (archival; 2005), *Last Call with Carson Daly* (2005), *BET Awards 2005, GMTV* (2005), *TV One on One* (2005), *At Large with Geraldo Rivera* (2005), *2nd Annual VH1 Hip-Hop Honors* (2005), *25 Strong: The BET Silver Anniversary Special* (2005), *The Mark Twain Prize: Steve Martin* (2005), *Glamour Magazine's Women of the Year Awards* (2005), *The Kennedy Center Honors: A Celebration of the Performing Arts* (2005), *Corazón de....* (archival: 3 segments; new footage: 1 segment, 2005–07), *Ellen* (4 segments; 2005–07), *106 & Park Top 10 Live* (2 segments; 2005–07), *The Oprah Winfrey Show* (3 segments; 2005–07), *What It Takes* (2006), *Inside the Actors Studio* (2006), *Today* (2006), *Independent Lens* ("Girl Trouble," 2006), *The 78th Annual Academy Awards* (2006), *The Insider* (2006), *The JammX Kids' All Star Dance Special* (2006), *The Second JammX Kids' All Star Dance Special* (2006), *The Daily Show with Jon Stewart* (2006), *Weekend Sunrise* (2006), *Getaway* (2006), *The Tyra Banks Show* (3 segments; 2006), *MTV Video Music Awards 2006, America's Next Top Model* (2006), *Entertainment Tonight* (13 segments; 2006–08), *Nickelodeon Kids' Choice Awards 2007, The 33rd Annual People's Choice Awards* (2007), *The 79th Annual Academy Awards* (2007), *HBO First Look* ("Welcome to the '60s: On the Set of Hairspray," 2007), *Access Hollywood* (2007), *Tavis Smiley* (2008), The *80th Annual Academy Awards* (2008), *E! True Hollywood Story* ("Renee Zellweger," 2008), *The 34th Annual People's Choice Awards* (2008), *Bridging the Gap* (documentary; 2008), *Larry King Live* (2008).

Video/DVD: *And Ya Don't Stop: Hip Hop's Greatest Videos, Vol 1.* (2000), *Through the Years of Hip Hop, Vol. 1: Graffiti* (2002).

Ralph, Sheryl Lee Born in Waterbury, Connecticut, December 30, 1956.

Sheryl Lee Ralph is known for many things, but perhaps foremost among them is her role as one of the original *Dreamgirls* on Broadway. She was Deena Jones, the one who breaks out of the trio and becomes a solo superstar, for which she was nominated in 1982 for Best Actress in a Musical and a Drama Desk Award. She made her Broadway debut in *Reggae* as Faith (March–April 1980). She was also the villainous Muzzy van Hossmere in the original cast of the Broadway hit *Thoroughly Modern Millie* (2002 Tony winner for Best Musical).

She is of half Jamaican heritage and was 1973 Miss Black Teen-Age New York. She has traditionally divided her time between Jamaica and the U.S., often spending time with her Jamaican-born father, Professor Stanley Ralph, in the States and her designer mother Ivy on the island. She graduated from Rutgers University at age 19 in 1975. She didn't attend the graduation ceremony because she had been hired to appear in a Skippy Peanut Butter commercial.

Significant film roles include her debut in the black buddy comedy *A Piece of the Action* (1987); *The Mighty Quinn* (1989), in which she played Denzel Washington's character's wife and got to use her flawless Jamaican accent; the highly regarded independent film about black family relations, *To Sleep with Anger* (1990), which won her the prestigious Independent Spirit Award for Best Supporting Actress; *Mistress* (1992), opposite

Robert De Niro; *The Distinguished Gentleman* (1992) with Eddie Murphy; and Disney's *Sister Act 2: Back in the Habit* with Whoopi Goldberg (1993).

Ralph first gained the attention of television audiences with her charming work in the ensemble comedy *It's a Living* (1986–89), playing the sexy waitress Ginger St. James. She co-starred with Phyllis Yvonne Stickney on the short-lived *New Attitude*, about two sisters who own a beauty salon (1990); she played the wife role (Maggie Foster) on the George Foreman sitcom *George* (1993); and was a hoot as the full-of-herself Etienne Toussaint Bouvier on *Designing Women* (1992–93). She had a long, successful series run on *Moesha* (1996–2000) in the stepmother role of Dee, but began to withdraw from the series when she disapproved of the direction it was taking. She segued from this to the role of Detective Dee Banks on *The District* (2000–01), and then was Claire on *Barbershop* (2005).

Ralph has made a major contributions to aids fundraising efforts. She produced and created the aids fund benefit *Divas Simply Singing!*, which raises money was well as awareness. In 2008 she wrote and performed in the one-woman show *Sometimes I Cry* (subtitled "The loves, lives, and losses of women infected and affected by HIV/AIDS.").

She is the founder of the very successful annual Jamerican Film and Music Festival, showcasing artistic achievement, fostering relationships, and building skills in acting, production and screenwriting. She was married to Eric Maurice from 1991 to 2000. Their two children are Etienne (1992) and Ivy-Victoria (1995). She married Pennsylvania State Senator Vincent Hughes in 2005.

Feature Films including Video and TV Movies: *A Piece of the Action* (1977), *The Neighborhood* (TV; 1982), *Pros & Cons* (TV; 1986), *Sister Margaret and the Saturday Night Ladies* (TV; 1987), *Oliver & Company* (voice; 1988), *The Mighty Quinn* (1989), *Skin Deep* (1989), *To Sleep with Anger* (1990), *The Gambler Returns: The Luck of the Draw* (TV; 1991), *Mistress* (1992), *The Distinguished Gentleman* (1992), *No Child of Mine* (TV; 1993), *Sister Act 2: Back in the Habit* (1993), *The Flintstones* (1994), *Witch Hunt* (TV; 1994), *White Man's Burden* (1995), *Lover's Knot* (1996), *Bogus* (1996), *Jamaica Beat* (1997), *The Easter Story Keepers* (voice; TV; 1998), *Secrets* (1998), *Unconditional Love* (1999), *Personals* (1999), *Deterrence* (1999), *Lost in the Pershing Point Hotel* (2000), *The Jennie Project* (TV; 2001), *Baby of the Family* (2002), *Kink in My Hair* (TV; 2004), *Odicie* (TV; 2007), *Frankie D* (2007), *Parallel Paths* (2007).

Sheryl Lee Ralph and Meshach Taylor in *Designing Women.*

TV: *A.E.S. Hudson Street* ("Shut Down," 1978), *Baa Baa Black Sheep* ("A Little Bit of England," 1978), *Husbands, Wives and Lovers* ("Murray Gets Sacked and Paula Gets Hired," 1978), *Good Times* ("J.J. and the Plumber's Helper," 1978), *The New Adventures of Wonder Woman* ("The Starships Are Coming," 1979), The Jeffersons ("Louise's Convention," 1979), *Search for Tomorrow* (recurring role as Laura McCarthy; 1983–84), *V* ("The Overlord," 1984), *Codename: Foxfire* (2 episodes in the role of Maggie Bryan; "Slay It Again, Sam," "La Paloma," 1985), *The 7th Annual Black Achievement Awards* (1986), *Hunter* ("The Return of Typhoon Thompson," 1986), *It's a Living* (recurring role as Ginger St. James; 1986–89), *L.A. Law* ("Beef Jerky," 1987), *Amazing Stories* ("Gershwin's Trunk," 1987), *19th Annual NAACP Image Awards* (1987), *Happy 100th Birthday, Hollywood* (1987), *The 42nd Annual Tony Awards* (1988), *Falcon Crest* (2 episodes as Mooshy Tucker; "Dark Streets," "Crimes of the Past," 1990), *New Attitude* (recurring role as Vicki St. James; 1990), *Story of a People: The Black Road to Hollywood* (1990), *Voices that Care* (1991), *Designing Women* (7 episodes in the role of Etienne Toussaint Bouvier; 1992–93), *Children of Africa* (1993), *The 7th Annual Soul Train Music Awards* (1993), *George* (1993), *Soul Train* (1996), *Wild On....* (1996), *The Rosie O'Donnell Show* (2 appearances; 1996–98), *Moesha* (4 episodes in the role of Dee Mitchell ("Mama Said Knock You Out," "Mentor," "Hello, What's This?" "Isn't She Lovely?" 1996–2000), *Oddville, MTV* (1997), *The Wild Thornberrys* (voice; "Flood Warning," 1998), *Sabrina, the Teenage Witch* ("What Price Harvey?" 1999), *The Parkers* ("Daddy's Girl," 1999), *Hollywood Squares* (3 segments; 1999–2001), *Acapulco Black Film Festival* (2000), *The Roseanne Show* (2000), *Recess* ("Me Know No," 2000), *The District* (4 episodes in the role of Dee Mitchell; "Imperfect Victims," "The L.A. Strangler," "Vigilante," "Rage Against the Machine," 2000–2001), *42nd Annual L.A. County Arts Commission Holiday Celebration* (2001), *The Proud Family* (2 episodes as the voice of Aunt Dee; "Romeo Must Wed," 2002), *Static Shock* (2 episodes as the voice of Trina Jessup; "Pop's Girlfriend," "Consequences," 2002 and 2003), *Justice League* (3 episodes as the voice of Cheetah; "Injustice for All," Parts I and II, "Kid Stuff," 2002–04), *The Wayne Brady Show* (2003), *Whoopi* ("She Ain't Heavy, She's My Partner," 2003), *Las Vegas* ("Luck Be a Lady," 2003), *101 Biggest Celebrity Oops* (2004), *E! 101 Most Starlicious Makeovers* (2004), *101 Most Unforgettable Saturday Night Live Moments* (2004), *E! 101 Most Awesome Moments in Entertainment* (2004), *Barbershop* (4 episodes in the role of Claire; "Madonna Is a Ho," "What's Good for the Cos...," "A Black Man Invented the Stop Light," "Debates and Dead People," 2005), *I Love the '90s: Part 2* (2005), *Entertainment Tonight* (2 segments; 2005–07), *In the Mix* (2 segments; 2006), *Bring that Year Back 2006: Laugh Now, Cry Later* (2006), *Exes & Ohs* (recurring role as Reverend Ruby; 2006–07), *7th Heaven* ("And Baby Makes Three," 2006), *ER* (2 episodes in the role of Gloria Gallant; "Strange Bedfellows," "21 Guns," 2006), *Angels Can't Help But Laugh* (2007), *Baisden After Dark* (2008), *Flavor of Love* ("Pimp My Gurney," 2008), *Broadway: Beyond the Golden Age* (2009).

Video/DVD: *The Directors: Norman Jewison* (1997).

Shorts: *Secrets* (also produced and directed; 1998).

Randle, Theresa Born in South Central Los Angeles, California, December 24, 1964.

Theresa Ellen Randle studied at Beverly Hills College with an early emphasis on dance and comedy. She got work at the Los Angeles Inner City Cultural Center. She also appeared in regional productions like *In Command of the Children, Sonata, 6 Parts of Musical Broadway*, and *Fight the Good Fight*. Her sole starring role to date was in Spike Lee's charming *Girl 6* (1996); earlier, she had had much smaller roles in his *Jungle Fever* (1991) and *Malcolm X* (1992). *Girl 6* was about a down-on-her-luck actress who becomes a phone sex operator to make ends meet. This doesn't sound like a light, Godard-influenced New Wave type comedy — but that's just what it is. Randle (and don't forget Lee himself, in what is perhaps his best acting role) gives a performance that is totally outside the box of what we're supposed to expect from a black actress. She's wistful, bemused, and arch.

Not shockingly, this did not lead to a flood of great roles for Randle, but she kept up her career in *Beverly Hills Cop III* (1994), *Bad Boys* (1995) and its sequel *Bad Boys 2* (2003), *Space Jam* (1996) and *Spawn* (1997). Recent years have seen a slowing down in her big screen appearances, but she has helped make up for the slack with her two appearances as Patricia Kent on *Law & Order: Criminal Intent* and Showtime's *State of Mind*, where she played Dr. Cordelia Banks.

Feature Films including TV Movies: *Maid to Order* (1987), *Near Dark* (1987), *Easy Wheels* (1989), *Heart Condition* (1990), *The Guardian* (1990), *King of New York* (1990), *The Five Heartbeats* (1991), *Jungle Fever* (1991), *Malcolm X* (1992), *CB4* (1993), *Sugar Hill* (1994), *Beverly Hills Cop III* (1994), *Bad Boys* (1995), *Girl 6* (1996), *Space Jam* (1996), *Spawn* (1997), *Livin' for Love: The Natalie Cole Story* (TV; 2000), *Partners and Crime* (TV; 2003), *Bad Boys 2* (2003), *The Hunt for Eagle One* (2006), *The Hunt for Eagle One: Crash Point* (2006), *Shit Year* (2009).

Theresa Randle in *Girl 6* (1996).

TV: *A Different World* ("Delusions of Daddyhood," 1989), *Seinfeld* ("The Apartment," 1991), *Duckman* (voice; "With Friends Like These," 1997), *Law & Order: Criminal Intent* (2 episodes in the role of Patricia Kent; "Tru Love," "Country Crossover," 2006), *State of Mind* (recurring role of Cordelia Banks; 2007).

Randolph, Amanda

Born in Louisville, Kentucky, September 2, 1896; died August 24, 1967.

Amanda Randolph was a singer and performer who appeared in Cleveland nightclubs and in musical comedy productions. Her sister Lillian also became a successful actress. During the 1930s Amanda Randolph partnered with the daughter of composer W.C. Handy to form the Dixie Nightingales.

When she segued into films she, like all black actresses, had two choices: play maids, or concentrate on black audience race films. Like some actresses, Randolph chose both paths. She appeared with Nina Mae McKinney and the Nicholas Brothers in the short *The Black Network*, and also appeared in several Oscar Micheaux features, including *Swing!* (1938), *Lying Lips* (1939) and *The Notorious Elinor Lee* (1940).

During the 1940s she and Lillian were on the exceedingly popular "Amos 'n' Andy" radio program. Amanda was only one of two performers from the radio show who transitioned to the television version. Due largely to protests from the NAACP, the show left the air in 1955. In the 1950s she also appeared in the Warner Bros. production *She's Working Her Way Through College* as Virginia Mayo's maid. She was cast as the housekeeper in *Make Room for Daddy* (later *The Danny Thomas Show*) starring Danny Thomas. The warm-hearted, funny show lasted for more than a decade (1955–64). At age 65, Randolph died after suffering a stroke.

Feature Films: *Swing!* (1938), *Lying Lips* (1939), *At the Circus* (1939), *The Notorious Elinor Lee* (1940), *Comes Midnight* (1940), *No Way Out* (1950), *Bonzo Goes to College* (1952), *She's Working Her Way Through College* (1952), *The Iron Mistress* (1952), *Bomba and the Jungle Girl* (1952), *Mister Scoutmaster* (1953), *A Man Called Peter* (1955), *Full of Life* (1956), *Heller in Pink Tights* (1960), *Pocketful of Miracles* (1961), *The Last Challenge* (1967).

TV: *The Laytons* (recurring role; 1948), *Amanda* (hostess; 1948), *The Amos 'n' Andy Show* (recurring role as Ramona "Mama" Smith; 1951–52), *The Beulah Show* (1953), *The Loretta Young Show* ("Something About Love," 1954), *Make Room for Daddy/The Danny Thomas Show* (recurring role as Louise; 1955–64), *Screen Directors Playhouse* ("Claire," 1956), *The Thin Man* ("The Screaming Doll," 1958), *How to Marry a Millionaire* ("What's Cooking with Loco?" 1958), *The Untouchables* ("The Dutch Schultz Story," 1959), *The Man from Blackhawk* ("The Ghost of Lafitte," 1960), *The Barbara Stanwyck Show* ("Big Career," 1961), *The New Breed* ("Sweet Bloom of Death," 1961), *Perry Mason* ("The Case of the Dodging Domino," 1962), *That Girl* ("Paper Hats & Everything," 1967), *CBS Playhouse* ("Do Not Go Gentle Into That Good Night," 1967), *The Danny Thomas Hour* ("Make More Room for Daddy," 1967).

Shorts: *The Black Network* (1936).

Randolph, Lillian

Born in Louisville, Kentucky, December 14, 1898; died September 12, 1980, Los Angeles, California.

A lot of Lillian Randolph's career has been censored or banned due to changing social tastes. Randolph is known for her role as the no-nonsense, downright kick-ass Madame Queen in both the radio and TV (1951–53) versions of *Amos 'n' Andy*. She was also the maid Birdie Lee Coggins on another popular radio comedy, *The Great Gildersleeve* (1941–54).

Her other great "heard but not seen" role was as the voice of Mammy-Two-Shoes in the *Tom and Jerry* cartoons of the 1940s and early '50s. Her voice was dubbed over by June Foray in 1960s TV showings of the cartoons, and the character was redrawn as an Irish housekeeper instead of as a black maid.

Her most famous film role was as Annie in Frank Capra's *It's a Wonderful Life* (1946). She made a guest appearance on *Sanford and Son* in 1972. She was the younger sister of actress Amanda Randolph. She sang at the funeral of Hattie McDaniel in 1952. Randolph died of cancer at age 81.

Feature Films: *Life Goes On* (1938), *Streets of New York* (1939), *Way Down South* (1939), *Mr. Smith Goes Ghost* (1940), *Am I Guilty?* (1940), *Little Men* (1940), *West Point Widow* (1941), *Kiss the Girls Goodbye* (1941), *Gentleman from Dixie* (1941), *Birth of the Blues* (1941), *All-American Co-Ed*

Left to right: Myrna Loy, Lillian Randolph and Shirley Temple in *The Bachelor and the Bobby-Soxer* (1947).

(1941), *Cooks and Crooks* (1942), *Mexican Spitfire Sees a Ghost* (1942), *Hi, Neighbor* (1942), *The Glass Key* (1942), *The Palm Beach Story* (1942), *The Great Gildersleeve* (1942), *Happy Go Lucky* (1943), *No Time for Love* (1943), *Gildersleeve's Bad Day* (1943), *Hoosier Holiday* (1943), *Gildersleeve on Broadway* (1943), *Phantom Lady* (1944), *Up in Arms* (1944), *The Adventures of Mark Twain* (1944), *Gildersleeve's Ghost* (1944), *Three Little Sisters* (1944), *A Song for Miss Julie* (1945), *Riverboat Rhythm* (1946), *Child of Divorce* (1946), *It's a Wonderful Life* (1946), *Pigmeat's Laugh Hepcats* (1947), *The Bachelor and the Bobby-Soxer* (1947), *The Hucksters* (1947), *Sleep, My Love* (1948), *Let's Live a Little* (1948), *Once More, My Darling* (1949), *Dear Brat* (1951), *That's My Boy* (1951), *Bend of the River* (1952), *Hush ... Hush, Sweet Charlotte* (1964), *The Great White Hope* (1970), *How to Seduce a Woman* (1974), *Miles to Go Before I Sleep* (TV; 1975), *The Wild McCullochs* (1979), *Jacqueline Susann's Once Is Not Enough* (1975), *Jennifer* (1978), *Magic* (1978), *The Onion Field* (1979).

TV: *The Amos 'n' Andy Show* (recurring role as Queen Madame; "The Young Girl's Mother," "Madame Queen's Voice," 1951), *The Great Gildersleeve* (recurring role as Birdie Lee Coggins; 1955), *Ben Casey* ("Allie," 1963), *Tom and Jerry* (voice; 1965), *The Bill Cosby Show* (recurring role as Rose Kincaid; 1969–70), *Mannix* ("The World Between," 1970), *Tenafly* (1973), *That's My Mama* ("Clifton's Sugar Mama," 1974), *Sanford and Son* ("Here Comes the Bride, There Goes the Bride," "The Older Woman," 1972–75), *The Jeffersons* ("Mother Jefferson's Birthday," 1976), *Roots* (miniseries; 1977), *Nashville 99* (1977).

Shorts: *The Mammy-Two-Shoes Cartoons: Puss Gets the Boot* (1940), *The Midnight Snack* (1941), *Fraidy Cat* (1942), *Dog Trouble* (1942), *Puss n' Toots* (1942), *The Lonesome Mouse* (1943), *The Mouse Comes to Dinner* (1945), *Part Time Pal* (1947), *A Mouse in the House* (1947), *Old Rockin'*

Chair Tom (1948), *Mouse Cleaning* (1948), *Polka-Dot Puss* (1949), *The Little Orphan* (1949), *Saturday Evening Puss* (1950), *The Framed Cat* (1950), *Casanova Cat* (1951), *Sleepy-Time Tom* (1951), *Nit-Witty Kitty* (1951), *Triplet Trouble* (1952), *Push-Button Kitty* (1952).

Rashad, Phylicia Born in Houston, Texas, June 19, 1948.

Phylicia Rashad graduated from Harvard University with a bachelor of fine arts and later taught drama there. She also studied at the New York School of Ballet. She will always be remembered as Clair Huxtable on *The Cosby Show* (1984–92), and she also co-starred as Ruth Lucas on *Cosby* (1996–2000). She even turned up on an episode of *The Cosby Mysteries* in 1994. Clair was the perfect balance to the more intense and opinionated Cliff Huxtable (Bill Cosby). She was Cliff's rock, a great TV mother in the classic tradition, and a winning role model for her five children in the series — and for America's children. She won the People's Choice Award in 1985 for Favorite Female Performer in a New TV Program, and in 1986 and 1989 for Outstanding Lead Actress in a Comedy Series. She was nominated for an Emmy in 1985 and '86 for Outstanding Lead Actress in a Comedy Series. In 1987 she was nominated for an NAACP Image Award for Best Actress in a Comedy Series, and again in 1997 for *Cosby*.

No matter how long-running and lasting her success on *The Cosby Show*, Rashad always returned to her roots in the theater. Her distinguished Broadway career began as an understudy and performer (in various roles) in *The Wiz* (1975–79); she was in the ensemble of *Dreamgirls* and understudy to the lead role of Deena Jones (1981–85); she was a replacement for the Witch in *Into the Woods* (1987–89); she was a replacement for Anita in *Jelly's Last Jam* (1992–93); she was Lena Younger in the revival of *A Raisin in the Sun* and reprised the role in a 2008 TV movie (April–July 2004); she was Aunt Ester in *Gem of the Ocean* (2004–05); she performed a one-night benefit of *A Wonderful Life* on Dec. 12, 2005; she was the Queen in Shakespeare's *Cymbeline* (2007–08); and she was Big Mama in the all-black revival of *Cat on a Hot Tin Roof*, directed by her sister, Debbie Allen (2008).

Rashad was nominated for a 2004 Outer Critics Circle Award for Best Actress for her performance as Lena Younger in the revival of *A Raisin in the Sun*. She was tied for the Drama Desk Award for Best Actress for *Raisin* (sharing the award with Viola Davis for *Intimate Apparel*). She also received a Drama League Award nomination for *Raisin*. She received a Tony Award nomination for Best Performance by a Leading Actress in a Play for *Gem of the Ocean* in 2005.

She was married to William Lancelot Bowles, Jr. (1972–75; they have a son named Billy, born in 1973); Victor Willis, lead singer of the group The Village People (1978–80); and Ahmad Rashad (1985–2001; they have a daughter named Condola Phylea, born in 1986). Her parents were Andrew Arthur (a dentist) and Vivian (née) Ayres, a Pulitzer Prize–nominated poet. She has two brothers, Andrew and Hugh, and a sister, Debbie, who went on to a major career in show business as an actress, director, producer, playwright, dancer and singer.

Feature Films including TV Movies: *The Broad Coalition* (1972), *The Wiz* (1978), *We're Fighting Back* (TV; 1981), *Uncle Tom's Cabin* (TV; 1987), *False Witness* (TV; 1989), *Polly* (TV; 1989), *Polly: Comin' Home!* (TV; 1990), *Jailbirds* (TV; 1991), *David's Mother* (TV; 1994), *Once Upon a Time ... When We Were Colored* (1995), *The Possession of Michael D.* (TV; 1995), *The Babysitter's Seduction* (TV; 1996), *Free of Eden* (TV; 1999), *Loving Jezebel* (1999), *The Visit* (2000), *A Raisin in the Sun* (TV; 2008), *The Middle of Nowhere* (2009).

TV: *Delvecchio* ("Wax Job," 1976), *Santa Barbara* (recurring role as Felicia Dalton; 1985), *One Life to Live* (recurring role as Courtney Wright; 1983–84), *The Cosby Show* (recurring role of Clair Huxtable; 1984–92), *The Love Boat* (1985), *Bob Hope's High-Flying Birthday* (1986), *The New Hollywood Squares* (1986), *The 39th Annual Primetime Emmy Awards* (1987), *The 13th Annual People's Choice Awards* (1987), *The 14th Annual People's Choice Awards* (1988), *Mickey's 60th Birthday* (1988), *A Different World* (4 episodes in the role of Claire Huxtable; "Clair's Last Stand," "Risky Business," "Forever Hold Your Peace," "Success, Lies and Videotape," 1988–90), *The Debbie Allen Special* (1989), *Reading Rainbow* ("Mufaro's Beautiful Daughters," 1989), *The Earth Day Special* (1990), *Blossom* ("Blossom Blossoms," 1991), *The Last Laugh: Memories of the Cosby Show* (archival; 1992), *A Bob Hope Christmas* (archival; 1993), *25th NAACP Image Awards* (1993), *TV's*

The cast of ***The Cosby Show*** (left to right): Sabrina Le Beauf, Lisa Bonet, Tempestt Bledsoe, Bill Cosby, Keisha Knight Pulliam, Phylicia Rashad, Malcolm Jamal-Warner.

Funniest Families (1994), *Touched by an Angel* (2 episodes; "Tough Love," "The Last Chapter," 1994 and 2002), *In the House* ("Sister Act: The Episode," 1995), *50 Years of Funny Females* (archival; 1995), *The Rosie O'Donnell Show* (1996), *Cosby* (recurring role of Ruth Lucas; 1996–2000), *28th NAACP Image Awards* (1997), *American Playhouse* ("Hallelujah," 1993), *The Cosby Mysteries* ("Expert Witness," 1994), *Intimate Portrait* (4 episodes; "Phylicia Rashad," "Madeline Kahn," "Florence Griffith Joyner," "Debbie Allen," 1998–2000), *The Kennedy Center Honors: A Celebration of the Performing Arts* (1998), *The 42nd Annual Emmy Awards* (1999), *Little Bill* (recurring role as Brenda; 1999), *Bull* ("What the Past Will Bring," 2000), *Happily Ever After: Fairy Tales for Every Child* ("The Princess and the Pauper," 2000), *Biography* (narrator; "Dionne Warwick: Don't Make Me Over," 2001), *PBS Hollywood Presents: The Old Settler* (2001), *Murder, She Wrote* ("The Last Free Man," 2001), *NBC 75th Anniversary Celebration* (2002), *The Cosby Show: A Look Back* (2002), *Great Women of Television Comedy* (2003), *The 58th Annual Tony Awards* (2004), *Character Studies* (series hostess; 2005), *The 59th Annual Tony Awards* (2005), *I Was a Network Star* (archival; 1996), *Russell Simmons Presents Def Poetry* (2005), *Legends Ball* (2006), *La tele de tu vida* (archival; 2007), *The 52nd Annual Drama Desk Awards* (2007), *The 61st Annual Tony Awards* (2007), *The Red Dress Collection 2007 Fashion Show* (2008), *The 60th Primetime Emmy Awards* (2008), *Broadway: The Next Generation* (2009).

Raven-Symoné Born in Atlanta, Georgia, December 10, 1985.

With a unique, vibrant style all her own, Raven is one of the very few performers who has made the leap from child star to teen star and now to adult star. Raven-Symoné Christina Pearman was a print model while still an infant, and by age two was appearing in nationwide ads for Ritz crackers, Jell-O, Cool Whip, and Fisher-Price toys. She launched her TV sitcom career in February 1989 at age three as the precious Olivia on *The Cosby Show*, and in 1993–97 she appeared on *Hangin' with Mr. Cooper* in the role of Cooper's cousin Nicole.

Unlike the vast majority of child actresses, she refused to fold her tent and disappear. Instead she found even greater fame and fortune as the star of the Disney Channel's *That's So Raven*, as the fast-talking, hyperactive teenager Raven Baxter. *That's So Raven* enjoyed tremendous popularity throughout the world, including Europe, Asia, Canada and Australia. She also appeared as Dr. John Doolittle's (Eddie Murphy) daughter Charisse in the hit film *Dr. Dolittle* (1998) and its sequel *Dr. Dolittle 2* (2001). Raven has recorded for MCA Records and later for Hollywood Records. A superb businesswoman as well as an adept comedienne, Raven has her own production company, That So Productions.

Feature Films including TV Movies: *Queen* (1993), *The Little Rascals* (1994), *Dr. Dolittle* (1998), *Dr. Dolittle 2* (2001), *The Cheetah Girls* (2003), *Kim Possible: A Stitch in Time* (TV; 2003), *The Princess Diaries 2: Royal Engagement* (2004), *Zenon: Z3* (TV; 2004), *Fat Albert* (2004), *For One Night* (2006), *Everyone's Hero* (2006), *The Cheetah Girls 2* (TV; 2006), *Madagascar 2* (2008), *Adventures in Babysitting* (2008), *College Road Trip* (2008), *Tinker Bell* (voice; 2008) *Further Adventures in Babysitting* (2010).

TV: *The Cosby Show* (33 episodes; 1989–1992), *A Different World* (1989), *The Oprah Winfrey Show* (2 segments; 1989–2008), *The Muppets at Walt Disney World* (1990), *ABC TGIF* (1990), *The Last Laugh: Memories of the Cosby Show* (1992), *Muhammad Ali's 50th Birthday Celebration* (1992), *It's Showtime at the Apollo* (1992), *The Fresh Prince of Bel-Air* (1992), *Soul Train Comedy Awards* (1993), *25th NAACP Image Awards* (1993), *Blindsided* (1993), *Hangin' with Mr. Cooper* (recurring role of Nicole; 1993–1997), *The Word* (1994), *ABC Saturday Morning Jam* (1995), *Happily Ever After: Fairy Tales for Every Child* (1995), *Space Ghost Coast to Coast* (1997), *All Star TGIF Magic* (1997), *Zenon: Girl of the 21st Century* (1999), *VH1 Where Are They Now: Former Child Stars* (2000), *The Proud Family* (voice; 2001), *My Wife and Kids* (2001), *Oh Drama!* (2001), *E! True Hollywood Story* (2 episodes; 2001 and 2005), *Express Yourself* (2001), *Live with Regis and Kelly* (5 segments; 2001–08), *NBC 75th Anniversary Special* (2002), *The Cosby Show: A Look Back* (2002), *Weakest Link* (2002), *I Love the '80s* (2002), *Kim Possible* (voice of Monique; 2002–07), *Totally Suite New Year's Eve* (2003), *The Teen Choice Awards 2003*, *The Nick at Nite Holiday Special* (2003), *Walt Disney World Christmas Day Parade* (2003), *That's So Raven* (100 episodes; 2003–06), *The Magical World of Ella Enchanted* (2004), *Nickelodeon Kids' Choice Awards 2004*, *Inside Dish with Rachael Ray*

(2004), *Macy's Thanksgiving Day Parade* (2004), *Total Request Live* (2004), *BET Comedy Awards* (2004), *MTV Video Music Awards 2004, The Teen Choice Awards 2004, On the Set: The Princess Diaries 2: Royal Engagement* (2004), *4th Annual BET Awards* (2004), *Motown 45* (2004), *Fillmore!* (2 episodes; 2004), *Dear Santa* (2005), *MADtv* (2005), *Biography* (2005), *The Teen Choice Awards 2005, Punk'd* (2005), *Higglytown Heroes* (2005), *For One Night* (2006), *I Was a Network Star* (2006), *The Tonight Show* (2006), *The View* (2006), *The Suite Life of Zack and Cody* (2006), *Everyone's Hero* (2006), *American Dad* (voice; 2 episodes, "Office Spaceman," "Stanny Slickers II: The Legend of Ollie's Gold," 2008), *Entertainment Tonight* (2 segments; 2008), *Come Feud with Me: The Top 10 Disney Channel Character Feuds* (2008), *Wrestlemania XIV* (2008), *Celebrity Family Feud* (2008), *Progressive Skating and Gymnastics Spectacular* (2009), *An Evening of Stars: Tribute to Patti LaBelle* (2009).

Video/DVD: *Kim Possible: The Secret Files* (2003), *That's So Raven: Supernaturally Stylish* (2004), *Kim Possible: So the Drama* (2005), *That's So Raven: Raven's Makeover Madness* (2006), *Raven's Postcards from Spain* (2006).

Ravera, Gina Born in San Francisco, May 20, 1966.

Gina Ravera originally wanted to be a lawyer and was taking pre-law courses when she started becoming interested in acting. She is still remembered for her role as Molly Abrams, the best friend of Nomi (Elizabeth Berkley), who is raped and beaten by an evil rock musician in *Showgirls* (1995), the cult film that wouldn't die. Like Berkley and Gina Gershon, her career has seen life after the infamous *Showgirls*.

Half Puerto Rican, half African American on her mother's side, Gina D. Ravarra (the original spelling) is also known for her role in the film *Soul Food* (1997) as the seductive Faith, and for her role in the Oprah Winfrey–produced *The Great Debaters* (as Ruth Tolson; 2007). These days she is best known for her role on *The Closer* as lapd Detective Irene Daniels (2005–08). This popular TNT series revolves around Deputy Chief Brenda Johnson (Kyra Sedgwick). It thrives because it is a character-driven show, mixing humor with the elements of a police procedural. Ravera fits in nicely on the program and gives a smooth, relaxed performance.

Feature Films including TV Movies: *Lambada* (1990), *The Five Heartbeats* (1991), *Steal America* (1992), *White Mile* (TV; 1994), *919 Fifth Avenue* (TV; 1994), *Illegal in Blue* (1995), *Showgirls* (1995), *W.E.I.R.D. World* (TV; 1995), *Soul of the Game* (TV; 1996), *Get on the Bus* (1996), *Kiss the Girls* (1997), *Soul Food* (1997), The Temptations (TV; 1998), *A Luv Tale* (1999), *Rhapsody* (TV; 2000), *Saint Sinner* (TV; 2002), *Chasing Papi* (2003), *Pryor Offenses* (TV; 2004), *Gas* (2004), *The Great Debaters* (2007).

TV: *The Fresh Prince of Bel-Air* ("Some Day Your Prince Will Be in Effect," Part II, 1990), *True Colors* ("Your Mamma's House," Part II, 1991), *Reasonable Doubts* ("Graduation Day," 1991), *Melrose Place* ("Second Chances," 1992), Frasier ("The Good Son," 1993), *Star Trek: The Next Generation* ("Phantasms," 1993), *Silk Stalkings* (recurring role of Dr. Diana Roth; 1993–94), *NYPD Blue* ("From Who the Skell Rolls," 1994), *In the House* ("Men in the Black," 1997), *Malcolm & Eddie* ("Dream Girl," 1998), *Time of Your Life* (21 episodes in the role of Jocelyn "Joss" House; 1999–2000), *The Fugitive* (recurring role as Sara Gerard; 2000), *Donny & Marie* (2002), *Miracles* ("The Patient," 2003), *Charmed* ("My Three Witches," 2003), *The Handler* ("Acts of Congress," 2004), *Boston Legal* ("A Greater Good," 2004), *Inconceivable* ("The Last Straw," 2005), *Everwood* ("Pro Choice," 2005), *The Closer* (recurring role of Detective Irene Daniels; 2005–08), *ER* (recurring role of Bettina DeJesus; "Heart of the Matter," "Family Business," Lights Out," "Sea Change," "In a Different Light," 2006–07), *Raines* ("Stone Dead," 2007).

Ray, Ola Born in St. Louis, Missouri, August 26, 1960.

One word for Ola Ray's career in show business: *Thriller*. Her conspicuous role in the landmark 1983 Michael Jackson video — now being reconceived as a Broadway show — has immortalized her. She was only 22 when she beat out hundreds of other girls for the role, and it *was* a role, since *Thriller* was more of a mini-movie than a music video. Directed by John Landis (then the hottest director in Hollywood, fresh off of directing *The Blues Brothers* movie), *Michael Jackson's Thriller* (the official title; 1983) was based on the hit song from the album of the same name (the best-selling album ever) and is the *Citizen Kane* of music video — slavish, atmospheric and electric. It won the Grammy Award for Best Video.

Neither Ray's acting career nor her financial situation flourished as a result of her appearance in *Thriller*. She had guest shots on the sitcoms *Gimme a Break!*, *Cheers*, and *What's Happening Now!* (all in the wake of her *Thriller* appearance). Her film roles were small and tended to focus more on her physical assets than her acting ability (Ray was *Playboy*'s Playmate of the Month in June 1980). She grew up in Japan since her father was in the U.S. Air Force. She has a daughter, Iam, born in 1995, with CBS cameraman Terry Clark.

Feature Films including TV Movies: *Body and Soul* (1981), *Night Shift* (1982), *48 HRS.* (1982), *10 to Midnight* (1983), *The Man Who Loved Women* (1983), *Fear City* (1984), *The Night Stalker* (1987), *Beverly Hills Cop II* (1987).

TV: *Automan* ("Murder MTV," 1984), *Gimme a Break!* ("The Center," 1984), *Cheers* ("King of the Hill," 1985), *What's Happening Now!* ("Married or Not," 1985), *VH1 Where Are They Now: Video Vixens II* (2000), *I Love 1980's* (2001), *Never Mind the Buzzcocks* (2002), *Video on Trial* (2006).

Video: *Michael Jackson's Thriller* (1983), *Making Michael Jackson's Thriller* (1983), *Michael Jackson: Video Greatest Hits: HIStory* (includes *Thriller*; 1995), *Michael Jackson: HIStory on Film, Vol. II:* (includes *Thriller* segment; 1997), *Michael Jackson Number Ones* (includes *Thriller*; 2003).

Reese, Della Born in Detroit, Michigan, July 6, 1931.

Born Delloreese Patricia Early, Della Reese was involved with gospel singing from age six, and at 13 sang with the Mahalia Jackson choir. Later she started her own female gospel group, The Meditation Singers, and was also a vocalist with Erskine Hawkins. She won a local talent contest, and first prize was a week's booking at Detroit's Flame Show Bar, which turned into several months when management got a taste of her ability.

In 1953 she relocated to New York City and signed a contract with Jubilee Records, a well-known label of the era. In tight, slinky evening gowns and with appealingly close-cropped hair, Reese was a visual as well as a vocal delight. She was recognized by *Billboard* as Most Promising Singer of the year, and she started charting singles, landing her first major hit, "And That Reminds Me (of You)." Her biggest hit came in 1959 with "Don't You Know," an anthemic ballad that was one of the best-selling songs of its era. She released many albums throughout the fifties, sixties and seventies, including *Melancholy Baby* (1957), *Amen* (1958), *A Date with Della Reese* (1958), *And That Reminds Me* (1959), *The Story of the Blues* (1959), *And What Do You Know About Love?* (1959), *Della* (1960), *Della by Starlight* (1960), *Special Delivery* (1961), *The Classic Della* (1962), *Della Reese at Basin Street East* (1964), *Black Is Beautiful* (1970), *Let Me Into Your Life* (1975), and *One of a Kind* (1978).

In 1969 she had her own variety series, *Della*, for one season. Then she started appearing on series like *Welcome Back, Kotter* and *The A-Team* and later in TV movies like *Mama Flora's Family* (1998) and *Having Our Say: The Delany Sisters' First 100 Years* (1999). She was a regular on *Chico and the Man* (1976–78) and starred with Redd Foxx on his short-lived sitcom *The Royal Family* (1991). Foxx died on the set shortly after filming for the series began.

Acting came relatively late in her professional life, and major acting stardom eluded her until she settled into a long Friday night run on *Touched by an Angel* (1994–2003), the refreshingly spiritual series on CBS. She starred as the character Tess and also the show's theme song.

Reese is of African American and Cherokee Indian descent. Her first husband was Leroy Gray, then she married Vermont Taliaferro. She married concert producer Franklin Thomas Lett, Jr., in 1983. She has two stepchildren from the marriage, Franklin and Dominique, and two of her own, Deloreese, adopted in 1961, and James, adopted in 1965, and now a doctor. Reese is an ordained minister in the Understanding Principles for Better Living Church in Los Angeles, a Christian, multiracial, nondenominational church.

Feature Films including Video and TV Movies: *Let's Rock* (1958), *The Voyage of the Yes* (TV; 1973), *Daddy's Girl* (TV; 1973), *Twice in a Lifetime* (TV; 1974), *The Return of Joe Forrester* (aka *Cop on the Beat*; TV; 1975), *Psychic Killer* (1975), *Flo's Place* (TV; 1976), *Nightmare in Badham County* (TV; 1976), *Harlem Nights* (1989), *The Kid Who Loved Christmas* (TV; 1990), *The Distinguished Gentleman* (1992), *A Thin Line Between Love and Hate* (1996), *A Match Made in Heaven* (TV; 1997), *Miracle in the Woods* (TV;

1997), *Emma's Wish* (TV; 1998), *Mama Flora's Family* (TV; 1998), *The Secret Path* (TV; 1999), *Having Our Say: The Delany Sisters' First 100 Years* (TV; 1999), *Anya's Bell* (TV; 1999), *Dinosaur* (voice; 2000), *The Moving of Sophia Myles* (TV; 2000), *Beauty Shop* (2005), *If I Had Known I Was a Genius* (2007).

TV: *The Ed Sullivan Show* (17 appearances; 1957–65), *The Lively Ones* (1963), *The Hollywood Palace* (1964), *The Hollywood Squares* (3 segments; 1966–68), *The Mike Douglas Show* (1967), *Girl Talk* (1967), *The Merv Griffin Show* (3 appearances; 1967–77), *The Mod Squad* ("Find Tara Chapman!" 1968), *Della* (series hostess; 1969), *Playboy After Dark* (1969), *The Bold Ones: The New Doctors* ("Killer on the Loose," 1970), *The Tonight Show Starring Johnny Carson* (29 appearances; 1970–75), *The Pet Set* (1971), *Mantrap* (1971), *Rowan & Martin's Laugh-In* (2 segments; 1972), *The Flip Wilson Show* (1973), *Match Game '73* (3 segments; 1973–75), *Police Woman* ("Requiem for Bored Wives," 1974), *McCloud* (2 episodes in the role of Police Sgt. Gladys Harris; "This Must Be the Alamo," "The Day New York Turned Blue," 1974 and 1976), *Rhyme & Reason* (1975), *Petrocelli* ("Once Upon a Victim," 1975), *Sanford and Son* ("Della, Della, Della," 1975), *The Rookies* ("Ladies' Day," 1975), *Chico and the Man* (recurring role of Della Rogers; 1975–78), *Medical Center* ("Major Annie, M.D.," 1976), *Vega$* ("Lost Women," 1978), *Welcome Back, Kotter* (2 episodes in the role of Mrs. Tremaine; "Come Back, Little Arnold," "The Gang Show," 1979), Insight ("God in the Dock," 1980), *Password Plus* (1980), *The Love Boat* (2 episodes in the role of Millie Washington; 1982), *It Takes Two* (recurring role as Judge Caroline Phillips; 1982), *The A Team* ("Lease with an Option to Die," 1985), *Crazy Like a Fox* (3 episodes; "Fox Hunt," "Is There a Fox in the House?" "A Fox at the Races," 1985–86), *ABC Afterschool Specials* ("The Gift of Amazing Grace," 1986), *Charlie and Co.* (recurring role as Aunt Rachel; 1986), *227* (2 episodes; "Far from the Tree," "Where Do We Go from Here?" 1987 and 1990), *Family Reunion: A Gospel Music Celebration* (1988), *A Pup Named Scooby-Doo* (voices; 1988), *Night Court* ("Auntie Maim," 1989), *The Young Riders* ("Born to Hang," 1990), *Married People* ("Dance Ten, Friends Zero," 1991), *McGyver* (2 episodes in the role of Mama Colton; "Squeeze Play," "The Coltons," 1990 and 1991), *The Royal Family* (recurring role of Victoria Royal; 1991–92), *Wonderworks: You Must Remember This* (1992), *Dream On* ("No Deposit, No Return," 1992), *Holiday Greetings from the Ed Sullivan Show* (1992), *Mo' Funny: Black Comedy in America* (1993), *Designing Women* ("Wedding Redux," 1993), *L.A. Law* ("Vindaloo in the Villows," 1993), *Picket Fences* ("The Lullaby League," 1993), *E! True Hollywood Story* ("Redd Foxx," 1993), *Touched by an Angel* (recurring role of Tess; 1994–2003), *Happily Ever After: Fairy Tales for Every Child* (as the Blues Fairy; 1995), *Promised Land* (5 episodes in the role of Tess; "The Motel," "Homecoming," "The Road Home," Part II, "Mirror Image," "Vengeance Is Mine," Part II, 1996–98), *CBS: The First 50 Years* (1998), *Journey to a Hate Free Millennium* (voice; 1999), *Intimate Portrait* ("Della Reese," 1999), *The Rosie O'-Donnell Show* (1999), *Biography* ("Redd Foxx: Say It Like It Is," 2000), *Getting Together* ("Singing the Blues," 1971), *Praise the Lord* (2002), *33rd NAACP Image Awards* (2002), *Rhapsody in Black* (2002), *The Wayne Brady Show* (2 appearances; 2003–04), *Larry King Live* (2 segments; 2003–05), *The Tony Danza Show* (2004), *CMT: 20 Greatest Songs of Faith* (2005), *Legends Ball* (2006), *That's So Raven* ("The Four Aces," 2006), *Miss HIV* (documentary; narrator; 2007), *Wise Women Speak* (documentary; 2009).

Video/DVD: *Guide to Healthy Living* (1998).

Reuben, Gloria Born in Toronto, Canada, June 9, 1964.

This biracial Canadian actress of Jamaican heritage resulted from the union of a gospel singer mother and an architect father. Reuben is the youngest of six children. Her brother Denis is also a stage actor and a children's TV show host. She studied music and ballet at the Canadian Royal Conservatory, got involved in modeling and TV commercials, and moved on to acting with a prominent role opposite Jean-Claude Van Damme in *Timecop* (1994) and TV guest spots on *21 Jump Street* (1988) and *China Beach* (1990).

She began her tenure on *ER* in the role of Jeanie Boulet in 1995 as a recurring guest star during the first season, joining the show as a full-time cast member in the second season, departed in the sixth season, and reprised her role as Boulet for a January 3, 2008, guest appearance. She earned two Emmy nominations for her work on the show, as well as a Golden Globe nomination. One of her best feature film performances is in *Indiscreet*

(1998), in which she got to play a venal femme fatale.

Other recurring series roles are Sabrina on *The Flash* (1990–91); Detective Theresa Walker on *Homicide: Life on the Street* (1995); Liza Fabrizzi on *The Agency* (2001–02) and one episode of *The District* (2002); the no-nonsense Brooke Haslett on *1-800-Missing* (2003–04), on which she was replaced by Vivica Fox in the second season; and her latest ongoing role, *Raising the Bar* (as Rosalind Whitman; 2008), which has turned into another hit for her.

Ever the frustrated rock 'n' roller and a talented singer and musician, in 2000 she fulfilled what must have been the dream of a lifetime when she sang backup for Tina Turner on the Twenty Four Seven Tour. In 2006 she played Condoleeza Rice in David Hare's *Stuff Happens*, a comedy-drama about the Bush administration and the war in Iraq, presented at the Public Theater in New York. She has been married to Wayne Isaak since 1999.

Feature Films including Video and TV Movies: *Immediate Family* (1989), *The Waiter* (1993), *Shadowhunter* (TV; 1993), *Percy & Thunder* (TV; 1993), *Timecop* (1994), *Confessions: Two Faces of Evil* (TV; 1994), *Dead Air* (TV; 1994), *Johnny's Girl* (TV; 1995), *Nick of Time* (1995), *Indiscreet* (TV; 1998), *David and Lola* (1999), *Macbeth in Manhattan* (1999), *Sara* (TV; 1999), *Deep in My Heart* (TV; 1999), *Sole Survivor* (TV; 2000), *Cold Blooded* (2000), *Pilgrim* (2000), *Shaft* (2000), *The Agency* (TV; 2001), *Feast of All Saints* (TV; 2001), *Little John* (TV; 2002), *Salem Witch Trials* (TV; 2002), *Happy Here and Now* (2002), *The Sentinel* (2006), *Kettle of Fish* (2006), *Life Support* (TV; 2007), *The Understudy* (2008).

TV: *Polka Dot Door* (host; 1985), *CBS Schoolbreak Special* ("The Day They Came to Arrest the Books," 1987), *Alfred Hitchcock Presents* ("World's Oldest Motive," 1987), *21 Jump Street* ("Slippin' Into Darkness," 1988), *China Beach* ("One Giant Leap," 1990), *The Flash* (6 episodes in the role of Sabrina; 1990–91), *The Young Riders* ("Between Rock Creek and a Hard Place," 1991), *Flash III: Deadly Nightshade* (in the role of Sabrina; 1992), *The Round Table* ("Yesterday We Were Playing Football," 1992), *Silk Stalkings* ("Team Spirit," "Schemes Like Old Times," 1993), *McKenna* ("The Pony," 1994), *Late Night with Conan O'Brien* (3 segments; 1994–99), *Homicide: Life on the Street* (3 episodes in the role of Detective Theresa Walker; "The City That Bleeds," "Dead End," "End Game," 1995), *ER* (recurring role of Jeanie Boulet; 1995–2008), *The Rosie O'-Donnell Show* (3 segments; 1997–98), *4th Annual Screen Actors Guild Awards* (1998), *1998 MLB All-Star Game*, *VH1 Divas Live 2* (1999), *The Oprah Winfrey Show* (2000), *On Tour with Tina* (2000), *The Chris Isaak Show* (2001), *The Agency* (recurring role of Liza Fabrizzi; 2001–02), *The District* (in the role of Liza Fabrizzi; "Shell Game," 2002), *Law & Order: Special Victims Unit* (2 episodes; "Dolls," "Snitch," 2002 and 2007), *1-800-Missing* (recurring role of Brooke Haslett; 2003–04), *Numb3rs* ("Noisy Edge," 2005), *This Week* (2006), *Positive Voices: Women and HIV* (2007), *Raising the Bar* (recurring role as Rosalind Whitman; 2008), *Memoires de la tele* (archival; 2008), *The Bonnie Hunt Show* (2008).

Music Video: *When the Heartache Is Over* (1999).

Richards, Beah Born in Vicksburg, Mississippi, July 12, 1926; died September 14, 2000.

Renaissance woman Beah Richards was an actress, but also a playwright, activist, and poet. Born Beulah Richardson, her parents were Beulah and Wesley; her father was a minister. She attended Dillard University in New Orleans, graduating in 1948. She moved to San Diego to study dance and drama and then to New York in 1950. After moderate success in theater with roles in plays such as *The Miracle Worker* (as Viney; 1959–61), *Purlie Victorious* (as Idella Landry; 1961–62), and as an understudy in *A Raisin in the Sun* (Lena Younger; 1959–60), her performance as Sister Margaret in James Baldwin's *The Amen Corner* (1965) earned her a Tony Award nomination for Best Supporting Actress.

She transitioned into films in the 1960s, and was known for her character roles, often in mother roles much older than her actual age. She was Reeve Scott's (Robert Hooks) mother in *Hurry Sundown* (1967), Otto Preminger's box office disaster, an exploitational look at race relations. She was the abortionist Mrs. Bellamy ("Mama Caleba") in Academy Award–winning Best Picture *In the Heat of the Night* (1967), a small but key role. She was James Earl Jones' mother in *The Great White Hope*.

In 1967, her role in *Guess Who's Coming to Dinner?* earned her an Academy Award nomination. It was one of the defining films of its era, the story of an interracial relationship and marriage and how it affected the families involved. Richards played the mother of Dr. John Wade Prentice, portrayed by Sidney Poitier, even though she was two years younger than Poitier. Prentice was a successful black physician who has to deal with liberal parents (Spencer Tracy, in his last film, and Katharine Hepburn) tested by their daughter's controversial relationship (at least by 1967 standards).

Richards received an Emmy Award for Outstanding Guest Appearance in a Comedy Series for the episode of *Frank's Place* titled "The Bridge." She was also in the key miniseries *Roots II: The Next Generations* (along with every other black actor and actress who was anybody in the business; 1979). She guest starred on *The Cosby Show*, and her final television appearance was on *The Practice*, for which she won a final Emmy Award days before her demise from emphysema. In 1974 Richards was elected to the Black Filmmakers Hall of Fame.

She was the subject of a documentary by actress Lisa Gay Hamilton—*Beah: A Black Woman Speaks* (2003). Hamilton had worked with Richards in the film *Beloved* (1998) and on the series *The Practice*, and was compelled to film 70 hours worth of interviews with the then ailing actress about her life, her philosophy, and a career that spanned 50 years. The film won the Grand Jury Prize at the AFI Film Festival. Many observers have pointed with pride at Hamilton's accomplishment. Here was a black actress acknowledging the achievements of a black actress who had gone before her—a truly refreshing gesture.

Feature Films including TV Movies: *The Mugger* (1958), *Take a Giant Step* (1959), *The Miracle Worker* (1962), *Gone Are the Days!* (1963), *Hurry Sundown* (1967), *In the Heat of the Night* (1967), *Guess Who's Coming to Dinner* (1967), *To Confuse the Angel* (TV; 1970), *The Great White Hope* (1970), *The Biscuit Eater* (1972), *Footsteps* (TV; 1972), *Outrage* (TV; 1973), *A Dream for Christmas* (TV; 1973), *Mahogany* (1975), *Just an Old Sweet Song* (TV; 1976), *Ring of Passion* (TV; 1978), *A Christmas Without Snow* (TV; 1980), *The Sophisticated Gents* (TV; 1981), *Generation* (TV; 1985), *Acceptable Risks* (TV; 1986), *As Summers Die* (TV; 1986), *Inside Out* (1987), *Big Shots* (1987), *Homer and Eddie* (1989), *Drugstore Cowboy* (1989), *Capital News* (TV; 1990), *One Special Victory* (TV; 1991), *Out of Darkness* (TV; 1994), *Beloved* (1998).

TV: *Dr. Kildare* (2 episodes in the role of Alice; "Gratitude Won't Pay the Bills," "Adrift in a Sea of Confusion," 1966), *The Big Valley* (2 episodes in the role of Hannah James; "Boots with My Father's Name," "Lost Treasure," 1965 and 1966), *I Spy* ("Cops and Robbers," 1967), *Hawaii Five-O* ("Once Upon a Time," Part II, 1969), *Ironside* ("Alias Mr. Braithwaite," 1969), *Room 222* ("Arizona State Loves You," 1969), *It Takes a Thief* ("To Sing a Song of Murder," 1970), *The Bill Cosby Show* (recurring role as Rose Kincaid; 1970–71), *Sanford and Son* (2 episodes in the role of Aunt Ethel; "By the Numbers," "The Light Housekeeper," 1972), *The Magician* ("Lightning on a Dry Day," 1973), *Apple's Way* ("The Witness," 1974), *Disneyland* (archival; "The Biscuit Eater," Parts I and II, 1976), *Roots: The Next Generations* (miniseries; 1979), *Vega$* ("The Hunter Hunted," 1980), *Palmerstown, U.S.A.* ("The Old Sister," 1980), *Benson* (2 episodes; "No Sad Songs," "Home for Christmas," 1981 and 1984), *Banjo the Woodpile Cat* (1982), *Capitol* (recurring role as Therese; 1982), *St. Elsewhere* ("Girls Just Want to Have Fun," 1984), *Wonderworks: And the Children Shall Lead* (1985), *Highway to Heaven* ("As Difficult as ABC," 1985), *Punky Brewster* ("I Love You, Brandon," 1985), *Hill Street Blues* (2 episodes in the role of Aunt Feeney; "Das Blues," "Scales of Justice," 1986), *The Hitchhiker* ("The Curse," 1986), *Hunter* (2 episodes in the role of Ella Mae Fuller; "Saturday Night Special," "Not Just Another John Doe," 1986 and 1987), *227* (3 episodes in the role of Carolyn Hurley; "Fifty Big Ones," "Happy Twentieth," "The Class of 90," 1986–90), *CBS Summer Playhouse* ("Barrington," 1987), *Frank's Place* ("The Bridge," 1987), *Beauty and the Beast* (5 episodes in the role of Narcissa; "Dark Spirit," "To Reign in Hell," "Dead of Winter," "When the Blue Bird Sings," "Ceremony of Innocence," 1987–89), *The Facts of Life* ("Present Imperfect," 1988), *Murder, She Wrote* (2 episodes; "Mourning Among the Wisterias," "Judge Not," 1988 and 1991), *L.A. Law* (2 episodes in the role of Alberta Williams; "Placenta Claus Is Coming to Town," "Blood, Sweat and Fears," 1989 and 1990), *American Playhouse* ("Zora Is My Name!" 1990), *My Designing Women* (3 episodes; "The First Day of the Last Decade of the Entire Twentieth Century," Parts I and II, "Wedding Redux," 1990–93), *Family Matters* ("I Should Have Done Something," 1991), *Hearts Afire* ("Bees Can Sting You, Watch Out," 1992), *Matlock* ("The Diner," 1993), *The John Larroquette Show* ("Amends," 1993), *ER* (8 episodes in the role of Mae Benton; 1994–95), *The Practice* ("Till Death Do Us Part," 2000), *Beah: A Black Woman Speaks* (archival; 2003).

Richardson, LaTanya Born in Atlanta, Georgia, October 21, 1949.

LaTanya Richardson graduated from the all-female Spelman College in Atlanta, Georgia, in 1971, and Samuel L. Jackson was a student at all-male Moorehouse (which is affiliated with Spelman). They married in 1980 and have a daughter named Zöe. She then received a master's degree in drama from New York University.

She began her career with the New York Shakespeare Festival after being seen at Spelman by festival director Joseph Papp. She appeared in the productions *Perdido* (1976), *Unfinished Women* (1977), *Spell #7* (1979), *For Colored Girls Who Have Considered Suicide/When the Rainbow Is Enuf* (1979–80), *The Trail of Dr. Beck* (1980–81), *Boogie Woogie and Booker T* (1987), *Ma Rose* (1988), *The Talented Tenth* (1989), and *Casanova* (1991).

She moved into feature films in the early nineties, including *Fried Green Tomatoes* (as Janeen), *Lorenzo's Oil* (as Nurse Ruth; 1992), *Malcolm X* (as Lorraine; 1992), *Sleepless in Seattle* (as Harriet; 1993), *U.S. Marshals* (as Deputy Marshall Cooper; 1998) and *Kill Bill* (as L.F. O'Boyle; 2003). She also appeared with her husband in *Freedomland* (2006).

She had a recurring role in the CBS series *Frannie's Turn* (1992), which led to her family moving to Los Angeles, after having been Harlem residents for many years. Richardson directed the film *Hairstory* in 2001 for the Lifetime Network. She and her husband were given the prestigious Frederick D. Patterson Award from the United Negro College Fund for their support of education.

Feature Films including TV Movies: *Hangin' with the Homeboys* (1991), *The Super* (1991), *Fried Green Tomatoes* (1992), *Juice* (1992), *The Nightman* (TV; 1992), *Malcolm X* (1992), *Lorenzo's Oil* (1992), *Sleepless in Seattle* (1993), *Shameful Secrets* (TV; 1993), *The Last Laugh* (1994), *When a Man Loves a Woman* (1994), *Midnight Run for Your Life* (TV; 1994), *Losing Isaiah* (1995), *The Deliverance of Elaine* (TV; 1996), *Lone Star* (1996), *Loved* (1997), *Julian Po* (1997), *U.S. Marshals* (1998), *Secrets* (1998), *Introducing Dorothy Dandridge* (TV; 1999), *Within These Walls* (TV; 2001), *The Fighting Temptations* (2003), *Freedomland* (2006), *Blackout* (2007), *All About Us* (2007).

TV: *A Man Called Hawk* ("Life After Death," 1989), *Law & Order* (2 episodes; "Life Choice," "Sisters of Mercy," 1991 and 1992), *Frannie's Turn* (recurring role as Vivian; 1992), *One Life to Live* (1992), *Civil Wars* ("Hit the Road, Jack," 1993), *Cheers* ("Woody Gets an Election," 1993), *Party of Five* ("Private Lives," 1994), *Earth 2* ("A Memory Play," 1994), *Baseball* (voice; "The Capital of Baseball," 1994), *Chicago Hope* ("Cutting Edges," 1995), *NYPD Blue* ("Heavin' Can Wait," 1995), *Homicide: Life on the Street* ("Betrayal," 1997), *Ally McBeal* ("Story of Love," 1998), *Any Day Now* ("Call Him Johnny," 1998), *Judging Amy* (pilot; 1999), *Once and Again* (pilot; "Boy Meets Girl," 1999), *Essence Awards* (2001), *100 Centre Street* (8 episodes in the role of Atallah Sims; 2001–02), *Boston Public* (2003), *Unchained Memories: Readings from the Slave Narratives* (2003).

Video/DVD: *RCS Meets USA: Working Shakespeare* (2005).

Shorts: *Secrets* (1997).

Richardson, Salli Born in Chicago, Illinois, November 23, 1967.

Salli Richardson is a versatile actress whose career has held steady since her beginnings in the Kuumba Workshop Theater in Chicago. She is the daughter of Marcia Harris, who ran a recording studio in Atlanta, and Duel Richardson, the director of Neighborhood Relations/Educational Programs and Office of Community Affairs for the University of Chicago.

Salli Richardson with Keenen Ivory Wayans in *A Low Down Dirty Shame* (1994).

She is best known these days as Allison Blake, head of Global Dynamics, on the Sci-Fi channel series *Eureka* (2006–09), but she has enjoyed success in motion pictures as well. She was good as a femme fatale in 1994's *A Low Down Dirty Shame*; she was in Mario Van Peebles' outrageous western *Posse* (1993), which showcased her singing ability with the soundtrack song "If I Knew Him at All"; and she was in the Denzel Washington–directed *Antwone Fisher* (2002).

Her other television credits include *Star Trek: Deep Space Nine*, *Silk Stalkings*, *New* York *Undercover* and *The Pretender*. Richardson is married to fellow actor Dondre Whitfield and they have one daughter, Parker Richardson Whitfield.

Feature Films including Video and TV Movies: *Up Against the Wall* (1991), *Prelude to a Kiss* (1992), *Mo' Money* (1992), *How U Like Me Now* (1993), *Posse* (1993), *Sioux City* (1994), *I Spy Returns* (TV; 1994), *A Low Down Dirty Shame* (1994), *Lily in Winter* (TV; 1994), *Once Upon a Time ... When We Were Colored* (1995), *Gargoyles ... The Heroes Awaken* (voice; 1995), *Soul of the Game* (TV; 1996), *The Great White Hype* (1996), *True Women* (TV; 1997), *Gargoyles: Brothers Betrayed* (voice; 1998), *Butter* (1998), *Gargoyles: The Force of Goliath* (voice; 1998), *Gargoyles: The Hunted* (voice; 1998), *Gargoyles: Deeds of Deception* (TV; 1998), *Lillie* (1999), *Baby of the Family* (2002), *Book of Love* (2002), *Antwone Fisher* (2002), *Biker Boyz* (2003), *Anacondas: The Hunt for the Blood Orchid* (2004), *I Am Legend* (2007), *Black Dynamite* (2008), *Pastor Brown* (2009).

TV: *Silk Stalkings* ("Wild Card," 1992), *Star Trek: Deep Space Nine* ("Second Sight," 1993), *Roc* ("The Last Temptation of Roc," 1994), *New York Undercover* ("Eyewitness Blues," 1994), *Gargoyles* (recurring role as the voice of Elisa Maza/Delilah; 1994–96), *Gargoyles: The Goliath Chronicles* (3 episodes as the voice of Elisa Maza/Delilah; 1996), *Stargate: SG-1* ("Bloodlines," 1997), *Between Brothers* ("The Player," 1997), *The Pretender* ("Gigolo Jarod," 1998), *Rude Awakening* (recurring role as Nancy Adams; 1998), *Mercy Point* (4 episodes in the role of Kim; "New Arrivals," "Last Resort," "Persistence of Vision," "Battle Scars," 1998–99), *The Jamie Foxx Show* ("Liar, Liar, Pants on Fire," 1999), *Family Law* (3 episodes in the role of Viveca; "The Nanny," "Media Relations," "Human Error," 1999–2000), *Secret Agent Man* ("WhupSumAss," 2000), *Acapulco Black Film Festival* (2000), *Pyramid* (2 segments; 2003), *CSI: Miami* (5 episodes in the role of Laura; "Bunk," "Forced Entry," "Evidence of Things Unseen," "Dispo Day," "Double Cap," 2003), *Line of Fire* ("The Senator," 2004), *Second Time Around* ("Coupling Up," 2004), *NYPD Blue* (2 episodes in the role of Bobbi Kingston; "My Dinner with Andy," "I Like Ike," 2004), *House* ("Sports Medicine," 2005), *1-800-Missing* ("Sisterhood," 2005), *The War at Home* ("Guess Who's Coming to the Barbeque," 2005), *Bones* ("Aliens in a Spaceship," 2006), *Eureka* (recurring role of Allison Blake; 2006–09).

Robertson, Georgianna Born in Port Maria, Jamaica, March 23, 1972.

Modeling queen Georgianna Robertson is of Jamaican heritage, born to a half–East Indian cosmetologist mother and a father of Scottish descent. She was raised as a Mormon when her mother brought her and two of her brothers to New York when she was 12 (two brothers and sisters remained in Jamaica). She attended Manhattan's Hunter College before her classic good looks began to attract the attention that led to a modeling career.

The 5'11" beauty modeled for Yves St. Laurent from the time she first went to Paris, when he chose her for his 30th anniversary show at the Paris Opera Bastille, until his death in 2008. St. Laurent was her mentor and helped define her as a model. She has been cover featured on scores of magazines, including *Paris Match* (in a memorable Marilyn Monroe pose with a blonde wig and white dress), *Amica*, *Elle*, French *Vogue* and *Town & Country*.

Her film debut was as Jack Lowenthal's (Rupert Everett) wife in director Robert Altman's *Prêt-à-Porter* (1994). She was then seen in the 1998 Italian TV movie *Un Nero per Casa*, a variant on *Guess Who's Coming to Dinner?* Her first major role in a feature film, *Rise Above the Silver and Gold* (2008), had been announced for at least two years before its completion, and eventually went directly to DVD. *Rise Above* is a comedy-drama about a rapper who decides that self-respect is more important than fame. Robertson has introduced her own swimwear line.

Feature Films including Video and TV Movies: *Prêt-à-Porter* (1994), *Un Nero per Casa* (TV; 1998), *French Spies* (2004), *Rise Above the Silver and Gold* (2008).

TV: *1997 VH1 Fashion Awards* (1997), *Oddville, MTV* (1997).

Short: *Save the Rabbits* (1994).

Robinson, Alexia Born in Ft. Lauderdale, Florida, January 1, 1970.

Robinson attended Florida State University with a major in business administration and a minor in theatre. She was Meg Lawson on the soap *General Hospital* in 1990; Akeesha Wesley on *Murder One* in 1996; Mona Phillips on *The Good News* in 1997; and Ashley on *Malcolm & Eddie* (1998–2000). Her feature films run the gamut from science fiction (*Total Recall*, 1990) to comedy (*The Nutty Professor*, 1996), to horror (*Candyman; Day of the Dead*, 1999). Theater credits include *Mother's Milk* (as Kay Carson; First Stage Theatre), *For Colored Girls Only* (as Lady in Orange; First Stage Theatre), and *A Raisin in the Sun* (as Beneatha Younger; Ruby Diamond Theatre).

Robinson received her acting and dance training from Roy London, the Vincent Chase Workshop, the Dupree Dance Academy, the John Sarno Workshop and the Tepper/Gallegos Commercial Workshop. She has opened her own studio in Burbank, California. The Alexia Robinson Studio encompasses acting studies for all ages and summer acting camp for kids and teens.

Feature Films including TV Movies: *Total Recall* (1990), *Last Detour* (1994), *The Nutty Professor* (1996), *Candyman; Day of the Dead* (1999), *MacArthur Park* (2001).

TV: *Fame* ("Team Work," 1985), *Rituals* (1985), *Hill Street Blues* ("The Cookie Crumbles," 1987), *General Hospital* (recurring role as Meg Lawson; 1990), *Freshman Dorm* ("Sex, Truth and Theatre," 1992), *Murder, She Wrote* ("The Sound of Murder," 1993), *Walker, Texas Ranger* ("Deadly Reunion," 1994), *Strange Luck* ("Over Exposure," 1995), *Murder One* (recurring role of Akeesha Wesley; 1996), *Savannah* (recurring role of Cassandra "Cassie" Wheeler; 1996–97), *The Good News* (3 episodes in the role of Mona Phillips; "Writing on the Wall," "A Joyful Noise," "A Christmas Story," 1997), *Getting Personal* ("Chasing Sammy," 1998), *Vengeance Unlimited* ("Dishonorable Discharge," 1998), *Malcolm & Eddie* (5 episodes in the role of Ashley; "Father of the Bribe," "Paint Misbehavin'," "B.S. I Love You," "Hanging by a Dred," "Swooped," 1998–2000), *Martial Law* ("Call of the Wild," 1999), *Veronica's Closet* ("Veronica's New Year," 1999), *V.I.P.* ("V.I.P., R.I.P.," 2000), *The Young and the Restless* (2001), *Haunted* ("Simon Redux," 2002), *CSI: Miami* ("Witness to Murder," 2004), *Eve* (3 episodes in the role of Tamara; "Prom Night," "Resident Aliens," "Three Divas, No Style," 2005).

Alexia Robinson.

Robinson, Mabel Date of birth unavailable.

Mabel Robinson is a choreographer and dancer (she danced with Alvin Ailey and Martha Graham) who has appeared in the theatrical films *Cotton Comes to Harlem* (1970) and *The Wiz* (as a Munchkin; 1978), and TV movies: *The Sister-in-Law* and *Dare to Love* (both 1995). Robinson was an actress on Broadway in *Golden Boy* (1964–66), *Murderous Angels* (1971–72), *Treemonisha* (1975), and *Your Arms Too Short to Box with God* (1976–78). *Kicks and Co.* (1961) closed on the road before it could get to Broadway.

She was assistant choreographer for *Purlie* (1970–71); choreographer and assistant director of the 1976–77 revival of *Porgy and Bess*; and choreographer of *It's So Nice to Be Civilized* (1980). She choreographed *Before the Flood* (1979–80) for the Amas Musical Theatre and directed and choreographed *Will They Ever Love Us on Broadway*

(1981). She was a faculty member of the North Carolina School of the Arts. In 2007 she worked with the National Black Theatre Festival in Winston-Salem, North Carolina.

Feature Films including TV Movies: *Cotton Comes to Harlem* (1970), *The Wiz* (1978), *The Sister-in-Law* (TV; 1995), *Dare to Love* (TV; 1995).

Robinson, Wendy Raquel

Born in Los Angeles, California, July 25, 1967.

Wendy Raquel Robinson is a graduate of the School of Fine Arts of Howard University. She is of African American and Native American descent. She is remembered for what is perhaps her best recurring role, Principal Regina "Piggy" Grier on *The Steve Harvey Show* (1997–2002). She received three NAACP Image Award nominations for Best Actress in a Comedy for her work on the show. She was also Kaylene on *Getting Personal* (1998) and Tasha Mack on *The Game* (2006–07).

Robinson tends to play "best friend' supporting roles in feature films — *Two Can Play That Game* (2001), *Something New* (2006) — that do not always take full advantage of her acting range. In 1995 she founded a theater arts school for children in Los Angeles called the Amazing Grace Conservatory. In 2001 she starred in *Black Woman's Blues* at the Regency West Theatre in Los Angeles. She married Marco Perkins in 2003.

Wendy Racquel Robinson on *The Steve Harvey Show.*

Feature Films including Video and TV Movies: *The Walking Dead* (1995), *A Thin Line Between Love and Hate* (1996), *Ringmaster* (1998), *Miss Congeniality* (2000), *Two Can Play That Game* (2001), *With or Without You* (2003), *Mind Games* (2003), *Reflections: A Story of Redemption* (2004), *Squirrel Man* (2005), *Rebound* (2005), *Something New* (2006), *Contradictions of the Heart* (2009).

TV: *Martin* ("Really, Gina Is Not My Lover," 1993), *The Sinbad Show* (pilot; 1993), *Thea* ("Artie's Party," 1993), *M.A.N.T.I.S.* (1994), *Dream On* ("The Homecoming Queen," 1994), *Me and the Boys* (recurring role of Amelia; 1994), *Sisters* ("Scandalous," 1994), *The Watcher* (pilot; 1995), *Vanishing Son* ("Long Ago and Far Away," 1995), *Minor Adjustments* (recurring role of Rachel Aimes; 1995), *NYPD Blue* (2 episodes in the role of Lucy; "Closing Time," "He's Not Guilty, He's My Brother," 1996), *The Steve Harvey Show* (5 episodes in the role of Regina "Piggy" Grier; "Whatever You Want," "My Left Gator," "No Free Samples," "Hate Thy Neighbor," "The Graduates," 1997–2002),*Getting Personal* (3 episodes in the role of Kaylene; "Chasing Sammy," "The Wedding Zinger," "Saving Milo's Privates," 1998), *Baby Blues* (2 episodes as the voice of Josie; "God Forbid," "The Bad Family," 2000 and 2002), *A Baby Blues Christmas Special* (voice; 2002), *Yes, Dear* ("Greg's New Friend," 2002), *Cedric the Entertainer Presents* (series regular; 2002), *Heroes of Black Comedy* (2002), *Pyramid* (3 segments; 2003), *The Parkers* ("The Accidental Therapist," 2003), *All of Us* (3 episodes in the role of Sarah Willis; "The Return of Mars Blackmon," "Handle Your Business," "Movin' on Up," 2004–05), *The New Adventures of Old Christine* ("The Other F Word," 2006), *In the Mix* (2006), *Girlfriends* ("The Game," 2006), *The Game* (recurring role of Tasha Mack; 2006–07), *Angels Can't Help But Laugh* (2007).

Shorts: *Keys* (2007).

Robinson Peete, Holly

Born in Philadelphia, Pennsylvania, September 18, 1964.

Born Holly Elizabeth Robinson, she is the daughter of Matt Robinson, the original Gordon (1969–71) on *Sesame Street*, the daughter of actress and producer Delores Robinson, and the wife of former NFL quarterback Rodney Peete of the Washington Redskins. Her father left the family when she was nine and her mother moved the family from Philadelphia to Los Angeles. She continues to have much respect for her father and sees him as a role model. She attended Sarah Lawrence College and later studied at the Sorbonne in Paris.

Her acting career has been centered in television. She was Officer Judy Hoffs, part of the young cop squad that included Johnny Depp in *21 Jump Street* (1987–91). She was the level-headed Vanessa Russell, roommate of the title character, on the gentle sitcom *Hangin' with Mr. Cooper* (1992–97) and had a featured role as Marlena Ellison on *For Your Love* (1998–2002). She also did one season as Clea on the UPN Network comedy *Love, Inc.*, but the network merged with the WB into the CW Network, and most existing UPN shows fell by the wayside.

An avid football fan, she is the author of *Get Your Own Damn Beer, I'm Watching the Game!: A Woman's Guide to Loving Pro Football* (Rodale; 2006). Robinson Peete is also an accomplished singer and has co-hosted a talk show with her husband on Oprah & Friends Radio.

She married Peete in 1995 and they have four children (fraternal twins Rodney James and Ryan Elizabeth, born in 1997; son Robinson James, born in 2002; and son Roman, born in 2005). Rodney was diagnosed with autism when he was three years old, and this put a strain on every aspect of Robinson Peete's life, but ultimately made her stronger and more focused than ever.

Feature Films including TV Movies: *Dummy* (TV; 1979), *Howard the Duck* (1986), *The Jacksons: An American Dream* (TV; 1992), *Killers in the House* (TV; 1998), *After All* (TV; 1999), *My Wonderful Life* (TV; 2002), *Earthquake* (TV; 2004), *Football Wives* (TV; 2007), *Matters of Life and Dating* (TV; 2007).

TV: *21 Jump Street* (recurring role of Officer Judy Hoffs; 1987–1991), *21st NAACP Image Awards* (1989), *The 61st Annual Academy Awards* (1989), *Booker* (2 episodes in the role of Judy Hoffs; "The Pump," "Father's Day," 1989 and 1990), *ABC TGIF* (1990), *Gabriel's Fire* ("Belly of the Beast," 1991), *The 6th Annual Soul Train Music Awards* (1992), *Circus of the Stars 18* (1993), *Intimate Portrait* (3 episodes; "Star Jones," "Lela Rochon," "Holly Robinson Peete," 1993), *Hangin' with Mr. Cooper* (34 episodes in the role of Vanessa Russell; 1994–97), *Off Camera with Dean Cain* (1995), *The Oprah Winfrey Show* (4 appearances; 1996–2007), *Sparkle Lounge* (1997), *Pacific Blue* ("Soft Targets," 1997), *Touched by an Angel* ("Smokescreen," 1997), *Late Night with Conan O'Brien* (1998), *The Rosie O'Donnell Show* (1998), *Hollywood Squares* (3 segments; 1998–2001), *For Your Love* (recurring role of Marlena Ellis; 1998–2002), *Strong Medicine* ("Donors," 2001), *One on One* (6 episodes in the role of Stacy; 2001–02), *33rd NAACP Image Awards* (2002), *Good Day Live* (3 appearances; 2002–04), *Essence Awards* (2003), *9th Annual Soul Train Lady of Soul Awards* (2003), *Pepsi Play for a Billion* (2003), *Like Family* (22 episodes in the role of Tanya Ward; 2003–04), *The Sharon Osbourne Show* (3 appearances; 2003–04), *The Wayne Brady Show* (2004), *The Tony Danza Show* (2004), *The View* (2005), *Love, Inc.* (5 episodes in the role of Clea; "Family Ties," "Hope & Faith," "One on One," "Three's Company," "Fired Up," 2005–06), *Dancing with the Stars* (2006), *I Was a Network Star* (archival; 2006), *Pepsi Smash Super Bowl Bash* (2006), *Larry King Live* (3 segments; 2007–08), *Entertainment Tonight* (4 segments; 2008), *An Evening of Stars: Tribute to Patti LaBelle* (2009).

Holly Robinson Peete.

Music Video: *Dance with My Father* (2003).

Rochon, Lela Born in Los Angeles, California, April 17, 1964.

Lela Rochon's career began while she attended Washington State University in Dominguez Hills. Between 1984 and 1986, she was a featured "Spudette" in the high profile "spokesdog" Spuds McKenzie Budweiser and Bud Light commercials. One of the most popular advertising campaigns of its era, it made Rochon's face (if not her name) known to the mass public. It was also during this era that she married Adolfo Quinones, a break-dancer she met while filming *Breakin'* and *Breakin' 2* (both 1984). They divorced in 1987.

She landed a role in *Harlem Nights* starring Eddie Murphy in 1989, but the outstanding role of her career to date was as Robin Stokes in *Waiting to Exhale* (1995), the box office smash that helped define a generation of black women. In addition to *Exhale,* she had a string of roles in lesser films: *Boomerang* (1992), again with Eddie Murphy, *The Meteor Man* (1993), *Why Do Fools Fall in Love* (1998), and *Any Given Sunday* (1999),

Rochon's career has been quiet in recent years, as she has concentrated on marriage and motherhood. In 1999, she married director Antoine Fuqua, best known for the film *Training Day*. They have two children, Asia and Brandon, and Antoine's son from a previous relationship, Zachary.

Feature Films including Video and TV Movies: *Breakin'* (1984), *Breakin' 2: Electric Bugaloo* (1984), *A Bunny's Tale* (TV; 1985), *Foxtrap* (1986), *Stewardess School* (1986), *The Wild Pair* (1987), *Into the Homeland* (TV; 1987), *Harlem Nights* (1989), *Extralarge: Black and White* (1991), *Boomerang* (1992), *The Meteor Man* (1993), *Waiting to Exhale* (1995), *Mr. and Mrs. Loving* (TV; 1996), *The Chamber* (1996), *Gang Related* (1997), *Legal Deceit* (1997), *Ruby Bridges* (TV; 1998), *The Big Hit* (1998), *Knock Off* (1998), *Why Do Fools Fall in Love* (1998), *The Charlotte Austin Story* (TV; 1999), *Any Given Sunday* (1999), *Labor Pains* (2000), *First Daughter* (2004), *Running Out of Time in Hollywood* (2006), *Balancing the Books* (2008), *Blood Done Sign My Name* (2009).

TV: *The Facts of Life* ("The Greek Connection," 1987), *The Cosby Show* ("The Shower," 1987), *What's Happening Now!* ("The Hat Comes Back," 1987), *Amen* ("Wedding Bell Blues," 1988), *21 Jump Street* ("A Change of Heart," 1990), *227* ("Gone Fishing," 1990), *1st & Ten* ("Don't Powerburst My Bubble," 1990), *The Fresh Prince of Bel-Air* ("Will Gets a Job," 1991), *Homefront* ("At Your Age," 1992), *Roc* ("Roc Throws Joey Out," 1992), *Tales from the Crypt* ("Werewolf Concerto," 1992), *The Sinbad Show* (pilot; 1993), *Hangin' with Mr. Cooper* (2 episodes; "On the Rebound," "The Courtship of Mark Cooper," 1992 and 1994), *The Wayans Bros.* (4 episodes in the role of Lisa; "Goop Hair It Is," "The Shawn-Shank Redemption," "ER," "Brazilla vs. Rodney," 1995), *Lauren Hutton and....* (1996), *The Rosie O'Donnell Show* (2 appearances; 1996), *The Outer Limits* ("The Awakening," 1997), *Essence Awards* (1998), *Intimate Portrait* (3 episodes; "Star Jones," "Lela Rochon," "Holly Robinson Peete," 1998), *The Division* (2 episodes in the role of Inspector Angela Reide; "Mother's Day," "Forces of Deviance," 2001), *Essence Awards* (2002), *Last Call with Carson Daly* (2003).

Roker, Roxie Born in Miami, Florida, August 28, 1929; died December 2, 1995, Los Angeles, California.

Roxie Albertha Roker was of West Indian heritage. Her role of Helen Willis on Norman Lear's *The Jeffersons* was a groundbreaker, since the character's husband was white (as was Roker's real life husband). *The Jeffersons*, a spin-off of Lear's *All in the Family*, ran from 1975 to 1985, and was a popular and influential sitcom.

Roker was married to TV producer Sy Kravitz; she is the mother of rock musician Lenny Kravitz, former husband of Lisa Bonet. She was born in Miami, but grew up in Brooklyn. She went to Howard University in Washington, D.C., receiving a bachelor of fine arts in 1952. She was an active member of the Howard Players drama group. Before her acting career took off, she was a correspondent for New York's channel 5, WNEW-TV, and hosted *Inside Bed-Stuy*, about the Bedford-Stuyvesant community in Brooklyn.

Her professional acting career began in earnest when she joined New York's Negro Ensemble Company. She won an Obie (off–Broadway) Award and was a Tony nominee for her portrayal of Mattie Williams in *The River Niger* (1974). She died of breast cancer at age 66.

Feature Films including TV Movies: *Change at 125th Street* (TV; 1974), *Claudine* (1974), *Billy: Portrait of a Street Kid* (TV; 1977), *The Bermuda Triangle* (TV; 1979), *Making of a Male Model* (TV; 1983), *Amazon Women on the Moon* (1987), *Penny Ante* (1990), *Statistically Speaking* (1995).

TV: *All in the Family* ("The Jeffersons Move On Up," 1975), *The Jeffersons* (recurring role of

Helen Willis; 1975–85), *Kojak* ("Law Dance," 1976), *Roots* (miniseries; 1977), *Fantasy Island* (1982), *Cagney & Lacey* ("Lottery," 1985), *Trapper John, M.D.* ("Strange Bedfellows," 1986), *Mickey Spillane's Mike Hammer* ("Esther," 1987), *ABC Afterschool Specials* (2 episodes; "The Celebrity and the Arcade Kid," "The Day My Kid Went Punk," 1983 and 1987), *227* ("Best Friends," 1988), *Punky Brewster* ("See You in Court," 1988), *Murder, She Wrote* ("Night Fears," 1991), *A Different World* ("Home Is Where the Fire Is," 1991), *Hangin' with Mr. Cooper* ("In Vanessa We Trust," 1993).

Rolle, Esther Born in Pompano Beach, Florida, November 8, 1920; died November 17, 1998, Culver City, California.

Esther Rolle was a multiple award winning actress who remains best known for her role of Florida Evans, first on Norman Lear's *Maude* (1972–74) and then on his forward-thinking, gentle spin-off about black family life, the admirable *Good Times* (1974–79). On *Maude*, the emphasis was on Florida as Maude's housekeeper; on *Good Times*, Florida and her extended family were the focus of the show. Rolle had a problem with what she perceived as the frivolous direction the show was taking, and the emphasis on Jimmie Walker's jive-talking J.J. character. Was it professional jealousy or genuine social concern? She did leave the show for a time late in the run (as did John Amos, who played Florida's husband), but returned for the final season.

She was the 10th child in a family of 18 children, the offspring of Bahamian immigrants. She relocated to New York City after high school graduation and attended Hunter College, Spelman College, and the New School for Social Research. For many years she held a job in the garment district, waiting for her passion for theater to turn into a viable, full-time income.

She did get her share of stage roles, including several prominent ones, often in plays produced by Robert Hooks and the Negro Ensemble Company. She made her stage debut in Genet's *The Blacks* (1962). She was also in *The Crucible* and *Blues for Mr. Charlie,* and was Miss Maybell in Melvin Van Peebles' *Don't Play Us Cheap* (1973). She won an Emmy for her performance in TV movie *Summer of My German Soldier* (1978) and an NAACP Image Award in 1975 for Best Actress in a TV Series (*Good Times*). She was also nominated for an Emmy for her work in the TV movie version of Maya Angelou's *I Know Why the Caged Bird Sings* (1979),

Roxie Roker.

She was given the American Federation of Teachers Human Rights Award in 1983. In 1990 the NAACP honored her with its Leadership Award. She died from complications of diabetes shortly after her 78th birthday. The actress, who had no children, was married to Oscar Robinson from 1955 to 1960. Her sisters, Estelle Evans and Rosanna Carter, were also character actresses.

Feature Films including TV Movies: *Nothing But a Man* (1964), *Who Says I Can't Ride a Rainbow!* (1971), *Every Little Crook and Nanny* (1972), *Don't Play Us Cheap* (1973), *Cleopatra Jones* (1973), *Summer of My German Soldier* (TV; 1978), *I Know Why the Caged Bird Sings* (TV; 1979), *See China and Die* (TV; 1981), *The Tragedy of Romeo and Juliet* (1982), *P.K. and the Kid* (1987), *A Raisin in the Sun* (TV; 1989), *The Mighty Quinn* (1989), *Driving Miss Daisy* (1989), *Age-Old Friends* (TV; aka *A Month of Sundays*, 1989), *The Kid Who Loved Christmas* (TV; 1990), *Blackbird Fly* (1991), *Color Adjustment* (documentary; 1992), *House of Cards* (1993), *Message from Nam* (TV; 1993), *To Dance with the White Dog* (TV; 1993), *How to Make an American Quilt* (1995), *My Fellow Amer-*

icans (1996), *Rosewood* (1997), *Down in the Delta* (1998), *Train Ride* (2000).

TV: *One Life to Live* (recurring role as Sadie Gray; 1968), *Maude* (7 episodes in the role of Florida Evans; 1972–74), *The 28th Annual Tony Awards* (1974), *Good Times* (recurring role of Florida Evans; 1974–79), *Match Game PM* (1975), *Celebrity Sweepstakes* (1975), *CBS: On the Air* (1978), *The Incredible Hulk* ("Behind the Wheel," 1979), *Darkroom* ("Needlepoint," 1981), *Flamingo Road* (2 episodes in the role of Julia; "The High and the Mighty," "The Harder They Fall," 1982), *The New Odd Couple* ("The Ides of April," 1982), *Fantasy Island* (1983), *The Love Boat* (2 episodes; 1983 and 1985), *Finder of Lost Loves* ("Goodbye, Sara," 1984), *Murder, She Wrote* ("Reflections of the Mind," 1985), *Ethnic Notions* (narrator; 1986), *Singer & Sons* (recurring role as Sarah Patterson; 1990), *The 11th Annual Black Achievement Awards* (1990), *Scarlett* (miniseries; 1994), *Nobody's Girls: Five Women of the West* (1995), *Touched by an Angel* (2 episodes in the role of Mary Harding; "Amazing Grace," Parts I and II, 1997), *Poltergeist: The Legacy* ("La Belle Dame Sans Merci," 1998), *The 51st Annual Primetime Emmy Awards* (archival; 1999), *E! True Hollywood Story* (archival; "Good Times," 2000), *TV's Greatest Sidekicks* (archival; 2004).

Video/DVD: *TV in Black: The First Fifty Years* (archival; 2005).

Rose, Anika Noni Born in Bloomfield, Connecticut, September 6, 1972.

Ah-*nee*-kah No-*nee* Rose is a Tony-winning Broadway star. She won Best Performance by a Featured Actress in a Broadway Musical for the role of Emmie Thibodeaux, the materialistic daughter of a black maid in 1963 Louisiana, in *Caroline, or Change* (2004). She also received a Theatre World Award, a Lucille Lortell Award and a Clarence Derwent Award, and was nominated for a Drama Desk Award for the play. When she reprised the role in Los Angeles, she won a Los Angeles Critic's Circle Award and an Ovation Award.

Rose graduated from Connecticut's Bloomfield High School in 1990, and she earned a bachelor's degree in theatre from Florida A&M University. She studied drama at the American Conservancy Theatre in San Francisco before moving to New York and landing a role in the short-lived and critically reviled musical *Footloose* (2000), based on the popular film. Other theater credits include off–Broadway's *Eli's Comin'*, which won her an Obie Award; the starring role of Lutiebelle in the Encore! Performances production of *Purlie*; and *Threepenny Opera* and *Tartuffe* at the American Conservancy's Geary Street Theater in San Francisco.

In 2008, she was Maggie the Cat in the black version of Tennessee Williams' *Cat on a Hot Tin Roof*. At 5' 2", and with rather wholesome good looks, Rose may not have connected quite as well as some actresses with the sheer seductiveness of the role, but her acting skills gave the role depth and humor.

She is well known for her role as Lorrell Robinson, one of the *Dreamgirls* (2006) in the film adaptation of the Broadway smash. Lorrell does not have the ample screen time or the big dramatic scenes given to Effie White (Jennifer Hudson) or Deena Jones (Beyoncé), but she's an appealing, charming character, and Rose makes her work. She provides the leading character Princess Tiana's voice in Disney's *The Princess and the Frog* (2009), the first time an African American actress has fulfilled such a role in a Disney film. She is the daughter of Claudia and John Rose, Jr.

Feature Films including TV Movies: *King of the Bingo Game* (1999), *From Justin to Kelly* (2003), *Temptation* (2004), *Surviving Christmas* (2004), *Dreamgirls* (2006), *Razor* (2008), *Just Add Water* (2008), *The Princess and the Frog* (voice; 2009).

TV: *100 Centre Street* ("Domestic Abuses," 2001), *Third Watch* ("Thicker Than Water," 2002), *The 58th Annual Tony Awards* (2004), *Black Theater Today: 2005*, *Broadway Under the Stars* (2006), *The Oprah Winfrey Show* (2006), *HBO First Look: the Making of Dreamgirls* (2006), *Dreamgirls: T4 Movie Special* (2007), *38th NAACP Image Awards* (2007), *Tavis Smiley* (2007), *The View* (2007), *The Starter Wife* (miniseries; 2007), *The No. 1 Ladies Detective Agency* (recurring role of Grace Makutsi; 2008).

Ross, Diana Born in Detroit, Michigan, March 26, 1944.

Those with even the slightest touch of "diva fever" must admit that Diana "The Boss" Ross is one of a kind. Diane Ernestine Earle Ross grew up in Detroit's tough-as-nails Brewster-Douglass Projects, the second of six children. She attended

Cass Technical High School. At age 15 she formed a girl group with Mary Wilson, Florence Ballard and Betty McGlown called The Primettes, the female answer to a hot new guy group called The Primes (later better known as The Temptations). Motown renamed the group The Supremes in 1961 and eventually turned them into a trio consisting of Ross, Wilson and Ballard. They charted ten #1 hits from 1964 to 1967, although the name of the group was changed to Diana Ross and the Supremes, and Cindy Birdsong replaced Florence Ballard.

Ross is a Tony and Golden Globe winner and an Academy Award nominee (for her haunting take on Billie Holliday in *Lady Sings the Blues* in 1972). She charted 70 hit singles both as a solo act and as the lead singer of the Supremes, the most successful girl group of the 20th century, and was able to bridge both the Motown and disco eras with a plethora of hit albums. Ross is the proud recipient of two stars on the Hollywood Walk of Fame, for her achievement as a Supreme and for her storied but brief acting career.

The Supremes recorded hits by the composer team of Holland-Dozier-Holland for Motown Records on what seemed like a monthly basis — spearheaded by Ross's thin but seductive voice. Even the titles are delightful: feisty teen anthems combining angst with girl power in equal measure. The list is a long one: "Baby Love," "Come See About Me," "Nothing but Heartaches," "Back in My Arms Again," "Stop! In the Name of Love," "My World Is Empty Without You," "I Hear a Symphony," "The Happening," "You Keep Me Hangin' On," "Love Child," "You Can't Hurry Love," "Love Is Here and Now You're Gone," "Reflections," and the sad, final hit, "Someday We'll Be Together."

Literally without missing a beat, Ross began to churn out an almost equally impressive string of solo hits: "Reach Out and Touch (Somebody's Hand)," "Ain't No Mountain High Enough," "Endless Love," the astonishing "Love Hangover," "Theme from Mahogany (Do You Know Where You're Going To?)," "Upside Down," and the beautiful "Missing You."

Her tenure as a Hollywood superstar was indeed a brief one. Much of the blame can be placed on two very bad film choices (*Mahogany*, 1975, and *The Wiz*, 1978) and her soaring career as a solo artist and concert star during the disco era, which must have soaked up a lot of her professional time. In *Mahogany*, Ross looked gorgeous as a superstar model — but the film was soap opera of the most simple-minded sort, and co-star Billy Dee Williams (here, as in *Lady Sings the Blues*), did know how to turn on his sex appeal and steal a scene. Ross put the damper on her acting career with this abysmally unsophisticated project. Following it with *The Wiz* was not a good move.

Diana Ross channels her Asian side in *Mahogany* (1975).

The film version of the Broadway smash *The Wiz* was one of the great critical and financial disasters of its time. Ross, as the world's oldest Dorothy, laid waste to the legacy of *The Wizard of Oz*. Shot on ugly stage sets, it was a chaotic, remarkably annoying film, and it was made even worse by the inept presence of Michael Jackson as The Scarecrow. Ross did appear years later in a couple of highly rated and critically well received TV movies: *Out of Darkness* (1994), for which she received a Golden Globe nomination, and *Double Platinum* (1999), a show biz mom and daughter story co-starring Brandy.

In 2000, Ross announced a Supremes reunion tour — but Wilson and Birdsong balked when they saw how little money they were being offered compared to Ross. The "Return to Love" Tour, as it was christened, went on anyway with two latter-day Supremes, Lynda Laurence and Scherrie Payne standing in for Wilson and Birdsong. The tour was a financial disaster and had to be cancelled after nine performances.

Ross was married to Robert Ellis Silberstein from 1971 to 1977, and Arne Naess, Jr., from 1985 to 2000. She gave birth to Rhonda Ross Kendrick with Motown mogul Berry Gordy; Tracee Ellis Ross and Chudney Ross with Robert Silberstein;

and Ross Arne Naess and Evan Ross with Arne Naess.

Feature Films including TV Movies: *The T.A.M.I. Show* (1964), *Beach Ball* (1965), *Lady Sings the Blues* (1972), *Mahogany* (1975), *The Wiz* (1978), *Out of Darkness* (TV; 1994), *Double Platinum* (TV; 1999).

TV: *Top of the Pops* (11 segments; 1964–99), *Ready, Steady, Go!* ("The Sound of Motown," 1965), *It's What's Happening, Baby!* (1965), *Hullabaloo* (2 segments; 1965), *The Mike Douglas Show* (2 appearances; 1965), *The Hollywood Palace* (4 appearances; 1965–69), *The Ed Sullivan Show* (6 appearances; 1965–69), *The Dean Martin Show* (1966), *T.C.B.* (1968), *Tarzan* ("The Convert," 1968), *The Dinah Shore Special: Like Hep* (1969), *Rowan & Martin's Laugh-In* (2 segments; 1969), *This Is Tom Jones* (1970), *Fight of the Century* (1971), *Make Room for Granddaddy* ("The Star," 1971), *Goin' Back to Indiana* (1971), *The Sonny and Cher Comedy Hour* (1972), *The Tonight Show Starring Johnny Carson* (2 appearances; 1972 and 1973), *The 45th Annual Academy Awards* (1973), *Soul Train* (1973), *The 16th Annual Grammy Awards* (1974), *The 46th Annual Academy Awards* (1974), *The 48th Annual Academy Awards* (1976), *The 2nd Annual Rock Music Awards* (1976), *NBC: The First 50 Years—A Closer Look* (1976), *An Evening with Diana Ross* (1977), *Diana Ross in Concert!* (1979), *The American Film Institute Salute to Alfred Hitchcock* (1979), *The 51st Annual Academy Awards* (1979), *The Muppet Show* (1980), *All-Star Birthday Party* (1980), *The 8th Annual American Music Awards* (1981), *Diana* (1981), *The 54th Annual Academy Awards* (1982), *Motown 25: Yesterday, Today, Forever* (1983), *The 11th Annual American Music Awards* (1984), *Motown Returns to the Apollo* (1985), *The Whimsical World of Oz* (1985), *We Are the World* (1985), *The 27th Annual Grammy Awards* (1985), *The 57th Annual Academy Awards* (1985), *The Muppets: A Celebration of 30 Years* (archival; 1986), *The 13th Annual American Music Awards* (1986), *Diana Ross: Red Hot Rhythm and Blues* (1987), *The 62nd Annual Academy Awards* (1990), *Primero izquierda* (1992), *Aspel & Company* (1992), *Muhammad Ali's 50th Birthday Celebration* (1992), *Diana Ross Live! The Lady Sings ... Jazz & Blues: Stolen Moments* (1992), *Apollo Theatre Hall of Fame* (1993), *Operalia* (1994), *All-Star 25th Birthday: Stars and Street Forever!* (1994), *Champions of the World* (1995), *Television's Greatest Performances I* (archival; 1995), *The History of Rock 'N' Roll, Vol. 3* (1995), *The 9th Annual Soul Train Music Awards* (1995), *Soul Train's 25th Anniversary* (1995), *The Greatest Music Party in the World* (1995), *Clive Anderson All Talk* (1996), *Super Bowl XXX* (1996), *Brit Awards 1997*, *The 39th Annual Grammy Awards* (1997), *Motown 40: The Music Is Forever* (1998), *MTV Video Music Awards 1999*, *TFI Friday* (1999), *An Audience with Diana Ross* (1999), *VH1 Divas 2000: A Tribute to Diana Ross*, *100 Greatest Dance Songs of Rock & Roll* (archival; 2000), *31st NAACP Image Awards* (2000), *The Oprah Winfrey Show* (2000), *The Howard Stern Radio Show* (2000), *We Are Family* (2002), *A Night at the Apollo* (2002), *It's Black Entertainment* (archival; 2002), *American Bandstand's 50th Anniversary Celebration* (archival; 2002), *Standing in the Shadows of Motown* (archival; 2002), *V Graham Norton* (2003), *E! True Hollywood Story* (archival; 2003), *50 Greatest TV Animals* (archival; 2003), *Celebrities Uncensored* (archival; 2003), *Good Morning America* (2004), *Inside Edition* (2004), *The View* (2004), *101 Biggest Celebrity Oops* (archival; 2004), *Sex 'n' Pop* (archival; 2004), *The 2004 Billboard Music Awards*, *Soul Deep: The Story of Black Popular Music* (archival; 2005), *Corazon de...* (archival; 2005), *50 y mas* (archival; 2005), *Tsunami Aid: A Concert of Hope* (2005), *This Morning* (2005), *Ant & Dec's Saturday Night Takeaway* (2005), *Inside the Actors Studio* (2006), *Be My Baby: The Girl Group Story* (archival; 2006), *The Best of the Royal Variety* (archival; 2006), *La imagen de tu vida* (archival; 2006), *The 4th Annual TV Land Awards* (2006), *Legends Ball* (2006), *La tele de tu vida* (archival; 2007), *BET Awards 2007*, *Late Show with David Letterman* (2007), *Live with Regis & Kelly* (2007), *American Idol* (2007), *Entertainment Tonight* (2008).

Video/DVD: *Visions of Diana Ross* (1985), *Michael Jackson: The Legend Continues* (archival; 1988), *Shindig! Presents Groovy Gals* (archival; 1991), *TV in Black: The First Fifty Years* (archival; 2004), *Soulful Sixties* (2004), *Behind the Blues: Lady Sings the Blues* (2005).

Rowell, Victoria Born in Portland, Maine, May 10, 1959.

Born to a Caucasian mother and an African American father, Victoria Rowell was raised by her foster parents, Agatha and Robert Armstead. Her mother was a schizophrenic, and when Rowell was 16 days old, she and two older sisters,

Sheree and Lori, were given to child care services. Rowell began studying ballet at age eight, and won a scholarship to the Cambridge School of Ballet. By age 17, she had also been offered scholarships to the School of American Ballet, the American Ballet Theatre and the Dance Theatre of Harlem. She danced with the American Ballet Theatre and the Juilliard School of Music Dance Program, and began teaching dance in New England.

In the 1980s she began a second career as a runway and print model, and then she found another world to conquer by turning her attention to acting. She attracted the attention of Bill Cosby and made two appearances on *The Cosby Show* in 1989–90, after having had appeared in his unsuccessful spy spoof *Leonard Part 6* (1987). Her association with the daytime drama *The Young and the Restless* and the role of Drucilla Winters began in 1990 and continued until 2007. She was nominated for three Daytime Emmy Awards (1996–98) and won 10 NAACP Image Awards for her work. Backstage politics eventually caused her to leave the role.

However, she had a wonderful working relationship with Dick Van Dyke on the prime time murder mystery *Diagnosis Murder* in the role of Dr. Amanda Bentley (1993–2001). One episode was about a murder on the set of *The Young and the Restless*, with Rowell playing both the role of Amanda and Drucilla.

Rowell's first marriage was to Tom Fahey in 1989; they produced a daughter, Maya, but the marriage only lasted one year. She has had a long-term relationship with jazz musician Wynton Marsalis, and they have a son named Jaspar. In 2007 Rowell published an autobiography entitled *The Women Who Raised Me: A Memoir*, and launched a national book tour on behalf of the critically acclaimed work. She is well known for her generous work on behalf of foster children and is the founder of the Rowell Foster Children Positive Plan.

Feature Films including Video and TV Movies: *Leonard Part 6* (1987), *The Distinguished Gentleman* (1992), *Full Eclipse* (TV; 1993), *Secret Sins of the Father* (TV; 1994), *Dumb & Dumber* (1994), *One Red Rose* (1995), *Barb Wire* (1996), *Eve's Bayou* (1997), *Dr. Hugo* (1998), *Secrets* (1998), *A Wake in Providence* (1999), *Fraternity Boys* (1999), *Feast of All Saints* (TV; 2001), *Without Warning* (TV; 2002), *A Town Without Pity* (TV; 2002), *Black Listed* (2003), *Motives* (2004), *Midnight Clear* (2005), *A Perfect Fit* (2005), *Home of the Brave* (2006), *Polly and Marie* (TV; 2007), *Of Boys and Men* (2008).

TV: *As the World Turns* (recurring role as Nella Franklin; 1988), *The Cosby Show* (2 episodes in the role of Paula; "Cliff's Wet Adventure," "Theo's Dirty Laundry," 1989 and 1990), *The Fresh Prince of Bel-Air* ("Clubba Hubba," 1990), *The Young and the Restless* (recurring role of Drucilla Winters; 1990–2007), *Herman's Head* (2 episodes in the role of Susan Bracken; "Bracken's Daughter," "I Wanna Go Home," 1991 and 1993), *Family Feud* (1993), *Diagnosis Murder* (recurring role of Amanda Bentley-Livingston; 1993–2001), *Soul Train* (1995), *Deadly Games* ("Divorce Lawyer," 1995), *The Rosie O'Donnell Show* (1998), *Late Show with David Letterman* (1998), *The 25th Annual Daytime Emmy Awards* (1998), *Hollywood Squares* (1999), *Penn & Teller's Sin City Spectacular* (2000), *Celebrity Profile* ("Scott Baio," 2000), *Family Law* ("Moving On," 2001), *18th Annual Soap Opera Digest Awards* (2003), *The Wayne Brady Show* (2 appearances; 2003 and 2004), *SoapTalk* (3 segments; 2003–06), *Pyramid* (2004), *The 31st Annual Daytime Emmy Awards* (2004), *Soapography* (2004), *36th NAACP Image Awards* (2005), *The 32nd Annual Daytime Emmy Awards* (2005), *Noah's Arc* (2 episodes in the role of Vonda; "Desperado," "Give It Up," 2006), *14th Annual Inner City Destiny Awards* (2006), *All of Us* ("He's Got Game," 2007), *2007 Trumpet Awards*, *The Morning Show with Mike & Juliet* (2007).

Shorts: *Midnight Clear* (2005).

Rowland, Kelly Born in Atlanta, Georgia. February 11, 1981.

Kelendria Trene Rowland was a founding member of Destiny's Child (along with Beyoncé Knowles and LaTavia Roberson), generally cited as the most popular female recording group of all time. Originally known as Gyrl's Time, the group was officially christened Destiny's Child in 1993 and released their self-titled debut album in 1998. Their second album, however, was the real breakthrough, selling over seven million copies. *The Writing's on the Wall* (1999) also yielded many single hits, including "Say My Name," one of the group's signature songs. Their third album, *Survivor* (2001) topped even that, selling over 10 million copies worldwide. Now the group consisted of Rowland, Knowles and Michelle Williams and, after concentrating on solo projects for three years, they released the album *Destiny Fulfilled* in 2004. The greatest hits compilation album *#1's* was released in 2005, and the following year the group received a star on the Hollywood Walk of Fame. Destiny's Child announced their disbandment at the end of their 2005 "Destiny Fulfilled ... and Lovin' It" world tour.

Rowland released her first solo album, *Simply Deep*, in 2002, which sold in excess of two million copies worldwide. It wasn't until 2007 that she released her second album, *Ms. Kelly*, which enjoyed moderately successful sales, debuting at number six on the *Billboard* album chart.

Rowland took her fresh-faced good looks and easy-going charm to the big screen in 2003 with a featured role in the horror film bash *Freddy vs. Jason*, following that with the lead in the romantic comedy *The Seat Filler* in 2004. She has also guest starred on TV sitcoms (*Eve, Girlfriends, The Hughleys*) and portrayed the great soul singer Martha Reeves of Martha and the Vandellas on *American Dreams* on two episodes of the show in 2003.

Rowland's parents are Doris Rowland Garrison and Christopher Lovett, who were married after the birth of Kelly. Her mother left her father when she was seven years old due to an abusive relationship. That's when Kelly and her mother relocated to Houston, Texas, and she made two friends named Beyoncé and LaTavia.

Feature Films including TV Movies: *Beverly Hood* (1999), *Freddy vs. Jason* (2003), *The Seat Filler* (2004), *Asterix aux jeux olympiques* (voice; 2008).

TV: *Smart Guy* ("A Date with Destiny," 1998), *The 1999 Malibu MOBO Awards, Pacific Blue* ("Ghost Town," 1999), *The Martin Short Show* (1999), *VH1 Divas 2000: A Tribute to Diana Ross* (2000), *Christmas in Rockefeller Center* (2000), *2000 Blockbuster Entertainment Awards, Walt Disney World Summer Jam Concert* (2000), *Making the Video* (2000), *100 Greatest Dance Songs of Rock & Roll* (2000), *The 2000 Billboard Music Awards, The Famous Jett Jackson* ("Backstage Pass," 2000), *Sen kvall med luuk* (2001), *The 43rd Annual Grammy Awards* (2001), *MTV Icon: Janet Jackson* (2001), *E! True Hollywood Story* ("Joan Rivers," 2001), *Destiny's Child Live* (2001), *The Record of the Year* (2001), *1st Annual BET Awards* (2001), *The Concert for New York City* (2001), *Michael Jackson: 30th Anniversary Celebration* (2001), *The Teen Choice Awards 2001, Intimate Portrait* ("Destiny's Child," 2001), *Nobel Peace Prize Concert* (2001), *Christmas in Rockefeller Center* (2001), *Pop Goes Christmas* (2001), *Saturday Night Live* (2 appearances; 2001–04), *Liza and David* (2002), *The 29th Annual American Music Awards* (2002), *The Victoria's Secret Fashion Show* (2002), *I Love the '80s* (2002), *Stjerne for en Aften* (2002), *The Hughleys* (3 episodes in the role of Carly; "Smells Like Free Spirit," "You've Got Male," "It's a Girl," Part II, 2002), *Saturday Night Live* (2002), *The Late Late Show with Craig Kilborn* (2 appearances; 2002 and 2003), *Top of the Pops* (3 appearances; 2002–04), *American Dreams* (2 episodes as Martha Reeves; "City on Fire," "Life's Illusions," 2003), *Star Search* (2003), *The Saturday Show* (2003), *2003 Trumpet Awards, The 45th Annual Grammy Awards* (2003), *The Michael Essany Show* (2003), *Born to Diva* (2003), *cd:uk* (4 appearances; 2003), *The Tonight Show with Jay Leno* (2 appearances; 2003), *Tinseltown TV* (2003), *I Love the '70s* (2003), *MTV Video Music Awards 2003, Boogie* (2 appearances; 2003), *Cribs* (2003), *Lighting Up Fifth* (2003), *The Sharon Osbourne Show* (2 appearances; 2003), *Eve* ("Twas the Night Before Christmas," 2003), *Celebrities Uncensored* (archival; 2003), *10 Things Every Guy Should Experience* ("Kentucky Derby," 2004), *Urban Soul: The Making of Modern R&B* (2004), *The 18th Annual Soul Train Music Awards* (2004), *Motown 45* (2004), *gmtv* (2004), *Ant & Dec's Saturday Night Takeaway* (2004), *The National Lottery: Wright Around the World* (2004), *Wetten, dass...?* (2004), *20/20* (2004), *The Record of the Year 2004, The Oprah Winfrey Show* (2 appearances; 2004 and 2005), *The View* (3 appearances; 2004–07), *Top of the Pops Saturday* (2005), *Diary* (2005), *106 & Park* (2005), *BET Awards 2005, Live 8* (2005), *ESPY Awards* (2005), *The 2005 World Music Awards, An All-Star Salute to Patti LaBelle* (2005), *2005 American Music Awards, Jimmy Kimmel Live!* (2 appearances; 2005 and 2007), *The 48th Annual Grammy Awards* (2006), *Girlfriends* (3 episodes in the role of Tammy Hamilton; "Oh, Hell Yes: The Seminar," "I'll Be There for You ... But Not Right Now," "I Don't Wanna Be a Player No More," 2006), *Video on Trial* (archival; 2 segments; 2006), *The Tyra Banks Show* (2006), *The 20th Annual Soul Train Music Awards* (2006), *Chancers* (2006), *The Story of Beyoncé* (2006), *Punk'd* (2007), *BET Awards 2007, Access Granted* (2 appearances; 2007), *The Beyoncé Experience*

(2007), *100 Greatest Songs of the '90s* (2007), *Clash of the Choirs* (2007), *Loose Women* (3 segments; 2007–08), *This Morning* (2008), *The British Soap Awards* (2008), *TRL Italy* (2008), *Good News Week* (2008), *T4 on the Beach 2008, Never Mind the Buzzcocks* (2008).

Video/DVD: *Survivor* (2001), *Destiny's Child: Live in Atlanta* (2006), *Destiny's Child: A Family Affair* (2006).

Rudolph, Maya Born in Gainesville, Florida, July 27, 1972.

The daughter of Minnie Riperton, one of the most distinctive and loveliest pop voices of the seventies, and composer, songwriter and producer Richard Rudolph, Maya Rudolph remains best known for her long stint on *Saturday Night Live* (2000–08). Fans of that show remember her best for her dead-on impersonation of Donatella Versace. Rudolph returned to the program just before the 2008 election to offer a rather generic impression of First Lady Michele Obama.

Riperton was only 31 when she died of cancer; Rudolph was just seven at the time. She attended St. Augustine by the Sea School, and later Santa Monica High School and the University of California in Santa Cruz. She graduated from Porter College with a bachelor of arts in photography. She joined *Saturday Night Live* after a stint with The Groundlings improv troupe, where she honed her talent for impersonation and characterization.

Like so many comediennes, Rudolph seems to be only tangentially concerned with an acting career. She has done guest shots on *City of Angels* and *Chicago Hope*, and what amounts to bit parts in films like *As Good as It Gets* and *Gattaca* (both 1997). She was also in Robert Altman's final film, *A Prairie Home Companion* (2006), and was quite at home with voice work in *Shrek the Third* as Rapunzel (2007). Rudolph is in a long-standing relationship with director Paul Thomas Anderson; they have a daughter, Pearl Bailey Anderson.

Feature Films including Video and TV Movies: *Gattaca* (1997), *The Devil's Child* (TV; 1997), *As Good as It Gets* (1997), *True Love* (TV; 1999), *A Glance Away* (1999), *Chuck & Buck* (2000), *Duets* (2000), *Frank's Book* (2001), *Duplex* (2003), *50 First Dates* (2004), *A Prairie Home Companion* (2006), *Idiocracy* (2006), *Shrek the Third* (voice; 2007), *This Must Be the Place* (2009).

TV: *Chicago Hope* (5 episodes in the role of Nurse Leah Martine; "Liver Let Die," "Higher Powers," "Mummy Dearest," "Split Decisions," "Growing Pains," 1996–97), *City of Angels* (recurring role of Nurse Grace Patterson; 2000), *Action* ("Dead Man Floating," 2000), *Saturday Night Live* (cast member; 2000–08), *VH1 Divas Live: The One and Only Aretha Franklin* (2001), *TV Funhouse* (voice; "Safari Day," 2001), *Saturday Night Live: Mother's Day Special* (2001), *NBC 75th Anniversary Special* (2002), *Heroes of Comedy: Women on Top* (2003), *Night of Too Many Stars* (2003), *Saturday Night Live Weekend Update Halftime Special* (2003), *The Ellen DeGeneres Show* (2003), *The Oprah Winfrey Show* (2004), *60 Minutes* (2004), *The Late Late Show with Craig Kilborn* (2004), *The Tonight Show with Jay Leno* (2006), *Campus Ladies* ("All Nighter," 2006), *HBO First Look* (2 episodes; "Shrek the Third," "A Prairie Home Companion," 2006 and 2007), *Shrek Movie Special* (2007).

Russell, Alice B. (aka Russell, A. Burton) Born in Maxton, North Carolina, June 30, 1892; died December 1984, New Rochelle, New York.

Like her husband, the great black film director Oscar Micheaux, Russell was a somewhat shadowy figure, who served as a producer and crew member as well an actress in her prolific husband's films. She was the older sister of Julia Theresa Russell, who had acted — for the first and apparently the last time — opposite Paul Robeson in Micheaux's *Body and Soul* (1925). Alice was a teacher who lived with her family in Montclair, New Jersey. The family had moved to Montclair from the small community of Maxton in Robeson County, North Carolina, when her father, Robert Burton Russell, had died abruptly around 1900. Her mother, Mary Malloy Russell, raised her five children well despite harshly limited financial resources. She worked as a laundress and later a school custodian to see to it that her children graduated from high school and settled into worthwhile jobs. After graduating high school in Montclair, Alice Russell studied music and gave voice and music lessons.

Micheaux was attracted to Alice and became a regular fixture in the Russell home. They married on March 20, 1926. She was the third Mrs. Micheaux. Russell soon became part of the financial as well as the creative underpinnings of the Micheaux motion picture operation. She began appearing in his films from *The Broken Violin* (1928) to Micheaux's final film, *The Betrayal* (1948). Russell was the one person Micheaux trusted most — the faithful and steadfast wife who anchored him and gave him something to believe in.

The quintessential Micheaux-Russell film is *God's Step Children* (1938). Russell wrote the source story "Naomi, Negress," and starred in the film, as well as being credited as producer. This is really Micheaux's take on *Imitation of Life* (1934), with Russell (Mrs. Saunders) in the mother role. Her lovely face is prominently featured in the upper left hand corner of the poster of the film, and she receives top billing. It seems that the Mrs. Saunders character — mother of a light-skinned daughter "too good" for her race — anchors this film the way Russell anchored Micheaux's life. She is stable, serene, and wise beyond words.

Feature Films: *The Broken Violin* (1928), *The Wages of Sin* (1929), *Easy Street* (1930), *Harlem After Midnight* (1932), *The Girl from Chicago* (1932), *Murder in Harlem* (aka *Lem Hawkins' Confession*; 1935), *God's Step Children* (1938), *Birthright* (1938), *The Betrayal* (1948).

Ryan, Roz Born in July 7, 1951

Rosalyn Bowen, better known by her professional name, Roz Ryan, is an actress and comedienne honored for her extensive Broadway work. Her vast array of Broadway roles includes *Ain't Misbehavin'* (Nell; 1978–82), *Dreamgirls* (Effie White; 1981–85), *Chicago* (Matron "MaMa" Morton; 1996), *A Christmas Carol* (Ghost of Christmas Present; 1998), *One Mo' Time* (Bertha Williams; 2002), and the revival of *The Pajama Game* (2006). Off–Broadway she was in *Violet* at Playwrights Horizon and was in the national tours of *Annie* (Miss Hannigan) and *Chicago*. She toured Australia, China and Thailand in *South Pacific* (as Bloody Mary), Israel and Europe in *Ain't Misbehavin',* and Japan in *Blues in the Night* (as Lady from the Road). Her regional theater credits include *The Old Settler, Seven Guitars*, and *Cole Porter Requests the Pleasure.*

She has done animation voice work in Disney's *Hercules* (1997) and on series such as *Buzz Lightyear of Star Command* (2000) and *Kim Possible* (2002–07). She has had recurring roles on TV series such as *Amen* as Sister Amelia Hetebrink (1986–91) and *Barbershop* as Mae (2005).

Feature Films including Video and TV Movies: *Hercules* (voice; 1997), *Went to Coney Island on a Mission from God ... Be Back by Five* (1998), *Nikita's Blues* (2001), *Kim Possible: The Secret Files* (2003), *I Think I Love My Wife* (2007), *Divine Intervention* (2007), *The Bobby Lee Project* (TV; 2008), *Steppin': The Movie* (2008), *This Side of the Truth* (2009), *Waiting for Forever* (2009).

TV: *Amen* (recurring role of Sister Amelia; 1986–91), *The New Hollywood Squares* (panelist; 1986), *The 11th Annual Black Achievement Awards* (1990), *Good News* (recurring role as Mrs. Dixon; 1997), *Sparks* ("Rehearsal of Fortune," 1997), *The Journey of Allen Strange* ("The Truth About Lies," 1998), *Buzz Lightyear of Star Command* (7 episodes; voice; 2000), *Danny* (recurring role as Chickie; 2001), *Kim Possible* (4 episodes; voice; 2002–07), *All About the Andersons* ("It's My Son, I Can Raise Him If I Want To," 2003), *Half & Half* ("The Big Practice What You Preach Episode," 2004), *JAG* ("Unknown Soldier," 2005), *Bid Whist Party Throwdown* (2005), *Barbershop* (3 episodes in the role of Mae; "Madonna Is a Ho," "Family Business," "Debates and Dead People," 2005), *Living in TV Land* (2006), *The Marvelous Misadventures of Flapjack* (voice; 2008).

Saldana, Zöe Born in New Jersey, June 19, 1978.

Zöe Saldana may become best known as the woman who replaced Nichelle Nichols as Uhura in the *Star Trek* series — but she had a varied career before that, and will no doubt continue to have one in the wake of her Uhura role.

Born Zöe Yadira Zaldaña Nazario, she is of Dominican heritage. The family moved from New Jersey to Queens, New York, then her father died in a car accident when she was a child and the family moved to the Dominican Republic for seven years. There Saldana studied at the ECOS Espacio de Danza Dance Academy, returning to the United States after her sophomore year in high school. She performed with Manhattan's Faces theater troupe, which presented productions about various social issues geared toward the teen audience.

Her first film role was as the ballerina Eva in *Center Stage* (2000), followed by a role in the Britney Spears vehicle *Crossroads* (2002) and a part in what turned out to be her early breakthrough film, *Drumline* (2002), a surprise box office hit about competing school bands. She had a small role as the pirate girl Anamaria in the mammoth success *Pirates of the Caribbean: The Curse of the Black Pearl* (2003).

After a series of indifferent films, she was cast in two of the biggest science fiction films of the era: J.J. Abrams' rebooting of *Star Trek* and James Cameron's *Avatar* (both 2009). Avatars are aliens who can possess human bodies. In *Avatar*, Saldana plays the alien Neytiri Nazachema, who is at first betrayed by the hero Jake, a paralyzed ex-marine, but then he comes to fall in love with her. The mega-budget spectacle was shot in imax 3d, and Saldana's character is a motion capture computer generated entity.

Star Trek goes back to the early days of the Enterprise officers and crew with a new cast of young actors stepping into the shoes of the iconic originals. Saldana's small screen roles have included guest spots on *Law & Order* (1999), *Law & Order: Special Victims Unit* (2004), and *Six Degrees* (2006).

Feature Films including Video and TV Movies: *Center Stage* (2000), *Get Over It* (2001), *Snipes* (2001), *Crossroads* (2002), *Drumline* (2002), *Pirates of the Caribbean: The Curse of the Black Pearl* (2003), *The Terminal* (2004), *Haven* (2004), *Temptation* (2004), *Constellation* (2005), *Guess Who* (2005), *Dirty Deeds* (2005), *La Maldicion del Padre Cardona* (2005), *Premium* (2006), *Ways of the Flesh* (aka *The Heart Specialist*, 2006), *Blackout* (2007), *After Sex* (2007), *Vantage Point* (2008), *The Skeptic* (2008), *Star Trek* (2009), *Avatar* (2009), *Bone Deep* (2010).

TV: *Law & Order* ("Merger," 1999), *Late Night with Conan O'Brien* (2003), *HBO First Look* ("Inside *The Terminal*," 2004), *Law & Order: Special Victims Unit* ("Criminal," 2004), *Los 50 mas bellos de People en espanola* (2005), *Punk'd* (2005), *106 & Park Top 10 Live* (2005), *Premios Fox Sports* (2006), *Six Degrees* (2 episodes; "What Are the Odds?" "What You Wish For," 2006), *The Late Late Show with Craig Ferguson* (2007), *19th Annual GLAAD Media Awards* (2008).

Diana Sands in ***Doctors' Wives*** (1971).

Sands, Diana Born in the Bronx, New York, August 22, 1934; died September 21, 1973, New York, New York.

Diana Patricia Sands was a beloved breakthrough actress of the 1950s–1970s who helped expand the kind of roles a black woman could play. Sands came from a middle class background: her mother was a milliner and her father was a carpenter. She was a graduate of Manhattan's High School of the Performing Arts.

Although she never duplicated her Broadway success in films, her brilliance is on display in the film version of *A Raisin in the Sun* (1961), where she recreated her role of Beneatha Younger from the original Broadway production.

Lorraine Hansberry's *A Raisin in the Sun* tells the story of a black family living on Chicago's South Side. When the family receives a check for $10,000 from the deceased Mr. Younger's insurance policy, the question of just what to do with the money causes serious soul searching and conflict. Beneatha is the Afrocentric, "militant" family member. This was a plum role for Sands, who knew a thing or two about what motivated Beneatha, and the play is now widely regarded as the vanguard production of black theater.

Sands worked as a keypunch operator for Con Edison while waiting for her acting career to take off. She made her professional debut — and a statement — by playing Juliet in the off–Broadway production *An Evening with Will Shakespeare* (1953), and a year later was in a production of Bernard Shaw's *Major Barbara* (in the late sixties she played Joan of Arc in the Repertory Theater at Lincoln Center production of Shaw's *Saint Joan*).

Other early stage appearances are *Land Beyond the River* (1957), and singing roles in *The Egg and I* (1958) and *Another Evening with Harry Stones* (1961), which also featured a young Barbra Streisand, who played the role of the prostitute Doris in the film version of *The Owl and the Pussycat*, originated by Sands on Broadway.

The list of awards and award nominations for Sands' theater work is a long one, including the Outer Critics Circle Award for *A Raisin in the Sun* (1959); a Theatre World Award for *Tiger, Tiger Burning Bright* (1962); two successive Tony Award nominations for James Baldwin's *Blues for Mister Charlie* (1964) and *The Owl and the Pussycat* (1965); and an Obie Award for *The Living Premise* (1964).

There was immense controversy — emphasis on "immense" — over Sands playing the role of a black prostitute involved romantically with the uptight, nerdy white character played by Alan Alda in *The Owl and the Pussycat*. The role had originally been written for a white woman, and no mention of Sands' color was written into the play.

Even though motion pictures did not provide her with the richness of roles she had in the theater, Sands did have an opportunity to make several memorable films. *The Landlord* (1970) heads the list. She played Francine Marie Johnson, resident of a rundown apartment building in Brooklyn, who gets impregnated by the naïve young white landlord who has bought the building. Racial politics abound in this cynical but very funny comedy. In *Doctors' Wives* (1971) she is Helen Straughn, a nurse who is the mistress of a married white doctor (Richard Crenna). Helen's drug problem only adds to her emotional turmoil as the "other woman." Sands never looked more beautiful on screen than she does here, and she gives an Academy Award–level performance in what is simply a big budget, big cast soap opera. (Unfortunately, great performances in bad films always get overlooked come Oscar nomination time.) *Georgia, Georgia* (1972) is an interracial love story with a screenplay by Maya Angelou. Georgia (Sands) is a singer who goes to Sweden to perform and falls in love with a Vietnam war deserter (Dirk Benedict). This is an interesting low-budget film in which Sands runs the emotional gamut, even though there is no chemistry with her bland co-star.

Another interesting low-budget film featuring she is 1963's *An Affair of the Skin*, written and directed by former documentary filmmaker Ben Maddow. Maddow's documentary influence is plain to see in his use of natural light and street locations. The film was not a critical or financial success at the time of its release, so Maddow re-released it in 1973 with a new title (*Love as Disorder*) and new off-screen narration. Sands plays a photographer observing the romantic ins-and-outs of the film's various characters.

In her last two screen appearances, the B-movies *Willie Dynamite* and *Honey Baby* (both 1974), we again see how Sands gave 100 percent to every role she played. In the former, she is a committed social worker, in the latter, she takes a rare comic turn as a reluctant adventuress: small films, large performances. Even though *Honey Baby* was clearly unfinished at the time of Sands' death — it has a lot of expository narration and still doesn't make much narrative sense — we are nevertheless grateful to see her final screen performance.

Her television credits yielded two Emmy Award nominations — for the "Who Do You Kill" episode of *East Side/West Side* (1963), in which she was the mother of a child bitten by a rat, and a special about black poetry, *Beyond the Blues* (1964). She also had guest star roles in major series such as *I Spy*, *The Outer Limits* and *Medical Center*. Sands had recurring roles on three series: Ollie Sutton on *The Nurses* (aka *The Doctors and the Nurses*) in 1964; Irene Rush on a 4-episode *Dr. Kildare* story arc (1966); and Cousin Sara on *Julia* (1970–71).

She was engaged to director Kurt Baker at the time of her death at age 39 from leiomyosarcoma, a very rare cancer that arises from muscle tissue and can occur anywhere in the body. She was preparing to star in the film *Claudine* (1974) at the time of her death. She was replaced by Diahann Carroll, who received an Oscar nomination for the role.

Feature Films including TV Movies: *Caribbean* (1952), *Four Boys and a Gun* (1957), *A Face in the Crowd* (1957), *A Raisin in the Sun* (1961), *An Affair of the Skin* (aka *Love as Disorder*; 1963), *Ensign Pulver* (1964), *The Landlord* (1970), *Doctors' Wives* (1971), *Georgia, Georgia* (1972), *The Living End* (TV; 1972), *Two's Company* (TV; 1972), *Willie Dynamite* (1974), *Honeybaby, Honeybaby* (aka *Honey Baby*; 1974).

TV: *East Side/West Side* ("Who Do You Kill," 1963), *The Outer Limits* ("The Mice," 1964), *Breaking Point* ("Never Trouble Trouble Till Trouble Troubles You," 1964), *The Nurses* (3 episodes in the role of Ollie Sutton; "Nurse Is a Feminine Noun," "The Imperfect Prodigy," "The Family Resemblance," 1964), *Dr. Kildare* (4 episodes in the role of Irene Rush; "A Cry from the Street," "Gratitude Won't Pay the Bills," Adrift in a Sea of Confusion," "These Hands That Heal," 1966), *I Spy* ("Turkish Delight," 1966), *The Fugitive* ("Dossier on a Diplomat," 1967), *ABC Stage 67* ("A Time for Laughter: A Look at Negro Humor in America"), *Snap Judgment* (1967), *Bracken's World* ("Will Freddy's Real Father Please Stand Up?" 1970), *Julia* (3 episodes in the role of Cousin Sara; "Sara's Second Part," "Cousin of the Bride," "Courting Time," 1970–71), *Medical Center* ("The Nowhere Child," 1971), *The Tonight Show Starring Johnny Carson* (1971), *The Flip Wilson Show* (2 segments; 1972–73), Free to Be ... You and Me (1974), *Lorraine Hansberry: The Black Experience in the Creation of Drama* (archival; 1975).

Scott, Hazel Born in Port au Spain, Trinidad and Tobago, June 11, 1920; died October 2, 1981, New York, New York.

Pianist and singer Hazel Scott was the first African American woman to have her own network TV show, *The Hazel Scott Show*, on the long-defunct but once prominent DuMont Network, from July to September 1950. She also appeared in feature films, including *Rhapsody in Blue* (1945), *Broadway Rhythm* (1944), *Something to Shout About* (1943), *The Heat's On* (1943) and *I Dood It* (1943).

Her mother, Alma, was a musician and leader of the All-Woman Orchestra, which Scott joined as a teenager, playing piano and trumpet. Her family moved to New York City when she was four years old. She was a child prodigy pianist and received training at the Juilliard School, later performing at Carnegie Hall. Her style of playing was the stride–boogie woogie technique so popular in the 1940s. By 1936, she was a star on the Mutual Broadcasting System at age 16. She played at the world-famous Roseland Dance Hall, jammed with the Count Basie Orchestra, was the opening act at Barney Josephson's Café Society Uptown, and toured Europe as well as the U.S. She appeared on Broadway in *Singing Out the News* and *Priorities of 1942*.

Scott's biggest hit was "Tico, Tico." Other signature songs included "There's Gonna Be a Great Day" and "Hazel's Boogie Woogie." Her most renowned album was *Relaxed Piano Moods* (with Charles Mingus and Max Roach; 1955). She was one of the many victims of Senator Joseph McCarthy in the 1950s. "Leftist" equaled "Communist" in the popular thinking of that era, and the McCarthy "witch hunt" was relentless until a saner perspective eventually prevailed.

She lived in Paris for five years in the 1960s. Upon her return, she acted on the TV programs *Julia* and *The Bold Ones* (both 1967). Scott was married to the charismatic congressman the Reverend Adam Clayton Powell, Jr., from 1945 to 1956; they had one child. She died of cancer at age 61. In 1978, she was inducted into the Black Filmmaker's Hall of Fame.

Feature Films including TV Movies: *Something to Shout About* (1943), *I Dood It* (1943), *The Heat's On* (1943), *Broadway Rhythm* (1944), *Rhapsody in Blue* (1945), *Le desordre et la nuit* (*The Night Affair*; 1958), *Une balle dans le canon* (*A Bullet in the Gun Barrel*; 1958), *Dead Ringer* (1964).

TV: *Toast of the Town* (2 segments; 1949–50), *The Hazel Scott Show* (1950), *Songs for Sale* (1952), *La grand farandole* (1962), *Aquì el segunda programa* (1966), *Trial Run* (1969), *CBS Playhouse* ("The Experiment," 1969), *The Bold Ones: The New Doctors* ("If I Can't Sing," 1970), *Brown Sugar* (archival; miniseries; 1986), *Scandalize My Name: Stories from the Blacklist* (archival; 1998),

Mamy scopitone: L'age d'Or du clip (archival; 2005).

Simms, Hilda Born in Minneapolis, Minnesota, April 15, 1918; died February 6, 1994, Buffalo, New York.

Hilda Simms was born Ethel Moses into a large family with three sisters (Evelyn, Laura and Rose) and two brothers (Richard and Emil). Primarily known as a theater actress, she dabbled in films and television, and made a lasting mark as a civil rights official for the state of New York. A graduate of South High School in Minneapolis, she migrated to New York and joined the American Negro Theater, where she was a publicist and doubled as the props and sound effects person.

She worked her way up to appear in the play *Three's a Family*, and then was given the keynote role of her career, the title role in *Anna Lucasta*. The play moved to Broadway starting in 1944 and ran for an impressive 950 performances. *Anna Lucasta* was a groundbreaking production about a young woman who drifts into a life of prostitution and who is haunted by a contentious relationship with her father. Later Broadway appearances include the searing drug drama *The Cool World* (1960), *Tambourines to Glory* (1963) and a revival of *The Madwoman of Chaillot* (1970). She gained international fame as a chanteuse in Paris nightclubs in the early fifties.

Simms was the creative rights director of New York State's Human Rights Division in the sixties. She called attention to and combated discrimination against black performers. She also earned a master's degree in education and worked for drug treatment programs in New York.

She played Nurse Ayres, a neurologist, on the CBS series *The Nurses* (1962–63). Her only two feature appearances were in *The Joe Louis Story* (as Marva Trotter Louis; 1953) and the murder mystery *Black Widow* (as Anne; 1954). She married Richard Angerolla in 1948. Her death was the result of pancreatic cancer.

Feature Films: *The Joe Louis Story* (1953), *Black Widow* (1954).

TV: *The Philco Television Playhouse* ("A Man Is Ten Feet Tall," 1955), *The Nurses* (3 episodes in the recurring role of Nurse Ayres; "Two Black Candles," "Image of Angela," "Night Sounds," 1962–63).

Simon, Josette Born in Leicester, Leicestershire, England, 1960.

British actress Josette Patricia Simon was trained at London's Central School of Speech and Drama. Simon is of Antiguan descent, best known for her role of Dayna Mellanby in seasons three and four of the science fiction series *Blake's 7* (1980–81). Danya is the daughter of Federation fugitive Hal Mellanby. The corrupt galactic Federation, with Earth at its center, drugs citizens into mindless submission. Other television work includes an episode of the detective series *Poirot* and a 1995 TV production of *Henry V.*

She has been a frequent performer with the Royal Shakespeare Company and the Royal National Theatre. She was nominated for a Best Actress Award for her performance in Royal Shakespeare Company production *Golden Girls*. She is also renowned for her role of Maggie in a revival of Arthur Miller's *After the Fall* (considering that the role was based on Miller's late wife Marilyn Monroe, this is a refreshing example of colorblind casting). She received the London Critics Circle Award and the London *Evening Standard* Theatre Award for this performance.

She received the Order of the British Empire for her acting career in 2000 and was given an honorary master's degree from the University of Leicester in 1995. She has been married to Mark Padmore since 1996; they have one child.

Feature Films including Video and TV Movies: *Aftermath* (1980), *Warlord* (1981), *Harem* (TV; 1986), *Cry Freedom* (1987), *Milk and Honey* (1988), *Somewhere to Run* (TV; 1989), *A Child from the South* (TV; 1991), *Seekers* (TV; 1992), *Bridge of Time* (TV; 1997), *The Extraordinary Equiano* (narrator; TV; 2007).

TV: *Play for Today* ("King," 1984), *Blake's 7* (recurring role of Dayna Mellanby; 1980–81), *Pob's Programme* (1985), *Thompson* (series regular; 1988), *Nice Town* (miniseries; 1992), *Performance* ("Henry IV," 1995), *Bodyguards* (1996), *Kavanagh QC* ("Blood Money," 1997), *Silent Witness* ("Divided Loyalties," 1998), *Dalziel & Pascoe* ("Bones and Silence," 1998), *Polterguests* (1999), *Celeb* ("The Guest," 2002), *Whitney Houston: The True Story* (narrator; 2002), *The Last Detective* ("Lofty," 2003), *The Way We Went Wild* (narrator; 2004), *Agatha Christie: Poirot* ("The Mystery of the Blue Train," 2005), *Midsomer Murders* ("Last Year's Model," 2006), *Casualty* (2 episodes; "The Sunny Side of the Street," Parts I and II, 2006),

Lewis ("Expiation," 2007), *The Whistleblowers* ("No Child Left Behind," 2007), *The Bill* ("Witness: Breaking Point," 2008), *Skins* (2008).

Sinclair, Madge Born in Kingston, Jamaica, April 28, 1938; died December 20, 1995, Los Angeles, California.

Madge Dorita Sinclair (née Walters) taught school in Jamaica until the age of 30. Finally she decided that she had to pursue her dream of being an actress. Her two boys stayed with their police officer father in Jamaica and she made the pilgrimage to New York to become an actress. She officially divorced Royston Sinclair in 1969, and the boys, Garry and Wayne, joined her in New York. She eventually acted with the New York Shakespeare Festival/Joe Papp's Public Theater, the holy grail of the New York theater scene at that time.

Sinclair was nominated for an Emmy for her role of Belle, wife of Kunte Kinte and grandmother of Chicken George in the epic ABC miniseries *Roots* (1977). She was diagnosed with leukemia in 1979 not long after being hired as a cast member on the medical series *Trapper John, MD*, but lived for many years after the diagnosis. In fact, she had a long run in the role of Nurse Ernestine Shoop (1980–86).

She was married to her second husband, Dean Compton, from 1982 until the time of her death in 1995. Sinclair loved life and squeezed every creative ounce out of her final years. In 1988 she was Queen Aoleon opposite King Jaffe Joffer (James Earl Jones) in Eddie Murphy's smash comedy success *Coming to America*. She also teamed with Jones in the series *Gabriel's Fire*, which earned her an Emmy for Best Actress in a Dramatic Series in 1991.

Star Trek fans know her well as the captain of the USS *Saratoga* in *Star Trek IV: The Voyage Home* (1986) and as Geordi La Forge's mother, the captain of the USS *Hera*, in the "Interface" episode of *Star Trek: The Next Generation* (1993). Her last film work was as the voice of Sarabi, Simba's mother, in Disney's animated classic *The Lion King* (1994). Her frequent collaborator, James Earl Jones, was the voice of Simba's father.

Sinclair wore many hats besides that of an actress: she was also a successful art dealer, owner of an income tax service, and chairman of the clothing manufacturer Madge Walters Sinclair, Inc.

Madge Sinclair with Doug McKeon in *Uncle Joe Shannon* (1978).

Feature Films including TV Movies: *The Witches of Salem: The Horror and the Hope* (1972), *I Love You, Goodbye* (TV; 1974), *Conrack* (1974), *Cornbread, Earl and Me* (1975), *Guess Who's Coming to Dinner* (TV; 1975), *Almos' a Man* (TV; 1976), *I Will, I Will ... for Now* (1976), *Leadbelly* (1976), *Convoy* (1978), *One in a Million: The Ron LeFlore Story* (TV; 1978), *Uncle Joe Shannon* (1978), *I Know Why the Caged Bird Sings* (TV; 1979), *High Ice* (TV; 1980), *Jimmie B. and Andre* (TV; 1980), *Guyana Tragedy: The Story of Jim Jones* (TV; 1980), *Star Trek IV: The Voyage Home* (1986), *Look Away* (TV; 1987), *Coming to America* (1988), *Divided We Stand* (TV; 1988), *The End of Innocence* (1990), *The Orchid House* (TV; 1991), *Jonathan: The Boy Nobody Wanted* (TV; 1992), *The Man with Three Wives* (TV; 1993), *The Lion King* (voice; 1994).

TV: *The Waltons* ("The Visitor," 1974), *Joe Forrester* ("Stake Out," 1975), *Doctors' Hospital* ("Come at Last to Love," 1975), *Medical Story* ("Wasteland," 1975), *Executive Suite* ("Re: Who Shall Hall Bring Mercy?" 1976), *Roots* (miniseries; 1977), *Serpico* ("One Long Tomorrow," 1977), *Grandpa Goes to Washington* (recurring role as Madge; 1978), *ABC Afterschool Specials* (2 episodes; "The Rag Tag Champs," "Backwards: The

Riddle of Dyslexia," 1978 and 1984), *The White Shadow* ("Sudden Death," 1979), *Roots: The Next Generations* (archival; 1979), *Trapper John, M.D.* (recurring role as Nurse Ernestine Shoop; 1980–86), *I Love Liberty* (1982), *19th Annual NAACP Image Awards* (1987), *Starman* ("The Test," 1987), *Ohara* (recurring role as Gussie Lemmons; 1987), *Midnight Caller* ("Take Back the Streets," 1989), *Gideon Oliver* ("By the Waters of Babylon," 1989), *Roseanne* ("Guilt by Disassociation," 1989), *21st Annual NAACP Image Awards* (1989), *Gabriel's Fire* ("To Catch a Con," Part I, 1990), *Pro and Cons* (3 episodes in the role of Josephine Austin; 1991–92), *L.A. Law* ("Diet, Diet My Darling," 1992), *Tales from the Crypt* ("Curiosity Killed," 1992), *Alex Haley's Queen* (miniseries; 1993), *Star Trek: The Next Generation* ("Interface," 1993), *A Century of Women* (1994), *Me and the Boys* (recurring role as Mary; 1994).

Smith, Bessie Born in Chattanooga, Tennessee, April 15, 1894; died September 26, 1937, Clarksdale, Mississippi.

Bessie Smith was born Elizabeth Smith and was the daughter of Laura (Owens) Smith and William Smith. Her father was a laborer and part-time minister who died when Smith was very young. Her mother passed when she was nine, so it fell to her older sister Viola to raise the other sisters and brothers. Smith and her brother Andrew became street performers to raise money. In 1912, she was hired as a dancer for the Moses Stokes troupe; her brother Clarence, who had left home in 1904, had already traveled with the troupe. By the early twenties, she made her first Broadway appearance in *How Come?* and began performing in East Coast black theaters.

Smith married Jack Gee, a security guard, in 1923. This was around the time Columbia started releasing her first recordings. She ended the stormy marriage in 1929, but there was never a legal divorce. By that time, she had become the highest paid and most renowned black performer in America. She later bonded for the remainder of her life with her common-law husband Richard Morgan.

She became known as the Empress of the Blues, and her best-selling Columbia recordings saw her accompanied by the top musicians of the day: Fletcher Henderson, Louis Armstrong, James P. Johnson, and many others.

In September 1937, Smith was severely injured in a car accident while traveling between Memphis and Clarksdale, Mississippi. She died at the Afro-American Hospital in Clarksdale within a matter of hours, after having her right arm amputated in an effort to save her life.

Her great songs included "Downhearted Blues" (1923), "St. Louis Blues" (1925) and "Empty Bed Blues" (1929). Smith is in the Blues Hall of Fame (1980), the Big Band and Jazz Hall of Fame (inducted in 1981), the Rock and Roll Hall of Fame (as an early influence; 1989), was given the Grammy Lifetime Achievement Award (1989), and was honored with a U.S. Commemorative Stamp in 1994.

Smith in included in this book because of her single appearance in a film. *St. Louis Blues* (1929) is a historically significant early two-reel talkie. It was directed by Dudley Murphy and filmed in Astoria, Queens, and shows her singing the W.C. Handy title song while accompanied by the Fletcher Henderson orchestra, the Hall Johnson Choir, and pianist James Johnson. Her charisma and dramatic eloquence was preserved for posterity, melding the fledgling art of the talking film with the essence of American popular music — and essentially setting the stage for the many black musicals to come. *St. Louis Blues* was later used as footage in *Bessie Smith* (1969), a tribute by filmmaker Charles Levine, with other Smith songs and a commentary included.

Feature Films including TV Movies: *St. Louis Blues* (1929), *A Huey P. Newton Story* (TV; archival; 2001).

TV: *Sanford and Son* ("Earthquake II"; archival; 1975), *Bessie Smith* (archival; 1969), *Before Stonewall* (archival; 1984), *Brown Sugar* (miniseries; archival; 1986), *The Ladies Sing the Blues* (archival; 1989), *That's Black Entertainment* (archival; 1990), *Bluesland: A Portrait in American Music* (archival; 1993), *The Century: America's Time* (archival; miniseries; 1999), *Jazz* (various segments; archival; 2001), *American Roots Music* ("When First Unto This Country"; archival; 2001); *It's Black Entertainment* (archival; 2002), *The Blues* (archival; 2003).

Video: *Hollywood Rhythm, Vol. 1: The Best of Jazz and Blues* (2001).

Smith, Dwan Born in Jackson, Tennessee.

Dwan Smith burned bright as one of the three Williams sisters in *Sparkle* (1976), the filmic forerunner to *Dreamgirls*, but her career was essentially over by the end of the seventies. The period story is about a girl group trying to make it in show business: Sparkle (Irene Cara), Sister (Lonette McKee), and Dolores (Smith). Dolores tries to get revenge on the gangster Satin (Tony King) who hooked Sister on cocaine. She seduces one of his men to set Satin up, but the sting backfires and Dolores decides to leave town and get away from the seedy world of show business. Although Cara and McKee continued to build on their careers after *Sparkle*, Smith was not able to do so. Or, like her character Dolores, maybe it was simply time for her to get out of the business.

Smith had a secondary role as Kendra in *The Brothers* (1979), unofficially based on the relationship between black radical Angela Davis and jailed Black Panther George Jackson (a subdued Bernie Casey). She was a flight attendant in the big budget *The Concorde ... Airport '79* (1979), the last — and least popular — entry in the *Airport* series that began in 1970. It was her last film role.

Her most conspicuous TV work was a recurring role on the well-reviewed but only marginally popular Lloyd Bridges cop drama *Joe Forrester* (1976–76). She also appeared on sitcoms like *Sanford and Son* and *The Jeffersons*. Her last work was a stint on the daytime soap *General Hospital* in 1987.

Feature Films Including TV Movies: *A Very Missing Person* (TV; 1972), *The Couple Takes a Wife* (TV; 1972), *Sparkle* (1976), *The Return of Joe Forrester* (aka *Cop on the Beat*, TV; 1975), *Brothers* (1977), *The Concorde ... Airport '79* (1979).

TV: *Room 222* (2 episodes; "The Valediction," "I Hate You, Silas Marner," 1970 and 1971), *Adam 12* ("The Adoption," 1972), *Emergency!* ("Audit," 1973), *Sanford and Son* ("Presenting the Three Degrees," 1973), *Joe Forrester* (recurring role as Jolene Jackson; 1975–76), *The Jeffersons* ("Lionel Gets the Business," 1978), *Barnaby Jones* ("The Final Victim," 1980), *General Hospital* (recurring role as Dr. Irma Foster; 1987).

Smith, Kellita Born in Chicago, Illinois, 1969.

Dignity, beauty and style are the watchwords for Kellita Smith. A bittersweet memory many of us have is of Smith on television reminiscing about Bernie Mac the day after his untimely death was announced. We saw an articulate, thoughtful woman sharing memories of the man she co-

Dwan Smith in *Sparkle* (1976).

starred with from 2001 to 2006 as his wife on *The Bernie Mac Show*.

Smith received numerous award nominations for her role of Wanda McCullough on the series, including four NAACP Image Awards for Outstanding Actress in a Comedy Series in consecutive years from 2003 to 2006, and two BET Award nominations for Outstanding Lead Actress in a Comedy Series in 2004–05.

Smith was the oldest of two siblings (her brother is named Eric). Her father served in Vietnam when Smith was a baby and was on tour of duty for 18 months. She moved to Oakland, California, with her mom, who had divorced Smith's father. She was educated at the Oakland Community Learning Center and graduated from Santa Rosa Junior College with a degree in political science in 1989. After secretarial and sales jobs, she decided to join an acting workshop. She got a role in the play *Tell It Like It Tiz* and toured with the show for two years. It was a great training ground for the young actress.

Although she has concentrated her career on television roles — guest starring on *The Parkers*, *Nash Bridges*, *NYPD Blue* and others, with recurring roles on *Martin*, *Malcolm & Eddie* and *The Jamie Foxx Show*— Smith has been in feature films as well. She made her film debut in *The Crossing Guard* (1995) with Jack Nicholson. She has also been featured in the black-oriented films *Kingdom Come* (2001), *Hair Show* (2004), *Roll Bounce* (2005), and *Three Can Play That Game* (2008).

Her theatrical work has centered around Los Angeles. She won an NAACP Theatre Award for Best Supporting Actress for her work in *Feelings* at the Hudson Theatre, and was nominated for the same award for *The Thirteenth Thorn* at the Complex Theatre. She was also in *No Place to Be Somebody* at the K.C. Theatre Company.

Feature Films including Video and TV Movies: *The Crossing Guard* (1995), *House Party 3* (20??), *Retiring Tatiana* (2000), *Masquerade* (TV; 2000), *Kingdom Come* (2001), *Hair Show* (2004), *Fair Game* (2005), *King's Ransom* (2005), *Roll Bounce* (2005), *Feel the Noise* (2007), *Three Can Play That Game* (2008).

TV: *Living Single* ("A Kiss Before Lying," 1993), *Hangin' with Mr. Cooper* ("Clothes Make the Man," 1994), *Martin* (recurring role of Tracy; 1994–95), *Sister, Sister* (3 episodes in the role of Tonya; "The Break-Up," "Thanksgiving in Hawaii," Parts I and II, 1995), *The Wayans Bros* ("Hearts and Flowers," 1996), *Dangerous Minds* ("Hair Affair," 1996), *Moesha* ("Women Are from Mars, Men Are from Saturn," 1996), *High Incident* ("Remote Control," 1997), *Malcolm & Eddie* (4 episodes in the role of Danielle; "Jugglin'," "Everynight Fever," "The Commercial," "Swappin'," 1997), *The Parent 'Hood* ("Zaria Peterson's Day Off," 1997), *The Jamie Foxx Show* (5 episodes in the role of Cherise; "The Employee Formerly Known As Prince," "Ain't Nothin' Happenin' Captain," "We Got No Game," "Fire and Desire," Parts I and II, 1997–99), *The Steve Harvey Show* ("Little Stevie Blunder," 1999), *The Parkers* ("And the Band Plays On," 1999), *For Your Love* ("The Special Delivery," 2000), *Nash Bridges* ("Kill Joy," 2001), *NYPD Blue* ("Under Covers," 2001), *The Bernie Mac Show* (recurring role of Wanda McCullough; 2001–06), *The 4th Annual Family Television Awards* (2002), *The Award Show Awards Show* (archival; 2003), *The Late Late Show with Craig Kilborn* (2003), *Biography* ("Bernie Mac: TV's Family Man," 2003), *The 6th Annual Family Television Awards* (2004), *35th NAACP Image Awards* (2004), *BET Comedy Awards* (2004), *TV Guide Close Up: From Comedy Club to Primetime* (2004), *Tavis Smiley* (2005), *Baisden After Dark* (2007), *CBS Early Show* (2008), *Larry King Live* (2008).

Video/DVD: *14th Annual Inner City Destiny Awards* (2006).

Smith, Mamie Born in Cincinnati, Ohio, May 26, 1883; died October 30, 1946, New York, New York.

Kellita Smith, Jack Nicholson and Priscilla Barnes in *The Crossing Guard* (1995).

Born Mamie Robinson, Mamie Smith was a noted blues singer who appeared in some "race films," mostly in the period 1939–41. Her recording of "Crazy Blues" (1920), which sold a million copies in one year, was inducted into the Grammy Hall of Fame in 1994 and was selected for preservation in the National Recording Registry of the Library of Congress in 2005. Smith was the first to record vocal blues songs, to tap into the hitherto ignored black audience for "race records," and to set the stage for the black music recording industry.

She appeared in the musical revue *Made in Harlem* in 1918. In 1923 she starred in the popular West Coast musical *Struttin' Along* (which also starred Carolynne Snowden). She toured throughout Europe with her orchestra, Mamie Smith & Her Jazz Hounds, with the *Struttin' Along Review*. She recorded for Okeh Records throughout the twenties and then for Victor.

Her first film appearance was in the early sound short *Jail House Blues* (1929). She returned to films in 1939 to appear in *Paradise in Harlem*, produced by her husband, Jack Goldberg. Smith was Madame Mamie, bar owner. A comedian witnesses a mob killing and flees town — but an opportunity to go serious and play Othello lures him back. In *Murder on Lenox Avenue* (1941), Smith is Hattie in a story of crime and corruption in Harlem. *Stolen Paradise* (1941) is the story of a troubled young soldier who eventually decides to join the priesthood. Smith had a small role. Her first husband was singer William "Smitty" Smith, whom she married in 1912.

Feature Films: *Paradise in Harlem* (1939), *Sunday Sinners* (1940), *Murder on Lenox Avenue* (1941), *Stolen Paradise* (1941).

TV: *American Roots Music* ("When First Unto This Country," 2001), *A Huey P. Newton Story* (archival; 2001), *The Blues* ("Warming By the Devil's Fire," 2003).

Shorts: *Jail House Blues* (1929).

Smith, Tasha Born in Camden, New Jersey, February 28, 1971.

She has been in a pair of Tyler Perry movies, *Daddy's Little Girls*, as the duplicitous Jennifer, and *Why Did I Get Married?* (both 2007), as Patricia, one of a three women (with Janet Jackson and Jill Scott) questioning their lives and marriages. She was Claire Plummer in *The Longshots* (2008), the mother of the Keke Palmer character, a girl who excels on the boys' football team. She was also in *Something Like a Business*, *Red Soil*, *ATL*, *The Good Mother*, *The Whole Ten Yards*, *Miles from Home*, *Playa's Ball*, and *Pastor Brown*.

Her most memorable role is perhaps as the drug addict Ronnie Boyce in the Emmy-winning HBO miniseries *The Corner* (2000). She has guest starred on *Without a Trace*, *Strong Medicine*, and *Girlfriends*. She has been a correspondent on *The Tyra Banks Show*. She appeared on *America's Next Top Model* as an acting coach for the models and runs Tasha Smith's Acting Workshop. Smith was raised by a single mother and has a twin sister, Sidra.

Feature Films including Video and TV Movies: *Twin Sitters* (1994), *Let It Be Me* (1995), *Max Q: Emergency Landing* (TV; 1998), *Chameleon II: Death Match* (1999), *Playas Ball* (2003), *The Whole Ten Yards* (2004), *Miles from Home* (2006), *ATL* (2006), *You, Me and Dupree* (2006), *Glass House: The Good Mother* (2006), *Love ... & Other 4 Letter Words* (2007), *Daddy's Little Girls* (2007), *Why Did I Get Married?* (2007), *The Longshots* (2008), *Something Like a Business* (2009), *Pastor Brown* (2009), *Red Soil* (2009).

TV: *Boston Common* (recurring role as Tasha King; 1996–97), *Chicago Hope* ("Brain Salad Surgery," 1997), *The Tom Show* (recurring role as Tanya Cole; 1997–98), *The Steve Harvey Show* ("Steve Don't Get Nun," 1999), *The Corner* (miniseries; 2000), *The Parkers* ("Knockout Times Two," 2001), *Intimate Portrait* ("Tisha Campbell-Martin," 2002), *Without a Trace* ("The Friendly Skies," 2003), *Nip/Tuck* ("Joan Rivers," 2004), *The Tyra Banks Show* (2 segments; 2005–06), *America's Next Top Model* (acting coach; 2 segments; 2004 and 2006), *Second Time Around* ("Big Bank, Little Bank," 2005), *Girlfriends* ("See J-Spot Run," 2005), *Angels Can't Help But Laugh* (documentary; 2007), *The Late Late Show with Craig Ferguson* (2007), *All of Us* ("The B-R-E-A-K-U-P," 2007).

Shorts: *My Purple Fur Coat* (2004).

Smollett, Jurnee Born in New York, New York, October 1, 1986.

Jurnee Diana Smollett (pronounced *small-let*) was a precocious child actress who seems to have been acting forever, although she is still a very young woman. Her performances as a child were vivid and indelible — especially in the modern classic *Eve's Bayou* (1998) — and she has made a successful transition to adult actress, despite having set the bar so high for herself. The daughter of Janet and Joel Smollett, she is of biracial heritage and comes from a family of young actors. Smollett's siblings are Jazz, Jocqui, Jake, Jojo, and Jussie.

Eve's Bayou is a haunting film. In rural Louisiana, 10-year-old Eve Batiste (Smollett) discovers her revered father Louis (Samuel L. Jackson), the town doctor, is having affairs with some of his patients, even though he is a pillar of the community and still loves his beautiful wife (Lynn Whitfield). Eve's sister Cisely (Meagan Good) tries to convince her that she is mistaken, but Eve keeps digging for the truth, knowing that it might destroy the family.

Smollett modeled diapers and appeared in a popular Pepsi commercial with football's Joe Montana at age three. She began her TV acting career with an ongoing role as Michelle Tanner's best friend Denise on *Full House* (the character was subsequently revived on *Hangin' with Mr. Cooper*).

She did a TV show with her brothers and sisters, *On Our Own* (1994–95). *On Our Own* did not find its audience, but it had a good initial premise. A family of seven brothers and sisters are raised by the eldest brother when their parents pass away. The authorities try to split up the children, but then things get a bit ludicrous when Josh Jerrico, the oldest brother, dresses in drag and tries to pass himself as an older aunt to the authorities. A kindly case worker sees through the ruse — it wasn't hard — and decides to help keep the family together. The drag aspect was wisely abandoned, and some characters were dropped and others added — but by then it was too late to save the show, even though Smollett was nominated for a Young Artist Award for her work.

Jurnee Smollett in *Eve's Bayou* (1998).

A more successful series role was on *Cosby* from 1998 to 2000, though it was the much less successful successor to *The Cosby Show* (the one everyone remembers). Smollett played a wise-beyond-her-years 11-year-old, also named Jurnee. She had a recurring role in the Wanda Sykes Comedy Central series *Wanda at Large* (2003). Guest star appearances have included *Strong Medicine*, *ER*, *House*, and *Grey's Anatomy*, on which she played a terminally ill girl.

Smollett has also done a lot of fine work in feature films. This includes *Jack* (her film debut, as Phoebe; with Robin Williams as a 10-year-old who looks 40 due to a rare aging disorder; 1996); *Beautiful Joe* (as Vivien; 2000); *Roll Bounce* (2005), a retro look at the "roller boogie" era, with Smollett as Tori, an ugly duckling who blossoms into a swan (she makes something of the role); and *Gridiron Gang* (as Danyelle Rollins; 2006). TV movies include *Selma, Lord, Selma* (1999), where she played a real life person, Sheyann Webb, a girl who befriended Rev. Martin Luther King during the march on Selma voting rights days of the sixties, and *Ruby's Bucket of Blood* (2001), as Emerald Delacroix, daughter of Ruby, a woman who falls in love with the white man who starts singing in her club.

She has been nominated for four NAACP Image Awards, winning three. She won Image Awards for Outstanding Actress in a Motion Picture for her role as student Samantha Brooke, part of the debating team in the Oprah Winfrey–produced *The Great Debaters* in 2008, which was nominated for a Golden Globe for Best Picture–Drama; and Outstanding Youth Actor/Actress for the *Cosby* series (in 1999 and 2000). She also won a Vision Award for her role on *Cosby*. She was nominated for Outstanding Youth Actor/Actress for *Eve's Bayou*. She was the winner of the Broadcast Film Critics Award for Best Performance by a Child Actor for *Eve's Bayou*, and also was nominated for a Young Artist Award for Best Performance in a Feature Film — Leading Young Actress for *Eve's Bayou*.

Smollet is active in the fight against hiv/aids; she spoke at the Ryan White Youth Conference (White was a beloved young AIDS victim). She is also on the board of Artists for a New South Africa (ANSA), an organization that is battling AIDS in Africa.

Feature Films including TV Movies: *Jack* (1996), *Eve's Bayou* (1997), *Selma, Lord, Selma* (TV; 1999), *Beautiful Joe* (2000), *Ruby's Bucket of Blood* (TV; 2001), *Roll Bounce* (2005), *Gridiron Gang* (2006), *The Great Debaters* (2007).

TV: *Sunday in Paris* (unsold pilot; 1991), *Hangin' with Mr. Cooper* (3 episodes in the recurring role of Denise Frazer; "Hangin' with Michele," "Please Pass the Jock," "Torn Between Two Teachers," 1992), *Martin* ("I Saw Gina Kissing Santa Claus," 1992), *Full House* (recurring role of Gina Frazer; 1992–94), *On Our Own* (recurring role of Jordee Jerrico; 1995), *NYPD Blue* ("Where's 'Swaldo?" 1996), *The Rosie O'Donnell Show* (2 segments; 1998), *Cosby* (recurring role of Jurnee; 1998–2000), *Happily Ever After: Fairy Tales for Every Child* ("Ali Baba and the 40 Thieves," 1999), *Strong Medicine* ("Positive," 2002), *ER* ("Next of Kin," 2002), *Wanda at Large* (recurring role as Holly Hawkins; 2003), *House* ("Fools for Love," 2006), *Kathy Griffin: My Life on the D-List* ("And the Award Goes To," 2008), *Grey's Anatomy* ("Freedom," 2008), *39th NAACP Image Awards* (2008).

Snowden, Carolynne (aka Snowden, Caroline)

Born in Oakland, California, January 16, 1900; died 1985.

Caroline (later Carolynne) Artiemessia Snowden had the ability and looks to be a superstar — and she refused to let the fact that she was black kill her dreams of Hollywood stardom. She was discovered in a high school production in San Francisco by the producing team of Fanchon and Marco. She began by dancing in the smoky jazz clubs of Los Angeles' Central Avenue. By the twenties she was a famous showgirl, blazing her way across the stage of Club Alabam and headlining at Culver City's Cotton Club, a whites-only establishment where her good looks garnered rapt attention and a world of respect. Who could resist an act called "Creole Carolyn Snowden with Her Dark-Town Tantilizers and Dancing Creoles"? Her friends of choice were the legendary Lafayette Players of Harlem, who toured and were known throughout the U.S.

Snowden's real dream was to break into Hollywood films — and she did, albeit slowly and with resistance. Like other black actresses after her, her sexuality was a weapon — a means to power. Her film debut was in Erich von Stroheim's *The Merry Widow* (1925) in an unbilled but conspicuous bit as a dancer, and she also appeared in von Stroheim's *The Wedding March* in 1928 as a prostitute. She had a private dressing room for *The Merry Widow*, getting her first taste of what it could be like to be a star. But after the von Stroheim films, maid roles were all that she was offered more often than not (*The Gilded Butterfly*, *The Jazz Singer*, *Nameless Men*) — although there were exceptions. She was in the one-reel short *Colored Syncopation* in 1927, directed by Bryan Foy and released through the Vitaphone Corporation. Another exception was *In Old Kentucky* (1927). As Lily May, she shared the first screen romance in a mainstream (indeed, big budget) Hollywood film with Stepin Fetchit as Highpockets.

After an appearance in *The Fox Movietone Follies of 1929*, Snowden's acting career was over except for an uncredited bit in *Playing Around* (1930). She performed at the annual meeting of the National Association for the Advancement of Colored People (NAACP) in Los Angeles in 1928 to help raise money and to entertain the attendees.

Feature Films: *The Merry Widow* (1925), *The Gilded Butterfly* (1926), *The First Year* (1926), *The Marriage Clause* (1926), *Orchids and Ermine* (1927), *The Jazz Singer* (1927), *In Old Kentucky* (1927), *The Devil's Skipper* (1928), *Nameless Men* (1928), *Sweet Sixteen* (1928), *The Wedding March* (1928), *Innocents of Paris* (1929), *The William Fox Movietone Follies of 1929* (1929), *Playing Around* (1930).

Speed, Carol

Born in Bakersfield, California, March 14, 1945.

Born Carolyn Stewart, Carol Speed had a picturesque early life that included the distinction of becoming the first black homecoming queen in Santa Clara County. She is the ultimate been there, done that girl. She is one of the queens of the blaxploitation film; she is a sharp social critic sensitive to the racism and lack of opportunity for talented artists in the film business; and she is a skillful writer (*Inside Black Hollywood, The Georgette Harvey Story*) acutely aware of the game playing and role playing in the publishing business.

She attended San Jose State University and San Jose City College, taught a drama course at the latter, and produced and directed a production of Sonia Sanchez's *The Bronx Is Next* with a student cast. She then received a scholarship to the San Francisco Conservatory Theatre — reportedly the first black student to do so.

Her film debut was as a blonde hooker in *The New Centurions* (1972). In *The Big Bird Cage* (1972), one of the early "women in prison" movies and an immensely popular drive-in movie, she was great as the savvy inmate Mickie. She was pimp Max Julien's girlfriend Lulu in one of the most famous and most financially successful blaxploitation films, *The Mack* (1973). She was the groupie Janyce in the white-oriented youth drama *Bummer* (1973). She was Samson's (Rockne Tarkington) lady friend in the rather pedestrian *Black Samson* (1974). *Savage!* (1972) was a Roger Corman New World picture filmed — like so many others — in the Philippines. Speed was an on-screen revolutionary, while genuine revolutionaries reportedly dotted the hills surrounding the shooting sites.

She played second fiddle to Rudy Ray Moore in the unfocused *Disco Godfather* (only the title was inspired; 1979). And she chewed up lots of scenery in *Abby* (1974), a black rip-off of *The Exorcist*, but fun nonetheless; it had a good cast — including William Marshall and Juanita Moore — but was done in by a low budget and a serious lack of sets. In recent years, she was in *Village Vengeance* (2006), a film about a community being terrorized by a rapist, and she was scheduled to appear in Quentin Tarantino's *Jackie Brown*— but that fell through at the last minute.

Carol Speed and James Iglehart in *Savage* (1974).

Speed added more to the frenetic culture of the sixties and seventies than just a spate of cult films. She appeared on seminal R&B–rock superstar Sly Stone's first album cover. At the start of her career, she was a backup singer and dancer for country star Bobbie ("Ode to Billie Jo") Gentry at Harrah's in Reno, Nevada. And she contributed to daytime culture as the Maidie Norman character's daughter on the famous soap *Days of Our Lives* in 1970.

Her varied TV credits include commercials (Gino's Pizza, Dolly Madison Pies, the Dodge Duster); sitcoms (*Sanford and Son, The Courtship of Eddie's Father, The Paul Lynde Show*); family shows (*Here Come the Brides*); and TV movies: *Love Hate Love* (1971) with Ryan O'Neal, *The Girls of Huntington House* (1973), and even *The Dating Game*.

Feature Films including TV Movies: *The Psychiatrist: God Bless the Children* (TV; 1970), *Love Hate Love* (TV; 1971), *The New Centurions* (1972), *Getting Away from It All* (TV; 1972), *The Big Bird Cage* (1972), *The Girls of Huntington House* (TV; 1973), *Bummer* (1973), *The Mack* (1973), *Savage!* (1973), *Dynamite Brothers* (1974), *Black Samson* (1974), *Abby* (1974), *Disco Godfather* (aka *Avenging Disco Godfather*, 1979), *American Pimp* (documentary; 1999), *Village Vengeance* (2006).

TV: *Sanford and Son* ("Here Comes the Bride, There Goes the Bride," 1972), *The Courtship of Eddie's Father* (1972), *The Paul Lynde Show* (1972–73), *Tenafly* (1973).

Spencer, Danielle

Born in North Trenton, New Jersey, June 24, 1965.

Danielle Spencer is best known from her childhood star days — she was nine when she began playing the role of the sharp-tongued, sarcastic Dee Thomas on *What's Happening!!* (1976–79), and in her reprisal of the role in that rarest of animals, a successful series sequel — *What's Happening Now!* (1985–86). Her catchphrase was "I'm gonna tell Mama!" She was so effective in this "bad seed" role that many viewers found Dee to be every bit as abrasive as the characters on the show did. She received a Nickelodeon TV Land Award in 2006 for the Brattiest Kid on TV and the Character Most in Need of a Time-Out.

Spencer was seriously injured in the car accident that took her stepfather's life in 1977. She recently started developing spinal problems, perhaps as a long-festering reaction to the accident (in which she had broken her arm and sustained facial injuries). She has had to receive therapy in order to walk again.

Spencer became a veterinarian in 1996, and has been married to Gary Fields since 1999. She played a veterinarian in *As Good as It Gets* (1997) and in the short *Peter Rabbit and the Crucifix* (2001). She was elected first national vice president of the Screen Actors Guild in 2005.

Feature Film: *As Good as It Gets* (1997).

TV: *What's Happening!!* (recurring role of Dee Thomas; 1976–79), *The Brady Bunch Hour* (1977), *NBC Special Treat* ("The Tap Dance Kid," 1978), *What's Happening Now!* (2 episodes, returning in the role of Dee Thomas; "Raj on the Run," "The Yard Sale," 1985 and 1986), *Christmas at Walt Disney World* (1987), *Soul Train* (1987), *Days of Our Lives* (2001), *Child Stars: Then and Now* (2003), *The 4th Annual TV Land Awards* (2006), *The 100 Greatest TV Quotes and Catchphrases* (2006), *TV Land Confidential* (2007).

Shorts: *Peter Rabbit and the Crucifix* (2001).

Stanis, Bern Nadette (aka Stanis, Bern-Nadette)

Born in Brooklyn, New York, December 22, 1953.

Bern Nadette Stanis is a graduate of Brooklyn's Erasmus Hall High School (1972). She appeared in a production of *The Three Faces of Eve* while there and was accepted at the Juilliard School of Performing Arts, receiving a bachelor of arts in drama. Her father was of West Indian heritage; her mother was from Louisiana. Stanis credits strong parental guidance as the foundation of her life.

She was the middle child — the female born between two brothers, the sometimes "in your face" Thelma Evans — on the hugely popular sitcom *Good Times*. Much of the show's longevity can be attributed to its strong cast (Jimmie Walker, Esther Rolle, John Amos, Ja'Net Dubois, Janet Jackson, Ralph Carter) and producer Norman Lear's insistence on creating a show that took place in a black milieu.

She appeared on an episode of *Girlfriends* that took an ingenious spin on her *Good Times* character. Will Dent (Reggie Hayes) is obsessed with the Thelma character, and has virtually convinced himself that she is real. Maya (Golden Brooks) informs him that Bern Nadette Stanis is her cousin — a flight of fancy by the show — and sets up a date for him. When they do meet, Stanis soon discovers that her real persona holds little interest for Will, so she morphs into the Thelma character — and for Will, this is the real deal. But Thelma charmed far more men (and women) than just Will. Stanis was chosen for the role of Thelma while competing in a beauty contest. She always found a way to put the exuberant, know-it-all J.J. in his place, and brought a little hint of black militancy to the sitcom world. Thelma is an important character in the historical development of black females on television.

Stanis is the author of the self-esteem book *Situations 101* (subtitled *Relationships: The Good, the Bad ... and the Ugly*), and has guest lectured at universities and other learning institutions, as well as at bookstore signings, throughout the U.S. She is also the author of the book of poems titled *For Men Only*. She is married to Kevin Fontana (her former husband is Terrence Redd), and has two daughters, Dior Revel and Brittany Rose Cole.

Feature Films including Video and TV Movies: *Hidden Blessings* (TV; 2000), *Land of the Free?* (2004), *Still 'Bout It* (2004), *The Engagement: My Phamily BBQ 2* (2006), *The Adventures of Umbweki* (2008).

TV: *Good Times* (recurring role of Thelma Evans Anderson; 1974–79), *Tattletales* (1975), *The Love Boat* (1980), *What's Happening Now!* ("Married or Not," 1985), *Family Reunion: A Gospel Music Celebration* (1988), *The Cosby Show* ("Adventures in Babysitting," 1991), *The Geraldo Rivera Show* (1992), *Good News* ("The Baby on the Doorstep," 1997), *The Wayans Bros.* ("Unspoken Token," 1997), *The Parent 'Hood* ("Mommy Dearest," 1999), *E! True Hollywood Story* ("Good Times," 2000), *Girlfriends* ("Where Everyone Knows My Name," 2003), *TV Land Confidential* (3 segments; "Breakout and Disappearing Star," "Changing Times and Trends," Oddballs and Original Characters," 2005–07), *BET Awards 2006*, *The 4th Annual TV Land Awards* (2006).

Video/DVD: *TV in Black: The First Fifty Years* (archival; 2004).

Stewart, Tonea (aka Stewart, Tommie) Born in Greenwood, Mississippi, February 3, 1947.

Tonea Stewart is an educator and actress who has concentrated on TV movies, but has done series guest star work as well (as Aunt Etta Kibbe on *In the Heat of the Night* from 1991 to 1993 and guest starring on *Matlock, ER, Walker, Texas Ranger*, and *Touched by an Angel*). She was associate producer of the TV movie *The Rosa Parks Story* (2002), in which she also acted. She also acted in the following TV movies: Maya Angelou's *I Know Why the Caged Bird Sings* (TV; 1979), *Don't Look Back: The Story of Leroy "Satchel" Page* (TV; 1981), *A Passion for Justice: The Hazel Brannon Smith Story* (TV; 1994), *Leave of Absence* (TV; 1994), and *Mama Flora's Family* (TV; 1998). Her most outstanding theatrical features are *Mississippi Burning* (as Mrs. Walker; 1988) and *A Time to Kill* (as Gwen Hailey; 1996).

The daughter of Hattie Juanita (née Leonard) and Thomas Ezekiel Harris, she was a high school teacher in Jackson, Mississippi, taught speech at Jackson State University, and became director of theater arts at Alabama State University. She is a graduate of Jackson State University with an arts degree in speech and theater. She received a master's degree in theater arts from the University of California at Santa Barbara and a doctorate in theater arts from Florida State University (the first black woman to do so).

She and her husband, Allen Stewart, have four children: two sons, a daughter and an adopted goddaughter. She was narrator of the memorable *Remembering Slavery* Public Radio International program in 1998.

Feature Films including Video and TV Movies: *Nightmare in Badham County* (TV; 1976), *I Know Why the Caged Bird Sings* (TV; 1979), *Don't Look Back: The Story of Leroy "Satchel" Paige* (TV; 1981), *Mistress of Paradise* (TV; 1981), *Courtship* (1987), *Mississippi Burning* (1988), *Unconquered* (TV; 1989), *Caroline?* (TV; 1990), *Love Hurts* (1990), *White Lie* (TV; 1991), *Livin' Large!* (1991), *Body Snatchers* (1993), *A Passion for Justice: The Hazel Brannon Smith Story* (TV; 1994), *Leave of Absence* (TV; 1994), *One Christmas* (TV; 1994), *Gramps* (TV; 1995), *The Sister-in-Law* (TV; 1995), *A Time to Kill* (1996), *My Stepson, My Lover* (TV; 1997), *Mama Flora's Family* (TV; 1998), *Hood Rat* (2001), *The Rosa Parks Story* (TV; 2002), *Baby of the Family* (2002), *Roper and Goodie* (2003), *Confessions of a Florist* (2003), *Constellation* (2005), *Love ... & Other 4 Letter Words* (2007), *Mississippi Damned* (2009).

TV: *Story of a Marriage* (1987), *American Playhouse* ("Courtship," 1987), *In the Heat of the Night* (recurring role as Aunt Etta Kibbe; 1991–93), *So Long on Lonely Street* (1988), *Hallmark Hall of Fame* ("Caroline?" 1990), "*Matlock* (2 episodes; "The Juror," "The Haunted," 1993), *ER* ("Middle of Nowhere," 1999), *Walker, Texas Ranger* (2 episodes; "Trial of LaRue," "Rise to the Occasion," 1997 and 1999), *Touched by an Angel* ("Living the Rest of My Life," 2000), *Still Holding On: The Music of Dorothy Love Coates and the Original Gospel Harmonettes* (narrator; 2000).

Stickney, Phyllis Yvonne Born in Little Rock, Arkansas.

Comedienne, actress, motivational lecturer, author, poet, fashion designer, world class beauty: these are all facets of Phyllis Yvonne Stickney. Her groundbreaking comedy routines at the Apollo Theater were a selling point for the long-running *Showtime at the Apollo* variety series. She made her television miniseries debut in Oprah Winfrey's *The Women of Brewster Place* (1989) as single mother Cora Lee. Her talents deeply impressed Bill Cosby, and she was a guest star on *The Cosby Show, Another World, New York Undercover, Linc's* (a recurring role as Yvette) and *Law & Order*. She was a regular, as well as a writer and creative consultant, on the short-lived ABC series *New Attitude* (1990). She played Yvonne St. James, who runs a beauty salon with her sister (Sheryl Lee Ralph). It was a good show with a good cast (including musician Morris Day), but it only lasted six episodes. She was on the PBS *Great Performances* presentation of George C. Wolfe's *The Colored Museum* (1991), and she was spotlighted on HBO's *Mo' Funny: The History of Blacks in Comedy* (1993).

Film roles include *New Jack City* (as Prosecuting Attorney Hawkins; 1991), *Jungle Fever* (as Nilda; 1991), *Malcolm X* (as Honey; 1992), *What's Love Got to Do with It* (as Alline Bullock, elder sister of Annie; 1993), and *How Stella Got Her Groove Back* (as Mrs. Shakespeare, mother of Winston, the young Jamaican man Stella Payne falls in love with; 1998), *Talkin' Dirty After Dark* (as Aretha, in a comedy about stand-up comics with Martin Lawrence; 1991); *The Inkwell* (as Dr. Wade; 1994); and *Die Hard with a Vengeance* (as Wanda Shepherd; 1995); and *Big Ain't Bad* (a black romantic comedy, as Mrs. Jordan; 2002).

Stickney is an accomplished writer who produced "The Upper Room," a weekly poet and writer's workshop in Los Angeles and New York, as well as *The Comedy Connection*, a weekly production at New York's resurrected Cotton Club in 1991. In 2001, she made her directorial debut when she starred in the gospel stage production *Been There, Done That.* She starred in *Where Eagles Fly* by Carole Mumin at the Lincoln Theater in Washington, D.C., as Ma Brown, who defends the history and legacy of what her granddaughter perceives to be an unsafe neighborhood (the real-life Shaw community, home to such icons as Langston Hughes and Duke Ellington). She was also in *Big Momma 'N' 'Em* (2008).

The second child born to Felix and Belle Stickney, she is the sister of actor Timothy Stickney (best known as R.J. Gannon on the soap *One Life to Live*). *Essence* magazine's 25th anniversary issue named her one of the 200 most influential African American women. She was the recipient of two audelco Awards for Excellence in Black Theater. She is the founder and executive director of the non-profit organization Alternative Careers in the Arts. She developed the "R U OUT OF ORDER" workshops for urban and suburban youths.

Feature Films including Video and TV Movies: *Talkin' Dirty After Dark* (1991), *New Jack City* (1991), *Clippers* (TV; 1991), *Jungle Fever* (1991), *Malcolm X* (1992), *What's Love Got to Do with It* (1993), *The Inkwell* (1994), *My Teacher's Wife* (1995), *Die Hard with a Vengeance* (1995), *Tendrils* (1996), *How Stella Got Her Groove Back* (1998), *Big Ain't Bad* (2002), *See Dick Run* (2008), *Haitian Nights* (2009).

TV: *The Cosby Show* ("Hillman," 1987), *The Women of Brewster Place* (miniseries; 1989), *New Attitude* (1990), *Great Performances* ("The Colored Museum," 1991), *Law & Order* ("Mother Love," 1993), *Mo' Funny: Black Comedy in America* (archival; 1993), *New York Undercover* (2 episodes; "After Shakespeare," "The Reckoning," 1994 and 1996), *ABC Afterschool Specials* ("Daddy's Girl," 1996), *Linc's* (2 episodes in the role of Y'vetta; "15 Seconds of Fame," "People Like Us," 1999 and 2000), *Acapulco Black Film Festival* (2000), *Essence Awards* (2002), *BET Comedy Awards* (2004).

Shorts: *Tendrils* (1996).

Madame Sul-Te-Wan

Born in Louisville, Kentucky, September 12, 1873; died February 1, 1959.

Considered to be one of the most prominent black actresses during Hollywood's burgeoning silent film era, Madame Sul-Te-Wan was the daughter of freed slaves. Her mother, Cleo de Londa, was a singer, and her father, Silas Crawford Wan, who abandoned the family early on, was a traveling preacher. After her husband left, Cleo went to work as a laundress for Louisville's theatrical actresses. Nelly's job was to deliver the laundry to the entertainers. She became enthralled with the theater. She would furtively watch the performers and copy their dance steps and routines. At the age of 15 she won first place in a buck-and-wing contest at the Buckingham Theater.

Nelly and her mother then moved to Cincin-

Madame Sul-Te-Wan. (Helen Armstead Johnson Photograph Collection, Photographs and Prints Division, Schomburg Center for Research in Black Culture, The New York Public Library, Astor, Lenox and Tilden Foundations).

nati, Ohio, and Nelly joined the Three Back Cloaks, using the name Creole Bell. She achieved minor success and began organizing her own theatrical companies that would tour the East Coast. She married Robert Reed Conley in the early 1900s and, after giving birth to two sons, moved the family to Arcadia, California. Two years later, her husband abandoned her when her third son was only three weeks old.

Desperately in need of income, she knew little about anything but show business. She heard that famous film director D.W. Griffith was making a movie in the area. At a time when most Negro roles were played by white actors in black face, Madame Sul-Te-Wan, as she was now calling herself, wrote a letter of introduction to the director and was given a contract and an onscreen role in *The Birth of a Nation*.

Subsequently, she had many uncredited roles in a host of Griffith's movies, but was fired from her five dollar a day contract because she was accused of stealing an actress' book. Undaunted, she hired the most prominent black lawyer of the time, sued to enforce her contract and won. She was featured in *The Marriage Market*, *Intolerance* and *Up from the Depths* for the D.W. Griffith studio.

Her transition into talkies was seamless in her career spanning over five decades. She worked alongside major actors of the day: Barbara Stanwyck, Fay Wray, Jane Wyman, Luise Rainer, Melvyn Douglas, Lucille Ball, Veronica Lake, and Claudette Colbert. However, she was limited to appearing in roles as minor characters who were usually convicts, native women, or domestic servants.

In 1954, Madame Sul-Te-Wan appeared in the Otto Preminger's *Carmen Jones* opposite Dorothy Dandridge, Harry Belafonte, Diahann Carroll, and Pearl Bailey as Dandridge's grandmother. There is still a widely believed rumor that Sul-Te-Wan was actually Dandridge's grandmother or great-grandmother, but there is no truth to this. In 1956, she had a stroke, but recovered to appear onscreen in small and often uncredited roles in a number of films such as *Something of Value* (1957) and *Porgy and Bess* (1959). Her last role was in 1959 in *The Buccaneer*, starring Yul Brynner and Charlton Heston. She had a second stroke and died at age 85.

Feature Films: *The Birth of a Nation* (1915), *The Cause of It All* (1915), *Hoodoo Ann* (1916), *Intolerance* (1916), *The Children Pay* (1916), *The Marriage Market* (1917), *Up from the Depths* (1917), *Stage Struck* (1917), *Who's Your Father?* (1918), *Manslaughter* (1922), *The Lightning Rider* (1924), *The Narrow Street* (1925), *College* (1927), *Uncle Tom's Cabin* (1927), *Queen Kelly* (1927), *Sarah and Son* (1930), *The Thoroughbred* (1930), *The Pagan Lady* (1931), *Heaven on Earth* (1931), *Ladies They Talk About* (1933), *King Kong* (1933), *A Modern Hero* (1934), *Black Moon* (1934), *Imitation of Life* (1934), *In Old Chicago* (1937), *Maid of Salem* (1937), *Island in the Sky* (1938), *The Toy Wife* (1938), *The Affairs of Annabel* (1938), *Kentucky* (1938), *Tell No Tales* (1939), *Torchy Blane ... Playing with Dynamite* (1939), *Safari* (1940), *Maryland* (1940), *King of the Zombies* (1941), *Sullivan's Travels* (1941), *Mokey* (1942), *Revenge of the Zombies* (1943), *Thank Your Lucky Stars* (1943), *Mighty Joe Young* (1949), *Carmen Jones* (1954), *Something of Value* (1957), *Tarzan and the Trappers* (1958), *Porgy and Bess* (1959), *The Buccaneer* (1959).

TV: *Medic* ("All My Mothers, All My Fathers," 1955).

Sykes, Brenda Born in Shreveport, Louisiana, June 25, 1949.

Brenda Louise Sykes made her film debut with a wordless, extraneous role in *The Liberation of L.B. Jones* (1970)—it looks like some dialogue scenes were cut, since a number of publicity shots of her were released at the time of the film's release, indicating that the original role may have been larger. She first made an impact as a student in the Elliot Gould film *Getting Straight* (1970), about a teacher who joins the ranks of the campus radicals. She was one of a multiracial cast of young beauties in *Pretty Maids All in a Row* (1971),

Brenda Sykes with Jim Brown in *Black Gunn* (1972).

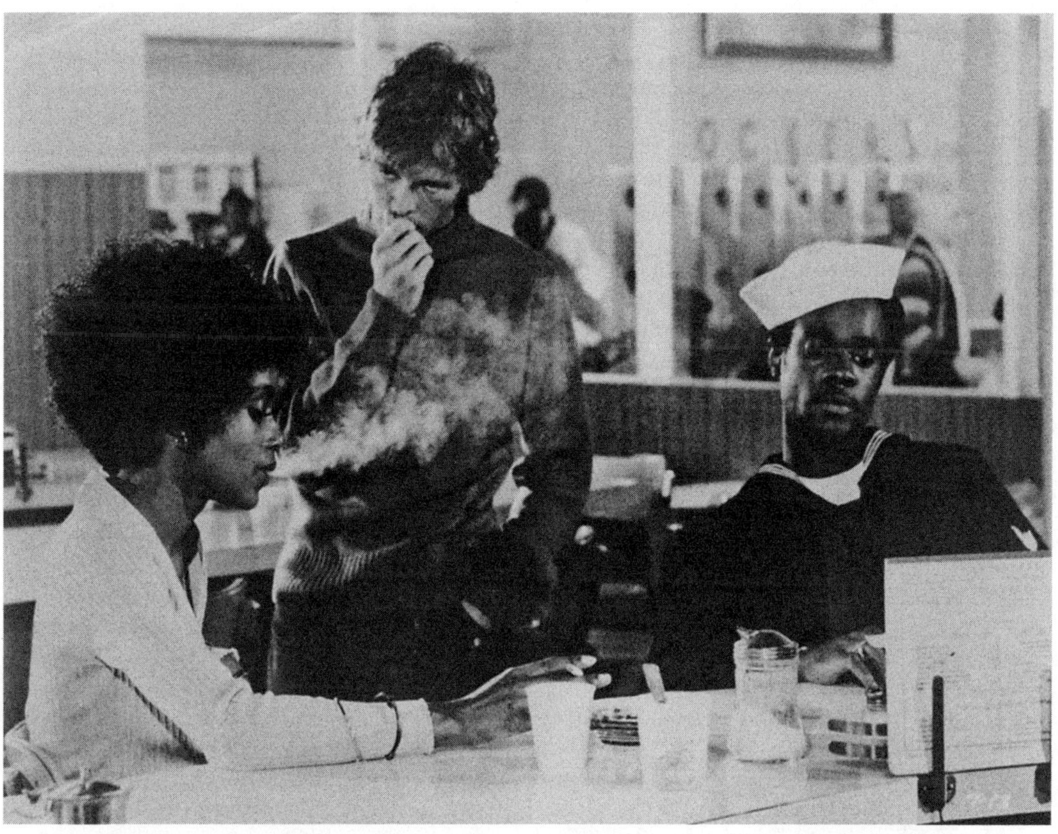

Left to right: Brenda Sykes, John Neilson and Glynn Turman in *Honky* (1974).

a dark comedy starring Rock Hudson and directed by France's Roger Vadim. All three of these films were box office flops.

Skin Game (1971) was a coy comedy with James Garner and Lou Gossett Jr. about interracial con men; Sykes was the slave girl Naomi who joins the con. She was Gunn's (Jim Brown) girlfriend Judith in the private eye action film *Black Gunn* (1972). Brown and Sykes made headlines when he was accused of physically abusing her and throwing her one story off a hotel balcony. She was Tiffany in the hit film *Cleopatra Jones* (1975), but all eyes were on Tamara Dobson in the title role.

What could have been an ongoing film career—*Honky* (1974), *Mandingo* (1975), and a bit role in its incoherent sequel *Drum* (1976)—suddenly stopped dead. Sykes segued into more TV work and then simply seems to have gotten sick of the Hollywood rat race. In *Honky* and *Mandingo*, Sykes became the poster girl for interracial sex—such as Hollywood had never seen before (and hasn't seen a whole lot of since). She is at the peak of her beauty in both films. In *Honky*, she was Sheila Smith, an upper middle class black girl (her dad is a physician, played by William "Blacula" Marshall) who does drugs and falls (rather inexplicably) for a lower-class white boy. She is raped by some white rednecks, and the relationship of the two young lovers becomes unbearably complex. The message of *Honky* seems to be stay away from black women. *Mandingo*, which was big box office, was a veritable festival of miscegenation, with Sykes as the slave girl Ellen, who is impregnated by plantation owner's son Hammond Maxwell (Perry King). Sykes' sizzling nude scene couldn't hide the fact that *Mandingo* was a violent, racist mess.

She was a regular on the series *Ozzie's Girls* with Ozzie Nelson, who had been a huge TV star in the 1950s and 1960s with *Ozzie and Harriet*—but the ratings showed that his star had set. Sykes also made guest star appearances on *Harry O*, *The Love Boat*, *Police Woman*, *The Streets of San Fran-*

cisco and *Love, American Style*. Her last professional acting credit was on an episode of *Good Times* in 1978. She was married to musician Gil Scott-Heron, and they had one child. She is now living out of the spotlight with her current husband, Paul C. Hudson, in Los Angeles.

Although her career spanned the so-called blaxploitation era, Sykes never played action heroine roles like Pam Grier. With her slim, girlish body and huge doe-like eyes, she was a sylph and a princess — more Audrey Hepburn than Tamara Dobson.

Feature Films including TV Movies: *The Liberation of L.B. Jones* (1970), *Getting Straight* (1970), *The Baby Maker* (1970), *The Sheriff* (TV; 1971), *Pretty Maids All in a Row* (1971), *Skin Game* (1971), *Honky* (1971), *Black Gunn* (1972), *Cleopatra Jones* (1973), *Young Love* (TV; 1974), *Mandingo* (1975), *Drum* (1976).

TV: *One Life to Live* (recurring role as Judy Tate; 1968), *Mayberry R.F.D.* ("Driver Education," 1969), *The New People* (1969), *Room 222* ("Triple Date," 1969), *The Doris Day Show* ("Young Love," 1971), *Love, American Style* ("Love and the Perfect Wedding," 1972), *Ozzie's Girls* (recurring role of Jennifer MacKenzie; 1973), *Soul Train* (1973), *The Streets of San Francisco* ("A Trout in the Milk," 1973), *Police Woman* ("Smack," 1974), *Harry O* ("Sound of Trumpets," 1975), *Mobile One* ("Roadblock," 1975), *Executive Suite* (recurring role of Summer Johnson; 1976), *The Love Boat* (1977), *Good Times* ("Where There's Smoke," 1978).

Sykes, Wanda Born in Portsmouth, Virginia, March 7, 1964.

Wanda Sykes is all about being funny: her expressions are priceless; her timing is superb; and she has evolved her comedic skills into a full-fledged acting career. She began doing stand-up comedy in 1987, but her day job was as a procurement officer for the National Security Agency. She relocated to New York, opened for Chris Rock at Caroline's Comedy Club (currently the foremost comedy club in the city), and in 1997 became a staff writer for *The Chris Rock Show*. She won an Emmy in 1999 (and received three nominations in other years) as part of the writing team.

She had her own sitcom, *Wanda at Large*, on the FOX Network in 2003, but the mainstream sitcom format seemed to visibly constrain the free-wheeling Sykes. Her character, Wanda Hawkins, was not the freshest, nor was the fish-out-of-water format new or interesting. Sykes was a down-on-her-luck comedienne working as a correspondent for a political talk show. She seemed more comfortable with her recurring role as Barb on the CBS sitcom *The New Adventures of Old Christine* (2001–05) and her work on HBO's *Curb Your Enthusiasm* (2006–08), which is "out there" by any standards, and suits her well. She also starred in and produced the Comedy Central series *Wanda Does It*, where she tried out a variety of jobs other than comedienne-actress. It never took off with audiences.

Her most uncharacteristic gig was as a correspondent on HBO's *Inside the NFL*. On more familiar terrain, she hosted Comedy Central's *Premium Blend* and was the voice of the character Gladys on Comedy Central's raunchy puppet show *Crank Yankers*, where comedians made prank calls while puppets acted out the scenarios.

Her 2006 HBO Comedy Special *Wanda Sykes: Sick & Tired* was based on material from her national tour, and was nominated for a 2007 Emmy Award for Outstanding Variety, Music or Comedy Special. Her first book, *Yeah, I Said It* (Simon and Schuster, 2004) was a popular collection of essays written from a Sykes' eye view of life.

Brenda Sykes.

Her increasingly busy motion picture career includes the outrageous *Nutty Professor II: The Klumps* (2000), *Pootie Tang* (2001), *Monster-in-Law* (2005), *Clerks II* (2006) and *Evan Almighty* (2007).

A new generation may know her best for her wonderful voice work on Applebee's commercials ("Get it together, baby!"). Sykes turns a one-minute commercial into a laugh-out-loud experience. Although born in Virginia, she was raised in Maryland. Her father was an army colonel and her mother was a banker. She is a graduate of Virginia's Hampton University.

Feature Films including Video Movies: *Tomorrow Night* (1998), *Nutty Professor II: The Klumps* (2000), *Down to Earth* (2001), *Pootie Tang* (2001), *Monster-in-Law* (2005), *The Adventures of Brer Rabbit* (voice; 2006), *Over the Hedge* (voice; 2006), *Clerks II* (2006), *My Super Ex-Girlfriend* (2006), *Barnyard* (voice; 2006), *Brother Bear 2* (voice; 2006), *CondomNation* (2006), *Hammy's Boomerang Adventure* (2006), *Evan Almighty* (2007), *License to Wed* (2007), *Back at the Barnyard* (voice; 2008).

TV: *Stand-Up Spotlight* (1988), *HBO Comedy Showcase* (1995), *The Chris Rock Show* (various episodes; 1997), *The N.Y. Friars' Club Roast of Drew Carey* (1998), *Dr. Katz, Professional Therapist* (voice; 1999), *Best of Chris Rock* (1999), *Late Night with Conan O'Brien* (5 appearances; 1999–2007), *American Comedy Awards Viewer's Choice* (2001), *The Downer Channel* (2001), *The Drew Carey Show* (3 episodes in the role of Christine Watson; "Eat Drink Drew Women," "Mr. Laffoon's Wild Ride," "Drew and the King," 2001), *Curb Your Enthusiasm* (recurring role of Wanda; 2001–05), *The Tonight Show with Jay Leno* (16 appearances; 2001–07), *VH1's 100 Sexiest Artists* (2002), *Comedy Central's Premium Blend* (hostess; 2002–03), *Crank Yankers* (2 episodes; 2002 and 2003), *Inside the NFL* (commentator; 2002) *The Award Show Awards Show* (archival; 2003), *Heroes of Comedy: Women on Top* (2003), *Good Day Live* (2003), *2003 MTV Movie Awards, 3rd Annual BET Awards* (2003), *Chappelle's Show: The Lost Episodes* (2003), *Wanda Sykes: Tongue Untied* (2003), *MTV Reloaded* (2003), *The Teen Choice Awards 2003, The 55th Primetime Emmy Awards* (2003), *MADtv* (2003), *The Sharon Osbourne Show* (2003), *Richard Pryor: I Ain't Dead Yet* (2003), *Comedy Central Presents: The Commies* (2003), *The Daily Show* (2 appearances; 2003 and 2005), *Comedy Central Presents: 100 Greatest Stand-Ups of All Time* (archival; 2004), *Celebrity Poker Showdown* (2004), *BET Comedy Awards* (2004), *Tavis Smiley* (2004), *Wanda Does It* (2004), *Jimmy Kimmel Live!* (2 appearances; 2004–06), *Last Call with Carson Daly* (2 appearances; 2004–06), *Ellen* (5 appearances; 2005–07), *106 & Park* (2005), *Costas Now* (2005), *The Early Show* (2005), *The 2nd Annual BET Comedy Awards* (2005), *Earth to America* (2005), *Richard Pryor: The Funniest Man Dead or Alive* (2005), *New Year's Eve with Carson Daly* (2005), *That's What I'm Talking About* ("Movers, Shakers and Playmakers," 2005), *HBO First Look* (3 segments; 2005–07), *The View* (2 appearances; 2005 and 2007), *The Late Late Show with Craig Ferguson* (2 appearances; 2005 and 2007), *Girls Who Do: Comedy* (2006), *The Megan Mullally Show* (2006), *Wanda Sykes: Sick & Tired* (2006), *Will & Grace* ("Bye, Bye Baby," 2006), *The New Adventures of Old Christine* (recurring role of Barb; 2006–08), *Entertainment Tonight* (2007), *Corazon de...* (archival; 2007).

Video/DVD: *Best of the Chris Rock Show* (2001), *Train Wreck!* (2006).

Taylor, Clarice Born in Buckingham County, Virginia, September 20, 1927.

Clarice Taylor was Anna Huxtable, Cliff Huxtable's mother, and wife of Russell (Earle Hyman), a touring musician, on *The Cosby Show* (1985–92), one of the longest running and most popular programs in TV history. She was nominated for an Emmy for the role in 1986. She also appeared as Harriet on *Sesame Street* for many years.

She grew up in New York City, and given the limited opportunities for African American actresses, she took a job at the post office in order to hedge her bets. She began her involvement with acting in the American Negro Theatre and was later one of the founding members of the landmark Negro Ensemble Company.

She broke through in feature films with the role of Minnie in director Otto Preminger's unpopular *Tell Me That You Love Me, Junie Moon* (1970) and as the ill-fated housekeeper Birdie in Clint Eastwood's influential *Play Misty for Me* (1971). She had a feminist-driven role lead role as Gladys Brooks in *Five on the Black Hand Side* (1973), a role she had originated off–Broadway. Her other notable role was as Addaperle, the Good Witch of the North, in the overblown film version of *The Wiz* (1978).

Her early '80s one-woman, Obie Award–winning off–Broadway show *Moms* later led to a national tour. *Moms*, a character study of comedienne Moms Mabley, led to a complex legal dispute between Taylor and playwright Alice Childress, who received sole copyright of the play, even though Taylor contributed much in the way of research and suggestions. Taylor eventually produced a new play on Mabley, but Childress cited copyright infringements and won her case.

Feature Films including TV Movies: *Change of Mind* (1969), *Tell Me That You Love Me, Junie Moon* (1970), *Play Misty for Me* (1971), *Such Good Friends* (1971), *Five on the Black Hand Side* (1973), *The Wiz* (1978), *Purlie* (TV; 1981), *Nothing Lasts Forever* (1984), *Sommersby* (1993), *Smoke* (1995), *History of the World in Eight Minutes* (1998).

TV: *Ironside* ("The Last Payment," 1973), *Sanford and Son* ("Hello, Cousin Emma," 1974), *Sesame Street* (recurring role of Harriet; 1976–90), *Beulah Land* (miniseries; 1980), *Nurse* ("The Gifts," 1981), *Lady Blue* ("Death Valley Day," 1985), *The Cosby Show* (recurring role of Emma Huxtable; 1985–92), *Spenser: For Hire* ("Rockabye Baby," 1986), *It's Showtime at the Apollo* (1987), *The Cosby Show: Looking Back* (archival; 1987), *Due South* ("An Eye for An Eye," 1995), *The Cosby Show: A Look Back* (2002).

Taylor, Libby Born in Chicago, Illinois, 1891; died 1973.

Legend has it that Elizabeth (Libby) Taylor was discovered by Mae West while Taylor was cooking barbeque at Harlem's Black and Gold restaurant. She was actually Mae West's real life maid, and she did appear with West in several films: *I'm No Angel* (1933) as Libby, a hairdresser-maid, and in *Belle of the Nineties* (1934), the maid of Mae West's character Ruby Carter.

Taylor began to get so much screen work that eventually West was waking her up in the morning, and it was then that they mutually decided Taylor should concentrate full time on her big screen maid roles. They must have paid better, since according to her manager, Ben Carter, Taylor was making better than $250 a week in the mid-thirties, having worked her way up from bit parts to billed roles. She also appeared in several Three Stooges shorts.

She was a close friend of Hattie McDaniel, the first African American actress to win an Academy Award. Her career spanned over 20 years, and she endured long enough to be cast in a non-stereotypical role in 1953's *Bright Road* with Dorothy Dandridge.

Feature Films including TV Movies: *Consolation Marriage* (1931), *The Cabin in the Cotton* (1932), *I'm No Angel* (1933), *Belle of the Nineties* (1934), *When a Man Sees Red* (1934), *Imitation of Life* (1934), *Society Doctor* (1935), *Ruggles of Red Gap* (1935), *Mississippi* (1935), *Star of Midnight* (1935), *Reckless* (1935), *Black Sheep* (1935), *Shanghai* (1935), *Diamond Jim* (1935), *Streamline Express* (1935), *Dangerous* (1935), *Sleepy Time* (1936), *Stage Struck* (1936), *Fury and the Woman* (1936), *Libeled Lady* (1936), *Camp Meetin'* (1936), *Three Smart Girls* (1936), *Mysterious Crossing* (1936), *The Good Old Soak* (1937), *The Last Train from Madrid* (1937), *Exclusive* (1937), *The Buccaneer* (1938), *The Toy Wife* (1938), *Woman Against Woman* (1938), *The Amazing Dr. Clitterhouse* (1938), *The Ice Follies of 1939* (1939), *Babes in Arms* (1939), *Broadway Melody of 1940* (1940), *The Great McGinty* (1940), *The Howards of Virginia* (1940), *Santa Fe Trail* (1940), *Blonde Inspiration* (1941), *Flight from Destiny* (1941), *My Gal Sal* (1942), *For Me and My Gal* (1942), *The Hard Way* (1943), *Coney Island* (1943), *And the Angels Sing* (1944), *This Is the Life* (1944), *The Adventures of Mark Twain* (1944), *Home in Indiana* (1944), *Saratoga Trunk* (1945), *Tomorrow Is Forever* (1946), *Cinderella Jones* (1946), *Swamp Fire* (1946), *The Perfect Marriage* (1947), *The Foxes of Harrow* (1947), *Another Part of the Forest* (1948), *You're My Everything* (1949), *Al Jennings of Oklahoma* (1951), *Two Tickets to Broadway* (1951), *Bright Road* (1953), *Stop! Look! and Laugh!* (archival; 1960).

Shorts: *Reckless* (1935), *Hollywood Hotel* (1938), *Calling All Curs* (1939).

Taylor, Regina Born in Dallas, Texas, August 22, 1960.

Born in Texas but raised in Oklahoma, Regina Taylor is a graduate of the Southern Methodist University. She brings a sensitivity and subtlety to her work and has juggled successful careers in theater, film, and television. Her quiet, reserved manner has been the foundation of a remarkably sustained creative effort.

On Broadway, she was one of the first African American women to play Juliet in *Romeo and Juliet* (at Joseph Papp's Shakespeare Festival). That same season she was Cecilia in *As You Like It* and

Left to right: John Aaron Bennett, Regina Taylor, Ashlee Levitch, Sam Waterston, and Jeremy London in *I'll Fly Away.*

the First Witch in *Macbeth*. She appeared in the original production of *The Vagina Monologues* (1999).

One of her pivotal roles—and perhaps the one for which she will always be most remembered—was as housekeeper Lilly Harper in the poignant period piece *I'll Fly Away*. The role earned her two Emmy nominations (1992–93) and a Golden Globe Award for Best Actress in a TV Series–Drama in 1993. She also received the

NAACP Image Award for Outstanding Lead Actress in a Drama Series for *I'll Fly Away*.

Taylor has two other Image Award nominations: Outstanding Actress in a Television Movie or Miniseries for *Children of the Dust* (1996) and Outstanding Supporting Actress in a Motion Picture for *Courage Under Fire* (1996). Theatrical films include *Lean on Me* (1989), *Losing Isaiah* (1995), *Clockers* (1995), *Courage Under Fire* (1996) and *The Negotiator* (1998). Memorable TV movies include *Crisis at Central High* (1981), *Howard Beach: Making a Case for Murder* (1989), *The Third Twin* (1997), *Strange Justice* (as Anita Hill; 1999), and *Cora Unashamed* (2000).

After several years' hiatus from acting, she returned to the small screen to play the recurring role of Molly Blane on *The Unit*, for which she received a 2008 NAACP Image Award for Best Actress in a Drama Series. (Fans of the series should check out Taylor's amusing and informative *The Unit* blog.)

Taylor is also a playwright, an Artistic Associate of the Goodman Theater in Chicago, and the writer-in-residence at the Alliance Theatre in Atlanta, Georgia. In 2000, she received the American Theatre Critics Association–Seinberg New Play Award for her play *Oo-Bla-Dee* (1999) about black female jazz musicians in the 1940s. In 2004, she received the Helen Hayes Award for Best Musical for her *Crowns* (2002), based on the book of photographs of black women's Sunday church hats by Michael Cunningham and Craig Marberry. *Drowning Crow* (2001), Taylor's variant on Chekhov's *The Seagull*, was performed on Broadway in 2004. Other plays by Taylor, some unpublished, include *Jennine's Diary* (1992), *Between the Lines* (1995), *Love Poems #97*, *Watermelon Rinds* (1993), *Inside the Belly of the Beast*, *Escape from Paradise*, *Mudtracks*, *Beside Every Good Man* (1999), *The Dreams of Sarah Breedlove*, *Urban Zulu Mambo*, and *A Night in Tunisia*. Her one-woman play *Millennium Mambo* included selections from the works of other African American writers.

Feature Films including TV Movies: *Nurse* (TV; 1980), *Crisis at Central High* (TV; 1981), *Concealed Enemies* (TV; 1984), *Lean on Me* (1989), *Howard Beach: Making a Case for Murder* (TV; 1989), *Jersey Girl* (1992), *Children of the Dust* (TV; 1995), *Losing Isaiah* (1995), *Clockers* (1995), *The Keeper* (1995), *Spirit Lost* (1996), *A Family Thing* (1996), *Courage Under Fire* (1996), *Hostile Waters* (TV; 1997), *The Third Twin* (TV; 1997), *The Negotiator* (1998), *Strange Justice* (TV; 1999), *Cora Unashamed* (TV; 2000), *In from the Night* (TV; 2006).

TV: *I'll Fly Away* (recurring role of Lilly Harper; 1991–94), *I'll Fly Away: Then and Now* (1993), *Law & Order* (2 episodes; "Mushrooms," "Virtue," 1991 and 1994), *Late Night with Conan O'Brien* (1995), *Feds* (recurring role as Sandra Broome; 1997), *The Education of Max Bickford* (recurring role as Judith Hackett Bryant; 2001), *Reading Rainbow* ("Uncle Jed's Barber Shop," 2006), *The Unit* (recurring role of Molly Blane; 2008), *Grey's Anatomy* ("Losing My Mind," 2008), *39th NAACP Image Awards* (2008).

Thigpen, Lynne Born in Joliet, Illinois, December 22, 1948; died March 12, 2003, Los Angeles, California.

Cherlynn Thigpen was a high school English teacher before she decided to try an acting career. She was also a talented singer, and it was her vocal expertise that landed her a role in the popular hippie musical *Godspell* in 1971 (she made her screen debut in the film version in 1973). Her Broadway career continued with Doug Henning's popular *The Magic Show* and the unsuccessful attempt to turn Studs Turkel's book *Working* (1978) into a musical. In 1979, she played Persona Non Grata in *But Never Jam Today*. In 1981, she earned a Tony Award nomination for her strong work in *Tintypes* (1980), which went from off–Broadway to Broadway. She waited until 1997 to win the Tony Award for Best Actress in a Featured Role in a Play for Wendy Wasserstein's *An American Daughter*. Thigpen played a black Jewish oncologist attempting to conceive a child in her forties. She also received two Obie (off–Broadway) Awards for her work in *Boesman and Lena* (1992) and *Jar the Floor* (1999).

Her emphasis was increasingly on feature films and television in the remaining two decades of her career, and she acted in an amazing variety of genres — from comedies, to police dramas, to children's programs. Feature film highlights include her powerful turn as an angry parent in the school drama *Lean on Me* (1989); the TV movie about *Brown vs. Board of Education*, *Separate but Equal* (1991); the political satire *Bob Roberts* (1992); and the remake of *Shaft* (2000), with Samuel L. Jackson. TV highlights include her recurring role as Nancy on *Love, Sidney*, arguably the first show centered around a gay character (as played by Tony Randall; 1982–83); Rosie on *thirtysomething* (1989); and her pivotal recurring role, the no-nonsense District Attorney Ruby Thomas on *L.A. Law* (1991–92). She received four Emmy nominations for her work as the Chief on the PBS children's series *Where in the World Is Carmen Sandiego?* (1991) and *Where in Time Is Carmen Sandiego?* (1996). Her other popular PBS children's series was *Bear in the Big Blue House* (as the voice of Luna; 1997–2003). Her last series role was on *The District*, as computer expert Ella Farmer, which she played from 2000 until the time of her death in 2003.

Thigpen died very suddenly of a cerebral hemorrhage. An elementary school in her hometown of Joliet is named for her.

Feature Films including TV Movies: *Godspell* (1973), *The Warriors* (1979), When Hell *Freezes Over, I'll Skate* (TV; 1979), *Amazing Graces* (1981), *Tootsie* (1982), *The Files on Jill Hatch* (TV; 1983), *Streets of Fire* (1984), *The Recovery Room* (TV; 1985), *Walls of Glass* (1985), *Rockabye* (TV; 1986), *Sweet Liberty* (1986), *Hello Again* (1987), *Running on Empty* (1988), *Lean on Me* (1989), *Fear Stalk* (TV; 1989), *Impulse* (1990), *Separate but Equal* (TV; 1991), *Article 99* (1992), *Bob Roberts* (1992), *Naked in New York* (1993), *The Paper* (1994), *Blankman* (1994), *Just Cause* (1995), *The Boys Next Door* (TV; 1996), *A Mother's Instinct* (TV; 1996), *Pretty Poison* (TV; 1996), *Chance of a Lifetime* (TV; 1998), *Night Ride Home* (TV; 1999), *Random Hearts* (1999), *The Insider* (1999), *Bicentennial Man* (1999), *An American Daughter* (TV; 2000), *Shaft* (2000), *Novocaine* (2002), *Anger Management* (2003).

TV: *The 35th Annual Tony Awards* (1981), *Broadway Plays Washington on Kennedy Center Tonight* (1982), *Freedom to Speak* (1982), *American Playhouse: Working* (1982), *Love, Sidney* (recurring role as Nancy; 1982–83), *The News Is the News* (1983), *Gimme a Break!* (3 episodes in the role of Loretta Harper; "Albany Bound," Parts I and II, "Family Reunion," 1985–86), *The Ellen Burstyn Show* ("Writer, Wronger," 1987), *The Equalizer* ("Blood and Wine," Part II, 1987), *Frank's Place* ("Dueling Voodoo," 1988), *Roseanne* ("The Slice of Life," 1989), *FM* (recurring role as Naomi Sayers; 1989), *thirtysomething* (6 episodes in the role of Rosie; 1989), *ABC Afterschool Specials* (2 episodes; "Private Affairs," "Girlfriend," 1989 and 1993), *Hunter* ("Where Echoes End," 1990), *The Days and Nights of Molly Dodd* ("Here's One Way to Fill Every Waking Moment," 1991), *The Cosby Show* (2 episodes in the role of Mrs. Hudson; "Theo and the Kids," Parts I and II, 1991), *L.A. Law* (recurring role of District Attorney Ruby Thomas; 1991–92), *Loving* (recurring role as Judge Hale; 1992), *Reading Rainbow* (voice; "The Salamander Room," 1993), *Where in the World Is Carmen Sandiego?* ("Cats Nipped," 1995), *Cagney & Lacey: The View Through the Glass Ceiling*, (1995), *Law & Order* (3 episodes in the role of Judge Ida Boucher; "Switch," "Savages," "Patsy," 1995–99), *Where in Time Is Carmen Sandiego?* (1996), *A. Philip Randolph: For Jobs and Freedom* (narrator; 1996), *The 51st Annual Tony Awards* (1997), *Homicide: Life on the Street* (3 episodes in the role of Regina Wilson; "Blood Ties," Parts I–III, 1997), *Promised Land* ("Take Back the Night," 1997), *All My Children* (2 episodes; 1997 and 2000), *Bear in the Big Blue House* (voice of Luna; 1997–2003), *King of the Hill* (voice; "Hank's Dirty Laundry," 1998), *Cosby* (2 episodes; "The First Gentleman," "Turkey Day," 1998), *The District* (recurring role of Ella Farmer; 2000–03).

Thomason, Marsha Born in Manchester, England, January 19, 1976.

Charming, low-key Marsha Thomason was born to an English father and a Jamaican mother. Thomason attended Holy Trinity Primary School in Blackley, and then the North Manchester High School for Girls. She has a bachelor of arts in English from Manchester Metropolitan University. Marsha Thomason joined the Oldham Theatre Workshop in England at age 12 and had her first professional appearance at age 14 on the BBC's *The 8:15 from Manchester*. She gained considerable fame with British TV audiences with recurring roles on the popular series *Playing the Field* (1997), *Where the Heart Is* (1998–99) and *Burn It* (2003).Thomason can play sexy or sweet roles, and uncomplicated or complex characters. She is well known in America for her two seasons as Nessa Holt on *Las Vegas* (2003–05) and Naomi Dorritt on *Lost* (2007–08). Her character was knifed in the third season finale and died of her wound in the first episode of the fourth season. She is also known stateside for her film roles in the pleasant *Black Knight* (2001) with an uncharacteristically low-key Martin Lawrence, and *The Haunted Mansion* (2003), an indifferent misfire with Eddie Murphy based on the Walt Disney theme park ride. Her considerable talents were also wasted in the puerile *My Baby's Daddy* (2004).

Feature Films including Video and TV Movies: *Safe* (TV; 1993), *Priest* (1994), *Prime Suspect 5: Errors of Judgment* (TV; 1996), *Brazen Hussies* (TV; 1996), *Swallow* (TV; 2001), *Black Knight* (2001), *Long Time Dead* (2002), *Pure* (2002), *The Haunted Mansion* (2003), *My Baby's Daddy* (2004), *The Nickel Children* (2005), *The Package* (2006), *Caffeine* (2006), *The Fast One* (2006), *The Tripper* (2006), *Tug of War* (2006), *LA Blues* (2007), *Messiah: The Rapture* (TV; 2008), *Into the Blue 2* (2010).

TV: *The 8:15 from Manchester* (1990), *Pie in the Sky* (recurring role as Sally; 1997), *Playing the Field* (recurring role as Sharon "Shazza" Pearce; 1997), *Where the Heart Is* (recurring role as Jacqui Richards; 1998–99), *Love in the 21st Century* (1999), *Table 12* ("Guess Who's Not Coming to Dinner," 2001), *Burn It* (recurring role as Tina; 2003), *Intimate Portrait* ("Vanessa Marcil," 2003), *Las Vegas* (recurring role as Nessa Holt; 2003–05), *The Wayne Brady Show* (2004), *The Film Programme* (2004), *Richard & Judy* (2004), *The Late Late Show with Craig Kilborn* (2004), *50 Hottest Vegas Moments* (2005), *Lost* (recurring role as Naomi Dorrit; 2007–08), *Life* ("The Business of Miracles," 2008), *Easy Money* (recurring role as Julia Miller; 2008).

Shorts: *Tug of War* (2006), *The Package* (2006), *The Fast One* (2006).

Thoms, Tracie

Born in Baltimore, Maryland, August 19, 1975.

Exuberant, versatile, and natural with a charmingly self-deprecating quality, Tracie Nicole Thoms has risen rapidly in the acting world. She is the daughter of Mariana and Donald Thoms; her brother is named Austin. She is a graduate of the Baltimore School of the Arts and Howard University in Washington, D.C., with a bachelor's in fine arts and a postgraduate acting diploma from Juilliard.

She got a role (as Sasha) on the quickly cancelled *As If* (2002), but had much more success with her role as Mahandra McGinty on *Wonderfalls* (2004). Kerry Washington played the role in an unaired pilot. Mahandra is the best friend of slacker Jaye Tyler, who works in a low-end gift shop called Wonderfalls. In 2005 she was added to the cast of *Cold Case* as homicide detective Kat Miller. She has also guest-starred on *The Shield* and *Law & Order*. She made her Broadway debut in actress-playwright Regina Taylor's *Drowning Crow* (2004), a modern variant on *The Seagull*. Other off–Broadway and regional productions include *Up Against the Wind* (New York Theatre Workshop), *The Exonerated* (New York's The Culture Project), and *The Oedipus Plays* (The Shakespeare Theater).

Her two best film roles to date are her delightful turn as the lesbian lawyer Joanne Jefferson in the underrated film version of *Rent* (2005), the lover of Maureen Johnson (Idina Menzel); and *Death Proof*, the second half of *Grindhouse* (2007), which was also released as a feature-length DVD later that year, with a considerable amount of new footage added. This woefully misunderstood paean to the 42nd Street films of the sixties and seventies showcased Thoms as foul-mouthed Kim, one of the women who teaches the sadistic Stuntman Mike (Kurt Russell) a violent lesson. This was Thoms at her most vivacious.

Feature Films including Video and TV Movies: *Porn 'n Chicken* (TV; 2002), *The Warrior Class* (2004), *Brother to Brother* (2004), *Everyone's Depressed* (2005), Rent (2005), *The Devil Wears Prada* (2006), *Grindhouse* (consists of two films: *Planet Terror* and *Death Proof*; Thoms is featured in the *Death Proof* half; 2007), *Death Proof* (expanded, feature-length version; 2007), *Descent* (cameo; 2007), *Sex and Breakfast* (2008), *Razor* (2008), *Jimmie* (2008), *Madness* (2008), *Peter and Vandy* (2008), *C.R.E.A.M.: The American Dream* (2009).

TV: *America's Most Terrible Things* (2002), *As If* (recurring role of Sasha; 2002), *The Shield* ("Dominoes Falling," 2003), *Wonderfalls* (recurring role of Mahandra McGinty; 2004), *Law & Order* ("Mammon," 2005), *Live with Regis and Kelly* (2005), *Today* (2 segments; 2005), *Ellen* (2005), *The View* (2005), *Cold Case* (recurring role of Kat Miller, 2005–08), *This Can't Be My Life* ("The Pink Pages," 2008), *Godfrey Live* (2008), *Entertainment Tonight* (2008).

Todd, Beverly

Born in Chicago, Illinois, July 11, 1946.

Beverly Todd is one of those excellent actresses who hasn't gotten the recognition she deserves. An early mentor was Sidney Poitier — at the height of his fame in those days. Todd did three films in a row with him: *The Lost Man* (1969), *They Call Me Mister Tibbs!* (1970), and

Brother John (1971), and later *A Piece of the Action* (1977). Other key films in Todd's career are *Baby Boom* (1987), *Moving* (1988), *Clara's Heart* (1988), *Lean on Me* (1989), and the Academy Award winning Best Picture *Crash* (2004), in a harrowing role as the pathetic mother of the Don Cheadle character. She had a recurring role on the popular daytime soap *Love of Life* (Monica Nelson; 1968–70) at the inception of her career. Soap operas were an excellent training ground for many actresses, and roles for black women in that genre were starting to open up by this time.

She was in the fifth segment of the epic miniseries *Roots* (1977), playing the role of Fanta as an adult. She was excellent as Mrs. Paige opposite Lou Gossett, Jr., in *Don't Look Back: The Story of Leroy "Satchel" Paige* (TV; 1981). Of more recent vintage, she was Mrs. Charles in the critically acclaimed series *Six Feet Under* (2002–03). Theater credits include *Deep Are the Roots* (1960) and the London production of *No Strings* (1974).

As her career moved on, Todd became involved in producing as well as in acting. Her production company is Carr, Todd, Warwick Productions. She was one of the writers and producers of *Tribute to the Black Woman* and co-produced *A Laugh, a Tear: The Story of Black Humor in America* (1990) with Whoopi Goldberg. She also produced the salute to Ella Fitzgerald called *Ella! 60 Years of Music: A Tribute*. She is a People's Choice Award winner and four-time NAACP Image Award nominee.

Todd is the co-founder of Sunshine Circle, a facility for preschoolers, and is founder and president of Hollywood Sisters, an organization that celebrates black achievement in the arts and provides scholarships to creative students pursuing higher education in the arts.

Beverly Todd in *Brother John* (1971).

Feature Films including TV Movies: *Deadlock* (TV; 1969), *The Lost Man* (1969), *They Call Me Mister Tibbs!* (1970), *Brother John* (1971), *A Piece of the Action* (1977), *The Ghost of Flight 401* (TV; 1978), *The Jericho Mile* (TV; 1979), *Don't Look Back: The Story of Leroy "Satchel" Paige* (TV; 1981), *Please Don't Hit Me, Mom* (TV; 1981), *Vice Squad* (1982), *Homework* (aka *Short People*, 1982), *A Touch of Scandal* (TV; 1984), *The Ladies Club* (1986), *A Different Affair* (TV; 1987), *Happy Hour* (aka *Sour Grapes*, 1987), *Baby Boom* (1987), *Moving* (1988), *Clara's Heart* (1988), *Lean on Me* (1989), *Class of '61* (TV; 1993), *Exquisite Tenderness* (aka *The Surgeon*, 1995), *Ali: An American Hero* (TV; 2000), *Crash* (2004), *Animal* (2005), *Ascension Day* (2007), *The Bucket List* (2008), *Miracle Mile* (2008), *The Lena Baker Story* (2008).

TV: *N.Y.P.D.* ("Which Side Are You On?" 1968), *Love of Life* (recurring role as Monica Nelson; 1968–70), *The Wild Wild West* ("The Night of the Diva," 1969), *Hollywood Television Theatre: Six Characters in Search of an Author* (1976), Barnaby Jones ("The Bounty Hunter," 1976), *Roots* (miniseries; 1977), *The Fantastic Journey* ("Turnabout," 1977), *Family* ("A Tale Out of Season," 1977), *Having Babies* (1978), *Having Babies III* (1978), *Lou Grant* ("Streets," 1980), *Benson* (2 episodes; "Benson in Love," "Benson's Groupie," 1979 and 1980), *Quincy M.E.* ("Seldom Silent, Never Heard," 1981), *Shannon* ("Secret Rage," 1981), *Falcon Crest* (2 episodes; "Cimmerean Dawn," Penumbra," 1983), *The Mississippi* ("Going Back to Hannibal," 1984), *For Love and Honor* (3 episodes in the role of Evie Yates; "The Big Party," "Mixed Signals," "Bloodline," 1983–84), *Blue Thunder* ("Payload," 1984), *St. Elsewhere* (2 episodes in the role of Corinne Close; "My Aim Is True," "Fade to White," 1984), *Otherworld* ("I Am Woman, Hear Me Roar," 1985), *Magnum, P.I.* ("The Treasure of Kalaniopu'u," 1985), *The Redd Foxx Show* (recurring role as Felicia; 1986), *Hill Street Blues* ("Days of Swine and Roses," 1987), *Wiseguy* ("Changing Houses," 1990), *A Different World* ("Almost Working Girl," 1991), *Sparks* (2 episodes; "Brotherly Love," "Cain and Abel Sparks," 1997 and 1998), *Six Feet Under* (4 episodes as Mrs. Charles; "The Plan," "Driving Mr. Mossback," "The Liar and the Whore," "Everyone Leaves," 2002–03), *Ghost Whisperer* ("The Night We Met," 2006), *House* ("House

Training," 2007), *The Closer* ("Grave Doubts," 2007), *K-Ville* (2007), *Lincoln Heights* (2007).

Torres, Gina Born in New York, New York, April 25, 1969.

Gina Torres is of Cuban heritage, the youngest of three children. She was born in Washington Heights; the family moved to the Bronx when she was young. Her father was a typesetter at the newspapers *La Prensa* and the *New York Daily News*. Torres attended Fiorello H. LaGuardia High School and New York's High School of Music and Art.

Many actresses specialize in — or are stereotyped in — one genre. In Torres' case, it is appropriate to say that her specialty has been science fiction. She was in *The Matrix Reloaded* (2003) and *The Matrix Revolutions* (2003), and in *Serenity* (2005), the big screen version of the cancelled-too-soon cult FOX network TV series *Firefly* (2002–03). She appeared in the superhero TV movie *M.A.N.T.I.S.* (1994), although not in the TV series that (briefly) followed. She also appeared in the *Dark Angel* TV movie (1996), but again not in the series. She had a recurring role on the supernatural series *Angel* (2003). She appeared on an episode of *Xena: Warrior Princess* (1997–99), and had a recurring role as Nebula on *Hercules: The Legendary Journeys* (1997). *Xena* producer Rob Tapert made sure that genre fans would really became aware of Torres when she co-starred on the syndicated *Cleopatra 2525* (2000–01), a tongue-in-cheek series about an exotic entertainer who finds herself transported to the far-flung future, where she fights bad guys with two other babes. The show was fun, but it did not last long. Torres was also the voice of Hispanic heroine Vixen on *Justice League* (2004–06), based on the DC Comics superhero group.

Those not inclined to science fiction can enjoy her skilled performances in *I Think I Love My Wife* (2007), as Chris Rock's "dull" but delightful wife, and in *South of Pico* (2007), as the sensitive waitress Carla. Other career highlights include recurring roles on *24* (2004), *Alias* (2001–06) and *The Shield* (2006). Her vocal talent is a well-kept secret. She is a gifted mezzo soprano, with training in opera, gospel and jazz. She is the wife of the distinguished actor Laurence Fishburne (married in 2002); they have one child, a daughter named Delilah.

Feature Films including Video and TV Movies: *Bed of Roses* (1996), *The Substance of Fire* (1997), *The Underworld* (TV; 1997), *The Matrix Reloaded* (2003), *The Law and Mr. Lee* (TV; 2003), *The Matrix Revolutions* (2003), *Gramercy Park* (TV; 2004), *Hair Show* (2004), *Soccer Moms* (TV; 2005), *Fair Game* (2005), *Serenity* (2005), *Jam* (2006), *Five Fingers* (2006), *I Think I Love My Wife* (2007), *South of Pico* (2007), *Don't Let Me Drown* (2008).

TV: *Law & Order* (2 episodes; "Skin Deep," "Purple Heart," 1992 and 1995), *M.A.N.T.I.S.* (1994), *NYPD Blue* ("E.R.," 1995), *One Life to Live* (recurring role as Magdelena; 1996), *Dark Angel* (TV; 1996), *Profiler* ("FTX: Field Training Exercise," 1997), *The Gregory Hines Show* ("Flirting with Disaster," 1997), *Xena: Warrior Princess* ("King of Assassins," 1997), *Hercules: The Legendary Journeys* (recurring role of Nebula; 1997–99), *La Femme Nikita* ("Open Heart," 1998), *Encore! Encore!* (pilot; 1998), *Cleopatra 2525* (recurring role of Helen "Hel" Carter; 2000–01), *Alias* (recurring role of Anna Espinosa; 2001–06), *2001 alma Awards*, *Any Day Now* (recurring role of Stacy Trenton; "It's Not Karma," "It's Life," 2001–02), *Firefly* (recurring role of Zoe Washburn; 2002–03), *Angel* (5 episodes in the role of Jasmine; "Inside Out," "Shiny, Happy People," "The Magic Bullet," "Sacrifice," "Peace Out," 2003), *The Agency* ("Absolute Bastard," 2003), *The Guardian* (2 episodes in the role of Sadie Harper; "Big Coal," "Shame," 2003), *CSI* ("XX," 2004), *24* (recurring role of Julia Milliken; 2004), *Justice League* (5 episodes as the voice of Vixen; "Wake the Dead," "Hunter's Moon," "Shadow of the Hawk," "Ancient History," "Grudge Match," 2004–06), *Sci Fi Inside* ("Serenity," 2005), *The Film Programme* (2005), *The Shield* (3 episodes in the role of Sadie; "Kavanaugh," "Smoked," "Of Mice and Len," 2006), *Without a Trace* ("More Than This," 2006), *Standoff* (recurring role of Cheryl Carrera; 2006–07), *Tavis Smiley* (2007), *Dirty Sexy Money* ("The Nutcracker," 2007), *Boston Legal* ("The Gods Must Be Crazy," 2008), *Eli Stone* ("Grace," 2008).

Toussaint, Lorraine Born in Trinidad, West Indies, April 4, 1960.

Lorraine Toussaint moved from Trinidad to Brooklyn, New York, at age ten. She is a graduate of Manhattan's School of the Performing Arts, as well as New York's Juilliard School. She is closely associated with the series *Law & Order* and

Crossing Jordan. She was assistant medical examiner Elaine Duchamps on *Crossing Jordan* in 2002–03, and was the incendiary Shambala Green on *Law & Order* opposite Michael Moriarty, and later Sam Waterston (1990–2003). But this is only the tip of the iceberg: she has had one of the most active television careers of any actress of her generation.

She has also had recurring roles on a variety of other series, including the soap *One Life to Live* (1988), *Bodies of Evidence* (1992), *Where I Live* (1993), *Amazing Grace* (1995), *Leaving L.A.* (1997), *Any Day Now* (as the driven attorney Rene Jackson, who grew up best friends with a white girl in the 1960s, and whom she encounters again 30 years later when Jackson moves back to the Alabama town where she grew up; 1998–2002), *Saving Grace* (2007–08) and *Ugly Betty* (2007). She also appeared in the miniseries Alex Haley's *Queen* with Halle Berry and the TV movie *Their Eyes Were Watching God* (2005), also with Berry.

She has been nominated for three NAACP Image Awards for Best Actress in a Drama Series and a TV Guide Award for Favorite Actress in a Drama Series (for *Any Day Now)*.

Feature Films including TV Movies: *The Face of Rage* (TV; 1983), *A Case of Deadly Force* (TV; 1986), *Breaking In* (1989), *Common Ground* (TV; 1990), *Hudson Hawk* (1991), *Daddy* (TV; 1991), *Red Dwarf* (TV; 1992), *Trial: The Price of Passion* (TV; 1992), *Love, Lies & Lullabies* (TV; 1993), *Point of No Return* (1993), *Class of '61* (TV; TV; 1993), *Mother's Boys* (1994), *A Time to Heal* (TV; 1994), *Bleeding Hearts* (1994), *Dangerous Minds* (1995), *It Was Him or Us* (TV; 1995), *Psalms from the Underground* (1996), *Jaded* (1996), *America's Dream* (TV; 1996), *Nightjohn* (TV; 1996), *If These Walls Could Talk* (TV; 1996), *The Cherokee Kid* (TV; 1996), *The Spittin' Image* (1997), *Blackout Effect* (TV; 1998), *Black Dog* (1998), *The Sky Is Falling* (2000), *Their Eyes Were Watching God* (TV; 2005).

TV: *One Life to Live* (recurring role as Vera Williams; 1988), *A Man Called Hawk* ("Hear No Evil," 1989), *227* ("Nightmare on 227," 1990), *Law & Order* (recurring role of Shambala Green; 1990–2003), *Tequila and Bonetti* ("The Red Cadillac," 1992), *Bodies of Evidence* (recurring role as Dr. Mary Rocket; 1992), *Queen* (miniseries; 1993), *Where I Live* (recurring role as Marie St. Martin; 1993), *The Sinbad Show* (pilot; 1993), *M.A.N.T.I.S.* ("Fire in the Heart," 1994), *Amazing Grace* (also known as *Wing and a Prayer*; recurring role as Yvonne Price; 1995), *Bless This House* ("A Woman's Work Is Never Done," 1995), *Murder One* (2 episodes in the role of Margaret Stratton; "Chapter Six," "Chapter Eight," 1995), *Mr. & Mrs. Smith* ("The Coma Episode," 1996), *Dark Skies* ("We Shall Overcome," 1996), *Promised Land* (aka *Home of the Brave*; "Running Scared," 1997), *Leaving L.A.* (recurring role of Dr. Claudia Chan; 1997), *Nothing Sacred* ("Signs and Words," 1998), *Cracker* (2 episodes in the role of Tisha Watlington; "If," Parts I and II, 1998), *C-16: FBI* ("My Brother's Keeper," 1998), *Any Day Now* (recurring role of Rene Jackson; 1998–2002), *Crossing Jordan* (6 episodes in the role of Dr. Elaine Duchamps; 2002–03), *Weddings of a Lifetime: Lifetime's Dream Weddings on a Budget* (2002), *This Far by Faith* (narrator; 6 episodes; 2003), *Threat Matrix* (5 episodes in the role of Carina Wright; "Doctor Germ," "In Plane Sight," "Alpha-126," "Cold Cash," "PPX," 2003–04), *Frasier* ("Boo!" 2004), *Judging Amy* ("The New Normal," 2005), *The Closer* (2 episodes as Deputy District Attorney Powell; "Fatal Retraction," "Standards and Practice," 2005), *Numb3rs* ("Bones of Contention," 2005), CSI (3 episodes in the role of Marla James; "Fannysmackin'," "Post Mortem," "Big Shots," 2006–07), *Saving Grace* (recurring role of Captain Kate Perry; 2007–08), *Ugly Betty* (recurring role of Yoga; "Secretaries' Day," "East Side Story," "How Betty Got Her Grieve Back," "Betty's Wait Problem," "A League of Their Own," 2007), *Rwanda Rising* (voice; 2007), *ER* ("Believe the Unseen," 2008).

Shorts: *The Gold Lunch* (2008).

True, Rachel Born in New York, New York, November 15, 1966.

Rachel India True was already almost 30 when she played her breakthrough role in the sleeper horror film *The Craft* (1996). She was one of a coven of four teenagers in what was one of the first films to tap into the "Goth" mentality that became so prevalent in our society not long after the film's release. This was also one of the first modern horror films to tap the post-boomer teen market. It was a nice showcase for True and helped launch a 20-year career in films and on television — and counting.

These days she's best recalled for her role on the UPN sitcom *Half & Half* (2002–06). Mona (True) and Dee Dee (Essence Atkins) are two half-

Clockwise from the top: Fairuza Balk, Rachel True, Neve Campbell and Robin Tunney in *The Craft* (1996).

sisters with the same father. They inadvertently become neighbors in the same San Francisco apartment building. Mona is in the music business and the younger Dee Dee is an honor role student. These two "intimate strangers" have essentially nothing in common, but they reluctantly learn to join forces and bond in certain respects as circumstances warrant. *Half & Half* was one of the finest black sitcoms of its era, and a nice showcase for True, whose character was quirky, vibrant and appealing. In 2006, she was nominated for an NAACP Image Award for Outstanding Actress in a Comedy Series for her work.

Of biracial heritage, she broke into television on the top level, with an appearance on *The Cosby Show* (1984). Many other roles on popular shows followed, including *Beverly Hills, 90210* (1990), *Boston Common* (1996), several episodes of HBO's *Dream On* (1994–95), as well as roles in TV movies such as *Moment of Truth: Stalking Back* (1993) and *A Walton Wedding* (1985). She had a recurring role on *The Drew Carey Show* as Janet Clemens (1997–98). She was in the rap music parody *CB4* (1993), which also featured a young Chris Rock, co-starred with Alyssa Milano in the sexy thriller *Embrace of the Vampire* (1995), and was Dave Chappelle's girlfriend in the drug comedy *Half Baked* (1998).

Feature Films including TV Movies: *CB4* (1993), *A Girls' Guide to Sex* (TV; 1993), *Moment of Truth: Stalking Back* (TV; 1993), *Embrace of the Vampire* (1995), *The Craft* (1996), *Nowhere* (1997), *Half Baked* (1998), *With or Without You* (1998), *The Big Split* (1999), *The Apartment Complex* (TV; 1999), *The Auteur Theory* (1999), *Love Song* (TV; 2000), *Groove* (2000), *Who Is A.B.?* (2001), *New Best Friend* (2002), *Pink Eye* (2006), *The Perfect Holiday* (2007), *Killing of Wendy* (2008), *Noah's Ark: A New Beginning* (2008).

TV: *The Cosby Show* (2 episodes in the role of Nikki; "Theo's Final Final," "Theo's Future," 1991 and 1992), *Hangin' with Mr. Cooper* ("Boyz in the Woodz," 1993), *Getting By* ("The Suit," 1993), *Renegade* ("Vanished," 1993), *Beverly Hills, 90210* (2 episodes in the role of Jan Myler; "So Long, Farewell, Auf Wiedersehen, Goodbye," "The Girl from New York City," 1993), *Thea* ("Artie's Party," 1993), *The Fresh Prince of Bel-Air* ("Take My Cousin ... Please," 1993), *Dream On* (2 episodes in the role of Linda Castorini; "From Here to Paternity," "The Weekend at the College Didn't Turn Out as They Planned," 1994 and 1995), *A Walton Wedding* (1995), *Family Matters* ("What's Up Doc?" 1995), *The Witching Hour* (1996), *Boston Common* ("To Bare Is Human," 1997), *The Drew Carey Show* (recurring role of Janet Clemens; 1997–98), *Damon* ("The Last Cub Scout," 1998), *Once and Again* (4 episodes in the role of Mali; "Let's Spend the Night Together," "Liars and Other Strangers," "A Dream Deferred," "Letting Go," 1999–2000), *Providence* ("Family Ties," 2000), *Dawson's Creek* ("Hopeless," 2001), *Half & Half* (15 recurring role of Mona Thorne; 2002–06), *My Coolest Years* (2004), *Kathy Griffin: My Life on the D-List* (5 segments; 2006–08).

Tunie, Tamara Born in McKeesport, Pennsylvania, March 14, 1959.

Tamara Tunie was the fourth of five children. Her father operates a funeral home in Pittsburgh, Pennsylvania. Both of her parents are morticians. She lived above the funeral parlor and grew up in an environment of wakes and funeral preparations. It doesn't seem to have darkened her disposition. She graduated with a bachelor of fine arts from Carnegie Mellon University in 1981. She was a Miss Black Teenage contestant in Pittsburgh in the early seventies.

With her refreshingly off-beat looks and "take no prisoners" acting style, Tunie has forged an impressive acting career, most notably in television and on Broadway.

She was lawyer Jessica Griffin on the soap *As the World Turns* (1986–95, and once more in 1999–2007). In 2003–04, she received two NAACP Image Award nominations for Outstanding Actress in a Daytime Drama Series and two *Soap Opera Digest* award nominations.

Tunie is also well known to fans from her long-running role as medical examiner Melinda Warner on *Law & Order: Special Victims Unit* (1999–present). Her other recurring roles of note are as Lillian Fancy on *NYPD Blue* (1994–97), and as Alberta Green on the first season of *24*. One of her most memorable guest star roles was as a power lesbian on *Sex and the City*. She was the off-screen narrator of director Kasi Lemmon's film *Eve's Bayou* (1997). Her superb narration — a rich underpinning to the story — is the unsung glory of *Eve's Bayou*. She had good roles in two Al Pacino films, *City Hall* (as his press secretary; 1996) and *The Devil's Advocate* (as the possessed wife of a partner in Pacino's law firm; 1997). In 2008, she produced and directed her first film,

See You in September, a romantic comedy that looks with a satirical eye at the world of therapy.

In her "other life," Tunie is a prominent Broadway producer, and in 2007 she received a Tony Award as co-producer of the Tony-winning Best Musical *Spring Awakening* (2006). She was nominated for a Tony Award for co-producing August Wilson's *Radio Golf* (2007). Her professional stage debut was in Richmond, Virginia, as Maggie the Cat in the first African American production of *Cat on a Hot Tin Roof*. She has also had a rich career as a Broadway actress. She was in the revival of the vintage musical *Oh Kay!* (1990–91), toured Europe with the troupe of *Bubblin' Brown Sugar*, and was in off-Broadway's *To Whom It May Concern* (1985). She was Helen of Troy in the New York Shakespeare Festival's Central Park production of *Troilus and Cressida* (1995). She was Calpurnia (the wife of Caesar) opposite Denzel Washington in the Broadway production of *Julius Caesar* (2005). She was Madame de Merteuil in *Les Liaisons Dangereuses* (2005) at the Shakespeare Theater of New Jersey. She also appeared in a special one-night benefit concert revival of *Dreamgirls* as Michelle Morris in September 2001. Her first husband was Greg Bouquett (1988–91). She is currently happily married to jazz vocalist Gregory Generet (since 1995).

Feature Films including TV Movies: *Sweet Lorraine* (1987), *Wall Street* (1987), *Bloodhounds of Broadway* (1989), *Rising Sun* (1993), *Quentin Carr* (1996), *Spirit Lost* (1996), *Rescuing Desire* (1996), *City Hall* (1996), *The Money Shot* (1996), *Rebound: The Legend of Earl "The Goat" Manigault* (TV; 1996), *Eve's Bayou* (voice; 1997), *The Peacemaker* (1997), *The Devil's Advocate* (1997), *Snake Eyes* (1998), *The Caveman's Valentine* (2001), *Showing Up* (documentary; 2010).

TV: *Spenser: For Hire* ("Shadowsight," 1986), *As the World Turns* (recurring role of Jessica Griffin; 1987–2007), *Tribeca* (2 episodes; "The Box," "Honor," 1993), *NYPD Blue* (5 episodes in the role of Lillian Fancy; "Up on the Roof," "Good Time Charlie," "Caulkmanship," "Tail Lights' Last Gleaming," "I Love Lucy," 1994–97), *SeaQuest DSV* ("The Siamese Dream," 1995), *I Love the '90s: Part 2* (1995), *New York Undercover* ("Bad Girls," "Sign o' the Times," 1995–98), *Swift Justice* ("Bad Medicine," 1996), *Law & Order* ("Deadbeat," 1996), *Prince Street* (pilot; 1997), *Feds* ("Missing Pieces," 1997), *Chicago Hope* ("Leggo My Ego," 1997), *Sex and the City* ("The Cheating Curve," 1999), *The American Experience* (voice; "Jubilee Singers: Sacrifice and Glory," 2000), *Law & Order: Special Victims Unit* (recurring role of Dr. Melinda Warner; 2000–08), *A Day's Work, A Day's Pay* (narrator; 2001), *24* (six episodes in the role of Alberta Green; 2002), *18th Annual Soap Opera Digest Awards* (2003), *Nefertiti: Resurrected* (narrator; 2003), *The 31st Annual Daytime Emmy Awards* (2004), *Law & Order: Trial by Jury* ("Day," 2005), *Party Planner with David Tutera* ("Tamara Tunie's Fire and Ice Party," 2005), *The Tony Danza Show* (2005), *Block Sorority Project: The Exodus* (voice; 2006), *After Hours with Daniel Boulud* (2008).

Shorts: *AfterLife* (2007).

Turner, Tina Born in Nutbush, Tennessee, November 26, 1939.

This musical titan will probably be best known on the big screen for the film about her life, *What's Love Got to Do with It* (1993), for which she provided the soundtrack vocals while Angela Bassett portrayed her on screen. Tina Turner's own infrequent forays into acting — the Acid Queen in *Tommy* (1975), small roles in *Sgt. Pepper's Lonely Hearts Club Band* (1978) and *Last Action Hero* (1993), and a villainous role in *Mad Max Beyond Thunderdome* (1985) — are not the stuff upon which legendary acting careers are made. But we'll always have Annie Mae Bullock (Turner's real name) the sexiest, leggiest diva in the history of rock 'n' roll.

"The Queen of Rock and Roll," who has been retired from major tours since 2000, began a new tour in 2008 called the *Tina: Live in Concert Tour*. Tickets were offered on eBay for outrageous amounts, rivaled only by tickets to the Barack Obama inauguration. It seems that retirement was not really in the cards for Tina Turner. She already holds the record for most concert tickets sold by a solo performer. She has had seven *Billboard* top 10 singles and 16 top 10 R&B singles in the U.S. She is the most successful female rock artist ever, with record sales nearing 200 million.

She is the daughter of Zelma (née Curry), a factory worker, and Floyd Richard Bullock, a deacon. Turner attended Flag Grove Elementary School in Haywood County, Tennessee. She and her elder sister Alline were deserted by their father, and briefly by their mother. The sisters reunited with their mother in St. Louis in 1956. It was in St. Louis that she met Ike Turner, and she convinced him to let her audition. She was attending Sumner High School at the time and began singing part-time with Turner's band when she was 18. In 1960, she substituted for another singer who was scheduled to record the song "A Fool in Love" but failed to appear. The record was an R&B smash, crossing over to reach number two on the national pop charts. Thus was born the Ike and Tina Turner Revue. The couple were married in Mexico in 1962.

It has long been felt that Tina Turner and the Ikettes (the girl back-up singers) popularized the miniskirt, or at least opened the world's eyes to its possibilities. As the group continued to grow in popularity throughout the sixties and seventies, they were frequent guests on *The Ed Sullivan Show* and popular teen shows like *Shindig!* and *Soul Train*, singing hits like "Proud Mary" and "River Deep, Mountain High."

The drug abuse and spousal abuse so graphically illustrated in *What's Love Got to Do with It* eventually took a toll on the couple's popularity and ended their marriage. Their divorce was finalized in 1978. Tina started a new life as a solo performer and began turning up in the mid-seventies on the variety shows of the era (*Donny & Marie*, *The Sonny and Cher Show*).

In 1984, Turner's solo career finally took off in a big way with the release of the album *Private Dancer* (and the hit single of the same name). The mega-hit "What's Love Got to Do with It" won Grammys for Record of the Year, Song of the Year and Best Female Rock Vocal Performance in 1985, and *Private Dancer* received a Grammy nomination for Album of the Year. Her role of Aunty Entity in *Mad Max Beyond Thunderdome* led to another big single, "We Don't Need Another Hero."

In February 2008, Turner performed with Beyoncé on the Grammy Awards, and in 2008, she celebrated her return to the stage with a concert with Cher at Caesar's Palace in Las Vegas, at which Oprah Winfrey also appeared. The diva had returned.

Feature Films: *The Big T.N.T. Show* (1966), *Gimme Shelter* (documentary; 1970), *Soul to Soul* (documentary; 1971), *Cocksucker Blues* (documentary; 1972), *Tommy* (1975), *Sgt. Pepper's Lonely Hearts Club Band* (1978), *Mad Max Beyond Thunderdome* (1985), *Last Action Hero* (1993), *What's Love Got to Do with It* (voice; 1993).

TV: *American Bandstand* (5 appearances; 1960–71), *The Cinnamon Cinder Show* (1963), *Shindig!* (3 segments; 1964–65), *Where the Action Is* (3 segments; 1965–66), *Ready, Steady, Go!* (1966), *Top of the Pops* (14 segments; 1966–2000), *Goodbye Again* (1968), *The Donald O'Connor Show* (1968), *The Hollywood Palace* (1968), *The Andy Williams Show* (2 appearances; 1969–70), *The Smothers Brothers Comedy Hour* (1969), *The Ed Sullivan Show* (1970), *Playboy After Dark* (1970), *The Everly Brothers Show* (1970), *It's Your Thing* (1970), *The Name of the Game* ("I Love You, Billy Baker," Parts I and II, 1970), *The Tonight Show Starring Johnny Carson* (9 appearances; 1970–81), *Kenny Rogers and the First Edition: Rollin' on the River* (1971), *Taking Off* (1971), *Starparade* (1971), *Beat-Club* (2 segments; 1971 and 1972), *Soul Train* (2 segments; 1972 and 1975), *The Midnight Special* (8 segments; 1973–79), *Don Kirshner's Rock Concert* (1974), *Countdown* (1974), *Whistle Test* (1975), *Ann-Margret Olssen* (1975), *Cher* (2 segments; 1975), *Poiret est vous* (1975), *Musikladen* (2 segments; 1975–78), *The Alan Hamel Show* (1977), *The Brady Bunch Hour* (1977), *The Sonny and Cher Show* (1977), *The Merv Griffin Show* (1977), *On the Road* (1979), *Olivia Newton-John: Hollywood Nights* (1980), *Rod Stewart: Tonight He's Yours* (1980), *Sound of the City: London 1964–73* (archival; 1981), *Saturday Night Live* (3 segments; 1981–97), *The Tube* (5 segments; 1983–86), *Estoc de pop* (1984), *MTV 1st Annual Video Music Awards* (1984), *The 12th Annual American Music Awards* (1985), *The British Record Industry Awards* (1985), *We Are the World* (1985), *The 27th Annual Grammy Awards* (1985), *Tina Turner: Private Dancer* (1985), *Live Aid* (1985), *Wogan* (5 segments; 1985–92), *The Prince's Trust Rock Gala: 10th Birthday* (1986), *The Max Headroom Show* (1986), *Brown Sugar* (archival; 1986), *Tina!* (1986), *Marvin Gaye* (archival; 1987), *Hysteria 2!* (1989), *Decade* (1989), *Big World Café* (1989), *The Royal Variety Performance 1989*, *Cilla's Goodbye to the '80s* (1989), *Des O'Connor Tonight* (3 appearances; 1989–96), *Aspel & Company* (1990), *Two Rooms: A Tribute to Elton John and Bernie Taupin* (1991), *The Grand Opening of Euro Disney* (1992), *The Who's "Tommy," The Amazing Journey* (1993), *Late Night with David Letterman* (2 appearances; 1993–97), *The 1993 World Music Awards*, *Surprise Surprise!* (1993), *This Morning* (1993), *Tina Turner: Nice ... and Easy ... and Rough* (1993), *The Best of the Don Lane Show* (archival; 1994), *Champions of the World* (1995), *The History of Rock 'n' Roll, Vol. 1* (1995), *GoldenEye: The Secret Files*

(1995), *Brit Awards 1996*, *Especial Tina Turner* (1996), *Tonight with Richard Madeley and Judy Finnigan* (1996), *The National Lottery* (1996), *Mundo VIP* (1996), *Wetten, dass...?* (3 segments; 1996–2004), *Larry King Live* (1997), *The 39th Annual Grammy Awards* (1997), *The Oprah Winfrey Show* (10 appearances; 1997–2008), *Tina Turner: Girl from Nutbush* (1998), *Eros & Friends* (1998), *VH1 Divas Live 2* (1998), *Elton John: With a Little Help from My Friends* (1999), *100 Greatest Women of Rock and Roll* (1999), *The 1999 Malibu MOBO Awards*, *TFI Friday* (1999), *Premios amigo 99* (1999), *Taratata* (1999), *The South Bank Show* (1999), *The National Lottery Stars* (3 segments; 1999–2000), *GMTV* (2 segments; 1999–2003), *On Tour with Tina* (2000), *Behind the Music* (2 segments; 2000), *On Tour with Tina* (2000), *Ally McBeal* ("The Oddball Parade," 2000), *Millionär gesucht!: Die SKL Show* (2000), *Playboy: The Party Continues* (archival; 2000), *It's Black Entertainment* (archival; 2002), *American Bandstand's 50th Anniversary Celebration* (archival; 2002), *The Wayne Brady Show* (2003), *Prey for Rock and Roll* (archival; 2003), *Cher: The Farewell Tour* (archival; 2003), *TeleVizierRing* (2004), *Star Academy* (2004), *Nordic Music Awards 2004*, *Parkinson* (2004), *The National Lottery: Wright Around the World* (2004), *Quelli che ... il calcio* (2004), *Les 40 ans de la 2* (archival; 2004), *Retrosexual: The '80s* (archival; 2004), *Canada A.M.* (2005), *Today* (2 appearances; 2005), *Live with Regis and Kelly* (2005), *The View* (2005), *The Ellen DeGeneres Show* (2005), *Once Upon a Time...* (2005), *Corazón de...* (2005), *The Kennedy Center Honors: A Celebration of the Performing Arts* (2005), *The Early Show* (4 appearances; 2005–08), *Legends Ball* (2006), *La imagen de tu vida* (archival; 2006), *Building a Dream: The Oprah Winfrey Leadership Academy* (2007), *Vivement dimanche* (2007), *Getaway* (archival; 2007), *La tele de tu vida* (2 segments; 2007), *African American Lives 2* (2008), *Banda sonora* (archival; 2008), *The 50th Annual Grammy Awards* (2008), *Entertainment Tonight* (6 segments; 2008), *Memories de la tele* (archival; 2008), *Oprah, Cher and Tina Turner at Caesar's Palace in Las Vegas* (2008), *The Early Show* (2008).

Video/DVD: *Cool Cats: 25 Years of Rock 'n' Roll Style* (archival; 1983), *Tina Turner: Rio '88* (1988), *Shindig! Presents Groovy Gals* (archival; 1991), *Shindig! Presents Soul* (archival; 1991), *Joe Cocker: Have a Little Faith* (1996), *Tina Turner: Live in Amsterdam* (1996), *Tina Turner: Celebrate Live 1999* (1999), *Tina Turner: One Last Time Live in Concert* (1999), *The Singer and the Song* (archival; 2004), *TV in Black: The First Fifty Years* (archival; 2004).

Tyler, Aisha Born in San Francisco, California, September 18, 1970.

Aisha Tyler is one of those "do it all" actresses with as varied a résumé as anyone in the entertainment industry. She is a stand-up comedienne; an actress; a film critic (she filled in for Roger Ebert on *Ebert and Roeper at the Movies*); TV host (*Talk Soup* in 2001 and *The Fifth Wheel* in 2002); author (*Swerve: A Guide to the Sweet Life for Postmodern Girls*, published in 2004, and a regular contributor to *Jane* and *Glamour* magazines); model (she appeared nude in *Allure* magazine in 2006 — the "Nude Issue" is an annual event, and raises money to fight skin cancer); political commentator (she was a guest on Bill Maher's *Politically Incorrect*); linguist (fluent in French, Russian and Swahili); and philanthropist (board member of the American Red Cross, advisor to the environmental organization The Trust for Public Land).

Her mother is Robin Gregory, a teacher, and her father is photographer Jim Tyler. Her parents divorced when she was 10, and she was raised by her dad. Tyler graduated from Dartmouth College with a degree in government and environmental policy. After briefly working for an advertising firm, she moved from San Francisco to Los Angeles in 1996. Even in high school, Tyler had a strong interest in comedy: she cut class to attend comedy improv classes. Eventually she began appearing at major stand-up venues like the Laugh Factory in Hollywood.

Her television work includes a recurring role as Charlie Wheeler on the ninth and tenth seasons of *Friends*; a recurring role on *Ghost Whisperer*, even though they killed her off after the first season; and recurring roles on *CSI* and *24* in 2004–05. She's had guest spots on *CSI: Miami*, *Nip/Tuck*, *Boston Legal*, *Reno 911!* and *Curb Your Enthusiasm*. She did voice work on the animated *Boondocks*.

In feature films, she was Mother Nature in the Tim Allen comedies *The Santa Clause 2* (2002) and *The Santa Clause 3: The Escape Clause* (2006). She was in the crime-action thrillers *Never Die Alone* (2004), *.45* (2006), and *Death Sentence*

(2006), a *Death Wish* type film starring Kevin Bacon. She brings real depth and authority to her dramatic roles and then turns around and takes another foray into wacky comedy, such as her role as Mahogany in the spoof of Asian martial arts films, *Balls of Fury* (2007). (Tyler is a big fan of the martial arts genre.) She married Jeff Tietjens in 1992.

Feature Films including Video and TV Movies: *Grand Avenue* (TV; 1996), *Dancing in September* (2000), *Moose Mating* (2001), *The Santa Clause 2* (2002), *One Flight Stand* (2003), *Never Die Alone* (2004), *For One Night* (TV; 2006), *The Santa Clause 3: The Escape Clause* (2004), *.45* (2006), *Death Sentence* (2007), *Balls of Fury* (2007), *Meet Market* (2008), *Bedtime Stories* (2008), *Black Water Transit* (2009).

TV: *Nash Bridges* ("High Impact," 1996), *The Pretender* ("PTB," 1999), *The Howard Stern Radio Show* (2001), *E!'s Live Countdown to the Academy Awards* (2001), *Weakest Link* (2001), *The Tonight Show with Jay Leno* (2001), *Off Limits* (cast member; 2001), *Curb Your Enthusiasm* ("Shaq," 2001), *The Fifth Wheel* (host; 5 segments; 2001–02), *Talk Soup* (host; various segments; 2001–02), *Howard Stern* (2 appearances; 2001–03), *Player$* (2002), *Last Call with Carson Daly* (2002), *Shirtless: Hollywood's Sexiest Men* (2002), *VH1's 100 Sexiest Artists* (2002), *The Sausage Factory* ("Purity Test," 2002), *Hollywood Squares* (2002), *I Love the '80s* (2002), *Friends* (recurring role of Charlie Wheeler; 2003), *VH1 Divas Duets* (2003), *2003 MTV Movie Awards*, *The New Tom Green Show* (2003), *9th Annual Soul Train Lady of Soul Awards* (2003), *The GQ Men of the Year Awards* (2003), *CSI: Miami* ("Body Count," 2003), *Spike 52: Hottest Holiday Gifts* (2003), *World Poker Tour* (2004), *Tavis Smiley* (2004), *On-Air with Ryan Seacrest* (2004), *The Sharon Osbourne Show* (2004), *MADtv* (2004), *The 18th Annual Soul Train Music Awards* (2004), *The Wayne Brady Show* (2004), *Last Comic Standing* (talent scout; various segments; 2004), *G-Phoria 2004*, *The Late Late Show with Craig Kilborn* (2004), *Nip/Tuck* ("Manya Manbika," 2004), *CSI* (recurring role of Mia Dickerson; 2004–05), *Comic's Climb at the USCAF* (2005), *Dennis Miller* (2005), *The 31st Annual People's Choice Awards* (2005), *Inside Dish with Rachael Ray* (2005), *24* (recurring role of Marianne Taylor; 2005), *The Ellen DeGeneres Show* (2005), *The Tony Danza Show* (2005), *The 19th Annual Soul Train Music Awards* (2005), *The Tyra Banks Show* (2005), *Ghost Whisperer* (recurring role of Andrea Moreno; 2005–07), *Live with Regis and Kelly* (2 appearances; 2005 and 2007), *The Late Late Show with Craig Ferguson* (7 appearances; 2005–08), *Ebert and Roeper at the Movies* (guest critic; various segments; 2006), *Comic Relief 2006*, *The View* (guest host; 2007), *Howard Stern on Demand* (2007), *Entertainment Tonight* (2 segments; 2007–08), *Boston Legal* ("Trial of the Century," 2007), *The Boondocks* ("Attack of the Kung Fu Killer Wolf Bitch," 2007), *Reno 911!* ("Dangle's Secret Family," 2008), *Top Chef* (2008), *History of the Joke* (documentary; 2008), *Super Password* (2009).

Aisha Tyler.

Video/DVD: *Kanye West: College Dropout Video Anthology* (2005).

Shorts: *The Whipper* (2000), *The Trap* (2008).

Tyson, Cathy Born in Liverpool, England, June 12, 1965.

The daughter of a Trinidadian lawyer father and a Caucasian social worker mother, Cathy Tyson made an auspicious screen debut as the ethereal but emotionally bereft black prostitute Simone in *Mona Lisa* (1986). She never quite connected with international audiences as deeply as she did in this film, but she has continued to have an impressive and varied career in the United Kingdom.

The family moved to Liverpool when she was two. She left college to join the Everyman's Theatre in Liverpool, and then won admission to the Royal Shakespeare Company. She has also performed at the Open Air Theatre in Regent's Park, and in 1998 was Cleopatra in Shaw's *Antony and Cleopatra* for the English Shakespeare Company.

Much of Tyson's latter day career has been on British television. She joined the hit series *Band of Gold* in 1995, and *Always and Everyone* in 1999. In 2007 she became a cast member on the BBC's academic drama *Grange Hill* as Miss Gayle, and that same year joined the cast of the British soap opera, *Emmerdale Farm*, as single mother Andrea Hayworth. She was married to Craig Charles from 1984 to 1989; the couple had one child, a son named Jack. Her second husband is Andrew Shreeves.

Feature Films including TV Movies: *Mona Lisa* (1986), *Business as Usual* (1987), *The Serpent and the Rainbow* (1988), *Turbulence* (1991), *Out of the Blue* (TV; 1991), *The Lost Language of Cranes* (TV; 1991), *The Golden Years* (TV; 1992), *Angels* (1992), *Barbara Taylor Bradford's Remember* (TV; 1992), *Priest* (1994), *Hidden Empire: A Son of Africa* (TV; 1995), *The Old Man Who Read Love Stories* (2001), *Perfect* (TV; 2001), *Forgiven* (TV; 2007), *Liverpool Nativity* (TV; 2007).

TV: *Horizon* (narrator; 1964?), *Scully* (recurring role as Joanna; 1984), *Lenny Henry Tonite* (1986), *Rules of Engagement* (miniseries; 1989), *Chancer* ("History," 1990), *TECX* ("Getting Personnel," 1990), *Medics* (1993), *Band of Gold* (recurring role as Carol Johnson; 1995), *Harry* (1995), *Always and Everyone* (recurring role as Stella; 1999), *Hope and Glory* (1999), *The Bill* (recurring role as Elspeth Wilkins-Barrister; 2000–05), *Night & Day* (recurring role as Reverend Stephanie MacKenzie; 2002–03), *Holby City* ("All the King's Men," 2004), *A Thing Called Love* ("The Lost Child," 2004), *M.I.T.: Murder Investigation Team* (2005), *Injustice* (narrator; 2001), *The Laurence Olivier Awards 2003*, *This Morning* (2006), *Inspector Lewis* ("Old School Ties," 2007), *Bonkers* (recurring role as D.I. Short; 2007), *Emmerdale Farm* (recurring role as Andrea Hayworth; 2007), *British Film Forever* ("Guns, Gansters and Getaways: The Story of the British Crime Thriller," 2007), *Grange Hill* (recurring role as Miss Gayle; 2007), *Doctors* ("What the World Needs Now," 2008).

Video: *RSC Meets USA: Working Shakespeare* (2005).

Cathy Tyson in *Mona Lisa* (1986).

Tyson, Cicely

Born in Harlem, New York, December 1933.

Cicely Tyson is the daughter of Theodosia and William Tyson, immigrants from the island of St. Kitts, West Indies. She began as a fashion model, after having been discovered by a photographer for *Ebony* magazine. She also worked as a secretary for the Red Cross to support herself until her acting career kicked in (which was hardly overnight).

Early in her career she had recurring roles on the daytime soap opera *The Guiding Light* (as Martha Frazier; 1966), and the critically adored but ratings-challenged *East Side/West Side* (1963–64) starring George C. Scott as a crusading social worker. Tyson was one of the first blacks to appear on television is a non-stereotypical dramatic role as secretary Jane Foster. *East Side/West Side* was nominated for eight Emmy Awards during its single season run (and won one for direction).

Her stage debut was in a production of *Dark Side of the Moon* at the Harlem YMCA in the mid–1950s. She was on Broadway in the original cast of Jean Genet's *The Blacks* in 1961, which became the longest-running off–Broadway drama of the sixties, for an amazing total of 1,408 performances. Featuring a black cast in white face make-up, this is an angry, uncompromising look at black rage that has come to be recognized as Genet's most significant work.

Her motion picture career began at a time when opportunities for black actresses were severely limited. She had uncredited roles in *Carib Gold* (1957), *Odds Against Tomorrow* (1959), and *The Last Angry Man* (1959), and was in the unsuccessful Sammy Davis, Jr., drama about a jazz musician, *A Man Called Adam* (1966). This led to featured roles in big budget financial flops like *The Comedians* (based on the Graham Greene novel, it took place in Haiti during the repressive "Papa Doc" Duvalier era, and starred Elizabeth Taylor and Richard Burton; 1967), and *The Heart Is a Lonely Hunter* (1968), a sentimental film based on the novel by Carson McCullers.

She was nominated for the Academy Award for Best Actress for her performance in *Sounder*. That was in 1972, the same year Diana Ross was nominated for her role as Billie Holliday in *Lady Sings the Blues*. It was the first time two black actresses had been nominated for Best Actress in the same year. *Sounder* finally gave Tyson the great role she deserved, as Rebecca Morgan, wife of sharecropper Nathan Lee (Paul Winfield) in 1933 Louisiana. The family faces a crisis when the husband is sent to a prison camp for a petty crime. Young David Lee Morgan (Kevin Hooks) is sent to visit his dad, and the journey becomes one of self-discovery for the boy. The scene where husband and wife are reunited is one of the great scenes in film history.

Tyson became the preeminent black actress in TV movies with appearances in some of the most extraordinary films of the seventies and eighties, most of them biographical studies of notable black women. She was the first black woman to win an Emmy Award for Best Actress (and, in fact, a second Emmy for Actress of the Year), for the deeply moving *The Autobiography of Miss Jane Pittman* (1974), which follows the evolution of the civil rights movement as seen through the eyes of one woman, born as a slave but living to be 110 and surviving into the civil rights era.

She was also in epochal miniseries such as *Roots* (appearing in the first two segments as Kunta Kinte's mother Binta; 1977), *King* (as Coretta Scott King; 1978), and *The Women of Brewster Place* (as Mrs. Browne; 1989); and the TV movies *A Woman Called Moses* (as abolitionist Harriet Tubman; 1978); *The Marva Collins Story* (as a dedicated teacher in an inner city high school; 1981), and *Oldest Living Confederate Widow Tells All* (1994), for which she received her third Emmy Award as the slave Castralia, owned by the Marsden family, whose lineage is traced by the film from the Civil War era to contemporary times.

She returned to the stage in 1983 after a long absence in *The Corn Is Green*. It received poor reviews and closed quickly, and Tyson was fired when she took a night off to attend a tribute ceremony for her husband (she was married to the great jazz trumpeter Miles Davis from 1981 to 88). She sued the producers for the full money due her in her contract, and after 15 years of litigation, she won the case.

Tyson has recently been seen in supporting roles in the TV movies *Mama Flora's Family* (1998) and *The Rosa Parks Story* (2002), and in the theatrical releases *Diary of a Mad Black Woman* (2005) and Tyler Perry's *Madea's Family Reunion* (2006). She co-founded the storied Dance Theater of Harlem in 1974 and was inducted into the Black Filmmakers Hall of Fame in 1977.

Feature Films including Video and TV Movies: *Carib Gold* (1957), *Odds Against Tomorrow* (1959), *The Last Angry Man* (1959), *A Man Called Adam* (1966), *The Comedians* (1967), *The Heart Is a Lonely Hunter* (1968), *Marriage: Year One* (TV; 1971), *Neighbors* (TV; 1971), *Wednesday Night Out* (TV; 1972), *Sounder* (1972), *The Autobiography of Miss Jane Pittman* (TV; 1974), *Just an Old Sweet Song* (TV; 1976), *The Blue Bird* (1976), *The River Niger* (1976), *Wilma* (TV; 1977), *A Woman Called Moses* (TV; 1978), *A Hero Ain't Nothin' But a Sandwich* (1978), *The Concorde ... Airport '79* (1979), *The Marva Collins Story* (TV; 1981), *Bustin' Loose* (1981), *Benny's Place* (TV; 1982), *Playing with Fire* (TV; 1985), *Acceptable Risks* (TV; 1986), *Samaritan: The Mitch Snyder Story* (TV; 1986), *Intimate Encounters* (TV; 1986), *The Kid Who Loved Christmas* (TV; 1990), *Heat Wave* (TV; 1990), *Fried Green Tomatoes* (1991), *Duplicates* (TV; 1992), *When No One Would Listen* (TV; 1992), *House of Secrets* (TV; 1993), *Oldest Living Confederate Widow Tells All* (TV; 1994), *The Road to Galveston* (TV; 1996), *Bridge of Time* (TV; 1997), *Riot* (TV; 1997), *Hoodlum* (1997), *The Price of Heaven* (TV; 1997), *Ms. Scrooge* (TV; 1997), *Always Outnumbered, Always Outgunned* (TV; 1998), *Mama Flora's Family* (TV; 1998), *A Lesson Before Dying* (TV; 1999), *Aftershock: Earthquake in New York* (TV; 1999), *Jewel* (TV; 2001), *The Rosa Parks Story* (TV; 2002), *Because of Winn-Dixie* (2005), *Diary of a Mad Black Woman*

(2005), *Madea's Family Reunion* (2006), *Fat Rose and Squeaky* (2006), *Idlewild* (2006), *Relative Stranger* (TV; 2008).

TV: *Frontiers of Faith* ("The Bitter Cup," 1961), *The Doctors and the Nurses* ("Frieda," 1962), *Naked City* ("Howard Running Bear Is a Turtle," 1963), *East Side/West Side* (recurring role of Jane Foster; 1963–64), *Slattery's People* ("Question: Who You Taking to the Main Event, Eddie," 1965), *I Spy* (2 episodes; "So Long, Patrick Henry," "Trial by Treehouse," 1965 and 1966), *Guiding Light* (recurring role as Martha Frazier; 1966), *Cowboy in Africa* ("Tomorrow on the Wind," 1967), *Judd for the Defense* ("Commitment," 1967), *Medical Center* ("The Last Ten Yards," 1969), *The F.B.I.* (2 episodes; "The Enemies," "Silent Partners," 1968 and 1969), *The Courtship of Eddie's Father* ("Guess Who's Coming for Lunch?" 1969), *Here Come the Brides* ("A Bride for Obie Brown," 1970), *The Bill Cosby Show* ("Blind Date," 1970), *Mission: Impossible* ("Death Squad," 1970), *Gunsmoke* ("The Scavengers," 1970), *Emergency!* ("Crash," 1972), *The Tonight Show Starring Johnny Carson* (1972), *Soul Train* (1972), *The Flip Wilson Show* (1973), *The American Film Institute Salute to James Cagney* (1974), *Free to Be ... You and Me* (1974), *The 46th Annual Academy Awards* (1974), *The 28th Annual Tony Awards* (1974), *The American Film Institute Salute to Bette Davis* (1977), *Roots* (miniseries; 1977), *The 49th Annual Academy Awards* (1977), *CBS: On the Air* (1978), *The 50th Annual Academy Awards* (1978), *The 30th Annual Primetime Emmy Awards* (1978), *King* (miniseries; 1978), *The 21st Annual TV Week Logie Awards* (1979), *The Television Annual: 1978/79* (1979), *Saturday Night Live* (1979), *The 34th Annual Tony Awards* (1980), *The Human Body: Becoming a Woman* (1981), *Night of 100 Stars* (1982), *The American Film Institute Salute to Lillian Gish* (1984), *Star Search* (1985), *An All-Star Celebration Honoring Martin Luther King, Jr.* (1986), *19th Annual NAACP Image Awards* (1987), *20th Annual NAACP Image Awards* (1988), *The Kennedy Center Honors: A Celebration of the Performing Arts* (1988), *The Women of Brewster Place* (miniseries; 1989), *B.L. Stryker* ("Winner Take All," 1990), *The Arsenio Hall Show* (1994), *A Century of Women* (voice; miniseries; 1994), *Sweet Justice* (recurring role as Carrie Grace Battle; 1994–95), *Flight to Freedom* (1995), *Celebrate the Dream: 50 Years of Ebony Magazine* (1996), *3rd Annual Screen Actors Guild Awards* (1997), *The Rosie O'Donnell Show* (1997), *CBS: The First 50 Years* (1998), *The 51st Annual Primetime Emmy Awards* (1999), *Intimate Portrait* ("Harriet Tubman," 2000), *Touched by an Angel* ("Living the Rest of My Life," 2000), *The Outer Limits* ("Final Appeal," 2000), *The Today Show* (2001), *Inside TV Land: African Americans in Television* (2002), *2002 Trumpet Awards*, *A Capitol Fourth* (2004), *The Black Movie Awards* (2005), *Higglytown Heroes* ("Wayne's 100 Special Somethings," 2005), *Tavis Smiley* (2 appearances; 2005–06), *Legends Ball* (2006), *AFI's 100 Years ... 100 Cheers: America's Most Inspiring Movies* (2006), *The 2006 Black Movie Awards*, *Rwanda Rising* (voice; 2007), *The 5th Annual TV Land Awards* (2007), *The 59th Primetime Emmy Awards* (2007), *Entertainment Tonight* (2008).

DVD/Video: *TV in Black: The First Fifty Years* (2004).

Shorts: *Clippers* (1991), *The Double Dutch Divas* (2001).

Cicely Tyson in *The Autobiography of Miss Jane Pittman* (1974).

Uggams, Leslie

Born in New York, New York, May 25, 1943.

Leslie Uggams might best be described as a quiet legend. She has gone about excelling in every aspect of the entertainment industry, she has broken her share of racial barriers, and she has had an outstanding, Tony Award–winning Broadway career. However, her generally low-key demeanor and her ability to make her extraordinary talent seem almost effortless is perhaps why this woman is a "quiet" legend. But a legend she is.

Her Tony Award was for *Hallelujah, Baby!* (1967) for Best Actress in a Musical. *Hallelujah, Baby!* follows four decades in the life of the beautiful Georgina (Uggams), a talented singer and dancer, as she struggles to attain stardom and becomes involved in a relationship with a white man, but discovers that the black man who also cares for her is capable of rising above his job as a porter and, like herself, can achieve higher goals. She was also nominated for a Tony for her role as Ruby in 2001 for Best Actress in a Play for August Wilson's *King Hedley II* (2001).

Uggams tried to follow up on the success of *Hallelujah, Baby!* with *Her First Roman* (1968). She was a sexy Cleopatra, but the critics hated it, and it closed in a couple of weeks. In 1985–86 she starred in *Jerry's Girls*, a musical revue featuring the music of Jerry Herman. In 1988 she was Reno Sweeney in the Lincoln Center production of *Anything Goes*, reprising her role at the Vivien Beaumont Theatre in 1989–90. She went on tour in 1991 with the play with music *Stringbean*, about the young Ethel Waters' rise to fame in the twenties. She was the Muzzy Van Hossmere in *Thoroughly Modern Millie* in 2003–04; although the show was a long-running hit, it had unappealing racist touches. In 2005 she joined James Earl Jones in a well-done revival of the touching *On Golden Pond*. She was in the off–Broadway revival of the 1975 black drama *The First Breeze of Summer* in 2008, which ran longer than the original production.

Her show business roots go back several generations — she appeared as Ethel Waters' niece on *The Beulah Show* in the early 1950s. She was six years old at the time. She also appeared on Johnny Olsen's *TV Kids*. In 1952, at age nine, she performed at the Apollo Theater, and in 1954 at New York's Palace Theater. As she grew into an adolescent and a teenager, she became a fixture on the most popular show on television in its day, *Sing Along with Mitch* (1960–64). Segments of the booming-voiced, all male chorus singing in incredibly precise harmony were interspersed with weekly appearances — she was the only African

Leslie Uggams at the height of her Las Vegas fame (*Hollywood Reporter*).

American regular on a TV show at that time — of a glove-wearing, sylph-like, young lady with a strange last name. But it was evident that Leslie Uggams could sing beautifully — mostly Broadway-style ballads and classics like "Someone to Watch Over Me."

In 1968 she became the first black woman since the days of Hazel Scott some 30 years before to headline her own variety show, *The Leslie Uggams Show*. It ran for three months from late September to late December, the victim of awful ratings in the time slot against the western *Bonanza*, the most popular show on TV. She replaced the controversial Smothers Brothers show. With a black cast and a weekly segment called "Sugar Hill" (also the title of a film in which she appeared in 1994), a comedy about a working-class black family, it was unlike anything the medium had ever seen before — or since.

Raised in the Washington Heights section of New York, she came from a show business family. Her father was a singer with the Hall Johnson Choir and her mother was a chorus dancer. Uggams has a rather spotty filmography. Motion pictures did not seem to know what to do with her. She sang in *Two Weeks in Another Town* (1962), then waited 10 years before her next two film appearances, in 1972. She was flight attendant Lovejoy Wells on a hijacked plane in *Skyjacked.* Her role as Netta in *Black Girl* was her first decent part in a theatrical film. The film centers on 17-year-old Billie Jean and her supportive yet insecure mother, Mamma Rose. Billie Jean dreams of becoming a ballet dancer, but first she must cope with a complex, dysfunctional family life. Uggams is the daughter away at college who comes home to visit and who wants Billie Jean to follow her path, to complete high school and apply for college. Directed by actor Ossie Davis, *Black Girl* is a complex, character-rich film, a refreshing change in the blaxploitation film era (even though the ad campaign showed Billie Jean wielding a knife!).

Uggams did appear — in what was her sole starring role in a motion picture — in one of the strangest films ever made. *Poor Pretty Eddie* (1975) was known under a slew of other titles, mostly retitlings for video and DVD. It has been titled *Black Vengeance*, *Heartbreak Motel* and *Redneck County Rape.* The film begins with Uggams singing "The Star-Spangled Banner" to a packed stadium, so it's clear she is a famous singer. Her car breaks down in the middle of nowhere in the "redneck" South — why she is traveling alone is never explained — and she finds herself held hostage by a deranged young Elvis-wannabe who beats and rapes her. (In an alternate, completely reedited version of the film, he's a good guy who eventually realizes his dream to be a singing star!) Academy Award winner Shelley Winters found herself in this offensive mess. It is surrealistic to see Uggams in what amounts to a sleazy drive-in exploitation film, but there is no denying the weird, hypnotic power the film exudes.

Leslie Uggams.

Sugar Hill (1994) is a neighborhood in Harlem. The film centers around Roemello Skuggs (Wesley Snipes), a drug dealer trying to change his life — but that is not to be. Uggams had a minor role (Doris Holly) in this overlong, rather predictable film, and acting honors belonged to Snipes, Clarence Williams and Theresa Randle. Uggams had much better luck with TV miniseries. She was Kizzy Reynolds in *Roots* (1977), the most famous miniseries — and one of the most famous programs — in TV history. Kizzy was the daughter of Kunte Kinte (the seminal character in the series) and Belle. Uggams was the lead character, Lillian Rogers Parks, in *Backstairs at the White House* (1979). Parks was a servant at the White House for 30 years and author of the book upon which the miniseries was based. Uggams has been married to Grahame Pratt since 1965; they have two children. She is a founding member of bravo Chapter/City of Hope, an organization dedicated to the eradication of blood-related maladies.

Feature Films including TV Movies: *Two Weeks in Another Town* (1962), *Skyjacked* (1972), *Black Girl* (1972), *Poor Pretty Eddie* (aka *Heartbreak Motel, Black Vengeance, Redneck County Rape*, 1975), *Sizzle* (TV; 1981), *Sugar Hill* (1994), *Toe to Toe* (2009).

TV: *The Beulah Show* (various episodes; 1950s), *TV Kids* (195?), *Ford Star Time* ("The Mitch Miller Variety Show," 1960), *Sing Along with Mitch* (series regular; 1961–64), *The Ed Sullivan Show* (10 appearances; 1964–67), *The Bell Telephone Hour* (3 episodes; "A Musical Tour of Tin Pan Alley," "The Music of Harold Arlen," "Music That Mirrors the Times," 1965–66), *The Girl from U.N.C.L.E.* ("The Jewels of Topango Affair," 1966), *The Hollywood Palace* (1966), *What's My Line?* (1967), *The Dean Martin Show* (3 appearances; 1967–72), I Spy ("Tonia," 1967), *The*

22nd Annual Tony Awards (1968), *The Leslie Uggams Show* (1969), *The 23rd Annual Tony Awards* (1969), *The Merv Griffin Show* (1969), *This Is Tom Jones* (1970), *Jimmy Durante Presents the Lennon Sisters* (1970), *The Andy Williams Show* (1970), *Swing Out, Sweet Land* (1971), *The Flip Wilson Show* (1971), *The 25th Annual Tony Awards* (1971), *The Ice Palace* (1971), *'S Wonderful, 'S Marvelous, 'S Gershwin* (1972), *Salute to Oscar Hammerstein II* (1972), *The Mod Squad* ("Kill Gently, Sweet Jessie," 1972), *The Tonight Show Starring Johnny Carson* (7 appearances; 1972–82), *The American Film Institute Salute to John Ford* (1973), *High Rollers* (1974), *Marcus Welby, M.D.* ("Feedback," 1974), *The Hollywood Squares* (2 appearances; 1976), *Perry Como's Spring in New Orleans* (1976), *Roots: The Next Generations* (archival; miniseries; 1979), *The 30th Annual Tony Awards* (1976), *Sinatra and Friends* (1977), *Roots* (miniseries; 1977), *The 31st Annual Tony Awards* (1977), *The 29th Annual Primetime Emmy Awards* (1977), *Julie Andrews: One Step Into Spring* (1978), *General Electric's All-Star Anniversary* (1978), *The Muppet Show* (1978), *A Special Sesame Street Christmas* (1978), *The Kraft 75th Anniversary Special* (1978), *Backstairs at the White House* (miniseries; 1979), *A Gift of Music* (1981), *The Love Boat* (2 episodes; 1981), *The 36th Annual Tony Awards* (1982), *Fantasy* (hostess; 1982), *Magnum, P.I.* ("Paradise Blues," 1984), *The 38th Annual Tony Awards* (1984), *Night of 100 Stars II* (1985), *Placido Domingo: Stepping Out with the Ladies* (1985), *The 39th Annual Tony Awards* (1985), *Christmas at Radio City Music Hall* (1986), *The 40th Annual Tony Awards* (1986), *Hotel* ("Discoveries," 1987), *The Kennedy Center Honors: A Celebration of the Performing Arts* (1988), *The 43rd Annual Tony Awards* (1989), *Reading Rainbow* ("Jack, the Seal and the Sea," 1990), *The Cosby Show* ("The Return of the Clairettes," 1991), *A Different World* ("College Kid," 1993), *Broadway at the Hollywood Bowl* (1994), *All My Children* (1996), *NY TV: By the People Who Made It* (Parts I and II) (1998), *Family Guy* (voice; "Mind Over Murder," 1999), *Biography* ("Ben Vereen: The Hard Way," 2000), *Inside TV Land: African Americans in Television* (2002), *Roots: Celebrating 25 Years* (2002), *Broadway: The Golden Age* (2003), *The Early Show* (2005), *The 59th Annual Tony Awards* (2005), *AFI's 100 Years, 100 Movie Quotes: The Greatest Lines from American Film* (2005), *Legends Ball* (2006), *The 60th Annual Tony Awards* (2006), *The 5th Annual TV Land Awards* (2007), *Roots Remembered* (2007), *The 59th Primetime Emmy Awards* (2007).

Union, Gabrielle Born in Omaha, Nebraska, October 29, 1972.

Gabrielle Monique Union is the daughter of Theresa and Sylvester Union. When she was eight, the family moved to Pleasanton, California. She excelled as an athlete at Foothill High School. She was an all-star point guard and participated in soccer and track.

At first Union wanted to go to law school, but she eventually found her way into acting, although she took a detour into modeling when she interned at a modeling agency. She attended a succession of schools (University of Nebraska, Cuesta College, UCLA, where she earned a degree in sociology), and after graduation began to get small roles in films like *She's All That* (1999), *10 Things I Hate About You* (1999), and *Love & Basketball* (2000).

She first attracted widespread attention with *Bring It On* (2000), a tale of cheerleaders who are more than a little on the competitive side. It was a surprise hit, and Union clearly showed that she was not just another pretty face. Then she got a prominent role as Dr. Courtney Ellis in *City of Angels* (2000), followed by a prominent guest star shot as the black romantic interest on the hitherto lilywhite *Friends* (2001) and a recurring role as Renee Slater, sister of the Vanessa Williams character, on *Ugly Betty* (2008). ABC's revived version of *Night Stalker* (2005–06) looked like it was going to be Union's ticket to major TV stardom, but even though she was quite good in it, it was a dark, depressing series that bore little re-

Gabrielle Union.

semblance to the original lighthearted Darren McGavin series and the *Night Stalker* TV movies of the 1970s.

Similarly, her feature film work has yet to yield the one big hit that would put her over the top, although she was charming as the bitchy Eva in *Deliver Us from Eva* (2003), and was matched by her smooth, charming co-star LL Cool J. The ill-advised *The Honeymooners* remake with an all-black leading cast deserved to crash and burn — and it did; *Meet Dave* (2008) was one of the biggest flops of Eddie Murphy's long career; and *Cadillac Records* did not do well and saw her playing second fiddle to Beyoncé (2008).

The female lead in *Bad Boys II* (2003), the box office smash starring Will Smith and Martin Lawrence, Tyler Perry's hit *Daddy's Little Girls* (2007), and the smooth Christmas film *The Perfect Holiday* (2007) were steps in the right direction. She has been nominated for four NAACP Image Awards: Outstanding Supporting Actress in a Motion Picuture (for *Bad Boys II*, 2004), Outstanding Actress in a Motion Picture (for *Deliver Us from Eva*, in 2004), Outstanding Actress in a TV Movie/Mini-series (for *Something the Lord Made*, in 2005), and Best Actress in a Musical or Comedy (for *Breakin' All the Rules*, in 2005). Union married NFL player Chris Martin of the Jacksonville Jaguars in 2001; they divorced in 2006.

Feature Films including Video and TV Movies: *She's All That* (1999), *10 Things I Hate About You* (1999), *H-E Double Hockey Sticks* (TV; 1999), *Love & Basketball* (2000), *Bring It On* (2000), *Close to Home* (TV; 2001), *The Brothers* (2001), *Two Can Play That Game* (2001), *Welcome to Collinwood* (2002), *Abandon* (2002), *Deliver Us from Eva* (2003), *Cradle 2 the Grave* (2003), *Bad Boys II* (2003), *Ride or Die* (2003), *Breakin' All the Rules* (2004), *Something the Lord Made* (TV; 2004), *Constellation* (2005), *Neo Ned* (2005), *The Honeymooners* (2005), *Say Uncle* (2005), *Running with Scissors* (2006), *Football Wives* (TV; 2007), *Daddy's Little Girls* (2007), *The Box* (2007), *The Perfect Holiday* (2007), *Meet Dave* (2008), *Cadillac Records* (2008).

TV: *Moesha* ("Friends," 1996), *Malibu Shores* ("The Competitive Edge," 1996), *Saved by the Bell: The New Class* ("The Long and the Short of It," 1996), *Goode Behavior* (3 episodes in the role of Tracy Monaghan; "Goode and Scared," "Goode Golly, Miss Molly," "Goode Grades," 1996), *7th Heaven* (in the role of Keesha Hamilton; "The Color of God," "America's Most Wanted," "Happy's Valentine," "The Tribe That Binds," 1996–99), *Smart Guy* ("Don't Do That Thing You Do," 1997), *Dave's World* ("Oh Dad, Poor Dad," 1997), *Hitz* ("The Godfather: Not the Movie," 1997), *Sister, Sister* (2 episodes; "Guardian Angel," "Show Me the Money," 1997), *City Guys* ("The Date," 1997), *Star Trek: Deep Space Nine* ("Sons and Daughters," 1997), *The Steve Harvey Show* ("The He-Man, Player-Hater's Club," 1998), *Clueless* ("Prom Misses, Prom Misses," 1999), *Grown Ups* (pilot; 1999), *ER* ("Family Matters," 2000), *The Others* ("Theta," 2000), *Zoe, Duncan, Jack and Jane* ("Too Much Pressure," 2000), *City of Angels* (recurring role of Dr. Courtney Ellis; 2000), *Young Hollywood Awards* (2001), *Friends* ("The One with the Cheap Wedding Dress," 2001), *The Tonight Show with Jay Leno* (2003), *The Daily Show* (2003), *HBO First Look* ("Bad Boys II," 2003), *Pepsi Smash* (2003), *The Proud Family* (voice; "Hooray for Iesha," 2003), *The Sharon Osbourne Show* (2003), *The GQ Men of the Year Awards* (2003), *Tinseltown TV* (2003), *Ellen* (2004), *On-Air with Ryan Seacrest* (2004), *The West Wing* ("The Benign Perogative," 2004), *4th Annual BET Awards* (2004), *Last Call with Carson Daly* (2 appearances; 2004 and 2005), *Jimmy Kimmel Live!* (5 appearances; 2004–08), *TV Land's Top Ten* (2005), *36th NAACP Image Awards* (2005), *Total Request Live* (2005), *Showtime Special: The Honeymooners* (2005), *The View* (2005), *Family Guy* ("Peter's Got Woods," 2005), *The Early Show* (2005), *BET Awards 2005, All Shades of Fine: 25 Hottest Women of the Past 25 Years* (2005), *Late Night with Conan O'Brien* (2005), *The Tony Danza Show* (2005), *Night Stalker* (recurring role of Perri Reed; 2005–06), *Showbiz Tonight* (2006), *Entertainment Tonight* (3 segments; 2006–08), *Late Show with David Letterman* (2007), *22nd Annual Stellar Gospel Music Awards* (2007), *Live with Regis and Kathie Lee* (2008), *BET Awards 2008, Ugly Betty* (recurring role of Renee Slater; "Burning Questions," "Twenty-Four Candles," "A Thousand Words by Friday," 2008).

Van Engle, Dorothy Born in Harlem, New York, August 14, 1910; died May 10, 2004, Ocala, Florida.

She was born Donessa Dorothy Van Engle. Her father, Fred, was a tailor born on the island of St. Kitts; her mother, Mynita, was a native of Massachusetts. Van Engle's stepfather was Arvelle

"Snoopie" Harris, a sax player with the Cab Calloway orchestra who had the connections that enabled her to meet black film director Oscar Micheaux.

She is best known for her appearances in the films of Micheaux, including *The Girl from Chicago* (1932), *Harlem After Midnight* (1934), *Murder in Harlem* (1935), *Swing!* (1938), *God's Step Children* (1938), and *Lying Lips* (1939). In *Swing!* she played Lena Powell, assistant to a producer (Carmen Newsome) striving to produce a black revue on Broadway. When the star is injured, Lena discovers that the seamstress has hidden talent, and the production is saved.

She had a key but small role in *God's Step Children* as the tragic mother abandoned by the white man who impregnated her. She makes the most of her haunting scene at the beginning of the film — it is one of the things about the film that sticks in the mind (the film is one of Micheaux's best and most controversial).

In *Murder in Harlem* (aka *Lem Hawkins' Confession*) she played Claudia Vance, a lead role as a young woman who hires a crusading black lawyer and helps him to find the real murderer of the white woman her brother is accused of killing. It turns out that the murdered woman was a secretary at the plant. The girl was accidentally killed by Mr. Brisbane, the owner of the plant, when she refused his advances and fell and struck her head. It was Brisbane and his accomplice, the janitor Lem Hawkins, who put her body in the basement. All ends well for Claudia's brother — and for Claudia and Henry as a couple.

Van Engle was married to Herbert Hollon from 1934 to the time of his death in 1992; they had two sons (Herbert and Marc). The Hollons originally lived in Brooklyn, then moved to Teaneck, New Jersey, and then on to Port Charlotte, Florida, where Van Engle worked for the public library. She died of emphysema at the Munroe Regional Medical Center at age 87. She was survived by her sons, five grandchildren and three great-grandchildren.

Feature Films: *Harlem After Midnight* (1934), *Murder in Harlem* (aka *Lem Hawkins' Confession;* 1935), *Swing!* (1938), *God's Step Children* (1938).

Vance, Danitra Born in Chicago, Illinois, July 13, 1954; died August 21, 1994, Brooklyn, New York.

Danitra Vance was the first African American woman to become a cast member on *Saturday Night Live* (for one season, 1985–86). She arrived in New York in 1981, after having performed with the Second City comedy troupe in Chicago. Vance had a unique look and style, and she had things to say. Her spiky hair and her wild eyes became a part of her comic persona. Her main *SNL* characters were Cabrini Green Harlem Watts Jackson, the black teen who gave dubious counsel on the art of getting pregnant (or not), and *That Black Girl*, a spoof of the white bread series *That Girl* with Marlo Thomas. Part of her reason for leaving *SNL* so quickly was her dissatisfaction with her limited role on the show.

She is most fondly remembered for her performance in two plays by George C. Wolfe. In *The Colored Museum* (1986), Vance is at her most arch as Miss Pat, the perky stewardess from hell on an airplane with a "fasten shackles" sign. *The Colored Museum* consists of 11 vignettes commenting upon and satirizing black life (including a dead-on satire of *A Raisin in the Sun*). The passengers on the plane visit different eras from slavery days to the present, represented as exhibits in the Colored Museum. She recreated the role on a PBS *Great Performances* telecast in February 1991.

She won an NAACP Image Award and an Obie Award for her performance in *Spunk* (1986) at the Public Theater, based on the short stories of Zora Neale Hurston. Vance played three roles in the three tales that made up the play, which was infused with music.

She was nominated for an Independent Spirit Award for her role in the film *Jumpin' at the Boneyard* (1992), in her last (and best) screen appearance as the cocaine-addicted Jeanette, girlfriend of Manny, another addict, whose brother is trying to get him into a rehabilitation facility.

Vance was just 40 years old when she died. She was diagnosed with breast cancer in 1990 and underwent a single mastectomy. The cancer reoccurred in 1993 and she passed away the following year at her grandfather's home. She was survived by her mother, Laura, and her sister, Latrice Lee. Her work was published in the collection *Moon Marked and Touched by the Sun* (1993), which included her one-woman sketch "Live and in Color!"

Feature Films including TV Movies: *Sticky Fingers* (1988), *The Cover Girl and the Cop* (TV; 1989), *Limit Up* (1989), *The War of the Roses*

(1989), *Hangin' with the Homeboys* (1991), *Little Man Tate* (1991), *Jumpin' at the Boneyard* (1992).

TV: *Saturday Night Live* (cast member; 1985–86), *Miami Vice* ("Child's Play," 1987), *Trying Times* ("Hunger Chic," 1989), *Great Performances* ("The Colored Museum," 1991), *Saturday Night Live Goes Commercial* (archival; 1991), *Saturday Night Live 25th Anniversary* (archival; 1994), *Retrosexual: The '80s* (archival; 2004), *Saturday Night Live in the '80s: Lost and Found* (archival; 2005).

Vanity (aka Matthews, Denise; Winters, D.D.) Born January 4, 1959, Niagara Falls, Ontario, Canada.

Denise Katrina Matthews was a Canadian model and sometime actress of German and African American heritage who was discovered by the musician Prince and was chosen to headline a group called Vanity 6. Prince had already devised the concept of the group and had chosen the original three members before Vanity (as she was now known) came on the scene. The group appeared in the film *National Lampoon's Vacation* and scored a major hit with their second single, "Nasty Girl." They also provided backup on the Prince albums released during their brief reign, went on tour with Prince in 1982–83, and saw their own self-titled album eventually go gold (it proved to be the group's only album).

Vanity was set to star with Prince in the film *Purple Rain* (1983), but before filming began she had a major rift with him and quit the project, as well as leaving Vanity 6 and severing any other attachment to the musician. She was replaced by Patricia Kotero (rechristened Apollonia). Vanity 6 became Apollonia 6, and they released only a single album. It outsold Vanity's album, largely because of the huge success of *Purple Rain*, especially the excellent soundtrack album, which contains some of Prince's finest music.

Vanity went on to have a decent albeit short-lived career in feature films, and proved to be a decent actress as well as a beauty and a sex symbol. She had already attracted attention among cult film devotees with *Tanya's Island* (1980), a strange, truly unique cross between an art film and a softcore sex film. Vanity played a young film sound assistant who dreams/imagines/is transported to an alternate reality (take your pick). In this realm she is an uninhibited but innocent island girl who is involved in a strange triangle with a jealous lover and an intelligent, sensitive ape named Blue. After awhile, she begins to prefer Blue. What it all means is a bit foggy, but many male fans were pleased that Vanity performed virtually the entire role in the nude or nearly so — an odd state of affairs for what some saw as a feminist statement (unless the nudity was part of the statement).

Another early although quite negligible appearance was in the 1980 B-horror film *Terror Train* (here, as in *Tanya's Island*, she was billed as D.D. Winters). She was also in the strange mixture of musical and martial arts film called *The Last Dragon* (1985), produced by Motown Records. *Never Too Young to Die* (1986) featured Gene Simmons of the rock group Kiss as a bad guy bent on world domination (or something to that effect), and John Stamos and Vanity as secret agents who interrupt his plans after Simmons kills Stamos' father (played by ex–James Bond George Lazenby), another weird addition to Vanity's very offbeat filmography.

Vanity closed out her career with a few good movies (and she was good in them). She was fine as an ill-fated stripper who helps blackmail victim Roy Scheider get revenge in the excellent film noir *52 Pick-Up* (1986); and was assured and glamorous as the nightclub singer and mistress who helps the hero *Action Jackson* (1988), played by Carl Weathers, nail her evil, controlling sugar daddy (Craig T. Nelson). She married Anthony Smith in 1995 and divorced him the following year. In the post–Vanity era, she became a born again Christian and a minister.

Feature Films including Video and TV Movies: *Klondike Fever* (1980), *Terror Train* (1980), *Tanya's Island* (1980), *The Last Dragon* (1985), *Never Too Young to Die* (1986), *52 Pick-*

Vanity and Kelly Preston in *52 Pick-Up* (1986).

Up (1986), *Deadly Illusion* (1987), *Action Jackson* (1988), *Memories of Murder* (TV; 1990), *South Beach* (1992), *Neon City* (1992), *Lady Boss* (TV; 1992), *Da Vinci's War* (1993), *Kiss of Death* (1995).

TV: *The Motown Revue Starring Smokey Robinson* (1982), *Soul Train* (2 segments; 1983–88), *The Noel Edmonds Late Late Breakfast Show* (1986), *Miami Vice* ("By Hooker by Crook," 1987), *Mickey Spillane's Mike Hammer* ("Green Lipstick/Mike's Daughter," 1987), *The Late Show Starring Joan Rivers* (1987), *Friday the 13th* ("The Secret Agenda of Mesmer's Bauble," 1989), *Booker* ("Deals and Wheels," Part I, 1989), *Tales from the Crypt* ("Dead Wait," 1991), *Sweating Bullets* ("Mafia Mistress," 1991), *Silk Stalkings* ("Powder Burn," 1992), *Highlander* ("Revenge Is Sweet," 1992), *Counterstrike* ("Muerte," 1993), *VH1: Where Are They Now?* (2002).

Video/DVD: *The Best of Sex and Violence* (1981), *Famous T&A* (1982).

Vaughn, Countess

Born in Idabel, Oklahoma, August 8, 1978.

Countess Danielle Vaughn is the daughter of Leo and Sandra Vaughn. She was born in a small Oklahoma town, but it wasn't long before she established herself as a presence in show business, initially as a singer. In 1988 she was junior vocalist champion on the show *Star Search*, but it was in the sitcom world that she became a star. Her rise started with appearances on *227*, *Hangin' with Mr. Cooper* and *Roc*. The big breakthrough was her long run on *Moesha* (1996–99) and the spin-off series *The Parkers* (1999–2004), as the clueless but confident Kimberly Ann Parker. She won the NAACP Image Award for Outstanding Supporting Actress in a Comedy Series for *Moesha*. She was so successful in the role of Kim that it seems to have kept her from crossing over into other roles — the "victim of her own success" syndrome.

She performed in *Mama, I Want to Sing, Part 2* (1990). Her album *Countess* was released on Virgin Records in 1992. She married Joseph James and they have a child (Jaylen James), but are now divorced.

Feature Films: *Trippin'* (1999), *Max Keeble's Big Move* (2001).

TV: *Star Search* (1988), *227* ("Double your Pleasure," 1988), *The Magical World of Disney* (1988), *Hangin' with Mr. Cooper* (2 episodes; "Cheers," "Warriors," Part I, 1992), *Thea* ("Danesha Project," 1993), *Roc* (2 episodes in the role of Carolita; "He Ain't Heavy, He's My Father," "The Last Temptation of Roc," 1993 and 1994), *Minor Adjustments* ("Witness," 1996), *Goode Behavior* ("Goode Lovin," 1997), *Moesha* (recurring role of Kimberly Ann Parker; 1996–99), *The Parkers* (recurring role of Kimberly Ann Parker; 1999–2004), *The Martin Short Show* (1999), *Mad TV* (2003), *TV's Greatest Sidekicks* (archival; 2004), *I Love the '80s* (2005), *I Love the '90s* (2005), *Cuts* ("Adult Education," 2006), *Thugaboo: Sneaker Madness* (2006), *Thugaboo: A Miracle on D-Roc's Street* (2006), *The Tyra Banks Show* (2006).

Music Video: *Hands Up* (2003), *Love Like This* (2007).

Vaughn, Terri J.

Born in San Francisco, California, October 16, 1969.

Terri J. Vaughn was the raunchy secretary Lovita Alizee Jenkins on *The Steve Harvey Show* (1997–2002), and Jonelle Abrahams on *All of Us* (2003–05), fellow teacher with and best friend of Tia Jewel (Elise Neal). Vaughn made her film debut in *Sister Act 2: Back in the Habit* (1993) and was China in *Friday* (1995) with Ice Cube. She was also in the Wayans Brothers' parody *Don't Be a Menace to South Central While Drinking Your Juice in the Hood* (1996). She was Brenda in Tyler Perry's *Daddy's Little Girls* (2007). She was in *Three Can Play That Game* (2008), the sequel to Vivica Fox's *Two Can Play That Game.*

She is divorced from Derrick A. Carolina, and they have a son, Daylen Ali (born 2001). Her husband is now football player Karon Riley, and they have a son, Kal'El Joseph Riley (born 2008). She has established the nonprofit Take Wings Foundation to provide opportunities for young women in public housing in the San Francisco area.

Feature Films including Video and TV Movies: *Sister Act 2: Back in the Habit* (1993), *Friday* (1995), *Black Scorpion* (TV; 1995), *Excessive Force II: Force on Force* (1995), *Friday* (1995), *Don't Be a Menace to South Central While Drinking Your Juice in the Hood* (1996), *Carnosaur 3: Primal Species* (1996), *8 Heads in a Duffel Bag* (1997), *Black Scorpion II: Aftershock* (TV; 1997), *The Smoker* (2000), *Detonator* (2003), *Fair Game* (2005), *Exposure* (2005), *Stick It* (2006), *Dirty Laundry* (2006), *Daddy's Little Girls* (2007), *Redrum* (2007), *I Wanna Dance* (2007), *Three Can Play That Game* (2008).

TV: *Living Single* ("Great Expectations," 1993), *The Sinbad Show* ("Strictly Business," 1993), *Married with Children* ("Business Sucks," Part I, 1994), *Family Matters* ("Beta Chi Guy," 1994), *Sherman Oaks* ("Attack of the Killer Tomatoes," 1995), *ER* ("Point of Origin," 1999), *The Steve Harvey Show* (4 episodes in the role of Lovita Jenkins; "Whatever You Want," "My Left Gator," "No Free Samples," "Hate Thy Neighbor," 1997–2002), *Girlfriends* ("Single Mama Drama," 2003), *Soul Food* (4 episodes as Eva Holly; "Stranger Than Fiction," "All Together Alone," "Shades of Grey," "Attracting Opposites," 2002–03), *All of Us* (recurring role of Jonelle Abrahams; 2003–05), *Angels Can't Help But Laugh* (2007).

Shorts: *The Smoker* (2000), *Exposure* (2007).

Voorhies, Lark Born in Nashville, Tennessee, March 25, 1974.

Though born in Nashville, Lark Voorhies grew up in Pasadena, California. She began as a child actress and was only 11 when she starred in *Small Wonder* (1985). Two years later she was in *Good Morning, Miss Bliss,* the forerunner to her popular 1989 sitcom *Saved by the Bell,* which was a Saturday morning ratings winner and made her a teen sensation of the era. She was fashion stylista and adolescent love goddess Lisa Tuttle, the obsession of Screech (Dustin Diamond), and about 10 million other love-starved "tween" guys.

Lark Voorhies.

Voorhies also had a good role as stuck-up socialite Wendy Reardon on the daytime drama *Days of Our Lives* (1993–94) and enjoyed a nice change-of-pace role as sweet fashion designer Jasmine Malone on another daytime drama, *The Bold and the Beautiful* (1995–96). She was in the *Star Trek: Deep Space Nine* episode "Life Support" (1995). She also guest starred on *Martin* (and was engaged for a time to series star Martin Lawrence), *Family Matters* and *The Fresh Prince of Bel-Air.* She married actor-producer Miguel Coleman in 1996; they divorced in 2004. She married Andy Prince in 2007. Voorhies is a talented screenplay writer and she has her own production company.

Feature Films including Video and TV Movies: *How to Be a Player* (1997), *Mutiny* (TV; 1999), *Jack of All Trades* (2000), *Fire & Ice* (TV; 2001), *How High* (2001), *Civil Brand* (2002), *The Next Hit* (2008), *The Black Man's Guide to Understanding Black Women* (2008).

TV: *Small Wonder* ("Vicki's Exposé," 1988), *Good Morning, Miss Bliss* (recurring role of Lisa Turtle; 1988–89), *Saved by the Bell* (recurring role of Lisa Turtle; 1989–93), *The Fresh Prince of Bel-Air* ("Mama's Baby, Carlton's Maybe," 1992), *Saved by the Bell: Hawaiian Style* (1992), *Martin* (2 episodes in the role of Nicole; "The Break Up," Parts II and III, 1993), *Getting By* (2 episodes in the role of Tasha; "Men Don't Dance," "Turnabout Dance," 1993), *Days of Our Lives* (recurring role as Wendy Reardon; 1993–94), *Saved by the Bell: The College Years* (1994), *Saved by the Bell: Wedding in Las Vegas* (1994), *Me and the Boys* ("Talent Show," 1994), *Saved by the Bell: The New Class* (1994), *CBS Schoolbreak Special* ("What About Your Friends?" 1995), *Star Trek: Deep Space Nine* ("Life Support," 1995), *Family Matters* ("Home Sweet Home," 1995), *The Bold and the Beautiful* (recurring role of Jasmine Malone; 1995–96), *Malcolm & Eddie* ("Club Story," 1997), *The Last Don* (miniseries; 1997), *In the House* (3 episodes in the role of Mercedes Langford; "Tito's in the House," "When Marion Met Natalie," "All's Fair in Love and War," 1997–98), *The Love Boat: The Next Wave* ("I Can't Get No Satisfaction," 1998), *The Parkers* (2 episodes in the role of Chandra; "Grape Nuts," "Scammed Straight," 1999), *Grown Ups* ("J's Pet Peeve," 2000), *Widows* (miniseries; 2002), *E! True Hollywood Story*

("Saved by the Bell," 2002), *Robot Chicken* (voice; "Boo Cocky," 2008).

Music Videos: *Never Too Busy, These Are the Times, On Bended Knee.*

Walker, Arnetia Born in Columbus, Georgia, 1956.

Arnetia Walker was only 16 and a drama major at the High School of Performing Arts when she landed a Broadway role in *The Sign in Sidney Brustein's Window* (it closed after a brief run on January 26–29, 1972). She also served as a replacement in *Two Gentlemen of Verona* (1971–73). She was a standby for Stephanie Mills as Dorothy in *The Wiz* (1975). Her most significant Broadway role was as Lorrell Robinson in the 1987 revival of Michael Bennett's *Dreamgirls*. She was also an understudy for the role of Effie, and eventually wound up playing all three of the lead roles in the *Dreamgirls*.

Her breakthrough film role was as To-Bel in director Paul Bartel's biting satire *Scenes from the Class Struggle in Beverly Hills* (1989). She was head nurse Annie Roland in the NBC sitcom *Nurses* (1991–93). She is currently featured as Ms. Ross in the WB comedy drama *Popular* (2008).

Walker is an accomplished singer as well as an actress. Her husband is news anchor and reporter Elliot Francis; they have a son named Trevor.

Feature Films: *The Wiz* (1978), *The Best Little Whorehouse in Texas* (1982), *Heart and Soul* (TV; 1988), *Scenes from the Class Struggle in Beverly Hills* (1989), *The Wizard of Speed and Time* (1989), *The Whereabouts of Jenny* (TV; 1991), *Cast a Deadly Spell* (TV; 1991), *Love Crimes* (1992), *Triumph Over Disaster: The Hurricane Andrew Story* (TV; 1993), *The Cherokee Kid* (TV; 1996), *Balloon Farm* (TV; 1999), *For Love of the Game* (1999), *Geppetto* (TV; 2000), *College Road Trip* (2008).

TV: *Midnight Caller* ("Take Back the Streets," 1989), *Quantum Leap* ("Disco Inferno: April 1, 1976," 1989), *Amen* ("I Can't Help Loving That Man of Mine," 1989), *227* ("Play Christy for Me," 1990), *Singer & Sons* (recurring role as Claudia James; 1990), *Nurses* (recurring role of Nurse Annie Roland; 1991–93), *The 5 Mrs. Buchanans* ("Alex, Then and N.O.W.," 1994), *The Fresh Prince of Bel-Air* ("The Wedding Show [Psyche!]," 1995), *The Cosby Mysteries* ("The Medium Is the Message," 1995), *Bless This House* (pilot; 1995), *Renegade* ("An Uncle in the Business," 1995), *Buddies* ("There Goes the Groom," 1995), *NYPD Blue* ("Ted and Carey's Bogus Adventure," 1996), *Living Single* ("Multiple Choice," "O Solo Mio," 1996–97), *Malcolm & Eddie* ("The Courtship of Eddie's Mother," "Mixed Nuts," 1997–98), *Just Shoot Me!* ("Rescue Me," 1998), *The Steve Harvey Show* ("And Injustice for All," 1998), *Touched by an Angel* ("The Perfect Game," 2000), *City of Angels* ("Cry Me a Liver," 2000), *Judging Amy* ("Human Touch," 2000), *Popular* (recurring role of Ms. Ross; 2000), *Some of My Best Friends* ("Scenes from an Italian Party," 200?), *Kate Brasher* ("Tracy," 2001), *Everybody Loves Raymond* ("Cookies," 2002), *The Big House* (recurring role of Tina Cleveland; "Hart Transplant," "Almost Touched by an Angel," "A Friend in Need," "The Kidney Stays in the Picture," "The Anniversary Party," 2004), *Popular* (recurring role as Ms. Ross; 2008).

Warfield, Marlene Born in Queens, New York, June 19, 1940.

Marlene Warfield has favored roles with depth and serious social underpinnings. She was critically lauded for the role of Clara Kerr in *The Great White Hope*, which she performed on Broadway (1968–70) and in the film version (1970). She won an NAACP Image Award and the Clarence Derwent Theatre World Award for her stage performance as the prostitute who is married to controversial heavyweight champion Jack Johnson.

She gave a compelling performance as the underground revolutionary Laureen Hobbs in the satirical, ahead-of-its-time *Network* (1976). She was the take-no-prisoners maid Victoria Butterfield on *Maude* (1977–78) in the final season of the long-running sitcom, succeeding Esther Rolle and Hermione Badderly in the plum role. Other guest star work on TV includes *Hill Street Blues, Perry Mason* and *The West Wing.*

Feature Films including TV Movies: *Joe* (1970), *The Great White Hope* (1970), *Goodbye, Raggedy Ann* (TV; 1971), *Cutter* (TV; 1972), *Across 110th Street* (1972), *Network* (1976), *The Sophisticated Gents* (TV; 1981), *Child's Cry* (TV; 1986), *Jo Jo Dancer, Your Life Is Calling* (1986), *How I Got into College* (1989).

TV: *The Name of the Game* ("The Time Is Now," 1970), *Madigan* ("The Midtown Beat," 1972), *Lou Grant* ("Hero," 1978), *Maude* (4 episodes in the role of Victoria Butterfield; "The New Maid," "Victoria's Boyfriend," "My Husband, the Hero," "Mr. Butterfield's Return," 1977–78), *The Jeffersons* ("Me and Mr. G.," 1979), *Little House on the Prairie* ("Dark Sage," 1981), *Hill Street Blues* ("Moon Over Uranus: The Sequel," 1983), *Cagney & Lacey* ("Old Debts," 1984), *Perry Mason* ("The Case of the Lethal Lesson," 1989), *Freddy's Nightmares* ("A Family Affair," 1990), *In the House* ("The Max Who Came to Dinner," 1996), *ER* ("Tribes," 1997), *The West Wing* (pilot; 1999), *So Weird* ("Blues," 2000), *Dead Last* ("The Crawford Touch," 2001), *The Shield* ("Dawg Days," 2002), *Cold Case* ("The Runner," 2003).

Warfield, Marsha Born in Chicago, Illinois, March 5, 1954.

Marsha Warfield is a stand-up comedienne who got her start on the short-lived Richard Pryor variety show as a performer and staff writer, which generated far more press than ratings. She is best known for her role as the poker-faced, in-your-face bailiff Roz on NBC's *Night Court* (1993–95). She was also prominently featured on the sitcom *Empty Nest* as Dr. Maxine Douglas (1993–95). Other TV appearances include *Family Ties*, *Clueless* and *Riptide*.

She even went the daytime talk show host route for a brief period (1990–91) with *The Marsha Warfield Show*. Despite Warfield's gruff image in her sitcom roles and as an onstage comic, this was "talk show light," with a basketball hoop as part of the on-camera set. Warfield enjoyed booking diverse guests on the same segment — people you wouldn't normally associate with each other (for example, British comic actor Dudley Moore and Marla Gibbs of *227*).

Warfield made appearances in a few feature films, most notably *DC Cab* (as Ophelia; 1983) and *Mask* (1985), in which she played a teacher in the story of a boy with a serious facial deformity and his indefatigable biker mom (Cher).

Feature Films including TV Movies: *The Marva Collins Story* (TV; 1981), *They Call Me Bruce?* (1982), *D.C. Cab* (1983), *Mask* (1985), *Anything for Love* (TV; 1985), *The Whoopee Boys* (1986), *Caddyshack II* (1988), *Doomsday Rock* (TV; 1997).

TV: *The Richard Pryor Show* (series regular; 1977), *That Thing on ABC* (1978), *Legends of the Superheroes* (1979), *Soul Train* (1981), *Riptide* ("Something Fishy," 1984), *Family Ties* ("Keaton and Son," 1984), *Cheers* ("The Belles of St. Clete's," 1985), *Night Court* (recurring role of Bailiff Rosalind Jane "Roz" Russell, 1986–92), *19th Annual NAACP Image Awards* (1987), *The 1st Annual Soul Train Music Awards* (1987), *Uptown Comedy Express* (1987), *Stand Up America* (1987), *Harry Anderson's Sideshow* (1987), *Motown Merry Christmas* (1987), *20th NAACP Image Awards* (1988), *Circus of the Stars 13* (1988), *Relatively Speaking* (1988), *The 10th Annual Black Achievement Awards* (1989), *Family Feud* (1989), *The Tommy Chong Roast* (1989), *The 4th Annual American Comedy Awards* (1990), *A Party for Richard Pryor* (1991), *The 6th Annual Soul Train Music Awards* (1992), *Saved by the Bell: The College Years* ("A Thanksgiving Story," 1993), *Mo' Funny: Black Comedy in America* (archival; 1993), *Soul Train Comedy Awards* (1993), *Hangin' with Mr. Cooper* ("Boy Don't Leave," 1993), *Comic Relief: Baseball Relief 1993*, *Empty Nest* (recurring role as Dr. Maxine Douglas; 1993–95), *The John Larroquette Show* ("Date Night," 1994), *Touched by an Angel* ("The Quality of Mercy," 1996), *Cybill* ("An Officer and a Thespian," 1996), *ABC Afterschool Specials* ("Me and My Hormones," 1996), *Dave's World* ("Does the Whale Have to Be White?" 1997), *Smart Guy* ("The Code," 1997), *Mad About You* ("Dry Run," 1997), *Goode Behavior* ("Goode Cop, Bad Cop," 1997), *Moesha* ("My Mom's Not an Ottoman," 1997), *Living Single* (2 episodes in the role of Agnes Finch; "Love Don't Live Here Anymore," Parts I and II, 1997), *Clueless* ("The Joint," 1998), *The Love Boat: The Next Wave* ("Divorce, Downbeat and Distemper," 1999), *Veronica's Closet* ("Veronica's Sliding Doors," 1999), *E! True Hollywood Story* ("Richard Pryor," 2003), *Star Dates* (2003).

Video/DVD: *I Be Done Been Was Is* (1984), *Truly Tasteless Jokes* (1987), *Paramount Comedy Theatre, Vol. 2: Decent Exposures* (1987).

Warren, Sharon Born in Opelika, Alabama.

Sharon Warren's father is a policeman and her mother is an administrator at the Tuskegee Institute. She graduated from Auburn University after attending Stillman College for three years. She is best known for her remarkable performance as Aretha Robinson, the mother of singer Ray Charles in *Ray* (2004). She is seen largely in flashbacks, but in one scene the adult Ray "meets" his mother in a vision, although she died when he was 14 years old. *Entertainment Weekly* campaigned for Warren to receive an Oscar nomination, but that was not to be, even though star

Jamie Foxx won the Best Actor Oscar for his remarkable performance as Ray Charles. Perhaps all the good performances by actresses in the film tended to cancel each other out come awards time. Warren did win Best Supporting Actress from the Boston Society of Film Critics, and was nominated for an NAACP Image Award.

In August 2002, Warren was doing local theater in Atlanta when she heard about auditions for the film. She deeply impressed director Taylor Hackford, who felt she was perfect for the role. She gives a performance infused with controlled frustration and rage. Before she appeared in *Ray*, Warren played Beneatha Younger in *A Raisin in the Sun* at the TeleFair Peet Theatre at Auburn University, and was Kat in *The Music Lesson* at the Alliance Theater Company in Atlanta. She is also a talented writer and poet. Warren's career has been quiet since her triumph in *Ray*, but she's far too good not to be heard from again.

Feature Films: *Ray* (2004), *Glory Road* (2006).

Warwick, Dionne (aka Warwicke, Dionne) Born in East Orange, New Jersey, December 12, 1940.

Dionne Warwick, born Marie Dionne Warrick, is fondly remembered for her great collaborations with songwriters-producers Burt Bacharach and Hal David. She has charted close to 60 singles in her storied career. These include "Walk on By," "I Say a Little Prayer," "Do You Know the Way to San Jose?" (garnering her first Grammy Award in 1968), "Anyone Who Had a Heart," "Alfie," "(Theme from) Valley of the Dolls," "A House Is Not a Home"— the list is virtually inexhaustible.

She began singing in church at age six and formed the Gospelaires with her sister Dee Dee and Cissy Houston, mother of Warwick's first cousin, singer Whitney Houston. In 1976 she earned a master's degree from the Hartt College of Music in Hartford, Connecticut. She had long tenures as a recording artist with Arista and Warner Bros. Records. Later hits include "Then Came You," "I'll Never Love This Way Again," and "Deja Vu."

In the tradition of many famous singers, Warwick took a stab at an acting career, but was less successful than most. She starred in *Slaves* (1969). Considering the presence in the cast of the great black actor and director Ossie Davis, and that Warwick was at the top of the pop charts at the time, it was reasonable to assume that *Slaves* would be a serious exploration of a towering historical issue. What it turned out to be was a low-budget black exploitation film with gratuitous nudity, a soap opera plot, and some of the worst acting of its era. That was the beginning and essentially the end of Warwick's film career. She did appear in a couple of TV movies (*The Return of Mickey Spillaine's Mike Hammer* (1986) and *Sisters in the Name of Love* (also '86), and two police films, *Rent-a-Cop* (1987) and *Extralarge: Black Magic* (1991). The second was an Italian film, virtually unshown in the U.S., featuring Bud Spencer, the charismatic but weight-challenged Italian film star known mostly for his westerns. It was part of a brief series of films with the detective.

In the 1980s Warwick served as the U.S. ambassador for health and in 2002 was named global ambassador for the United Nations Food and Agriculture Organization (FAO).

Her first book, *My Point of View*, was published in 2003.

She was married to William Elliot from 1967 to 1975. They have two sons, David and Damon.

Feature Films including TV Movies: *Slaves* (1969), *The Return of Mickey Spillane's Mike Hammer* (TV; 1986), *Sisters in the Name of Love* (TV; 1986), *Rent-a-Cop* (1987), *Extralarge: Black Magic* (1991).

TV: *Hullabaloo* (2 segments; 1965–66), *Thank Your Lucky Stars* (archival; 1965), *The Bacharach Sound* (1965), *The 39th Annual Academy Awards* (1967), *The Merv Griffin Show* (1967), *The Joey Bishop Show* (1967), *Noche del sábado* (1967), *Upshaw* (1967), *Dream Girl of '67* (1967), *The Ed Sullivan Show* (4 appearances; 1967–70), *The Best on Record* (1968), *The Beautiful Phyllis Diller Show* (1968), *Romeo und Julia '70* (1969), *The Best on Record* (1970), *The Name of the Game* ("I Love You, Billy Baker," Parts I and II, 1970), *The Tonight Show Starring Johnny Carson* (5 appearances; 1970–73), *Top of the Pops* (3 segments; 1970–82), *The Dean Martin Show* (2 appearances; 1973), *The Fifth Dimension Traveling Sunshine Show* (1971), *The Flip Wilson Show* (1972), *The Great American Music Celebration* (1976), *The CBS Festival of Lively Arts for Young People* (1976), *The Stars and Stripes Show* (1976), *Switch* (3 episodes in the role of Sherri; "The Case of the Purloined Case," "Legend of the Macunas," Parts

I and II, 1976–77), *In Concert Classics Featuring Dionne Warwick* (1977), *The Day the Music Died* (1977), *The Rockford Files* ("Second Chance," 1977), *The 4th Annual American Music Awards* (1977), *The Captain and Tennille* (1977), *Happy Birthday, Las Vegas* (1977), *The 20th Annual Grammy Awards* (1978), *The 21st Annual Grammy Awards* (1979), *Sinatra: The First 40 Years* (1980), *The 22nd Annual Grammy Awards* (1980), *The 52nd Annual Academy Awards* (1980), *Barry Manilow: One Voice* (1980), *The Big Show* (1980), *Solid Gold* (co-host; 1981), *A Gift of Music* (1981), *The 23rd Annual Grammy Awards* (1981), *The 53rd Annual Academy Awards* (1981), *Debbie Boone ... One Step Closer* (1982), *I Love Liberty* (1982), *Aplauso* (1982), *The 25th Annual Grammy Awards* (1983), *We Are the World* (1985), *Star Search* (judge; 1985), *The 27th Annual Grammy Awards* (1985), *Circus of the Stars II* (1986), *The 1st Annual Soul Train Music Awards* (1987), *The Fall Guy* ("Tag Team," 1986), *Super Password* (1986), *Live from Her Majesty's* (1988), *Aretha Franklin: The Queen of Soul* (1988), *Especiale nochevieja 1987: Super 88* (1988), *The 14th Annual People's Choice Awards* (1988), *The 2nd Annual Soul Train Music Awards* (1988), *Family Feud* (1989), *The Probe Team* (1989), *The 3rd Annual Soul Train Music Awards* (1989), *Captain Planet and the Planeteers* (voice of Dr. Russell; 1990), *Sammy Davis, Jr. 60th Anniversary Celebration* (1990), *The 4th Annual Soul Train Music Awards* (1990), *Dionne and Friends* (host; 16 episodes; 1990), *The 5th Annual Soul Train Music Awards* (1991), *The Oprah Winfrey Show* (1991), *The 34th Annual Grammy Awards* (1992), *Guest Night* (1992), *Out All Night* ("That's What Friends Are For," 1992), *Child of Mine: Songs to Our Children* (1992), *Children of Africa* (1993), *Noche, noche* (1993), *The Jackson Family Honors* (1994), *Great Love Songs* (1995), *Burt Bacharach ... This Is Now* (1996), *The Wayans Bros.* ("Grandma's in the Hiz-House," 1996), *Mundo VIP* (1997), *Close to You: Remembering the Carpenters* (archival; 1997), *Pauly* ("Through the Ringers," 1997), *The Drew Carey Show* ("Drew's Brother," 1997), *VH1's Behind the Music* (2 episodes; "The Carpenters," "Gladys Knight," 1998), *League of Legends* (1998), *Burt Bacharach: One Amazing Night* (1998), *Arista Records' 25th Anniversary Celebration* (1999), *So Weird* ("Lost," 1999), *Happily Ever After: Fairy Tales for Every Child* ("The Bremen Town Musicians," 1999), *The Beth Littleford Interview Special* (1999), *Top Ten* ("Heartbreakers," 2000), *Walker, Texas Ranger* ("Faith," 2000), *The 72nd Annual Academy Awards* (2000), *Walk on By: The Story of Popular Song* (archival; 2001), *Rhythm and Blues 40: A Soul Spectacular* (2001), *Michael Jackson: 30th Anniversary Celebration* (2001), *Biography* (3 segments; "Dionne Warwick: Don't Make Me Over," "Burt Bacharach," "Lesley Gore; It's My Party," 2001), *Christmas at the Vatican* (2001), *We Are Family* (2002), *The Brian Conley Show* (2002), *Tupac: Resurrection* (archival; 2003), *Top of the Pops 2* (2003), *Parkinson* (2003), *American Juniors* (judge; 2003), *MADtv* (2003), *Soul Man: Isaac Hayes* (2003), *Hollywood Squares* (2004), *Intimate Portrait* ("Dionne Warwick," 2004), *Straight from the Heart: Timeless Music of the '60s & '70s* (2004), *AFI's 100 Years ... 100 Songs* (2004), *The View* (2004), *The Heaven and Earth Show* (2005), *Life & Style* (2005), *Avenue of the Stars: 50 Years of ITV* (2005), *Saturday Swings* (2005), *UK Music Hall of Fame* (2005), *The 8th Annual Soul Train Christmas Starfest* (2005), *Entertainment Tonight* (2006), *Legends Ball* (2006), *American Idol* (2006), *Celebrity Duets* (2 segments; 2006), *The Paul O'Grady Show* (2006), *Ein herz fr kinder* (2006), *Soapstar Superstar* (2007), *2007 Trumpet Awards, Dancing with the Stars* (2007).

Video/DVD: *Do It Debbie's Way* (1983), *Whitney Houston: The Greatest Hits* (2000), *The Best of Music Flashback Television Shows* (2001), *The Songmakers Collection* (2001), *Luthor Vandross: From Luther with Love—The Videos* (2004), *Soulful Sixties* (2004), *The History Makers* (2005).

Washington, Fredi Born in Savannah, Georgia, December 23, 1903; died June 28, 1994, Stamford, Connecticut.

Fredericka Carolyn Washington was the oldest of nine children. When her mother passed away, she was sent by her father along with her sister Isabel to study at St. Elizabeth's Convent. She moved to Harlem when she was still a teenager, lived with her grandmother, and worked as a bookkeeper and secretary at Black Swan records. She danced with the troupe The Happy Honeysuckles and then went on tour with the hit show *Shuffle Along*. After that she became a chorus girl at New York's Club Alabam. Producer Lee Shubert saw her at the club and got her a role opposite Paul Robeson in the play *Black Boy* (1926).

Bandleader Roger Wolfe Kahn—whose father Otto was obsessed with Washington—hired her and her dance partner Al Moiret to appear at his club Le Perroquet. They toured all the major capitals of Europe as Moiret and Fredi.

Fredi Washington is best known for the role of Peola, the light-skinned black woman who decides to "pass" and turns her back on her darker-skinned mother Delilah in the Best Picture Oscar nominee of 1934 *Imitation of Life*.

Director John Stahl, in a quest that was well publicized in the press, was determined to find a black woman to play Peola, although the role was played by a white woman (Susan Kohner) in director Douglas Sirk's 1959 remake. This was *the* Hollywood role for a black woman — the role that would possibly swing open the gates of Hollywood stardom. Stahl found his Peola in a young New York woman who had already had some success as a dancer and an actress — she was in the visually striking Duke Ellington short *Black and Tan Fantasy* in 1929, and had appeared in a small role as a prostitute with Paul Robeson in *The Emperor Jones* in 1933). She looked more like Joan Crawford than a black woman. Indeed, she'd had to darken her skin for the role in *The Emperor Jones*.

With *Imitation of Life*, Fredi Washington was chosen for the role that forged a link for all black actresses to come. Peola Johnson was a haughty, self-centered character, but also a pathetic and a star-crossed one. There was nowhere in society for her to turn without selling her soul in the process. And although Washington was nothing like her character — in fact, she was a bastion of black pride — she could surely relate to Peola in that she was too black for Hollywood and too white for race pictures. It soon became clear that the film world had no place for Washington. It's interesting to think what might have happened if she had explored doing films in Europe, in the footsteps of Josephine Baker — but this was not an option that interested her.

The studio heads at Universal were taken aback when Washington was quite insistent on getting well paid for her role in *Imitation of Life* (she wound up receiving a substantial salary of $500 a week). Also, she had problems with some of the dialogue and certain scenes in the film — specifically one where she is discovered to be black while working as a cashier in a ritzy white restaurant when it is seen that she has no "half-moons" on her fingernails. Washington pointed out that this was ridiculous, and refused to do the scene. Nor did she want to commit to an extended contract with the studio, feeling that, not far down the road, she would have been stuck in demeaning maid roles.

When *Imitation of Life* opened, Louise Beavers received more than her share of the critical acclaim, given her sympathetic role. Some critics — especially ones in the black press — were not happy that the film was basically recycling the same old "passing" theme and the black mammy stereotype. Oscar Micheaux's *God's Step Children* (1937) was the black director's answer to *Imitation of Life*, with racial politics that were more complex and closer to what the black audience was used to seeing reflected in their lives. Two years later, Washington was already relegated to the low-budget voodoo drama *Ouanga* (aka *Love Wanga*; 1936). She gives an overzealous performance as a black plantation owner who casts a voodoo curse when the white owner of a neighboring plantation chooses to share his affections with a white woman rather than her.

Her only significant role after *Imitation of Life* was in 20th Century–Fox's *One Mile from Heaven* (1937). She was a nurse who had raised a white child and found herself in a dramatic court battle for the child. At least this was a role in a decent Hollywood production, and Washington got good reviews for her work. It would be her last film. After a part she was being considered for in *The Foxes of Harrow* fell through, she decided that enough was enough, and turned her back on Hollywood — not with anger or sadness, but rather as a woman who had other doors to knock on and other things to do.

She helped to found the Negro Actors Guild and wrote articles about prejudice against black actors in *The People's Choice*, a newspaper published by her brother-in-law, future congressman Adam Clayton Powell (who was married to her sister Isabel). Washington dedicated much of her time and energy to civil rights activism. She also appeared in Afro-centric stage productions such as an all-black version of *Lysistrata* in 1946 with Etta Moten, and productions of *A Long Way from Home* (1948) and *How Long Till Summer* (1949).

In the 1940s and '50s, she was active in the cultural division of the National Negro Congress and the Committee for the Negro in the Arts. During the McCarthy era, Washington was one of many African Americans entertainers suspected of being Communist sympathizers. In 1953, she served as a casting consultant for *Carmen Jones*, the film that would propel her successor Dorothy Dandridge to full-fledged (if fleeting) stardom.

Washington had her share of relationships and marriages. She had a passionate affair with Duke Ellington in the late twenties, but he was married, and Washington — unlike Peola, she was a clear-headed realist — knew that nothing could come of it. She married a member of Ellington's band, trombone player Lawrence Brown, in 1933. Following their divorce in 1951, she married dentist Hugh Anthony Bell. She died of a stroke at age 90. It wasn't really until after her death that Washington finally received her due as a film icon. She was inducted into the Black Filmmakers Hall of Fame in 1975.

Feature Films: *Black and Tan Fantasy* (1929), *The Emperor Jones* (1935), *Mills Blue Rhythm Band* (1935), *Imitation of Life* (1934), *Ouanga* (aka *Love Wanga*; 1936), *One Mile from Heaven* (1937).

Video/DVD: *Hollywood Rhythm, Vol. 1: The Best of Jazz and Blues* (2001), *TV in Black: The First Fifty Years* (2004).

Fredi Washington (Fredi Washington Photograph Collection, Photographs and Prints Division, Schomburg Center for Research in Black Culture, The New York Public Library, Astor, Lenox and Tilden Foundations).

Washington, Kerry Born in the Bronx, New York, January 31, 1977.

Washington is one of the most prominent African American actresses of the post–Halle Berry generation. She is of African American and Native American descent. Her father is a real estate broker; her mother is a professor. Washington performed in children's musical theater with the TADA! Youth Theater. She attended the Spence School in Manhattan (graduated 1994) and earned a theater degree from George Washington University (1998).

In feature films, she first attracted attention as Chenille Reynolds in the teen romantic drama *Save the Last Dance* (2001), for which she won for the Choice Breakout Performance Award at the Teen Choice Awards. She was Della Bea Robinson, the long-suffering wife of singer Ray Charles, in the excellent bio pic *Ray* (2004). This was a rather passive role, but Washington handled it well, and she was given an NAACP Image Award for the performance. She had the somewhat thankless role of the blind Alicia Masters, girlfriend of The Thing, the mutated superhero of *Fantastic Four* (2005), and was given a bit more to do in the sequel *Fantastic Four: Rise of the Silver Surfer* (2007).

She gave a heartbreaking performance as the ill-fated wife of Ugandan dictator Idi Amin in *The Last King of Scotland* (2006), featuring Forrest Whittaker's textured and complex Academy Award–winning performance as Amin. This was Washington's coming of age as a serious actress. She was excellent as "the other woman" Nikki Tru in Chris Rock's underrated *I Think I Love My Wife* (2007), steadfastly refusing to let the role sink into cliché. She was a black woman married to a white man in the pedestrian *Lakeview Terrace* (2008); the couple moves next door to a racist "neighbor from hell" (Samuel L. Jackson). She had a recurring role as Chelina Hall on ABC's *Boston Legal* (2005–06) and guest starred on all manner of series, including *NYPD Blue*, *Law & Order*, *100 Centre Street*, *The Guardian* and *Psych*.

Despite her relatively brief career, she has received many award nominations: a BET Award Best Actress nomination for *The Last King of Scotland*; a Screen Actors Guild Award nomination and a Satellite Award nomination for *Ray*; an Independent Spirit Award nomination for Best Female Lead for *Lift* (2002); and NAACP Image Award nominations for Outstanding Supporting Actress in a Motion Picture for *The Last King of Scotland*; and Outstanding Supporting Actress in a Drama Series for *Boston Legal* in 2006.

Feature Films including Video and TV Movies: *Our Song* (2000), *3D* (2000), *Save the Last Dance* (2001), *Lift* (2001), *Take the A Train* (2002), *Bad Company* (2002), *The United States of Leland* (2003), *The Human Stain* (2003), *Sin* (2003), *Against the Ropes* (2004), *Strip Search* (TV; 2004), *She Hate Me* (2004), *Ray* (2004), *Sexual Life* (2005), *Mr. & Mrs. Smith* (2005), *Fantastic Four* (2005), *Wait* (2005), *Little Man* (2006), *The Last King of Scotland* (2006), *The Dead Girl* (2006), *I Think I Love My Wife* (2007), *Fantastic Four: Rise of the Silver Surfer* (2007), *Lakeview Terrace* (2008), *Miracle at Santa Anna* (2008), *Mama Black Widow* (2009), *Life Is Hot in Cracktown* (2009), *A Thousand Words* (2009), *Bury Me Standing* (2010).

TV: *ABC Afterschool Specials* ("Magical Make-Over," 1994), *Standard Deviants* (1996), *NYPD Blue* ("'Franco, My Dear, I Don't Give a Damn," 2001), *Law & Order* ("3 Dawg Night," 2001), *100 Centre Street* (5 episodes; "Joe Must Go," "No Good Deed Goes Unpunished," "Queenie's Tough," "Daughters," "Andromeda and the Monster," 2001), *The Guardian* ("The Next Life," 2002), *Wonderfalls* (pilot; 2004), *The Sharon Osbourne Show* (2004), *The Late Late Show with Craig Kilborn* (2004), *36th NAACP Image Awards* (2005), *Boston Legal* (5 episodes in the role of Chelina Hall; "'Til We Meet Again," "Tortured Souls," "Let Sales Ring," "Death Be Not Proud," "Race Ipsa," 2005–06), *Late Night with Conan O'Brien* (2006), *Last Call with Carson Daly* (2006), *The View* (2007), *Tavis Smiley* (2007), *The Late Late Show with Craig Ferguson* (2007), *Entertainment Tonight* (2007), *Psych* ("There's Something About Mira," 2008), *Jimmy Kimmel Live!* (2008), *From the Mouthpiece on Back* (narrator; 2008), *Real Time with Bill Maher* (2008), *Le Grand journal de canal +* (2008), *The People Speak* (documentary; 2009).

Shorts: *3D* (2000), *Wait* (2005), *Woman in Burka* (2008).

Music Video: *I Want You* (200?).

Washington, Mildred Born in 1905; died September 7, 1933, Los Angeles, California.

Kerry Washington.

Mildred Washington graduated with honors from Los Angeles High School and spent two years at the University of California at Los Angeles. She also attended Columbia University for a time. Quite apart from her sexy stage image as a dancer and entertainer, Washington was an intellectual who spoke French and Latin, and who was well acquainted with the works of Milton and Homer. Her dance mentor was Carolynne Snowden, also an entertainer of considerable acclaim — another black woman who was in the vanguard of those who were trying to break through Hollywood's color barrier.

She performed at the Apex, a black club in Los Angeles that opened in 1928 and was owned by bandleader Curtis Mosby. In conjunction with Mosby, she produced elaborate shows at the Apex such as "A Night at the Orient." She also performed her sexy reviews at the Legion Club and Jazzland. Washington appeared in the landmark *Hearts in Dixie* (1929), the first black cast talkie, but the producers decided she was too light-skinned for the production, so they darkened her skin, in a strange variation on "blackface." While she did appear in some maid roles — *Torch Singer* (1933) is one example — her sexy, confident persona was more in keeping with her high standing as an entertainer in sophisticated, exclusive clubs.

When an earthquake hit Los Angeles in 1933, Washington was rehearsing with other performers for *King Kong* at the Egyptian Theatre (Washington does not appear in the film itself). She had a fall outside the theater either from the earthquake vibrations or while running for cover, and she was taken to White Memorial Hospital, where it was diagnosed that she had appendicitis. She contracted peritonitis after being operated on and passed away soon after at age 28.

Feature Films: *Tenderfeet* (1928), *The Shopworn Angel* (1928), *Hearts in Dixie* (1929), *The Thoroughbred* (1930), *Blonde Venus* (1932), *Bed of Roses* (1933), *Morning Glory* (1933), *Torch Singer* (1933), *Only Yesterday* (1933).

Waters, Ethel

Born in Chester, Pennsylvania, October 31, 1896; died September 1, 1977.

Ethel Waters is one of those performers whose amazing career is waiting to be discovered by new generations. She is considered by many to be the first black superstar. She made her film debut in the talkie *On with the Show* in 1929 (remade as *42nd Street*). She sang "Am I Blue?" and "Birmingham Bertha." Her second film role was in the all-black satirical film *Rufus Jones for President* (1933).

Waters was, after Hattie McDaniel, the second African American to be nominated for an Academy Award. She was nominated for a Best Supporting Actress Award in 1949 for her role in *Pinky*, the still-touching tale of a light-skinned black woman doing a balancing act between the black world and the white world. Her measured, subtle performance provides quite a contrast to the theatricality of Ethel Barrymore, who is also in the film. A lovely but miscast Jeanne Crain does her best with the title role.

Brandon DeWilde, Ethel Waters and Julie Harris in *The Member of the Wedding* (1952).

Born to a 13-year-old mother who had been raped, Ethel Waters was raised in a violent, impoverished Philadelphia ward. Even though she was eventually adopted by her grandmother, she never lived in the same place for more than 15 months. She married at age 13, but soon left her abusive husband. At 17, she sang in an amateur contest and was offered professional work in Baltimore. She was billed as "Sweet Mama Stringbean" at the amateur night contests. Despite her early amateur success, she soon fell on hard times again and joined up with a carnival. Later she headed to Atlanta. There she got a hint of the glory to come when she worked in a club with blues icon Bessie Smith.

Waters fell in love with a drug addict, but their stormy relationship ended with the advent of World War I. Around 1919, she moved to Harlem and became part of the legendary Harlem Renaissance. There she obtained a job at Edmond's Cellar, a black club. She also appeared in a blackface comedy called *Hello 1919*.

Waters, who had by now morphed into a blues singer, was only the fifth black woman ever to make a recording. She later joined Black Swan Records, where bandleader Fletcher Henderson was her accompanist. Her sweet, low-pitched, crystalline voice was blessed with perfect tone and a formidable range. Few vocalists then or now could interpret a song like Ethel Waters — she could live inside the song and give it three-dimensional life.

In 1924, Waters played at the Plantation Club on Broadway (where she introduced the Song "Dinah"). She also toured with the Black Swan Dance Masters. She first recorded for Columbia Records in 1925; this recording received a Grammy Hall of Fame Award in 1998. "His Eye Is on the Sparrow" became her signature song, remaining her best-loved song throughout her life.

Waters started working with Pearl Wright, the pianist who would become her long-time accompanist, and together they toured the South. In 1929, Harry Askt helped Waters and Wright create a version of "Am I Blue?" that became another of Waters' signature tunes. Also during the 1920s, she performed with and was recorded with the ensembles of Will Marion Cook and Lovie Austin. As her career evolved, she began performing with the likes of Duke Ellington, becoming a star at the Cotton Club in the 1930s.

In 1933, she appeared in the Broadway musical revue *As Thousands Cheer* (singing "Heat Wave," and "Suppertime"). Her Broadway career began to escalate with major shows such as *Africana*, *The Blackbirds of 1928* (and *1930*), *Rhapsody in Black*, *At Home Abroad*, and *Mamba's Daughters*. At one point, she was the reportedly the highest paid performer on Broadway. As her career as a vocalist gradually faded, she was able to take advantage of opportunities in film and on stage. She also starred on a national radio program (the first African American to do so) and continued to sing in clubs.

She starred for MGM as Petunia in *Cabin in the Sky* (1942), an encore of her Broadway role of 1940. *Cabin in the Sky* is a hard film to watch these days (for many, it was probably a hard film to watch even then!). Despite a big budget and newcomer Vincente Minnelli at the directorial helm, it plays as an unintentionally racist film, with Waters as a stereotypically supportive black woman determined to stand by her no-good man (Eddie "Rochester" Anderson) at any cost. Every offensive stereotype is trotted out, right down to the inevitable conclusion that black people are — literally — better off dead. Only intermittent appearances by Louis Armstrong in a minor role and the appearance of a sexy Lena Horne make this painful exercise fitfully bearable.

Waters, offended by the smash success of newcomer Horne, and starting by this time to feel her age, went into a temporary career decline. After a lull, Waters began to work with Fletcher Henderson again in the late forties. Then *Pinky* came along, and in 1950 she won the New York Drama Critics Award for her performance opposite Julie Harris in the Broadway adaptation of Carson McCullers' "The Member of the Wedding." Waters and Harris repeated their roles in the set-bound 1952 film version.

In 1950, she starred in the TV series *The Beulah Show*, but quit after the first season, complaining that the scripts were degrading to African Americans. More bad news followed: she lost tens of thousands of jewelry and cash in a robbery, and the IRS was beginning to hound her for back taxes. Her health suffered. She began to work only sporadically. She died in 1977 at the age of 80 from heart disease. She had been staying at the home of a young couple that was taking care of her, and this is where she died.

Waters wrote two autobiographies, *His Eye Is on the Sparrow* (1950) and *To Me It's Wonderful* (1972). In the period before her death, she toured with the Reverend Billy Graham, singing "His Eye Is on the Sparrow" as such major venues as Madison Square Garden — performing for some of the largest audiences of her life.

Feature Films: *On with the Show* (1929), *Rufus Jones for President* (1933), *Bubbling Over* (1934), *Gift of Gab* (1934), *Tales of Manhattan* (1942), *Cairo* (1942), *Cabin in the Sky* (1943), *Stage Door Canteen* (1943), *The Voice That Thrilled the World* (archival footage; 1943), *New Orleans* (archival; 1947), *Let's Sing a Song from the Movies* (archival; 1948), *Pinky* (1949), *The Member of the Wedding* (1952), *Carib Gold* (1957), *The Heart Is a Rebel* (1958), *The Sound and the Fury* (1959), *That's Entertainment II* (archival; 1976), *That's Dancing* (archival; 1985).

TV: *Toast of the Town* (1949–50), *The Beulah Show* (title role; 1950–52), *Songs for Sale* (1951), *The Jackie Gleason Show* (1952), *Climax* ("The Dance," 1955), *GE Theater* ("Winner by Decision," 1955), *Playwrights '56* ("The Sound and the Fury," 1955), *The Steve Allen Show* (1956), *Saturday Spectacular: Manhattan Tower* (1956), *Whirlybirds* ("Copter Patrol," 1959), *Route 66* ("Good Night, Sweet Blues," 1961), *The Great Adventure* ("Go Down, Moses," 1963), *Vacation Playhouse* ("You're Only Young Twice," 1967), *Daniel Boone* ("Mamma Cooper," 1970), *Owen Marshall: Counselor at Law* ("Run, Carol, Run," 1972), *The Hollywood Palace* (1969), *The Tonight Show* (1972), *The Ladies Sing the Blues* (archival; 1989), *That's Black Entertainment* (archival; 1990), *The Nightclub Years* (archival; 2001), *Jazz* (archival; 2001), *Great Performances: The Great American Songbook* (archival; 2003), *Broadway: The American Musical* (archival; 2004).

Watson-Johnson, Vernee Born in North Trenton, New Jersey, January 14, 1954.

Vernee Watson-Johnson began appearing in TV commercials at age 19. She's also done a lot of voice work in animated films, most notably as Dee Dee Sykes in the various Scooby-Doo incarnations, including *Scooby's All-Star Laff-A-Lympics*, *The All-New Scooby and Scrappy-Doo Show*, and *A*

Pup Named Scooby-Doo. She has also done voice work involving the DC Comics stable of characters, including the video movies *Batman: Mask of the Phantasm* (1993), *Superman: The Last Son of Krypton* (1996), and *Batman Beyond: Return of the Joker* (2000). In addition, she has done voice work in major theatrical features such as *Garfield: A Tale of Two Kitties* and *The Ant Bully* (both 2006).

She had recurring roles in the series *Carter Country* (1977), *Welcome Back, Kotter* (1975–78), *Foley Square* (1985–86), and *Baby Talk* (as the voice of Baby Danielle; 1991). Her most remembered series work was as Viola "Vy" Smith, mother of Will Smith, on *The Fresh Prince of Bel-Air* (1990–95). She has done guest spots on dozens of top series, among them *That's My Mama, What's Happening!!, Vega$, Fantasy Island, Eight Is Enough, The Jeffersons, The Love Boat, Punky Brewster* and *Benson*. More recently she's been on *Dharma & Greg, ER, The West Wing, CSI* and *Without a Trace*. On the soap opera front, she was Dr. Ella Kraft on *Days of Our Lives* (2007).

Watson-Johnson once ran an acting school for children. She continues to teach acting to all ages with private sessions, workshops and seminars. She generated some real life news when she testified for the defense at Michael Jackson's child molestation trial in 2005.

Feature Films Including Video and TV Movies: *Cotton Comes to Harlem* (1970), *Trick Baby* (1973), *Norman ... Is That You?* (1974), *The Boy in the Plastic Bubble* (TV; 1976), *Death Drug* (1978), *Love's Savage Fury* (TV; 1979), *All Night Long* (1981), *The Violation of Sarah McDavid* (TV; 1981), *G.I. Joe: The Movie* (voice; 1987), *Over My Dead Body* (TV; 1990), *Showdown in Little Tokyo* (1991), *The House on Sycamore Street* (TV; 1992), *Caged Fear* (1992), *Batman: Mask of the Phantasm* (voice; 1993), *Angie* (1994), *Superman: The Last Son of Krypton* (voice; 1996), *The Kid* (2000), *Batman Beyond: Return of the Joker* (voice; 2000), *No Turning Back* (2001), *Baby of the Family* (2002), *Home Room* (2002), *Antwone Fisher* (2002), *Christmas with the Kranks* (2004), *The Celestine Prophecy* (2006), *Garfield: A Tale of Two Kitties* (2006), *The Ant Bully* (voice; 2006), *Applause for Miss E* (TV; 2009).

TV: *The Corner Bar* ("Cook's Night Out," 1972), *That's My Mama* ("That's Earl, Brother," 1975), *Welcome Back, Kotter* (recurring role of Vernajean Williams; 1975–78), *Scooby's All-Star Laff-A-Lympics* (voice of Dee Dee Sykes; 1977), *Good Times* ("Thelma's African Romance," Part I, 1977), *What's Happening!!* ("Nice Guys Finish Last," 1977), *Captain Caveman and the Teen Angels* (voice of Dee Dee Sykes; 1977), *Carter Country* (recurring role as Lucille Banks; 1977), *Vega$* (2 episodes; "The Eleventh Event," "The Hunter Hunted," 1979 and 1980), *Fantasy Island* (3 episodes; 1979–81), *Eight Is Enough* ("Welcome to Memorial, Dr. Bradford," 1980), *The Jeffersons* ("I've Still Got It," 1981), *American Playhouse: Working* (1982), *The Love Boat* (4 episodes; 1978–84), *Punky Brewster* ("Visit to the Doctor/Go to Sleep," 1984), *Benson* (2 episodes as Benson's Sister; "Taking It to the Max," "The Reunion," 1984), *Hill Street Blues* ("Passage to Libya," 1985), *Foley Square* (recurring role as Denise Willums; 1985–86), *The All-New Scooby and Scrappy-Doo Show* (voice of Dee Dee Sykes; 1986), *Mr. Belvedere* ("The Trip," Part II, 1988), *A Different World* ("My Dinner with Theo," 1988), *A Pup Named Scooby-Doo* (1988), *TV 101* ("First Love," Part I, 1989), *Murphy Brown* ("My Dinner with Einstein," 1989), *Married with Children* ("He Ain't Much, But He's Mine," 1989), *L.A. Law* ("Armand's Hammer," 1990), *Over My Dead Body* ("A Passing Inspection," 1990), *Baby Talk* (voice of Danielle Craig; 1991), *Diagnosis Murder* (1992), *Empty Nest* ("Sayonara," 1992), *Animaniacs* (voices; 1993), *Batman* (voices; 2 episodes; "Fire from Olympus," "The Worry Men," 1993), *Roc* ("Labor Intensive," 1993), *Grace Under Fire* (2 episodes in the role of Vicki Hudson; "Grace Under Oath," "Simply Grace," 1993 and 1994), *Me and the Boys* ("Your Cheatin' Heart," 1994), *CBS Schoolbreak Special* ("What About Your Friends?" 1995), *Party of Five* ("All-Nighters," 1995), *The Fresh Prince of Bel-Air* (recurring role of Viola "Vy" Smith; 1990–95), *Sister, Sister* (5 episodes in the role of Patrice; "Boy from the Hood," "Ch-ch-ch-changes," "Model Tia," "Guardian Angel," "Designer Genes," 1996–97), *Profiler* (2 episodes; "Night Dreams," "On Your Marks," 1996 and 2000), *Suddenly Susan* ("It's a Mad, Mad, Mad, Maddy World," 1997), *Superman* (voice; 1997), *The Steve Harvey Show* ("Every Boy Needs a Teacher," 1998), *Martial Law* ("How Sammo Got His Groove Back," 1998), *Batman Beyond* (2 episodes as the voice of Lorraine Tate; "Spellbound," "Armory," 1999 and 2000), *The Young and the Restless* (recurring role as Birdie; 1999–2002), *JAG* (2 episodes; "Front and Center," "Crash," 1999 and 2004), *Chicken Soup for the*

Soul ("A Pearl of Great Value," 2000), *Dharma & Greg* ("Let's Get Fiscal," 2001), *Any Day Now* (2 episodes; "It's Not Just a Word," Parts I and II, 2001), *The District* ("Lost and Found," 2001), *That's Life* ("Something Battered, Something Blue," 2001), *ER* (2 episodes in the role of April Wilson; "Start All Over Again," "Supplies and Demands," 2001), *NYPD Blue* ("Mom's Away," 2001), *Static Shock* (2 episodes as the voice of Mrs. Watson; "Tantrum," "Consequences," 2001 and 2003), *The Guardian* ("Causality," 2002), *The X-Files* ("Audrey Pauley," 2002, *Presidio Med* ("This Baby's Gonna Fly," 2002), *MDs* ("Time of Death," 2002), *Hidden Hills* ("The Concert," 2003), *Judging Amy* ("Wild Card," 2003), *Malcolm in the Middle* (2 episodes; "Malcolm Holds His Tongue," "Future Malcolm," 2003), *The West Wing* ("Twenty Five," 2003), *The Lyon's Den* ("Duty to Serve," 2003), *Two and a Half Men* ("Ate the Hamburgers, Wearing the Hats," 2004), *Soul Food* ("Two to Tango," 2004), *Jack & Bobby* ("Better Days," 2004), *CSI* ("Snakes," 2005), *Eve* ("Kung Fu Divas," 2005), *Desperate Housewives* ("Listen to the Rain on the Roof," 2006), *Ghost Whisperer* ("Giving Up the Ghost," 2006), *Studio 60 on the Sunset Strip* (2 episodes as Zelda; pilot; "The Harriet Dinner," Part I, 2006 and 2007), *Days of Our Lives* (9 episodes as Dr. Ella Kraft; 2007), *The Big Bang Theory* (2 episodes as Althea; pilot; "The Peanut Reaction," 2007 and 2008), *Cold Case* ("Wednesday's Woman," 2008), *Shark* ("One Hit Wonder," 2008), *Without a Trace* ("Driven," 2008), *Good Behavior* (2009).

Watts, Rolonda Born in Winston-Salem, North Carolina, July 12, 1959.

From local New York news anchor to actress and syndicated talk show host, Rolonda Watts has parlayed an authoritative yet sympathetic manner, charisma, good looks, a keen intelligence, and a way with words to a major multi-media career. She started in broadcasting as a local reporter in Greensboro, North Carolina. Then she was a fixture at the anchor desks at *News 4 New York* (1980–85, earning an Emmy for her reporting) and *Eyewitness News* (anchor; 1985–93), and hosted a lifestyle show, Lifetime Television's *Attitudes* (earning a Cable Ace Award nomination for Best Talk Show; 1987), and *Inside Edition* (1988). She parlayed these credentials to become host and supervising producer of *The Rolonda Show*, a free-wheeling, syndicated effort by King Features, which had also syndicated *First Edition*. This audience participation talk show with a "town hall" format allowed her to interact with people, as she does best. *Rolonda* ran for an impressive four seasons.

She is a graduate of Spelman College in Atlanta, Georgia (1980), and New York's Columbia University Graduate School of Journalism (1981). She was trained as an actress at the Howard Fine and Aaron Speiser Acting Workshops in Los Angeles. She has played a variety of roles on dramatic series, sitcoms and soaps: *One on One* (Dr. Taylor); *The Steve Harvey Show* (marriage counselor); *Smart Guy* (Lydia Carter); *Yes, Dear* (Sylvia); *The Bold and the Beautiful* (recurring role as Attorney Julie Shoemaker); *The District* (Mrs. Waters); *JAG* (Judge Deborah Mayfield); *The West Wing* (Melissa); *Sister, Sister* (recurring role as Vivica Shaw); and *Days of Our Lives* (recurring role as Attorney Cameron Reese).

She also does voice-over and announcing work (she is the announcer on *The Judge Joe Brown Show* and the game show *Temptation*), including commercials (Alka-Seltzer, Wendy's) and children's animation (*Curious George*). She was a radio talk show host for Green Stone Media in 2006–07 and finished her first novel early in 2008. She is CEO and president of her own production company, Watts Works Productions.

Feature Films including TV Movies: *Girl 6* (1996), *The Stupids* (1996), *Maniac Magee* (TV; 2003), *Meet Wally Sparks* (1997), The *Best Actress* (TV; 2000), *Shackles* (2005).

TV: *News 4 New York* (anchor; 1980–85), *Eyewitness News* (anchor; 1985–93), *Attitudes* (host; 1987), *Inside Edition* (1988), *Life Stories: Families in Crisis* ("Blood Brothers: The Joey DiPaolo Story," 1992), *Rolonda* (hostess; 1995–98), *New York Undercover* ("You Get No Respect," 1995), *Sister, Sister* (recurring role of Vivica Shaw; 1997–98), *Smart Guy* ("That's My Mama," 1998), *The Jamie Foxx Show* ("Fire and Desire," Part II, 1999), *The Steve Harvey Show* ("Guess Who's Not Coming to Counseling," 2000), *The West Wing* ("The White House Pro-Am," 2000), *The Division* ("Secrets and Lies," 2001), *7th Heaven* (2 episodes in the role of Sylvia Carter; "Chances...," "Are," 2001), *Days of Our Lives* (recurring role of Cameron Reese; 2001–08), *The District* ("Thursday," 2001), *For Your Love* ("The 'What I Done' Show," 2002), *One on One* ("The Test," 2003),

Boston Public ("Chapter Sixty-Four," 2003), *Dorothy Dandridge: An American Beauty* (2003), *The Bold and the Beautiful* (recurring role of Attorney Julie Shoemaker; 2003), *The Proud Family* (voice; "Election," 2003), *Ned's Declassified School Survival Guide* ("Teachers and Detention," 2004), *My Wife and Kids* ("Pokerface," 2004), *JAG* ("Camp Delta," 2004), *Yes, Dear* ("Dead Aunt, Dead Aunt...," 2004), *Complete Savages* ("Bad Reception," 2005), *Lie Detector* (hostess; 2005), *14th Annual Inner City Destiny Awards* (2006), *Bring That Year Back 2006: Laugh Now, Cry Later* (2006), *Can You Teach My Alligator Manners?* ("Classroom Manners," 2008), *The Judge Joe Brown Show* (announcer; 2005–present), *Curious George* (voice of Professor Brown; 2006), *Temptation* (announcer; 2007).

Video/DVD: *TV in Black: The First Fifty Years* (2004).

Wayans, Kim Born in New York, October, 1961.

Kim Wayans is part of the huge (and successful) Wayans comedy family, which includes brothers Keenen Ivory, Damon, Marlon, Shawn and Dwayne, and sisters Nadia, Elvira, Deidre and Vonnie. Wayans grew up in the Chelsea section of Manhattan. Her mother was a social worker and her father was a supermarket manager. She is a graduate of Wesleyan University.

She had her first taste of breakout fame with *In Living Color* (1990–93), a Sunday night comedy sketch review headed up by her brother Keenen Ivory and prominently featuring another brother, Damon, that helped put the fledgling FOX Network on the map. Her best ongoing skit was probably "I Love Laquita," a wacky variant on *I Love Lucy*. She has also lent her manic comic style to some of brother Keenen Ivory's feature films: *I'm Gonna Git You Sucka* (1988), a very funny parody of the blaxploitation era; *A Low Down Dirty Shame* (1994), an appealing private eye take-off; and *Don't Be a Menace to South Central While Drinking Your Juice in the Hood* (1996), a parody of the black social realism films epitomized by the work of director John Singleton.

She also had a recurring role at the start of her career as Allison on *A Different World* (1987–88) and was Tonia Harris on the sitcom *In the House* (1995–98) with LL Cool J. In recent years, she was a story editor on brother Damon's hit sitcom *My Wife and Kids*.

In 2008 she appeared in the performance art presentation *A Handsome Woman Retreats* (*...a seriously funny journey to inner peace*), about a woman who undertakes a ten day period of silent meditation to root out her anxieties; the performance included autobiographical insights into what it was like growing up funny in the Wayans family.

Feature Films including Video and TV Movies: *Eddie Murphy Live* (1987), *Hollywood Shuffle* (1987), *I'm Gonna Git You Sucka* (1988), *Talking About Sex* (1994), *Floundering* (1994), *A Low Down Dirty Shame* (1994), *Don't Be a Menace to South Central While Drinking Your Juice in the Hood* (1996), *Critics and Other Freaks* (1997), *Juwanna Mann* (2002), *What News?* (2007).

TV: *A Different World* (recurring role of Allison; 1987–88), *China Beach* (2 episodes in the role of Cameo Candette; "Lost and Found," Parts I and II, 1988), *Dream On* ("Over Your Dead Body," 1990), *In Living Color* (cast regular; 1990–93), *The Best of Robert Townsend and His Partners in Crime* (1991), *Wisecracks* (1991), *Soul Train Comedy Awards* (1993), *In the House* (recurring role of Tonia Harris; 1995–98), *The Wayans Bros.* (2 episodes in the role of Sheila; "Farmer's Daughter," "A Country Christmas," 1995 and 1998), *Waynehead* (recurring role of Mom; 1996–97), *Getting Personal* ("There's Something About Rhonda," 1998), *Random Acts of Comedy* (1999), *The Oprah Winfrey Show* (2004), *Thugaboo: Sneaker Madness* (voice; 2006), *Thugaboo: A Miracle on D-Roc's Street* (voice; 2006), *What's News?* (2007), *Why We Laugh: Black Comedians on Black Comedy* (2009).

Webb, Veronica Born in Detroit, Michigan, February 25, 1965.

An intellectual as well as a supermodel, Veronica Webb is also an actress, writer, journalist and television host. She grew up in a middle class milieu, reading comic books and dreaming of being a model. Her father was an electrician for Chrysler and her mom was a nurse at Detroit General Hospital. She has three sisters. She is a graduate of New York's Parsons School of Design (with a major in animation) and the New School.

Webb was the first black model to sign a contract with a major mainstream cosmetics company (Revlon). She has been on the covers of every major fashion magazine, including *Vogue* and *Elle*, and has modeled for Chanel and Victoria's Secret and designers Karl Lagerfield, Isaac Mizrahi, and Todd Oldham.

On screen she has mostly played smaller roles (or appeared as herself) in films about the fashion industry — *Unzipped* (1995), *Catwalk* (1996), *Zoolander* (2001) — and she was in two Spike Lee films, *Jungle Fever* (1991) and *Malcolm X* (1992). On television, she has guested on *Damon*, *The West Wing* and *Becker*, and was most recently on *Tim Gunn's Guide to Style* (2007). She was an editor-at-large for *Interview* magazine and wrote a column for *Paper* and for *Panorama*, the Italian news magazine. She is also the author of the autobiographical book of essays *Veronica Webb Sight: Adventures in the Big City*.

She married George Robb in 2002; they have two children, Leila Rose, born in 2002, and Molly Blue, born in 2004.

Feature Films including TV Movies: *Jungle Fever* (1991), *Malcolm X* (1992), *For Love or Money* (1993), *Unzipped* (documentary; 1995), *Catwalk* (1996), *54* (1998), *Holy Man* (1998), *The Big Tease* (1999), *In Too Deep* (1999), *Zoolander* (2001), *Someone Like You* (2001), *Dirty Laundry* (2006).

TV: *The Word* (1994), *Ford Supermodel of the World* (1995), *The 9th Annual Soul Train Music Awards* (1995), *Politically Incorrect* (1995), *People Yearbook '95*, *Clueless* (2 episodes; "Do We with Bad Haircuts Not Feel?" "Fixing Up Daddy," 1996 and 1997), *Just Shoot Me!* ("The Devil and Maya Gallo," 1997), *Howard Stern* (3 segments; 1998), *It's Like, You Know...* ("Hoop Dreams," 199?), *Damon* (2 episodes as Tracy Warren; "The Apartment," "Chasing Tracy," 1998), *The West Wing* ("200 Hours in L.A.," 2000), *Miss Universe 2001*, *Becker* ("The Princess Cruise," 2001), *VH1: Where Are They Now?* ("Ford Supermodels," 2002), *The Isaac Mizrahi Show* (2002), *Retrosexual: The '80s* (2004), *Real Life Divas* (various segments; 2006), *Tim Gunn's Guide to Style* (co-host; 2007).

Welch, Elisabeth Born in New York, New York, February 27, 1904; died July 15, 2003, Northwood, Middlesex, England.

Although American born, Elisabeth Welch made her career (and life) largely in Britain. She was of mixed African, Native American, Irish and Scots blood. The career of Elisabeth Margaret Welch shows that the egregious racial stereotyping that was so much a part and parcel of Hollywood's treatment of blacks was not necessarily reflected in British films. She was presented with dignity onscreen, if only to sing a song in a cabaret that had nothing to do with the plot of the film.

She starred in two back-to-back films with Paul Robeson: *Song of Freedom* (1936) and *Big Fella* (1937). In *Song of Freedom*, she's Ruth Zinga, the wife of Johnny (Paul Robeson), a dockworker who becomes an international opera star but chooses to return to his African roots. In the musical drama *Big Fella*, she's Miranda, a café singer and Robeson's girlfriend. Again playing a dockworker, Robeson is asked by the authorities to help find a missing child who disappeared while on an ocean liner. Both Robeson and Welch have some fine song numbers in this film. She is also in the great (and rare, in that not too many horror films were made in England until the great Hammer Films output of the 1950s) British omnibus horror film *Dead of Night* (1945). She plays Beulah, the nightclub owner-hostess.

She was also popular in Paris and sang in nightclubs there (often performing at the Moulin Rouge). She first went to Paris as part of the tour for the revue *Blackbirds of 1928*. Welch made many recordings throughout her life. She entertained the troops during World War II in Malta and Gibraltar. She was nominated for a Tony Award for Best Actress in a Featured Role in a Musical for *Jerome Kern Goes to Hollywood* (1986). Her Broadway career went all the way back to *Liza* in 1922–23, *Runnin' Wild* in 1923, and *Blackbirds of 1928*. She was also in *The New Yorkers* (1930–31).

Later productions she appeared in were *Pippin* and *Cindy-Eller*. She presented a one-woman off–Broadway show in 1986 at the Lucille Lortel Theatre, earning an Obie and an Outer Critics Circle Award. She was married to jazz musician Luke Smith from 1924 until his death in 1936.

Feature Films including TV Movies: *Death at Broadcasting House* (1934), *Soft Lights and Sweet Music* (1936), *Song of Freedom* (1936), *Big Fella* (1937), *Calling All Stars* (1937), *Around the Town* (1938), *Over the Moon* (1939), *This Was Paris* (1942), *Alibi* (1942), *Fiddlers Three* (1944), *Dead of Night* (1945), *Our Man in Havana* (1959), *Girl Stroke Boy* (1971), *The Man Who Came to Dinner* (TV; 1972), *Revenge of the Pink Panther* (1978), *Arabian Adventure* (1979), *The Tempest* (1979).

TV: *Not So Much a Programme, More a Way of Life* (1965), *BBC 3* (1966), *Play of the Month* ("The Moon and Sixpence," 1967), *Jackanory* (10 episodes as the Storyteller; 1968–69), *The Royal Variety Performance 1979*, *Joyce Grenfell 1910–1979* (1980), *This Is Your Life* (1985).

Video/DVD: *The Jerome Kern Songbook* (1990).

Whitfield, Lynn Born in Baton Rouge, Louisiana, May 6, 1953.

Class, bearing and intelligence are the key qualities Lynn Whitfield brings to every role. Born to a distinguished, ambitious family with roots in southern black royalty, she has always projected an aristocratic mien and a formidable sense of style. Her father was Valerian Smith (1926–92), who founded the Baton Rouge Playhouse in 1952, and who worked on the scores of such films as *Band of Angels* (1957) and *Hurry Sundown* (1967). He also composed musical stage productions such as *Supper*, *Earl K. Long*, *Creole Baby* and *Tribulations*.

Whitfield graduated with a bachelor of arts degree from Howard University. She performed with the Black Repertory Company in Washington, D.C., and co-starred in the Los Angeles, London and Australian companies of Ntozake Shange's *For Colored Girls Who Have Considered Suicide/When the Rainbow Is Enuf.* Whitfield first attracted national attention during the PBS *American Playhouse* telecast of *For Colored Girls....*

Lynn Whitfield and Martin Lawrence in *A Thin Line Between Love and Hate* (1996).

Her off–Broadway roles have included *The Great MacDaddy* and *Showdown*. In 1979, she began her film career under a talent development program at Columbia Pictures. Early roles included the Dan Aykroyd comedy *Dr. Detroit*, where she was mere window dressing; and the eccentric, lively western *Silverado*, in the sketchy, improbable role of a dancehall girl.

In HBO's *The Josephine Baker Story*—her signature role—Whitfield was as beautiful and sensual as the actual Josephine (although, unsurprisingly, she lacked Josephine's comedic charm and dazzling dance talent). Aging from 18 to 68 during the course of the film, her interpretation suggests rather than slavishly duplicates the real Baker. The film pointedly presents Baker as a symbol and an icon as well as an individual. Amazingly, Whitfield captures the aging Baker of the Rainbow Tribe and late-career comeback years, as well as the vital Baker of the Folies-Bergére era. Indeed, it is her scenes as the mature Josephine that ring most true and touch the heart in surprising, original ways. Her superb evocation of Baker, however, proved both a blessing and a curse, as Whitfield becamc so identified with the Jazz Age superstar that other opportunities proved limited.

But there were a few other big screen highlights—the brilliant, haunting *Eve's Bayou* (1997) and the underrated cautionary tale *A Thin Line Between Love and Hate* (1996). On the other side of the ledger, some truly awful TV movies (*Taking the Heat*; 1993) and theatrical features (*Gone Fishin'*; 1997) did not help her cause. Whitfield has had a varied love life. Her first marriage was to Vantile Whitfield of the D.C. Black Repertory. Her second was to Brian Gibson (1990–92), the British director of *The Josephine Baker Story*. This marriage produced a daughter named Grace. Whitfield was also the companion of Kweisi Mfume, former head of the NAACP and chairman of the Congressional Black Caucus.

Feature Films including TV Movies: *Doctor Detroit* (1983), *The Slugger's Wife* (1985), *Silverado* (1985), *Johnnie Mae Gibson: FBI* (1986; TV), *The George McKenna Story* (aka *Hard Lessons*) (1986; TV), *Dead Aim* (1987), *Jaws: The Revenge* (1987), *The Women of Brewster Place*

(1989; TV), *The Josephine Baker Story* (1991; TV), *A Triumph of the Heart: The Ricky Bell Story* (1991; TV), *Stompin' at the Savoy* (1992; TV), *Taking the Heat* (1993; TV), *Thicker Than Blood: The Larry McLinden Story* (1994), *In the Army Now* (1994), *Sophie and the Moonhanger* (1996; TV), *A Thin Line Between Love and Hate* (1996), *Gone Fishin'* (1997), *The Planet of Junior Brown* (aka Junior's Groove) (1997), *Eve's Bayou* (1997), *The Wedding* (1998; TV), *Stepmom* (1998), *The Color of Courage* (1999; TV), *Deep in My Heart* (1999; TV), *Dangerous Evidence: The Lori Jackson Story* (1999; TV), *A Time for Dancing* (2000), *Head of State* (2003), *That's So Raven: Supernaturally Stylish* (TV; 2003), *The Cheetah Girls* (TV; 2003), *Redemption: The Stan "Tookie" Williams Story* (2004; TV), *Madea's Family Reunion* (2006), *The Cheetah Girls 2* (2006; TV), *The Women* (2008), *Kings of the Evening* (2009), *Mama I Want to Sing* (2009), *The Rebound* (2009), *Pure Shooter* (2009).

TV: *Hill Street Blues* (recurring role as Jill Thomas; "Chipped Beef," "Second Hand Rose," "Can World War III Be an Attitude?" 1981), *American Playhouse: For Colored Girls Who Have Considered Suicide When the Rainbow Is Enuf* (1982), *This Is the Life* ("Certain Arrangements," 1983), *Matt Houston* ("The Centerfold Murders," 1983), *Cagney & Lacey* ("Who Says It's Fair?" Parts I and II, 1985), *Miami Vice* ("Bought and Paid For," 1985), *The Fall Guy* ("Escape Clause," 1985), *Mike Hammer* ("Harlem Nocturne," 1986), *Shelley Duvall Presents: American Tall Tales and Legends: John Henry* (1987), *St. Elsewhere* ("Curtains," 1988), *HeartBeat* (series regular in the role of Dr. Cory Banks, 1988), *Equal Justice* (recurring role of Maggie Mayfield, 1990), *American Playhouse: Zora Is My Name!* (1990), *Matlock* ("The Informer," Parts I and II, 1990), *The Trials of Rosie O'Neill* ("Real Mothers," 1991), *State of Emergency* (1994), *The Cosby Mysteries* (recurring role of Barbara Lorenz, 1994), *Martin* ("Goin' Overboard," Parts I and II, 1997), *Touched by An Angel* ("Amazing Grace," Part I," 1997), *Intimate Portrait: Josephine Baker* (1998), *Intimate Portrait: Patti LaBelle* (1998), *Love Songs* ("A Love Song for Jean and Ellis," 1999), *A Girl Thing* (miniseries, 2001), *Boston Public* (3 episodes in role of Louanna Harper), *Biography* ("Martin Lawrence: Comic Trip," 2002), *Lost in Oz* (2002), "Suspect," 2002), *Without a Trace* (recurring role as Paula Van Doren: "Lost and Found," "Fallout," Parts I and II, 2004; "Are You Now or Have You Ever Been?" 2003), *Strong Medicine* ("Race for a Cure," 2004), *The Tyra Banks Show* (2006), *Tavis Smiley* (2006).

Whitten, Marguerite (aka Whitten, Margaret) Born in Mississippi on February 23, 1913; died Los Angeles County, December 25, 1990.

Marguerite Whitten is a primary example of a black actress whose career should be re-evaluated and reassessed. She had a striking screen persona, one quite ahead of its time. Even when she played a maid, that maid was sexy and quick with a retort. Through her screen work, we get an important sense of what many young black women of the era were really like (especially when the "man" wasn't looking).

It's great fun watching her exchange comedic barbs with Mantan Moreland in the campy but entertaining *King of the Zombies*. It is probably for her role of Samantha, the cocky maid, that she is best remembered today. Other roles include her screen debut, *Spirit of Youth*, with heavyweight champion Joe Louis, and the entertaining *Two-Gun Man from Harlem* with Herb Jeffries. In *Spirit of Youth*, Marguerite (billed as Margaret) appears as the sister of Louis — called Joe Thomas — in what is little more than a thinly disguised bio pic. Both *Spirit* and *Two-Gun* also featured the omnipresent Mantan Moreland, the actor she worked best with, especially in the surrealistic *Mr. Washington Goes to Town* (1941).

Feature Films: *Spirit of Youth* (1938), *Two-Gun Man from Harlem* (1938), *The Toy Wife* (1938), *Bad Boy* (1939), *Way Down South* (1939), *Mystery in Swing* (1940), *King of the Zombies* (1941), *Mr. Washington Goes to Town* (1941), *Let's Go Collegiate* (1941), *Cadet Girl* (1941), *Sleepytime Gal* (1942), *After Midnight with Boston Blackie* (1943).

Williams, Cynda Born in Chicago, Illinois, 1966.

Cynda Williams is another of those "had the talent, didn't get the recognition" actresses, but her sultry yet compassionate screen persona has stayed in the minds of many a film buff who saw her in contemporary classics like the ultra-suspenseful *One False Move* (1992) and the hypnotic *Caught Up* (1998). For these and other films, such as *Black Rose of Harlem* (aka *Machine Gun Blues*; 1996), she should be considered the uncrowned black queen of film noir. Her acting style is ideal for the genre.

Top: Left to right: **Florence O'Brien, Mantan Moreland, Marguerite Whitten, and Clarence Hargrave (in gorilla suit) in *Mr. Washington Goes to Town* (1941). *Left:* Cynda Williams in *Black Rose of Harlem* (*Machine Gun Blues*) (1996).**

Cynthia (Cindy, then Cynda) Williams is a graduate of Indiana's Ball State University. She made her film debut in director Spike Lee's *Mo' Better Blues* (1990) and enjoyed some commercial success with the song "Harlem Blues." Williams is a talented singer and can be heard extensively in the film *Black Rose of Harlem*. The song "Harlem Blues" went to number 9 on the R&B chart. She was scheduled to produce a jazz album with Sony, but it fell through.

Theatrical credits include Richard Wesley's *The Talented Tenth* (Los Angeles) and *Langston Is My Man*, an original musical performed in Richmond, Virginia. Williams has appeared in several significant made-for-TV movies: Oprah Winfrey's production *The Wedding* (1998) and *Introducing Dorothy Dandridge* (1999), as Dorothy's sister Vivian. Williams has had three husbands: the talented actor Billy Bob Thornton, with whom she starred in *One False Move* (married 1990–92); Arthur Louis Fuller (1993–98); and TV producer

Roderick Plummer (2001–present), with whom she has one girl.

Feature Films including Video and TV Movies: *Mo' Better Blues* (1990), *One False Move* (1992), *The Killing Box* (1993), *Condition Red* (1995), *The Tie That Binds* (1995), *Gang in Blue* (1996), *Spirit Lost* (1996), *Tales of Erotica* ("Wet" segment; 1996), *Black Rose of Harlem* (aka *Machine Gun Blues*; 1996), *The Sweeper* (1996), *The Wedding* (TV; 1998), *Caught Up* (1998), *Relax ... It's Just Sex...* (1998), *The Last Call* (aka *Stingers*, 1998), *Introducing Dorothy Dandridge* (TV; 1999), *The Courage to Love* (TV; 2000), *Hidden Blessings* (TV; 2000), *March* (2001), *MacArthur Park* (2001), *Violation* (TV; 2003), *With or Without You* (2003), *Shooter* (2004), *When Do We Eat?* (2005), *Our House* (TV; 2006), *Divine Intervention* (2007), *Frankie D.* (2007), *Tru Loved* (2008), *Beautiful Loser* (2008).

TV: *Tales of the City* (1993), *Fallen Angels* ("Fearless," 1995), *New York Undercover* ("Hubris," 1997).

Williams, Kiely Born in Alexandria, Virginia, July 9, 1986.

Kiely Alexis Williams has enjoyed popularity as a member of the Disney-created group The Cheetah Girls and prior to that was a member of the girl group 3LW (their debut album in 2001 went platinum, but the group has since disbanded). Although Williams was born in Alexandria, her family later relocated to Newark, New Jersey.

She was cast as Aquanetta Waker (Aqua) in the first Disney Channel Original Movie, *The Cheetah Girls* (2003), with Raven Symoné, Adrienne Bailon (who was also a member of 3LW), and Sabrina Bryan. The successful film, based on the young adult books by Deborah Gregory, spawned two sequels, *The Cheetah Girls 2* (2006) and *The Cheetah Girls: One World* (2008), which did not feature Raven Symoné. In addition to the popular best-selling soundtracks from the three films (their first album sold over three million copies), the group released the albums *Cheetah-licious Christmas* (2005), *In Concert: The Party's Just Begun Tour* (2007), and *TCG* (2007). In addition to close to 20 singles with The Cheetah Girls (including "Cinderella [The Cheetah Girls Song]," "I Won't Say [I'm in Love]"), Williams has released several singles of her own, "I Know What Boys Like," "Make Me a Drink,"), and a solo album. There is a Cheetah Girl doll line, clothing line, and toys and video games based on the group.

In November 2008 an announcement was made that The Cheetah Girls would break up at the end of their One World Tour in December. However, with her burgeoning solo music and acting career (she had a role in the popular comedy *The House Bunny* in 2008), Williams can look forward to an extended run in show business.

Feature Films including TV Movies: *The Cheetah Girls* (TV; 2003), *The Cheetah Girls 2* (TV; 2006), *The Sisterhood of the Traveling Pants 2* (2008), *The Cheetah Girls: One World* (2008), *The House Bunny* (2008), *The Science of Cool* (2009).

TV: *The Making of "Jimmy Neutron,"* (2001), *Taina* ("Blue Mascara," 2001), *The Nick Cannon Show* (2002), *All That* (2002), *9th Annual Soul Train Lady of Soul Awards* (2003), *The Cheetah Girls* (11 episodes in the role of Aqua; 2004), *79th Annual Macy's Thanksgiving Day Parade* (2005), *Walt Disney World Christmas Day Parade* (2005), *The Teen Choice Awards 2006*, *Arthur Ashe Kids' Day* (2006), *The Cheetah Girls: In Concert* (2006), *The View* (2006), *Martha* (2006), *The Tonight Show with Jay Leno* (2006), *2006 American Music Awards*, *Good Morning America* (3 appearances; 2006–08), *Good Day L.A.* (2007), *The Early Show* (2007), *ktla Morning Show* (2007), *Kristi Yamaguchi Friends and Family* (2007), *A Hollywood Christmas Celebration* (2007), *Entertainment Tonight* (2 segments; 2007–08), *The Suite Life of Zack and Cody* ("Doin' Time in Suite 2330," 2008), *Extra: The Entertainment Magazine* (2008), *American Idol* (2008), *Wal-Mart Soundcheck* (2008), *E! News Live* (2008), *Mi TRL* (2008), *Total Request with Carson Daly* (2008), *The Disney Channel Games* (5 segments; 2008), *ktla Morning Show* (2008), *Studio DC: Almost Live '08*, *2008 alma Awards*.

Video/DVD: *The Cheetah Girls: Behind the Spots* (2004), *Cheetah Tips! How to Be Cheetah-licious* (2006), *The Today Show* (2006), *Blue Peter* (2007), *The Disney Channel Games* (2007), *Meet the Cheetahs* (2007), *The Cheetah Girls in Concert: The Party's Just Begun Tour* (2007).

Williams, Tonya Lee Born in London, England, July 12, 1958.

Tonya Maxine Williams is of Jamaican heritage. Her father was a Supreme Court justice who served with the United Nations as a judge on the

Rwanda tribunals, the African nation of Rwanda being the scene of much internecine strife. Her mother is a retired nurse. Williams is a graduate of Ryerson University's Theater School in Toronto. Born in London, she moved to Jamaica at one year of age, then to Birmingham, England, when she was five, and then to Oshawa, Canada, at age 12.

She is best known stateside for her role as Dr. Olivia Barber Winters on the soap *The Young and the Restless* (1990–2005, 2007–08). The "Lee" part of her name was made up on the spot when she applied for her Screen Actors Guild card. There were already several Tonya Williamses recorded, so she was asked to change the spelling of the name or add a middle name. Her real middle name (Maxine Gwendolyn) was too long, so she settled for Lee, and it stuck.

She has combined appearances on American TV with shows in Canada. She has been on such U.S. series as *Hill Street Blues, Matlock,* and the special *A Very Brady Christmas* (1988). Williams also briefly had a recurring role as Linda Dukes on the unsuccessful soap *Generations* (1989–90). In addition to her acting work, she was the director of the pilot of *Kink in My Hair* (2004) with Sheryl Lee Ralph and the hostess of *Tonya Lee Williams: Gospel Jubilee* (2004).

She is the founder and president of the well-known ReelWorld Film Festival, an annual event in Toronto. She was married to Robert Simpson from 1983 to 1991.

Feature Films including TV Movies: *Skullduggery* (1983), *As Is* (TV; 1986), *The Liberators* (TV; 1987), *Spaced Invaders* (1990), *The Borrower* (1991), *Seventeen Again* (2000), *A Perfect Note* (TV; 2005), *Poor Boy's Game* (2007).

TV: *Polka Dot Door* (hostess; 1971), *Check It Out* ("No Cause for Alarm," 1985), *What's Happening Now!!* ("The New Employee," 1987), *Street Legal* (2 episodes; "A Little Knowledge," "Tango Bellarosa," 1987), *Hill Street Blues* ("It Ain't Over Till It's Over," 1987), *Falcon Crest* (3 episodes as Chase's secretary; "Hat Trick," "Battle Lines," "Redemption," 1987), *Captain Power and the Soldiers of the Future* ("And Study War No More," 1987), *A Very Brady Christmas* (1988), *Matlock* ("The Starlet," 1989), *A Peaceable Kingdom* (pilot; 1989), *Nasty Boys* (pilot; 1989), *Generations* (recurring role as Linda Dukes; 1989–90), *The Young and* the *Restless* (recurring role of Dr. Olivia B. Winters; 1990–2008), *Counterstrike* ("The Contender," 1993), *Getting By* ("Shop 'Til You Drop," 1993), *Silk Stalkings* ("The Last Campaign," 1994), *PSI Factor: Chronicles of the Paranormal* ("Bad Dreams," 1998), *The 27th Annual Daytime Emmy Awards* (2000), *SoapTalk* (2003), *Tonya Lee Williams: Gospel Jubilee* (hostess; 2004).

Video/DVD: *Seeking Salvation* (2004).

Williams, Vanessa (aka Williams, Vanessa A.) Born in Brooklyn, New York, May 12, 1963.

Two fine actresses share the name Vanessa Williams, with a different initial that sets them apart on their Screen Actors Guild card. This Vanessa Williams was born in the Bedford-Stuyvesant section of Brooklyn. She was a member of the New York Opera's Children's Chorus and did television commercials prior to attending the High School of Performing Arts and earning a bachelor's in theater and business from Marymount Manhattan College.

She first attracted major public attention when she was cast on *The Cosby Show* as a student schoolmate of Theo, aspiring actress Jade Marsh, from 1989 to 1991. She returned to the series in another role, as Theo's girlfriend Cheryl Lovejoy from Barbados. Her theatrical credits include *Death and the King's Horseman* (ensemble; 1987) at Lincoln Center, and the Broadway productions

Vanessa A. Williams in *Candyman* (1992).

Sarafina! (as Vanessa; 1988–89) and *Mule Bone* (as Bootsie; 1991).

Her feature film output has been busy and varied, starting with the crackerjack crime thriller *New Jack City* (1991), where she played the deadly Keisha, security for Wesley Snipes' drug czar Nico Brown. She followed that the next year with *Candyman*, the first in the popular horror film series with Tony Todd. Here she gave an unusually insightful performance for the genre as the single mother Anna-Marie McCoy, who is menaced by the creepy title character.

Williams continued to work a combination of theatrical, TV and direct to video movies, but it was four TV series that cemented her fame. The first was *Melrose Place*, the popular FOX nighttime soap. She played Rhonda Blair in 1992–93. Then she was Lila on Steven Botchco's *Murder One* in 1995–96, for which she earned her first NAACP Image Award. Her role as Dr. Grace Carr in *Chicago Hope* (1996) earned her a second Image Award nomination. This was followed by her finest role of Maxine Joseph Chadwayon Showtime's *Soul Food* (2000–04), a continuation of the 1997 film about black family life in Chicago, centered around the Joseph family. *Soul Food* was authentic, insightful and deeply involving. Williams was the series' resident sex bomb and was nominated for three NAACP Image Awards (2001, 2004, 2005) and won one (2003). The series received over 30 other NAACP nominations for Outstanding Drama (winner 2002–04) and for various other individual cast members. (The other Vanessa Williams had appeared in the original movie, in the role of Teri Joseph, played on the series by Nicole Ari Parker). *Soul Food* remains the most successful black cast drama in television history.

She received a Daytime Emmy Award nomination for her role in *Our America* (as Sandra Williams; 2002), which was also shown at the Sundance Festival. Two Chicago teens investigate the murder of a child. Williams is the author of a collection of poetry and prose titled *Shine*. She has also written essays and poems for *Essence* magazine. She is also a talented singer-songwriter and has performed at venues such as the Temple Bar in Santa Monica, California. She married Andre Wiseman in 1993; they have one child.

Feature Films including TV Movies: *New Jack City* (1991), *Fatal Bond* (1992), *Candyman* (1992), *Drop Squad* (1994), *Mother* (1996), *A Woman of Color* (TV; 1997), *Breakdown* (1997), *Incognito* (TV; 1999), *Playing with Fire* (TV; 2000), *Punks* (2000), *Afrocentricity* (2000), *Baby of the Family* (2002), *Our America* (TV; 2002), *Like Mike* (2002), *Black Listed* (2003), *Allergic to Nuts* (2003), *Gift for the Living* (2005), *Contradictions of the Heart* (2006), *Drawing Angel* (2007), *Ice Spiders* (TV; 2007), *Jimmie* (2008), *Flirting with 40* (TV; 2008), *Nowhereland* (2009), *Contradictions of the Heart* (2009).

TV: *The Cosby Show* (4 episodes; "Theo's Women," "What He Did for Love," "Theo's Final Final," "No More Mr. Nice Guy," 1989–91), *Law & Order* ("Happily Ever After," 1990), *The Jaleel White Special* (1991), *Melrose Place* (recurring role of Rhonda Blair; 1992–93), *NYPD Blue* ("Don We Now Our Gay Apparel," 1995), *Living Single* ("Another Saturday Night," 1995), *Murder One* (19 episodes in the role of Lila; 1995–96), *Buddies* ("Marry Me ... Sort Of," 1996), *Malcolm & Eddie* ("Big Brother Is Watching," 1996), *Chicago Hope* (4 episodes in the role of Dr. Grace Carr; "Out of Africa," "Back to the Future," "Liver Let Die," "Liar, Liar," 1996), *Between Brothers* ("The Interview," 1997), *The Pretender* ("Collateral Damage," 1998), *The Steve Harvey Show* ("Rent," 1998), *Total Recall 2070* ("Self-Inflicted," 1999), *Heavy Gear: The Animated Series* (voice; 2001), *Acapulco Black Film Festival* (2000), *Soul Food* (recurring role of Maxine Chadway; 2000–04), *E! True Hollywood Story* ("Melrose Place," 2003), *Happy to Be Nappy and Other Stories of Me* (voice; 2004), *The Bachelorette* (2005), *In the Mix* (2006), *2006 American Music Awards*, *Angels Can't Help But Laugh* (2007), *Cold Case* ("Shuffle, Ball Change," 2007), *Video on Trial* (archival; 2007), *Entertainment Tonight* (2007), *Knight Rider* (2 episodes; 2008), *Baisden After Dark* (2008).

Shorts: *Breakdown* (1997), *Driving Fish* (2002), *Gift for the Living* (voice; 2005), *Drawing Angel* (2007), *Hummingbird* (2008).

Williams, Vanessa L. (aka Williams, Vanessa)

Born in Tarrytown, New York, March 18, 1963.

Vanessa L. Williams is the daughter of music teachers Helen and Milton Augustine Williams. She and her younger brother Chris grew up in the middle-class community of Millwood, New York. Her early interest was primarily focused on singing. She was a theater arts major at Syracuse University from 1981 to 1983, but interrupted her education to concentrate on her Miss America duties and her career in show business. She received an honorary degree in 2008 and delivered the convocation address at the College of Visual and Performing Arts.

Williams started competing in beauty pageants in the 1980s. Her otherworldly good looks and music talent held her in good stead as a competitor, and she won the Miss New York contest as preparation for Miss America. She had won the preliminary talent and swimsuit competitions, so she went into the contest on pageant night as the forerunner and entered the record books in 1983 when she became the first African American Miss America.

A series of explicit nude photographs published in *Penthouse* magazine was a major scandal in the wake of her victory, forcing her to surrender the Miss America crown in a press conference on July 23, 1984. Today, this incident isn't even a blip on the cultural radar screen. Grammy, Emmy and Tony Award nominee Williams is more known more for her acting than her singing these days, due in measure to work in the hit series *Ugly Betty*.

But first came her major singing career. Her debut album was *The Right Stuff* in 1988, which yielded the R&B hit "(He's Got) the Look" and her first *Billboard* Hot 100 hit "Dreamin.'" The album was a success; it went gold, and earned her three Grammy nominations (including the prestigious Best New Artist). Her second album, *The Comfort Zone* (1991), was even bigger, including her giant hit "Saving the Best for Last," which was number one in the U.S. for five weeks, and number one or top ten all over much of the rest of the world. *Comfort Zone* sales reached triple platinum

Vanessa Williams and Arnold Schwarzenegger in *Eraser* (1996).

in the U.S. and the album was nominated for five Grammy Awards. Her third album, *The Sweetest Days* (1994), saw her experimenting with different musical styles, including jazz and hip-hop. It too was certified platinum and garnered two Grammy Award nominations.

To fully appreciate Williams' dynamic talent you are best served by seeing her on Broadway. Her Broadway triumph is *Kiss of the Spider Woman* (1994–95), as the iconic Hollywood "dream woman" of the homosexual Latin political prisoner. Williams was also astonishing as the Witch in the revival of *Into the Woods* (2002). She was in the off–Broadway productions *Checkmates* (1985) and *One Man Band* (1989); played *Carmen Jones* at the Kennedy Center; and starred in New York City Center's Encores! Concert of *St. Louis Woman*.

Feature films have not been Williams' venue — roles for black actresses are scarce at any rate. She was really good opposite Arnold Schwarzenegger in *Eraser* (1996) and nailed the role of "first daughter" Teri Joseph in *Soul Food* (1997), her best motion picture showcase. After a story arc as Elizabeth Bauer on *South Beach* in 2006, Williams found the TV role of her career with her performance as the evil but vulnerable fashion doyenne Wilhemina Slater on *Ugly Betty*, starting in 2006. Her Emmy-nominated work has boosted her career to a new level.

Her first marriage was to Ramon Hervey II; they had three children: Melanie (1987), Jillian (1989) and Devin (1993). She married NBA player Rick Fox in 1999, but filed for divorce in 2004. Their daughter Sasha was born in 2000.

Feature Films including TV Movies: *The Pick-up Artist* (1987), *Under the Gun* (1988), *Full Exposure: The Sex Tapes Scandal* (TV; 1989), *The Kid Who Loved Christmas* (TV; 1990), Another You (1991), *Harley Davidson and the Marlboro Man* (1991), *Stompin' at the Savoy* (TV; 1992), *The Jacksons: An American Dream* (TV; 1992), *Score with Chicks* (1994), *Nothing Lasts Forever* (TV; 1995), *Bye Bye Birdie* (TV; 1995), *Eraser* (1996), *The Odyssey* (TV; 1997), *Hoodlum* (1997), *Soul Food* (1997), *Dance with Me* (1998), *Futuresport* (TV; 1998), *The Adventures of Elmo in Grouchland* (1999), *Light It Up* (1999), *The Courage to Love* (TV; 2000), *Don Quixote* (TV; 2000), *Shaft* (2000), *A Diva's Christmas Card* (TV; 2000), *WW3* (aka *WWIII*; TV; 2001), *Keep the Faith, Baby* (TV; 2002), *Beck and Call* (TV; 2004), *Johnson Family Vacation* (2004), *My Brother*

(2006), *And Then Came Love* (2007), *Hannah Montana: The Movie* (2009), *Phenom* (2009).

TV: *Late Night with David Letterman* (2 appearances; 1983–96), *The Love Boat* (2 episodes; 1984 and 1986), *Partners in Crime* ("Celebrity," 1984), *The 5th Annual Black Achievement Awards* (1984), *T.J. Hooker* ("Partners in Death," 1986), *Soul Train* (2 segments; 1988–92), *The 16th Annual American Music Awards* (1989), *Family Feud* (1989), *It's Showtime at the Apollo* (1989), *Perry Mason: The Case of the Silenced Singer* (1990), *MTV Video Music Awards 1992*, *The 34th Annual Grammy Awards* (1992), *The Tonight Show Starring Johnny Carson* (1992), *The 6th Annual Soul Train Music Awards* (1992), *Top of the Pops* (2 segments; 1992), *The Fresh Prince of Bel-Air* ("A Funny Thing Happened on the Way Home from the Forum," 1992), *Free to Laugh: A Comedy and Music Special for Amnesty International* (1992), *The Word* (1992), *Saturday Night Live* (2 segments; 1992–98), *The 35th Annual Grammy Awards* (1993), *David Foster's Christmas Album* (1993), *Ebony's 15th Annual Black Achievement Awards* (1994), *Carnegie Hall Salutes the Jazz Masters: Verve Records at 50* (1994), *The 48th Annual Tony Awards* (1994), *Some Enchanted Evening: Celebrating Oscar Hammerstein II* (1995), *Star Trek: Deep Space Nine* ("Let He Who Is Without Sin," 1996), *Super Bowl XXX* (1996), *The 68th Annual Academy Awards* (1996), *Vanessa Williams and Friends: Christmas in New York* (1996), *The Rosie O'Donnell Show* (9 appearances; 1996–2002), *The Tonight Show with Jay Leno* (1997), *Between Brothers* ("The Interview," 1997), *Pavarotti and Friends for the Children of Liberia* (1998), *A Very Special Christmas from Washington, D.C.* (1998), *I'll Make Me a World: A Century of African American Art* (6 episodes; 1999), *L.A. Doctors* (3 episodes in the role of Dr. Leanne Barrows; "O Captain, My Captain," "Que Sera, Sarah," "Every Picture Tells a Story," 1999), *Style World* (hostess; 2000), *The 72nd Annual Academy Awards* (2000), *2000 Blockbuster Entertainment Awards*, *Our Favorite Things: Christmas in Vienna* (2000), *Donny Osmond: This Is the Moment* (2001), *The Making of "Jimmy Neutron"* (2001), *Christmas in Rockefeller Center* (2001), *The American Experience* (archival; "Miss America," 2002), *Ally McBeal* ("Another One Bites the Dust," 2002), *Cool Women* (2002), *It's Black Entertainment* (2002), *The 56th Annual Tony Awards* (2002), *The View* (5 appearances; 2002–06), *Unchained Memories: Readings from the Slave Narratives* (2003), *Boom Town* (6 episodes in the role of Detective Katherine Pierce; 2003), *Great Performances* ("30th Anniversary: A Celebration in Song," 2003; archival; "Broadway's Lost Treasures III: The Best of the Tony Awards," 2005), *101 Most Shocking Moments in Entertainment* (archival; 2003), *Living It Up! with Ali and Jack* (2004), *The Sharon Osbourne Show* (2004), *35th NAACP Image Awards* (2004), *MADtv* (2004), *On-Air with Ryan Seacrest* (2004), *Fashion in Focus* ("Compassion in Fashion," 2004), *Retrosexual: The '80s* (2004), *Vanessa Williams Christmas: Live By Request* (2004), *Christmas in Washington* (2004), *The Tony Danza Show* (4 appearances; 2004–06), *Jimmy Kimmel Live!* (2 appearances; 2004–07), *The Late Late Show with Craig Ferguson* (2005), *Tavis Smiley* (2005), *Howard Stern* (2005), *Cinema mil* (archival; 2005), *Entertainment Tonight* (archival, 2005; 5 segments, 2007–08), *Fashion Week Diaries* (2005), *Geraldo at Large* (2005), *The Kennedy Center Honors: A Celebration of the Performing Arts* (2005), *La imogen de tu vida* (archival; 2006), *Greatest Miss America Moments* (2006), *South Beach* (8 episodes in the role of Elizabeth Bauer; 2006), *A Capital Fourth* (2006), *Rehearsing a Dream* (2006), *Ugly Betty* (recurring role of Wilhemina Slater; 2006–

Vanessa Williams.

08), *Live with Regis and Kelly* (2 appearances; 2006–07), *The Beautiful World of Ugly Betty* (2007), *Al rojo vivo con Maria Celeste* (archival; 2007), *The 64th Annual Golden Globe Awards* (2007), *38th NAACP Image Awards* (2007), *Expos* (2007), *The 61st Annual Tony Awards* (2007), *E! True Hollywood Story* (2007), *39th NAACP Image Awards* (2007), *The 60th Primetime Emmy Awards* (2008), *Jimmy Kimmel Live!* (2008), *AFI's 10 Top 10* (2008), *Extra* (2008), *The 6th Annual TV Land Awards* (2008).

Wilson, Ajita Born in Brooklyn, New York, 1950; died May 26, 1987, Rome, Italy.

Most of Ajita Wilson's popularity was centered in Italy, Spain and Greece, where she made a nonstop series of films in the seventies and eighties. Apparently, she never met a script she didn't like, since the films themselves are a mix of mainstream genre films and softcore or hardcore pornography. Wilson was both a presence and an actress, and she did a professional job in many genres, from horror films (*Macumba Sexual*) to espionage thrillers (*Black Aphrodite*) to anachronistic historical epics (*Messalina*).

Ajita Wilson was born a male named George Wilson. She was a full-fledged transsexual, although this was not a huge issue in terms of her screen career. She made her screen debut in director Cesare Caneveri's *La Principessa Nuda* (*The Nude Princess*) in a leading role as Miriam Zamoto, an African princess on a fund-raising mission who encounters Italy's *La dolce vita*. The film is a light comedy with a slight satirical tinge that pokes fun at celebrity and the jet set.

Wilson was a top-billed cult star by the time the Italian-Greek co-production *Black Aphrodite* was released, but today she is best known stateside for her films with prolific Spanish cult director Jess Franco. *Sadomania* (*Hölle der Lust*; 1981) is a German-Spanish co-production, a women-in-prison film that was widely distributed in the U.S. on video and later on DVD. Wilson is quite good as the sadist warden Magda, and the film benefits by clearly not taking itself too seriously. Also worth seeing is Franco's *Macumba Sexual* (1983), essentially a remake of Franco's *Vampyros Lesbos* (1971), where a mysterious woman begins to possess the body and soul of another woman. Visually this almost resembles an art film, and the scarcity of dialogue works in its favor (as was the case with *Vampyros Lesbos*).

In May 1987, Wilson was in a terrible auto accident and died of a cerebral hemorrhage. In recent years, more American fans are discovering her on DVD and falling under the spell of her curious but undeniable mystique.

Feature Films: *Gola profonda nera* (1976), *La principessa nuda* (*The Nude Princess*, 1976), *Mavri aphrodite* (*Black Aphrodite*, 1977), *Candido erotico* (1977), *La bravata* (1977), *Sylvia im reich der wollust* (1977), *Proibito erotico* (1978), *Bactron 317* (1978), *Le notti porno del mundo 2* (1978), *L'amour chez les poids lourds* (1978), *La pitoconejo* (1979), *Pensione amore servicio completo* (1979), *Libidine* (1979), *Eros perversion* (aka *Twelfth Night*, 1979), *Los energeticos* (1979), *Una donna di notte* (1979), *Pasiones desenfrenadas* (1980), *Orgia stin kerkyra* (1980), *Erotiki ekstasi* (1980), *Femmine infernali* (aka *Escape from Hell*, 1980), *Luca il contrabbandiere* (1980), *Orinoco prigioniere del sesso* (1980), *Eva Man* (1980), *Erotiko pathos* (aka *Blue Passion*, 1981), *Sadomania, Holle der lust* (aka *Sadomania, Hellhole Women*, 1981), *I eromeni* (1982), *Apocalipsis sexual* (1982), *Bacanales romanas* (1982), *Catherine Cherie* (1982), *La doppia bocca di Erika* (1983), *Anomali erotes sti Santorini* (1983), *Macumba Sexual* (1983), *Stin athina simera ... oles ton pernoun fanera!* (1984), *Ke to proto pinelo* (1984), *Idones sto egeo* (1984), *Perverse oltre le sbarre* (1984), *Detenute violente* (aka *Hell Penitentiary*, 1985), *Savage Island* (1985), *Bocca bianca, bocca nera* (1986).

TV: *Joe D'Amato Totally Uncut* (archival; 1999).

Winfrey, Oprah Born in Kosciusko, Mississippi, January 29, 1954.

Oprah Gail Winfrey is a worldwide icon who, in addition to having the most successful talk show career in the history of the medium, has also had notable success as an actress and producer. Born in Mississippi to an unwed teenaged mother (Vernita Lee), she grew up in an inner city Milwaukee neighborhood and then moved to Tennessee to live with her father, Vernon.

She was still in high school when she began her broadcasting career at WVOL radio in Nashville, Tennessee; she became the news anchor at Nashville's WTVF-TV at age 19; and then went to Baltimore's WJZ-TV to anchor the news and co-host a local show, *People Are Talking*. In 1984 she made the move to Chicago as host of WLS-TV's morning show, *A.M. Chicago*. The ratings took off almost immediately and within a year it was renamed *The Oprah Winfrey Show*. It entered the syndication market in 1986 and went on to become the highest rated talk show in TV history.

Winfrey established her own production facility, Harpo Studios, in 1988. Her program is broadcast internationally to about 134 countries. Harpo Films is her company's film division and it has produced many notable TV movies under the "Oprah Winfrey Presents" banner, including *The Wedding* (1998), *Tuesdays with Morrie* (1999), *Their Eyes Were Watching God* (2005) and *For One More Day* (2007). Harpo Films has also produced the theatrical features *Beloved* (in which she also starred; 1998), *The Great Debaters* (2007), and the musical film version of *The Color Purple* (2010).

Winfrey has also excelled as an actress. Many of us first became aware of her through her heart-rending performance as Sofia in *The Color Purple* (1985), for which she received a Best Supporting Actress Academy Award nomination and a Golden Globe nomination. The wife of the cruel Harpo, she endures spousal abuse as well as the abuses of a racist society, paying a great physical and psychological price in the process, but remaining true to herself, and eventually triumphing. She has also given well received performances in the TV movies *The Women of Brewster Place* (1989) as Mattie Michael, denizen of a rundown housing project; *There Are No Children Here* (1993) as Lajoe Rivers, in a tale of children growing up in a Chicago housing project; and *Before Women Had Wings* (1997) as Zora Williams, a positive force who helps the abused wife of an alcoholic husband; as well as in the theatrical feature *Native Son* (1990) as Mrs. Thomas, mother of Bigger, who kills a white woman.

Harpo Productions, Inc., also syndicates the *Dr. Phil* talk show and *The Rachael Ray Show*, both of which have gone on to outstanding success in the daytime market. Winfrey is one of the partners in Oxygen Media, Inc., creators of the Oxygen Channel, and is preparing the launch of her own network, in conjunction with Discover Communications, to be called *OWN: The Oprah Winfrey Network*. In April 2000, *O, The Oprah Magazine* was introduced, reaching a circulation of 2.3 million readers a month.

Winfrey is an outstanding philanthropist, having awarded hundreds of grants through the Oprah Winfrey Foundation and Oprah's Angel Network. She has also established the Oprah

Oprah Winfrey, Daytime Emmy Awards, 1987.

Winfrey Leadership Academy for Girls in South Africa, which opened in January 2007. Her many awards include the Peabody Award for Individual Achievement (1995); the National Academy of Television Arts and Sciences Lifetime Achievement Award (1998); the United Nations Global Humanitarian Action Award (2004); and The Elie Weisel Foundation for Humanity Humanitarian Award (2007).

Feature Films including TV Movies: *The Color Purple* (1985), *Native Son* (1986), *Throw Momma from the Train* (1987), *Lincoln* (voice; TV; 1992), *There Are No Children Here* (TV; 1993), *Before Women Had Wings* (TV; 1997), *Beloved* (1998), *Bolero* (2004), *Charlotte's Web* (voice; 2006), *Ocean's Thirteen* (2007), *The Princess and the Frog* (TV; 2009).

TV: *The Tonight Show Starring Johnny Carson* (1985), *The 58th Annual Academy Awards* (1986), *Saturday Night Live* (1986), *The Oprah Winfrey Show* (host; 1986–2007), *The 59th Annual Academy Awards* (1987), *Dolly* (1987), *Christmas at Pee Wee's Playhouse* (1988), *20th NAACP Image Awards* (1988), *The 10th Annual Black Achievement Awards* (1989), *Diet America Challenge* (1989), *The Women of Brewster Place* (miniseries; 1989), *Listen Up: The Lives of Quincy Jones* (1990), *Grammy Legends* (1990), *Brewster Place* (recurring role as Mattie Michael; 1990), *Gabriel's*

Fire ("Tis the Season," 1990), *The Arsenio Hall Show* (1992), *Scared Silent: Ending and Exposing Child Abuse* (1992), *The Fresh Prince of Bel-Air* ("A Night at the Oprah," 1992), *ABC Afterschool Specials* (4 episodes; "Surviving a Break-Up," "Shades of a Single Protein," "Learning Not to Hurt," "I Hate the Way I Look," 1992–94), *Michael Jackson Talks to Oprah* (1993), *10th Annual TV Academy Hall of Fame* (1994), *All-American Girl* ("A Night at the Oprah," 1995), *The 67th Annual Academy Awards* (1995), *Celebrate the Dream: 50 Years of Ebony Magazine* (1996), *The Tonight Show with Jay Leno* (2 appearances; 1996 and 2005), *About Us: The Dignity of Children* (1997), *Ellen* (2 episodes; "The Puppy Episode," Parts I and II, 1997), *Behind the Music* (archival; "M.C. Hammer," 1997), *The 23rd Annual People's Choice Awards* (1997), *E! True Hollywood Story* (archival; "Elizabeth Taylor," 1998), *The Rosie O'-Donnell Show* (2 appearances; 1998–2000), *Quincy Jones: The First 50 Years* (1999), ABC 2000: *The Millennium* (archival; 1999), *Celebrity Profile* ("Danny Glover," 19??), *Home Improvement* ("Home Alone," 1999), *Parkinson* (1999), *A Celebration: 100 Years of Great Women* (1999), *The 26th Annual Daytime Emmy Awards* (1999), *The Hughleys* ("Milsap Moves Up," 1999), *Our Friend Martin* (voice; 1999), *It's Good to Be...* (archival; 2000), *Mundo VIP* (2000), *Bette* ("Two Days at a Time," 2000), *Use Your Life* (2001), *A Prayer for America: Yankee Stadium Memorial* (2001), *American Masters* ("Quincy Jones: In the Pocket," 2001), *The Kennedy Center Honors: A Celebration of the Performing Arts* (2001), *The Cosby Show: A Look Back* (2002), *Oprah After the Show* (2002), *The 54th Annual Primetime Emmy Awards* (2002), *MADtv* (2002), *Entertainment Tonight* (8 appearances; 2003–07), *Unchained Memories: Readings from the Slave Narratives* (2003), *100 Years of Hope and Humor* (2003), *Celebrities Uncensored* (archival; 2003), *200 Greatest Pop Culture Icons* (archival; 2003), *ABC's 50th Anniversary Celebration* (2003), *Second Opinion with Dr. Oz* (2003), *Extra* (2003), *Nobel Peace Prize Concert* (2003), *Larry King Live* (6 appearances; 2003–07), *Entertainment Tonight* (8 appearances; 2003–07), *Brothers of the Borderland* (2004), *Biography* (archival; "Bette Midler," 2004), *Good Morning America* (2004), *The 76th Annual Academy Awards* (2004), *On-Air with Ryan Seacrest* (2004), *Cristina: El 15 aniversario* (2004), *E! True Hollywood Story* ("Oprah Winfrey," 2004), *The Barbara Walters Special* (2004), *An Evening of Stars: Tribute to Quincy Jones* (2005), *Emmanuel's Gift* (narrator; 2005), *Michael Jackson's Boys* (archival; 2005), *36th NAACP Image Awards* (2005), *Sign Chanel* (2005), *36th NAACP Image Awards* (2005), *Corazón de...* (2005), *Out of Africa: Heroes and Icons* (archival; 2005), *Late Show with David Letterman* (2005), *The Kennedy Center Honors: A Celebration of the Performing Arts* (2005), *CMT Greatest Moments: Dolly Parton* (archival; 2006), *Showbiz Tonight* (2006), *African American Lives* (4 episodes; "The Promise of Freedom," "Listening to Our Past," "Searching for Our Names," "Beyond the Middle Passage," 2006), *Legends Ball* (2006), *The View* (2006), *The 60th Annual Tony Awards* (2006), *Forbes Celebrity 100: Who Made Bank?* (2006), *Rachael Ray* (2006), *The 2006 Black Movie Awards*, *Inside Edition* (2006), *Forbes 20 Richest Women in Entertainment* (2007), *Building a Dream: The Oprah Winfrey Leadership Academy* (2007), *Oprah's Roots: An African American Lives Special* (2007), *The Film Programme* (2007), *The Big Give* (9 segments; 2008), *The Insider* (2008), *We Have a Dream '08.*

Video/DVD: *Dangerous: The Short Films* (archival; 1993), *Tina Turner Celebrate Live 1999*, *Larry King Live: The Greatest Interviews* (2007).

Winston, Hattie Born in Lexington, Mississippi, March 3, 1945.

Sincerity, commitment, kindness: these are key words in the persona of Hattie Mae Winston. Although born in Lexington, Mississippi, she was raised in Greeneville. Her parents are Selena Thurmond and Roosevelt Love Winston. After graduating from Howard University in Washington, D.C., she joined the prestigious Group Theatre Workshop in New York and was a member of the venerable Negro Ensemble Company.

Much of Winston's acclaim has been on Broadway; she made her debut in the epochal *Hair* (as Dionne/Member of the Tribe; 1968–72) and with featured roles in *The Me Nobody Knows* (as Nell; 1970–71), *Two Gentlemen of Verona* (as Silvia; 1971–73), and *The Tap Dance Kid* (as Ginnie; 1983–85). She was also in *Does a Tiger Wear a Necktie?* (Linda; 1969), a revival of *Scapino* (as Zerbinetta; 1974–75), and *I Love My Wife* (Cleo; 1977–79). Off-Broadway, she received Obie Awards for her work in *Mother Courage, The Michigan*, and *Billy Noname*.

She adapted Langston Hughes' *Black Nativity* at the Master Theater in New York in 1990 in conjunction with her husband, James Stovall, and Phylicia Rashad in 1990. The off-Broadway production was called *Nativity: A Life Story.*

The National Black Theatre Festival in North Carolina has twice declared a Hattie Winston Day (in 1993 and 1997). Winston has served as National Co-chair of AFTRA's Equal Employment Opportunities Committee. The University of Louisville (Kentucky) was the recipient of the Hattie Winston Collection, including over 250 books, scripts and pieces of theater memorabilia, most of them contributed by Winston.

In television, she is best remembered by many for her role as Margaret Wyborn on *Becker* (1998–2004), but children knew her as the librarian on *The Electric Company* (1973–77), the compatriot of Easy Reader (Morgan Freeman), and as the voice of a variety villainesses on the "Spidey Super Stories" sketches. Daytime drama fans knew her as Veronique on *The Edge of Night* (1976), and she also had recurring roles on the soaps *Ryan's Hope* (1987) and *Port Charles* (1998). And for others she was the voice of Lucy Carmichael in *The Rugrats Movie* (1998) and the Nickelodeon series *All Grown Up*, a *Rugrats* spinoff. Older fans remember her fondly as Toni Gillette on *Nurse* (1981–82) or, a generation or so later, as Gloria Davis on *Homefront* (1991–93).

In films, she was Simone in Quentin Tarantino's *Jackie Brown* (1997); Angela Russell in *True Crime* (1999), with Clint Eastwood, and Principal Holmstead in *The Battle of Shaker Heights* (2003). She is married to composer Harold Wheeler; they have one child. Wheeler is the musical director on *Dancing with the Stars.*

Feature Films including Video and TV Movies: *Ann in Blue* (TV; 1974), *Out to Lunch* (TV; 1974), *Hollow Image* (TV; 1979), *Good to Go* (1986), *Clara's Heart* (1988), *Runaway* (TV; 1989), *A Show of Force* (1990), *One Woman's Courage* (TV; 1994), *Beverly Hills Cop III* (1994), *Sunset Park* (1996), *The Cherokee Kid* (TV; 1996), *Jackie Brown* (1997), *Meet the Deedles* (1998), *Living Out Loud* (1998), *The Rugrats Movie* (voice of Lucy Carmichael; 1998), *After All* (TV; 1999), *True Crime* (1999), *Unbowed* (1999), *The Battle of Shaker Heights* (2003), *All Grown Up* (2003).

TV: *The Electric Company* (recurring role as Sylvia/Valerie the Librarian; 1973–77), *The Edge of Night* (recurring role as Veronique; 1976), *The Dain Curse* (miniseries; 1978), *3-2-1 Contact* (2 episodes in the role of Jessica; "Hot/Cold: Heat and Work," "Crowded/Uncrowded: Human Crowding," 1980), *Les uns et les autres* (miniseries; 1981), *Nurse* (recurring role of Toni Gillette; 1981–82), *Ryan's Hope* (recurring role as Carol Bruce; 1987), *CBS Summer Playhouse* ("Coming to America," 1989), *Reading Rainbow* ("Galimoto," 1991), *Homefront* (recurring role of Gloria Davis; 1991–93), *The Little Mermaid* (voice; "King Crab," 1994), *Step by Step* ("Adventures in Babysitting," 1995), *Nick Freno: Licensed Teacher* ("Dance Fever," 1996), *Duckman* (voice; "Coolio Runnings," 1997), *Malcolm & Eddie* ("Jugglin'," 1997), *Arsenio* ("Throw Momma from the House," 1997), *The Parent 'Hood* ("Wendell and I Spy," 1997), *Smart Guy* ("Rooferman, Take One," 1998), *Port Charles* (recurring role as Alice Burgess; 1998), *Becker* (recurring role of Margaret Wyborn; 1998–2004), *Cosby* ("The Vesey Method," 1999), *To Tell the Truth* (panelist; 2000), *5th Annual Prism Awards* (2001), *The Proud Family* (voice; "Teacher's Pet," 2001), *Hollywood Squares* (2 segments; 2001 and 2003), *Scrubs* (2 episodes in the role of Margaret Turk; "My Old Man," "My Best Friend's Wedding," 2002 and 2004), *The Late Late Show with Craig Kilborn* (2003), *SoapTalk* (2003), *Pyramid* (2003–04), *ER* ("Twas the Night," 2004), *Girlfriends* ("With a Twist,"

Hattie Winston.

2005), *Numb3rs* ("Jack of All Trades," 2008), *All Grown Up* (voice of Lucy Carmichael; 20??).

Shorts: *Deathdealer: A Documentary* (2004).

Woodard, Alfre Born in Tulsa, Oklahoma, November 8, 1952.

Alfre Ette Woodard is a contemporary Renaissance woman — actress, philanthropist, activist, mother and wife (her husband is writer Roderick Spencer; they have two adopted children, Mavis and Duncan). She is the youngest of three children. She was sports oriented at Bishop Kelley High School in Tulsa — track and cheerleading — but became interested in acting and went on to study it at Boston University.

Woodard has won a record number of primetime Emmy Awards and a record amount of Emmy nominations for an African American actress. In 1984 she was Outstanding Guest Actress in a Drama Series for *Hill Street Blues*. In 1986 she was Outstanding Supporting Actress in a Drama Series for the pilot of *L.A. Law*. In 1997 she was awarded her third Emmy for the TV movie *Miss Evers' Boys* (as Eunice Evers; 1997). She received an Emmy nomination as a cast member on *St. Elsewhere* (Dr. Roxanne Turner). She also received two Emmy nominations for *Desperate Housewives* (for ensemble acting and Outstanding Supporting Actress in a Comedy Series; 2005–06), and another for the miniseries *The Water Is Wide* (2006). Other Emmy nominations include Outstanding Supporting Actress in a Limited Series of a Special for *Words by Heart* (*Wonderworks*) in 1985; Outstanding Lead Actress in a Miniseries or a Special for *Unnatural Causes* (1987); Outstanding Lead Actress in a Miniseries or a Special for *A Mother's Courage: The Mary Thomas Story* (1990); Outstanding Lead Actress in a Miniseries or a Special for *The Piano Lesson* on *Hallmark Hall of Fame* (1995); Outstanding Supporting Actress for a Miniseries or Special for *Gulliver's Travels* (1996); Outstanding Guest Actress in a Drama Series for *Homicide: A Life on the Street* (1998); and Outstanding Guest Actress in a Drama Series for *The Practice* (2003). She has also won three Screen Actors Guild Awards. These were for her work in *The Piano Lesson* (1995), *Miss Evers' Boys*, and as part of the ensemble cast of the series *Desperate Housewives*.

Woodard's lengthy film career contains many highlights. In 1984 she received an Academy Award nomination for Best Supporting Actress for *Cross Creek*. She was delightful in quirky roles in the independent films *Miss Firecracker* (as Popeye Jackson; 1989), *Passion Fish* (Golden Globe nominee as Chantelle; 1992), and *How to Make an American Quilt* (as Marianna; 1995). She was Lily Sloane in *Star Trek: First Contact* (which netted her an NAACP Image Award; 1996); Carolyn Carmichael in Spike Lee's touching, sorely underrated *Crooklyn* (1994); Loretta Sinclair, a drug-addicted single mother in *Down in the Delta* (1998), and Camille Wright in the African American romantic comedy *Love & Basketball* (2000).

Her most recent recurring TV series role was as Mavis Heller on NBC's *My Own Worst Enemy* (2008), which fell victim to scant ratings. Her stage work includes *Map of the World, Me and Bessie, Drowning Crow* and *The Winter's Tale*. Woodard is a founder and board member of Artists for a New South Africa.

Feature Films including TV Movies: *The Trial of the Moke* (TV; 1978), *Remember My Name* (1978), *Freedom Road* (TV; 1979), *Health* (1980), *The Sophisticated Gents* (TV; 1981), *Precious Blood* (TV; 1982), *The Ambush Murders* (TV; 1982), *Cross Creek* (1983), *Sweet Revenge* (TV; 1984), *The Killing Floor* (TV; 1985), *Go Tell It on the Moun-*

Alfre Woodard in *Grand Canyon* (1991).

tain (TV; 1985), *Extremities* (1986), *Unnatural Causes* (TV; 1986), *Mandela* (TV; 1987), *The Child Saver* (TV; 1988), *Scrooged* (1988), *Miss Firecracker* (1989), *A Mother's Courage: The Mary Thomas Story* (TV; 1989), *Blue Bayou* (TV; 1990), *Pretty Hattie's Baby* (1991), *Grand Canyon* (1991), *The Gun in Betty Lou's Handbag* (1992), *Passion Fish* (1992), *Rich in Love* (1993), *Heart and Souls* (1993), *Bopha!* (1993), *Aliens for Breakfast* (TV; 1994), *Blue Chips* (1994), *Race to Freedom: The Underground Railroad* (TV; 1994), *Crooklyn* (1994), *Statistically Speaking* (1995), *The Piano Lesson* (TV; 1995), *How to Make an American Quilt* (1995), *Follow Me Home* (1996), *Gulliver's Travels* (TV; 1996), *Special Report: Journey to Mars* (TV; 1996), *Primal Fear* (1996), *A Step Toward Tomorrow* (1996), *Star Trek: First Contact* (1996), *The Brave Little Toaster to the Rescue* (voice; 1997), *The Member of the Wedding* (TV; 1997), *Miss Evers' Boys* (TV; 1997), *Down in the Delta* (1998), *Secrets* (1998), *The Wishing Tree* (1999), *Funny Valentines* (TV; 1999), *Mumford* (1999), *John Henry* (voice; 2000), *What's Cooking?* (2000), *Love & Basketball* (2000), *Dinosaur* (voice; 2000), *Lost Souls* (2000), *Holiday Heart* (TV; 2000), *K-PAX* (2001), *Baby of the Family* (2002), *Searching for Debra Winger* (documentary; 2002), *The Wild Thornberrys Movie* (TV; 2002), *The Singing Detective* (2003), *The Core* (2003), *A Wrinkle in Time* (TV; 2003), *Radio* (2003), *The Forgotten* (2004), *Beauty Shop* (2005), *Something New* (2006), *The Water Is Wide* (TV; 2006), *Take the Lead* (2006), *20 on 20* (2007), *Pictures of Hollis Woods* (TV; 2008), *American Violet* (2008), *Reach for Me* (2008), *The Family That Preys* (2008), *Tempting Hyenas* (2009), *Bury Me Standing* (2009).

TV: *The White Shadow* ("Reunion," 1980), *Enos* ("Forever Blowing Bubbles," 1981), *American Playhouse: For Colored Girls Who Have Considered Suicide/When the Rainbow Is Enuf* (1982), *Tucker's Witch* (recurring role as Marcia Fulbright, 1982), *Hill Street Blues* (3 episodes in the role of Doris Robson; "Doris in Wonderland," "Praise Dilaudid," "Goodbye, Mr. Scripps," 1983), *Wonderworks: Words by Heart* (1985), *Sara* (recurring role as Rozalyn Dupree; 1985), *Faerie Tale Theatre* ("Puss in Boots," 1985), *St. Elsewhere* (recurring role of Dr. Roxanne Turner; 1985–88), *L.A. Law* (pilot; 1986), *20th NAACP Image Awards* (1988), *The 65th Annual Academy Awards* (1993), *The Arsenio Hall Show* (1994), *Frontline* ("In the Game," 1994), *A Century of Women* (voice; miniseries; 1994), *Countdown to Freedom* (narrator; 1994), *Frazier* ("The Botched Language of Cranes," 1994), *Frederick Douglass: When the Lion Wrote History* (narrator; 1994), *The American Experience* (narrator; 2 episodes; "Malcolm X: Make It Plain," "Eleanor Roosevelt," 1994 and 2000), *Happily Ever After: Fairy Tales for Every Child* (1995), *People's Century* (narrator, various episodes; 1995), *The Wizard of Oz in Concert: Dreams Come True* (1995), *2nd Annual Screen Actors Guild Awards* (1996), *Wild On...* ("Wild on Jamaica," 19??), *Cadillac Desert* (narrator; miniseries; 1997), *Adventures from the Book of Virtues* (voice; "Faith," 1997), *The 55th Annual Golden Globe* Awards (1998), *Homicide: Life on the Street* ("Mercy," 1998), *Celebrity Profile* ("Danny Glover," 1998), *The Underground Railroad* (1999), *The Directors* ("The Films of Spike Lee," 1999), *The 56th Annual Golden Globe* Awards (1999), *The Tulsa Lynching of 1921: A Hidden Story* (2000), *The Kennedy Center Presents: Speak Power to Truth* (2000), *Half Past Autumn: The Life and Works of Gordon Parks* (narrator; 2000), *Dennis Miller Live* (2001), *American Exile* (narrator; 2001), *Unchained Memories: Readings from the Slave Narratives* (2003), *Nat Turner: A Troublesome Property* (narrator; 2003), *Tribeca Film Festival Presents* (2003), *The Practice* (2 episodes in the role of Denise Freeman; "Down the Hatch," "Final Judgment," 2003), *Static Shock* (voice; "Flashback," 2003), *The 55th Annual Primetime Emmy Awards* (2003), *All Our Sons: Fallen Heroes of 9/11* (narrator; 2004), *Reading Rainbow* ("Visiting Day," 2004), *Tavis Smiley* (2005), *The View* (2005), *Inconceivable* (2 episodes in the role of Dr. Lydia Crawford; "Secrets and Thighs," "Pilot," 2005), *Desperate Housewives* (recurring role of Betty Applewhite; 2005–06), *HBO First Look* (2 episodes; "16 Blocks," "Take the Lead," 2006), *Corazon de...* (archival; 2006), *Legends Ball* (2006), *King Leopold's Ghost* (voice; 2006), *The 60th Annual Tony Awards* (2006), *Kathy Griffin: My Life on the D-List* (2006), *The 58th Annual Primetime Emmy Awards* (2006), *The Oprah Winfrey Show* (2006), *The Megan Mullally Show* (2006), *Nefertiti and the Lost Dynasty* (hostess; 2007), *My Own Worst Enemy* (recurring role as Mavis Heller; 2008), *Entertainment Tonight* (2008), *The 60th Primetime Emmy Awards* (2008), *For Love of Liberty: The Story of America's Black Patriots* (voice; 2009).

Woodard, Charlayne (aka Woodard, Charlaine) Born in Albany, New York, December 29, 1953.

Charlayne Woodard is a playwright as well as an actress.

She was nominated for a Tony Award as Best Actress in a Featured Role in a Musical for *Ain't Misbehavin'* (1978–79). Her performance was preserved in the PBS telecast of the play in 1982. On TV she is best known as Janice, aunt of Will Smith, on *The Fresh Prince of Bel-Air* (1991–93). She has also had recurring roles on *Roseanne* (as Vonda Green; 1988–89); *Days of Our Lives* (as Desiree McCall; 1991–92); and *ER* (as Angela Gilliam; 2006–07).

She made her film debut in the memorable "White Boys" number in the film version of *Hair* (1979). Her best film work is in Arthur Miller's *The Crucible* (1996) as Tituba, a slave from Barbados who leads a group of impressionable young girls into "consorting with the devil." They are promised forgiveness if they promise to implicate their friends and neighbors. She was the Samuel L. Jackson character Elijah's mother in director M. Night Shamalyan's *Unbreakable* (2000). It's a flashback role, but Woodard is superb as the doting mother who nurtures her physically fragile son. She also played the inspiring Olympic sprinter Gail Devers in *Run for the Dream: The Gail Devers Story* (1996). This was some of her best acting work in any medium.

She trained at the Goodman School of Drama and is a member of The Actor's Studio. If there aren't enough good roles for black actresses, write some. Woodard is the author of three plays: *Pretty Fire*, *Neat* and *In Real Life*, and has starred in all three. *Pretty Fire* won an L.A. Drama Critics and NAACP Image Award. *Neat* received the Irving and Blanche Laurie Theatre Vision Award and an Outer Critics Circle Award Nomination. *In Real Life* was nominated for Drama Desk and Outer Critics Circle Awards for best solo performance and received an Audelco Award, Backstage West Garland Award and NAACP Image Award for best playwright and actor.

Her extensive theater credits include the long-running off-Broadway production *Don't Bother Me, I Can't Cope* (1975), *Hair* (1977), *A ... My Name Is Alice* (1984), *Twelfth Night* (1989) and *The Caucasian Chalk Circle* (1990) at the New York Shakespeare Festival, and her solo show, *In Real Life* (in which she debuted in Seattle in 2000–01 and then took to New York in 2002). Other credits include her *Pretty Fire* (another solo show, with which she toured extensively, but began at L.A.'s Odyssey Theatre in 1992) and *In the Blood*, performed at New York's Public Theatre in 2000. Woodard is married to lawyer Alan Harris.

Feature Films including TV Movies: *Cindy* (TV; 1978), *Hair* (1979), *Hard Feelings* (1982), *Crackers* (1984), *Me and Him* (1988), *God Bless the Child* (TV; 1988), *Buffalo Girls* (TV; 1995), *Run for the Dream: The Gail Devers Story* (TV; 1996), *Touched by Evil* (TV; 1997), *The Wedding* (TV; 1998), *Twister* (1989), *He Said, She Said* (1991), *One Good Cop* (1991), *The Meteor Man* (1993), *Angie* (1994), *Babyfever* (1994), *Eye for an Eye* (1996), *The Crucible* (1996), *Around the Fire* (1999), *The Million Dollar Hotel* (2000), *Unbreakable* (2000), *H.M.O.* (TV; 2001), *Sunshine State* (2002), *D.C. Sniper: 23 Days of Fear* (TV; 2003), *Lackawanna Blues* (TV; 2005), *Southern Comfort* (TV; 2006).

TV: *Ain't Misbehavin'* (1982), *Taxi* ("Nina Loves Alex," 1982), *Spenser: For Hire* ("Blood Money," 1985), *Wise Guy* ("Blood Dance," 1988), *Roseanne* (5 episodes as Vonda Green; "Life and Stuff," "Radio Days," "Let's Call It Quits," "Guilt by Disassociation," "Sweet Dreams," 1988–89), *A Different World* ("21 Candles," 1990), *Days of Our Lives* (recurring role as Desiree McCall; 1991–92); *The Fresh Prince of Bel-Air* (4 episodes in the role of Janice; "Guess Who's Coming to Marry?" "Christmas Show," "Mommy Nearest," "The Baby Comes Out," 1991–93), *Frasier* ("Flour Child," 1994), *Sweet Justice* (2 episodes as Harriet Battle-Wilkins; "The Power of Darkness," Parts I and II, 1994), *Bless This House* ("The Bowling Method," 1996), *Chicago Hope* (10 episodes in the recurring role of Gina Wilkes; 1994–2000), *Law & Order: Special Victims Unit* (recurring role of Sister Peg; 2002–06), *Boomtown* ("Fearless," 2003), *Strong Medicine* ("The Real World Rittenhouse," 2004), *The Division* ("Lost and Found," 2004), *Declarations of War* (2004), *Great Performances* ("Broadway's Lost Treasures III: The Best of the Tony Awards," 2005), *In Justice* ("The Public Burning," 2006), *Shark* ("Fashion Police," 2006), *ER* (7 episodes in the role of Angela Gilliam; 2006–07), *Terminator: The Sarah Connor Chronicles* (2 episodes in the role of Terissa Dyson; pilot, "The Turk," 2008), *Broadway: Beyond the Golden Age* (2009).

Wright, N'Bushe Born in New York, New York, September 20, 1970.

N'Bushe (nuh-*boo*-shay) Wright made her film debut in *Zebrahead* (1992), a sensitive, realistic story of an interracial relationship — there have been few such admirable presentations of the subject before or since. She is the daughter of a jazz musician and a New York City Board of Education psychologist. She is a graduate of the High School for the Performing Arts. Wright was originally a dancer, training at the Alvin Ailey Dance Center and the Martha Graham School of Dance. She studied acting at the top-drawer Stella Adler Studio.

After good roles in *Fresh* as a drug addict (1994), *Dead Presidents* as a passionate Black Panther (1995), and *Blade* as an ally to a half-vampire, half-human vampire hunter played by Wesley Snipes (1998), her film career seemed to peter out, but she sustained a viable career on television and seems to be showing renewed activity after about a five-year lull.

One of her best TV roles was in fact her TV debut, Claudia Bishop, a civil rights activist, on the admirable *I'll Fly Away* (1992–93), one of the few great network shows about the black experience. Guest star series work includes *Homicide: Life on the Street, New York Undercover* and *Chappelle's Show.*

Feature Films including TV Movies: *Zebrahead* (1992), *Fresh* (1994), *Dead Presidents* (1995), *Johns* (1996), *His and Hers* (1997), *A Woman Like That* (1997), *Close to Danger* (TV; 1997), *Squeeze* (1997), *Blade* (1998), *3 Strikes* (2000), *Civil Brand* (2002), *MVP* (2003), *He Say ... She Say ... But What Does GOD Say?* (2004), *God's Forgotten House* (2005), *Restraining Order* (2006), *A Talent for Trouble* (2008).

TV: *I'll Fly Away* (5 episodes in the role of Claudia Bishop; "Comfort and Joy," "Small Wishes," "What's in a Name?" "Commencement," "State," 1992–93), *Homicide: Life on the Street* ("Night of the Dead Living," 1993), *Lifestories: Families in Crisis* ("power: the Eddie Matos Story," 1994), *American Gothic* ("Eye of the Beholder," 1995), *Swift Justice* ("Takin' Back the Street," 1996), *New York Undercover* (4 episodes in the role of Carol; "Checkmate," "Andre's Choice," "No Greater Love," "Deep Cover," 1996), *Subway Stories: Tales from the Underground* ("The Red Shoes," 1997), *Third Watch* ("History of the World," 1999), *UC: Undercover* (3 episodes in the role of Keisha; "Amerikaz Most Wanted," "Honor Among Thieves," "Nobody Rides for Free," 2001), *Widows* (miniseries; 2002), *The Award Show Awards Show* (archival; 2003), *Platinum* (recurring role as Maxine "Max" Colt; 2003), *Chappelle's Show* (2004), *Widows* (miniseries; 2008).

Yancy, Emily Born in Brooklyn, New York, January 16, 1979; died August 25, 2002.

Singer, film and TV actress, Broadway star: Emily Yancy has had a long and rewarding career. Her most famous film role is as the camera girl in the nightclub who takes a picture of Prince Mamuwalde, better known as *Blacula* (1972). When she develops the photo in her home darkroom (still wearing her sexy nightclub costume), she notices that here is an empty space where Blacula sat. She is then attacked by Blacula, who drains her blood, turning her into one of the living dead. Many who saw this popular film at the time of its release did not realize that Yancy was a popular jazz and pop singer who had also appeared in major Broadway shows. Another memorable film role is as Mabel Hill in *Cotton Comes to Harlem* (1970), as one of the many characters in search of a bale of cotton that contains a fortune in stolen money collected as part of a "back to Africa" scam.

Her Broadway career began as a replacement in the role of Irene Malloy in the original *Hello, Dolly!* (she was attached to the show from 1964 to 1970). She was an understudy for and replacement for the role of Dulcinea in the original Broadway run of *Man of La Mancha* (she was attached to the show from 1965 to 1971). When the show was revived in 1977, she starred as Dulcinea for 124 performances. She starred as Seena in the expensive flop musical *1600 Pennsylvania Avenue* (politics and music didn't mix), which opened May 4, 1976, and closed on May 8.

Yancy appeared on two episodes of *Frasier* (2002 and 2003) as Cora, the mother of Frasier's contentious neighbor Cam Winston. She also did guest star work on *Love, American Style, Sanford and Son, Emergency!, The Mod Squad, That's My Mama, Police Story, Starsky and Hutch, It's a Living, Dallas, Diff'rent Strokes, Punky Brewster, Knots Landing, MacGyver, Picket Fences* and *Cold Case.*

Feature Films including TV Movies: *What's So Bad About Feeling Good?* (1968), *Tell Me That You Love Me, Junie Moon* (1970), *Cotton Comes to Harlem* (1970), *Second Chance* (TV; 1972), *Blacula* (1972), *Poor Devil* (TV; 1973), *The Sword and* *the Sorcerer* (1982), *The Abyss* (1989), *Heat Wave* (TV; 1990), *Nine Months* (1995), *Jasper, Texas* (TV; 2003).

TV: *The Tonight Show Starring Johnny Carson* (2 segments; 1962–72), *The Merv Griffin Show* (2 segments; 1967–68), *Love, American Style* ("Love and the Mystic," 1972), *Sanford and Son* ("Sanford and Son and Sister Makes Three," 1972), *Emergency!* ("Dinner Date," 1972), *The Mod Squad* ("Run, Lincoln, Run," 1973), *A Touch of Grace* ("The Working Girl," 1973), *Here We Go Again* ("The Times They Are A-Changin'," 1973), *The Rookies* ("Johnny Lost His Gun," 1974), *That's My Mama* ("Stephanie's Boyfriend," 1975), *Police Story* ("Oxford Gray," 1976), *Starsky and Hutch* ("Huggy Bear and the Turkey," 1977), *It's a Living* ("R-E-S-P-E-C-T," 1981), *Dallas* ("Goodbye, Cliff Barnes," 1982), *Diff'rent Strokes* ("Arnold and Lisa's Mother," 1984), *Punky Brewster* ("I Love You, Brandon," 1985), *Knots Landing* ("Merger Made in Heaven," 1989), *Father Dowling Mysteries* ("The Substitute Sister Mystery," 1991), *MacGyver* ("Walking Dead," 1991), *Picket Fences* ("The Dancing Bandit," 1993), *The Practice* ("Gideon's Crossover," 2001), *Even Stevens* ("Stevens Manor," 2002), *Frasier* (2 episodes as Cora Winston; "The Love You Fake," "Fraternal Schwinns," 2002 and 2003), *Cold Case* ("Glued," 2004), *The Unit* ("Silver Star," 2006).

Yarbo, Lillian Born in Brooklyn, New York, January 16, 1979; died August 25, 2002.

In James Whale's *Wives Under Suspicion* (1938), one of the characters, referring to the Creola the maid character played by Lillian Yarbo, says, "She certainly can cook — that's more than what most of them can do." In one of her last maid roles, *A Date with Judy* (1948), Yarbo's maid character apparently spends most of her time walking around singing "Sing Low, Sweet Chariot."

Like Louise Beavers, Theresa Harris, Marietta Canty and Libby Taylor, Yarbo spent much of her career playing domestic servants in the 1930s and '40s. Given the temper of the times and the very limited opportunities for black actresses of the era, the reader has to make a personal judgment call whether to accept the path Yarbo and others took, or whether they side with the actresses (Dorothy Dandridge, Francine Everett, Nina Mae McKinney, et al.) who refused to go that route.

Yarbo was in Frank Capra's *You Can't Take It with You* (1936), appearing with Eddie "Rochester" Anderson as the servants of the homespun Vanderhoff family. This uneasy mix of Depression era politics and Andy Hardy posturing had little of the bite of the George S. Kaufman and Moss Hart Broadway hit upon which it was based. But Capra was at the peak of his popularity, and the film won Oscars for Best Picture and Best Director. She was also in *Way Down South* (1939), a vehicle for child star Bobby Breen, also featuring Clarence Muse, and with a screenplay by no less than Langston Hughes. This tale of a little white master who fears that his slaves are about to be sold is not the sort of film you're likely to see at your local multiplex these days.

Feature Films: *Rainbow on the River* (1936), *Stella Dallas* (1937), *Big Town Girl* (1937), *Wives Under Suspicion* (1938), *You Can't Take It with You* (1938), *Up the River* (1938), *Kentucky* (1938), *There's That Woman Again* (1939), *Persons in Hiding* (1939), *Café Society* (1939), *Society Lawyer* (1939), *The Story of Vernon and Irene Castle* (1939), *The Family Next Door* (1939), *Boy Friend* (1939), *The Jones Family in Hollywood* (1939), *The Gracie Allen Murder Case* (1939), *Way Down South* (1939), *Destry Rides Again* (1939), *Honeymoon Deferred* (1940), *They Drive By Night* (1940), *The Return of Frank James* (1940), *Sandy Gets Her Man* (1940), *Buy Me That Town* (1941), *Henry Aldrich for President* (1941), *Moon Over Her Shoulder* (1941), *Wild Bill Hickok Rides* (1942), *The Great Man's Lady* (1942), *Footlight Serenade* (1942), *Between Us Girls* (1942), *Presenting Lily Mars* (1943), *Redhead from Manhattan* (1943), *Swing Shift Maisie* (1943), *The Gang's All Here* (1943), *Whistling in Brooklyn* (1943), *Music for Millions* (1944), *The Naughty Nineties* (1945), *Saratoga Trunk* (1945), *The Sailor Takes a Wife* (1945), *No Leave, No Love* (1946), *The Time, the Place and the Girl* (1946), *My Brother Talks to Horses* (1947), *A Date with Judy* (1948), *Night Unto Night* (1949), *Look for the Silver Lining* (1949).

Bibliography

"All-Colored but Not Much Different: Films Made for Negro Ghetto Audiences, 1913–1928." *Phylon*, vol. 36, no. 3 (3rd qtr., 1975): 321–339.

Angelou, Maya. "Cicely Tyson: Reflections on a Lone Black Rose." *Ladies' Home Journal* 94 (February 1977): 40–41.

"Barbara McNair: Twelve Years to Broadway." *Ebony* 13 (May 1958): 69–74.

Beckford, Ruth. *Katherine Dunham: A Biography*. New York: Marcel Dekker, 1979.

Black Films and Filmmakers. New York: Dodd, Mead, 1975.

"Black Women in Film." *Jet*, June 29, 1972.

Bogle, Donald. *Blacks in American Films and Television: An Encyclopedia*. New York: Garland, 1988.

_____. *Brown Sugar: Eighty Years of America's Black Female Superstars*. New York: Harmony Books, 1980.

_____. "The Dorothy Dandridge Story." *Essence* 48 (October 1984).

Bronner, Edwin. *The Encyclopedia of the American Theatre 1900–1975*. New York: A.S. Barnes, 1980.

Buckley, Gail Lumet. *The Hornes: An American Family*. New York: Alfred A. Knopf, 1986.

Carroll, Diahann, with Ross Firestone. *Diahann!* Boston: Little, Brown, 1986.

Cole, Natalie. *Angel on My Shoulder*. New York: Warner Books, 2000.

Contemporary Black Biography, vol. 1. Michael L. LaBlanc, ed. Detroit: Gale Research, 1992.

Dandridge, Dorothy, and Earl Conrad. *Everything and Nothing: The Dorothy Dandridge Tragedy*. New York: Abelard-Schuman, 1970.

Directory of Blacks in the Performing Arts. 2d ed. Metuchen, N.J.: Scarecrow Press, 1990.

Egbert, Alan. "Pam Grier: Coming into Focus." *Essence* 43 (January 1979): 107–08.

Encyclopedia of African-American Culture and History. New York: Macmillan, 1996.

Facts on File Encyclopedia of Black Women in America: Theatre Arts and Entertainment. Darlene Clark Hine, ed. New York: Facts on File, 1997.

"Gail Fisher: The Girl from Mannix." *Ebony* 24 (October 1969): 140–44.

"Gail Fisher's Bid for Stardom." *Sepia* 13 (October 1964): 48–51.

Gross, Linden. "Oprah Winfrey: Wonder Woman." *Ladies' Home Journal* 105 (December 1988): 40.

Horne, Lena. "Believing in Oneself." In *Many Shades of Black*. Stanton L. Wormsley, Lewis H. Fenderson, eds. New York: William Morrow, 1969.

IMDBPro.com

Inside the Actors Studio. "Halle Berry." New York: Bravo, 2007, 10–29.

Jones, G. Williams. *Black Cinema Treasures: Lost and Found*. Denton: University of North Texas Press, 1991.

Kitt, Eartha. *Alone with Me*. Chicago: Regnery, 1976.

_____. *Thursday's Child*. New York: Duell, Sloane and Pierce, 1956.

Klotman, Phyllis Rauch. *Frame by Frame: A Black Filmography*. Bloomington: Indiana University Press, 1979.

Lamparski, Richard. "Butterfly McQueen." In *Whatever Became of...?*, 2d series. New York: Crown, 96–97.

Leab, Daniel J. *From Sambo to Superspade: The Black Experience in Motion Pictures*. Boston: Houghton Mifflin, 1976.

MacDonald, J. Fred. *Blacks and White TV: Afro-Americans in Television Since 1948*. Chicago: Nelson-Hall, 1983.

Mapp, Edward. *Directory of Blacks in the Performing Arts*. Metuchen, N.J.: Scarecrow Press, 1978.

McGilligan, Patrick. *Oscar Micheaux: The Great and Only*. New York: HarperCollins, 2007.

McNeil, Alex. *Total Television: A Comprehensive Guide to Programming from 1948 to 1980*. New York: Penguin, 1980.

Notable Black American Women, Books II and III. Jessie Carney Smith, ed. Detroit: Gale Research, Int. Thomson, 1996.

Notable Names in the American Theater. Lindsay Patterson, ed. Clifton, N.J.: James T. White, 1976.

Null, Gary. *Black Hollywood: The Negro in Motion Pictures*. Secaucus, N.J.: Citadel, 1975.

Richards, Larry. *African American Films Through 1959*. Jefferson, N.C.: McFarland, 1998.

Sampson, Henry R. *The Ghost Walks: A Chronological History of Blacks in Show Business 1865–1910*. Metuchen, N.J.: Scarecrow Press, 1988, 34–35.

The Scribner Encyclopedia of American Lives, vol. 2. New York: Charles Scribner's Sons, 1999.

"She Sings Along with Mitch." *Ebony* 17 (March 1962): 40–46.

Stewart, Leisha. "Esther Rolle: Good Times Continue for *Good Times* Star." *Ebony* 46 (June 1991): 64–66.

Variety Obituaries, 1957–1963. New York: Garland, 1988.

Waters, Ethel, with Charles Samuels. *His Eye Is on the Sparrow*. Garden City, N.Y.: Doubleday, 1951.

Watts, Jill. *Hattie McDaniel: Black Ambition, White Hollywood*. New York: HarperCollins, 2005.

Who's Who Among Black Americans, 1994–95. 8th ed. Edward Mapp, ed. Detroit: Gale Research, 1994.

Index